MORNING STAR OVER AMERICA

The New Millennium
AD 2003-2005

Anthology of Messages
The Blessed Virgin Mary

William L. Roth, Jr.
Timothy Parsons-Heather

The Morning Star of Our Lord, Inc. is a nonprofit, tax-exempt, (501)(c)(3) religious, charitable organization that is incorporated under the laws of the State of Illinois. It has been created for the dissemination of various apologetic works in defense of the Holy Gospel of Christianity. It is the role of this Roman Catholic corporation to provide pastoral consolation to those lacking in faith, the infirm, homebound, incarcerated, deprived, dejected and those who are otherwise suffering-humanity for the Glory of the Kingdom of Jesus Christ. All proceeds from this book are being donated to other charitable causes to help feed, clothe and house the poor, and for the reproduction of Christian media for distribution across every continent of the world. If anyone would like to contribute to this worthy cause, you may do so through the following website address.

The Morning Star of Our Lord, Inc.
Springfield, Illinois
www.ImmaculateMary.org

Published by The Morning Star of Our Lord, Inc.
Used with permission.
Copyright © 2008
William L. Roth Jr. & Timothy Parsons-Heather
All rights reserved.

Publish date: September 8, 2008

ISBN10: 0-9793334-0-7
ISBN13: 978-0-9793334-0-8

Cover Image
Copyright © 2008 Michael Bath
www.LightningPhotography.com

The Morning Star of Our Lord, Inc. has published ten works to date by William L. Roth Jr. and Timothy Parsons-Heather, the initial being their sixteen hundred page, two volume diary which meticulously chronicles the opening days of the miraculous intercession of the Most Blessed Virgin Mary in their lives. These men are under ecclesial obedience to His Excellency, Bishop George J. Lucas, of the Diocese of Springfield in Illinois who reserves final judgement concerning their disposition.

Dedicated to all who ever said,

...I've lived my whole life for this moment.

Consider, O human being, in what great excellence the Lord God has placed you, for He created and formed you to the image of His beloved Son according to the body and to His likeness according to the Spirit.

- Saint Francis of Assisi

Morning Star Over America

The New Millennium
AD 2003-2005

Table of Contents

Essays
by
William L. Roth Jr.

I. A visitation from the beatific realms
II. Building unity on a foundation of miracles
III. Abortion and the cultural extinction of America
IV. Virtue, the Commandments and evangelic grace
V. To whom much is given, much is required
VI. The Primacy of the Roman Catholic Church
VII. Protestantism as a reactionary ideology
VIII. Methinks thou are protesting too much!
IX. The Woman Clothed with the Sun
X. Twelve Apostles, Three Persons, One Church
XI. The Eucharist is the authentic Bread of Life
XII. Mary, poised in grief, hopeful for humanity
XIII. The purifying mandates of God's Kingdom
XIV. Jesus, Son of the Matriarchal Intercessor
XV. Sung with an eloquence few have ever heard

Page sequence continues from previous Anthology

AD 2003 399

AD 2004 509

AD 2005 621

Three things are necessary for the salvation of man: to know what he ought to believe, to know what he ought to desire, and to know what he ought to do.

- Saint Thomas Aquinas

I. A visitation from the beatific realms

    I have begun compiling this work in the beautiful fall of the year 2007, nearly seventeen years advanced in time since the inception of our Holy Virgin Mother's messages which compose our manuscripts. I feel a deep nostalgia and contentment as I reminisce the events of those earlier days, even while so much more has occurred for the enlightenment of humankind since those times. At the completion of our initial diary titled *Morning Star Over America* in 1997, my perception was limited to the preceding six years of Our Lady's immaculate grace and the mystical events that had inundated the lives of my brother and me since February 22, 1991. As I recall our disposition and state of anticipation in those dawning stages, our hopes were enormous, being friends who wished so deeply for the world to finally change. We were maneuvering our daily lives unaware of the spiritual magnitude which would blossom from our obedience to the Mother of Jesus Christ. I was genuinely thankful for the progression of my personal relationships and the prayerful events that we attended prior to the soul-shattering thunderclap of Her supernatural appearance, but life took on a profound new meaning on that cold winter day in the same way the Old and New Covenants were separated in time by the virginal Birth of the Messiah in Bethlehem. A new morning had dawned in the middle of the night; a Light had begun to flicker in the cryptic vaults of mankind's veiled existence. I realized a new possibility for Christian evangelization had been conceived which would inevitably promote the deliverance of the Earth's inhabitants from the lethargic rancidness of repeated human error to a bold conviction of life altering Truth. The evidence to sustain a thorough reawakening of our spiritual identity had been dispensed. The ethereal unseen became concrete reality for us. Life was irrevocably transfigured where the substantive essence of our motivations and consciousness was enlightened by the undeniable Truth of Deific Love. Even as we were immersed in those unfolding moments of spiritual lucidity, we were nonetheless oblivious to the permanence of our timely transformation and the impenetrable longevity of the Most Blessed Virgin's loving succor that now reverberates in its original clarity throughout our entire existence, even to this day. We were in possession of a nearly 1600-page diary which is a singularly-unique historical "re-declaration" of what God wishes the world to know, accept and obey in our age, but we were otherwise unaware of the additional magnification that Our Lady intended to subsequently amplify. The Mother of Jesus desired that the scope of our writing not be limited to a word-for-word, faceless dictation of Her messages, but that it proffer a more comprehensive circumspection of the intentions of God within the context of our daily lives in exile. She asked that we synthesize Her guidance through the framework of our understanding as children of faith in every sense of the word. My brother and I stood at the threshold of a prefigured future, eager, excited, fulfilled, accomplished, tempered, tested, abused and fearless, and without the faintest realization of the stratospheric heights to which those sentiments and emotions would be further catapulted in the ensuing years. She has made our faith-spirits indomitable, our conviction impregnable, and our devotion and deference to Her Motherhood as gentle and supple as the lighting of a dove. Our part has always been to lash our flesh and egos, while demanding they comply with Her Immaculate grace. I remember kneeling in tears one night after our pilgrimages to Medjugorje, sometime in 1990 before Our Lady began appearing to us more definitively. I was pouring-out my heart to our Virgin Mother in recognition of the obstinate disbelief and scandalous arrogance that people level against Her miraculous intercession. I recognized the astounding measures of supernal grace that She was offering to the world with so few humbling themselves to receive these gifts from Her sinless hands. Overcome by the immense pain that She was experiencing, my compassion transcended deeply into Her Immaculate Heart where I told Her I would accept and obey everything that others refused to believe. I promised Her that I would embrace the panoramic scope of Her assistance to humanity, even if there would never be another soul who would stand alongside me with such bold conviction. I petitioned God that none of Her aid would ever be lost as a revelation to mankind through a deficit of faith by any seer, congregation, or ecclesial body. I told Her that I would believe and support Her messengers, no matter who they were, with a further petition that I would be protected from ever being deceived by charlatans. And, even as I prayed, it never occurred to me that any one of those mystical graces would ever descend and overwhelm my life. Such patterns of thought never existed within my soul. They were gifts that were given only to saints, and I knew that I did not merit standing in their ranks. I simply felt that I had one power that I controlled, and that was my own will to choose to believe. I summoned the courage to make my heart stand at the ready to invoke any sacrifice in order to accede to the Will of God on the Earth through Her intercession. I knew with all my heart that I wanted this beautiful Virgin from Heaven to feel loved and appreciated with absolute perfection by at least one person on the face of the globe in our time. I wanted Her to be able to tell Jesus that She had found a son who would never utter the word "no" to Her, notwithstanding the cost. Only "yes," only willingness, only obedience, perpetually to the Mother of God and to the Christ whom She serves. Thus, here we are, bearing our fair share of the sacrificial responsibility for the advancement of the Holy Gospel and the building up of the Kingdom of God for the ages.

II. Building unity on a foundation of miracles

Our Holy Mother has provided my brother and me one thing above many others, and that is a sense of moral perspective, some might call it wisdom, regarding the unapologetic priorities of Heaven over the ad hoc whims of sinners upon the Earth. When the Holy Spirit envelops a person, the entire constitution of the human psyche begins to complement, cascade and resonate in a beatifically regenerative way that, first of all, obliterates the irrelevant obstacles of the material world, then transforms infinite possibilities into eternal realities right before the eyes of our soul. This perception of life brought by Our Lady's miraculous presence forces us to be brutally honest with ourselves about our interior motivations, long held beliefs, and the bases of our disposition toward untold numbers of circumstances that are encountered during life. She brings righteous clarity by removing the obtrusive clutter from our spiritual sight so that we can discern rightly by Heaven. Hence, the spiritual integrity of our souls demands that we imitate Her uncompromising candor in many instances while realizing that it can create deeply sacrificial circumstances which ultimately lead to one sharing in the Cross of Calvary. There is a battle being waged by the Hosts of Heaven within the heart and soul of humanity against those whose haughty egos have been unleashed upon the historical majesty of Christianity who are rending unity, virtue and reason like rapacious wolves while fabricating and defending a spiritless wasteland of selfish pride, sensuality, immorality and materialistic greed in allegiance to a demon whose name is "Diversity." But let it be known that there is not the remotest possibility of their victory because the Most Holy Virgin has been interceding for humanity throughout salvation history with the full brilliance of Heaven's power, and She is not inclined to abandon us now. The Immaculate Mother has miraculously appeared the world over in unprecedented ways, particularly during the past 150 years, from the most notably approved shrines of Lourdes and Fatima to the worldwide phenomenon of Medjugorje, with a relentlessly welcome barrage of dozens of yet undecided intercessions occurring in this highly technological age of the last three decades. Why? Cardinal Ivan Dias, Prefect of the Congregation for the Evangelization of Peoples, stated the reason with righteous clarity during his December 8, 2007 homily at the opening of the 150th anniversary celebration of the Apparitions of Lourdes, France. He said:

After her apparitions at Lourdes, the Holy Virgin has not ceased to manifest her great maternal concerns for the fate of mankind in her several apparitions worldwide. She has everywhere asked for prayers and penance for the conversion of sinners, for she predicted the spiritual ruin of certain nations, the sufferings that the Holy Father would face, the general weakening of the Christian faith, the difficulties of the Church, the rise of the Antichrist and of his attempts to replace God in the life of men, attempts which, despite their instant success, would nevertheless be destined to fail. Here, at Lourdes, as everywhere in the world, the Virgin Mary is weaving an enormous web of her spiritual sons and daughters in the whole world in order to launch a strong offensive against the forces of the Evil one, to lock him up and thus prepare the final victory of her divine Son, Jesus Christ.

The Virgin Mary invites us once again today to be a part of her combat legion against the forces of evil. As a sign of our participation in her offensive, she demands, among other things, the conversion of the heart, a great devotion to the Holy Eucharist, the daily recitation of the rosary, unceasing prayer without hypocrisy, the acceptance of suffering for the salvation of the world. Those could seem to be small things, but they are powerful in the hands of God, to whom nothing is impossible. As the young David who, with a small stone and a sling, brought down the giant Goliath who came to meet him armed with a sword, a spear, and a shield (cf. 1 Sam 17,4-51), we will also, with the small beads of our rosary, be able to heroically face the assaults of our awesome adversary and defeat him.

The struggle between God and his enemy still takes place, even more so today than at the time of Bernadette, 150 years ago. Because the world finds itself stuck in the swamp of a secularism that wishes to create a world without God; of a relativism that stifles the permanent and unchangeable values of the Gospel; and of a religious indifference that remains undisturbed regarding the higher good of the matters of God and the Church. This battle makes innumerable victims within our families and among our young people. Some months before becoming Pope John Paul II, Cardinal Karol Woytjila said (November 9, 1976) "We are today before the greatest combat that mankind has ever seen. I do not believe that the Christian community has completely understood it. We are today before the final struggle between the Church and the Anti-Church, between the Gospel and the Anti-Gospel." One thing remains certain: the final victory belongs to God, and that will happen thanks to Mary, the Woman of Genesis and of the Apocalypse, who will fight at the head of the army of her sons and daughters against the enemy forces of Satan and will crush the head of the serpent.

And now, the Mother of God is addressing those who stand at a distance from Roman Catholicism under the title *Morning Star Over America*. From the heartland prairies of the United States, here in the capital of the State of Illinois, a couple furlongs away from the burial tomb of this nation's slain emancipator, the Matriarch of Creation has launched Her mystical oratory for the divine liberation of humanity from the decadence of this world, an epic battle that She is willing to engage for the unity of mankind beneath the Salvific Cross of Her Son. She has chosen this symbolic setting and these ominous days to declare the highest cause of God, the most profound, amendatory and everlasting petition for conversion short of divine chastisement. Through the power of Jesus Christ, She intends to set the world aflame in Love with the Divine Truth of Christianity because humankind would be lost to the fires of a desolate holocaust if She did not. For my part, the Holy Mother has delivered me from a state of unfocused devotion that I could not have brought to precision in a hundred years of the most severe penances had I to rely solely upon the spiritual guidance availed to me prior to Her miraculous appearance in my life. I am in obedient legion, heart, soul, mind and strength with millions who recognize the signs of the times and realize that America has become an arid wasteland of spiritual desolation in many regions of our once hallowed greatness. But now, the rains have arrived. Rivers of light will flow again, and floods of purification will inundate and overwhelm the sweltering arrogance of the wretched because the Virgin of Nazareth is powerful and unrelenting. She will not accept *no* for an answer to the question, *Will you become like Jesus and render God the honor of attending Me in Paradise?* Heaven's Queen is gracious and speaks softly, endearingly and tenderly, reluctant but not unwilling to offend, patient with the temperaments of Her lost children, and meek to the harsh effrontery leveled against Her Immaculate stature as the Matriarch of Humanity. Our Holy Mother is filled with reverence and gratitude for the growing remnant who have invoked their valorous faith and given their hearts unconditionally to Her guidance, burning-out their lives in sacrifice, prayer, dedication, and obedience to the Catholic Church like candles flickering in perpetual expectation of Jesus' Return. And, while Heaven wishes to show us its gentlest side through Her supernatural presence, the Third Person of the Most Holy Trinity wishes to be more frank to the masses of sinners who have habitually ignored the call that God is issuing forth through Her mystical venues. Heaven demands our change of heart and conformity with the Holy Gospel, both in this world and the next, while testifying that horrific chastisement and the fires of Hell await us if we do not retrace our wilful steps and ponder anew where we have gone so wrong in our relationship with God in this postmodern menagerie of secular relativism. We are being given the opportunity for our ultimate success as a collective humanity; a chance that has never been afforded to mankind in the history of the world on such a grand and revelatory scale. Everyone is being enjoined to accept the laurels of eternal victory and move to the side of history that will be the only record of mortal man which will be perpetuated into Eternity. The Heavenly Father has spoken peacefully and fluently to the ages through His Holy Spirit since the earthly life of the Lamb of God, but as we move ever closer to the inevitable Second Coming of the Messiah, He is being forced by the obstinance of mankind to assert His Dominion over Creation and speak more powerfully through every venue at His disposal, whether it be Nature, human events, the authoritative voice of Catholic Pontiffs, the miraculous intercession of angels and saints, or the salvific shockwaves raised by the appearances of the Queen of Heaven upon the Earth. God is rendering the veil ominously *translucent*, reserving the complete devastation of our capacity for faith for the striking moment of Jesus'

Glorious Return. The Virgin Mary's intercession is a revelatory prelude to the opening of that Eternity, just as Her life was the precedent to the timely Birth of our Salvation. The King of Creation is attempting to awaken a virtuous recognition in His redeeming overtures so that the farthest away may embrace His Divine Mercy and be saved before it is too late to greet His righteous Dominion beneath the forgiving canopy of His Sacred Blood. It serves not the cause of human sanctification or Redemption for those already possessing a virtuous and lively faith to say, *Well, I already believe, so I don't need these extraneous intercessions.* This may be technically correct according to the theological bent of the professional gnat strainers, but it is a gross act of negligence and dereliction of religious duty to possess the convalescent remedies bestowed by the Great Physician upon the ages and then deprive the lost who require the healing salve of miraculous grace to soothe their lacerated hearts. Most people do need miracles, and therefore Jesus worked them, and God grants them. And, we are the ones who live amongst their flourishing contemporary essence who recognize them for what they are. The Catholic Church is surely the grand city which possesses the seven salvific thoroughfares of redemptive grace from the Throne of God, but those graces are irrelevant to sinners who are too far away to notice that there is even a city to behold. If our Heavenly Father has been gracious enough to ignite a beacon for all humanity to see, has He not likewise called us to lift it high above the skyline as a beckoning invitation to every earthly wayfarer, inspiring them to come and walk our golden streets? What will the judgement of the ages be for those who are determined to keep the bushel basket of their faithless indifference over this light, especially when their sacred vocation is to remove these hampers and fill them with the Bread of Life to dispense to the multitudes who would see the Will of God for what it is: indisputable, immutable, and inevitable?

I must attest that intellectual arguments rarely impress Our Lady because they flourish in the realms of pride. She does not change our hearts with rational discussion or win us over with promises of unrivaled intelligence or unearned rewards. She promises instead that we will experience ill-winds, abuse, rejection and loneliness, but a joy that can be surpassed by no earthly satisfaction, and the experience of being triumphant at last. Cerebral themes rarely convert anyone because the human brain is too adept at defending its own temporal assets and interests. The transfiguration of man comes when the miraculous presence of God paralyzes worldly intellectualism, creating an epiphany of holy transcendence. This is the fertile ground of conversion that produces instances of spiritual transformation on a universal scale. Consider the biblical miracle of Pentecost when God's Divine flame came down upon the Church and the driving wind of the Holy Spirit roused the consciences of the citizens of Jerusalem. It was the action of the Apostles in cooperation with the supernatural impetus of the Holy Paraclete that effected the conversion of thousands in one day and sent transformation to the Earth like a bolt from a storm sets a forest ablaze. If the disciples of the Lord had not manifested evangelic action within their heroic faith and witnessed with the hearts of lions in response to the grace of God, those multitudes of curious people would have been scattered amidst the intellectual quandary of what had just taken place. The Apostles of the Messiah gave meaning and stability to the infant faith that had just been ignited by God's miraculous intervention. The people saw the resurrected faith of a body of convicted believers, and mass conversion was drawn forth from the tomb. And, that is what we are to imitate in response to His action flourishing from Our Lady's immaculate intercession. Sadly, few are the cases where trust in our Almighty Father has been so strong as to battle away the expedient excuses that have shorn faith of its unimaginable power. Is it not incumbent upon every person of Christian belief, especially those who have the responsibility for shepherding the Church, to call upon the courage of the original Apostles and witness openly and confidently to the miraculous intercession of the Woman Clothed with the Sun? Her gifts are like divine lightning strikes whose beatific luminescence can slice through any darkness generated by man. They rearrange priorities and sweep our intellects into realms that transcend our personal prejudices and disputes. They are the hope and guidance in the storm, just as those fiery braziers illuminate an entire countryside in the middle of the night. If Catholics refuse to invoke their faith and draw the converting grace of God the final distance through the veil, in effect rendering it fully *transparent* so that Heaven becomes a convincing and flourishing reality before the eyes of all humankind, surely we will collectively endure the horrific suffering and desolation that will be greeted upon our rejection. The faithless ones do not have a chance while floundering in the secular humanist swamp that surrounds us if they cannot draw strength from those who believe in something far more grand; and it is we who know the truth who will be held accountable for not carrying His mystical water to them. It is sorrowful to imagine what could have been accomplished in the last 90 years since the great Solar Miracle of Fatima, or even the previous 27 years of Our Lady's continuous presence in Medjugorje, had the collective body of our religious leaders invoked a more abundant faith in God, marshaled the evangelic witness of the Catholic Church, lifted our obedience to the Mother of Creation to saintly new heights, and attested to the miraculous to our last dying breath as did Peter, James, John and all the Saints. Indeed, why are not 1.3 billion Catholics praying the Rosary as our divine mandate and testament to the miraculous in response to our Queen's requests in all of Her supernatural appearances? We have more power at our disposal than could possibly be conceived by the enemies of Christianity. While some would claim that their stoical prudence serves as protection against the Catholic Church being deceived, I respectfully ask how anyone can believe the Church is protected if it is not gathered beneath the verifiable confirmations of the hand of God being bestowed by the Holy Spirit through the miraculous intercession of the Virgin of Nazareth? The Heavenly Father has an agenda in which He asks us to cooperate that has both mystical and material components. It is not enough that He is on our side; we must display our faith and testify to the world that we are on His side. It has never been possible to remain beneath the Mantle of the Mother of God and also reject the mystical guidance She articulates. The Church must subsist definitively beneath that canopy of Immaculate protection. I say to you, it is the stronghold of beatific grace and Salvation. Satan would sooner annihilate the universe before getting anywhere near God's children who are nestled beneath Her immaculate grace. There is no safer place in Creation! If we would unite beneath the Virgin Mary's mystical presence in the epicenter of the Roman Catholic Church, there would be no more enemies of Catholicism; the Triumph would be made manifest because those who oppose the Church would be conquered by the overwhelming composure of the Virgin's Immaculate Heart. The world would join us with a newfound ecstasy beneath the charism of Her Maternal Love, worshiping the Son of God and receiving His Sacred Body and Blood from the Altar of Sacrifice. Our Almighty Father asks us to trust in His salvific designs and effect this allegiance to the Matriarch of Creation with prayerful dispatch, because the Triumph of Her Most Immaculate Heart belongs to our generation the moment we come into alignment with His Will for this final age of man.

III. Abortion and the cultural extinction of America

My brother and I labor beneath the Mantle of Wisdom adorning the Queen of Heaven, humbly serving the Universal Truth which rests beyond the abridgement of men with an unyielding preeminence that is more secure than the trajectory of the Moon from the meddling arrogance of our greatest scientific minds. The intelligence of contemporary Americans cannot fathom the degree to which they are subject to God's absolute Kingship. The idea of a definitive truth by which we will ultimately be judged and a Supreme Being who owns us outright are abhorrent concepts to the mind-set of our secular American nation. Our consciences are pilloried every day with derision of all that portends our responsibility as human beings to any higher order than wandering beasts. For all the prevaricating, posturing and pontificating regarding civil rights by social appraisers, democracy is still nothing more than a grace-filled opportunity bestowed upon the ages. God has expectations for our spiritual greatness, but are we remotely directed toward fulfilling His hopes? With our penchant for trotting-out the accomplishments of the most gallant of our countrymen to obscure our guilt when confronted with our personal moral deficiencies, can any of our lame excuses mitigate the abominations that have been perpetrated, perpetuated and praised within our borders, especially legalized infanticide. Fifty million is the number. Hear me again, fifty million is the number. Each millennium has been replete with those whose hopes could never have towered high enough to envision the unfettered nature of our American nation. Yet, democracy is only the arena that was carved-out of a turbulent world by the hand of Divine Providence where a perfect union of humanity with its God could transpire. Still, this republic is not the ultimate goal or a success in itself. Can we look over our shoulders at the history that lies in our wake and truly say that the aspirations of God have been fulfilled at any time within our chronicled scrutiny? Our country was meant to be a sacred place of collegial possibility where the enfeebling forces that might inhibit our elevation toward social perfection would be vanquished by new generations conscientious enough to shepherd this nation's progeny past the travails that evil could attend upon them. But, what do we see most clearly? Our experience of freedom is being terminally despoiled by those who believe that liberty is their personal possession which grants them license to any debauchery that their putrid souls can wallow in for financial gain or the satiation of their passions. They are waging a fanatical revolution against virtue and reason in the name of some libertine irreverence to the flesh, while our culture is floundering in rebellion with multitudinous positions of societal influence seated with those who are unwilling to engage the moral conflict raging in our time. The scourge of infanticide has left the corridors of American history standing in solitude, their hallowed walls etched with a lesser witness than was ascribed for their pages. Our mystical porticos have been depopulated of their grandest definition, whistling a dirge past their columns that marks time to a divisive nightmare where our helpless progeny have been struck down at their pristine moment of conception with the indignant approval of our republic's elite. Among those fifty million souls purloined from their mothers' wombs were presidents and statesmen, journalists and jurists, doctors and scientists, poets and pastors, athletes and composers, soldiers and sailors, teachers and artists, and the ambassadors who would have possessed the diplomatic grace needed to mediate our disputes before they could abscess into war. America has been deprived of the inspiring mosaic of what each of these children of God would have grown, developed and matured to be. Lost to humanity are the flavorful triumphs, contributions, successes, discoveries, solutions, and stories that would have defined the American landscape with the tenor of virtuosity that our cultural palate will now never taste. All of this has been irretrievably forfeited amidst the diabolical demagoguery that tries to justify terminating human life whether it be a sparkling flash of brilliant purity ignited in a mother's womb or a soiled and forsaken cinder on death-row. The complete vitae of America originates at the moment of conception of its children, and so does our future. Fifty million human lives have been deprived their intended appearance upon this earthen stage in the fullness of their mortal glory; and the flourishing essence of their lives along with the reproductive, regenerative, expanding and magnifying consequences of their existence have been excised from the script of the mortal ages. The incalculable loss to humanity that we have so far reaped can be gleaned from any genealogical family tree by retreating five generations and reflecting on the cultural and human dimensions that would have been lost if anyone's great-great grandfather had been killed at birth, then multiply this horror by fifty million grandfathers and grandmothers. Abortion is effecting the cultural extermination of America, and the silence of our secular leaders is deafening because they are cowards whose souls have already been enslaved by Satan; their righteous essence purchased by the diabolic silver of worldly prestige. We are presently flush with venues where unprincipled opportunists speak authoritatively before the nation as though their hollow arguments contribute to the highest ideals of our democratic human family. The benevolent shackles of principled reason have been discarded, spawning an arrogant temporal relativism where every last strand of spiritual morality is questioned, soiled, and spate upon in defiance of the age-old demands of moral excellence, virtue, and self-restraint. This messenger of the Gospel is warning our country that it is damning itself one pundit, judge, entertainer and politician at a time. Moral relativism is an unprincipled deception from the mouth of the serpent of Eden, clad in the shimmering lie that it grants our liberation from sorrow and misfortune. Let it be known instead that suffering and sacrifice in union with Jesus Christ Crucified is our victory! Satan's illusion cannot withstand the confrontation with the Salvific Cross of the Lamb of God; therefore the eternal genius of the King of kings is not allowed its podium within realms coopted by evil. The greatest human person who ever walked this planet is hated now as much as He ever was, and He is preparing to respond by appearing again in His righteous glory. Christian religiosity is the sole repository of the honored sanctifying virtues which are learned nowhere else in our culture, save our faith-filled upbringing or the purifying agony of our missteps. Is the latter not an awful way to discover the beauty of life? The ethical brilliance within moral vision has been banished ex post facto from our civilized order and is being deprived from our children. Spiritually impoverished, they wander life seeking the meaning of existence, absent the guidance they should have inherited by universal mandate. They are taken hostage before the age of reason by the infernal forces of depravity, depression and death which are marketed to them by Satan's legions through the entertainment industry. Is sanity not appalled when people perpetrate immoral acts as validation of their freedom? Does liberty demand that one verbalize profane public utterances as evidence of a person's right to speak? Do such artists and entertainers actually accept the blasphemous credo that being radical provocateurs lifts their prestige to the realms of the never forgotten? Is freedom actually authenticated if one dives to where the devil would tremble? Verily I inquire, is something not lost when sewage is flushed into a crystal clear lake? Living beneath the civic mantle of the U.S.

Constitution is not a moral achievement, but what we accomplish from that station can be if we accept the wisdom of the Holy Spirit as the motivating force behind our excellence. It is both ethical and demanded by reason that we engage, subdue and extinguish through every righteous, lawful, and benevolent means available those actions which are an affront to the dignified nature of man. Logic demands that we wage this battle against human dignity. Every person who chooses to abuse the blessings of freedom to pollute our nation with any artifice that impugns holiness, sanctity, or our dignity as children of God is a domestic enemy of the union that we must defend ourselves against with our right hand raised and the other placed faithfully and heroically upon the New Testament of Jesus Christ. The long-hailed patriots whose blood soaked many a battlefield did not forfeit their lives defending our sacred shores so baneful social revolutionaries could abuse the entitlements that their heroic sacrifices secured. Neither did the Messiah die on the Cross so that evil would be allowed a voice in the outcome of the ages. Woe to those who wish to make a hedonistic wreck of this country, absent of all moral virtue. They will one day meet the Crucified Lamb, along with the signatories of our declaration of freedom and the battalions of warriors who line the hilltops of our American heritage. The cold stare of Valley Forge is the lesser gaze that will fall upon them as they are shaken-down by Divine Truth for an answer as to why such crimes against human sanctification were allowed to stain the garment that was sewn for our immortal destiny.

Our democratic culture is being led to desolation and damnation by those who believe there are no standards of spiritual and moral excellence to which they must adhere. A large segment of our population is living in harsh contradiction to the realization that God is uncompromising in His call for universal unity, human sanctity, and perfect love. For all the demagoguery regarding how elitist and alienating Christianity is portrayed to be, when has it ever been divisive to articulate the truth at any time in the history of the world? The division has always come through those who have rejected it, with the separation being between each soul and his eternal reward. I repeat, the Most Holy Trinity is not negotiating with the surly egos of men, neither does that Triune Divinity perceive a righteous rebuke of the self-possessed as a violation of charity. The Almighty Father has dictated the terms of eternal Redemption in the Crucifixion and Resurrection of His Son Jesus with mankind having been granted no voice, view or opinion regarding that universal act of forgiveness. There is only one option for the people of the Earth, and that is to comply with the mandates of the Messianic Gospel advanced to every generation by the Church founded upon the Rock of Saint Peter. Our pluralistic culture seems to demand that a potpourri of conflicting opinions must be embraced for the maintenance of peace, the elevation of personal dignity, and to assuage the vanities of men. There is neither peace nor dignity outside the boundaries of

God's tenets, and certainly no vanity exists inside them. The Messiah serves no pluralism and is definitely unafraid of men! What more could we do to Jesus that He has not already conquered? Therefore, He reveals His will and our destiny according to His own unilateral inclination. Christianity is the order of Eternal Life that is promised to us through our repentance, reorientation, acceptance, baptism, and devotion to the mind and intentions of the Almighty Father in the workings of the Church that His Son founded. Man has no say in that divine ordination without complete surrender to Christ; only then will God ratify and magnify our sanctified intentions, incorporating them into His Divine Will for the culmination of the world. We reside between the artistry of angels and the diablerie of demons; and if we continue to allow and defend the despicable, our country will plummet into an abyss from which it will not recover in a thousand years. Fifty million is the number.

IV. Virtue, the Commandments and evangelic grace

Effective communicators routinely develop a proficiency in the art of speaking to the masses, often learning to gracefully adjust their linguistic styles to comport with the sensibilities of the individual audiences they address. Notwithstanding the contemporary mechanics of communication, advancing the message of the Holy Gospel through the miraculous intercession of the Holy Spirit brings its own unique problems because its authoritative power engages our self-identity at its deepest levels; and rarely are our sentimental thoughts balanced sufficiently to peacefully assimilate newer perspectives after the world has formed us with its depleting artifices. Our sense of discernment is often intertwined too delicately with our perception of our essential dignity and our inflated estimation of our self-laudability; meaning if one's ideas are attacked, we invariably believe that our worth as a human being is also under assault. So, how is one to declare a Truth that is impervious to human opinion, indestructible by any force known to man, and by its very essence demanding of its rightful place of supremacy in a world that it already governs? If one speaks through a voice of self-abasing deference, the seriousness that God wishes to convey is often lost amidst the indignant pluralism fortressed by those harboring a dismissive arrogance. If the definitive work of the Holy Spirit is related respectful to the opinions of manifest reprobates, the realization that He has sent the Immaculate Virgin to petition for our conversion and that humanity is being placed on notice before the final ages is eclipsed by their argumentative babblement. And, if anyone rises with thundering conviction, the godless giggle and walk away when other indignant Christians dignify their cause and lambaste the messengers for being self-righteous and off-putting for reasons none other than they also refuse to heed the evangelistic voice of the Holy Spirit, take-up their own crosses, and follow Jesus into higher planes of sanctity. The natural inclination for self-defensive posturing when the human ego confronts foreign viewpoints routinely produces a state of rebellion against anything requiring due self-sacrifice, whether it be the surrendering of wealth, materials, or pseudo-sacrosanct attitudes. It is a wonder to behold how people will insist that others give wholesale deference to their errant opinions before they will consider the Truth of the Almighty whom they are forcing to grovel and negotiate with the musings of their sin. This inane tendency is the contemporary Passion and Crucifixion of Jesus Christ. The Resurrected Messiah will not subordinate Himself to any melange of worldliness again. Need one ask where Christian evangelization has gone in the midst of such flying flak and ornery opposition? It is cowering in the shadows, afraid of rousing the normal belligerent response from those who reject what the King of Creation desires of them. Our Savior says that He did not come to bring peace, but division. No one should misconstrue this to mean that we are authorized to cause fights at the drop of a hat. But, let us be truthful. When anyone reminds others how Jesus commands us to live, calls anyone else to conversion, or admonishes one to holier conduct, it is none other than the voice of the Holy Spirit speaking. And, when that evangelic grace is met by rebellion, shouting, manifest derision and violence, who caused the destruction of peace? Jesus said, "If they hated Me, they will hate you." Virtue and the fruits of the Holy Spirit do not reside in allowing others to forward lives of depravity, blasphemy and irreverence, but rather in conscientiously and firmly guiding our brothers and sisters to higher levels of sanctity, even if it requires drawing a line in the sand which you will not permit them to cross in your presence without a fight. Many people would alter their illicit conduct if they knew that they were going to be required to make an accounting for it. How many Catholic politicians would rethink their public support of abortion if they were told faithful Catholics would allow them to take the Most Blessed Sacrament only over their dead bodies? No one has the right before God to soil sanctity or pollute this sacred vineyard, no matter what they believe a venerable 230-year old piece of paper says. Happy the man who is found defending the gates with every spiritual weapon at his disposal upon the return of the Son of God. Creation does not belong to licentiousness or murderous evil.

Our Lady has allowed us to run the gauntlet of human opinion so that we could experience firsthand the oppressive manipulation that is inflicted upon anyone who bears the truthful message of the Messiah. The times that we have been called down or slandered by our fellow Christians for boldly speaking the truth of Our Lady's intercession are beyond numerous. One would think that the most aggressive opposition would come from those who refuse to accept that there is a God. Contemporary Catholics, in particular, are not accustomed to anyone defending the Faith that the Apostles bequeathed to them because too many have been indoctrinated in a false ecumenism by illicit opportunists who have contrived it to mean that all denominations claiming to be Christian are equally valid and additionally that there are an infinite number of paths to our perfect union with God outside the downpour of Jesus' Sacred Blood. For the record, they aren't and there isn't. Pope John Paul II and Pope Benedict XVI in succession have definitively refuted these ideas in their response to the theology of religious pluralism in the papal encyclical "Dominus Jesu." Nonetheless, the Blessed Virgin has taken us into the jaws of fear and asked us to resolutely engage the backlashing against our faith, oftentimes by those closest to us, in order to bring the realization to everyone that it is better to wage the moral battle for the Truth than slink off into compromise to preserve a false peace. Our Lady has taught us to be unafraid of what human beings may say about us or do to us, and care instead only whether we are paying homage to the Cross and would be judged worthy of being placed upon it for the same reason that the Lamb of God died there. Christians must never allow evil to selfishly dominate any arena where we are present. Bring the Light of Christ to bear upon every situation with all the grace the Holy Spirit dispenses at that moment, remembering prudently that there is a difference between being surrounded by darkness which is a result of naivete and that which is rearing its arrogant sophisticated head. My point could be no better illuminated than in a news article that appeared while I wrote these words. There was an elderly Catholic priest who was faithfully and responsibly articulating the teaching of the Church regarding human sexuality from his pulpit when two lesbian parishioners stood, interrupted the Holy Mass, and ridiculed him during his homily. The event provoked the removal of the priest from the parish by his bishop. What message was sent to every person of faith by this incident? All Satan has to do to extinguish Christian evangelization is throw a fit when confronted with the Truth, and another disciple of the Lord will be spiritually crucified. Does anyone really believe that imitating those who killed Jesus is the most productive way to enhance the propagation of His message throughout the world? There is no doubt that the Apostles were tempted with this same inordinate trepidation when Jesus aggressively addressed the immorality of His day, believing it was no way for a prince of peace to go about spreading a message of forgiveness and mercy. The priest who courageously spoke the truth of our sexuality should have been hailed by his parishioners while the ushers should have escorted the manifest blasphemers into the streets until they converted their hearts and humbled themselves enough to reenter full communion with the Church through the Sacrament of Reconciliation. It is an act of mercy to disallow such damning conduct, while never being cowed from spreading the Gospel, even from the housetops. These indignant and calculated affronts to the hallowed sanctity of the Catholic Church must be engaged and brought swiftly to an end. Jesus removed less when He drove the money changers from the Temple with epitaphs of white-washed tombs. Our Faith is something we surrender to with all our being in sacrificial love, leaving our old selves and donning the mantle of Christ. We convert ourselves into union with the Church's infinite well of sanctity through the Sacraments, rather than demanding it declare us acceptable saints while remaining manifestly obstinate in our unrepentant sins. Therefore, I say, defend the Catholic Church with the power of the Gospel, and let them drag you in chains before the courts of human opinion. It is then that the Holy Spirit will give voice and volume to your testimony to declare to the world what you are defending.

While it is easy for many people to lament helplessly over the sinister individuals who seem to be such an impediment to the procession of sanctity, we feel merciful pity for them, knowing that their influence is the most fleeting illusion. They truly do not know what they are doing. Those who oppose the tenets and disciplines of Roman Catholic Christianity clearly do not have the transcending vision that would convince them as to just how blind, weak and vulnerable they truly are. The Universal Truth of Roman Catholicism is readily apparent before the purview of every person in our age whether they are willing to see it or not. It has been revealed with laser-precision clarity on a worldwide scale upon the passing of Pope John Paul II, justified in the elevation of a theological giant to the Papacy as his successor, and providentially validated through the numerous miraculous intercessions of the Blessed Virgin Mary across Catholic culture. Our Lady has hailed each Vicar of Christ and the Catholic Church in Her appearances, knowing fully whom they have been for the ages, having accompanied each Roman Pontiff with certitude as he brought the true Light before men. Through many events, the Original Apostolic Church is being glorified and elevated as a sign of the imminent Return of Jesus Christ in Glory which is approaching with prophetic thunder. But sadly, the Church is also being maligned, impugned, slandered, and hated by those who serve the Antichrist. Soon, each of these people will realize that the Truth of God is not something that is deferential to them. It is a monolithic, impenetrable giant of verity that will crush the pride of men at the instant the veil is pulled back between time and Eternity. I have experienced dimensions of this finality, and my heart has been catapulted into ecstasy knowing that I am nestled within the Sacred Heart of Christ from my position as a common parishioner within the bosom of the Catholic Church. I have also experienced great dread for those who vocally make themselves adversaries of the Church, especially secular progressives who attack Catholicism with insane fanaticism and outlandish impunity, and particularly those who are holding the noose of the sexual abuse scandal around the neck of the Magisterium. Our Lady knows that at present, far too many of them will stand horrified upon realizing just how shabbily they are dressed for the Banquet of the Living. They will hate themselves with the same fervor that they detested the Original Apostolic Church and those whom the Holy Spirit charged to lead it. They will judge themselves according to the same measure that they have maligned the Mystical Body of Christ. Their souls will scream in repulsion of themselves, and their consciences will drive them to the darkest realms to avoid the stare of the Sacred Lamb whom they crucified. They should be advised that this gaze is the thinnest of veils away from them at this very moment. Unbeknownst to their pride, their lives hang in a balance being held by the King of Creation who is mercifully restraining their self-annihilation a hairs-breadth below their awareness, granting them additional moments of life to come to conversion of their own free will because He loves them. He restrains His glorious triumph for the same reason that He did not descend from the Cross in response to those who jeered Him to prove His power. There will be no excuses that matter on the day of judgement because each of us will know that an infinite allotment of grace and an ample amount of time was dispensed to us for our conversion and sanctification. If we do not respond, we will recognize that we dismissed the call of God as irrelevant to us through the direct act of our will. Nevertheless, we are asked to surrender nary a soul to the darkness until this age of Divine Mercy is culminated.

It is our humble duty to live with the grace and love that we have received from the Immaculate Heart of the Mother of God. We do in fact love our enemies. It is characterized and manifested in our hope that all see the ultimate success of their lives in the peace of God. Every living soul should both desire and be given the opportunity to walk this Earth with the bearing of kings and queens. This is what we want for our brothers and sisters, and it is why we fight for the highest truths of revelation. Jesus and His Mother love us beyond the combined affections of mankind, and they challenge us to engage with sacrificial courage any impediment to the triumph of divinity where others with fainter hearts would compromise. Christians are commanded to invoke righteousness and dislodge with angelic veracity any obstacle attempting to veil the beatific vision of the unseen dispensed to us from the Hosts of Heaven. There is no hint of audacity in this, but rather a prodigious allegiance to the Mighty One who is Righteous and True, and who died on the Cross that we might experience the beatitude of Heaven's glory. Our evangelistic vocation has its precedent in the lives of every Saint, many who struggled and suffered amidst far greater adversity and torment than we might ever witness in our contemporary culture. It is the prayers of our triumphant predecessors that carry us aloft toward a new springtime that Our Lady is tilling to a blossom within our midst during these closing moments of human existence. I am convinced that nearly anyone in our position would immediately comply with every intention set forth by the Most Blessed Virgin, many doing so in more perfect ways than our faith has generated. There has never been any difference between my brother and me and any of those confirmed by the Holy Spirit through the maturing Sacrament of the Church. I am heartened by the Christian faith that is displayed upon every continent, and am thankful for the heartfelt sacrifices contributed by each and all. Yet, despite such good works on behalf of the Son of God in fulfillment of His Gospel, we must ask ourselves, why does the world remain in such dire straits among the nations? Why is the faith which Christians profess held in such contempt? Why is there such disunity? Why is spiritless relativism becoming so prevalent? Why do so many Christians no longer feel humbled and thankful at the opportunity to receive the true Bread of Life that Jesus offers? And, why is the miraculous intercession of the Woman Clothed with the Sun being routinely ignored? I am ever conscious that people of many differing dispositions will ultimately read our books and unleash monsoons of personal criticism against what has been related between their covers. I urge them to remember that the Queen of Heaven has never asked sinners to critique Her work, but rather for us to absolutely comply with what they reveal. It is never Our Lady's intention to offend when She speaks, but She is courageous enough to engage any topic, no matter the response, because She knows that Her children have already been assaulted too egregiously by the enemies of human salvation. She will no more back down to spiritual toddlers than any mother would retreat from a three year old. You see, the earthly playpen is being dominated by bullies, biters and hair-pullers. Cantankerous immoral anarchy has ensued from Her perspective, and She cares little about the infantile platitudes of those who believe they will never be held accountable to the authoritative Kingship of Her Son. There is no future for humanity outside the beatific doctrines of Christianity because sinners will descend into nightmares and horrors as they reject the noble course of holy virtue, retreat into worldliness according to their whimsical passions and diabolical ideologies, and fail to preserve the inherent dignity of every person. Therefore, She will not step back one micron from the Truth, even if the entire body of mankind collectively shakes its fist at Her in one blasphemous moment and chooses to wage war against the Roman Catholic Church for having the audacity to declare Her the most blessed among women. Even then, Our Lady would control the winds of war to our favor and see us to peace once again where everyone would have a renewed appreciation for why we should have listened to Her pleading from the beginning.

V. To whom much is given, much is required

Our existence on Earth in the flesh is a precious commodity of limited duration. It is a time of preparation for the moment of Truth when we will be exposed to the blast furnace of Infinite Love beyond the veil of time. Some would retort by asking how this could possibly be an uncomfortable encounter. I would respond by asking everyone to imagine walking through a wooded valley and happening upon an immense concrete wall that disappears past the treetops. You have no idea what it is, but realize immediately that you cannot go over or around it. Upon noticing a small stream of water trickling from a tiny crack in the edifice, you stretch out your hands and allow its cool refreshment to wash the dirt from your palms as it soothes the scratches you acquired from your travels. Now, imagine hearing someone call you from a nearby cliff, petitioning you to join them at their higher position because you are about to get wet. You look back at your hands in befuddlement, wondering how getting wet could be so urgent. In fact, you believe that it is rather refreshing. Then, the dam bursts and a wall of water hundreds of feet high crashes down upon you. It is the same liquid that soothed your hands moments before, but is now gushing upon you in a magnitude that is beyond your imagination. Humanity does not understand what lies beyond the veil of death. But, Our Lady does, and so does Jesus who died because it was so important for us to become holy people in order to greet that moment! Shadrach, Meshach, and Abednego offer us a prophetic vision. *(Daniel 3)* We will judge ourselves while being consumed by an unyielding and unrelenting perfection that has already been defined in the bedrock of Creation and unveiled as a reality within the history of men through Jesus' Life, Death, and Resurrection. Only this perfection is granted entrance into Paradise; there is nothing soiled there. That should be a sobering thought that can place our materials in their proper perspective. Our possessions are no more than a pile of dirt if they are not surrendered as a charitable tool throughout our existence, benefitting the least among us. Yet, we watch people destroy their families, friendships, cities, and countries to gain these decaying artifacts solely for themselves. What does it profit a man to gain the whole world and suffer the loss of his soul? How will the rich judge themselves when faced with the desolate family of man they ignored their whole life long?

Our work consists of helping everyone realize that God communicates with His children in many prolific ways within the realms of faith and beyond our ability or authority to deride Him for doing so, and usually in manners that call for the sacrifice of our personal druthers. Faith, and the Truth revealed through it, are very mysterious things. Truth is impenetrable and protected by the walls of faith because one must have the transcendent quality of belief in the unseen elements of our existence to get anywhere near the Truth. Yet, the Truth resides before us in elegance and certitude, open and apparent, reaching into the world at every point on the globe and at every moment in time, beckoning humanity to rise above the mundane servings of sin and realize with each morning sunrise the shimmering essence of our noble identity which lies within the glory and dignity of the Most Blessed Trinity. What then causes so many to misconstrue their own selfish interior babbling as the voice of God? What provokes us to deny an immediate conversion into compliance with the provisions set forth by His Will? Why do so few listen to the words of those who are bearing the unadulterated Truth to mankind? Is it because we do not like what we are being asked to believe and do? Do we love the fallacy of the present more than the facts of the future? Our fallen nature is characterized by the prideful obsession to "decide," and an attitude that proclaims, "I am master of my life, and no one has the authority to require anything of me!" Well, Our Lady has news for us. The Master of Creation has set requirements for the eternal salvation of men. The prescription for the Redemption of Humankind has been decided—by God! For my part, I simply wish that I could inspire every person on the planet to be silent for a moment, irradiate their souls with gentle good will, consider their place in the unfolding of the universe, embrace humanity as one family, and recognize the miraculous intercession of the Virgin Mary throughout the world as God's authentic sign for the reconciliation of men within Christianity in mystical preparation for the Second Coming of the Son of Man. The God of our fathers is calling from the core of the universe to the center of our being through the voice of His Immaculate Mother for His children to seek reconciliation with the heavens. Our hearts would be filled with goodness if we would reach for those new heights. We are all proceeding toward the same end that is none other than a new beginning, unfettered by human sin, partisan division, prideful arrogance, and material gain. Oh, that the thinking would stop, and the praying would start! If only our useless attitudes and haughty opinions would extinguish themselves, our childlike hearts could emerge from their hiding, and then Our Lady could transform the Earth into a paradisial garden that would reflect the glorious landscape of Paradise before its next rotation. Our difficulties lie in that we are not fully cognizant of humanity's indistinguishable nature with the Father, that the Truth is a Person whose name is Jesus Christ, or that mankind's King has definitive commands regarding the vineyard He owns. When we fail to realize there is a classical, knowable, universal structure of Truth ordained from outside our physical existence, we invariably refuse to accept that anyone may have knowledge of it or be in union with it. Thereafter, in the absence of our collective recognition of the immutable truths governing Creation, fallible human opinions are allowed to compete on levels of credibility to which they are not entitled. Hence, we become closed-off from accepting any person the Holy Spirit might use to deliver sanctifying clarity about God's wishes. Our positing of reality becomes nothing more than a battle of finite opinions whose circumference and scope never transcend into the realms of eternal "livingness" where we discover the ultimate reason for our being brought from nothingness by our God. The Most Blessed Trinity has never been afraid to engage humanity, in spite of the evidence that too many people revel in their role as modern day renegades shouting, "Show us a miracle, then we will believe." And, even though the Heavenly Father realizes that they have the cart of their arrogance before the stallions of His genius, He responds nonetheless with Divine Mercy and allows the appearances and messages from His Immaculate Queen, accompanied by numerous confirming supernatural signs such as the prophesied Great Solar Miracle of Fatima in 1917 witnessed by 70,000 people, but seemingly to no avail for those who had no intention of believing anyway. You see, God usually requires faith to be preserved even through His miraculous acts because faith is the definitive requisite for mercy, while the faithless will meet the full brunt of His Divine Justice. Therefore, we must begin by trusting God—not that He will affirm us in our whims, but that He will assist us with every grace, power and gift so that our faith might be strengthened in the direction of His Holy Will. Our Lady's intercession is His most genteel effusion of divinity inundating the Earth from the highest vault of Heaven, creating purified messengers and evangelists by the thousands. Unknown people with no theological credibility have begun to experience the beatitude of Heaven on plateaus which supercede intellectualism and are thereafter witnessing in the simple Spirit of the Gospel writers. Saint Thomas Aquinas, himself, experienced this transformation at the close of his life at the pinnacle of his intellectual prowess. He exhausted his mortality in the honorable vocation of writing voluminously as a philosopher and theologian in the thirteenth-century. And yet, on December 6, 1273, he encountered the unbounded Love of God in a beatific vision while offering the Holy Sacrifice of the Mass, after which he left unfinished his greatest work, the *Summa Theologiae*, saying *"I cannot go on.... All that I have written seems to me like so much straw compared to what I have seen and what has been revealed to me."* He died three months later, on March 7, 1274, a spiritual giant who entered Paradise with the disposition of a child, unencumbered by the cerebral weight which he was forced to bear so that the pagan intellects throughout the ages could find a path to Christianity marked out for them. He laid low every stumbling block that they ever created. Even so, the foregathering with the supernatural power of God overwhelmed the giant intellect of this Doctor of the Church. Multitudes recoil upon being asked to believe these edifying mystical occurrences because they awaken the reality that Truth exists beyond the mortal constraints of our own intellectual reason. Saints such as Thomas have maintained that *"...faith is higher than reason, but reason trumps all else."* Therefore, is it not reasonable to immerse ourselves in the genius flowing from heavenly revelation, especially when it is the Queen of Paradise from whom it is emanating? Relativism takes a broadside bashing by the miraculous intercession of the Holy Spirit in whatever form God chooses to reveal Himself; and many a hell-bent agenda are impeded through the immutable call of the conscience before the august majesty of His Dominion. Quite frankly, there are far too many speaking for the Savior of the world who do not have the foggiest notion about who He is, what He wants, or why He died; and as long as they wantonly evade the mystical reasoning behind Roman Catholic Christianity, they continue to hoodwink everyone they encounter into believing that no one possesses knowledge of the definitive Truth revealed by God, leaving open the lie that anyone can determine their personal version for themselves, no matter how contradictory it may be to the Church instituted by Christ. And, while enacting this diabolical charade, the highest reality of our collective human nature is obscured from their spiritual senses. When one states that no ultimate authority exists to which we must submit, all anyone has to do is gather a few initials after his name, throw in a speculative pretense as an option, and the flock will be divided. Add a few more complex intellectual alternatives, and they will be completely scattered. This egotistical cafeteria phenomenon of intellectualism has caused distinctions, distrust, division, disunity and destruction in every generation. One need look no further than the competing and conflicting schools of religious thought over the past 500 years to see the degradation and distortion of the message of Christ. What did Saint Thomas Aquinas see in his moments of divine light that they have not? Is it any wonder that such a large cross-section of the populace is skeptical of institutionalized religion when its hallowed credibility has been scattered to the winds by innumerable individuals with their own partisan religious agendas? Do our hearts not testify instead that the Truth is found in unity and a concise vision of reality that comports with reason, goodness, tradition, and revelation? Indeed, how does the verifiable miraculous intercession of the Virgin Mary comport with our personal vision of God's divine will for us? Everyone can envision what an awesome gift that universal Christian unity would be for the world today, but there seems to be too many egos, both inside and outside the Church, that have to be satisfied to ever achieve it. And, it can be argued that it is not those in the pews who are causing the separatism because the vast majority are simple children who will humbly follow where they are led. It is those who ignore the wisdom and perspective in the miraculous graces of God that inordinately stake their pastoral careers within the prideful autonomy of their own disparate theological ideologies. This insipid dispersal is a disdainful affront to the Gospel of Jesus Christ, and these men and women will someday answer to God for their ego-stricken misdeeds. Plainly, this is why Our Lady passionately petitions for our humility. She honestly and meekly asks who we think we are? A forest of thought has been created and cultivated that should never have been planted where it could becloud the simple spiritual expanse which reveals to us the countenance of God's glorious face. We must cut down our intellectualism and vaporize the battery of arguments lacking divine reason, and allow ourselves to be lifted by the revelations of the Holy Spirit above what separates us. Not every argument has to be settled if we decide preemptively to purge from our minds what we were arguing about. All theological difficulties do not have to be reconciled before one embraces the Most Blessed Sacrament of the Altar and unites as one body at one table of faith. It simply requires an invocation of faith and a profession of allegiance and obedience to the Faith of the Vicar of Christ. There is so much negotiation, very little faith, and almost no loving abandonment or obedience. This is why God has allowed the Virgin Mary to intervene in a way that still requires humanity to collectively summon belief from the deep recesses of its soul. Our Lord is transcending our irrelevant deliberations and stewing dialogue with His miraculous grace, and He is unilaterally calling the world to solidarity beneath the maternal guidance of His Immaculate Mother. Blessed are those who respond, for they will be granted heavenly protection during the coming storm. For those who believe this is not biblical, they should deeply contemplate and pray over the significance of these times and the relevance of the sign that appeared in the heavens in the twelfth chapter of the Book of Revelation, a Woman Clothed with the Sun. While the last book of the Bible is of deep symbolic imagery that most decipherers of Scripture are haphazardly stumbling over, is it truly beyond consideration that the explosion of Marian apparitions in our contemporary age may be the redemptive portent that is fulfilling the prophecies in the writings of the Apocalypse? I declare that it is She who is giving humanity a reason to believe in the imminent Return of the Son of Man and the simple answers to the only questions that will ever matter. Her intentions are not to satisfy the 'whys' that people can generate, but to elicit an 'I will' and 'I do' from each of Her children. We are headed for a bath whether we like it or not; and it is evident that some will be dragged into these purifying waters by their ears. Our Lady says that we will hear the kicking and the screaming, the splashing and the spitting of water, but humanity entire will become cleansed before we appear before the Son of God. The spiritual darkness that has been inflicted upon masses of people by false teachers is approaching its eradication through the miraculous light that God is placing on a lamp stand before the nations. The Most Blessed Virgin's pedestal is coming to full bloom in the Triumph of Her Immaculate Heart. I would hope that no one would refuse to hear me out or consider the supporting evidence put forth in Our Lady's messages simply because I am called to unveil a picture that is not altogether rosy. There are better fortunes for humanity than to be a prodigal child living in a muddy pigsty, enticing everyone to also leave the Father's house and join them in the mud. Sinners immersed in the materials of this world have yet to don their robes for the Feast of Paradise, and are desperately in need of conversion.

All that weighs upon me now is summed up in the declaration: To whom much is given, much is required. When the Truth has been confirmed in miraculous dimensions of experiential grace to any age of humankind, it rises with supremacy above the morass of mediocrity, complacency and compromise, elevating itself beyond the competition and debate, and advancing a moral supersession over the bantering opinions of feckless men. Wisdom refuses to soil itself attempting to either untangle or satisfy the theological problems generated by intellectual gymnastics. How many complications which arrogantly demand an answer should never have been conceived! How much unity has been dissipated by haughty egos thrusting illicit hubris into the decisional vat of human attention! Our Lady wants to know the number of human falsehoods which have previously suffered defeat at the hands of moral reason that have been irresponsibly resurrected and given venue, voice, and pen. So much is made of the statement that the Truth will set you free. Before Our Lady made Her presence seeable to me, I believed I understood what that meant, but I was nonetheless confused by the conflict among so many people with disparate opinions about what denotes their freedom. I know now without doubt that no one has been emancipated from the darkness who rejects the liberating vision of the Roman Catholic Church. They are factually incarcerated in some measurement of error whether they recognize it or not. Our Holy Mother's intercession polished this profound revelation in my soul. If worldliness is a fog obscuring our vision of Paradise, Her grace is the sunlight which is burning it away.

VI. The Primacy of the Roman Catholic Church

By God's divine ordination, my being bears the confirmation that the Woman who birthed the Savior into the world; the same Mother whom humanity entire recognizes on Christmas eve, is alive and has been mystically engaging our age in an effort to dispense the unequivocal wisdom of Heaven to a seemingly-faithless humanity languishing in the consequences of its own misdeeds. The Immaculate Virgin who knelt before the Manger, the undefiled Mother who fled into Egypt, the compassionate intercessor who petitioned at the wedding feast of Canaan, the sorrowful Co-Redemptrix who endured the horrific Sacrifice of Her Son on Mount Calvary, the steadfast Matriarch of the Apostles who was present at Pentecost is clarifying the Truth about Her own life and that of Her beatific Son. Humanity is presently experiencing a concrete connection with redemption history in Her supernatural appearances throughout the world. She is igniting devotion to the Catholic Church to full flame, making it more important than the air we breathe. The body of work advancing under the flying banner, *Morning Star Over America*, is a testimonial to an "experiential" charism which offers the transfiguration of personal belief and simple faith into an all-consuming conviction that transcends the intellectual opinions of postmodern relativists, the protestations of religious pluralists, and the actions of those who would obliterate faith in Jesus Christ from the face of the Earth if they could muster the power. It matters not whether our physical brains can recall the pastoral perspectives of all the reverend theologians and Popes, Doctors and evangelists of the Church from former ages; we must concur with the panoramic scenery of their ethical brilliance nonetheless. Through Our Lady's immaculate grace, we gain the sense of the Holy Spirit to recognize wholeheartedly what their enlightened hearts were set upon through the finite adequacy of earthly languages that know not how to speak to the infinite scope of the celestial heights. The Virgin Mary asks us to realize that our penitential allegiance lays open our hearts to the same Deific Love that each of these great Saints was serving in their attempts to unveil the spiritual realities of Creation to a lost world of mortals who could not conceive that they were children of an Omnipotent God. Our mutual admiration for the Saints and the acclamation of their sacrifices and angelic wisdom come from our spontaneous gratitude for the faith they advanced into our time, as we petition them to assist us in succeeding for future generations with the same honorable integrity by which they secured the triumph for ours, and all for the Glory of God. These giants of faith gave their lives defending the Truth that the Most Blessed Trinity implanted into Creation with the Blood of Jesus Christ, knowing that anything, however benign, either within or without, that would instigate separation from the original Apostolic lineage or soil the professions of their testament before men was either a work of ruthless disregard for the truth or outright evil, no matter how inadvertent it may be. Our Lord prayed that we may be one; and He instituted and has nurtured a Church into the present age where that grace could be sustained by the Bread of Life which is His own Flesh and Blood given for the life of the world. Heaven is united in one mind and one vision; and since God's Kingdom is to be manifested in its fullness on Earth as it is in Heaven, humanity entire must unite within the Roman Catholic Church under the Vicar of Christ. The salvific wholesomeness of humankind will occur no other place during the age of mortal man. Many would counsel me to gloss over this declaration of supreme Catholic universality and remain inattentive to the roots of our divisions, especially with those who presently cannot conceive surrendering their fealty to the Roman Pontiff. However, our Holy Mother is poised to mature any perception at odds with the Truth, and She has instructed me to courageously address the catastrophic errors that have separated Christian brothers and sisters one from another. Therefore, I broach many winnowing subjects so that everyone may have the opportunity to receive the infinite grace offered by the Almighty Father through the Most Blessed Sacrament from the Catholic Altar before they see Him face-to-Face, and furthermore, so that no one will ever be able to say that they were not told when on Judgement Day they are forced to cough-up a response to the question, ***What kept you from accepting the miraculous guidance of My Immaculate Mother?***

Please let it be understood that I recognize and admire the loving hearts and faithful dedication that each of my non-Catholic brothers and sisters portrays. Some might claim this hard to believe since I am required to speak so bluntly about the substance of higher realities, ones which they have been enculturated to see as subjects for their malleable personal interpretation. It is not a difficult concept to accept that we must encourage people who are on a ladder to ascend to its next higher rung while concurrently being ever thankful that they at least have their feet affixed to one of them. While peace and the perfection of every virtue reside at the pinnacle of our ascension, there are too many presumptuous individuals who believe they are already standing on their tippy-toes at its highest elevation instead of realizing they are squatting on their haunches toying with the footpads at its base. We must remember that it is a flawed perspective to assume that the people who love us the most are the ones who do nothing more than reaffirm everything we happen to believe. This is why the Catholic Church recognizes the Spiritual Works of Mercy, in particular that we instruct the ignorant, counsel the doubtful, and admonish the sinner. Every mature Christian recognizes that the Holy Spirit is at work in each person who is breathing the air of this world. The proof for those reading this book are the words flowing in front of your eyes. While no one is exiled from the purview of the Light of Divine Truth, nothing but our sacrificial conformity with the Wisdom of Jesus Christ impregnates our lives with divine meaning and sanctifies our existence with heavenly perfection. Even so, our love and support for all that anyone has accomplished in the realms of virtue through the venues they have been offered is authentic and immense. Yet, Our Lady asks each and all to humbly realize that the human ego is the enemy of our redemption. It is fundamentally at odds with God's wishes to lift the family of man ever higher, to the ultimate plateau of unified sanctity in fulfillment of His original plan. No worldly man can take us into the romantic sphere of Heaven's indivisible love; it is rather God's divine action that is accomplishing this final congregation of humanity beneath His Holy Cross, a divine ordination which is presently being manifested through the miraculous intercession of the Queen of Heaven. So, let he who feels the smallest twinge of conscience believe anew and accept now! The Immaculate Virgin is an unabashed apologist for the Roman Catholic Church because it alone bears the highest and most concise revelation of the Father through Jesus Christ. It alone possesses and emanates the unity, sanctity, power, scope and dominion directly from the Sacred Heart of Jesus Christ to every age of man. Notwithstanding the personal mistakes that some of Her Catholic children have made throughout the centuries, whether they be the venial missteps of the least in the flock or the thrice-denial of the first Pope, Our Lady is the most ardent defender of the Church that Her Son instituted on Earth. She asks those who find it difficult, or maybe think it impossible, to accept the cleansing disciplines of the Original

Apostolic Church to forgive their brothers and sisters as Christ will someday forgive them within the penitential Sacrament, remembering that their brethren's errors were only temporary stumbles which have been forgiven and redacted from the history that God is recording; infractions they suffered while attempting to serve a perfection that none of them had yet attained in a world that was clawing and condemning the Truth with every heathen breath. If one can make a partial analogy, consider the United States of America in the ethereal essence of what it is, the values she holds, the liberty that she secures, and the longevity she hopes to sustain. There have been miserably corrupt presidents; and the politicians of this day are wallowing in their most diabolic moments while refusing to stop the scourge of infanticide; yet none of them have degraded, hampered, or diminished the essence of America. The ideals of this republic are embodied within the hopes, vision, faith and legacy of every honorable American who has ever labored to sustain its communal grace. This body of noble humanity underpins our identity, just as the entire two-thousand year strong Communion of Saints upholds the grace and dignity of the Roman Catholic Church. That is why we revere the Saints. Our nation's declarations of independence and governance are thus far the pinnacle achievement of secular governing unity which has yet to be overthrown either from within or without. No person can legitimately come forward and say that they hate America in toto simply because a certain segment of their countrymen have failed to live up to its ideals. Nor can they coopt the Constitution, delete its amendments, keep only the Preamble, and claim they represent the authentic United States within our borders according to the designs and traditions of its original framers. They would all be seen as separatists, truly unAmerican, and likewise be considered truly disproportional in their judgement and absent the truest sense of social justice. It is much the same in regards to the Roman Catholic Church. Two thousand years is a long time, a length of time that is truly incomprehensible to the fleeting awareness of our modern psyche. Yet, there are demagogues who have selected moments of no more duration than the flash of a camera bulb who disingenuously proclaim through every medium they can coopt that these departures of Christians from the highest grace generally characterize the expanse of Catholicism, rendering it corrupt, and thereby requiring the forfeiture of its primacy and supremacy in the annals of history and the eyes of God. The Blessed Virgin Mary believes that each of these people would better find their own perfection before the eyes of divine scrutiny before throwing stones so large. During the expanse of twenty-four thousand months of human corruption, weakness and fallibility, surely anyone would expect instances where the flesh has overwhelmed the spirit, especially in the face of so much generational oppression and murderous evil. But, the essence of perfection that Jesus instilled within the Church that He founded is still present, living, thriving, and unending. This Truth lives within the Papacy, Dogma, Traditions, Magisterium, and the bosom of faithful Roman Catholics, all encompassing past and present; resting beyond the heavenly firmament and the defilement of the sin of history's Judases in union with the sacrificial nature of those who face the contemporary onslaught against Jesus Christ in our day. Therefore, it is a malfeasant act of outright malevolence and a mortal sin against justice to summarily indict the Roman Catholic Church for the misjudgements of its members at any particular moment through the ages. They were simply people who neglected to grasp perfection in their time in much the same ways that each of us is failing to appreciate it in ours. Our Lady asks each of Her children to weep instead for their own sins, and thereafter lay them before a Catholic priest in a confessional in order to receive Divine Absolution; then we will begin to see clearly enough to accept our responsibilities to engage Creation to its higher states of grace. Further, those who would have an inclination to spontaneously deride Catholicism for any historical actions should ponder whether the Church's staunch defense of itself and its people through the last 2,000 years has actually been the stately vindicating work of the Holy Spirit guaranteeing that Hell shall never prevail against what God has established on Earth for the Salvation of men. Can anyone be taken seriously who denies the right of the Messiah to both absolve His people and defend His Original Church; a right that any king in history has claimed in defense of his kingdom? The mystically-guided St. Joan of Arc is historical proof that God will ultimately cut down unrepentant evil in its tracks in defense of His Church and the dignity of His faithful children. The King of Calvary is alive again! But, oh how many wish that the Catholic Church was not standing in their way, bearing its tenets of human excellence aloft! We see this so clearly in our modern secular culture which seethes with contempt for everything the Church of Rome stands for. Men who have been possessed with self-serving pride and sinister intentions have always wished that the Holy See would speak with no more than a whisper so they could spread their self-serving worldly empires with unchecked volume and domination. Materialistic capitalism will share in the demise of atheistic communism; and by way of the same Immaculate Virgin Mary who took down the Union of Soviet Socialist Republics through Her Polish son during the Pontificate of John Paul the Great. The dictatorship of relativism is destined to collapse before the transcendent certainty of Our Lady's ongoing miraculous intercession.

So, what is the lot of those who have died before uniting themselves with the Catholic Church, and thus deprived themselves of the Bread from the Altar of which Jesus spoke, "...Unless you eat the flesh of the Son of Man and drink His Blood, you will not have life in you...?" *John 6:48-58.* Is it that they are all damned? Perish the thought, instead! This intellectual dilemma is one of the primary sources of rejection of Christianity, particularly the Catholic Church, because too many believe that they are being forced to reconcile an infinitely merciful God condemning to eternal fire their loved ones whom He created that may have been lost in the world and failed to apprehend His Sacred Mysteries. We must take heart and realize that the redemption of these souls who lived outside the boundaries of the Catholic Church's definitively-redemptive Sacraments subsists in the personal judgement that each of these people leveled against themselves at the Throne of God when they faced the astral beauty of Jesus' Church arrayed in suffering and sacrifice out of love for them while simultaneously confronted and compelled by Divine Truth to confess all the reasons they refused to invoke their faith and return their love to His Mystical Body while they lived on Earth. These departed members of the human family realized with perfect clarity in those enlightening moments that the Catholic Church is truly Christ's Mystical Body which has been hanging on the Cross for 2,000 years in the suffering and sacrifice of His faithful people who loved humanity enough to endure the onslaughts of the ages against the Savior's testament to human spiritual perfection, salvific faith, comprehensive forgiveness, and fraternal love. Those who passed the veil unconverted are faced with the reality that those who accepted the sanctifying disciplines of the Universal Church and received the Bread of Life are affixed with Our Lord in His agony because we believed, though we had never seen; that if we died to ourselves with Christ, so too will we be resurrected with Him in His Glory. So, are all those who are not Catholic damned? The decision rests in the Divine Mercy of Jesus Christ, their response, and the sacrificial invocation that is yet to be manifested by the Catholic faithful which will complete Christendom's petition to the Father, because "we" as the co-redeeming Mystical Body of Christ united in Jesus' suffering through the Most Blessed Sacrament are the mitigating entity of salvation for many during each moment of time through the power of our love, knowing that millions who arrive at their judgement outside allegiance to the Universal Church will not refuse our love when they see it from the mystical purview of the Salvific Cross outside of time. This is why we forgive our enemies and pray so fervently for those who have died. Our devotion to the Original Apostolic Church is our love for humanity because the prayers, desires, and hopes that we generate amidst our unity with the sufferings of the Sacrificial Lamb are becoming the Savior's will as He listens and grants the fruit of our petitionary love by incorporating our sentiments into the completed nature of Heaven. And, since our prayers are for the deliverance of those who do not believe, He fulfills our prayers by dispensing infinite Divine Mercy upon them at their judgement and granting them the opportunity to embrace our eternal unity in the inexcusable light of their full understanding. Their door to Paradise becomes fully ajar, the mountains laid low, the pathway strewn with roses, and convalescent light illuminating the thoroughfare to the center of Jesus' Sacred Heart where the Catholic Church subsists in the fullness of its Eternal Glory. Our love preserves our wayward brothers and sisters from dooming themselves because it renders Heaven so beautiful that it would be nearly unthinkable for them to ever entertain a condemning thought about themselves, notwithstanding the egregiousness of their sins over the expanse of time. They realize that Heaven has truly forgiven them for crucifying the Mystical Body of the Church because they see that it was Christ alive saving the world as one body unified with Him in supernatural grace through the unilateral dispensation of the Bread of Life! This is the "life in us." We "put on Christ" through a oneness with divinity so profound that the world is redeemed through His Church as an extension of His Living Sacrifice through time—we confer salvation by proxy through our communion with the power of Jesus' Sacred Body and Blood from the Hill of Mount Calvary. The faithful gain this beatific stature, undeserved and unearned, upon the reception of the Most Holy Eucharist during our profession of solidarity with Christ's Crucifixion during the Holy Mass. When those who have passed through the veil are shown the day the Lamb of God died, the parameters of the material world and their mortal vision are breached, and those souls openly see the reality of the Crucifixion with timeless vision. They see everything in the Victim of the Cross that was united with Him in love by the Bread of Life from the Catholic Altar. On that Cross before them hangs the Roman Catholic Church, every Pope, the Magisterium of every age, two millennia of Catholic faithful, every saint, all the reverend doctors and theologians, each priest and nun, the faithful husbands and wives, visionaries and seers, converts and custodians, miracle-workers and penitents, the sufferers, the vision of every sickness and infirmity, every child injured or born less than whole, all the debilitating accidents laid upon the best among us, those who grieved undeserved pain, every selfless act offered to God for sinners, each sentiment of penance, all the intentions of the humble, the repulsiveness endured, the injustices borne, the depression sustained, the poor afflicted, the martyrs murdered, and every child stolen from their mother's womb. All those who have died have seen this, and most have asked through tears, "Why, Lord, so much suffering and desolation?" And, He answered them, "So you could be saved. All that you see has paid the price in union with Me for your eternal redemption because you are loved." Then, the decision is present with the gravity of their lives placed inconsequentially in the balance of the ages that is filled with the salvific love of the Communion of Holy Saints of Christendom with Jesus being the universal Lamb who endured and encompassed it all within His faithful people while hanging on the Holy Cross. So you see, there truly is no Salvation outside the beatific conception of the Catholic Church; it all occurs within it because all who are saved ultimately unite themselves within the mystical entity which is conferring Redemption by its hypostatic union with the Savior of the world. And, at the inauguration of this transfiguration in the souls of the departed, those who were saved became engulfed in a passionate fire of desire to suffer in thanksgiving for all those who loved them during the mystery which encompassed this mortal life, and their purgative agony commenced unto Eternal Life amidst their great joy. Unbelievably and mysteriously, there have been those who cursed everything they witnessed on the Cross and rejected it as their gift outright just as they did in life—and they plummeted to their place of torment in the fires of Hell to remain there gnashing their teeth over the decision they made forever-to-come. When every person finally accepts the gravity of this decision and is granted this visionary epiphany of redemptive love while uniting with Christendom at the Altars of the Catholic Church, suffering will be no more because there will be no need for God to ask the innocent to suffer any longer for the guilty in the image of His Son. Thanksgiving will reign because Love will claim its victory from Eternity to Eternity. Love will be one in itself, fully flourishing unimpeded among the hearts that God created. Therefore, I ask everyone to come to the Catholic Altar so that the suffering of humanity may become complete in the Cross. It is a horrible moment to be granted the vision of Good Friday and be unable to find yourself adorned in Jesus' Wounds, sharing in all that He accomplished, and finding peace and fulfillment in the reason why you were born. This is why Our Lady appears and declares that the Most Blessed Sacrament is the Bread of Life which confirms our presence with Our Lord Jesus Christ in the Mystery of the Cross. The unalterable conclusion as to why we so passionately engage the indifferent and the arrogant is that we know that each time we see one of our brothers or sisters suffering, it is because humanity has thus far refused to unite at the Altars of the Roman Catholic Church. A sinner needs someone to suffer for him so that he can be saved. The Crucifixion is becoming ever more beautiful by the moment. This is the reason for the history of the Church's agony on the Earth, and why She is pummeled and mocked to this day. God will wipe every tear from our midst if we unite and faithfully receive the Most Holy Eucharist. Who could possibly say no, and why would they?

VII. Protestantism as a reactionary ideology

When striving for our goal of unity, it is a rather difficult prospect to gracefully engage the proud thinkers who head many Christian denominations when they are bantering on a plane of individual perspectives without the experiential vision that would elevate them into a more profound union with Divine Wisdom. Five centuries of division is proof that very few of them are actually searching to be united in the truth of Jesus' words—*that they may be one*—; most are insecure and simply looking for validation of the perspectives they already hold, or worse, constructing and construing further theological complexities on erroneous foundations to justify themselves in the next battle that they wage against the unifying action of the Holy Spirit. The heavens see their preaching more as a product of human pride based upon how many people they can subordinate to their theological and pastoral views under the guise of being "saved" than being an effusion of humble divinity which makes princes of paupers in a united kingdom. This is why it is so important for each of us to honestly consider the authenticity of the Virgin Mary's miraculous intercession and the messages contained herein our body of works or one of many others throughout the globe. These writings are the ominous confirmation of the defeat of every ego at odds with Her sublime intentions because Our Lady's supernatural intervention is the broomstick that God has thrust into the whirling spokes of their tricycle wheels. I have found, and often lamented somewhat unjustifiably, that there is nothing more difficult than altering what another person has come to accept as reality in their own world view. Jesus' Crucifixion proves the point with perfect clarity—and He was raising people from the dead! Our dispositions are often like cement that has hardened into concrete, whereupon we are offended when God is finally required to use a jackhammer to reach us. When faith becomes limited to the static acceptance of the conclusions of other fallible mortals who have been impressed with perspectives unworthy of the highest reality of God, the living dynamics of faithful communion and apostolic action are atrophied; the organic growth toward the fullness of life is terminated, bearing the rotten fruits of dictatorial ideology and generating mere conscription into a mindless herd. Intellects become warped into parochial steel traps with conditioned retorts blocking any avenue where the Holy Spirit might try to touch them with more edifying grace. This darkened condition beckons to the enlightened remainder with convincing expediency to compromise the highest truths simply to find a modicum of common ground upon which to base the remnant of our unity. When faith cannot transcend the undergirding of our personal perspectives and step outside the trappings that lost sinners have created, our beliefs will never incorporate the allegiance that the Holy Spirit desires of us in the current moment. How many are liberated from their egos to a sufficient degree where they allow themselves to move at the slightest wisp of the Holy Spirit, especially if God is asking that they tread a path that is repulsive to their mental constitution? The number of years of Our Lady's appearances set against the response by mankind that we have thus far witnessed provides its own revelation in answer to this question. There are religious schools across this country which believe honestly and sincerely that they are educating the children of men in the truth of God and instilling in them a multi-dimensional platform of spiritual awareness in preparation for their engagement with the world, who are in actuality programming their charges with little more than sophisticated rejoinders in opposition to the Will of God. Cases in point are the fundamentalist Protestant universities in America whose echelons are courted by presidential candidates in every election cycle, who are teaching each of their students that the Holy Father in Rome is in legion with the Antichrist! Think about it! There are ideologues who are instructing their children that the

Papacy was conceived by the devil, that Pope John Paul the Great was an adversary of Jesus Christ, and that Mother Teresa was a deluded insignificant in the history of the world. And, they believe they are giving glory to God by professing as much. Sorrowfully, many of their children will carry this burden of darkness their entire lives. This is an example where the light within is actually darkness, and oh how deep that darkness will become. Everyone has seen the old western movies where the townspeople pile wagons, water troughs, barrels, tables, and every other type of obstruction across their city streets at the warning of approaching outlaws. They cower behind these rickety ramparts with weapons shouldered at the ready to launch salvo, slander and smoke at any at-large suspect who appears on their self-constructed wanted posters. Those who have a negatively biased view of Catholicism are prone to erect just such obstructions which they fail to realize do nothing more than separate them from the panoramic universality of Christendom; in fact, they have been initiated into a spiritual stupor where they have stopped believing that this beatific state of moral excellence is even the goal. They are crouching behind their biases looking outward at a land of spiritual freedom which they will never allow themselves to participate in because of the fears indoctrinated in them by others who are as terrified as they are. While I passionately wish to refrain from being accused of deriding the dignity of any of my brothers and sisters, the errant views they hold are not off-limits, especially when one considers the beauty that Our Lady is attempting to wrest from the diabolical grip of darkness. Sentiments that vilify any Successor of Saint Peter, whether they be from priest, parishioner, pilgrim, Protestant or pagan, render the Truth obscured from those who hold them. Our Lady provides the example we must follow as She hails the succession of Pontiffs, no matter what any mortal might say in derision of them. She believes in Divine Mercy; She believes in forgiveness; She believes in the unity of mankind. She has also seen the authentic history of the world and recognizes the self-possessed and often abridged verdicts which sinners have leveled against the Original Apostolic Church, and She counsels humanity nonetheless to be true to the Magisterium who is guiding us all with the grace of God. The Roman Catholic Church did not stumble and cede its ecclesial authority upon the religious rebellions of the tumultuous past. While our faith asks us to bear the weaknesses of others with grace, compassion, forgiveness and love, ecumenical dialogue is not a table for bartering over the Dogmas of Christianity in an attempt to persuade our detractors to like the Catholic Church any better than they have been taught to disparage Her. Nor is it a condition where all religious ideologies of the world come together, disavow everything they disagree about, and create a new religion based only upon those few things where beasts would find agreement. With all due respect, Our Lady would love to see Protestantism as something other than a five century aberration that has been splintering and disintegrating since its inception. She would be heartened to know that the authority that

Jesus Christ invested within His Apostles had not been rejected, and that the interpretation of the Gospel had never been surrendered into the hands of individual sinners. Oh, how She would be bathed in ecstasy to know that the beatific Testament of Christianity had remained within the collegial discernment and judgement of the successors of the Apostles anointed by the Holy Spirit. Jesus and Our Lady respect that portions of the faultfinding basis for Protestant grievances were founded in the Truth of the Gospel and the difficulties of the times, yet they also realize that the remedy sought was neither prayer, sacrifice, fasting, self-denial nor penance, but instead an ill-conceived exodus from the authoritative mechanism instituted by the Holy Spirit for the propagation of the definitive nature of Divine Truth throughout the ages. And, as an unfortunate result, Protestantism has defined itself in history as the original source of moral relativism through which the prince of darkness has advantageously proliferated disunity, disloyalty, and disarray within the body of Christendom throughout the globe. Five hundred years ago, a group of confused and frustrated sinners lost their patience and decided in restless futility that the yoke was neither easy nor the burden light, thereafter filtering God's Sacred Word through their prejudices instead of leaving that sacred revelation within the unified sphere of the enlightened discernment of the Magisterium who held the keys to the real and authentic historicity of Christianity. Protestantism is a reactionary ideology that has been fragmenting from its cradle where, inadvertent or not, the acerbic rhetoric of an Augustinian monk imprudently incited the nationalistic grievances of the German people, whereupon he offered the Roman Pontiff as the sacrificial lamb for the altar of their scorn, causing the destabilization of an entire cultural region which led to the incalculable bloodbaths of partisan war for nearly a century, and solidifying our unfortunate division to this day. These are the facts of history. The imperfect Christian philosophy underpinning Protestantism is easy to embrace if a person has an aversion to surrendering their will to the Faith of the Original Apostles and the Church they founded, notwithstanding the moral lapses of the leaders of any particular age. It is a separation from the legacies of the Saints and all they held dear unto their deaths, sometimes in the teeth of lions or at the point of swords. The Dogma and Traditions of Roman Catholicism are undeniably standing the test of time and the howling winds of human derision. They are the Rock of God which is the cornerstone upon which His earthly Kingdom is built. Without the sacrificial emulation of Christ Himself, religious belief becomes marked by personal interpretation and self-will instead of heroic virtue, loving abandonment, seamless unity, and selfless charity within the collective body of Christian believers. There have always been Judases, but the Roman Catholic Church has no more been sullied by them in the estimation of God than Jesus was corrupted by the Iscariot.

VIII. Methinks thou are protesting too much!

I have always been perplexed by spiritual petrification, meaning people could encounter reports of the greatest miracles witnessed by millions, and yet they would reject the testimony of each and every one of these multitudes because their spiritual consciences have been formed by falsehoods that have destroyed the living dynamics of their faith, making their dispositions nearly impenetrable to the signal graces which God dispenses to His people by the power of Holy Spirit. They will not believe anybody who challenges how they have been indoctrinated, even if one were to work a miracle in front of their eyes. We call this state of unbelief "invincible ignorance." People with such a spiritual affliction believe they have too much to lose by surrendering their present views to a higher state of grace, whether it be their congregation, their prestige, or the financial windfall that comes from the previous. A myriad of otherwise faithful people are spiritually numb, doing no more than repeating out-of-context mantras that are incapable of satisfying their hunger to be liberated from their misdeeds. Furthermore, there are throngs who exhibit a brainwashed euphoria where they passionately profess how in love with Jesus they are, but snarl and turn-up their noses at any grace He wishes to dispense to awaken them to the sanctification of their souls. Still others are simply terrified that they may be required to sacrifice their pursuit of the materials of this world; yet all are incarcerated in mental prisons from which they need to be freed. It is an empirical fact that those who are outside full communion with the Catholic Church while living in these states of darkness will never come any closer to the authentic Bread of Life spoken of in the Sacred Scriptures unless they shake themselves with a leap of faith, reconsider the significance of Our Lady's miraculous intercession, and realize that the Catholic Church and the veracity of its spiritual thinking existed 1,500 years before the wanting Five Pillars of Protestantism distracted them from the truth. By whose authority did those who led the Protestant uprisings demarcate and consign five pillars of belief for anyone? They were not commissioned through any miraculous sign, nor were they recipients of the laying-on of hands that would confirm their identity as witnesses for God. No appearance of an angel, no sign in the skies, no apparition, no locution, no miracle, no healing, no justifying grace of any kind signaled the approbation of Jesus Christ for their deeds. Yet, we can contrast this deprivation with the true action and ordination of the Holy Spirit. What was God saying to humanity in 1858 when four years after the Catholic Church declared the infallible Dogma hailing the Immaculate Conception, the Blessed Virgin Mary miraculously appeared to an illiterate child in Lourdes, France, confirming Her identity as the "Immaculate Conception," and initiated a miraculous spring of water which runs to this day that possesses the grace to have healed thousands of people of physical and emotional infirmity to prove it? Did He not say to His Church, "I concur with your infallible declaration!

What you have bound on Earth, I have also bound in Heaven!" The record of Catholic history is replete with the verifiable signature of God in events such as these, where He has miraculously confirmed His Will and reaffirmed His promise to redeem the world through His sacramental dominion. God never signed such a pact with the founders of Protestantism because its bedrock principle—*sola scriptura*—Scripture alone—has no basis in the Bible and no communion with the thinking of the original Apostles or their sacrificial lives. The Five Pillars were an ill-conceived necessity by those religious revolutionaries who knew a competing authority must be erected in order to sever the allegiance of the faithful from the Magisterium of the Original Apostolic Church in perpetuity. The revolutionaries of the Reformation were a group of disciples who walked away from Peter, James, and John and embarked upon a mission of prodigal evangelization founded on the pretext that everyone ignore the traditions of the original Apostles and the immaculate grace of the Mother of Jesus, Herself. This is why the Protestant faithful have shown almost no respect for the Queen of Heaven in the last five hundred years, errantly believing it obscures devotion to Jesus, whereupon they deliberately counsel their flocks away from Her miraculous shrines which would confirm their error. Neither the Apostles nor the Church ever believed that the Bible alone was the sole repository of what could be known about the Most Blessed Trinity, nor was it the liturgical foundation upon which Christianity would spread the Truth to the ends of the Earth. To the contrary, the Apostles themselves knew that *they* were the living repositories for the propagation of the Holy Gospel of the Deliverer of Humankind, and their actions of worship were the unifying catalyst which would enshroud humanity in grace as one body beneath the Divine Mercy of the Savior. And yes, the Bible has remained an efficacious instrument for developing faith in Our Lord within every culture and civilization since, but that sacred text is not the Church which He instituted. It is the collection of writings inspired by the Holy Spirit from the Apostolic age which the collegial body of the Catholic Church secured and certified as authentic nearly 1,700 years ago to be protected from the willful influence of sinners and other forces like those which have repeatedly attempted to alter its text through the ages to fit their selfish agendas. Some are even plotting to do this in our day, such as the forces who are removing all masculine references from its texts and those who are creating cinematic religious fiction to marginalize its content. The greatest Saints the world would ever know could fill every seat of the hierarchy within the Catholic Church, and the basic principles of Protestantism would never bless anyone wishing to live life under their holy stead. Jesus stated clearly in Matthew 16:18-19, *"And I say also unto thee, That thou art Peter, and upon this rock I will build my church; and the gates of hell shall not prevail against it. And I will give unto thee the keys of the kingdom of heaven: and whatsoever thou shalt bind on earth shall be bound in heaven: and whatsoever thou shalt loose on earth shall be loosed in heaven."* Read attentively—Jesus Christ established a Church that no power could bring down, and endowed His apostles with His authority over it through the stead of Peter. Nowhere in the Bible does He say that He would establish a book and that the world should be unilaterally bound and loosed by its multiplying interpretations through time. No amount of exegesis can alter this declaration of truth. But, look what has been built upon that falsehood in the last five centuries. Oh, how many people have been deprived the authentic Bread of Life from the original lineage of Jesus Christ because of this misdirection! Therefore, my beloved Protestant brothers and sisters, in the Name of Jesus Christ and with all the pleading and tears of the Immaculate Virgin Mary, this authentic messenger of God calls you to reunite yourselves with the Church that Jesus Christ founded. Allow the Mother of Our Lord to set you free and lead you to the Promised Land. Do not wait for pestilence, plagues and fire from the skies before you open your hearts to the Queenship of the Matriarch of Creation. If the children of God ever needed a mother, it is now! You have innocently and unwittingly inherited the error of your forbears, and have allowed yourselves to be lured away from the only Bread which gives Life by well-meaning people holding Bibles in their hands. I petition you with deep humility to consider the identities of those who said to the King of kings, "Lord, have we not prophesied in thy name? and in thy name have cast out devils? and in thy name done many wonderful works?" These words are the scriptural prophecy of what will one day be uttered by some of you! My prayer is that God will know each of us personally, and that He will find that we came to full countenance in His divine Light while here in this world because we loved one another so much. Many of you are like the eunuch who after Jesus' Resurrection was reading the Scriptures but confounded by their meaning, yet this eunuch's great witness to the ages is that he was humble to the direction of a true disciple of the Lord. Allow Our Lady's words to open your clouded eyes to the beaming truth of Jesus' Life and the fulfillment of His Truth within His Apostolic Church. It is now time for the Protestant world to be called home and surrender its unfortunate and misbegotten understanding of the Sacred Scriptures into the hands of the Queen of Calvary, thereby allowing Her to refocus the Truth of the Life of Her Son upon all our souls, because no one knows Him better. She is the heroic Samson who is going to liberate and unite us all by bringing down the Five Pillars with nothing more than Her presence and the grace of Her Immaculate Heart.

IX. The Woman Clothed with the Sun

The clearest vision and the antidote to the sickness of our spiritual confusion, hapless division, and moral apathy lies beneath the Mantle of the Virgin Mary's intercessory Wisdom. She can demolish and reconstruct in the blink of an eye because Her dominance and grace are beyond the load-bearing weight of any man's mental constitution or religious ideology. She cares not whose pride She offends. Her supernatural presence is the actuator of unity in this final age of men. Above all others, She is the authority on the Life of the Messiah. As an example of greatness, Popes lay their pontificates at Her feet, knowing that She is the Universal Queen of The Living Sacrifice of Calvary! And, with that primacy in the salvific drama of the Lamb of God, it behooves humanity to listen to the Woman Clothed with the Sun through every authentic messenger that She has commissioned throughout the world. It is not we who speak, it is the very intentions of God, validated and confirmed through Her miraculous charisms. The Most Blessed Trinity is calling to the entire spectrum of humanity. Not only are agnostics, atheists, and materialists asked to believe and reorient themselves for the sake of their deliverance, but Cardinals, Bishops and priests of the Catholic Church, along with the rest of Christendom, are being petitioned by the heavens to invoke their faith, believe more deeply, engage the heights more intimately, surrender more profoundly, and act more courageously. We are crossing the mighty stream of time terrified to take any step until another faith-effacing intellectual stone appears from beneath the current. There we are, each man, family and denomination, standing isolated and separated on our particular rock, paralyzed by how deep the water may be. But, Our Lady has called us out upon the waves, caring not whether we can swim, asking us to be unafraid of what separates us, to confess Her miraculous assistance, align ourselves with the Apostolic Church, and fearlessly stride atop the fathoms into an embrace with one another as true brothers and sisters for the first time in five centuries. Our Lady wishes the 500th anniversary of the Protestant Reformation to be a reunion celebration of Her prodigal children with the Father of Christendom upon the sacred grounds of His earthly estate which their forbears vacated. The Most Blessed Trinity desires open, public, and passionate allegiance to the miraculous guidance of the Blessed Virgin Mary in a tangible way as witness to the world of His redeeming agenda. We must show the world that our faith is perfected in One, Universal, Roman Catholic and Apostolic Church, and not in a cacophony of useless, diverse mantras pealing repetitively through our minds which have no power to unite us as one kingdom of people in His sacramental grace. By our faith, we profess that we believe in a potent mightiness that is altogether present and overwhelming, a Love so immeasurable and eminently profound that we cannot help but be conscripted into its grace and loose our vocal chords proclaiming the good that God is accomplishing in our midst.

X. Twelve Apostles, Three Persons, One Church

When the original Apostles fanned out into the world, they did not witness in terms of faith as it has been metastasized to mean in our day by the many varying sects who proclaim their individual allegiances to the Bible. Nor did they speak from an intellectual position of personal belief, as if their thoughts were to respectfully rank in competition with those of all other men. They stood before kings and conquerors, and principalities and powers with supremacy and spoke with humble conviction through an absolute vision of reality that was a product of their factual experiences. Their personal lives testified and embossed a concrete truth that transcended the whims of most everyone they engaged. They were proficiently evangelistic in the Universal Truth articulated by God Himself, applicable to everyone, amendable by no one, and on a collision course with the ends of the Earth and time; and they knew it, believed it, and were willing to die for it. Triumphalism, indeed! The solidarity of the original Apostles and disciples was impregnable because they knew what it meant to sacrificially mount the Cross out of love for their enemies, whereas they had seen that deific witness firsthand through the sparkling agony of their tears. And, they defended each other, corrected one another, and knew that they had the affirmation of God in all they did with the keys they held. They engaged the world with the merciful grace and righteous fortitude that emanated from the maternal guidance of the Most Blessed Virgin who was the birthing fount of the Revelation of God on Earth, while the Holy Spirit enveloped them with His power. And, as their witness to the Father in human flesh through Jesus' Life propagated into the world, it steam-rolled the attitudes of men with a warming display of evidentiary potency and angelic wisdom that could be surpassed by no living creature. They no more respected the debilitating and errant ideas of sinners than they regarded their own former dispositions. In fact, they were trying to liberate humankind en masse from the darkness in which it was engulfed. They were intent upon setting a spiritual fire upon the Earth with the kindling being the broken hearts of the least among men. Groundswells of goodness were launched through their courage which broke upon the consciences of the proud like mighty sledgehammers taken to splintering granite. They confronted injustice and superstition with honorable audacity at every turn, determined that every person hear what they had to say, not because they wanted to be right, but because they loved humanity enough to confront them with the celestial wisdom that would free everyone from the ageless iniquity that had perpetuated agony upon the face of humankind since the first man was set free in the flesh. Their inspirited souls commanded them to do no less out of the same Love that beamed into their hearts from the Cross of Calvary. In their world, religious pluralism did not exist because they superceded it. They compromised their witness and knowledge of Jesus Christ with no one, taking their mission seriously to build a church in which all men could take refuge against the ultimate revelation of God's majestic justice. A new day had dawned in history, and they were the custodial mouthpieces of the Heavenly Father for a world that required redemption in every sense of its meaning. Their commission was to foster and ignite a supernatural faith in the transfiguring parameters of Mount Tabor; to unveil the truest reality past the limitations of man's physical sight into the depths of the Sacred Heart of the Messiah who would respond from the Cross with an influx of "experiential truth" into each and every person who would believe His Word, and by His grace, recognize their stature as His divine children. In sure succession, new generations of original Catholic conviction arose, and being more than simple belief, crashed against the shores of the future with sign, wonder, wisdom, sacrament, healing, blessing, and perseverant determination for the sacrificial advancement of the Spirit of Infinite Love. It is the *experiential truth* that we must be open to receive in our time, but faith is the enlightening prerequisite to this divine order. When one embraces the evidentiary intercession of the Most Blessed Virgin Mary with complete submission and heroic response, life explodes with new purpose, vision, conviction, signal graces, gifts, answers to prayers, and every other kind of confirming grace because we are swept up in the original tsunami of redemption that the earthquake of the Son of Man lifted long before these days; the same tidal wave that flows down upon this world from the Altars of the Catholic Church at the Moment of Consecration to this very day. It is there that the past, present and future become one as we take-up residence within the realms of the miraculous which surge past us toward the end of time, where existence pours over the precipice between this world and the next into the bay of Jesus' Divine Mercy and the Salvation of the world.

Now, I humbly ask; has there been a breach that has occurred; and where are we today along this mystical continuum? Between our sense of awareness and the unimpeachable reality of God lies an obscuring veil that is called the "world," this darkened place of sacrificial exile which assaults faith at every moment through its bounded essence. Where there should exist a crystal clear panoramic scene into Eternity lies a human mortality polluted with the crass regurgitations from the minds of men, arrogant distortions of reality, pontifications from the secular wasteland, material and sensual distractions, and blinding wickedness fomented by people who have outright disdain for the sacrifices that sacred Love commands. There are many truths that need to be embraced by humanity, and far more misconceptions that must be rescinded for the manifest advancement of society in holy virtue. I have wrestled with the dilemma of simply stating the Truth that Our Lady has revealed to me before moving on or allowing myself to become more cerebral in an attempt to explain what is impeding our elevation. Although the Immaculate Virgin has blessed both of my intentions, I have been encouraged not to attempt a personal invasion of the brains of other people in an effort to reconstruct their thoughts.

She said this is the work that each person must do for themselves in response to the fusillade of Truth that She has launched through Her many miraculous appearances. I have always been a person who desired deeply to know the most profound truth, no matter what former position had to be adjusted. I believe God admires a disposition that He can easily influence, while I do not wish to find at the end of time that I lived life as an unwitting dupe, or worse, an arrogant snob. My personal ideas have never been entwined with my self-identity where my sense of dignity would be impugned if someone were able to show me where I may have been somewhat misguided. I am convinced that we are children of God, possessing dignity, no matter what ideas flow through our minds. I simply ask, who really wishes to walk around ignorant or in the dark, not to mention being an adversary of God, inadvertent or not? It is like mingling during a cocktail party with your pants unfastened, but no one in the room having the courtesy to tell you. I always believed that if I was not in the light, I wished God to help me because I wanted to know what it is, and become united with Him more deeply as quickly as possible, no matter what sacrifice I had to make. It is not a great act of self-immolation to admit that human beings are quite fallible and our world views and attitudes intrinsically malleable beyond reason according to either who influenced our thinking first or who offended us last. So, where do we place our abandonment; in whom do we entrust our eternal lives with complete faith? I declare that Our Lady is more qualified for that epic responsibility than anyone alive, especially because it is She whom God has allowed to appear throughout the world to encourage our faith. She will tell us what to believe and where to go to enter into the Light. Honestly, can any man's vision compete with Hers? Her eyes saw the Messiah crucified; Her Heart grieved the pain; and still Her being flawlessly executed His Will! That is the original resume of salvation which every Saint has pined to share. Faith, belief, and unquestioning courage is what Jesus wished to draw forth from the souls of His Apostles, knowing in advance that only one would dare confront the world and stand with His Mother beneath the Cross as He died. Diabolical forces are attempting to kill the living faith within the Mystical Body of Christ by discrediting and usurping the authentic vision of His Kingdom, instilled by the Crucified Lamb within the Roman Catholic Church. Our Lady has appeared to scatter them in their conceit.

XI. The Eucharist is the authentic Bread of Life

The parable in the Gospel where Jesus refers to the impossibility of pouring new wine into old wine skins *(Matthew 9:16-17)* is an allegory that I never really understood until our Holy Mother's intercession began to unfold in our lives. The Blessed Virgin has taught me that the mortal receptacle in which our spirit is encased is a very suppressing entity. Our thoughts, demeanor, and sense of self are highly susceptible to being secluded on obscure plateaus of composure, meaning that our places of interior peace often become nothing more than lairs where we avoid sacrificing our druthers to the higher work of striving for the excellence of human perfection. These are our wine skins where many people often believe that they are resting in the affirmation of God, when they are actually sequestered in the darkness listening to the solitude of their dead souls, hoping that the Holy Spirit will never come calling. I have encountered multitudes who have been exposed to Our Lady's miraculous intercession, especially through our works, who wish to do no more than debate the credible worth of these mystical appearances, notwithstanding whether they believe them or not. Each of these individuals is quartered within their own bunker behind various reasons which describe their inability to move in faith beyond the circumference of their exilic perception. It is immaterial whether the excuse is that they refuse to believe that the Matriarch of Humanity would ever actually intercede to advance God's wishes or that Her instructions may not be a definitive requirement of their faith. They nonetheless dismiss all miraculous occurrences that they do not personally witness, and even some they do witness, which bear a message that contradicts their thinking or dares to encourage them out of their complacent state of spirituality. They are truly in a place where they would have dismissed the original Apostles happening into their town, clothed in the power of God Himself. Thus, when they peruse the contents of witnesses such as ours, they do so with the disposition of arguing every point that does not settle in their personal perspectives, those with theological training oftentimes being the worst. The composition of their identity is an old wine skin whose interior stability they sense will burst should they honestly attempt to assimilate the genius that Our Lady dispenses within their spiritual constitution. Indeed, the truth that they must become a Roman Catholic, or at least a better one, and receive the Most Blessed Sacrament (the authentic Bread of Life) to have the fullness of life and come into complete conformity with the Holy Gospel begins to haunt their conscience. And, they fight-off this prompting of the Holy Spirit by rejecting the miraculous assistance that God dispenses to them in our time, leveling absurdities that all messages and appearances of the Mother of Jesus are the work of the devil, and repeating the blasphemy of those who hissed the same epitaph about Jesus in response to His miraculous works. And, since they do not wish to place themselves in the unenviable predicament of one day being seen as having attacked the Blessed Virgin Mary's work directly, it is left for the messengers to endure the sacrificial onslaught against their good character, honesty, reputation, mental stability, intellectual depth and person. So, you can see how lost and afraid some people can truly be while still quoting the contents of the Bible. The wine skins of these doubters are composed of simple intellectual opinions, unsupported by God and the experiential power that He bestows, which is derived from being in consonance with the manifestations of the Holy Spirit they scorn. Then, there are the blessed who may be completely blind at first, but humbly abandon everything they have previously known because their childlike hearts realize they are being touched by a loving power from beyond the ages that no man could generate on his own; and they wish to be united with it, making it the living essence of their born-again beings. They are the ones who trust Jesus more than they trust themselves. They shall arrive in Heaven to the accolades of God and receive titles of *The Courageous, The Indomitable*, and *The Faithful* because they were unafraid to transfer their lives into the supernatural reign of the Holy Spirit and lay themselves out according to the prescriptions that God would accomplish through their sacrificial love.

XII. Mary, poised in grief, hopeful for humanity

It can be recalled by many people yet alive, the poise and grace by which Jacqueline Kennedy endured the assassination of her husband, President John Fitzgerald Kennedy, in November 1963. Her strength, composure, and determination while processing the valley of his death were a profound manifestation of her Catholic identity which she inscribed upon the pages of American history in an heroic act of matrimonial love and defiant preservation of the greatest spirit of our nation. Only President Kennedy's most ferocious partisan enemies refuse to acknowledge her unassailable grace in those dark hours. Therefore, is it a symptom of willful human arrogance or merely a stumbling of fallible mortal judgment that religious partisans, cultural artists and theological pundits parse, critique and mischaracterize the stratospheric spiritual composure of the Most Blessed Virgin Mary for their post-enlightenment descriptions of Her authentic life and historical character? Count the movies, as well as documents and articles, that depict nothing more than sin-bound renditions of Her magnificent life, portraying Her as being just another woman who bore a child into the world that responded to his death with incapacitating grief and nominal disposition. Cinematographers and storytellers routinely obscure the grace of Heaven's Queen as if She were some helpless insignificant in the unfolding of time; a bit player of scant mention. They devolve Her sanctified bearing to the level of our mundane helplessness, mimicking common themes of human sinfulness to ratify their paltry estimations of a salutary life. The world must know instead that the Immaculate Mother of

Jesus Christ is of a plateau where all the Jacqueline Kennedys in history are merely Her children from whom they received a portion of Her Immaculate grace. On the day they lifted our Crucified Redeemer from the lap of the Pieta and carried our Savior away to His Tomb, the Queen of Calvary did not need to be assisted to a place of rest, nor was She so weakened by grief to need ambulatory care or medicinal aids. No, Our Lady stood erect, powerful and undaunted in the face of the flushed bowels of Hades which were evacuated upon the Earth to assail the believers of Christ in the darkest hour of Creation. She panned Jerusalem with a vision of majestic solicitude as if She presciently knew that She was its forgiving Queen. She gazed into the desolate eyes of those around Her, beckoning the flames of expectation to match the fires of anticipation that raged in Her crucified Heart. She knew Her Son was going to rise from His grave and claim victorious dominion over all the Earth. Grieved, yes; emotionally assaulted, most certainly; subdued and defeated—never in all Eternity. Her perfect soul contemplatively accompanied Her Son into the pit of Hell with the same triumphant bearing that He wielded against its damning gates. Filled with life-giving hope in the face of the permanency of primordial death, She was the only Light left at the total eclipse of the mortal world. The radiance of everlasting life beamed from Her Immaculate Heart because She still believed in the testimonial power of Her Lord and God who had just been murdered before Her grief-stricken eyes. The immortal soul of the world was faltering; all the faith in Creation was dying before Her pleading gaze like a flower wilting in the scorching heat. Yet, She alone held back Hell's blast, refusing to succumb to the terminal nature of man; buoying Her Son's newly-ignited dream for the everlasting ages from descending into oblivion beneath the primeval depths of Adam's sin, holding it aloft before the history of mankind, unyielding, unafraid, and victorious. There is a line of spiritual and mental composure that mothers instinctively know not to cross during the agony of childbirth for the sake of the life they are bearing into the world. If they succumb to the pain and refuse to sustain the birthing process, oftentimes neither themselves nor their offspring survive. The Mother of human Salvation had no line where Her composure could be struck down. She was complete maternal Redemption who was bearing the moment of birth for all the children of God as the Matriarch of kings and queens, the life-giving entity of the universe whose parental spirit was ignited by the words of Her dying King and Redeemer on the Cross. Her Love for the children of Heaven obliterated any temptation where She might stumble. Her power was so great that hopelessness, sin and death could not touch Her unblemished spirit. She did not lash out, She did not condemn, She did not look for justice to consume Her Son's executioners and the hate-mongers that herded Him to Calvary because She could see the Triumph of the Cross spreading out through time right before Her prophetic watch. She was the consummate emulation of Mercy,

Light, Redemption, and Deliverance in the Divine Image of Her Son; the Complete Reflection, Magnifier, Mediatrix, Co-Redemptrix and Mother of Paradise standing yet on mortal soil, within reach of the hearts who had heretofore unperfected Her spiritual power. No woman in history has ever come close to responding as She did to such a personally excoriating event as the Crucifixion of Her sinless Child. And, none ever will! Therefore, Jesus Christ desires everyone who refuses to concede the Virgin Mary's exalted station in Heaven and on Earth to come forward and answer this question, **"What more do you want to convince you of My Queen's station amongst the history of this world's Eves?"**

All mankind, especially those who diminish the Virgin Mary to being nothing more than another sinner in salvation history, should reject the diabolical assertion that Jesus is somehow offended by the elevation of His Mother as the most blessed among women. Every person who allows such indignity to pass their lips is violating the Holy Spirit, and is likewise under the influence of the Antichrist. They should realize that it is the Lamb of God Himself who is elevating His sinless Mother above all women, just as the Holy Scriptures prophesy. Remember the Magnificat uttered through the inspiration of the Holy Spirit—*"All nations shall call me blessed!"*, and the prophetic utterances of Elizabeth, *"Blessed are you, and blessed is the fruit of your womb."* Both are Blessed! God is confirming the Bible true in its every word through Her miraculous intercession across every landscape of this planet. Jesus is the Sacrificial Lamb and our only Redeemer, but Mary is His perfect Mother who taught Him how to die with a Love so blinding brilliant that the eternal corona of God pierced the bonds of Creation and obliterated every last vestige of human sin that could be conceived by the darkened heart of man. Her soul has magnified His Light, and magnifies it still. Jesus could not be more ecstatic with any other human being as He inspires Her appearances and locutions, and commands us through His Holy Spirit to obey Her before He is instructed by the Father to come as the Just Judge. She is the magnificent Evangelizer of the End Times. This Immaculate Virgin who gave the Messiah life in this world has power that is beyond the collective witness of all the ages of evangelists. Every one of them fell at Her feet in thanksgiving the instant they saw Her. Imagine what She suffered for humanity—and She said 'yes' willingly and heroically! What faith! What devotion! What power! And, She accomplished and completed Her life perfectly. We must comport with biblical prophecy through our manifest recognition of Her grace, instead of remaining as an impediment to the Gospel that She is mystically advancing in measures that are leaps and bounds ahead of us all. If one admits that the original Apostles experienced and possessed the experiential truth of Jesus Christ, and we are to imitate their convictions which have become our faith, does anyone believe that they did not revere the Most Holy Virgin beyond all telling as the Mother of our Salvation? How do we suppose they treated Her so that we can offer Her at least as much gratitude, reverence, and respect? They recognized that She was the experiential miracle still in their presence after Jesus rose into Heaven and sent His Holy Spirit upon them. And, She is ours now! Before their very eyes, Our Lady came to full-revelation as the woman-prodigy spoken of by the great Prophet Isaiah. She is Paradise's mystical presence emanating from the vaults of God's Kingdom in which all the early apostles and disciples conjoined themselves as they processed across the globe, shining the Light of the Messiah before men. She is the knowledgeable source which completed His identity to the Evangelists so the Scriptures could be written. His entire Life is contained in Her. The Son can still be seen in the Mother. When the Mother is touched, it is the Sacred Heart of the Son who is touching back. When the Mother speaks, the Word of God is reverberating from each syllable. When the Mother appears, it is She who is center stage before our devotions as we assume Her posture in giving Glory to the Son. Would anyone care to imagine what would happen this day if the Virgin of Bethlehem were to appear on Christmas eve in flesh and blood within any Christian religious gathering? Would any man diminish Her then? If not, what is the motivation for devaluing Her royal dignity now? It could not possibly be a reflection of the Will of God. I tell you in truth, each and every man and woman would fall to their knees and weep at the radiant beauty that would overwhelm them at the appearance of Heaven's Queen, while the children would scamper in one giggling torrent into Her embrace. I have seen this heart-rending Matriarch of Perfection, and Her beauty is why I scurried to Her bosom where She began talking to me. Her arms are the dais from which I speak. From that perch, I am smiling and waving my arms for everyone to come closer because Her embrace is universal, Her love is boundless, and the Truth that She extols is unequivocal and everlasting.

XIII. The purifying mandates of God's Kingdom

We must begin to see the assaults against human sanctity, moral reason and motherhood, in particular, for what they are. Our morally-stricken popular culture has immersed this generation so deep in sins of the flesh that multitudes cannot conceive the beauty of virginal purity, while the minds of secular politicians, ambassadors, sociologists, psychiatrists, educators, and activists dismiss and mock holiness as if it could not possibly be a plausible achievement for the human species. The attack against motherhood perpetrated by radical feminist ideologues has been particularly damaging to the graceful psyche of the western world, leaving the feminine grace of the Virgin Mother which the Catholic Church has always lifted before the world as God's testament to womanly perfection replaced by a template of sinful human characteristics that are no more than skin deep and wrought with the vanity of a dying gender.

Our image makers have abandoned any conception of purity, and thus devalued human sexuality and the spiritual dignity of the human person to the base tendencies and natural inclinations of propagating beasts with the approving applause of those whose souls are perishing in this darkness. And, how did it happen? Our destruction has not been planned through an immediate strike of obliterating proportions which would appall the global gallery and rouse our defensive retaliations like a bugle to its legions. No, it has happened through the simple compromises of otherwise righteous people over segments of time that were beyond their prescient gaze. Those who are immersed in the temporal world perceive their lives in terms of days, hours and minutes, instead of the seasons, decades, and generations that lie open before the regard of spiritual men. The seeds for the devastation of any civilization are planted sometimes centuries before its fall is ever realized in its most horrific consequences. Any historian will tell us that every societal collapse through the ages, save natural disasters, did not just happen unawares, but was a product of the destabilization of the underpinnings of a just and orderly society through the disregard for righteous reason, moral integrity, and the stabilizing traditions of justice that are the cohesive elements for its fraternal fabric. Our Lady warned me in some of the first sentiments that She ever offered in 1991 that Satan works as a fine grindstone who hones away our virtue and peace at a pace which renders his baneful stratagem for our damnation imperceptible to our sensibilities because, absent the cultivation of our visionary spiritual identity, we cannot see the aftermath in time of vacating our good senses and better motivations to the wiles of expedient selfishness and materialistic gain. It has been written before that nothing is accomplished by compromising with unscrupulous malcontents except the surrender of those portions of our greatness which are required to momentarily placate their ravenous appetites. The single act by the devil which has been accomplished with due diligence and precise success over the last century is the calculated deception thrust upon American women that bearing children is more of a burden than it is worth, a form of bondage, and that there is more fulfillment offered by our materialistic society than could ever be gained by cultivating a paradisial relationship with a husband and conceiving a family within the sanctifying vocation of motherhood. The family is a baby church, and it is being aborted along with the children in their mothers' wombs because vast throngs of women refuse to engage their responsibilities in the hierarchy of God's kingdom. These misguided ladies are awash with contempt for their sacrificial surrender in the spirit of Love to the Vicars of the Family, even though Our Lady provides them the example where She pines to remain perfectly submissive to Her Son out of Her great Love. This Love is why She is beautiful. Bearing new life into the world is the unique act of woman that consecrates her existence in the creative genius of God at the summit of Paradise. Incarnate Motherhood stands upon the peak of Creation along with the feminine nature that serves it.

The entire rebellious mind-set at war with the Patriarchy of the Roman Catholic Church to the dereliction of motherhood and the sanctified female nature is directly from the Prince of Darkness because once you detach a woman's affections and sensibilities from enwombed children, that civilization is doomed in time. Many an Eve has been seduced by the fruit offered by the serpent of the Garden, and she is trying to stuff it down Adam's throat through claims of victimhood when she should be concentrating instead upon the Victim of the Cross and the Queen who stood before Him. It is the definitive act of woman unredeemed by Christ. There is no excuse for young ladies to pine for the glamour and riches of the world or to believe that any accomplishment in any field or endeavor ranks as high in the estimation and judgement of God as loving a husband and bearing new life into the world through that union, and nurturing those children to sanctity in preparation for their reception of the rewards of Heaven. Multitudes have set out to conquer the world, and will in the end lose their souls. Is every woman required by God to become a mother? Certainly not. But, Our Lady's response to those who choose not to bear children is that they clothe themselves in the robes of holiness, piety and purity nonetheless, and burn-out their lives serving Jesus Christ in humility, chastity, prayer, and contemplation in whatever portion of the vineyard they choose to serve. The Heavenly Father thinks more of a pauper than a president, and the rowers in the hold of a slave ship over the tyrants who placed them there. He cares not about our conquest of space or our scouring for treasure on the ocean floors. He abhors the domination of societies and countries by corporate lords who are buzz-cutting human dignity from the face of the Earth for profit. He cares not who owns the most, who is in control of what, how the cheering throngs adore us, or whether we have secured the riches of the planet at our own feet. All men die and come before Him to make an accounting of their lives according to the prescriptions of Jesus' Life, Death, and Resurrection, even those who never knew Him. No one escapes the revelation of their deepest secrets, clandestine motivations, and hidden acts before the Throne of God. Everything which is done in the darkness will be displayed in the Light for what it is. The works and intentions of men will be smelted in the Furnace of the Eternal Ages with only the gold of charity and the sparkling clarity of our most heroic sacrifices surviving the holocaust. Some of the harshest judgement will come to those who claimed they followed Jesus Christ, but sought to gain the whole world and wilfully abandoned their responsibilities to humanity and the life that God intended they serve within His Church.

    I pray every day that these sentiments will greet the fertile ground of compliant and heroic hearts who do not resent being offered a more noble itinerary for the unfolding of civilization. While Our Lady is extending the ultimate peace of God through Her intercessory guidance, my brother and I offer our simple humility to Heaven's holy commission by testifying that we are

Her messengers fulfilling our duty through the impetus of the confirming power of the Sacraments of the Roman Catholic Church. It is the miraculous anointing of the Most Blessed Virgin Mary that strengthens us to counter the world and its most ferocious opposition, and offer it instead the opportunity for the Truth to be seen for the wisdom it contains. While we have trusted God, he has trusted us in a reciprocal embrace of fidelity which flourishes from our relationship with the Immaculate Virgin of Bethlehem. Humility before the Most Blessed Trinity compels us to advance His holy will, aggressively if need be. It is never a lacking in humility for anyone to speak to any point where we may be failing our Lord God, maligning the canvas of history, or planting seeds of desolation for the future ages of our children. Consider the repercussions and outcomes of the rebellious upheaval of the 1960s and how so many misguided children were incubated in their rogue university settings, but were deprived the Christian wisdom to envision the inevitable effects that they were launching into our day with their naive social arrogance. We went from the honorable character of the men and women of the greatest generation whose calloused hands knew hardship, who revered the composed families they represented, who accepted their moral responsibilities with saintly honor, who filled their church pews every Sunday in record numbers, who tendered their ultimate sacrifices and delivered the world from the grip of Fascism and Nazism to gansta-rappers destroying the character of a generation of children, the instigation of rampant divorce through the wholesale attack on every form of patriarchy, millions of deranged women screaming for their right to exterminate the children of their wombs, legalized sodomy sweeping the nation, the disintegration of marriage and its definition, rampant promiscuousness and sexually transmitted diseases, pornography mainstreamed to our entertainment palate, multinational corporate greed of a colossal scale, and young men desensitized to violence through gruesome video games; the latter entertained by the insanity of the New Coliseum of cage fighting, satiated by women who have objectified themselves as fleshed-crazed "booty," and nearly every civic and governmental organization abandoning all sense of honor and nobility before God to whom we will all someday answer. And low and behold, church pews stand fallow because we have neither the courage nor the righteousness to admit that a sinister relativistic worldly mentality vacated of faith swamped the implementation of the Second Vatican Council in America, flushing away our disciplined sense of the mystical and the miraculous, and in essence thrust 2,000 years of Sacred Tradition to the margins like a pauper thrown to the gutter, leaving decimated our faithful devotion to the divine institution of the Magisterium which concretizes our relationship with the Redeemer who was bloodied beyond horror and nailed to a Cross to save us all. The time of reserved silence hoping that the Heavenly Father will singlehandedly make it miraculously go away before it devours all humanity yet on the Earth is over! Righteousness is His Will! We are participants in the redemption of the world, advancing the same unequivocal message of human deliverance that the Saints died for, declaring the unadulterated Truth of conversion which could not be destroyed even by Crucifixion, and calling the world to repentance and acceptance of the Gospel of the Messiah because the Dominion of Heaven is preparing to call us to an accounting of our moribund deeds. We are our brothers' keepers along with being custodians of this earthly vineyard which is the vestibule of God's Kingdom. Therefore, hear me now, and hear me well! Our Lady is ready to assault our senses with the grace that will liberate us from our despotic futility! The Almighty God of our fathers is bringing about the definitive eradication of every godless agenda at this very moment through the Queen of Heaven who is present and arrayed in a power that is beyond the sensual imagination of man. The Judgement of the Ages is imminent! The Lord God is mercifully restraining the manifestation of His Divine Triumphant, waiting for the last human soul who will surrender to Him, the one who will tip the scales of influence and favor in the direction of His Kingdom for all Eternity. And, the instant that last soul converts, the heavens will open and the obliteration of evil will commence at the hands of the Saints, Seraphim, and Sovereigns unto the cleansing of the Earth. Through the Divine Mercy of Jesus Christ, Our Lady is appearing and asking for our collective allegiance to Her immaculate grace and the courage to lift it with convicted determination within every venue of man for the sake of those last fortunate souls who are destined for the heights of Paradise. It is time for Holy Christendom to come to its feet and declare with the righteousness of Heaven that the Reckoning is on its way because God is coming off the mountain with all the fury of an enraged Moses. He is going to break His law across the keel of this Earth—and then we will love Him again.

XIV. Jesus, Son of the Matriarchal Intercessor

What is the Truth that God desires every man, woman, and child to know? Divine Love manifested as universal unity within the bonds of Christ's Deific perfection beneath the authority of the Vicar of Christ whom He has seated in His earthly stead at the pinnacle of His Church on Earth. The Truth and all blessings that will ever flow upon mortal humanity originate in the congregation of one Body, partaking of one Bread at one Table of belief in all that is of God who is both real and the adjudicator of our ultimate fate. Jesus Christ is alive, and His Mother is appearing throughout the world as the grace to unite Christendom within the bosom of the Catholic Church in preparation for the final christening of man's eternal destiny. The Second Coming of the Son of Man has been imminent for two millennia, and is closer now than at any time in human history. The world must openly confess in unity and with passion that God has manifested Himself to humanity as a Trinity of Persons;

1 The New Millennium

Father, Son and Holy Spirit. Jesus Christ is the Personified Truth, the Messiah, our Redeemer and only Advocate before the Father; there is no other who has preceded, superceded or succeeded Him; nor are there any authentic messengers of God other than those under the testament, tutelage, discipline, and discipleship of Jesus Christ. The Truth is the revelation of what is and shall always be. It demands that we believe the Messiah was born of the sinless Virgin Mary who has miraculously remained ever-virgin, before, during, and after His Birth in Bethlehem. She is the Matriarchal Intercessor before the affections of Her Son, validated from the wedding feast of Canaan to the foothills of Medjugorje to the Altar beneath St. Peter's dome. The Crucifixion of the Lamb of God redeemed humanity from eternal oblivion outside of time; and this Triumphant King of Peace rose from the Tomb on the third day, ascended into Heaven, sent the Holy Paraclete at Pentecost, and instituted His Catholic Church from the onset of His Will for its epochal mission of evangelizing Christian Truth and preserving the world from Eternal Damnation. From this pinnacle of Creation, the Catholic Church dispenses the Bread of Life which is *actually* and *truly* the Body, Blood, Soul and Divinity of Jesus Christ, handed to us from the Table of the Last Supper.

*Now as they were eating, Jesus took bread, and when he had said the blessing, he broke it and gave it to the disciples. 'Take it and eat,' he said, **'this is my body.'** Then he took a cup, and when he had given thanks, he handed it to them saying, 'Drink from this, all of you, **for this is my blood**, the blood of the covenant, poured out for many for the forgiveness of sins.   Matthew 26:26-28*

This Most Blessed of all Sacraments unilaterally sustains our unity and without reservation grants Eternal Life to all the penitent. Heaven is mystically and perfectly present on the Earth within the bonds of the Roman Catholic Church, notwithstanding the sinful lapses of its members. The Risen Christ has taken His seat at the right hand of His Father in Heaven, and will, sooner than anyone realizes, return to judge both those who have loved and obeyed Him and those who have hated Him, administering justice and reward upon each according to His own Divine Mercy and righteous Judgement. Hell has yet to prevail against the Original Apostolic Church, and it never will. For nearly seven hundred thirty thousand days, the Faith of Saint Peter has endured, declaring to humanity, *thou art the Christ, the Son of the Living God,* with the power and beatitude of Jesus' Sacrifice on the Cross manifested in every Holy Mass. It alone empowers mankind with the ultimate sacramental graces for the advancement of civilization into the heights of deliverance. His Triumphalism lives! God cares not about any other philosophies or ideologies other than His own because only His Love can cleanse, sanctify, and redeem us into the everlasting beatitude of Paradise for all the ages to come. Indeed, no other doctrines can compete; they are all obliterated in His Light and self-destruct in time. He does not respect the arrogant whims of men and women. Anything not in perfect alignment with the Truth of His Universal Act of Redemption through His Son Jesus is both humiliated and extinguished in the flames of His righteous Love. What man can hold any other idea next to the Deific Brilliance exhibited in His Passion, Death, and Resurrection and still believe he holds a greater intelligence or more profound prescription for the elevation and unification of humanity? Yet, Our Lady is appearing the world over in one Catholic venue after another, validating this very fact, and the faithful seem reticent at best to trumpet this fantastic revelatory prodigy. We are restrained in our abandonment to Her guiding grace because too many are afraid that we are going to offend the sensibilities of people who detest Roman Catholicism anyway. These are not fighting words; they are a slicing sword of truth across the neck of a beast. A young French maid named Joan of Arc faced greater adversity and with far more heroism. Liberation is going to come at the cost of the egos of men. The pathway to Christian unity is through Our Lady's intercession and leads into the very heart of the Roman Catholic Church. I tell you now, the only solidarity that matters in the sight of God is hereby convening under the Mantle of the Woman Clothed with the Sun. We must be unyielding, speak powerfully, peacefully, potently and more prophetically, and sacrifice and pray as if the future of the world depends on it. The children of Mary are poised to enlighten this age; and the Light will actually taste sweet. Humanity is about to be catapulted into a new state of awareness by the grace of the Most Blessed Trinity. Ecstatic fulfillment will be the lot of those who heed the signs of the times. All the long-held dreams of broken men will be accomplished in the blinking of an eye because in God's design, no one loses in order for others to win. His Victory will be that overwhelming.

XV. Sung with an eloquence few have ever heard

We have been placed in this alcove of the ages—together—for only a brief flash in the unfolding millennia. Amidst the enthralling and alluring spectacle of the Earth, there is but one simple message. It is Jesus Christ who is the Supreme Love of God. While human beings too often manifest imperfection, the true power resting peacefully in communion with our spirit must be called upon to make-up the distance from where we are at present to the pinnacles of human excellence that our Creator calls us to inhabit in perpetuity. We must enshrine the parameters of our fraternal unity in a macroscopic script, distinguishable beyond our generation by anyone who would someday survey our times for the most breathtaking examples of our era. It is for each of us to discern our most prolific sacrifices, embrace them with courageous humility, and advance our contribution to the elevation of our brothers and sisters above the demagogic darkness that diminishes us all. We must synthesize dogma and platitude into dignity and power, and allow it to emanate from our hearts. This potency radiates from the invocation of our love for those we do not even know or with whom we are at odds. We must stop offending, vilifying, persecuting, and prosecuting the Truth through some false sense of preservation of our freedom to choose. And, choose wisely we must. Our choices must take the form of accepting our pious responsibilities and the burden of our difficulties as opposed to embracing the temptation to selfishly jettison them through some immoral expedience. If we do not always commit ourselves to the highest good that has been revealed to mankind, we will not ascend from the mire, but taken down instead into the horrific consequences that have repeatedly plagued humanity throughout the ages. Those who are indulging in lesser actions than those befitting their dignity as human beings, and inflicting these sad choices with reckless disregard upon us all, are truly spiraling toward the demise of themselves and that portion of society that they are driving into the depths. Somewhere and at some time, each person commits themselves to the trek of noble greatness, lest they find at the last that their lives were irrelevant at best, and no more than an impediment to the stellar hopes of a collective human species. We must arrive at that glistening future arm-in-arm, our hearts aglow with compassion and caring based upon the highest principles we can articulate and emulate, rather than being forced into daily increments of recurring tension, generated and inflicted upon our societies by people who care only little about themselves, and surely nothing for their fellow citizens. Civility and the unity which blossoms from its fertile environment are a far more pleasurable state of existence than the compaction and grief we inflict upon one another at the rejection of these wiser courses of life. There are wars of truth to be fought, but they are in the realms of virtue and the righteous dignity that each person should require of themselves and demand for others. The combatants we will face always bear banners articulating their rights and license as human beings to sin and degrade as they wish, but we must engage them nonetheless.

Our cinematographers have honed an amazing artistic ability to create moments on the silver screens that help us experience very heartfelt and deeply moving emotions. Most of us have seen movies where the actors have played-out their storylines of grief, desolation and drama, overcoming insurmountable odds and claiming peaceful success at the close of their epics. The outcomes of these sagas often metaphorically depict their characters relaxing beside one another, perched on rails of old wooden fences, surveying the newly-liberated countryside with their faces awash in the comforting glow of the flat light of a setting sun, while heart-rending melodies wisp hauntingly through the air. We are caught-up in their emotions as they reminisce the vivid memories that fate etched upon their souls, awed by the spirit that rose from their nondescript essence which convened their determination and conscripted them as custodians and defenders of truth for their time amongst the rolling ages of tyranny. It is therein as we witness their lives that we sense the peace of our own existence, the purpose of our convictions, and the renewed hope which testifies to us that holiness is prevailing, despite the fictitious facade that Satan splays before us. In these aesthetic scenes, we are reinvigorated by the knowledge that a new beginning always flourishes, notwithstanding the biting memory of the carnage of our tribulations. It is there we sense our wounds exploding like the sun and gratitude falling upon our lesser angels like morning dew upon the meadows, permeating our beings with the satisfaction that we were chosen to engage the sanctification of men as their catapults to perfection. It does not matter whether the moment is composed of a survivor looking aft from the stern of a ship, recalling the tragedy of a luxurious steamer interred beneath the waves, or the son of a champion standing in victory atop the roof of his automobile, taking-in the thundering approval of a sympathetic nation after conquering the raceway that claimed the life of his iconic father. It is all about the heroic sanctity of the human heart triumphing over its most afflicted day, where courageous resilience outlasts the howling winds of ill fortune and sinister intention. It is mystically engraved in the legacy of the children of God who have lifted their gaze from many a pit of despair and stared into the face of the unmitigated evil who placed them beneath their dignity, and declared in union with the one universal body of righteousness that their will remained as newborn in amazing grace as an infant just baptized and placed in its father's arms. It is about believing in the supremacy of the beautiful, residing like the sun above the most menacing storms, obscured only for its time-measured moment, while we patiently engage the mystical pilgrimage beneath their shadows in a cadence of divinity, knowing the ultimate end bears the eclipse of God's genius over every mortal encounter with iniquity. It is the confident testament that an ultimate Triumph is in the offing, one so unfathomable that God will close-out the ages and seal for Eternity the immaculate victory that every created soul has longed in succession to secure from the first day of the world. Our scientists tell us, based upon the facts of the universe and the probabilities of chance, that our life-giving planet will someday succumb to the ages where forces of galactic destruction clandestinely lurk beyond our vision. No matter whether our Creator preempts or perpetually delivers this world from these occurrences, there is a concluding day reserved for it nonetheless where the last Roman Catholic priest will lift a simple piece of unleavened bread above the altar and say for the final time amidst this purifying trial of sanctification, *Take this all of you and eat, this is My Body which will be given up for you.* And, then the salvific drama of the Creation, Fall and Redemption of mankind will be complete. The universe will reverberate with the words, *It is finished.* And, at that opening strike of Everlasting Life, the Holy Mass will be accomplished, and all of history in the heavens and what was once upon the mortal Earth will take its seat atop the palisades of Paradise in the Spirit of

Resurrection. The eyes of the redeemed will peer back across the millennia to the first horizon of human existence; to the gestating cradle where the children of God began their engagement between Heaven and Hell, good and evil, righteousness and diablerie; where the battle for survival and dignity ensued, and we will reminisce in the full light of omniscient Glory the story of suffering humanity who conquered in solidarity with the poignant reality of Jesus' Crucifixion which will rise with grandeur before our beatific affections as the sole event in those millions of years which declared with preeminence beyond the heavens that mankind in the flesh was special in the universe. The Light of Christ beaming from the Cross of Calvary through the prism of His Mystical Body will be the bathing spectacle of ecstasy that will radiate from those treacherous ages upon our tear-drenched faces, wiping away the pain and the horror from our souls, and lauding us instead for believing that Love was our thoroughfare in transcending death. Our Lady wishes us to take heart now and realize that She is already bathing in that glow, taking-in our lives as our proud Mother, assisting us during our passion with all the affections of Her Immaculate Heart, and calling us to process through the butchery and banality of these years with the valor and strength of warriors whose legacies can never be struck down in the annals of Paradise. Our lives of holiness are flushing evil from Creation through the corona of our beatific intentions and the bull-nature of our hearts which are blinding the starlit heavens to the lesser actions of compromising men, rendering their nefarious infractions the unseens of Eternity, replacing and overwhelming the legacy of these unrepentant Adams with the hidden light of the human heart. God will satiate our souls with the knowledge that the passion, endurance, trust, commitment, and devotion of the meek of the Earth were the furnace of deliverance that He kept burning through the expanse of the eons, waiting for the curtain to rise on the hopes and dreams that we were tempted to believe would never come, but knew in our beings were already here.

We hold to this Truth that is filled to brimming with perfection. What price would we pay for a good hero in a world of timid creatures wrapped in Nature's songs? Humanity's fate is the prerogative of God, lest we find ourselves witless about the impending concession of the castigating years. We recognize our Redemption with adequacy overflowing, goodness anointed, and atonement exposed atop an Earth whose coarse face was secretly conceived, forever living and always dying, imprisoned by the druthers of men, and shattered beneath a blanket of broken dreams, and whose beauty and destiny have been encrypted among the lineage of stars. Come, true hope!-amidst the glaring sword's piercing sovereignty, where brides and grooms are tossed to the wind, where the faint-of-heart devour affection and the mind slowly fades, where lost societies meander aimlessly toward the sculpting of the ages at the hands of our compassionate Lord who has too brilliantly concealed His Face to suit our wincing eyes. Our spirits will soon be subdued by a lethal dose of

Heaven's resolve to sift us from the ashes of our burned-out sins! Would God not remind us that living freer than death implies that we not grovel too low among the perpetually condemned when He bestows Eternity upon His people who are clad in the Blood-soaked raiment of His Offspring's Death? Put on Christ, indeed! How do we know when we have sufficiently deferred to the Cross where our Salvation was publicly impaled? *Gentlemen of the republics, what say you?* With what urgency do we examine our beaming addictions and ocean-quipped fondness for the anatomical depths, our smoldering funeral pyres, and flickering cumulus skies? All hail our baptisms galore; reconcile us with the King! Low and behold, we awaken from our sepulchers repeating the question we put to our forbears; when will you enter your Kingdom?

MORNING STAR OVER AMERICA

The New Millennium
In the Year of Our Lord
AD 2003

Wednesday, January 1, 2003
Solemnity of Mary, Mother of God
7:19 p.m.

"My beloved children, Eternity looms and Salvation calls, and your future depends on your willingness to be remade into the holiness of My Son. I appear before you to speak of the reunification of the nations and the abhorrent condition of the spirit of America. The mystifying absence of moral courage in the United States is an utter shame, and the civility and good will you once espoused is nearly extinct. God's Triune Love and your own intuitive loyalty comprise the fealty to Heaven that lives inside your hearts, and it must be shared equally with strangers and enemies as with your families and friends. I implore you to not withhold this creative coalescence from them; do not keep the best for yourselves, believing that there is insufficient goodness in the universe to share. The Father will bless you if you do this, if you reject looking glibly at commoners as being insignificant, if you do not study the isolationism that has made such a shipwreck of the western hemisphere. Engage others in the context of what they endure, and remember that they are often more weak than malevolent. I beg you not to force Me to come calling upon you by saying 'My dear woefully embittered children.' Those who are young and capable must defend the Church with innovative vigor, while your grandfathers recline in their fruitwood chairs beneath boxelder trees, ruing the inequity of your republic with their health waning and death approaching. When history knocks at your door, what will you tell it? If you succumb to the impulses that devalue your faith, you will be hidden from the Cross; and good Christians are above such distractions. Your generation must learn why Truth is the Will of the Father. It is not because He takes pleasure in someone else's sorrow. Anyone who speaks with spiritual insight already knows that there is enough suffering in the world, that you have sufficient poetic rituals, verses, unspoken eulogies, and unsung dirges to last until the end of time. You must realize that you are engaged in a battle against the adversaries of common sense. Secular humanism suborns everything ill-founded from the sultry to the bizarre, while poverty in the masses perpetuates infirmity, disquietude, anguish, aggression, and despair. Progressive materialism is no more than a fable, while some Americans seem to have lost their moral compass somewhere between pragmatism and vengeance. Christians know that secularism is riddled with irrelevance, that the enemies of the Church have resorted to deceptive hyperbole in an attempt to discredit the Truth of the Gospel and draw generalizations about the faithful by citing the aberrations of a few. You experience the whole spectrum of emotions in anger, pride, sorrow, and joy before finally acknowledging that the only sensation that matters is being at peace with God. If you are prone to tears, remember that weeping out of love for humanity is the greatest sign of His presence. Since you are a nation that espouses religious freedom, conditions should not require that the Lord's Mother should tell you that America's perception of equality is manifestly unfair. To remedy this, you should return to your Christian origins and address the problems that are plaguing your land. You must shine the Light of Love through Creation with speeches pealing the oratorical eloquence of the Kingship of Christ. You must protect the dignity of the heart because it is the steward of your faith. You need not worry that the Lord will become intolerant of His creatures or that one among you will be the proverbial last tired soul whom Jesus will suffer gladly. His Providence is unique to each person and universal for all humanity. When you intone the melodies of life, Jesus will help you through the mourning bars to the glorious refrains, and this is why you have been given the faculties of the intellect and moral judgement for the cultivation of the world. It is also the reason I come to you, My children, because God scatters the seed that makes the villages grow.

Will history prove that holiness demanded more than most Americans were willing to pay? Do you find any imperative in leading lives of sacrifice and self-denial? When righteousness came in the form of a Dove to elevate your land with Wisdom, did you set a snare to inhibit its flight? When justice called, did you respond with clemency? When paupers pleaded for relief, did you lift them up? Jesus knows that you will falter unless you enlist His Kingdom, and for this you require vision, energy, strength, and commitment. God does not always slumber you gently to numb the sting of your overwhelming sacrifices, but when you stand in the meadow and look at the blue forest mountains, do you not gain a sense for the majestic that expands your hopes for something greater than death? Do you realize that the United States is off-center from redemptive piety? When passels of foreign dignitaries visit your most venerated public shrines, do they know the depths of your immorality? To help you ponder your response to these questions, allow the love and unification between you to be served, that peace shall prevail around the globe, and Christ Jesus will have the last word. All things are pressing toward the engagement between time and Eternity, and I have come at this hour to teach you how to pray while humankind, with sea waves crashing, pursues its primordial origin. Do not panic or leap to conclusions about what I am saying to you. Remember that it is not impossible for someone to be late in coming but still ahead of his time."

Sunday, January 5, 2003
Solemnity of the Epiphany
3:32 p.m.

"Dear children, My messages are a spiritual poultice for your world-weary souls, and they give you strength during the unprecedented sanctification of the existence of men. Remember that the Lord lends you a Christian heart to be the chaplaincy of your moral conscience. Today, you commemorate the journey of the Magi to visit their newborn King. What a transformation for them and their successors. Imagine the scene as their hearts shuddered in wonderment that the Lord God deigned to become Incarnate as Baby Jesus. They represented the faith and trust that millions are practicing today. They brought gifts that portended the unfolding of Jesus' Life, Crucifixion, and entombment in the Sepulcher. My little children, as difficult as it may seem to believe, as horrible as the condition of the world now stands, and as far from Divine Love that so many people are, these are among the gladdest days that humanity has ever known. Every promise that the Child in the Manger oathed during His earthly life is 2,000 years closer to reality. I assure you that many aspects of this age will be contemporary when the Son of Man returns in Glory. I have told you this before, and I reconfirm that it is true. I pray unceasingly that your fellow countrymen will relinquish their penchant for pursuing disordered behaviors that run contrary to the Holy Gospel. You must petition the Father along with Jesus to procure this blessing. Absent the human heart, your intentions are only strains of falsetto, only superficial phrases without eternal meaning. You must maintain a loving relationship with God because the Son of the Most High will soon return and the Earth's mortal framework will be repealed. We must pray to transform your brothers and sisters' faithlessness from an icy floe of indifference into living waters of belief. Millions of Americans saw the biography of a Hollywood entertainer who was given four minutes on a stage, a minuscule period that will allow him to depart this mortal world a millionaire. I have been speaking to you for generations about others who have devoted their entire lives of seventy and eighty years in the service of Jesus, and they will leave their years as paupers. Why is this so? Because they warehoused their riches in the Kingdom of Heaven where they will flourish beneath God's Triune Providence forever. This is a prospect that not many consider, neither do they meditate upon the effectiveness of self-denial. As striking as it may seem, the richer you are in love, the less you sense a need for material artifacts. You understand more clearly that Jesus hears your plaincry to shelter you from the throes of daily life. I assure you that praying the Holy Rosary is a priority that I commend all My children to embrace, especially during this Year of the Holy Rosary as has been proclaimed by Pope John Paul II. I urge you to recite all twenty Sacred Mysteries to alleviate the suffering of those who are still living in poverty, neglect, and pain. They share Jesus' suffering on the Cross for the same reason that He so copiously bled for the Redemption of the lost. Please remember to petition not only for those who are agonizing, but for the many whose selfishness is causing such torment. My hope as AD 2003 opens is that the evolution of the conscience of humanity will broaden so that political borders no longer cause divisions among men. Yes, it is true that the Earth appears to be unified from the heights of the horizons. The forests and mountain ranges run smoothly and without demarcation from one republic to the next. It is only by the transits of geographers that such distinctions exist. When every nation of peoples is brought before the Cross, the vision of entire regions will become distinct. And, the older you grow in years, the better you are capable of knowing that there are too many fallacious vacuums that separate mortal men. Too much arrogance and too little meekness have caused political upheaval on every corner of the globe, even as United States' capitalists ply their wily skills of skimming the wealth of foreign patrons in the interest of national defense. Why would you fear your enemies' arsenals if by spreading the Holy Gospel you can disarm them from the heart? No trigger can be tripped if it is not the will of the weapon bearer. These thoughts should be part of peacemaking everywhere. If heads of state and hardened negotiators would cease skewing the definition of victory, humanity would not reach the brink of war. In this spiritual context about which I speak, the slogan of 'I win' is supplanted by 'We all win!' Indeed, there are tens-of-thousands of innocent lives in jeopardy where war is imminent. I tell you, the Son of Man will avenge every one of them should they be sacrificed in the resultant melee. Condoning collateral damage is nonsensical in the prosecution of war. Anyone whose life is taken, whether or not they are the direct target, is a life that was not loved enough by their attackers to preserve. Too many leaders hold to the belief that their pride and patriotic reputations are more important than the casualties that are inflicted while defending themselves. This has been true throughout human history, and it is the case in these times.

My Special son, I know that you are wondering what My messages about such wars can do to stop the bloodshed before it is too late. For this, there is only your prayers to preclude them because humanity is frequently loath to heed the admonishments of the Mother of God. While it is better to prevent such atrocities from the start, My words to the world that I am dispensing at your hands will have converting influence precisely because the response of Jesus to the arrogance of humanity will be as I am telling you now. In this, the Earth is bringing certain annihilation upon itself. Once the human race is privy to My messages to you, they will make more sense because they will be outlaid in a context that is more comprehensible. It will not be upon deaf ears that your warnings will fall that the Immaculate Virgin Mary has appeared before you to relate what might occur if humanity does not refrain from the prosecution of war. Sadly, some will not stop through this admonition alone! Hence, you are seeing the pitiable result of the conduct of men when they take it upon themselves to stain the future. How easily they forget that they are saved by Grace that is larger than life. To be clear, this is not unlike the feeling I had during Jesus' Passion and Crucifixion on Good Friday. I knew, however, that He would be resurrected from the Tomb and that the fullness of His Wisdom would subsist through Eternity. If not for the tragedy of His death, the Earth for all history would never have known. This will be the effect of the wars to come, those that are being provoked by such countries as the United States of America. It is a nation eerily reminiscent of the Roman soldiers who are crucifying the Mystical Body of Christ in your day. Please pray for peace! This is the crucial factor in whether you accord humanity the opportunity to heed what I am saying. If you admonish them more about peace than prophesies of doom, you are likely to instill in them the notion that Jesus is a loving King, not filled with vengeance in the face of their errors. Prayer and forgiveness are central to these things, and this is where we direct their attention. This is the strength and facility of your writing. Thank you for entering this new year with such hope for the success of sharing the New Covenant of Jesus with the lost and despairing, those whose happiness has been destroyed by the schemes of partisans, and the little ones who have no one to care for them. Your new book will be a segment of immortal history to soften hundreds-of-millions of hearts before the Throne of the Father. Let us watch with anticipation what Jesus does. I know that whatever the outcome of your efforts, the work you are doing will reflect a positive light. As you have seen, such reaching-out has always been a blessing. Your books are food for peace for proceeding generations, but it takes time to make them part of the human record. How could Russia have been converted and the USSR disbanded if not for God's willingness to await the papacy of Pope John Paul II? *(I spoke to Our Lady about the downfall of European Communism not coming more swiftly.)* Does it in hindsight seem a missed opportunity for God to have prohibited Marxism to fester from the beginning? How else do you suppose the Gospel can be fulfilled? It is occurring today. You are speaking about events that have been ongoing for centuries, while I am referring to the transformation of an entire human species that will be converted and redeemed for the expanse of Eternity. I have told you about the Sacred Mysteries, and that endless numbers of intellectuals throughout history have attempted to rationalize the Salvation of God's creatures. Please read and absorb the Sacred Scriptures, and you will discover your answers there. The human language through which I am speaking is much too exhaustible for Me to explain the facets and parameters of the sublime expulsion of evil from the Earth. It is not a matter of how many centuries expired or the billions of souls who have died, it is whether everyone who has participated, the good and the bad, will at last yield their hearts to the Savior of the Ages and enter Paradise as one united family. Having said this, the acclamation that you have made that there should be no more wars on Earth because of the fidelity of the Love of God is as true as Truth can be. He has provided for the Salvation of the souls of mankind by Jesus' Sacrifice on the Cross, and the Divine power that is needed to mend Creation has previously been handed to you. Jesus is waiting for His disciples to do precisely what you are suggesting. This is what the New Covenant is for; it is why the Holy Spirit is convening righteousness through everyone who will listen, and it is the reason I am speaking to you now.

There is never a purpose for war other than that the parties are telling each other that they are disdained. When humanity becomes evolved to the point that they assert that they will war no more, you will see the indivisible union between Heaven and Earth. What more do you wish God to do? Do you not know that the human will was destined to be a part of His plan since Adam and Eve? You are asking for more miracles, more signs, more pious destruction, more revelations from Heaven. You are wishing for lightning bolts to strike and holy disintegration to befall the Earth because your brothers and sisters will not listen to what the Holy Spirit has been telling them for centuries. God is asking when it will be His people's decision to respond and accept the holiness that He has been seeking in them. The fuller point you are making is that you are tired of humanity's lack of spirituality and their reticence to accept the Sacraments whose origin they cannot see. In essence, you are calling upon God to punish them for their lack of faith—a faith that He is offering freely as their gift for the taking. Should He come to the Earth in the form of Angels and tell those who are rejecting His benisons that they do not have the will to do so? This would not be true. I lack the means to provide an appropriate response to your question because it would require you to see life from the other side and comprehend the faculties of suffering. It is the Will of God that you live on Earth as Jesus did for the purpose of altering the orientation of His people by everything you are saying, writing and accomplishing, to usher His Kingdom to its fullest extension in the consciences of mortal men. You are doing so, and much more. I cannot fault you for being impatient because you are only asking God to be God, to destroy the enemies of righteousness and spare the innocent lives that are lost. I pray for this as well. I have the same hopes that live in your humble heart, but the destruction of the adversaries of holiness prior to their realizing that there is such a thing as righteousness would deprive them of the choice to convert with volition. See Saint Paul. Again, the constraints of time and the elements of your exile preclude Me from making this point more clearly. *(I asked Our Lady to provide a greater sign to convert lost sinners.)* Wherever did you get the idea that such a sign will not be given? Have you heard of Medjugorje? *(Our Lady was being facetious, as She is aware of my two pilgrimages there.)* Where is there a place in the world where a great miracle will be manifested, not the least of which is the vision restored to a sightless man in his elder years? Why have you forgotten about these things?

There is a history of this. What has become of the memoirs of the 70,000 people who saw the miracle of the sun at Fatima in 1917? What impact did it have?... Each and every sinner who lives on the face of the globe is the holy soul you are seeking. They do not know it, and this is what your writing is for, indeed it is what your life is for. Jesus is not only the Master of the Ages, He is the Master of good timing. You could not have asked Me these issues if the Holy Spirit had not prompted you from the depths of your heart. Imagine with what utter frustration I have gone to Him to ask these things, and the Father looked into the sorrowing eyes of His Son and Myself and said, *But there are just a few more that I know I can reach!* And then, He begins to weep because He realizes that He is like Oskar Schindler who can rescue many more before the final hour comes. This is why He allows Jesus to be Crucified on the altars of the Catholic Church, because there are millions who can know, and they will know. He is longing for the opening hearts of His people that only they can effect, that they will be converted by the good offices of their trust. Are you beginning to see this more clearly? It is a matter of the will. The response you are seeking is that you wish to know when it will be time for God's flock to take hold of the Earth and shake it like a pillow to loosen every form of evil from its fabric. Your hopes are of the Eternal Victory that lives in the Triumph of My Immaculate Heart. Do you not realize that you are reciting your greatest prayers from which you are weeping with enlivened hope? Your expectation is that of the Saints who believed the Second Coming of Christ would arrive in their day. If it should not occur in your earthly tenure, please know that God has a reason that you will see. Would your spirit and all Creation not be poorer if you did not seek the alleviation of suffering? Is it not true that the Salvation of humankind came at the price of the Crucifixion of the only perfect Man who ever lived? What is emanating from you is your desire to see the Lord set things right according to the Books of the Bible, and this is a perfectly proper thing for you to do. You pray to perpetuate Heaven here on the Earth, and His wish is that humanity will welcome Him from the heart. His worst enemy is the stubbornness of mortal men; it has been this way since the Fall of Adam. If you are searching for someone to blame, look to the wretches who despise the Savior with whom you will soon share Paradise. It is not unreasonable for the faithful to inquire when God will do something more, but am I not enough? Are My Shrines insufficient? Are My apparitions too few? All Jesus wants to know is when will be humanity's decision to convert. He performed miracles while on Earth, and what happened? They crucified Him anyway. Thus, it is not by miracles or chastisements that the world is transformed into the likeness of Heaven, but in the sharing of its people with the Holy Cross and forging the fathoms of self-sacrifice. I am not suggesting that such is inevitable or that there is enmity between God and man, I am saying that humanity must pray, do penance, fast, receive the Sacraments of the Church, and fall to their knees asking the Lord to restore peace and order to the universe from within the hearts of the creatures He deigned to give life. Is this not what we are fostering? There are words to express what Jesus seeks from His people, and I remind you time and again what they are. But, what lives in the Will of the Father is a far higher Love than you can see. He is waiting for His people to repent so they will not cast themselves into Hell when He sends Jesus back again. What happens during the interim? The sinners who are not converted are causing suffering in the lives of the innocents. If this seems like a paradox, it is because you are viewing it through the element of time. Every Saint who has been canonized and those whom God knows to be His own has asked the same question that you put before Me; this is not unique to you. While the answers are never simple and the solutions slow to come, I ask that you walk in faith with the knowledge that God does everything perfectly, and what He allows during the sanctifying of the world is mitigated by Christians with faith like yours. Every person who was martyred because of the sins of heathens, hypocrites, and warmongers was delighted to greet Jesus with thanksgiving that they suffered a hero's death. You will understand once you see this from the other side of time. No life sacrificed for the Salvation of the lost is surrendered in vain. Please wait a moment."

My dear brother! This is Jesus! I will soon dispatch the millions of souls who were aborted in their mothers' wombs to conquer the evil about which you have spoken. They are that covenant of miracle workers you are hoping to see! And, you will! They are the martyred innocents who will soon destroy My enemies on the Earth! Please continue to pray with patient anticipation! Do you remember when I thought that the Cup might pass Me by? I am overjoyed that it never did! You will see! I love you. You are My Fathom!

"It has been My joy to speak to you. Thank you for sharing the intricacies of your heart. This has been fulfilling for Me, educational for you, and cleansing for the world!..."

Sunday, January 12, 2003
The Baptism of Jesus
3:22 p.m.

"Now, the festive Season of Christmas has come and gone for another year, and the Church will begin preparing for the arrival of Ash Wednesday. However, there is much more to be done by then. I ask you to ponder your own baptism on this holy day because it is the anniversary of the grace-filled blessing of Jesus by John the Baptizer. I wish to make clear that baptism is more than the symbol that some ecclesiastics have described it to be. The sacramental relinquishing of the human will to be nothing less than the perfect poverty of Jesus commences at the moment of baptism. Upon being blessed, the water is no longer its parenthetical chemical sufficient, it is the perfume of your concession that Jesus Christ is your new reason for living, that the Holy Spirit is your guide, and that the mission of the Church has supplanted every other purpose for your existence on Earth. Your makeup comprises a spiritual one upon your baptism because your soul becomes the property of the Lord. You reject Satan and his evil works, and you labor both physically and prayerfully to defeat his effects in your life and of your brothers and sisters. My children, knowing that Satan has been lurking in the shadows of the world for thousands of years, and that most of you are less than five decades old, I can see how you might believe that defeating his legions is a tall order at times. However, if you embrace the vows of your baptism, attend the Holy Sacrifice of the Mass every day for peace and strength, receive the Sacrament of Penance at least once a month, and recite the Sacred Mysteries of the Holy Rosary seven days per week, Satan will not wish to approach you because he knows that such are the disciples of God and lethal to his demonism from the underworld. I assure you that yours is the miraculous revelation of the Cross in your Christian faith, and God has made no reason for such beauty to be put asunder or defeated by those who refuse to believe in Him. And, with this, your victory is only a matter of time. So, pray and be thankful that you belong to Jesus. Recall forever what I have told you, that baptism is more than a symbol; it is your profession, your avocation, and your destiny in Christ. Thank you for having responded to My call. My Special son, after the eloquent way you addressed the Heavens last week in our message and your absolutely profound writings for your books since then, we will speak only briefly today. I have come to pray with you today because there is never a time when I do not. I see the visions and hopes in your heart that you poured-out before Me last week; and you can see more clearly now that many questions are never easy to answer. Let Me tell you, however, of a matter that is for sure. Yesterday, January 11, 2003, the Governor of the State of Illinois, USA, pronounced both Mercy and Pardon upon the lives of every single person who had previously been condemned to die by the courts, executed outright for their crimes. There is no doubt that you listened to a speech that will live-on until the end of the world. It rivals the deliverance of the Sacred Beatitudes by Jesus Christ on the side of the Mountain. It reflects with precision the Holy Gospel of Christianity in its most essential form. This is a man who has risked scorn, rejection, ridicule, and physical danger to his life. I tell you today that Jesus Christ has gained another Saint and Doctor of the Church, a man of great means who has absolved the poor and wretched who have been given very little. I speak of a man who wept at the loss of someone very dear to him from his own hometown, and then boldly told the world that these criminals who flank him on both sides, all of them, would not die for their sins. Does this sound familiar? Governor George Ryan, whose original signature you have on a letter he sent to you, is being lauded by the greatest Angelic Courts ever to have sung the praises of a mortal man. It is both clear and obvious what the followers of evil, especially the media and the courts, will try to do to him now. I am telling you that as he leaves office tomorrow at midday, he will not only take his dignity with him, but the blessing of the Son of God that is so profound that his mortal soul will glow with Light. Imagine how the Holy Trinity has wept in thanksgiving of the change of heart of My little boy, My George, who is now the conqueror of the wretchedness of vengeance and hate. His power and conviction are nearly unparalleled in the annals of history, and certainly in the time of modern man. Forget about the Nobel Prize for Peace, this man is a walking Saint of Holy Christendom, and all should fall at his feet and wish to emulate his Grace! I thank him for his wisdom and strength, Jesus offers His Love for his every loving act, and God the Almighty Father will soon deliver him to the highest pinnacle of the Heaven He has promised. Yes, His soul will bask in a land of milk and honey with the greatest among men who ever set foot on the face of the globe... What a day!—this January 11, 2003! What a humble man! What a moment! What a Saint! What a bountiful heart! I wish only that you would someday make My remarks public so all in the world can understand... Thank you for helping Me to do so. Please do not be too disappointed by some of the actions of a humanity who has been taught by their predecessors to be like they are. Every time someone like your Governor, who leaves office tomorrow, stands-up against the howls of evil that come from those who espouse hatred and revenge, it drowns-out the declaration from centuries-past of, ...*What I have written, I have written...*"

Sunday, January 19, 2003
2:47 p.m.

"I hear your angelic voices crying in the darkness of exile while you suffer the effects of the transgressions of your brothers and sisters against you. With all the wonder in your hearts, there is plentiful Grace to make you strong in the Spirit of Truth, rendering you no less than valiant warriors whom Jesus has enlisted to fight for purity and justice worldwide. Please remember to pray for the straying ones in your midst because deep inside, they are beautiful too. Too many of your peers are influenced by the temptations through which they are impacted by an environment of shameless indifference and hatred. I implore humanity to place a moratorium on weakness and disavow sin altogether, promising Jesus that you will not surrender to it again. In Him, you never engage life with the expectation that your errors are inevitable, but that your slate is clean from the moment you accept His Blood as expiation for your transgressions. My children, I speak of a happiness that can be found in no other origin than your conversion to Christian Truth. For all the drudgery you see in Creation, the lack of your volitional love is the greatest wrongdoing. My call is to those whose consciences are being awakened by the Holy Spirit to rise again and be renewed by the Crucifixion of Jesus on the Cross. In the Son of Man, the consistency of your Christian conscience grows beyond the bonds of fear so you become the heroes you have always dreamt to be and sought from others. After all, is this not the kind of deliverance that so many have prayed for during the past 2,000 years? It is written in the Scriptures that God has visited His people, and this is your time to respond. The measures by which you judge one another are the criteria by which you shall also be judged. Even in this, I implore you to command much from yourselves in the realms of Christian righteousness! If it burdens you to adhere to the Commandments or believe in the Holy Sacraments, give your worries and trust to Jesus, and He will be your assurance that these are true Absolution. The Church is not only your sanctifying Mother, it is the reason you were born and baptized to be the children of God. I cherish these moments when I offer you Jesus' Truth in clement ways. He is the Holy One in whom the Judgement of the Earth has been bestowed. When the collective sins of humanity were heaped upon Him and He paid the price for your Redemption, all knowledge and vision coalesced to extricate you from the fate of eternal death. For those who aspire to become prophets, Jesus is your reason to prophesy. To the honorable ones who wish to become the conquerors of evil that is wreaking such havoc upon the lives of the innocent, your power and Wisdom reside in Christ's Crucifixion and Resurrection. These are not hollow gestures or smithing of oratory from empty rhetoric, they are the Gospel Truth that has been handed down throughout the ages. Men and women from all avenues of life have fought to the death defending what they know to be the Messianic Truth, which through God's Mystical Grace is the Salvation of humankind. Is He searching for martyrs in this age? To the capacity that you would lay-down your lives to those who oppose Him, the answer is yes. It is imperative that whenever a man ponders the sacrifices that Jesus asks him to make through the journey of life, the response to His call must be from this affirmation. Every time He hears your fiat reechoing Mine, the Father is glorified to an infinite degree. This, My children, is instilling purpose to your living and your compliance with the requests of Heaven so you are the healing of the sick and comfort for the dying. All this has come to you so you will open your hearts in supplication, that you will serve God in the multitude of ways to which the Holy Spirit summons you. Your predecessors from previous generations are waiting like angels for you to take to Creation's fore and finish their designs with such profundity that they will be like gleeful children whose lost puppies have come home.

    Now, My Special son, the time has arrived for Me to speak in briefer terms because you are becoming weary. I know that you will ask Me to respond to the prettiness of your writing, and I wish I had the appropriate words to tell you how beautiful it is. It is important that you rest your thoughts after this message. Each of your books is special because they address a different segment of society and the tenets of Christianity in their unique ways. Your deposit of works will have the converting power that you and your brother desire. Jesus is pleased because you love Him with a loyal alliance. The winter is passing quickly, and 2003 will have plentiful blessings. I know you are grateful to the Lord for every one of them. Can you sense the pious presence that your heart is wielding against the evil in the world?..."

Sunday, January 26, 2003
SS. Timothy & Titus
12:24 p.m.

"To the extent that there is Divine Mercy for those whose hearts are given to God in contrition, there shall likewise be vindication for the victims who have suffered at the hands of the last to concede. Please listen carefully to the words of your Mother. The peril in which the world finds itself in this nuclear age is as nothing compared to the Final Judgement of My Son. Therefore, I plead with you to become more loving, more holy, and less dependent on the temporal things of Earth. I am encouraged that most of My children are reciting the Holy Rosary as a matter of course because such is the Grace through which the Wisdom of the Holy Spirit abounds across the globe. Now, you are given by Christ's Vicar five Sacred Mysteries of Light upon which to ponder, taking humanity ever closer to finishing your mortal exile through the Holy Eucharist. It is imperative that the leaders of nations learn that there can be no victory for the people they represent unless that leadership takes massive populations to the Cross. It is futile for a public servant to believe that any true peace can last without the justification for the battle arising from the Holy Gospel of Christianity. I am the Mother of the Church; I am the Immaculate Queen of the only Heaven the Saints will know, and it is through My intercession that the Earth will comprehend matters of peace and Justice in the context of Divine Truth. From whom does My commission come? Jesus Christ. This is what you must acknowledge. All prophecy, progress, peace, Salvation, and the fruitful begetting of the Light of Eternity are found in Him. Let the people who oppose the Cross be on notice that their defeat is at hand because the Kingdom of God has inherited the Earth. This is not an hour for anxiety, but one of joyous Revelation. There is sufficient time for those sinners who have not converted to repent. Am I suggesting that anyone who is not Christian will be condemned to the fires of Gehenna? Certainly not. This is a blessing of the same Crucified Messiah. His Divine Mercy pervades deeply the essence of Creation that He shall raise all mankind by the overwhelming pardon that resides in Him. Conversely, it is imperative that His Mystical Body grows to its finest, that no soul should be shorn of their prefigured participation in the Gospel Covenant. Other religions may practice peace, justice and self-denial, but these are only portions of the Truth. The Body of Salvation for the sinful nature of humankind is Jesus Christ; there is no other expiation for the transgressions of the created world, past, present, or the remaining parameters of the future. I assure all who will hear that gladness and joy of heart are the bountiful blessings of the Christian who suffers because he is chosen to glorify the Lord. This, My children, is the emergence of Light. While the Heavens are asking the followers of the Messiah to alleviate the suffering of their broken brothers and sisters, this is the reflection of that same Light. There would be no need for suffering in a world where the Kingdom of God is wholly embraced because the Creation He fills with plenteous Redemption would be saturated by perfection. It is the depravity of sinners who reject Jesus that causes human suffering. Therefore, we pray together so the conversion of the lost will arrive. It is with this hope that I appear around the world, knowing that none of this is simple. My intercession is irrefutable evidence that God matters, and that He has definitive goals in mind. He is a working Lord whose Prophets have foretold humanity for centuries about the inevitable future. Those who have listened have surrendered treasure and flesh in favor of Truth and spiritualism. In effect, they have become the perpetual victors that those who embrace themes of corporeality will never inherit, for the latter will be vanquished, defeated, and rejected. I do not wish for this to happen to My children! These are the days and moments when we can make a difference together; and we are surely doing this, that those who subscribe to Divine Truth will gain even more, and the ones who own little will lose their paltry amount so that all that remains will be men's souls laid bare before Jesus and His pardoning for you before the brilliance of the Cross. It is toward this juncture that Heaven is inspiring and that humanity should be seeking. I know it is difficult for many to perceive this through the distractions of marketers and atheists, but the vision of righteousness will eventually come for those who seek the Lord while He can be found. Deep inside the conscience of everyone rests the capacity to know this. My Special son, I need not tell you these things over and again because you already realize them. You have come so close to permeating the veil of mortality through your thoughts, prayers, and actions that your identity in Jesus is crystal clear. However, there are millions who do not see, and it is for them that I exhort you to finish your work. I know that you have been doing so with anticipation, and for this reason, I will speak briefly so you can rest. Please make no issue of your brother's birthday because he wishes it to pass without notice. He is gratified that he is able to spend his mortal years with you, regardless of the age, no matter what the circumstances..."

Sunday, February 2, 2003
Feast of the Presentation of the Lord
3:57e/2:57c

"My dear little children, Jesus has asked Me to tell you that on this day of the Commemoration of a Sword which has pierced My Immaculate Heart, as America's culture of death is still doing; that during the sixteenth hour along its eastern seaboard and to an obedient messenger who has knelt to pray within a few hundred yards of the tomb of its sixteenth President, Heaven is confirming after a space vehicle was launched on the sixteenth day of 2003, completed a mission of sixteen days, and that perished within sixteen minutes of its return to the ground, God has decided that if the United States of America wishes to continue to inject poison into penitent sinners' veins to execute them in the name of secular justice and strew their corpses in dark graves all across its breadth and length—if you wish this retribution to be the legacy of your nation—then God has been moved to complement your wishes by allowing even more corpses from the heights of the skies to be strewn across the expanse of your vast and vengeful acreage. They are more innocent victims of a republic of unmitigated hatred. When He commissioned you to be fruitful and multiply, He did not intend for you to do so corruptly or with the same pride and vengeance that has brought such evil into the lives of the suffering. Were it not for the Grace of His Almighty Love, He would have heretofore allowed the destruction of many more of your institutions and social cliques. Why are these things occurring? Because the people of America are still too far from holiness. Your designs are always to the advancement of the self and rarely for the care, teaching, and nourishment of the helpless. Be sure to remember that Jesus had proclaimed that vengeance belongs to Him, and He is on the brink of claiming it on behalf of the billions throughout history who have been forced to agonize in other parts of the world because the USA has been so absorbed in garnering as much materiality as possible. These are perilous times, not because of the wrongful things that foreign legions might do, but by virtue of the Divine Justice that has made the Kingdom of God the place of blessing and exaltation to the followers of Christian Truth.

I have spoken at length to you before about Truth and Love because too many among you have mistaken them for posterity and patriotism. The ways that the Western world has skewed the meaning of Love has brought devastation upon the entire globe—so much so that the errors of Russia which had been put down at My intercession pale by comparison. The Soviet republics embraced atheism in an outward way, while the United States of America has espoused Christianity while deceivingly living in a way that despises its very tenets. This, My children, is why the American republic must be humbled, and humbled it will become! How far? Completely to its knees and flat on its belly so it can crawl around like the Reptile it has so egregiously embraced! You must know that this process has already begun. When hundreds-of-thousands of American people turn their heads to the skies and ask God why such torment is being brought upon their nation, He is silently but assuredly responding that it is because the United States has become a companion of evil! The way your impressionable youth are being scandalized is an outright abomination! Could it be true that the Mother of God would come before you through the kindness of a humble messenger and tell you that your God is not pleased? Yes! As surely as the Son of Man died on the Cross to save you from the fires of Hell, I am telling you that masses of your citizens are unfit and undeserving of such an absolution. These are difficult things for Me to tell you because you know that I am the Patron Saint of America and your Protectress from harm. I wish to protect you by asking you to avoid the perils of your own error! In its simplicity, is this too difficult for you to understand? Those who claim to be fair upholders of the public law are as corrupt as the criminals they are attempting to capture. Their discriminatory practices, vices, hatred, and outright sorcery in the name of some blind civility that has nothing to do with the Love of the Son of God will make for a great fire in which the chaff will burn! Indeed, such error and corruption are more fuel for this inferno of Justice. If anyone whose eyes fall upon the text of My messages should become afraid that they are among the guilty, then let them convert to the Sacred Heart of Jesus before it is too late!

    My Special son, I am not unmindful of the injustices you see, and we have discussed before your assertion that their end should come. There is no mortal who is living on the side of Truth who disagrees with you. There are many things that are being done and will happen in the hours of the ensuing week. God wishes you to endure a portion of the pain I suffered when the Sword of Sorrow pierced My Immaculate Heart. With your permission, please allow Me to be more clear. Knowing Jesus the way I have since He was born of My Womb, and rearing Him with the love and compassion that I have for Creation even today, and seeing that He was despised, ridiculed, chided, scourged, beaten, bludgeoned, and executed on the Cross as an innocent man, how do you think I felt? What thoughts do you suppose passed through My mind when this occurred? Many of the same ones that you now feel. Some of the conditions are identical because the Holy Spirit in your heart has been rejected by those with whom you come into contact. None of this is easy. The love you offer humanity in the likeness of Jesus is discounted and disdained. You know what it means to have your dignity impugned by haughty politicos and wealthy conglomerates. I have not come to say that this will be punished some time in the future, but now! They will be heaved into the inferno of God's Wrath today. They will be consumed by flames and spate into the pit of the netherworld where they can no longer cause a despondent feeling to enter gentle hearts like yours. Your suffering has aided in your understanding of the

Passion and Crucifixion of Jesus by means that are relevant to anyone who is predisposed to Christianity. You are not alone; your suffering does not go unnoticed, those who hate Jesus will be cast into the fires of Hell, and the righteous shall prevail; they are beginning to do so already. You sense it in your heart and feel it by the impressions you know from matters that are rarely seen in the media. When seven astronauts lost their lives in the fiery stream of twisted shards and gaseous fumes overhead, another seven teenage children were buried by an avalanche in Canada. The first was heard by most within the hour, but the media declined to broadcast the latter because they believed the lives of the young were not as important. This is the inequity about which you have spoken regarding the American media, and it is being addressed during these moments. I encourage you and give you strength. Please know that everything I have told you is true. I realize that you feel a sense of urgency since AD 2003 has arrived. Please do not become emotionally trapped in the rapid fire because it will diminish your peace. The battle between good and evil is playing-out, and I wish not that your emotions to become a casualty of this..."

Sunday, February 9, 2003
3:08 p.m.

"My dear children, O' that you would awaken in the morning filled with the goodness of the Holy Spirit and pour it over God's Creation before you retire for the night! My peace is with you during these frightful hours when the warring of men is imminent and ongoing. I pray with you for peace, and this is our promise to God that you shall remain loyal to Him through the Grace of My Sacrificed Son. The dimensions of the years take your hearts ever closer to seeing Him with your eyes—the all loving and omnipresent perfection that is being sought from within you. Thank you for listening and responding, for the cultivation of the Earth is dependent upon the participation of the righteous in the pious prayers and dutiful sacrifices that repudiate evil works wherever it is found. My little ones, such is the means of enlivening your faith that was sought from men of old, and the Truth for which they lived and died is the same Love to which you are called, for whom you are asked to live. This is not only your Redemption, it is the transformation of the Earth into the pristine beauty that if seen with the naked eye would be recognized as the innate beatification of your Christian faith about which I spoke before. Far and wide I have searched for My wayward children who have been hiding in the darkness of sin and corruption. And, aided by the Holy Spirit, the Angels and the Saints, I have been rooting them out and exposing them to the Sacrifice by which humankind is purified. These are the most amenable profits of your supplications on their behalf. I will reveal these things to you by vision and action when the time is full, but now I ask your continued participation in leading lives of holiness, evangelizing the Holy Gospel in your own righteous ways, and being the simple offspring of a single-minded world. If you can imagine the combined sorrow and gladness that comprises the years of mortal men, think about how My Son feels that He has provided your venue for Salvation on the Cross, and the jubilation He has in realizing that you are only a measure of time from coming to Heaven. And yet, too many millions are disrespectfully resisting Him because they boast of being proudly self-sufficient. These people's hopes are built on the shifting sands of an exasperated Earth; they have no bedrock on which to stand because their consciences are dead. The year 2003 is an intense time of revelation for humanity, not in the sense that the Holy Gospel will be appended, for the entire deposit of Christian Redemption has already been divulged, but in the means by which the Will of God is still unfolding before the Earth. If too many are afraid that they can make no difference in the outcome or destiny of their friends and neighbors, they should take solace that their courage and strength are found in Jesus' Most Sacred Heart. Men with wives and wives with husbands should reexamine their lives in accordance with the Wisdom of the Holy Paraclete. In this is discovered the key to making your children the holy souls you have pined for them to be. I beseech humanity not to grieve over the obsolescence of the Earth because the Kingdom of God is at hand. What does this foretell? What could it have meant when Saint Paul wrote so prolifically to his own contemporaries? It means that perfect Love, Divine Love, has come into the world in the Persons of Jesus Christ and the Holy Spirit to reclaim everything that has been lost. In this, the age of Saint Paul and the 21st century coexist in the same crucible. Jesus holds you in His hands; for all who have died alone in their beds or from spontaneous violence in the streets, those wearing uniforms in battle or by misfortune and accident, all of these have been witnessed and adjudicated by the Son of Man. Why? How has it come to be that humankind has endured such tragedy and loss? Why death? My children, the answers to these questions are found in your hearts. You see by the influence of the human will that great catastrophes have come. There is no peace in a heart where Jesus is not allowed to reign. Living prayerfully and safely not only implies that you accept Him, but that you have served notice upon devilish forces to never approach you again. You suffer death because you shall rise again in Glory in the Son of Man. Henceforth, do not fear nightmares that you might die a thousand times or that the torture of mortality will last forever. In Jesus, you are taken from the burden of your crosses into the limelight of happiness and peace. Give your souls to Him and this will occur.

    The Mother of God has appeared today in this central American home to plead for your hands. I wish to walk you through the dark valleys and beyond the horrors that terrify you. There are too many shadows lurking nearby, and you are too timid to bear them on your own. God is your Light and Life, and Mine is the happy role of seeking your hearts and exhuming you from beneath the pall of your transgressions. With these things in mind, please approach 2003 with hope and a sense of spirituality that you have never known before. The world is wicked and the enemies of Love are many, but Satan was dealt a death sentence when Jesus cast him into Hell on the Cross. I ask each of you to ensure that he stays there by denying him access to your lives, and remember to call upon Saint Michael the Archangel for help. By His Sword, evil spirits are cast into the Abyss where they belong. I remind you again today, and I shall repeat it redundantly, that Saint Michael can drive-out any demon, on any day, during any hour. God has vested him with the authority to do what mortal men have declined to attempt. Take-up the Sword of Saint Michael by emulating the Love of the Angels! When the devil strikes at your heels, force him into the dungeons of the netherworld by your indomitable faith. This is how the Earth is remade like Heaven, and impending wars are averted. This is how the ferocities of Nature are suspended, and failing health is restored. Perhaps My children do not understand the trueness of the Will of the Father in defending you! I assure you that the tenets of your faith are real. Live in this hope and remember that Jesus is your guard, shield, and protection in times of trouble. Your enemies will do their worst because they do not know love, and they are destined for eternal morbidity rather than Everlasting Life. My Special son, I ask you to remember these things because many will call upon you, wondering where they will capture the strength to sustain their faith. I know that you are a witness for God's Kingdom; you have proven it time and again for 41 years. These are the golden days that you did not believe would come. I beg you not to allow the naysayers in your midst to dampen your aspirations or make you believe that your dreams will not survive the battle for lost souls. What is the New Covenant about which I speak? It is changing everything you ever wanted to be different, but somehow lacked the proficiencies to accomplish. It is the power to strike men dead in their tracks when their hatred is all that seems to be living in them. It is the Wisdom to know how to repudiate the babblers of the world who wish nothing to do with Jesus Christ. It is the ability to make pleated threads unravel instantaneously and cause corrupt constables to stand bare in the streets. I am telling you these things not as figurative imagery, but the veritable essence of your faith by which the Lord has tendered your heart to Me. He will bestow these gifts upon you when the fullness of time arrives. I know this requires your continued trust, but by what other price has the souls of the millions before you been given to the Light of the Cross? Thank you for accepting your mission for Jesus..."

Sunday, February 16, 2003
3:18 p.m.

"It is with comfort and joy that I have come to speak to you today because I know the intensity of your holy labors for Jesus. He has asked that I tell you that His Kingdom is overwhelmingly pure and that the hope you have espoused for humanity by finishing your work for God portends good things for Creation. My Son boasts of your sacrifices through Eternity because He is aware of the lives you might have otherwise led. Indeed, too many of your peers are doing so presently. The Lord is princely kind, profoundly genius, divinely perfect, sublime in Love, and as inspiring as the constellations. It is obvious why He has sent Me to your community and into this household because He realizes that your devotion is magnanimous and true. You are prepared to take *Babes in the Woods* for its first publication and will soon work on your other manuscripts. These are the making of the conversion of millions of misguided souls. You are doubtlessly aware that their placement in history cannot be expunged because they are of the final works of the Son of Man before He returns in Glory. I assure you that the sinners they are intended to touch will be exposed to their beauty before the end of time. What a brilliant way for Jesus to reach His lost brethren! With the Holy Spirit in your hearts and in your midst, you are reaping the most from your years. The fruits of your labors are the nourishment for your famished brothers and sisters in their journey toward Heaven. Thank you for having responded to My call. At the end of this week, you shall mark the twelve-year anniversary of the beginning of My messages. There is no question that the Earth has changed in deprecating ways, but your prayerful lives have been the mitigation of wrongs and the reason why conditions in America have not worsened. The untimely warfare that your public officials are planning has nothing to do with peace or justice because it is based upon gross vengeance. If they wish to preempt future violence, they should pray on their knees before the Most Blessed Sacrament, taking their suffering to the Holy Cross, and thanking God that He has suspended the horrors that could have come. Together, we pray with the Saints that national leaders will come to their senses and realize that the Love of Jesus Christ is the amelioration of every illness in the world. I bring you further blessings from your deceased relatives who are living with Me in Heaven. They are humbled by your untiring labors for God, the Maker of Creation. You will someday see the world from their purview in Eternity and realize that your years on Earth were far too brief, that they passed like a flash of lightning through the darkness. All the Heavens appeal to you to go forward with the assurance that there is not a second on the clock that you do not live for Jesus. If they could speak to you in one collective voice, you would hear them say with chiming clarity that everything for which you are working in

Jesus' Name is worthy of your untiring discharge. They ask for your commitment to the poor and helpless. Prayer from the heart is the key to understanding these things because it connects you in supernatural ways with the Divine unseen. We pray together when I appear to you and speak on behalf of the Father because the timelessness from which I hail and the mortality in which you live are eminently unified in His Kingdom. Jesus seeks in you the understanding that the destiny of human souls resides in Him. If the entire Earth would surrender the fight for materials in favor of the spiritual Truth that will take them to perfection, all men would live the good will that most seek during the Season of Christmas. My children, let us pray for this as the future is splayed before you. I hold your hopes and aspirations within the perfection of My Heart. I understand with arithmetic conciseness that your brilliance in doing holy works cannot be put asunder by the evildoers in your path. When I enlisted your participation in cultivating humanity, it was not only toward the goal of making you purer in the sight of God, but that you would help Heaven in the struggle to reach your own families, friends, and enemies to take you by the hand and walk in unity to your Salvation in the Cross.

    I wish for you to get plentiful rest when the opportunities arise because the strain of your labors is relentlessly manifest. You will be rewarded not only with the accolades of Paradise, but with peaceful comfort and the guarantee that nothing you despise on Earth will encroach upon your eyesight again. You are elevating humankind in the integrity of the Lord when you travel through your mortality with patience and perseverance. Remember that Jesus is among you in the Sacraments of the Church and in the Holy Spirit who empowers them. Let no one take away your happiness or the intentions of your hearts to make your faithfulness the truest remnant of Jesus' Sacrifice you can muster. It is not required that you should lay down your lives to prove your faith in Him because there are many agonies you could suffer that are worse than death. Be pleased that you have been asked to saturate your neighborhoods and cities with the fruits of your works. I assure you that you are blessed beyond any measure you are capable of conceiving. Thank you for allowing Me the opportunity to speak to humanity in the Light of God's Divine Glory. With Jesus in My arms, I outstretch My Holy Mantle to protect you as My children and preserve you from harm. My Angels are also in your presence, exalting the Sacred Beatitudes that Jesus gave upon the Mount. Summon them when you feel far from Grace or fear anything that causes you to weep. There are millions of Angels in your midst; Jesus dispatches them as your advocates before God's Throne. It is with humility, thanksgiving, gratitude, and prayerfulness that I offer My blessing for your service to humanity and the mission of Jesus Christ. You will be repaid a hundredfold for the lives you are leading now..."

Sunday, February 23, 2003
3:49 p.m.

"Hear, dear children, your Mother who loves you without ceasing has come to pray with you for all who have declined God's invitation to join Him in Grace. I do this with emphatic fervor because of your diligent work for Jesus, now into thirteen fruitful years. I prefer that you receive My intercession as a gift and not a sign from Heaven that you are chosen by any merit of your own. Thank you for the allegiance you have devotedly offered the Kingdom of God on Earth. As we begin another series of messages, I draw you to a Biblical passage that opens to the future. It is Isaiah 43:19 wherein the Holy Spirit tells you that He is springing-forth something new. You will see the variations of the same themes of holiness and servitude that you have afforded Jesus being borne in more bountiful ways. Thank you immensely for your patience as your apostolate is enhanced. I cannot overstate the importance of your Christian knowledge about the exoneration of Creation and the spiritual things of life. The more you record in your published manuscripts, the greater number of people will believe you. The fruit of this is that more will approach the Holy Cross for Salvation. My children, I am sure that you can discern the many ways that your lives from the past, in the present, and your hopes for the future are interconnected. I have told you on several occasions that all Love is one, and that time has no effect on the constancy of Truth. The older you grow in years, and the nearer you move toward Heaven, you will better understand that this is true. Your faith is not in its infancy as when I came to you twelve years ago. I am pleased that you sense that there are many dimensions of Divine Love for you to extrapolate beyond this world. I am even more happy that you realize that you can personify Jesus' righteous perfection by emulating His holiness. We must pray for the infirm, the homebound, the lame, the indigent, and for the helpless unborn innocents. While there are many who have accepted the mission of eradicating abortion in America, their pleas are being muffled by those who are clamoring for expanded international war. Hence, you can see that our prayers are as important as ever. We began this year speaking about the Light of Truth because too many people are still groveling in the darkness of sin. They do so willfully because most have never been taught that such is an obstacle to a grace-filled life. There are even more who reject righteousness outright because they have sworn an oath to Satan. I call each and every one of My children to pray for these miserable souls. While God has never forsaken them, they are hurting themselves and the innocent victims of their wantonness. This too is why I have come to you today. I wish to never refrain from speaking about the goodness that the future brings because your hearts are an important part of it. By the designs of Heaven, you have been chosen to participate in this process.

The dialogue between Heaven and Earth will never end because the Holy Spirit is attuned to the needs of God's people. I remind you that when it seems as though suffering and neglect are overwhelming to endure, Jesus is your companion. Repose in Him for peace and ask Him to dispense His healing to your friends through the felicity of your hearts. The Lord seeks no more than this from the converts who are beginning to comprehend the vastness of His Will. Indeed, it would not be improper to reconfirm that this is a jubilant hour! Even with the inequities and debauchery of so many wayward lives, their sanctification blossoms through the Children of Light. I wish you could see beyond the Firmament the many ways that your prayers and servitude are setting the world aright. When you rise each morning, remember that your piety is refashioning the surface of the Earth; your attendance at the Holy Sacrifice of the Mass is the mainstay of subsistence that redefines the lives of your prodigal friends, and your recitation of the Holy Rosary has procured their spiritual confessions.

My Special son, I realize that you feel warmed by giving your life to Jesus. He accepts your sacrifices, offerings, and services in the interest of God because He has every intention of reconfiguring Creation as you see it in your heart. Yes, you speak of miracles. Such supernatural events as the gift of your faith is one of them, one that you are wielding for the advancement of human exculpation and the destruction of evil. Your legacy of decades on behalf of Divine Love is already bearing sweet fruits. Thank you! There are goals that I wish for your brother to accomplish for the purpose of outfacing the American media. There is no doubt that they are an adversary of Christianity. If he should be so fortunate as to infiltrate their ranks, you will see the end of their corruption. Again, this will require patience on behalf of you both, but it is certainly a goal worth pursuing. When the soldiers raised the United States flag at Iwo Jima many years ago, the basis you used for a parable in *Morning Star Over America*, they did not realize that they were laying the foundation for other ways to refer to the Victory of Jesus and the Triumph of My Immaculate Heart. Therefore, we shall proceed in the hope that you remain strong and faithful not only to God, but to yourselves. What is it that the poet said? 'Patience and patience, we shall win at the last.' I am gratified that you have kept your promise by remaining beneath My Mantle for so long. Words cannot describe My thankfulness. *(We began our personal conversation at this point.)* Can you see the tangled logic that has been the downfall of marriages today? Well over three-quarters of American women have concluded that they must become wage earners to be freed from the responsibilities of rearing children. An example of this delusion is in the acts of many you have known. These women know that you will never relinquish your Christian conviction. They feel affronted by religiosity because they know that it will always be more important than your relationship with them. In other words, they will never come before man's faith in Jesus. Hence, some of them feel betrayed. They fear Christianity because they know that if they give their hearts and souls to God, they will never be lukewarm again, and they will choose the virtues of motherhood over autonomy in wealth. Sadly, some would rather remain ignorant than obedient to the Truth. This does not infer that they will never follow the proper course. *(We changed our topic to speaking about our newest book.)* Indeed, you have written another good book! Your family will be elated, proud, humbled, and brought to tears by celebrating your nephews on the cover. They are precious in this picture, and are perfect for the subject of your text. You are correct; it is in the innocence of their faces and the poverty of their posture. Who could not love little children such as these?..."

Sunday, March 2, 2003
1:27 p.m.

"Now, you have come to the Season of Lent during which for forty days you will perform your personal examen to clarify your lives and willingness to accede to the burdens of Christian refrains. My children, whenever you work for holiness, you give venue to the breezes of peace through the fruit-blossom trees promised by the Angels. Your happiness is assured because you know that you have given your doubts and despair to Jesus. I beseech you kindly to remember these things come Wednesday; and not only that, but to observe the period of Lent as a time of gratitude for the graces the Lord has accorded you to be sustained in your faith. Remember the miracles He has wrought because you believe in Him. There is no doubt that self-denial and almsgiving are intrinsic portions of Lent, and I am asking you to be holier and humbler in a way that lends to your understanding why. Your petitions transfer the forsaken into the Kingdom of Light. Your good works make practical reparation for thousands of unchaste lives. The peace you seek spares untold casualties of war, and all these things are the purpose in your yearning to bask in the Truth of the Cross. My children, it is not enough that you simply know God, but you must engage Him in every way availed and revealed. The Sacred Liturgies, your own intonations of praiseworthy virtues, your Marian cenacles, and the dailiness of your charitable gifts compose the ratification of your lives in Jesus. He wishes that your years be filled with the integrity that comes in communion with Divine Love. To My two children who live on the avenue to the tomb of the fallen American president, I remind you that your freedom to rise in the dignity of God comes not from patriotism or secular strife, but in His Will to bring you to the land of milk and honey beyond the gateway of Heaven. It is only there that you will comprehend the implications of being free. You live atop the soil of a nation that permits the espousing of religion as long as you do not teach it in public institutions. Is this the utility of the Bill of Rights? Jurists hand-down decisions to petitioners who propagate atheism by denying the mention of God in your patriotic pledge. Is there a semblance of freedom in this? If it were put by referendum before your people, do you suppose that the majority would uphold the tradition of stating that your country lives under God? The answer is that they would hail their Lord and Maker, but this seems not sufficiently important to ask the electorate to decide. We pray together for these things as Lent arrives because God knows who is denying His Word; and to declare that He is dismayed by the penchant of Americans to reject Christianity would be putting it mildly. You have been told about seers and locutionists who have heard the voice of the Holy Spirit warning about the horrible events that will befall your nation. I need not repeat them here, nor do I wish to dwell upon them because My intentions are to seek the cultivation of the heart that will stir the compassion from God who has every reason to be filled with righteous indignation. I wish to tell you about My Son the healer, the comforter, and the giver of solace. My intent is to induce from you the desire to seek the Divine Mercy that He wishes to dispense upon the penitent and contrite. However, where can they be found in a country of lavish lifestyles and licentiousness? Too many in America who hear My messages about these things look around at those in their company and say, *...surely the Mother of Jesus Christ cannot be speaking about me!* I am referring to people who attend Church on Sunday and live like despots and harlots the rest of the week. Jesus is plentifully angered by such hypocrisy; you can see the suffering of the innocents whom these sinners are exploiting. There are only few more moments in the history of man like this one today—one during which Heaven is forewarning not about specific chastisements, but of the call to holiness before it is too late. Many that have been prophesied in private revelations can be averted if the indicted will heed My call. Again, we pray not only for this possibility, but that they will comply with the swiftness of the Archangels to allay the suffering of their hundreds-of-thousands of victims who are agonizing during the wait.

    My Special son, I speak to you briefly to say that Jesus is a loving Savior, a sublime Redeemer, and a benign deliverer. You have always known these things, but many around whom you live seem not to care. Your litanies and sacrifices are fostering the mitigation of these errors. Jesus told humanity that by His Death and Resurrection, you are freed from sin and morbidity. The Holy Gospel is the irreproachable avenue through which God's Will is dispensed, and the giving of souls to the Cross is the catalyst for healing the face of the Earth. You are one of the fortunate ones who have lived the Truth all your life. I know that it is difficult to look at the awkward ways of America with its lying and deception, materialism, lust, and outright evil works. These are in no way aspects of being a superpower in the sight of Heaven. All of this will be drawn down—and you and your brother will witness it—because the Savior you know will not permit it to remain. Please pray that the principals will incorporate only the guilty. Having an awareness that miracles do occur and hopes for the future come true, I know that you understand the necessity for the conversion of the multitudes who will stand by you in faith when the world's dying hours arrive. What about ending the scourge of abortion? What of the throes of poverty into which so many paupers are cast by greedy Americans? All hellfire, brimstone, Justice, Wrath, and Holy Judgement will befall their lives. I tell you this because by finishing your mission, you can spread the message of Salvation before it is too late. By building your volume of works, as I indicated last week, you will have a corpus of Wisdom upon which they may depend to know what Heaven commands them to do..."

Sunday, March 9, 2003
4:03 p.m.

"Mine is the call of the holy into the service of humanity, where the concept of Suffer the Children will have no longer a fashionable age. My little ones, your prayerfulness is the alleviation of torment and the grand catalyst for sanctifying Grace that is given to those who honor God. Please remember during this Season of Lent that there are people who are praying for you. This makes your role in the conversion of humanity important because your contributions are counted among the blessed. This communication is the networking about which I have spoken before, and this is a day of gladness because so many are recognizing the need for prayer on the eve of what will soon become a strategic military blunder. How can the nations speak of peace when they are battling with bombshells and rocketry? Please remember the souls of the tens-of-thousands who are about to die because of the naked offensive aggression of the United States of America. Campaigns of war are never about peace; they cannot be disguised as such. I pray that the Feast of the Annunciation will transform the Earth where there are no battlegrounds or deep-seated issues of contention. I urge My children to join Me in the future to strive to make this a viable component of the final age of mankind, and I offer My Motherly affection and gratitude to those who understand that Christian Love is always a greater force for change than hatred. When the wise speak of discretion, they refer to the same people who despise them for not hoisting arms against their neighbors. The call for human decency is the beginning of new negotiations for peace above warfare, and this My children is what is lacking in this modern age. I again call for your petitions as the months unfold, and in the meantime, rejoice! Offer thanks that God has given you Jesus through Me so that you can know the validity of sinlessness in your extraordinary lives. Give thanks for Jesus' Passion by which your sins against Heaven have been mitigated and for His Crucifixion by which they are expunged. These are gruesome times for the millions of souls who do not yet understand that the Love of God is the resilience they seek to live-out their days in prudence and goodness. This is the epoch in history where the true distinctions between darkness and Light are being revealed. My Special son, how pleased I am to come pray with you and your brother today. With what great warmth in My Immaculate Heart do I speak with fond thankfulness for the gifts you are giving to the Lord. This week will bring the publication of another of your great works, one that will touch millions of hearts before time is through. Your books are your offshoots of love that God is dispensing to the world through your holiness and determination. This must make you feel valued in evangelizing His Kingdom. I cannot overstate how important it is for you to remain anonymous in this process, lest you become too distracted to go on. There will be a day when you will speak from places like the Chandler Cenotaph, just as I promised, but you have work to do on a more practical plane. You and your brother are having an influence on humanity's spiritual deficit that is too overwhelming to describe... This is an auspicious moment for the world because of all you have incorporated in *Babes in the Woods*. No Christian has written about abortion this way or offered My messages in the tenor you have taken in Chapter XVI. You are similar in your reproaches of indignant sinners as Saint Timothy when his soul was glowing with pious justice! I will stand beside you in whatever you do toward making the Earth more holy because I realize that it is near the end of time. Many secularists prefer for you to be inordinately mild in upholding the virtues of Christianity because they know that in due season, you might train your weapons on them. This has exacerbated the problem with your friends who have forsaken you. Stand your ground and make them practice their faith. These are not the times during which the disciples of Jesus should yield to cowardice. I pray with you as I did Saint Joan of Arc because you are a visionary warrior. As for your brother, he is simply your brother; that is about as benign as I can convey it. He gleans a great deal about faith and morality from you because you are a commendable example. You are the one person on Earth who gives him strength, leading him to repose in the sanctuary of the Lord's spiritual hospice, My Most Immaculate Heart..."

Sunday, March 16, 2003
2:38 p.m.

"With all the loveliness of the Paradise you seek, I come to pronounce you in good favor with the Lord. Little ones, My beauty is as profound as you have attested because I am the Mother of Christ. We pray together because the world is in great peril; innocent people are suffering everywhere, and lost souls must be converted. I tell you that there is resilience in the divinity of the Almighty Father, and His beauty outshines the seas. Please accept My blessing upon His praying couple of children in this humble home. Thank you for allowing the Holy Spirit to become the reason for your lives. As you realize, there are more hearts to open and families to bless. Too many on Earth are hungry, naked, diseased, and dying. God wants to know from where will arise the contemporary Saints to alleviate this pain. I would ask for you to remember that the conversion of humanity is like the ebb and flow of waves against a shoreline because some people relapse into their everyday insolence after their extraordinary reorientation of accepting Jesus deep inside. I see it much like a baker preparing dough on a table. Once it is pressed and the roller is lifted, the dough loses its expanse until another pass is made. We are mindful that Christian conversion cannot be brittle, but must remain firm in the Truth so that there is no compromise in the defense of God's Plan. I urge this age to remember that the Church Militant is the Original Catholic and Apostolic Mystical Body of My Son. I pray with you and on your behalf, and I seek for you the sanctification that will make you the Children of Light. Therefore, it is My joy and happiness to speak to you on this occasion. If you believe that humanity will never be purified, remember the prophecies of My Son. When it appears too dark in the world to be real, recall that the break of dawn is only mere moments away. There is hope in this because Jesus inundates your hearts with sublime nostalgia and gladness. Remember that living in perpetual expectation means trusting His Word, knowing that your labors for Him will always bear the fruit of enlightened souls. My Special and Chosen sons, I realize that you internalize the future with more hope than before. You sense the destiny that the accomplishment of your mission is at hand. There is no doubt that the days seem to expire without your peers seeing your progress, but this is of benefit to you. The deposit of works that you are upbringing for God's Kingdom is one that will never be cast aside or put asunder. These are blessed times and holy hours. They are a gift for humankind that will be revealed with power and authority; and for these good things, I know that you are righteously proud. I thank you as your Advocate in Heaven for being God's healers in a fragmented world. You shine His Light by imitating His Love. As has been foretold in many places around you, where else would you go for the beatific essence that is seeking a presence in you? Only to Jesus, My little ones, only to Jesus! As this Spring blooms, remember that your hearts must open to all the possibilities that accompany your service for Jesus—joy, Wisdom, happiness, suffering, prayerfulness, and reparation. You embrace these things because you are the inheritors of a bountiful Providence. You belong to the immortal ages that are coming of their own through the accordance of time. Be stouthearted because you know the culmination of the Earth and the future of your souls. Today, I wish to tell you that an extreme number of people are opening their hearts to your work that they have seen in writing and the electronic sites to which they have access. It is a gift from God that they are hearing My messages around the globe. People are speaking about Me on walkways because of the *Morning Star Over America* books that you have dispensed. I tell you over and again, it is imperative that they become hungry for Truth and that it be satisfied by their decision to pray. I hope you understand that you should remain anonymous to the multitudes in order for your mission to succeed. My Special son, I have shed grateful tears because you consented to do this, not because it is easy, but because holiness is difficult. I am heartened because your love for God cannot be suspended by your enemies. My Soul sings because you feel His Light inside you and are eager to emit it into the foggiest valleys of night. Could you have imagined that your signature on human existence would be this ennobling? It is important for you to remember that the greatest apostolates to ever blossom were given venue by their own simplicity. Thank you for extolling the humility that is making your works the envy of men. This will be a favored Spring for you, but a horrid one for those whom your government sees as its enemies abroad. The battle of military might will be won by the United States, but the war against terrorism still lays in question. I know that you see your nation as being arrogant, as does Jesus. Please pray for the errors of the western hemisphere to be brought to a halt. And, to those who are about to end one procedure of abortion, they will take their message into the streets and proclaim that the fight on behalf of unborn children has been won. Of the two-million abortions perpetrated in the United States each year, partial-birth infanticide represents a fraction of them. Sadly, you will hear politicians hailing themselves as gladiators to their voting constituents, proclaiming that they have conquered the last foothill against abortion, when in truth they will have only placed themselves in the position they were before. Do not let them deceive you. If they are real Christians, they must end abortion and capital punishment altogether. Thank you for allowing Me to speak to you and for writing your sentiments with your brother. This is how the elation of the Angels is wrought..."

Sunday, March 23, 2003
2:18 p.m.

"With all the Grace from Heaven by which Creation has been blessed, I have come to pray with you for world peace. These are the difficult hours about which men of peace have told you since the first shot was fired in the war of human sinfulness so many ages ago. My children, when we pray for the reaffirmation of the hearts of the lost to be regained by Glory again, let us not forget to include those who claim to be united in the Sacred Heart of Jesus who are only murmuring His Holy Name while they seek materialism and disgrace for themselves. It is a very dangerous world where there lives a lot of free people whose culture does not allow them to see the reasons for defense of the enemies they despise. Such is the misunderstanding that accompanies a globe so large, with so many regions, and with so many values and assumptions about the role of God in the reclamation of man. Today, you can readily see the ongoing conflagration about which I spoke on September 16, 2001. Why has this come to be? Because of the vengeful nature of humanity. It has come because too many will not exhaust all avenues of peaceful unity. And, now, too many thousands of innocent people are paying a terrible price. The ongoing war that the United States and its allies are prosecuting in the Middle East is an outright mortal sin. It is the collective efforts of a republic which has given its wiser side to the skullduggery of Hell. While I am the Patroness of America, I am weeping mournful tears of sorrow because My people will not heed My call for peace and unification. My little ones, please keep this message in a place of safe keeping because, soon, the United States will pay deeply and dearly for this onslaught of naked military aggression. How can the leaders of the West be so adamant about eradicating the oppression of other societies when its own people are enchained in the horrific effects of material wealth, lust, arrogance, and lack of spirituality? How dare anyone proclaim that God has shed His Grace on Thee! You will see more accurately that He will dispense His Holy Wrath upon your lands instead! I do not bring messages of doomsday cults or the rubbish of the darker age. I am speaking about the Truth of the present-day world in which the haughty isolationists who inhabit the United States of America are fighting only for the right to spread its capitalism to the rest of the continents... People will say '...How can the humble and meek Mother of Jesus Christ issue such a stern condemnation of the freest nation on the Earth?' My response to them is that I have seen the very God whose Wrath is justly waiting in the wings. I have heard the mourning of the pious little children of Light all over the world who look to the West in sorrow. I hear the groaning of Creation under the burden that the United States of America has placed upon it by the horrendous weight of it sins against the dignity of life! Americans kill helpless unborn children in their mothers' wombs and call it the right of free choice. They allow the poor to die of starvation in their own streets and in ghettos around the globe and call it self-imposed poverty. They inject poison into the veins of poor lost sinners and call it secular justice. My children, I have been dispatched by the God of your fathers to tell you without equivocation that He calls all of these the actions of a country that is wholly under the influence of Satan. All the speeches about freedom and international dignity are the product of a hollow rhetoric that is dying into the dust. Indeed, tell those who might proclaim that the Mother of their God would not be filled with such disdain for America that they have never been more wrong in their lives! I will weep! I will cry tears of sadness when God allows His Holy Justice to rain absolute horror onto the land of the free and home of the brave. You are the land of the obstinate and the lifeless! You espouse the culture of death so that you can nourish only your own life! Yes, I will weep because too many generations have passed without any response to My apparitions. I am telling you that the future will be filled with deep agony for Americans everywhere, and it will be a necessary function of the cultivation of the West that so many will suffer. Am I telling you this so as to prophesy a new kind of chastisement? Please pray with Me, and God will give you the answer.

My Special one, you have seen with your own eyes the destruction and lack of concern for innocent human life that is ongoing in the war in Iraq. This entire conflict is based upon political and financial motivations! We pray together that more and more will come to understand this as the weeks ahead continue to unfold... Thank you for saying your prayers together with Me today. I will ensure that you receive a special blessing on the Feast of the Annunciation! This is My blessing for you both now. ✝ I will speak to you again next week! I love you. Goodnight!"

Sunday, March 30, 2003
3:03 p.m.

"My little children, I ask you to see the future as the culmination of your past because it holds many facets of the victory you are claiming in My Immaculate Heart, and because God has deigned it, you have accepted it, and My Soul magnifies the Lord in the union we share. Thank you for adhering to the sacred principles that are already healing the Earth, as difficult as this may seem. My children, I come before you with an aura of elation today because so many of your friends are changing. I am not telling you that My message last week was impertinent, but the movement of sinners to the Holy Cross as a result of your providing the offices to express My concerns is a miracle itself. Someday, My little ones, you will see how important this is. Your relations with the Hosts of Paradise represent much more than the single dimension of My speaking and your hearing. Indeed, I began offering My messages to humanity the hour when the Son of Man was Resurrected from the Tomb. The world of AD 2003 took its new shape when Jesus awakened from the dead into the Light of Everlasting Life, taking you with Him as He stands tall in Truth. My Motherhood reigns beyond Jesus' Life, Crucifixion, and Resurrection. I am providing the same direction that I offered Him, the same affection, and the same vision that was accorded Him from the holiness of My Immaculate Heart. It is proper that this be true because you are His Mystical Body on Earth. What mother would abandon her children during these times, the most important years of your lives? Therefore, I teach you about the ways in which God has chosen to conclude the ages and ask for your prayers with the Angels and Saints to ensure that the most good is made of these years to effect the transference of the millions of unconverted souls to the Sacred Blood of My Son. It is for this that I raise My head and realize that the hope by which you live is true. Never mind the passing of time or whether you believe your brothers and sisters are living the image of Jesus quickly enough. The most important matter is that they will do so because the Christians of the Earth are leading them there. Your examples, prayerful acts and pious works, the meditations of your hearts, and the extension of your faith beyond this place into the Light of immortality are portions of the transformation of the world into the likeness of Heaven. Therefore, while My Heart is burdened by the wars and tribulations of humanity and by the blinded people who are still trying to climb to their feet, I live in the same hope that you embrace. It is a trust whose reality has been fulfilled. My purpose here and wherever I go is to instill in you the understanding that the Lord is in control of the transpiring cultivation of humanity. You are still laboring in His earthly vineyard, and the work of your hands is a discernable power that is making your age one of the finest of the whole. If this were untrue, I would have told you. Many followers of God fail to understand that such service is greater than the age in which they offer it. You are ameliorating the suffering of millions of sinners not only where you live, not just during these hours, but for all who failed to pray when they were mortals among you. You are amending the facets of human life that passed unnoticed in bygone marketplaces and forgotten street corners. You are reconfiguring created men for all seasons, futures, and the history of all recorded histories; and in this, you must know that I am pleased. I tell you one week about the Wrath of God, and another about the reasons why He dispenses ample measures of Divine Mercy upon His people. This is done by the way you live. If anyone chooses to record the effect of these days upon the epilogue of Creation, let them say with accuracy that the Children of Mary spared humanity from the holocaust that would have otherwise ensued.

These are among the reasons why I am happy beyond the facility of words and that My Immaculate Heart overflows with gratitude for the means by which you are dispatching the Angels in honor of God to those for whom you pray. Yes, these are dark and perilous days. There are wars and casualties too numerous to count, but the fact that you do not question the Father as He allows Creation to unfurl is an attribute of your subsistence in His Grace. Behold this portion you are sustaining in the sanctification of humankind! Align yourselves not with the constellations, but with the Truth! God is divinely in love with your souls because you remain as warriors for His Kingdom where your forefathers died. Be at peace knowing that He is glorified by your lives and your deposit of works upon which His people's spirit will feed until the obsolescence of time. This is a moment of jubilation, accomplishment, power, harvesting, and invigoration. You belong to Heaven because you are My responsive children! You recite the Holy Rosary in reparation for humanity's sins. You speak aloud about the Christian Gospel while others are muted by their own indifference. You give generously of your time and resources to the evangelization of Salvation and Truth. I ask you today, therefore, to understand the opportunities by which you are effecting the changes that have been too long in coming. Join Me in this happiness and know that the unfolding of the future is on course and attuned to the piety of the Saints who have tread the paths of righteousness on which you now proceed. My Special son, it is you who make Me happy because you are allowing Jesus to reign freely and abundantly in this place, around the American cities, in corridors where He would not otherwise be known, and within the hearts of the thousands who are being touched by your writings. This Spring 2003 is not only opening as one of Grace and peace, but of contemporary revelation because the contiguous societies in your midst are finally understanding who God is. As your bibliography grows, you must surely be able to see that your peers are taking notice. Who else has written a book about the inordinate hunt for sinners in the priesthood when the substance for which they seek does not even exist? Who in the world understands the minds of children the way you have written in the book that you will receive from the printer in less than ten days? And, as I have indicated, the best of your wares is yet to come... I hold high hopes that you will accomplish these things during the period of time when you work on the manual tasks that you wish to complete on your home and elsewhere. You have seen the way that half the marriages in America have ravaged hearts and destroyed the spiritual lives of hundreds-of-thousands of your peers. Be thankful that you have not become one of them. If anyone should question who owns your heart, please do not hesitate to remind them that you have given it to Me. I have claimed you as My holy son, and your brother alongside you. The two of you are pillars of Christian strength in a world where spineless materialists live. And, please remember to discuss with others the importance of the Sacrament of Confession. The Confession about which I speak is an eternal one! Exiled people are required to confess their sins through the Sacrament of Penance, and this is especially true during Advent and Lent..."

Sunday, April 6, 2003
3:51 p.m.

"Regaling the revelations of the Sacred Mysteries of Christ's Kingship, I appear in this holy place in peace. My children, there is a sense of urgency with which you must pray because of the untold number of lives being sacrificed in the name of international war. Let us plead for lasting unity to cease the fighting and instill a new sense of civility that those whom are so engaged have never known. My Special son, rather than seeing the children of America seated like olive plants around their parents' tables, the scene I wish to show you is the horrible one that exists. *(Our Lady presented a vision of a contingent of U.S. Marines carrying a flag-draped coffin containing the remains of a fallen comrade at a funeral in Illinois.)* This is what is happening to young people in America, in the foreign battles in which they are being killed. I beseech you to pray for the cessation of conflicts that have nothing to do with the propagation of Christianity. I realize that the grotesque scenes of war impact your consciousness every day because they are on television and in the newspaper. This is an historical moment not only because of this, but because such fighting is an unprecedented distraction for people who have no spiritual foundation by which to facilitate its end. We pray for them to come to the Cross with peace in their hearts. I call the American nation to rise against the atrocities that its military forces are causing in other lands because aggression is not the means to foster the changes that the United States is seeking. While I have told you that your country will prevail, it will only bring further terror to your homeland. It is more about revenge and materialism than justice, reparation, and peace. We must pray for those who are prosecuting the war against Iraq because their motivations appear to change with the wind. And, who have you been told will rebuke the Earth in these latter times in the name of My Son? The Children of Mary. You bear My messages to reprove those who use warfare to induce social progress. Such are not Christians, no matter if they call themselves followers of Jesus. It is critical that you record My sentiments for distribution at a later time because it will not be too late for millions of partisans to rethink their stance. The victims of unjust wars die in vain. The victims of unjust wars die in vain. *(Our Lady said this twice.)* Let no one from any walk of life say anything otherwise. The culture of death that the United States espouses appears to be spreading to other parts of the globe because of the wealth that America has to protract it. I bear no specific message about chastisements that will result, but the people of the West are placing themselves in a precarious position before the Justice of our sovereign God, and I promise that this must be atoned before time is through. While I am speaking, dozens more innocent lives are being taken in Iraq by the explosions of weaponry made in the United States. Children are being orphaned, expectant mothers are dying in their beds, water and food systems are being disrupted, and medical centers destroyed. Innocent people are being terrified because of the aggression of the United States. Civilian personnel, media employees, and others who are supposed to be disinterested and independent are being lost in the fight. Is this the same America who says that it values peace over all else, and on whom the Lord has shed His Grace? The hypocrisy and evil being manifested by the American government are too unscrupulous to ignore, and a day of reckoning will come. I will protect those who call upon My Immaculate Heart when that time arrives. I also ask you to pray for a better conscience in those who are dispensing your nation's wealth. Many are profiteering who do not need any aid, and others are becoming rich because of their relationships with those in power. To suggest that there are shared assets and equal rights in the United States is a fabrication. Why do not the citizens of your nation see this more clearly? Because the struggle for wealth is blinding the people who must see the best. I am not speaking about the meek ones or paupers, or the hundreds-of-thousands who are shivering in the cold. I am referring to the social elite, capitalists, atheists, and the recalcitrant youth who believe that they can conquer the travails and setbacks of living in exile from Heaven on their own.

My children, God is seeking more than the modification of the conduct of individual people, He demands the cultivation of the hearts of the entire body of American citizens. He implores the mass conversion of whole societies who have claimed their share of the goods and commodities that are available to all, while not turning their heads to see who they are forcing into poverty. This selfishness shall not prevail! I ask for the petitions of the faithful so the conduct of America will change. Thank you for saying your prayers for the millions who do not realize that they are offending God and punishing poor people. A new spring has come in the nation I love! Please realize that I will never surrender the fight to claim the hearts of My lost children. These are the times about which the Prophets spoke. These days and hours are more than a driving force that will precede the future promised; your actions in this age are the premonition that will open the door for the coming of the last. Please seek it with the awareness that God shall separate the sheep from the goats without inhibition. Let there be no mistake, My Son has no hesitation in defending His Truth, and those who are not in compliance will perish in the end. You have been warned many times in the Sacred Scriptures. If there is anyone who feels that he is not purified in the eyes of the Father, then he should run to the Holy Cross for the cleansing of his soul. If there is a person among you who lay in sin, they must receive the absolving Sacraments. Time is of the essence because the Truth about which I speak has closed-in on humanity in a way that cannot be reversed. My Special son, I know that you are reciting the Rosary devoutly and with love in your heart. Together with your brother, you are helping the change that is required in America. There are many who disbelieve what you have been saying, but there are multitudes who accept. I have captured them by the heart and guided their lives by the intercession I offer through My messages. It is My intention to keep you isolated so your progress can proceed. You should be thankful that you have this way of life. I will tell you, however, that the time will come when you will be sought by many. To prepare, you must live-out your years in simplicity and humility. I will do the rest. Thank you for your willingness to help the priests from India seek financial help from foundations in America to improve the lives of the children in their nation. This is another fruit of your apostolic heart. The priests are having difficulty speaking the way you prefer because the secular void will not give them venue. The people attending Holy Mass are not the only ones who need to hear. Centuries ago, Roman Catholic priests were summoned to speak at almost every public function as a signal of the Lord's presence. Now, however, the malevolent media have convinced most Americans that they can be more productive living in autonomy from the Church. The media have persuaded the U.S. populace that the Church is a subpart of a graded plane of worldly components of which secular humanism and relativism maintain a part. This is what their sensationalism was about regarding the errors of a few priests in 2002. Now, when the clergy speak out, they are maligned not only through the media, but by the public that has been hoodwinked into believing what the media spews. Do you see that this has tended toward that end? How can it be reversed? We are doing it now. The fact that you have placed My messages into print is God's way of showing them that the Gospel of Salvation cannot be destroyed. This is a laudable time for you and your brother, for your work, for My intercession, for America, and for the Kingdom of Heaven..."

Palm Sunday, April 13, 2003
1:58 p.m.

"Dear children, this is the liturgical anniversary of the Palm Sunday miracle that I provided at the Saint Augustine cemetery in March of 1991. Much has been accomplished since then, and we have a great deal more to do for Jesus before your Marian mission is concluded. As your Bishop said to you this week through a written letter, *thank you for promoting the sanctity of human life*. This is the grand declaration that Roman Catholic Bishops all over America wish to tell their flocks who are serving in Washington DC, but they are unable to do so because the latter will not uphold their promise to obey the Commandments of God. Your work is of tremendous presence in teaching them that real discipline in Christian Truth cannot be separate from their secular affairs. I am pleased because of the prayerful sacrifices you have given My Son during this Lenten Season. Many hearts have been touched by your efforts. And, you have undergone the examen of your own piety to ensure that your thoughts and actions are in alignment with the Will of the Father. Whenever you see places where you appear lacking in the virtues of patience and self-control, this is where you must direct your petitions to Jesus to give you the strength to overcome your weaknesses. Even though you may not have committed sin just because you are shorn in something, you must be able to attain a level of confidence so that you will not be caught off-guard. So, all in all, this has been a revealing Lent for you. I am pleased that you understand that the Lord God teaches you in ways that most mortals would not expect. This, henceforth, is a beneficial time! I am preparing your hearts and thoughts for the onslaught of enemies who are about to assail your recent book for the content of Chapter XVI. As you can see, you are unprepared for it. I will pray with you and work through the love in your heart to help you understand that such adversity is rarely an assault against your private person. Also today, we are praying for the conversion of the politicians who have conducted the war in Iraq, those who feel that a great objective for justice has been achieved. Such a position could not be further from the truth. The media broadcasts in America are as biased and filled with half-truths as those they claim to be their enemies. Where are the films of the multiple-thousands of Iraqi troops whose dismembered bodies have been strewn across their acreage by U.S. military bombs? Where is the footage that depicts the devastation that has been wrought in the lives of the indigenous civilians whose children have been killed and their homes destroyed? Indeed, what has been the boasting of the American warmongers during the recent days? That their enemy did not set their oilfields afire; this is their measure of success. I promise that the flaming derricks of Kuwait twelve years ago will look like candles on a birthday cake compared to God's response to the calculated aggression of the United States of America.

My dear children, you live in a nation filled with freedom lovers and foreign nation haters. Such isolationism is unworthy of an open republic that purportedly espouses Christianity. You have spoken and written about these things, now you will witness some of the most conceited braggadocio and haughtiness that has ever been heard from the western world. Your leaders will declare their mission to be accomplished. There will be a tone of opportunism from America to appeal to its enemies to lay down their weapons or risk further perils of war. What kind of diplomacy is this? The Arab nations who hold to their Christian beliefs and those elsewhere around the globe who live according to the Holy Gospel compose the authentic City on a Hill that Jesus seeks from His people. Satan has America in a trance, and the first thing he has done is place blinders over the consciences of its leaders so they cannot see it. I pray devoutly for the republic for which I am Patroness Saint. If I were not, God would surely have annihilated it by now. I do not wish for you to look disdainfully upon all the good that your predecessors have done, nor do I wish you to become paranoiac about what your government will do next. My only purpose is to describe the distinctions between the way America ought to behave and the actions it is presently undertaking..."

Easter Sunday, April 20, 2003
2:31 p.m.

"I realize that it is with intense jubilation that Christians around the world are celebrating the Resurrection of Jesus from the Tomb, and it is especially more fruitful for My Roman Catholic children who receive the Eucharistic Body, Blood, Soul and Divinity of the Messiah who redeems all believers. I come to you with hope this Easter to enjoin your prayers during Jesus' Paschal Resurrection. What does this Feast mean to you? Not unlike a description of Heaven, it can scarcely be put into words. Hence, I will say that it is an articulation of the anniversary of Jesus' Resurrection in your modern continuum and a precursor to His Return in Glory when all who have died in Him will be raised, and all who believe in Him shall have Everlasting Life. Throughout the ages, this has been called The Good News because, as you see by the conditions unfolding around you, there is much torment in the lives of those who do not have love. Their news is only poor, and oftentimes growing worse by the hour. I bid you to remember all of them as you pray in thanksgiving for your Christian faith on this most auspicious day in the Church's Liturgical Year. I assure you that many will be delivered from the throes of Purgatory today because of the manifold prayers of the faithful. And on Earth, tens-of-thousands have joined your faith anew. These are My children who have charted a course of purity and humility, a means of living that most of them have heretofore never known. I beseech the Church to embrace and guide them, take them by the hearts and hands, and hold them dear as your renewed brothers and sisters in Jesus. You see every day the poignance of life in the agonies of the lost, forsaken, grieving and ignorant, but this Feast marks the deliverance of untold numbers from the darkness into the Light. My good wishes are with them, and My prayers to the Father on their behalf multiply. Indeed, I have been praying for them to become members of the Mystical Body of Christ for years. I accept the children who have been converted and confirmed; I offer My Mantle to protect their wisdom, asking them to be given in consecration to My Immaculate Heart throughout and beyond the element of time. You have listened to Easter homilies and testimonials by priests and the elect for centuries. While the message of the Resurrection of Jesus has remained the same, the sense of urgency for humanity to embrace it has never been prompter. You have heard the Prophets, read their premonitions, and seen them permeate the majestic ages. I wish to remind you that you are their heirs and successors. By the power of the Holy Spirit, you are the prophets of the End Times—to teach, admonish, lead, console, and deliver. Jesus lives in your hearts not only to make you holy, but that you might be His messengers for universal humanity. You have the Wisdom and wield the power from old, and now is upon you that fateful series of moments during which you must assert your finest courage. I assure you that the Grace and Peace of Jesus is within you, that these are the solemn years in which you have been declared idyllically separate from the world and freed from the effects of mortality. You are My Christians! Thank the Lord, Almighty! You are My Christians! I beg you to be dressed in the holy attire that has been fitted for you. Shed the darkness and enter the brightness of eternal perfection! Prepare for the arrival of the final dawn that will usher you to the foyer of Divine Truth! These wishes are achievable in your mission of humanizing the Sacred Beatitudes. Allow this hope to be your vision and purpose, the way you walk and speak, the reason for your rising in the morning, and your vespertine petitions at night. I am happy on Easter because I understand its imperial impact on humanity. A billion Catholics who live on the continents stand and resoundingly applaud the Heavens to proclaim in one voice, *He is Risen!* And with this, your Savior spreads His blessings across the globe to comfort every contrite heart who accepts Him. These are among the reasons why I have hope today. I stand with elation beside the Angels and Saints to whom you call for intercession before the Almighty Father. What a courtly contingent of love! What a holy and magnificent assemblage of living perfection!

Therefore, My Special and Chosen ones, you must realize that I have taken these moments to embrace you in ways that you have never before understood. The times in which you live are changing, and so is the Earth beneath your feet, but your love for My Son shall never die, and your allegiance to your Heavenly Queen will thrive forever. I thank you not only because I know these things to be true, but because the decisions and sacrifices that make them possible are made by you. Through the suppliance of your will, you have said 'yes' to God when many others surrounding you are saying 'no.' I embrace not only your hearts and souls, but your words and actions, your very lives! I harbor the dreams that you yearn for in My Immaculate Heart, knowing that in time they will come true. If only you will accept that what I am telling you will come to pass, you would never have another negative thought again. Your brothers and sisters will eventually believe your messages, the lost will be found, the hungry will be fed, the naked clothed, and the arrogant will be broken like vases of clay. And, the seed beneath the soil will grow into bountiful fields of green! I have brought a mirror today into which I would like you to look at the brilliance of your souls. With My words and blessings, you are peering into it now. See how obedient you are! Perceive the sacred beauty that makes the Archangels leap with joy! See the anticipation that cannot be tarnished by the tawdriness of life or the faithlessness of other men. These are not only the new beginnings to which you committed in 1991, but are the finishing complements you will carry with you when you appear before the Father's Throne. If you must be sad, know that it is only because the passage of time seems too sedentary for you. Everything that you wish for at its completion has already been prepared. This, My children, is My Easter message for 2003. It is one of hope and promise, of expectation and purpose. I give you My assurance as your Queen of Love that you will see these things soon. Please remember My words, and you will never lose hope. Your writing will continue to be as profound as it has been and as effective in converting the hearts of those who read it. The paragraphs that you and your brother completed yesterday and a few days past are more beautiful than I have ever seen. I wish for you to enjoy Easter as I bless My other children in distant parts of the world..."

Sunday, April 27, 2003
Feast of Divine Mercy
10:30 a.m.

"My dear children, today's celebration is about human forgiveness. Yes, I say to you that it is about The Divine Mercy of the Son of Man, bestowed upon all the faithful who plead to Him for an Absolution that is forever perfect. Within the submission of the humble heart rests the reason for the remaking of the soul because the newness of Everlasting Life begins to bloom therein. I have told you before that the most egregious blasphemy against the Holy Spirit by humanity is to refuse to forgive other sinners. My presence here is another call for My children to pardon the trespasses of those who have offended them. In this, and only in this, can an individual be given energy to seek the Light of Heaven. I have come to speak to My Special and Chosen ones because there is much work to do toward the conversion of souls to the Holy Cross. You must remember that time is of the essence in this seriously penitential matter. It has been years since we began this process together, and Jesus will tell us when your work is complete. Today, I refer to the surety of the impending perfection that is come into the world through the Christian heart. Many people maintain that they are not yet there, and that they probably never will be. These people are correct only in the first. Through the Grace of God, My intercession, their contrition, and the passing element of time, each soul shall make it to the Paradise that is sought by the faithful. Jesus knows His sheep; He pines for your return to the fold, and He searches for you with Eternal Love in His Being. I pray that His Word will go forth into every hamlet and sector so that peace and justice will reign on every continent through the end of time. What do I proclaim about The Divine Mercy of Jesus? It is imperative that everyone bows before the Calvarian Cross and realizes that the exculpating reflection of My Son's Crucifixion shines redeeming Light upon them. This is the first premise that must be accepted. Second and simultaneously, each soul must know that every sin has been expunged from the face of the Earth by that same Crucifixion. There is no one who is incapable or unqualified for the forgiveness of sins in the Sorrowful Sacrifice of Jesus. My children, I wish for you to pray with Me in terms that are larger than the dimensions by which you are receiving this message. Contemplate the fulcrum about which you spoke in your Diary. The interconnection between Heaven and Earth is the precise point where the Blood of Jesus makes contact with the human soul. As you have stated, and as you are presently writing, this cannot be observed with the naked eye. The universe of graces that are blessing the nations are knowable by your faith in the Christianity you profess. This is the corridor into which I wish to direct your attention. One might say that it is a peak between two valleys or the eye of a storm. It is the calm between the signatures of all eternal manifestations and the summit from which you perceive the remainder of your lives. My Special son, if you place the instincts you possess that bring you to ask various questions into this new dimension, you will better comprehend what I am saying. It is similar to your brother looking at a two-dimensional scene in 1991 and feeling the wind blowing against his collar at the same time. Every facet of intellectual thought is eclipsed by the Glory of Jesus' Resurrection from the Sepulcher in this corridor. In other words, certain persuasions that ordinarily or pragmatically lead to popular conclusions do not always apply in this timelessness, and the sense of inevitability that circumstances and conditions exist because of your previous knowledge and experiences does not either. I am raising your sense of awareness to this purview, even though your mind and body have not exited your prayer room. Can you discern this aura of freedom and peace that you have never felt before? And, the most important thing is why you feel it. The insights of your soul are more important to this exercise than whether you can analyze what I am saying. I am aware that this is difficult because you are not undergoing the physical bilocation that is often experienced by other visionaries. However, the attributes of the Truth are independent of your position in time and space.

The Easter Octave in which you are participating is the perfect time for you to comprehend that things are not always as they seem. Life's tragedies are real and true; human suffering is never symbolic, the grotesque nature of mortal sin is an egregious affront to Jesus, and the spiritual needs of the world's population must be met. However, the foreboding misdeeds of your sworn enemies, be they strongly perceivable or subtly ambiguous, the opinions expressed by secularists in public fora, the so-called 'personal plight' of those who complain that they do not have the freedom to be atheists, and all other malfeasances of this nature are from the disillusionment that Satan casts upon humanity. According to this premise, you know that grave transgressions such as abortion and murder are condemning sins, ones that must be stopped. When someone approaches you and says that it would be better if the Faith Church were no longer patriarchal, this is an equally evil illusion. If you believe that the sacred priesthood has been diminished by anything you have seen in the history of man, you have again fallen into this illusion. If you think that ten million people have not seen your works, you are under the illusion still more. If it is your opinion that your labors with your brother have not brought them to better understand their Heavenly Mother as Co-Redemptrix of the world, then you are suffering an even greater illusion. Let us speak about the eclipse of the present and the 'other present' that you cannot yet see. Time is a catalyst, as I have said. It is a place where everything you have ever sought from the Lord will be granted, and it is universally happening at this moment. You are asked to endure this exile for the conversion of your lost brothers and sisters. You have been accorded foresight and been privy to information about

Heaven, the Earth, and the consciences of men that they would give life and limb to know. The Divine Mercy of Jesus Christ is about this eclipse. It is about a retroactive transformation of the existence of humanity that you cannot see because you are living in the material world of thought and action. This is why you do not know not to be worrisome when you should be more confident. It is why you oftentimes become despondent when you are praying the Holy Rosary before Mass. You have not fully understood the congruence between the imminence that Jesus dispenses over the Earth and the Consecrated Love brought forth by His Sacrifice and Resurrection. You are only now learning to see that millions before you have grieved over an apparent loss of valuable time before God changed the world for the better. He has done so, it is ongoing, your prayers are being answered, and by your faith you know this to be true. I am telling you these things not only so you will comprehend, but that you can make this much clearer to My lost children in your next books. It is imperative that we address your preliminary questions about what I have told you. Do you remember when I said that the entire world became the Holy Cross on Good Friday? Can you see that the Earth about which I spoke is this one in the fullness of time? In other words, the Mystical Body of Jesus Christ, humanity itself, is being crucified with Jesus at this moment, and this is the eradication of the effects of human sin. Hence, when you say...*how can we make the future come now?* are you not asking God to neutralize the vestiges of linear time? When Jesus comes again in Glory, the passages of human history in which the transgressions have occurred will be wiped from the memories of the absolved. This is His deliverance of the future to you now. It has been done... *it is finished.* Does it not make sense for Heaven that still sees the Crucifixion of its King to see humanity on the Cross? And, how does one witness this sacrifice of blessed creatures in the most tangible terms? By living in mortal exile inside the context of time. Hence, this is where you are stationed. I am not telling you that all the anti-Christian errors you are seeing in your life do not exist, I am saying that they are a portion of humanity that is not converted bearing heavily against the dignity of your purpose in the flesh. The concept you are thinking about is spiritual darkness that exists because the lack of your brothers and sisters' faith in Salvation prohibits God's Light from touching their souls. This is why we have been working for the past twelve years; Heaven's converting presence has arrived. Who was spoken about in the Gospel at Holy Mass today? Saint Thomas. How do you believe he felt about the solvency of his faith once he touched Jesus' side? Are you asking Christ to allow everyone on Earth who does not yet believe to feel as chagrined as Thomas that day? The miracle is not only in the wonders you are seeking; human conversion is not just the result of supernatural events, it is in faith that is self-tested before the fact. If you believe that darkness prevails over the Earth and is not a function of sequestered quarters, then you are under the misperception that Christianity has failed. You are victimized by a lack of information based upon the way you receive it. The American media, heresies spoken on the street, the negativity of your colleagues, the reluctance of the impassioned to approach you on a humble basis; all of these problems have given you the impression that the world is not moving in the direction of the Cross. There is so much pressure to be diverse that the accomplishments of Christians are not being made known. This is part of the darkness and a function of the illusion. Let us refer to the eclipse again. Can you see that such falsehoods cannot permeate the filter through which every facet of righteousness will be glorified before the Throne of the Father? Will men disavow them then? We are fighting back. Humanity's heart is being purged, cleansed, refined, remade and reconstituted; this has been ongoing for 2,000 years. The evangelization of lost sinners, the administration of the Holy Sacraments, the sharing of agape about which many people speak, the turning of the tide against evil, and the inexorable march of the ages toward the Second Coming of Jesus Christ are the harvests of this gift. You are basing your observations about the effectiveness of Christianity upon two phenomena, your knowledge of historical events from the 20th century and the world you see with your eyes. I am beseeching you not only to point your vision beyond these earthly concourses, but past your own mortality. The people living on the continents around you are moving like a priceless gem toward the spires of Heaven; they always have been, and they always will be. Again, I repeat, this is not something you can see with the trammeled eye. Did Jesus not tell you that there would always be the poor in your midst? He did so because He knew that the cultivation of the Earth and the conversion of humanity would be such a gradual progression that His return in Glory might preclude the elimination of all the ills that existed during His earthbound years. If He returned tomorrow, what would you declare to Him? That you did not have sufficient Light? That there were not multitudes of Angels in your midst? There were not enough people in the Church helping you understand, or that the evil and indifference around you seemed too tumultuous to overcome? Are these the things you would cite? Jesus invites you to take comfort; they nailed Him to the Cross.

What more would you have the Lord do for you? Do you wish for the power to awaken people from the dead? Do you want to heal every person confined to a hospital bed? Do you yearn for the authority to speak in Jesus' name and the world say,...*he speaks the Truth, let's follow Him?* Jesus has already done these things, and they crucified Him. You could miraculously raise every soul who ever died from their grave, and lost sinners would still despise you. I am saying that the good offices that would come to be, those for which you are asking, will occur even so. We pray that the world ends in the condition Jesus desires when He returns in Glory; this is every Christian's desire. Short of the miracles you are seeking, how can this happen? The expiration of time. Sadly, you have made the element of time your enemy, for only through time will the world change; not by striking your foes with lightning bolts, not by knowing every broken heart, not by delaying the sun from setting. Without holy hours, there is no prayer. The governor about whom you speak feels the same heaviness that Jesus felt that was placed upon Him by those who refused to believe. The entire prospect of this discussion revolves around the love that you espouse, and few in history have understood love better than you. How can you and your fellow Christians embrace a humanity whom you will not allow sufficient time to approach God in a way that would not make them feel like Saint Thomas? The new day about which you speak has already come. It seems that you cannot draw the connection between the world that is passing away and the New World about which Jesus speaks. The momentum of the Earth is in the direction of Salvation. Your faith and knowledge of the Kingdom of Heaven allows you to see the eclipsing corridor about which I spoke to begin this message. You have better patience than before because you understand that the eminent Truth of the Holy Gospel is the impending culmination of the Earth. Within this is the Good News that you have lauded since you were an adolescent boy. I have a final parable for today, one that is rather poignant, but will help you understand. Please recall the date of August 14, 1989 when you stood at the mountaintop in Medjugorje. What would have happened if one of the visionaries had turned to the crowd and said while searching for you, ...*the Blessed Mother has just told us that She is not going to give us any other messages or appear again unless we make that person over there get off the mountain. He seems to be quite repulsive to Her.* How would you have felt? There are millions of sinners around the globe who believe that this is what God has done to them. They are wrong, and they need the experience of their lives in order to refine their faith and deploy their trust to prove it. What does this mean for our discussion? During the wait, the sinful nature of fallen humanity is causing other transgressions to be committed. They will eventually accept the holiness that belongs to them, brought forth from Heaven in the timeless Sacrifice of Jesus' Crucifixion. God desires that no one feel as though they are being asked to leave the mountain, and it is imperative for everyone to know that they are My children and not succumb to the effects of their sins. Do you understand? I am asking you to practice the faith you have professed. The conversion of sinners is a portion of that process, but other errors, as inadvertent as they may be, occur along the way. I wish for you not to concede and say that you understand just to make Me feel better. Never say resignation. You must say...*there is another inequity that has been resolved in the Cross!* It may take months before you fully internalize what I have told you. I have not seen a Saint expend more energy to prove his love for humanity or desire for the atonement of the Earth than you. The fruits of this message will be savored by many for as long as the Earth shall last..."

Sunday, May 4, 2003
2:01 p.m.

"The brilliant splendor of the eternal ages is shining deeply upon your souls with graciousness and peace. These are the moments in which the cultivation of humanity abounds through the piety of your hearts and the fruitfulness of your prayers. Join Me in supplication to the Father so He may fashion the Earth into the likeness of Heaven in your day. I have mighty blessings to dispense to those who will listen. Indeed, My messages are one of those gifts. My children, as you live according to the Holy Gospel during this new springtime of hope, please call to mind the generations who have passed away. Remember the plight imposed upon them because of the lack of amenities that you enjoy. It has been said that they seemed closer to Heaven than you, but it need not be this way. It is obvious that God's Truth is the mitigation of everything that ails you, and that your calling Him elicits His response. Modern man is much more distracted from holiness because of the rapidity by which you live. If you make peace for reasons of love, then you will be as near God as your predecessors. I am but a simple Handmaid arriving at your door, seeking to touch your hearts so you will know the contrition that Jesus desires. Who is bold enough to say that a lowly Maiden cannot be the Queen of Heaven? I am the Lady of Perpetual Help for all who are in agony, for the lanced and suffering, and for the millions who do not know God. My mission is clear. If there is grief, disharmony and torment, it is because your brothers and sisters have not responded to My call. We pray so they will assemble beneath My Mantle where I nurture their hearts. I am a Mother who requires reciprocation from My children. The disciples of Jesus have no other mother than Me. I hold you in My Immaculate Heart and enshrine you inside the Sacred Heart of My Son. When you attend the Holy Sacrifice of the Mass, you often hear of the Good Shepherd. Jesus is this Holy Manna who is calling you, guarding your lives, and feeding you the Bread of Life. Will everyone come into the fold and begin life anew? Can this hope be spread across the seas, mountains, and mainland acres so humanity will be united as one? Proof that this can be done is that I am still praying, beseeching your assistance, receiving your petitions, and prompting you to hold to the virtues of the Cross. I ask you to cling not only to Jesus' legacy, but to the eternal signs that He is giving. I come in joy because of the opportunities He offers the world to be remade in His likeness, to become cultivated so you will not be cast into the flames of perdition alongside the heathenish and their hatred. I promise as your Mother that Christ Jesus is generous in Absolution and Grace. Everyone can live a new life through His suffering on the Cross, for He bled and died for you. Let us pray that billions of lost sinners discover Christianity and that the nonbelievers who have heard and rejected it will have a change of heart. It is the latter whose souls are in the gravest danger. As I said last week, Jesus' Divine Mercy is a healing balm. His Crucifixion is the antidote for death. You should live as though you have seen Heaven because your hearts are reinvigorated. My response is of favor and gratitude, and My success in converting My lost children is dependent upon whether you permit God's Living Waters to irrigate your lives. The Holy Spirit implants Divine Truth in you, but you must ask Jesus to quench your thirst for Salvation through faith. My Special one, the fruits of your writings are saturating the Earth, and the universe is unfolding as it should. I am heartened that you recite the Sacred Mysteries of the Rosary, and that you attend the Holy Mass. These things keep your heart aloft in the sanctity of the Cross. This is God's message to the ages in reparation for the transgressions of the boastful, arrogant, haughty, loathsome, and proud. You will not discover anything in the world so opposed as your love for the Mother of God. Jesus has surrounded you with spiritually famished people for reasons to do with your sacrifices. There are signs and wonders for them everywhere. Do you sense that this is entwined with God's blessings for the world He loves, and that you are His disciples? My messages offer a protocol through which He is deigning goodness, and for you to recognize His confidence in you. These blessings mitigate the wrongs about which we have spoken. Never surrender your dignity to the netherworld because victory is yours. Those who live around you cannot see this, but you are waiting for the years to expire. Do you remember that Bishop Lucas said that the poor hold a claim over the rich? This is the same principle. Your enemies will always be in your debt unless they submit to the righteousness you espouse. The Lord will not allow the eclipse of Heaven and Earth to capitalize until you have experienced these victories because He wants you to live them over and again in Paradise. The purpose of these exercises is to enlighten you about the improprieties of humanity. This will help you become a better teacher of men and will assist your defense of the Gospel. Your response has placed you at the fore of the battle for wayward souls. Thank you for enlisting Jesus' power while the epilogue of Creation is being inexorably inscribed..."

Sunday, May 11, 2003
Mother's Day [secular]
3:03 p.m.

"The Mother of all humanity has come to speak to you today because I wish to bring My Holy Love into broken hearts who have never known the true meaning of Divine affection before. Yes, this is a day that has been set-aside for the admiration of human mothers, but I am calling even these to take refuge beneath the protection of My Mantle and in the sweetness of My Immaculate Heart. My children, I wish to tell you on this special occasion what it means to be the Matriarch of Creation. My role as Queen of Heaven and Earth is one of particular strength and compassion, much like the bearers of children on the Earth. But, I own the title of Mother of God, and there is no other. It gives Me great honor for My children to remember Me, therefore, on this day as well. I have seen through the vision of Wisdom and the benefit of the blessings of Eternity that your human hearts are still aching. And, this need not be true. Temptation, sin, impatience, and greed are the cause of such torment. When you enlist the Holy Spirit to be your guide through mortal life, you will see that only your relationship with God is what matters the most. When mothers and fathers love God with the fidelity of the Angels, He will ensure that your children follow alongside you. Being a mother means tending to the needs of her children, but being the Mother of God gives Me the capacity and authority to shape the spiritual goodness of their souls. A mother in the world provides food, clothing, and filial affection. This Mother of God gives the Bread of Life, Eternal guidance, ecclesiastical Wisdom, and compassion for the heart. I am known for all time and beyond the everlasting ages as the Benevolent Consoler because I accept and embrace the people of the Earth, even in their weaknesses. I understand what causes the agony in your lives without your having to explicate it to anyone else. You need not even utter audible groanings with your voices for Me to know that you are in pain. Do you not remember the Sacred Reproaches upon which you meditate during the Season of Lent? Such are also the pleadings of the innocent human heart! The benign nature of little children lives inside everyone, begs to come out, and cowers in the darkness of the brutal world. It is to this intrinsic simplicity that I have come, offering the Peace of God where there is sorrow and regret. My children, I am the only mother in Creation who can do these things.

    I thank all of My faithful children for acknowledging My Grace during the month of May, and for all of time. I am grateful for the many prayerful ceremonies where a statue of Me receives a crown of flowers. Each 'Hail Mary' of the Most Holy Rosary is a reciprocal kiss on My cheek by the humanity whom God has deigned to call His children. We share a unique and spectacular relationship that transcends the history of the world, which cuts through the darkness of the lost mortal ages, and that pays no mind to matters of the flesh. Together, we form a spiritual bond of Divine Love that cannot be put asunder or affected in any malevolent way by forces of the world. We share goodness, peace, joy, sanctity, purity, and Light through the Resurrection of Jesus from the Sepulcher; and we understand the motivations of God by the power of the Holy Paraclete. Why have I come seeking you with such great intensity? Because you are My babes who are yet calling-out from your nests in the world, craning your necks to see where your Mother may be. I am here, My little children! Your Mother is at your side, and I will never leave you to suffer harm anymore! I am the same Blessed Virgin Mary who bore your Salvation in My

Womb, now holding the Lamb of God who takes away the sins of the world in My Arms as the Thrice-blessed King of all Creation. His Will is to be done in your time! His little eyes are glowing in acknowledgment that it is coming true! Do not be sorrowful that the unification of the world seems not to be at hand because, in the end, it has already been achieved. Imagine the sorrow I have had for the wait! I watched sadly as My Son was Crucified on the Earth. My Immaculate Heart was pierced with a sorrow that has passed beyond the veil. Why? Because too many who are living sinful lives are still crucifying Him! And, I cry compassionately for unborn children in their mothers' wombs whose lives will be ended much too soon. I weep for victims of war and crimes of the heart. I sorrow because there are too few who will turn to Jesus for the eradication of pestilence, disease, famine, plight, and nakedness. Yes, all of these things cause the Mother of God great pain.

And, if this is not enough, I am sorrowful because even those who have faith in My Son will not wield its power to admonish and rebuke the enemies of the Cross. They cower in the back pews of their parishes and watch as though they are casual spectators while the Holy Sacrifice of the Mass is offered. I ask My little children to participate more fully in the cultivation of humanity in the way of the First Apostles and Saints! Be the activists for the conversion of the world to the Cross, and counteract all the clamoring of the millions who are seeking to abandon the alone, dying, unkempt, disheveled, and misled. Become the new Saints Francis, Augustine, Matthew, Mark, Luke, John, Juan Diego, Pio, and all the Saints! Pray from your hearts that your next-door neighbors will abandon their lives of drunken licentiousness and turn their lives over to upholding the Gospel of Christianity. Call upon them to embrace the spiritual goodness that has brought many wretched sinners to the contrition that saved their souls! Ask them to espouse the Holy Virtues and the Sacred Beatitudes that Jesus proffered the world in the Sermon on the Mount. Then, when you turn to your Heavenly Mother and ask how you can better please Me, bear these fruits in your hands as you raise them in faith. If you seek more graces for your friends and enemies too, let us meet at the intersection of Heaven and Earth on Mount Calvary, upon the Sacred Altars of the Roman Catholic Church! Come there and tell Jesus that you have brought your gifts of contrition and reconciliation in exchange for His benisons upon you! Be the blessers of other lives, of terrified human hearts, of dying men, of broken families, and of timid little children. Become the health of the sick and consolers of the grieving by making this age of humankind better than any that has ever lived before! And, yet, too many come to Me and say '...but Dear Mother, how do we do these things?' And, My response to the millions who are waging war instead of seeking peace is to ...*become every good thing that you are not now allowing to live!* I have great patience for the humanity that is Mine, and I will wait through all Eternity if this is what God has planned for you.

On this Mother's Day, the greatest burden that I bear is the lukewarm faith of Christians everywhere. If only My children would adopt the same patience that has become the forte of the Savior of the world, they would try harder to ameliorate the ills of their peoples because they would know that there is sufficient time to succeed. Never believe that it is a contradiction to also know that the Son of Man might return before dawn tomorrow! And, what will He discover you doing? What will the Master of the House find when He enters the door? He is seeking your Love, My children, in exponentially viable quantities! He is seeking the Love in your hearts to be flooding the Earth as in the days of Noah! My Son is a good swimmer! Make the Earth to be the vast ocean of miraculous human affection in which He would like to plunge and take you all under His arms to the safe shores of Paradisial jubilation! When you make the cause of your days the pursuit of this Love, you will lose your desire for the mortal. You will drop the materials in your hands. Your eyes will begin to see the Glory of the Coming of the Lord! Hallelujah! You will learn what it feels like to be Saints before you ever die! When you raise-up the Cross of the Son of God and His Glorious Resurrection too, all Creation will come running to stand beside you as you elevate the very purpose of your having been given the gift of human life. I am hopeful and joyous at the same time that I hold the sorrow in My Heart for those who have not yet tried because I know, above and beyond the pondering of any modern prophet, that everything I have ever sought in My children of the Earth will come true! I have seen it, and I ask you to believe that I have.

My Special son, it gives Me great pleasure to speak to you with high hopes because, as you know, you and your brother are already two of the most successful of My children. There are still many things yet to do, notwithstanding those who behave as though they are your enemies; for many of them are not, they are only feeding their own indignant pride. You had a very good conversation with your relatives; you are continuing to be the spiritual mentor for tens-of-thousands in this modern day; and, by your courage and perseverance, you are becoming the conqueror for Jesus whom you have always prayed to be... My son, you have said on any number of occasions that you and your brother are living in a world where there seems to be nobody else. Never be resigned to the unfortunate fate to which so many have subjected themselves in blind errancy! God is always with you, Jesus is your best friend, and the fellowship of the Holy Spirit will be with you always, even past the cleft between your mortal nature and Eternal Life. I have also told you that self-compassion is one of the greatest gifts you can give of yourself to the God who lives in your heart... Thank you for your prayers today... This is My holy blessing for you and your brother now. ✞ Please continue to be happy that you are doing God's Will. I love you. Goodnight!"

Sunday, May 18, 2003
3:18 p.m.

"This is a beautifully resilient and righteous way for you to pray with your Mother on this blessed Sunday. Indeed, this is the 83rd birthday of Pope John Paul II. My Special son, do you have a prayer that you wish to uplift on behalf of the Holy Father today? When do you wish to commence reciting it? *(I offered the prayer that I had prepared in thanksgiving for the greatness that Pope John Paul II has advanced into our age.)* Such would be a welcome salutation. I come to remind you about the powerful ways that you have converted the world to the Cross by petitioning God with altruistic piety. As we speak, Creation is being purified by your posture at My feet. Does it surprise you to know that John Paul II has arranged to beatify Mother Teresa on October 19, 2003? *(I offered very special prayers and penances for the intentions of Our Lady on October 19, 2002. She is alluding to the fruit which is coming in response to these prayers.)* These are the plans as announced, and they were fashioned into being because of our intentions. I join the Lord in offering you the benisons of Eternity for believing in the awesome stature of your role in the transformation of Earth into the likeness of Heaven. You know that this same jubilation, fulfillment, and anticipation are thriving in you. We pray together because we love—we who are loyal to Christ and the sanctification of humankind for whom He was Crucified. Remember in your glorious meditations that He was raised from the dead so you can have the strength, Wisdom, courage, and foresight to defer to the Holy Spirit in the ways you discern. I am pleased that you allow Me to amplify your petitions with the essence of Truth issuing from your heart. I bear the Good News because this is an opportune time for Creation. Your soul is unified with the fermentation of the spirit of the nations into the holiness of Paradise. You give your life, efforts, materials, and the center of your spirit so those who are falling can rise up again. I commend you for knowing why the Almighty Father does what He does, that His hope as our Creator is derived from the fact that you and all Roman Catholics stand beside the Church without wavering. I humble Myself before Him to offer thanks that He has deigned souls such as you to be My children. You console Me by means that are unbeknownst to others. I gain strength from your strength with the same providing that you grow holier by My Wisdom. You are a child of faith, the exculpating venue of Divine Love. I can go few places and see the beauty that I perceive in your bountiful heart. I hope this gives you consolation when you feel downtrodden by the errors and vices of your lost brothers and sisters who refuse to offer reparative sacrifice. I know that your determination flows from the filling of your heart with the Truth of the Holy Spirit. This is a good time, a good day, an invincible hour, and a moment for the ages. I assure you that you are one with Jesus during times like these, and I exhort you to be convinced of this because it yields the fruits of many blessings. The lives of millions will be taken to the Blood of Jesus as a result of your fostering the changes, effects, and forces that exemplify your holiest acts. And, as I have indicated, you cannot fall from Grace because you are absorbed by it. I am the Lady of Perpetual Help, and I am in unity with you. I share the prudence that My Son gives to those who are one in Him, who comply with the Will of the Father, and who pour-out their lives so the starving can be fed. Can you see that Paradise abounds through you? Do you sense Jesus' presence touching you? I am the Queen of Love, and I ask God to hear you so the infirm can be healed, the dying comforted, the afflicted brought to the fullness of life, the naked clad, the homeless sheltered, and everyone who suffers to facilitate human Redemption delivered to everlasting peace. You are My Special one, My elation, My joy, My child. There are mysteries you cannot decipher, but you will know all these things when you arrive in Heaven with Me, the Angels and Saints, and the Most Blessed Trinity. Thank you! The Holy Spirit is with you. My son, the petitions that you and your brother have raised are the alleviation of problems that you did not know had solutions. I bless humanity because their prayers augment ours. God will use them to the enlightenment, healing, and sanctification of the world..."

Monday, May 26, 2003
Memorial Day [secular]
4:36 p.m.

"My dear children, for all the motivations by which you shall recollect the brilliance of these days in future years, you will hold this one special to your hearts because the Mother of God has come to bless you. I present Myself through the holiness you are seeking as I have borne the perfection of your souls in My Womb. Jesus is My Son, your Savior, and the Wonderful Counselor whose almighty Truth has given you the Promised Land you desire. As you realize, My prayers are in unison with your petitions for the conversion of the world, indeed they are much greater than this. We ask the Lord to heal the sick, comfort the dying, console the grieving, and alleviate all forms of human suffering. I call you to remember these intentions during the coming month of the Sacred Heart of Jesus. Today, I have seen many memorials celebrated in America for the tens-of-thousands killed in international wars. Tragically, the one that has recently been declared to be over is still consuming innocent victims. Could not a humanity that is purportedly so given to the Grace of God see that war is an act of futility in seeking peace? When you remember your fallen heroes with poignant eulogies, are you not saying that they are the casualties of your reluctance to pursue it? I assure you that many of them have come to Salvation early in their lives. Their work was finished, and it is your duty to rear their orphans in their stead. You have mourned their passing without questioning the reasons why they are gone. It is because nations refuse to love. Sovereign states are reluctant to share their material goods. I am praying this Memorial Day that My dear children will not forget that Christianity calls for reconciliation over confrontation. When humanity understands this, there will be no more dead to mourn. My Special son, I am pleased by your writing. You are too self-critical along these lines. The Holy Spirit assists your development of the proper things to say, and it makes Me sorrowful when you believe that you have not written well enough. Can you use your ingenuity to write about the reasons why Jesus laid the Commandments and Beatitudes at humanity's feet? What would Creation be like without them? These are positive and constructive themes about which you can speak without seeming cynical. Include the writings of the Saints whose lessons are in your library. Cite your feelings about the meditations of Saint Augustine and others. What are your remembrances of Mother Teresa? How does her life compare to yours? What of Pope John Paul II? What does your heart tell you about this holy man whose service has meant the propagation of the Catholic Church? Go into the Hierarchy and glorify the effects of its institutions. What about the Traditions of Catholicism? What does your faith tell you about the enlightenment you felt as you grew into adulthood? You can meditate upon these things and not seem controversial. What do you feel when laying prostrate before the Altar during the Exposition of the Blessed Sacrament? What connections can you draw between piety and such sanctiforms as the relics of the Saints, their statues, the Rosary, My Marian shrines, and the homilies about the Cross that you would have offered if you were given the opportunity in the past and the future?

You know the world the way it is and the one yet to come. Without being critical of the first, explain your vision of the New Earth Jesus has wrought—His Kingdom without end that keeps your hopes alive. Reach into the depths of your spirit and describe how the transformation of sinners should come to pass in their day. Ponder intricately what will make their perfection a reality, whether through offerings of sacrifice, the miracle of a new birth of freedom in the revelations that grow from My Immaculate Heart, and your impressions of their capacities for change. These can be your examples for others around the globe. You are unlimited as to what you can write. You have been given a blank palette and a brush with which to illustrate the beauty in your heart. Your faith is inspired by the parables and images I have offered. I have given you the foundation to see Creation in reflection of Jesus without demanding retribution against those who spurn Him. I realize that you wish for your tone to be positive; and to achieve this, describe how you expect to become. Can you imagine what your soul should look like when you stand before Jesus in Heaven? What do you want Him to see?... It will be a new month when I speak to you again, but I will be with you every day, every hour, and every sleeping and waking moment..."

Sunday, June 1, 2003
1:34 p.m.

"Wishing is all that many of your brothers and sisters can do, My children. They peer upward and outward from their plagues of poverty and loneliness, but there are few stooping to comfort them. Not only are their lives wracked by the selfishness of others, they endure the egregious neglect that has become such a deficiency of the American way. I pray with you that My children in the United States will share and share alike those things that bring consolation to the less-fortunate. The insolence of their enemies makes this a difficult prospect. Even when you look beyond your borders, you see millions of indigents who are crying-out for help, but Americans are too interested in patriotism and capitalist wealth. Most will reach-out only when there is a benefit to be reaped. I wish for My words to be heard throughout the Earth and until the end of time. The political savagery of the President of the United States to take his irreverence to the homeland of Pope John Paul II is one of the most brazen insults ever perpetrated in the history of the universe. I assure you that goodness and Mercy follow those who fear the Judgement of the Lord, but this man is in need of reproval from people of faith. Indeed, the entire American nation requires reparative prayer for repentance and conversion. One faction declares that they have the right to kill children in their mothers' wombs, while another claims that the unborn should be protected, yet the latter does little to make it happen. The atrocity against enwombed American children is the horriblest scourge since the summary genocides of World War II. Their future has been fodder for partisan debate by those who have no intention of carrying-out their promises. This hypocrisy cannot be tolerated, and it will not go unpunished. Therefore, by the time the multitudes in America hear the words I have spoken today, the worst catastrophic events in this century will have begun. And, after I am heard, know that the conflagration was caused by the deliberate refusal of Americans to protect their unborn children. Justice is as simple as this. My Special son, please remember to pray for the poor souls in Purgatory. They are comprised of the anguished souls of the Church Suffering. Please be clear in knowing that the Church Triumphant has no such boundaries. Human life is a condition, and Purgatory is a condition, but Heaven is unconditional... You are living specific lives, and your residence will be remembered as a shrine. I ask you to realize that your brother's work is done to his joy and is never a burden on him. The Holy Spirit is alive in you..."

Sunday, June 8, 2003
Feast of Pentecost
2:19 p.m.

May the hope, peace, and healing of the Holy Spirit be with you! This, My children, is My wish as we begin our prayers on the birthday of the Church. I bid you happiness because these are the blessings bestowed upon all who love God. It is through the Holy Spirit that you are brought to Christian sanctity. God has given you many gifts under the Third Person of the Trinity, and you have power in you. Whatsoever you do for His Kingdom, the Lord offers His benedictions. Please love Him, O' children! Seek Him as your Guiding Light in the darkness of the years. Your lives are products of the Holy Spirit. Your knowledge is borne throughout the timelessness of Heaven. All this God gives those who love Him. Every transcription, inspiration, ejaculation, recitation, and prayer is manifested by the Holy Spirit. Therefore, be children of God by inviting the Holy Paraclete to take refuge in your hearts. I have told you on many occasions that the reason for your conversion is this Wisdom. You are given nourishment and peace as you pray. I have also told you about new beginnings. By the power of the Holy Spirit, each hour is a new one because the old world is passing away. These things have been revealed in the Sacred Scriptures, and the Scriptures are your blueprint for success. I have watched you since you were conceived in your mothers' wombs. I lay claim to you because I am your Immaculate Mother of graceful pleasance. I ask that you become devoted to Me by the Light of Paradise sustaining our unity through the Holy Spirit. My Special son, your life is on course, and there is much work to do. I have no lesson today. I have no particular message for the world, and I have no requests. I simply come to pray with you and your brother on this Feast because I am moved by the dignity in which you live, the dutiful efforts you pour-forth for God, and the dedication that you have afforded the transformation of the Earth into the likeness of Heaven. Thank you! Be assured that I am with you, as is the Holy Spirit who empowers the faithful. I am above you where you work and play, when you ponder and write, when you rise and rest, and whether you are in joy or angst. I am the Mother of Jesus whom His disciples must come to know. Your brother will write many things that can be utilized for the purification of humankind. You have known him for decades. God has given him another goal to reach in the next few months, and he will do what is necessary to achieve it. I will tend to My other children while you enjoy this Sunday. Please know that there is never a time when you are beyond My sight or the means through which I hear My children calling for the intercession of their Mother..."

Sunday, June 15, 2003
Feast of the Most Blessed Trinity
3:47 p.m.

"In the name of the Father, the Son, and the Holy Spirit. Amen. Thus, we invoke the Holy Trinity on behalf of Creation that is blessed by the Dominion of God. I pray with you because My children must remember how special they are, for this is the way happiness begins. The Blessed Trinity. What a sacred mystery and grand feasting to beatify the world. Is it possible for exiled sinners to know that the Trinity existed before the Earth? If you recall that you are thrice-loved, then you will understand with assurance that God is a sovereign Father, Jesus is your brother and Savior, and the Holy Spirit is the Wisdom in your hearts and Advocate before the Throne of Heaven. You have heard the analogies offered by the Saints to describe how they pondered the Blessed Trinity. If there is a clover on Earth that can encapsulate the magnificence of the Blessed Trinity, let it grow to the heights of the stars. If there are concentric circles to explain what the Holy Trinity is, then let those circles be the circumference in which all other centers reside. If there is a number one and a number 111, then let them be conjoined so all that is of Heaven lies within its toll. My children, you understand the Blessed Trinity by the vision in your hearts. What thoughts you might have about seeing God, His Only Begotten Son, and the Holy Paraclete as though they could rest on the surface of a plane, remember that the Blessed Trinity cannot be measured by such things. You are loved and brought to perfection by Truth. Please remember that this Feast is about God's definition of Himself, where others are about what He has done. It is in His Being that you understand, and Eternity is real and in your lives by the faith sustaining you. These Mysteries are sacred because they are of the mystical Creation that you recognize as the affection of the Lord for His people. Thank you for praying for the invocation of the Paraclete to infiltrate your hearts. You may remember an effective way to parablize the Blessed Trinity. My Special son, do you recall? Yes, that is one means. And, another way to show the presence of three under one is three straws that you view one atop another with a space between them. Closing one eye and peering down with the other, you see the concept of the Holy Trinity. Do you remember that this is one reason for the eye configured atop the architecture of churches and cathedrals? This cannot be examined in one-dimension. It simply implicates the distance between the Earth and the celestial realms above. *(Our Lady had me place one straw on a table while holding one in each hand. Then I was to hold one a few inches above the other lying on the table, and the last straw, a few inches higher above the second straw, in a way where none of them were physically touching. I was then told to look down through them from above and align their tips in the form of a triangle within my vision.*

Then, I closed one eye to eliminate my depth perception that they were on different planes atop one another, giving them the appearance that the three straws were actually one geometric object. In this, one can see an image of three separate entities forming a unified Trinitarian image on a plane of awareness that is outside our normal spacial perception.)

I have come to say that God has brought another of His children to Heaven, Eddie Dean Thomas. His soul is saved in Glory. Please bring your Morning Star book to your prayer room and turn to June 9, 1994. There, you see the date Eddie came to Heaven, and on the opposite leaf, you see his grieving mother traveling by that mode of transportation to tell her beloved son goodbye. This has been in God's plan since the foundation of the Earth. You may tell his mother about this if you wish. Assure her that Eddie is with Jesus, that he is resting in living peace with his Grandma and Grandpa. Tell her that Eddie has asked that they do not grieve his death because they will see him again with all the Angels and Saints. Thank you for praying for everyone who has brought new life into the Church by their faith and for the millions who fight for righteousness when their brothers and sisters turn away. It is difficult when people are aggrieved by the sorrow of death. However, it is opportunity for celebration, dignity, deliverance, freedom, and the culmination of the hopes of the human spirit in the Sacred Heart of Christ. Yes, Eddie is with Me and is embracing Jesus with thanksgiving for forgiving his sins. His vision is perfect, his eternity has begun, and he waits with all who have fallen asleep in Jesus for the arrival of the Messiah into His Kingdom to end the ages. Thank God! Thank God that He deigned to absolve the souls of sinners who have succumbed to death! The Lamb of God who has taken away the sins of the world is holding Eddie Thomas in His arms like a newborn child. My Special one, I know that you weep not from sorrow, but from joy for the new life that Eddie has gained. You knew him, you saw the facets of his spirit, and you were kind to him when he needed you most. For these things, Saint Eddie will intercede for you as he has since the moment last Monday when you were told that he slipped through the veil of the exiled world into the Eternal. My son, this can only be a good thing for those who know the Lord and accept Jesus' Blood as expiation for their sins. Therefore, when you think about the Holy Trinity, when you wonder how there could ever be a God so great, think about how happy Eddie is. Yes, he realizes now that I am his Mother. I wish to tell you something more about the Mercy of God. Whatever sinner you bring to mind, no matter who it is, just ask Jesus to forgive them in Heaven, and He will hear. When you pore over the annals of history from the ancient days, the Middle Ages, the Crusades, the Inquisition, and the world wars, no matter how large or small, all you need to do is think of these souls, not even knowing their names, asking Jesus to remember them in Paradise, and He will listen. This is your advantage over those who do not believe in God. Your heart, your love, your sacrifices, and your intentions are their deliverance.

Your brother has been asked to earn another college degree. His mind is as strong as when he was young, his integrity is intact, his capacity to discern the enemies of righteousness just as sound, and his desire to remain at your side as profound as ever. None of this has changed. It has been the same for decades. Inside you in communion with your brother, God is still reigning, converting, transforming, cultivating, and purifying His people. The beauty of Creation is revealed by the supplications you offer for the Salvation of humanity. Wretches are falling prostrate before the Risen Christ. Marriages are being repaired, vows reaffirmed, the health of the sick restored, and the legacy of those who have been cast aside for their faith preserved. All of these manifestations are occurring while you go about your work, seeing the same faces, looking into the same screens, commuting the same avenues, and entering the same doors. The underworld is brawling with the misdeeds of the multitudes being trumped by your righteousness. You and your brother have consecrated a movement that cannot be impeded. Before the Son of Man reinstitutes the Earth, there will be hundreds-of-thousands pleased to call themselves My Eucharistic Fidellites. How strong their witness is beyond the element of time! Fathers Ken and Kevin will hail their chastity at the front of the parade to the joy of the Saints! People who have hidden in the darkness, addicted to contraband, and groveled in gutters of despair will use the cutting edge of their rejuvenated spirits to excise their tattoos from their flesh. Be prepared, for this will happen earlier than you believe, when your heart is despondent, when you think that not a man, woman, or child is listening. Be ready because the Coming of the Son of Man is nigh. My Special son, I hold great hope not only because it is intrinsic to My Immaculate Heart, but because I see it in the lives of My children. I hear the cries of My lost little ones in the same way that you hear thunder in the night. I pray with you for the forthcoming graces that millions have already received by accepting the peace of reconciliation. You are not at the beginning of this transformation, but past its midpoint and near the Narrow Gate through which the saved will walk. It is this Redemption that overtakes the world, defeats evil, and brings enlightenment to your hearts about the Kingdom of Heaven. It is the Blessed Trinity that provides the foundation upon which you stand in Jesus Christ. If you were a bird capable of flying above the lands where your fathers played as children, would you not tell them of the lofty things you have seen? Would you beckon them to look into the upper realms to realize their hopes and dreams? You bear the Holy Spirit in your heart, and it is this Advocate from the Father who is elevating you so you will not be so sorrowful. Your Mother offers the visions that you gain nowhere else. They are perceptions that you have seen by your faith. My Special son, these are not daydreams, they are the Wisdom of the Blessed Trinity providing the Truth as you endure your remaining years. This is why all who have died in God's favor are savoring His presence in Heaven where there are no tears. I give you My promise that the world in which you live will conclude as you have prayed. If you do not believe this to be true, you are suffering the illusion under which other lives have been palled. We have spoken about this before. In the name of the Father, the Son, and the Holy Spirit, we have come to the conclusion of another message..."

Monday, June 23, 2003
6:42 p.m.

"My cherished children, I wish for you to hear a song for your transition to prayerfulness. It has such elegance and majesty. Thank you, My Special one, for writing your consoling words in the guest book for Eddie Thomas. When you receive notice that it has been posted, have your brother read it to you, and Jesus will help his inflections so you will realize how it will be received by the world. You speak about hope and eloquence, and your writings are much the same because the Holy Spirit has taken abode in your heart to change the world for the better, to mend the divisions between races, to offer your Christian love to those who are abandoned, and to teach the ignorant about their Salvation in the Blood of the Holy Cross. Even though I have spoken to you for over twelve years, I have only just begun. The Eternity we shall spend together has opened while you reside in mortal flesh on Earth. The brightness of the Light which has shined on you is of the Divine Providence of God, the Angels, and the Saints. I assure you that you will experience this as you advance in years. I have come to speak about the Love you seek because it is inside you that Heaven is manifested. Why does it come to the heart? Because it is the sustenance of your life and the origin of your righteousness. I have reflected upon the heart on many occasions, of pretty ones, inspirited ones, broken ones, and those whose thoughts ache deep inside from the burdens of sin. I have spoken about the transgressions that your brethren have committed and the ones that have been perpetrated against them. It is to this pain that I speak, and it is about the transformation of the heart into Divine Love that My intercession is about. Mending the ills of humanity begins at the core of the heart, and this month of June, of the Most Sacred Heart of Jesus, has been another during which He is offended by the wretched and comforted by the righteous. I assure you that the special kind of Light whose origin you yearn to see is guiding you now. My children, Creation is more than a place of doing, it is a perpetual state of Divine Love. When you come to the understanding that the element of time cannot affect it, you will realize what it means to deflect the worries of the world. Perfect Love is the Kingdom of God. As I told you, it is not a facet of human intuition or a longing for contemporary fads. It is an affirmation of everything that is true, an affection for the Savior who paid your passage into Heaven. When you yearn for peace, you are pining for Jesus. If your lives seem filled with inexplicable darkness, it is the Light of the Son of Man you are seeking. When I declare that you are under His Dominion, He has you in His sights. Your souls have come out of hiding from the shadows of the Earth. This is the source of trust that all is well in His Holy Kingdom. All comprehension, understanding, patience, and genius are wrought from your acceptance of all that Jesus' Most Sacred Heart contains. Its pulse is the Breath of Life to those who are suffocating in the secular void, so be religious and be righteous! Be Christians and be happy! Demand that the Gospel be a catalyst for change, personal and social, the kind of change that leads tyrants to the Cross. My children, I have imagined what this would be like, and I have seen it with My eyes. It is closer than the distant offing and is ongoing as we speak. This is the hope through which you rest during the night and awaken with a sense of purpose. It is brilliance, authority, perpetuity, and cleanliness. This is the hope that casts away doubts about the present and the future. It is the healing of every ailment and the raising of throngs from their fathoms of despair. Jesus has given you these things not only for you to ponder, but to live with purpose and judgement. I am always pleased when accorded an opportunity to speak to My messengers. As I say, it is as though I just began, that this is the first day when you were so timid, curious, and somewhat afraid. This newness never expires. You live in the perpetual bliss of the Divine Love of God in your hearts. Thank you for letting Me speak to you! Please remember that whenever you are in pain or sorrow, anguish or frustration, or loneliness or sadness, I am here for you. I am with you because Jesus lives in you..."

Sunday, June 29, 2003
Feast of Saints Peter & Paul
4:21 p.m.

"The infinite realms of Eternal Glory are emanating the Divine perfection of God, little children. Heaven is within you, everlasting Dominion engulfs you, perpetual Wisdom comforts you, and beatific brilliance surrounds you. I give you the ascending power of the Sacred Heart of My Son on this Feast of Saints Peter and Paul who are sources of true enlightenment for people of faith everywhere. With their preface of piety as your guide, be strong in your beliefs that the Son of Man has shined His Deific approval upon His disciples of righteousness. This Mother of Holy Truth has come speaking to you about His Love because, absent My intercession, you would not offer the obedience you have been giving to heed the summons of the Holy Spirit. Therefore, I ask that you open your hearts wide. Be people! Be My holy people! During these hours while the extreme darkness of human sin is corrupting the world, I implore your petitions for your conversion. The impiety that has encompassed the globe is perpetuating violence and casting doubt upon the safety of millions of citizens. We must pray for them! I deign to seek your supplications for the purification of the hearts of sinners in every land, foreign and domestic. Yet in all of this, I come today as a happy Mother because I know that My Crucified Child has redeemed you through His Sacrifice on the Cross. When you sense that eternal victory is yours, it makes the fight worthy for Christians from all walks of life. Thank you for believing! I am heartened today because Christians are seeing the higher purpose of God's Justice and that He has accorded it to those whose faith perseveres. In the final hours, your trust becomes your ultimate freedom. Even as your good works suffice your honor, the authentic faith in your hearts is your Salvation. Remember that Jesus Christ is the Savior of the human race; and believe it with the entirety of your humanity, and you will be redeemed. This is the source of My peacefulness, My children. I have seen the Lord. Unlike you, I have already joined Him. The time you labor in His earthly vineyard is imperative. You must not only be led by the Holy Spirit, you must be beacons of hope for your prodigal brothers and sisters. This is the acceptance and reflection of God's divinity that has become your meaning in life and the purpose of these days. We share one great passage of historical revelation—yours from the vantage-point of exile, and Mine from the pinnacle of Truth as Queen of Heaven. You see how the world is changed when we allow our love for humanity, for God, and for the Angels and Saints to be commingled with the miraculous gifts that the Father ordains. It is bettered because the focus of human hearts is clarified and sustained. When you accept Jesus as your Savior and Wonderful Counselor, you know beyond doubt that your actions and reactions have influence. The essence of purpose for the humble human is to be strong in this faith. It is a blessing from God in Heaven for which you must pray. My children, I ask that you be unafraid of things that might harm you. Do not cower from assaults against your holiness and struggles for peace. Do not hinder your progress toward the perfection that Jesus seeks by stoning the devil's dogs. It is better to fire a lamp than curse the darkness. Be with Me in every way through the elevation of your prayers, and in the knowledge that you stand in favor of Truth. Be confident that you are beneath My Mantle. With these expressions of assurance, carry-on with the strength of the Holy Spirit to whom your lives are given. Herald the teachings of Peter and Paul. Remember the reflections of faith that they gave you. Imagine the holiness they brought to Earth by their allegiance to the Son of Man. Their memoirs echo the persistence of loyalty that is lacking in those who impugn the Vicar of Christ and the Roman Catholic Church.

    My Special son, how pretty are your writings for your next book. You know that your sacrifices and appreciation for God's gifts are the origin of your spiritual health. Thank you for seeing what consoles you in the Truth and Wisdom of God. The sights you behold comfort Me because you understand what it means to trust in faith. You witness beauty, Providence, sanctification, destiny, humility, peace, and virtue. Can you see how this gives your holiness wider parameters by which you write the sentiments of your love for Jesus? I come to say that I love you, and I will give you in the future some intense and beautiful messages to reaffirm My support, offer My advice, and seek in you the peace you have accepted from Heaven. Know in this that your kindness bears sweet fruits. My dear William, this is a hopeful time for you and your brother because auspicious events are happening and new manifestations are unfolding. You should be grateful for these gifts from God. Your faith is secure in the knowledge that you have been given signs that would prompt other men to fall to their knees in ecstasy. I have witnessed the rest of your life. There will never be a moment when you are other than thankful for the blessings that God has dispensed. If you could sense Jesus' appreciation, you would never see sacrifice the same way again. I have much to do in guiding you because I know that the ways of the spatial world are treacherous. You are gifted because you lead a righteous life, and you are the focus of the Lord's adulation. You are the esteemed Special one upon whom the Mother of God comes calling for the conversion of humanity... Thank you for taking care of your brother and tending to him with such devotion. Like you, he is close to the Father..."

Sunday, July 6, 2003
3:38 p.m.

"May the Peace, Love, and Grace of God be with you always! My children, I come to remind you about the Glory of Heaven because within the brief passing of time, it shall be the final resting place for your souls. It is with delight that I speak to you because I share the gifts of Grace that are pouring-down on you from Paradise. It has been said that the Throne of God is not a place because He is a Spirit. I remind you that the Throne of the Father is a tangible location in Heaven from which He authors your lives, presides over Creation, and hails with Jesus to await the close of the ages. What a telling revelation this is for the unsuspecting! I have told you about His Love for more than twelve years, and you have listened ardently and intently. Forever will I be grateful that you recognize the Truth after all this time, for it is Truth in your hearts that tells you when your brothers and sisters are failing to practice it. The Holy Spirit within you reveals that there are weaknesses in the Church, lukewarm parishioners, clergy who have betrayed their vocations, and others behaving as though they will never be asked to answer for their transgressions. My dear children, it is not a sad day when you realize these things, it is an indication that additional prayer is needed. You cannot recollect history that is anything other than the way it unfolded. If there were moments of chastening and strife, your hearts will tell you. If you have endured any indignity, your spirit will remember. These thoughts allow you to examine yourselves as the Mystical Body of Christ and the reasons you seek the studious element of change. I am heartened when I see you reprove secular institutions because you contrast them to God's Truth. I am likewise pleased when you upbraid the failings of your brothers because it is your prayer to facilitate their conversion. Do not despair that conditions do not seem as they should. You would have a right to dejection if you lacked the vision to know the difference. I exhort you to continue praying, surveying, and scrutinizing the implications of humanity's insufficiencies and be careful that they do not befall you. When I speak about graces, I refer to blessings you are receiving. You employ your vision for the good of humanity when you scrutinize the contradictions between what people say and what they eventually do. These distinctions allow you to see hypocrisy, desecration, schism, and a lack of righteousness in other men. Be thankful that your faith is so strong that you are uncomfortable with the worldliness of lost sinners. It is when you see this that you ask Jesus to come to their aid. When you petition the Father to send the Holy Spirit to infiltrate estranged hearts, He will respond. He is doing so as we speak; and speak we must, and pray we shall. Drawing battle lines against indifference is a righteous undertaking. Refusing to accept your brothers' lukewarmness is not only your right, it is the duty of the Church. Is this not why you write about Truth and the Second Coming of the Messiah? When the Earth looks like a wasteland in which the dregs of society have sunken to the bottom of the seas, you lift them to the surface where Jesus resuscitates them. You are not commoners in God's Kingdom, He has created you to be the chosen elect. You are not pacifiers, you are subscribers to His revolution. This is what He mandates and the reason you were given your faith. I assure you that you are succeeding in ways you cannot see, while others approach Him in the dark of night pleading, *I want to know! I wish to identify the effects of my efforts for the conversion of humanity now!* My response is that I do as well, but you must patiently fight to purify the Earth and number your successes later. You are the Mystical Body of My Son. I bring signs of Providence and the liveliness of the Most Blessed Trinity, engaging humanity as dramatically as miracles from other worlds, imploring your servitude on behalf of His Eternal Kingdom.

My little children, the Grace I offer is higher than any summit you will ever ascend. It is more viable than any prophecy foretold. The Grace I give is more supple than a rose. Inside the Grace that you cannot earn but will always receive resides the reprieve for which you hunger and your hopes thirst. If you follow Me; if you cast aside the distractions of Earth, if you permit Me to be your Mother for everything you will become, then Jesus' Crucifixion and Resurrection will be clear to you. Your Christian faith will have new meaning. The essence of life will be born into your consciousness like the lifting of a veil. If you call me Mother, the Savior whom I birthed at Bethlehem will purify your souls, preserve your dignity, provide your strength, and predestine your days so the victory of Salvation will be visited upon you with Truth and Light. If you accept Me as your Mother, you will understand the reason for suffering with the precision of a jeweler, and you will breathe as if your soul had wings. You will challenge the world by speaking about what is wrong; this is your prayer for making it right. My children, if you call Me Mother, God will elevate you to new heights with such expedition that you will believe that Eternity has begun before the backdrop of your grandest hopes and dreams. This is the freedom for which you are searching; this is the Wisdom that makes you whole. You discover Creation's benevolence in Me. I am your Mother whose eyes have seen more than the dignity of the Lord, I have greeted the Saints from the past. I have heard the cries of the poor, the lamenting of the wicked, the wailing of those in pain, and the footsteps of the penitent walking in contrition to the Holy Cross. I have seen giants fall to their knuckles before the Fount of Life so precipitously that the Earth shuddered in their dust. I have seen Angels by the millions comforting them, whispering in their ears that it is time to begin anew. Never mind the Lilliputians, linger among the Leagues of Angels! Listen to My Winged Pearls tying the heartstrings of humanity into a new accord, fit for the Son of Man. When I speak about Grace, My children, I instill hope deep inside your hearts so that out springs the holiness that God has seeded there. I promise you My Motherhood if you become My children. I will lead you through the darkness into Eternal Light because you cannot get there on your own. If you sense that there is a Triumph in the offing, believe that it is of My Immaculate Heart. Be confident that the Beatific Light surrounding you is the brilliance of Jesus Christ! He is perpetuity, invincibility, Absolution, deliverance, renewal, and Messianic Truth. Pursue His excellence and He will take you to Heaven before the sun slips past the horizon on the last day of the world. My Special son, it is a privilege to visit you because you live in the Grace about which I speak. You are enriched by the fruits that the Saints celebrate in their prayers. There is one reclamation of the souls of humanity, and you know it to be the Crucifixion of My Son. In this, you must never fret because the issues ladening your heart are passing. Your hopes rest in the Holy—

TRVTH

When I ask you to see the universe concisely, I call you to be My visionary, and you and your brother are doing this to perfection. You are the inspiration for My speech because you have never surrendered your hopes for humanity to change. You have been obedient to Me, embracing the miracles that others have maligned. You are yearning for the Second Coming of the Son of Man..."

Sunday, July 13, 2003
3:33 p.m.

"When you ponder the starry hosts about which you were speaking earlier, please remember to glorify the Creator who placed them there and fashioned the cynosure of the cosmos in whose vastness they are gleaming. My children, it is the smallness of your spirits that makes you magnanimous among men. As I said previously, everything you do for Jesus is heightened through the reflection of the ages. I come calling humanity to see the poverty in which many in your number are living. Pray for the patients who are dying from disease. Ask Jesus to mend broken people whom you have never met in countries whose inadequacies you do not know. I beg My American children to live simply so the impoverished around the world can simply live. We assemble in the presence of the Angels and Saints, in the Name of Jesus, and through the power of the Holy Spirit to invoke God's blessings, to bring urgent healing to the millions upon millions who require His intervention. The western world lives at such a pace that it does not take time for prayer. There is a vision-blurring agendum in the people of the United States that casts a malevolent shadow over the entire western hemisphere. I pray that these things will change, that the children of God will awaken from their slumber and realize the sanctity of life through the Holy Trinity. My Special son, I will speak only briefly because you have declined to rest, although your labors and writings are venerable and powerful. I do this by design because you do not require My words to pamper you. I am forever in your company, and I intend to employ your talents this autumn to record some crucial messages for the Mystical Body of My Son. There will be other tragedies in America before then, ones that will reveal to you the purpose of the Cross. The moral fabric of the United States is frayed, and something must be done. The Supreme Court bears no honor in the mind of God. Something must be done! I ask for the prayers of the faithful because they suspend the Wrath of God. Many are turning deaf ears to My call, violating the Commandments, spurning the Beatitudes, and ignoring the Scriptures dealing with chastity, the sanctity of life, charity of the spirit, and openness of the heart. Indeed, something must be done. As you look around your nation that is called land of the free and home of the brave, what do you see? Yes, and who are these enslaved cowards you mention? You are correct. The disheartening silence of Christians is bringing the United States to ill-repute. There may be annihilations, castigations, and chastisements to follow. Imagine a marriage of sinners of the same sex. This is an outright evil that Satan has concocted. I know you share the sentiment that America is deserving of this punishment; you are accurate in your assessment. While we pray for your nation to change, vengeance belonging only to the Lord will force it. Do not be afraid, you and your brother will be unharmed, but tolls of innocent people will be affected. This is how America will recognize that God's Grace is not shed on thee! Please remind your countrymen about My September 16, 2001 message when these events occur. Call on everyone for fasting and prayer. Be assured that Jesus will not permit the perversions corrupting His people to stand. Something must be done! The writing of your sixth and seventh manuscripts are part of His plan. You will place them in the proper location when the time is right, just as you have the prior five. Your readership understands that your writings with your brother are shared. Remember that those who suffer persecution are mitigating the errors about which you have spoken. When they arrive in Heaven, they will be grateful that they were granted the opportunity to convert the lost. Their portion of the Cross has been a fruitful one. Remain close to Timothy, recite your prayers, attend Holy Mass, perform your duties, write your books, send your brother to school, and do the other things around which your life is centered, and the result will be the jubilation of your soul in the Triumph of My Immaculate Heart..."

Sunday, July 20, 2003
"One Giant Leap for Mankind"
2:09 p.m.

"Please remember Me when deep in your prayers, little children, for I will amplify them with My exemplary Grace before the Almighty Father. My intentions are benign, My purposes are always benevolent, My Immaculate Heart is sincere, and My power to effect the change you are seeking on Earth is unprecedented in the Sacred Heart of Jesus. I call upon you so that you will reciprocally call upon Me to be your holy guide in living-out your days. How I truly wish for you to be happy! I have told other messengers throughout the ages that I cannot make you happy here on the Earth compared to the rejoicing you will do in Heaven. However, compared to the dismal lives many people have led before, I can assure you that your blissful faith will open the doorway for your anticipation of the Eternal Salvation of your soul. My children, God has granted Me the gift of being your benefactor so that you will be fully prepared to accept this Salvation. What is it that I give to you? I bring you Wisdom in the form of undying Love. I offer you the compassion of a Perpetual Mother. I console your hearts when you are in pain. And, with the Light of the Love of Jesus, I make your pathway clear to the Holy Cross. You surely must remember that I stood beneath that same Cross on Good Friday when My Loving Son was Crucified. What does His Sacrifice tell you? That you are saved by the power of His Blood! And, that you know that human life is never wholly shed of sorrow, but such sorrow need not give you cause to surrender the fight for righteousness. You are more than conquerors in Him who has Redeemed you! Your dignity has been regained in the indignity of the Passion of My Slain Son. I am the Mother of all of this supernatural Grace, and My call is for you to be strengthened in your sorrows. Never give-up or give-in to the sadness of the world, because the happiness and joy of Life Eternal has vanquished it for the good of your future. There is hope in these things, there is new life, Resurrection, and the knowledge that you are free to choose the holy pathway of mortal life. This is the goodness to which you are called. My children, if this were not true, I would have told you very plainly heretofore.

I am calling upon My humanity to come to its feet for the change that is needed all around the world. You are but little children, and you have done many mighty things in technology, medicine, communication, and travel. You have taken that very small step for (a) man, but have you chosen as a collective people to make that giant leap for mankind? Have you decided for God as a unified species? Do you acknowledge Jesus Christ as the Savior of humanity from every hamlet, borough, city, suburb, and summit? Are you yet so divided that you cannot see past your own indignance? Time is a very short passing for you to endure. You see the ages which are affected by the elements and edifices. Your hearts are buffeted by rejection and sorrow. To what do you attribute these things? Is the world so blind that its inhabitants assume that human suffering is inevitable? If so, then you must open your eyes to the Truth which has been borne to Creation in countless miracles throughout the history of all histories. I give you My solemn Word, My Son—your Savior; and your reaction and response must be one of peace and hope; for if you do not, your future is indeed hopeless! Every venue by which you can see the fruitful beginnings you have been seeking for centuries is available to you now in the Salvation you have gained in the Cross of My Son. You must crucify your own will so that it can be raised again in unity with God through the Resurrection of Jesus from the Tomb. This is what it means to be holy people. When you see tragedies and losses occurring around you at a seemingly more regular pace, do not place their attribution at the doorstep of your Loving God! Humanity is to blame for every teardrop that has ever been shed! When you turn inside to ask yourselves why, you will see your absence of holiness there, completely banished from your spirits in favor of the grief that you have asked the Almighty Father for instead. Call upon the Angels to give you comfort! Ask the Holy Spirit to guide you through the darkness! Become filled with allegiance to the Crucified Son of God, and anything that burdens you will be lifted from your shoulders, cleared from your pathway, and erased from your recollection.

I have also told My people that if you pray with the intensity of the Saints, you will not realize your passing from this life into the next. I have asked you to be united as one humanity under the Holy Cross in the likeness of no other age. And, if you continue to decline to do these things, you will make no giant leaps in any direction that has anything to do with Divine Love!

All of your accomplishments in the past are only metaphors for your own vanity and the way for you to say 'We are proud!' Your Almighty God is asking you to answer the question, ...proud of what? Please tell Me that you have not spent the past 2,000 years pining to seek other worlds when you have yet to perfect the unity of the very one on which you stand! Please tell Me that it is not true! Please assure the millions of Holy Saints who reside in Heaven that your purpose in being the leader of the nations is not to become better at making war, fabricating pretenses to conquer your foreign neighbors, cheating the very friends upon whom you have relied so many times before out of their very next meal, and self-aggrandizing your capacity to wave a red, white, and blue flag and say 'I'm free!' My people, tell the Mother of your Omnipotent God that your intentions are more benevolent than this! I pray you, tell Me that it is not true! What about the giant leap of faith that My Son has asked you to make headlong in knowing that His Life, Death, and Resurrection is God's gift to you in absolute Love? This is the priceless act that He is seeking in you now. Give your souls to Him as though you were diving into a deep ocean from atop a towering cliff! This is the giant leap! This is where your courage lies! The stern admonishments that your Immaculate Mother might give you now are nothing compared to the division of the sheep and the goats which will occur come the end of time. I am kind and gentle, and God is fair and mild. And, Jesus is very much filled with Divine Mercy for those who can read the signs that are ongoing on the Earth today. Indeed, the many who understand the Truth of the Holy Gospel and reject it anyway are in grave trouble! We must pray for them! We must pray for them! Someday, the sizzling sound you will hear will be the agony of their souls in the blazing flames of Hell! We must pray for them!

    Therefore, when you see suffering, loss, tragedy, and sorrow in your midst today, remember that it is the egregious arrogance of a lost humanity that is making it so. And, the obvious question of millions in your midst '...when will all of this end(?)' is entirely dependent upon when the sinners decide to relinquish what they are doing and turn their lives over to Jesus. It could happen by the end of today if only everyone would believe. Or, it could occur tomorrow if Jesus decided to provide a large enough miracle. Is this any way to urge a people to embrace their faith? Is fear the only way to guide the lost into the righteousness of the Light? These are such questions to which humanity, itself, must respond. I will tell you something that may give many of My children great hope, others apprehension, and millions a signal of a long-earned sense of relief... *(Our Lady prophesied the coming of horrific events that pertain to the annihilation of evil which I am not allowed to reveal.)* Please read the Book of Revelation! The righteous shall have their fill! I promise that this is what will happen if the millions who have rejected the Cross of their Salvation do not bend in contrition before it, amend their lives, and never return to such baneful ways again. And, for those who know the Mother of

God as the Gentle Maiden who reigns as the Queen of Peace over Heaven and Earth, I assure you that there will be irrevocable peace on Earth once this righteous purging has been done. I give you My solemn promise that all of these things are true. Lucky will be the villains who will die between now and then of their own accord!

My Special son, it has not been My purpose to frighten you today. The historical nonsense that happened on this day 34 years ago has nothing to do with human Salvation. I am calling for a '...giant leap' that involves the surrendering of the will to God, of sacrifices from the wealthy on behalf of the poor, and the deposing of popularly-elected democratic leaders in countries whose agenda are to only profit for themselves. You have been told that the world is upside down, and Jesus is about to invert it to the pleasure of every Martyr who ever died trying to prove it in their day. Thank you for allowing Me to speak to you with such profound seriousness today... Thank you for doing your part in a very holy way. You have been a very easy little boy for Me to guide. And, your brother has been one as well... Yes, it is true. Some of the things I told you today were also told to Saint Joan of Arc... This is now My holy blessing for you. ☥ I love you. Goodnight!"

Sunday, July 27, 2003
3:22 p.m.

"It is with happiness and peace that I share the splendor of God's Love with My American children. If you believe My intercession to be a miracle, then you have arrived at the appropriate conclusion. No one can earn the gifts that My Son dispenses to His chosen people because they are a manifestation of the Grace by which you are saved. You are loved in essence, and it is with this Love that you are afforded every good thing. My children, My Immaculate Heart is filled with gratitude for the goodness of the Church and the services that are rendered by the missions to end the suffering of paupers who live in poverty around the globe. My eyes beam with admiration as I see My holiest ones eradicating crippling diseases and making way for the purity of the soul that is manifested through the Wisdom, power, and Light of the Cross. My messages are about gentleness, reconciliation, piety, wholesomeness, and charity. There is a true bond of unity between Heaven and Earth that is given by God in the Resurrection of Jesus from the Sepulcher. There is renewed vigor in the air and promise that change for the better is in the offing and rightfully ongoing. Your petitions are heard by God. He listens to His people who speak with humility in Jesus' name, and this is why I am encouraged. I know that He loves you in ways that you do not have the capacity to discern. I speak in every tongue to convey the message to the world that Jesus is your King. He is the begetting of Absolution and the remaker of the face of the globe. Please call your hearts to the Sacrifice by which you are reconciled with God. Thank you for the gift of your lives this day, in the past, and the future in which you serve in His vineyard. I offer My assurance and blessings from Jesus because He wishes you to move forward in His Truth. This is how thousands are fed by the Grace you personify as Christians. My Special son, no matter what men believe, Jesus' Divine Mercy is greater than any transgression humanity can commit. I have told you some revealing facts the past weeks because I desire you to know the extent to which My Son is ambitious to sanctify Creation. Together, we mitigate errors and restore the decency that has eroded because humanity has turned away. Your prayers can preempt catastrophic events and reverse the flow of waterways. They have the ability to rewrite history so the atrocities you are expecting will not occur. Do you remember that I told you that evil influences can cast illusions over the consciousness of sinners? Suffering is not an illusion. It is real agony, and the errors of humankind are repealed by suffering. Did not My Crucified Son amend the future of your existence on the Cross? He not only forgives sins, He expunges their vestiges from the record. This, My Special son, is saving power! You and your brother reflect this same Divine Light by praying the way you do. You are beneficiaries of God's Triune Grace and are His peacemakers, teachers, leaders, advocates, and friends of tens-of-millions of Christians who are clinging to their faith. Hence, do not fear My warnings about chastisements and reproaches. Be joyful that such manifestations are the way sinners are converted to the Cross, even if at the moment of their death. We pray well together, My Special son! With your brother, we suspend, remove, and right the wrongs that plague Creation. You have written, admonished, absolved, and authored authentic prophecy. You have garnered Jesus' favor in so many ways that it would take Me until the end of time to count them. Be satisfied knowing that My predictions and proclamations are true, and accept in your heart that you are already succeeding. Your writings are beautiful, filled with the contrition and conversion that I have asked you to extol, and directed in a simple way to the lost sinners who need it. I am moved by your expertise. The Lord is generous to allow the Holy Spirit to speak to you, and you are hospitable to receive Him. Can you see the preface of His Kingdom from your station on Earth? I ask others to pray with you on their journey of righteousness because you are a blessing to them. You help their hearts grow tall as mountains, dignified, accepted, and viewed with respect. These are the fruits of the Love you inherited from Jesus. What do you feel when I assert that God understands the circumstances in which His children have been reared? He asks you to call-out His name, Abba! Father! Papa! He seeks in you the innocence that allows men to return to their childhood years, only this time through the rewritten history that Jesus' Crucifixion provides. There is no greater recourse than this. Thank you for being kind to your brothers and sisters. You are welcoming to My priests from India, those who traveled to

America to share in the Lord's plenty. Your conduct allows My intercession, the Eucharistic Fidellites, and your Diary to be known in foreign countries, especially the tens-of-millions who yearn for God's compassion. This is the generosity that elevates humanity high above the Earth. This is your mark on Creation that many are seeing as one of the grandest, and it is centered around your compliance with the Gospel, your love for Jesus, and your obedience to Me. The Indianese priest at the Cathedral is offering morning prayers for the success of your Marian Apostolate. He hails from a poor nation where people are starving and dying from the heat. God's response is the providing of relief for his countrymen and the advancement of your mission. When he communicates with his friends in India, he tells them about you and your brother. He is composing a diary about his experiences that will be evocative reading. The friendship you offer him and his brother priests is unprecedented in the relationship between your dioceses. The month of August will be upon you before I speak again. You will see the propagation of your books to make the world a holier place. Your demeanor is considerate, professional, and charitable because you are a child of Mine..."

Sunday, August 3, 2003
'They shall all be taught by God' [John 6:45]
2:31 p.m.

"My precious children, I visit you in principled Truth to propagate the Love of Jesus' Sacred Heart to satisfy your yearnings. My mission is one of goodness, Light, the conversion of men, and the mitigation of wrongs that are being forced against the Kingdom of God. I come seeking your help in the eradication of the darkness that blinds humanity from seeing the signature of the Holy Spirit in their midst. My desire to address you is a manifestation of the beauty that I possess as your Immaculate Mother. Thank you for welcoming Me to pray with you. I am your Protectress who has come to teach you about humility. I am the Mother of the Messiah and the sanctification you inherit by opening your hearts to receive Him. When Jesus says that you shall be taught by God, He likewise refers to Me, the Mother who nurtured, guarded, and taught Him from whence He was a fair-faced Child. I hold as much esteem for you as I had for Him while we were on Earth and in the Eternity since His Ascension into Heaven. You suffer His same anguish when you see His Truth absent in others. You pray with authenticity to the Father to intercede for the helpless who are crouched in ghetto-like slums in your neighborhoods, for the end of war, aggression, licentiousness, and gluttony. I know that you beseech the Father to make perfect your lives, purify your hearts, sanctify your marriages, and bless your children. Jesus has accorded these things because through you, His goal is to ensure that the Earth becomes like

Heaven. I remind you, little ones, that this can occur because it is flowing through Me. Be thankful that the Lord is with you, that Jesus lives in you, and that He sends Me to teach you to blossom in His likeness while you are exiled on Earth. Therefore, when you read John 6:45, you see evidence of My role in the End Times. 'They shall all be taught by God.' This is an impelling benediction, My children. It is a holy fact. Yes, My intercession is more than symbiotic paraphrases and stern admonishments, and My lessons are greater than the syllables with which they are constructed. I speak every language known to man, and the reason is the most important. I bring you messages and teachings from Christ, and there can be no clearer enlightenment than this. I seek your patience during your trials, good judgement in public affairs, perseverance in times of trouble, prayer in stressful hours, and an inner-peace that rivals no other. I have told you that these things begin with the reconciliation between God and man, which itself is a product of regaining the trust, affection, and respect of other people. No more war! This is what Pope Paul VI declared to the United Nations. I am humbled that you have joined Me in prayer for the censuring of society's obscenities because prayer is the solution to every corruption known to the world. You must be pleasing to God. My messengers are a family of faithful believers. You come to the conclusion that life means only to be obedient to Him, and that your impending death does not imply anything more. There are billions of variables, reactions, emotions, and tribulations in life; this is what makes it unpredictable and removes any doubt that God is in command. If it seems as though you are not in control of your future, this is the helplessness about which I spoke in the 1990s. You must call on Jesus; this is how God asks you to remain. My Special son, thank you for your piety, your friendship with your neighbors, taking care of your brother, and for remembering that you belong to Jesus. The Angels protect you, but you have the responsibility of being careful on your own. Please never forget that the Dominion Angels rebuke the world's heretics. O' how I adore the Angels!..."

Monday, August 11, 2003
Anniversary of the Death of Saint Clare [1193-1253]
7:12 p.m.

"Good evening, My precious children! What a glorious moment has come because I have visited from the Light of Paradise to herald Jesus' Sacrifice! I sent a double rainbow this evening as a sign that you are receiving this message on the proper day. Jesus is glorified by your courtesies. As you see, the Faith-Church on Earth is observing the Feast of Saint Clare whose biography you were offered by Father Titus during the Holy Sacrifice of the Mass today. You are correct in your assessment that it was the homiletics of

Saint Francis of Assisi that prompted her to lead an austere life. She made herself materially impoverished to preserve her riches in the Kingdom of Heaven. Saint Clare is an intercessor whom I urge you to summon because she possesses power to rebuke the American media. This is the reason why I wish you to record My message about her. Saint Clare is with Me, and she hears your petitions for the social propriety that is lacking in the venues about which you have been speaking, the printed and electronic media. I have told you what will become of their empire. Also, today I call upon your patience as the cultivation of the world continues according to God's Plan. *Why must He wait(?)* you are prone to inquire. Because everyone who approaches His Table must do so of their own accord. As you realize, this has taken a long time, but the future will be short. This is why My messages are so urgent. Jesus is utilizing your lives for the conversion of humanity in ways that you do not fully comprehend. My Special son, when your brother completes his studies next year, you will notice My intentions for this segment of your lives play-out to the extent that you may wonder what is next. He will suffer physical ailments in 2005 and 2006. You must be prepared for this and continue to live peacefully. *(This prophecy was fulfilled. Timothy underwent surgery to remove his gallbladder, and experienced serious post-operative complications which nearly ended his life. It took him several months to recuperate.)* I know that you are skilled in adapting to life's challenges because you have faith that Jesus is with you. I am moved by your manuscript that you entered in your computer. It is concise and forthright. Its tone is precisely what humanity needs in this age. Please do not dilute your writing style. You make Me jubilant that you maintain your candor as My Special child. I know that there will be an increase of activity at your workplace, but nothing we do will impede you from completing it. These are good times you are living, very good times. I wish only to remind you that Saint Clare and the Poor Nuns are praying for you and to affirm that Jesus is My Love for you. It will be a brief period before your brother resumes his schooling, and you see the effect that his performance has had on their academic standards. This is good news. You make your brother special; only you do these things. He can do nothing without you because God planned it that way. He cannot survive without you. When the future comes and you observe the fruits that your work is bearing, you will understand with clarity. You need not vacate your home. It is a monument to Christianity where My weekly messages have been dictated for the conversion of lost sinners to the Holy Cross. Please remember September 25, 1992 as a special day regarding the sanctity of this house..."

Friday, August 15, 2003
Feast of the Assumption of Mary
7:15 p.m.

"Thank you, My children, for invoking the sanctifying Grace of the Sacred Mysteries of the Most Holy Rosary on this Feast of the Church. I am honored to speak with you about your Salvation. My holy ones, please remember that Mine is a message of Love. God's mandates are dictated in Love. You are sanctified in Love, provided spiritual happiness as a gift of Love, and brought together on your journey to Paradise in Love. Today, Roman Catholics have entered their chapels, churches, cathedrals, and basilicas to recognize their Mother consecrated to them by Jesus during His Crucifixion on Good Friday. Lest there be any mistake, that Holy Lady of Love is Me. I humbly remind you that I am worthy of the accolades showered upon Me by priests and clerics, and by Christians everywhere. How can I be this honored? Because I am the Queen of Creation, and My intentions are benign before the Father. Come unto Me! It is with joy that I share His Wisdom about the Redemption of humanity with the same devotion that I offered Him My life as a simple Handmaid. Be assured that I am the most benevolent Woman to be given the breath of life. While My Soul Doth Magnify the Lord, My purpose is gathering sinners beneath My Mantle for protection against the evil forces that are trying to lure you away from the Cross. I urge you to depend on the Archangel Michael to assist your struggles in conquering the devil. Saint Michael casts evil spirits into Hell at the issuance of your prayers. Heaven sees everything that God has made. We see the hills and plains you travel, and we know the obstacles that cause you to stumble. Call on us for Divine intervention! God deigned us to be your guidance in the same way the Holy Spirit gives you discernment. This is free for the taking because you are loved. Life is all about Love! My Special son, I am pleased that you are before Me to hear My words because the work you and your brother are completing is on course, and you will eventually capture the venues to deliver the speeches about which you have dreamed. Once this is given, there will be countless souls around you with open hearts to listen to your preamble, *...I say to you, let me tell you what Immaculate is!* The Saints whose mortal frames are entombed near the Chandler Cenotaph are waiting like children for you to step to the lectern overlooking the spacious Illinois River valley and exalt the Truth that Jesus offers. I have told you that this will come, and it is coming. Every time you rise in the morning to prepare for work, you are another day closer to the end of the ages. This is what makes Me joyful, because I have seen the grande finale for which you are praying, that you anticipate with guarded hope. God cannot fail you. Your petitions are never in vain. It is with the impression of victory that you should live, for you are touching exiled men one heart at a time. Thank you for being My obedient servant. And, My Special one, these are days that you will look back upon with a feeling of accomplishment because they are milestones to the spiritual resolutions that you wish for in life. You can do no wrong when you commit your words and actions to Christian righteousness. You are unlike those hypocrites who claim to be dedicated to God, but are only liars. Why are they not lined shoulder to shoulder at the entrance of the Supreme Court demanding that abortion be declared against the law? Because they are too distracted spending their fortunes holidaying in Europe, Antarctica and the Carribean Isles, buying vehicles at $50,000 apiece, and counting their stocks and bonds. I wish to invoke your memory of your 1989 Medjugorje pilgrimage on today's Feast. Please try to remember what you felt when the moment arrived for you to return home. Can you describe your feelings to Me? You found your purpose in life; you discovered the reason you were born, and you thought you were leaving Me behind when you boarded the airplane. The latter is the point I wish to discuss. What happened after you landed in Illinois? You went back to Medjugorje in December. What were your feelings when you departed a second time? Yes, you are remembering everything. My presence is worldwide, and My Grace is everywhere. You are still experiencing Medjugorje! This is the exculpating Love that has defined you, but has been stifled by malevolent forces in America. And, this is the reason why you must hope, because you are living at the center of its States and Commonwealths where your holiness is the conversion of its people. You are situated at the heart of America to open it to the Motherly guidance that I accord the nations. Your mission, thesis, and purpose are to live in the simplicity to which I have called you so your friends and even your enemies know that they can kneel before the Cross without relinquishing their identity. You have written profoundly about this in *Morning Star Over America*. You must be able to see that the prophecies in its text are being fulfilled. I am happy because your life has become everything you desired. Imagine the joy that I hold for you. My intercession has taken you where you are today, and your obedience has shaped it into being. Thus, you feel the reciprocity that we share. I remind you that this will never end; it is as perpetual as Eternity. Can you see that I have more reason to be thankful for the years you have given the Lord than you might be? I guide you through prayer every day of your life. I am the Queen of Peace! It gives My Immaculate Heart even greater peace knowing that you love Me. Please always love Me! You sense the depth in which your brother loves you. Without you, he cannot survive. I have said this in successive messages. This means that you must choose wisely, never go where there is danger, and get your rest. If not for you, he would have no way to convert his friends, and you are providing these things. The request you make for Me to nurture the hearts of your family is one I offer all My children. There will be months when I shall offer daily messages like I did in 1991. You will know why this is necessary, but it is nothing to fear. Imagine the jubilation

I have had for 2,000 years knowing that on this day in 2003, I would speak to you, that you would hear My voice, and the entire world will listen. Thank you for being My child. I will approach Jesus on behalf of everyone you have asked Him to bless. You will see Me many times before your spirit departs the Earth..."

Sunday, August 24, 2003
Saint Bartholomew, First Century Apostle
3:25 p.m.

"I greet My saintly children with a kiss of love and Wisdom that keeps you holy. I bring you tidings from the Lord and bless you with His righteousness. All this is befitting of His little darlings! Please pray for the coming of a gentler age of peace and good will because the Earth is at war with itself. We ask My Son to implant sublime reason in the hearts of all involved for their conversion, healing, teaching, discernment, and contrition. My children, Creation cannot condone the onslaught against its dignity that people who practice evil are perpetuating. I seek in you the desire to build a better world founded in Jesus. Why do I appear in this place and extol His Grace? Because His Truth is living in your hearts, and I ask you to be the practitioners of the justice that effects the peace that humanity is lacking. I have fostered the struggle for holiness for centuries. The first decade of this millennium has begun with sparse evidence that lost sinners have turned their hearts to God. Members of the Church are fighting among themselves; the desecration of the Liturgies is rampant, a lack of prayer is causing the refusal of forgiveness, and too many claiming to be Christians are perverting the meaning of the Sacraments. Allow Me to be clear. Anyone who claims to be Christian, but believes that God would ratify a union between people of the same sex is under the influence of Satan. Such are among the grievous abominations that I have sought humanity to renounce for generations. How can holiness survive through such heresy? Amid the sins of abortion, apostasy, homosexuality, and feminism, how can the Truth be told? Hear, I will respond to My query. Once the plumes of smoke have dissipated from Jesus having obliterated His enemies, those who survive will see Him. The flames of His Sacred Heart are cleansing and revealing. They are purifying and castigating. Indeed, the parable of heatwaves around the globe is benign compared to the conflagration about to ensue. I do not mean to frighten you in your fight against evil. I am asking My Army of Marian Christians to stand upright because the Son of Man will conscript you into mightier things. Speech about tolerance for anything other than Christianity is the babbling of the beast described in Sacred Scriptures. There is only one Cross, one Salvation in the Blood of Jesus! Thousands of Martyrs in twenty centuries have surrendered their lives attesting to this. Be assured that their bloodshed was not in vain. God has accomplished great things with small people in remote places for His Kingdom. He has made seers of the blind. He commissioned a young maiden to conquer a European empire. His intentions are to take America to its knees by similarly meek people, poor and anonymous men. Multitudes of sinners will turn skyward and ask the Lord in whom they refused to believe, ...*why are you doing this? In the name of mercy, what have we done wrong?* My children, it is then that secular imperialists will fall because these wretches will see the record of their lives. They will feel aghast by the way they mistreated those whom Jesus placed among them as Himself. They will know that they persecuted the blessed, shunned the sacred, lanced the innocent, and condemned the pardoned. Warn your friends to awaken from their slumber, take-up the torch of righteousness, and accept the Cross. I have told you that time is short, even more brief as we speak. How long will My children wait to accept their Savior with sincere hearts? Many among you are so obstinate that they do not know what this means, but they will learn because no one can deny the Judgement of God; none can survive before Him without Jesus' Absolution. My Special son, this is a good day because we are hailing the Blessed Trinity. I know you are strengthened by what I say, and I promise that everything is true. I have beckoned you to have high hopes and know deep in your heart that your brothers and sisters are changing. You realize that I seek your help because you and your brother strive to eliminate the heresies I have mentioned. This proves that your work excels in spiritual Truth, and you are not fanatics in the battles against secularism. I am convinced that you understand the importance of ensuring your safety so you do not fall into the hands of villains. I will protect you, but you must give your Guardian Angel reason to remain with you. I will pray that you return safely from your travels. You must always make intelligent decisions..."

Sunday, August 31, 2003
1:25 p.m.

"To Crispen Courage"

"Now comes your Holy Mother to speak to you again inside the wonder and splendor of the loveliness of God. I have blessed your lives since before the very hour you were born, and long since you have been raised into adulthood. Please understand that these are only timely things because your soul belongs to the Eternal. My purpose is to call you to holiness so that you will be fully prepared to be reunited in the perfection of Heaven. My children, you are also My teachers of your brothers and sisters on the Earth for Jesus—His Voice, Wisdom, Light, and Peace. He has made you these things in your acceptance and imitation of Him. This is the last Sunday of this month, meaning that time will go onward tomorrow, and you will be able to rise from your beds with the purpose of the conversion of the world in mind. Yes, you must go about your daily chores to sustain yourselves, but you must never forget that your prime mission in life is to follow the call of Jesus that you hear interiorly. For, what else would I do with My gratitude if I did not offer it to you? And, too, I realize that your mortal existence is a very difficult process. There are too many distractions, and you have far too many enemies of the Holy Cross with which to cope and battle. Never mind that they do not accept what you already know to be the Truth! Converting them does not imply that you will see its immediate effects. Your lessons and legacies are their conversion, for each of them must comprehend your emulation of Jesus through their own set of eyes. This takes time, and such time is always on your side. This is another reason why I have come to speak to you today about the tenacity that you must embrace if your goals are to succeed. When I speak of being tenacious, I am attesting to the fact that you are My soldiers of righteousness for Jesus on the Earth. He has sent you into battle against both evil and indifference, the latter being as great an enemy as the first. God is asking you to be His carpenters for His Kingdom, the potters of His works of clay that He has placed into your hands upon the spinning world. Above all this, My children, you must have courage. You must be strong and brave, determined, perseverant, prayerful, and always ready to make the most of every situation you are proffered to exalt the message of the Holy Gospel.

My Special son, please take your dictionary in hand. Search for the word 'crisp.' Brisk, sharp, decided. Invigorating, firm and fresh. Now, look at the definition of the word 'crispen.' What am I asking you to do with the courage of other men? To make it brisk, sharp, decided, invigorating, and fresh. Hence, I am asking all of My children, especially My messengers and seers, *'To Crispen Courage.'* No one has ever thought that this would become the title of a magnanimous work about the conversion of the world to the Cross of Jesus Christ. I am giving it to you for such a purpose. It is very important that you know what this really means. Does it imply to you that you must make rank-and-file warriors of everyone you meet? No. (Because) this is a choice that must be made by the individual human will, as much as accepting human Salvation in the Blood of the Cross must be done by each and everyone. To become a warrior for Christianity implies that their courage has become crisp according to the way that only the brave-of-heart can truly understand. I am telling you these things because I wish to support and ratify the tenor of your present writing. It is the true warriors for Divine Love who will eventually defeat the forces of evil in their most physically prevalent form. Your writing is in the process of giving untold numbers of sinners the courage to rise above their own faults, enter the ranks of soldiers for the Kingdom of God, and stand tall in the Grace that I am dispensing to them. You see, therefore, that the mission of your present writing is *'To Crispen Courage.'* Please do not be concerned that your writing will be offensive to those to whom it is directed. Indeed, I wish it to be! Time is now very short, I have told you this before. This is not the time to be shy about your transmission of the serious nature of the Judgment of God and the sorrowful condition of His Church on Earth. I support the work that the Holy Spirit is penning through your humble heart as it is transcribed by you onto the page.

I have come to speak to you only briefly today... You will continue to do the work that God has given you to do, *'To Crispen Courage'* wherever you see that it may be weak, and to never surrender to the dailiness of mortal life. You are strong and still very young. You and your brother have a great deal of work yet to do for Me before your days are done... You are My children, you are worthy of the dignity that you are refused in certain circles, and I will not send you into places where your honor is under attack... I give you both now My humble blessing. ✞ Thank you for offering Me your obedient hearts! I will speak to you again at the beginning of the new month of September! I love you. Goodnight!"

Saturday, September 6, 2003
Saint Donatian, [5th Century]
3:41 p.m.

"The Mother of God loves Her children! I hold you near Jesus and pray for you, bringing you blessings, interceding on your behalf, calling you to repentance, and offering My messages by which your hearts are opened. Today, you share the Glory of His Kingdom. Here in this place and in your time, Heaven is unfolding by your lives of prayer. To say 'thank you' for the Saints insufficiently expresses their gratitude. Hence, I say 'bless you' and all Creation understands. My little children, you have much to be thankful for. God provides the means to maintain your dignity against the adversaries of your faith. He calls on you to help those who have no hope, nothing to eat, no place to sleep, and no garments to wear. He gives you Jesus to open your hearts to the holiness He extols. God does not weigh goodness in pounds, but by self-sacrifice. God is good, and He requires you to espouse this goodness. The virtuous life has little to do with academic aptitude, secular victory, or triumph in battle. Indeed, it is comprised of your confidence in God in such a way that the world becomes more holy. In these waning summer days, please remember the achievements you have made for the millions who would not have known Salvation in the Cross. Your petitions have lifted them from despair. Your acts of kindness have restored their happiness. You do these things not only because you are obedient to Jesus, but because He dignifies His people from your hearts. By allowing Him to take residence there, you augment the reconciliation between Heaven and Earth that has been ongoing for 2,000 years. Indeed, to say 'thank you' is not enough, I say 'bless you' for all you do for the Cross. There is much more to My benedictions than you realize. My Special son, I see the happiness you feel as you shall enter autumn soon, which is your favorite time of year, because it reminds you of the harvest of your labors. It is a precursor to the Midwestern snows. You greet your neighbors at festivals as they look to the skies as if to thank the sun for giving them another year of light and hope. My Special one, you have pleasant memories from your childhood that are founded in the fall. This is true for everyone who lives in Illinois. Can you sense that the peace you feel is the closeness that Jesus seeks in His relationship with the rest of the world? You have no anxiety when autumn comes, and His wish is for you to see this as a metaphor for the ages. You will be prepared for that day; you and millions of others are ready for it now. I will dictate more messages in the next weeks that will assist your writing. They will be comprised of visions to harken your childhood whose innocence you never lost. With your brother, there are simple affairs occurring in your lives; there is no tension in you now. You are finishing your work for Jesus on course. Can you see the doctors of philosophy calling on your brother for counsel and advice? Please do not compliment him; it is I who have taught him. He knows this to be true, and he wishes all praise to be given to Me. Having said this, I remind you that you are the support for your brother's labors; you have always been, and you shall be until the end of time. You are his sustenance because you said 'yes' to Me. There will never be a time when I ask you to be separated. You garner pious concepts for your writing when you pray at the front portico. When winter arrives, you will kneel indoors where your messages come, and Jesus will place images in your mind. You can discern that the Holy Spirit helps your brother with his lessons for school. Always remember that if he is called visionary, genius, or one in a million, it is because Jesus is his other self. I have fashioned him this way. The Holy Spirit lives in his heart as the Holy Spirit flourishes in you. This is the Wisdom of the Lord, His Paraclete, His Advocate for humanity pervading the framework of your spiritual conscience. Heaven's Grace is personified by those who aspire to this perfection. God has given you a clement day, and you have planned an enjoyable evening. I could speak for hours, but to supplant the peace you are living by My intonations would be a disservice. It is obvious by the melody in your heart that you know that I am pleased with you. All Glory and honor belong to Jesus! I am happy that you are situated beneath My Holy Mantle. We need each other because I am your Mother and you are My son. Can you tell Me what will happen two weeks from today? *(My birthday is on September 20.)* Oh, but you are still quite young! You will always be My innocent little boy. Thank you for taking care of your brother..."

Saturday, September 13, 2003
Vigil of the Triumph of the Holy Cross
2:51 p.m.

"Little children, I speak of the saliency of hope and give you reason to have expectations. Welcome to the resplendence of My Immaculate Heart. Remember that I intercede for you before Jesus when you pray the Rosary. Never forget that your Mother hears your every word and marks your piety with Grace. Thank you for adoring Jesus in the Most Holy Sacrament of the Altar. Today, I refer to the Spiritual and Corporal Works of Mercy, the moral imperatives to be embraced by humanity, because conversion is fostered by them. Be satisfied knowing that you are of profound assistance to your brothers and sisters, and they for you. Open your hearts to holiness, confession, prayer, and sacrifice. I have told you that I wish for little girls to become like Me, and I request everyone on Earth to share in Jesus' kindness. I tell you over and again that your life is about embracing His Love, of longing to see the Glory of God. When you pray for peace, you discover its seeds there. Please have no despair that some gifts do not come immediately. There are distractions in the world that keep your friends from hearing. Do not desist! Maintain faith and perseverance in all things that reflect the brilliance of Heaven. Be righteous people! God has given you untold gifts and manifest ways to enhance His Kingdom. Time is pressing, but do not relinquish your patience. This is the Vigil of the Triumph of the Holy Cross, known as the Exaltation of the Cross. Know that your victory of faith is found in Jesus' Crucifixion. Your storied beginnings that you have dreamed are born and prosper in Him. The fullness of Truth is there, and deliverance, nourishment, sanctification, and reconciliation. Jesus is everything that prepares you for Salvation, and those who love Him know it. My Special son, I wish to take your thoughts to your childhood when you sat in the back yard of your parents' home and watched the sunsets, heard the birds chirping and dogs barking, and wondered how you could understand the subtly of these. Your heart was tender even as it was subjected to trials. You were giddy in your demeanor, filled with vigor, looking any direction for a source of fun. This innocence still lives in you. Now, however, you have a keener perception of the purpose of trees and birds; you see with clearer vision the facets of Nature, and your heart has brought you to comprehend that the meaning of life is to strive for Redemption. Your prayers, your attendance at the Holy Sacrifice of the Mass, the Most Blessed Sacrament, and the presence of the Angels have guided you to this poise. You and your brother are workers in the fields that cultivate the hearts and minds of humanity. It is not difficult to realize that this is true because you trust in Jesus; you are obedient to your Mother; you serve humanity in the likeness of the Saints, and you wait in joyful hope for the

Coming of the Lord to take you to Heaven. In these things, you are that child of your youth. When you penned your memory of falling from a tree in *Babes in the Woods*, you allowed Creation to share your joy. You sense the presence of holiness in you today as prolifically as you did then. When I urge you to recall the moments when you were a child, I am not asking you to be immature, but to remember that this is the innocence I am seeking from humanity. If your lost brothers and sisters meditate on the Sacred Mysteries of the Holy Rosary, their hearts will open to the possibility that they can become blameless again. Prayer is the providential Grace that erases the scars of time and places in you the thoughts of the little ones who see and hear only what the Holy Spirit is saying. It is possible to be this simple and remain grounded in faith. I have been showing you and your brother how to prevail by this benignity for more than twelve years.

In looking comprehensively at life, you become prescient about how your best years will unfold. You are confident in your decisions, assured of the benefits of your labors, wise in anticipating the response of your friends, wary about the tactics of your foes, and prepared to greet Jesus with calmness instead of anxiety when your earthly journey is through. These are appeals of Wisdom by which you live through God's Plan. And, when you offer your brothers and sisters the moral imperatives of the Works of Mercy, you dispense this Wisdom in the lineage of the Saints. You do as millions of pilgrims in places like Medjugorje; you become the presence of Jesus and the reflection of Me. As I have said, this can be a lengthy transformation for those who are fixed in sins of the flesh, materialism, and other abominations. For some, adopting a spiritual context to human life seems light-years away. But for you, it is clear that Divine Love can be engaged while you are still tethered to mortality. When others suggest that it is impossible to be perfect or purified, they are misconstruing the point. I am not asking them to be flawless in ways other than what God instills, neither am I demanding their compliance with perfection in mechanical terms. I am seeking perfection in Love! Love is the beatific property of mystical existence that transcends time and unites you with Heaven. Do not let anyone tell you that a person cannot be perfect in Love. You may never be infallible in your judgements or resurrect a soldiers' line, or read a transcript at seventy paces, but you can become perfect in Love! This is the Truth as I have spoken it since the First Century. It is a spiritual apocalypse in union with the Messianic Return that is nigh. When you pray, God issues the presence of mind and sureness of heart to know how to act. He spreads the future before you like a tapestry so you can see Heaven hemmed by the Cross. When you pray for discernment, you discover that it has been yours all along. Therefore, clarify your petitions to My Son and shape your prayers in alignment with the Will of the Father. His omnipotence gives your heart the Wisdom to foresee the future like reaching through a portal. There is power knowing how to serve the Lord that is dispensed by the Holy Spirit during your holiest hours. There is healing for the broken when your pity moves you to tears. The surfacing of Truth must be the goal of all peoples. This revelation is found not only in your prayers, but through the Exaltation of the Cross and the Triumph that has belonged to the ages since Jesus was Crucified. Hence, please have hope not only because there is reason, but because the future is saturated with His promise. If you wish to be part of the celebration, be righteous in Jesus and you will see for yourself. If others scoff or approach you with disdain, see the Light breaking past the dawn. Listen for the melodies of the songbirds again, just like you did in your backyard swing. Your Mother asks you to never surrender this hope. Be glad in anticipation, pleasing to God, and confident under oppression, and the Cross will touch those around you with your perfection in Him. I beseech Jesus to help you accomplish these things. My Special one, I spare no words to help you recognize that the Triumph of My Immaculate Heart and the Triumph of the Holy Cross are from Heaven. I wish for you to be comforted by your writing and heartened that you walk with God's Kingdom. If you did not, I would have told you. Thank you for rebuking the followers of existentialism, pragmatism, and secular humanism. These works are fastened in error, and you have the authority to admonish them. Pay no mind that your excellences may not be told; God will ensure that your adversaries hear them. As I have said, this takes time. This is the matter that you must place into perspective, the element of time. Please do not feel alone; sometimes the wait is difficult. My children are not moving toward Heaven swiftly enough, and this is why I weep. Your words stop My tears and help Me not to cry. What a gift to Heaven you are. Your generosity will be repaid a hundredfold..."

Sunday, September 21, 2003
St. Matthew, First Century Apostle
2:10 p.m.

"The reason for your sentence in exile is to correct the unjust and cultivate the purification of human souls. My children, once you understand the fruits of these, you will see with the Light of Truth. I commend you for reproving your lost brothers and sisters about their shortcomings. Your righteousness is the means to assure them that you harbor no hypocrisies. We pray together so the nations will listen, heed My messages, and unite beneath the Cross of Salvation. Today, I again call you to recollect your youth so you can accept the Dominion of God as your provider in faith. God gives you faith as a blessing from Heaven, and it is by believing in Jesus that you are forgiven of your sins and delivered to Redemption. Thereafter, you must accomplish the rest; it is you who must accept. I remind My children that time is a remedial element for change. The vastitude of your years is not intended to cause anxiety, but to allow you to know that humanity seems far from holiness. Through the power of the Holy Spirit, I ask you to apply your love for Jesus as a response to His suffering people. He elevates the downtrodden through your lives. When you do good things for '...the least of these,' you are comforting Him. The crying of an infant is a sign that the souls of the innocent are still restless. When you enfranchise the weak and lift-up the lowly, you are the presence of the Lord for His creatures. You realize this because you are bearers of peace and prudence to sinners who do not know Him. Thank you for being Christians so the Earth can be transformed into Heaven. When you ponder your childhood memories, do you sense the carefree days when it seemed as though your elders' problems were miles away? Were most people not shielded from the deceitful liberality that has led many sinners away from the Cross? I call on you to restore the world's decency by the Holy Gospel so your brothers and sisters will be pure. Teach them in the name of My Son! Admonish them through the moral imperatives that you have learned. This is the Feast of Saint Matthew the Apostle. Like Jesus, he lived in austerity, self-discipline, and sacrifice for those who did not comprehend God's Kingdom. I call on you to emulate the life of Saint Matthew. Touch unconverted sinners. Evangelize the Truth. Accept the Cross. Bask in the Resurrection of Jesus from the Sepulcher! We pray that everyone will make their purpose in life the realignment of their priorities to those of the Holy Scriptures. Material possessions are a fallacy; temptations of the flesh are a ruse; haughtiness of the heart is a sin, and wise people know these to be true. The sincerity of your faith, My children, is not only to realize this, but to actively pursue the Firmament that eradicates sinfulness from your lives. Please believe Me when I say that the most powerful means to cleanse the Earth is to pray for God's intervention. Yes, you have spoken of signs and wonders, and have hailed miracles. It is heartening that you recognize the way God manifests His Kingdom in the physical world. However, your penchant for surrendering to impatience causes others to look at these gifts with doubt. Be confident in your knowledge! Satan tells his followers that you are not sure in your trust if you buy the falsehood that Jesus is not doing enough to heal the Earth. My Son has accorded His flock every tool to conquer evil, and you are succeeding in time. What do you believe the world would be like if you were not accomplishing this? There would be such hellish travesties that it would seem as though there is no light of day. You are ringing the clarion that is foretelling the Kingdom of God to the billions who must hear it. And, for the millions who choose not to listen, their fate is etched in the fiery Abyss. Do not pity them if they spurn the Blood of Salvation. Convert as many as you can, but they must submit to your witness if they expect to reside among the Saints at the moment they succumb to death.

You remain inside your hearts those little children who sat on river banks and in park swings and watched with innocence the rest of the world go by. You must marry this happiness with the responsibility you have assumed as Christians to deliver the Truth to the untold pagans who are lost. If you offer the Holy Spirit to your neighbors by the orthodoxies in your teaching and they continue to resist in obstinance, then this is where your commission ends. When you refer their fate to the Judgement of God, this does not imply that you have forsaken them. Quite the contrary, it is your petition to Jesus to dispense His Mercy upon their souls. You are not expected to incessantly knock on their doors or call with bullhorns across ravines. Each man, woman, and child wields an inherent conscience with which they discern the possibilities of life. Influence them toward the path of the Everlasting Way, and Jesus will redeem them for God, for His Kingdom, and for you. I am motivated and hopeful because you have received the benediction and benison of the benevolent Savior who loves you. I am a fortunate Mother who has seen your vindication with the propensity of My eyesight, and I am elated to know that you will soon view it clearly. For My children who have been obedient to Me, this will be a moment of immense jubilation, but for those who have scoffed at the Laws of God, it will be an hour of agony and gnashing of teeth. This is why I call you to complete your work while not counting the cost, never-minding the lack of response of your friends, peers, and family. Allow My Crucified Son to achieve the rest. If you hope to arrive in Heaven and hear *...well done, good and faithful servant*, you must realize that your spirit is not to be disturbed if your message of conversion is shunned. I have told you that you will pander to the devil's dogs if you stop to survey the measure of your success. It is vain to wonder whether you will persuade a given number of sinners to the cause of the Just. Tend to your work, and Jesus will bring them to Paradise by the concordance of your faith. My Special son, how uplifted I am to speak to you. I offered a blessing yesterday on your 42nd birthday that I know you received. I need not remind you how special are these times during which you and your brother are pouring-out your lives for God. Every new year, you see the inevitability of your victory over everything that opposes you. Like Jesus as an adolescent, you have grown in strength to face the realities of life with trust, hope, charity, and sacrificial love. I am pleased by your progress. Your manuscripts have brought the Angels and Saints to tears. Please proceed with your humble supplications for the Prelates and Cardinals, the Princes of the Roman Catholic Church! You are anticipating the Victory of Truth with dignity and eloquence because I have been preparing you. Thank you for reciting your prayers..."

Sunday, September 28, 2003
Saint Wenceslaus [AD 903-929]
2:38 p.m.

"My little children, you are created only a little lower than the Angels, and I have visited you in tranquility and Providence to pray for the sanctification of the Earth. Humanity must accept the Blood of the Cross as expiation for your sins. Please remember that God the Father does not wish that you would condemn yourselves at your final hour, but that you will appeal to Jesus for Redemption. I speak of Salvation because I am the Matriarch of Paradise. We pray so all world wars will cease, for the protection of unborn children so they will be given birth, for the eradication of poverty and disease, and for all the other intentions that will make the world a holier domain. We have discussed the purpose of suffering and the purification of humanity. There is agony and anguish in all nations. Please join Me in asking God to lend His healing to these souls. It may often seem that your prayers are becoming routine, or they are having no benefit at all. I beg you not to entertain such doubts. God knows the world that you wish to see when you rise from your beds. He is aware of the excruciating persecution that you undergo for His sake. Heaven is engulfing the Earth with piety that is born into Creation from the bounty of your hearts. Let us be united in the Holy Spirit so My children will listen and comply. When Pope John Paul II delivers his homilies across the hemispheres, humanity should realize that he is speaking with the fullness of God's Wisdom. I beseech good citizens everywhere to imitate his kindness and authenticity. This Pontiff will receive a reward in Heaven, and those who remain will propagate his legacy. He has taught the Messianic Truth in regions that have espoused only atheism. He has dared to challenge the fads and fashions of the secular void. He has shamed heretics, conquered wolf-packs of evil, and has been a shining beacon in lands of blinding darkness. When he passes into Jesus' arms, remember that he has been a unifier of humanity in the lineage of Saint Peter. My Special son, I am honored to pray with you. As you know, I am giving your brothers and sisters unprecedented signs and wonders as gifts for their faith. The atmosphere around you is replete with evidence that Jesus is blessing His people. The Angels and Saints are interceding during every minute of your life, and the ploughshares of Paradise are cultivating the world. These manifestations occur every day just beyond your recognition, and they encourage millions of Christians in America and around the globe to rise-up and conquer the Earth's darkness with the same power, vision, and invincibility that instilled such valor in Saint Joan of Arc. My miracles touch everyone this way. The essence of My speech is that Christian mightiness seems subliminal to you now, but it is becoming more obvious by the hour because I am configuring God's disciples into armies of love. You bear a sense of dignity that draws other people in because you and your brother are approachable children of Heaven.

You are speaking with the Mother of God, and I will help if you let Me. My gratitude and adulation are yours. I simply ask you not to feel as though your life after February 22, 1991 is burdensome, routine, repetitious, or anything other than evocative joy. If you believe otherwise, then I have failed. Do you see that My Immaculate Heart is open for you to know that your life is brilliant, that it is only your imagination that makes you think it could be mundane? I am pleased with you, and I am sorrowful when you are unhappy. Mother Teresa and other Saints endured extreme periods of despondence in their lives, but they prevailed because they inscribed their impressions in letters and personal diaries, and did not dwell on it anymore. Writing purges the mind. Can you see that you have been better able to devote your heart to Me? For this, I am grateful, Jesus is elevated before humanity, and God the Father is glorified..."

Sunday, October 5, 2003
St. Flora of Beaulieu [1309-1347]
1:51 p.m.

"My pretty children, I pray for your souls, for the conversion of humankind to Christianity, for purity, and the Eternal Salvation of the world in the Blood of Jesus. It is for these reasons that I approach you, and it is a sacred parenthesis in time when I appear. You are worthy recipients of the miraculous intercession of the Mother of God because you dare to fathom the ways you are encompassed by My Son. We search for lost souls who are famished for the Truth. Hence, we will proceed in the ways God allows to reach them because as unknowable as it might seem, they are worth the fight. Please lift your hearts to the gladness that I bring. Remember the gift of the Holy Rosary, another great Feast of the Church that you shall celebrate this week. Thank God for the power of the Rosary! Indeed, thank Him for the Most Blessed Sacrament of the Altar, the Holy Eucharist. Autumn of the year brings the clemency of Nature and the bounty of harvests. It harbors moments for reflection and renewal because you sense the perseverance of the heart and the changing of the guard during God's constant vigil for humanity's enlightenment. While you may not believe the years have been good, please never forget that the Almighty Father is forever merciful and benevolent. When you see the yields of the harvest in the work of human hands and the Providence of God, you are recognizing the oneness of Heaven and Earth. My Special son, you pray to hear My messages because you admire your Mother and seek My intercessory Wisdom. I am grateful to you and your brother for remaining this way. When you imagine what a gift you are to each other, you will recognize why your friends enjoy spending time with you. You lend them strength, direction, and support in wholesome ways. My Special son, I must remind you that it is important that you rest when you are working additional hours, even if you do not feel tired. Your system is fighting a cold virus that will worsen if you get insufficient sleep. I will dictate a longer message later, but it is appropriate that you enjoy the weekend. Thank you for bringing the gifts to the Altar during the Holy Sacrifice of the Mass. Please pray for Pope John Paul II as he observes the anniversary of his election in October 1978, and thank you for remembering your family and friends..."

Sunday, October 12, 2003
St. Maximilian of Lorch, Martyr [d. 284]
2:08 p.m.

"Welcome to the consolation of My Immaculate Heart! What Divine Love blossoms there! Thank you, dear children, for dedicating your lives to Jesus as I assist your understanding of the Most Blessed Trinity. I am the Matriarch of the Trinity, the Mother of God, the Mother of Jesus and Spouse of the Holy Spirit. In this is your Salvation procured. Today, I ask you to embark on a journey of the faithful through the Sacred Scriptures. The failure of anyone to be obedient to the Father is the origin of sin. You remember that sin stands in diametric opposition to Heaven. Most everyone who is given the breath of life will make it there, but not before intense sanctification is wrought through the atonement manifested by Jesus' Blood on the Cross. There have been wars, famine, and untold agony that have occurred because millions of people have not comprehended, never believed, or willfully accepted that humanity can be spiritually reborn. This is illustrated by world conflicts and even in the microspace of a disconcerted heart. My role is to address the latter so the former becomes extinct. I bring the peace of My Son, the Prince of Peace, who was born at Bethlehem. It is obvious that you now have power and immeasurable vision by virtue of Pentecost and Jesus' Crucifixion and Resurrection from the Sepulcher. And, this has preserved billions of people down through the centuries, and overwhelming consolation has been brought to them by Christian believers. However, these Christians resided among heathens who denied the Holy Cross. This is the embedded life that Jesus endured after He was birthed from My Womb. He donned the Flesh to teach humanity that to be sown to the Spirit is the purpose of life. Christians know that the successful remaking of Earth into the image of Heaven implies the relinquishing of human cravings. God does not force this into the actions of men because He wishes His devotion to be reciprocated by His creatures. It is a measure of trust that defines how this is demonstrated in each person. Every heart must accept God's Love for the soul to be open to the piety that Jesus teaches. I personify Heaven's beauty because I am the Mother of Divine Truth. The Earth is fortunate for this, but is lacking in the willpower to tender itself to My care. The contradictions in the motivations of men are the genesis of war, hunger, and fear. I say to those who know Me, you will reap a great reward in Heaven for helping convert the lost. And, I declare to the lost, whether or not they accept what I say; the reign of God is at hand, and My children are your conquerors! You will be vanquished from the Earth by the Children of Mary and herded into the netherworld by Saint Michael, mannered by their petitions to Heaven. I am a gentle Mother with no tolerance for wickedness. I protect My children with Truth and Light. No evil shall overcome them, and no darkness will dampen the Spirit in their hearts. I come as the Triumphant Mother of the Victorious King! Holy Christendom has arrived! Glory, honor, and praise shine like the sun from the crests of Jesus' disciples. Paradise is on the move, and those who identify themselves as atheists, millionaires, and secularists should take warning because the Son of Man is on the way. God will censure and rebuke you! Heaven will refuse you! Hell will devour you! And, the Christians who are living in your midst will come to the Salvation they deserve!

My Special son, God is not finished sanctifying the souls He will bring to Heaven and not completely collected those whom Jesus will hurl into the Abyss. Remember that time is on your side. Jesus knows that your heart has been broken by the arrogant and audacious, but you react with discretion at every turn. There is no blame in you. You are a farsighted prophet. You are William the Conqueror! Lift up your heart! Be emboldened that such occasions open the eyes of the blind. Although it seems as though the answers to your prayers are long in coming, how do you think I have felt knowing that 50 million children have been aborted from their mothers' wombs? And, how I have grieved seeing the Church maligned by fortune-seeking capitalists whose gods are their lawyers and media consultants. My Special son, you know what Saint Michael would do if I sent him to expunge these rogues from the face of the Earth. He would do it instantly, but I believe that these lost sinners are salvageable. Their souls can be rescued from the wreck they have made of their lives. Is this not why Jesus was Crucified? Are you not bearing your crosses for the same reason? You are playing the part that the Lord asked of you since you accepted Him. Your questions are legitimate ones. When do we expel the malevolent influences from your midst and usher human decency there? How much more must we condone before denying the forces of evil room to move? How do you know who will be saved and who is destined for Hell? My son, these are among the questions whose answers shall come. I am beyond time because My existence is eternal. I can reveal who is in Heaven, and those who are not. Some of your adversaries will be great Saints! I know that this is difficult to believe, but what of the early years of Saint Paul? You must remember that some people will be brought to their knees by suffering so profound that you will weep for them in pity. Should this be the measure of Christians as to whether another soul is worthy of the Cross, that you see them break under the throes of agony? Is this not retribution that belongs only to the Lord? Your suffering is the grace that nullifies the impiety of wayward sinners, and their excruciating future makes reparation for others like them. I am telling you that everyone shares in situations like these for the consecration that God evokes from the Church. You will watch your enemies on their suffering trails. You will see their torments. You will know why this has come, and you will prohibit them from being embittered toward God. Be their friend, become their advocate, and let them know that divinity is made of these things. Your actions are vindicated by the righteousness of Jesus that you espouse. I reassert, there is no blame in you. You are a magnifier of God's Truth, a facilitator of change, an agent for forgiving sins, and a player in the conversion of the millions who are reading your writings, messages, and testimonies. Monsters are meant to be slain, and we shall slay this one together. Do not worry, and get sufficient rest. You will never leave this world alone. Please be strong for all the Saints. I declare to you, they are worth it!..."

Sunday, October 19, 2003
Saint Paul of the Cross [1694-1775]
1:53 p.m.

"Welcome to the endearing consolation of My Immaculate Heart! We are elated upon the auspicious occasion in the Roman Catholic Church and all of Christendom because Mother Teresa of Calcutta is being beatified. Thank God for her life and her blessings upon humanity. I assure you that her prayers for the poor accompany your petitions, and the Son of Man hears them. I speak to you as a gift for lifting your hearts to Heaven. I wish you to know that you are loved, and that God hears your pleading. Together, we elevate the destiny of humankind so those who do not know Jesus will accept Redemption in His sanctifying Blood. And, what of these prayers? Why do I call you to meditation every hour? Because you know not when might come the last, and every moment of your prayerful lives is a reflection of Heaven that is eclipsing and consuming the Earth. Your Mother approaches you pleasingly because one of the greatest adversaries of the Catholic Church, the American media empire, is being forced to grapple with the reasons why a humble nun in India has overshadowed their secular headlines. They reap millions of dollars celebrating anything that is impious, but this time, they report the fitting homage that Mother Teresa has earned. Sadly, they speak of her to enhance their coffers, and what a deplorable shame. My children, I offer you the opportunity to make reparation for their sins in the depths and intentions of your supplications. Remember the poor to God when you ask for help for yourselves. Be the Divine Love of Jesus in your lives and you will possess the power to cast-out demons. Stand before Creation and 'will' your love into being, never leaving a creature behind. Do Jesus' bidding in bereft and dreary places. Remember to the Savior by whom you are blessed the lost who cannot see beyond the darkness of their own errors. You harbor the princely power and kingly domain of the Son of Man inside your hearts, and I ask you to wield His righteousness with authority and purpose, never compromising with the devil. You must remember this until you die. The Mother of God is proclaiming that you can be, indeed you must be, perfected in the likeness of My Son. Hope springs with amplitude for the world in this. My Special son, it is a bright and cheerful day in Illinois where you live. It is telling of the warmth and peacefulness about which I have just spoken. Even though winter is about to arrive, know that the comfort of My Love will keep you sheltered through the good graces of God. Join Me in the happiness that I bring. Thank you for making piety the purpose of your life. With your brother, you are renewing the face of the Earth with your timely writings and sacrifices for Jesus. You share love because you have become an inherent portion of the greater Glory of God in the temporal world. The reward that you and your brother will receive is great, and is waiting your passage into Heaven. I ask you to remember that you have a modest amount of work to accomplish before then. Thank you for praying for Pope John Paul II, God's imminent Saint, who is beatifying Mother Teresa. His mind is as keen and his willingness to lead the Church as sincere as they were on October 16, 1978. You know that your gift a year ago helped make these events possible. What a mystical blessing! Pay no attention to the radical demonstrators outside the ceremony who falsely maintain that there was no miracle given to the sufferer who sought Mother Teresa's intercession for healing. It is paranormal in every sense of the word. I will tell you about another miracle. It is a miracle that God has not sent fires from the skies and incinerated these faithless pagans where they stand. Someday, they will see everything with clarity, but some will continue to disbelieve. Do not pity them for what will happen. Focus your attention upon the Mystical Body of Christ in whom you and your brother are a part. It is for this reason that you offer oblation and thanksgiving. Be joyful that you belong to Me. Pray for the lost sinners who have separated themselves from Heaven by rejecting their Salvation in the Cross. The more receptive you are to the difficulties you face, the more the Lord will free you from them, and you will live in peace and joy. Vacate your anxieties and God will build a New Kingdom there. Obedience means that you not only have conquered this world, but disciplined yourself as well. The latter is the most important. Oh, My Special son, I am unsure that you realize how important are these days! I am convinced that you love God, Jesus, the Holy Spirit, and all the people on Earth. But, you have yet to know the reasons why you are living for the glory of them all. Your life is patently miraculous, engorged with gladness, meaningful in ways that your senses cannot grasp, foretelling of the future, and lasting beyond the ages in the Divine Love that God has for you. Thank you and your brother for saying yes, for inspiring My Immaculate Heart, and for being Mine!... Please pray for the unborn. They are still a treasure to Mother Teresa..."

Sunday, October 26, 2003
St. Rusticus, Bishop of Narbonne [d. 461]
2:49 p.m.

"My faithful children, the primacy of human sanctification runs through the repudiation of the flesh. Your Blessed Mother has arrived in the splendor of God's Truth to share His vision of holiness. I bring you peaceful wishes and the healing comfort of My Immaculate Heart. You must remember that when your soul has been perfected in Jesus, all that composes you is of pious accord. My cherished ones, I am trying to make Saints of you before you die. Can you understand what this means? Do you realize what an accomplishment this would be for Creation, for the litany of actions and principles by which you live, and for the broadness of Eternity? Henceforth, My message is about the purification of the soul that comes through the mortification of the flesh and the humiliation of your pride. You will never lose your dignity by following Jesus because you are elevated beyond your loftiest dreams. There is a stark difference in perfecting the soul and the things that make you physically attractive. Indeed, being perfect in Love has nothing to do with how provocative you appear. Once you are perfected, you use your body for holy things that serve to propagate God's Kingdom over the Earth. Thus, the invincible Holy Spirit is hard at work sanctifying you. Some of My children have asked 'what is the purpose of the temporal world?' My response is as it has always been. Your Savior was born Incarnate to prove to you that Salvation begins here. This is your preparatory ground, the place where you rid yourselves of everything that makes your souls less than the image and likeness of Jesus. The purpose of the Earth is to reveal that tangible space can be exercised to tool your perfection. Your spirit thrives on ameliorating everything that is wrong; and giving yourselves to one another in humility and servitude is sheer excellence for the soul. You are building-up the Mystical Body of Christ by praying with them. This intertwining nature of fellowship is good not only for the individual who gives, but for all who receive. Be kind to others, and they will learn the meaning of kindness. Be pure, and they will be pure. Pray deeply and heartily for the conversion of sinners, and the Light of Truth shall be shined upon them. There has never been a connection between sanctity and sinful human flesh that Eternity has avowed. You must be sown to the Spirit to see beyond your death. Jesus came to Earth in perfect Flesh, and He reigns among you in the Eucharist, the Most Holy Sacrament of the Altar. His Gospel helps you pursue the virtues of the Spirit over the cravings of the body. When you undergo anguish and pain, remember that your soul is not subject to these things because you belong to God, and your soul aspires to Salvation. There are no human tears in Heaven. Embrace your sufferings because they are living evidence that your spirit is bound for

Paradise. Jesus is the epitome of everything I am telling you. He sorrowed knowing that there were lost sinners in His midst, everyone in His company except Me, but He took joy that His life, Death, and Resurrection would become their exposure to all that lives and reigns in Him. It would seem that His Sacred Heart was torn between this sorrow and joy, but the jubilation He harbored for the arrival of God's Kingdom that is eclipsing the Earth brought Him to the same peace to which He is calling you. My urging is that you remember that the mission of the Church is to align you in flawless unity with the Most Blessed Trinity, and that by giving your will over to the Father, you shall remain as esteemed as Jesus. You must be wary of the skepticism attempting to lure you away from making the judgements that hold you fervent in sanctity. This is rarely easy, and it is why I counsel and guide you. My Special son, I have the honor of addressing you because My Immaculate Heart pines for your simplicity. You have told others that I have taught you many holy lessons through the years and shared visions that bring you tears of happiness. Yes, this is true. However, My joy is knowing that you believe what I have said. You have dedicated yourself to the Holy Spirit residing in your heart. You and your brother have made great strides in altering the face of the Earth. The fruits of your labors are ripening, and they will be sweet to the taste of the new Saints whom you are converting for God. You have known this for a long time..."

Sunday, November 2, 2003
Merciful Feast of All Souls
3:46 p.m.

"The righteousness and servitude of the Children of Light are the healing balm and deliverance of the people who are trapped in the dungeon of their sins. My little ones, I call upon you to celebrate the Divine Mercy of Jesus as you pray for the repose of the souls of those who have died. Pray for your beloved families, your departed friends, the millions who have crossed the threshold to the celestial shores. I assure you that the Saints are pouring-out their supplications for people who remain on Earth. So many times, I have referred to the reciprocity between Heaven and the ground upon which you walk. The Faith-Church owes intense allegiance to the Church-Suffering in Purgatory and the Church-Triumphant in Heaven. Please remember those in Purgatory in your petitions for Divine Mercy. As you keep your hopes alive for entrance into Paradise, so do the Saints wish you to be there. But for the expiration of time, you have already arrived. Remember these joyous things as you serve in God's vineyard, tending to His straying sheep, feeding His lambs, healing the sick, comforting the dying, and all you have been afforded as the Spiritual and Corporal Works of Mercy. When you 'put on Christ,' you wear the dignity that is yours to keep through Eternity, even in this life. Your Christian commission is not to seek happiness through the flesh or pursue goals that are not of Salvation. As My children, you are commended to elevate Creation in the holiness that the Love of Jesus places in you. Thus, become the singers and players of the angelic strains that soothe the savage beast in your brothers' hearts and purge ruination from their beings. Become God's healers and peacemakers. Walk a jaded mile with them twain over and again until your sandals wear paper thin. Grasp the hands of the wandering-lost and lead them upon the narrow path. And, dry the tears from their eyes with the hope that lives in you, the Resurrection and Life that you anticipate with the vision of the Saints. Be the jubilation of the Angelic Courts along the dark alleyways and creaking boardwalks of desperation that take so many sinners to despair. Tell them about your Immaculate Mother! Tell them that through the Light of the Holy Spirit, they are not orphans anymore. Then, they will be fulfilled; they will close ranks with you, and they will sing and dance to the music of the Most Blessed Trinity echoing Thrice-Glory through the swamps, in the dales, and from the snowy mountaintops. Your Mother has come to speak about hope and anticipation; about Justice, peace, reward, awakenings, deliverance, and destiny. I ask My children who have been christened in the Love of the Holy Spirit to bring your baptismal gowns back with you on the last day when your Savior appears a second time in resplendent Glory. My darlings, go out and greet Him with confidence in the company of the Angels and Saints. Tell Him that you belong to Heaven when He says that He recognizes who you are. Say that you did your best to fend-off the dogs, to fight the good fight against evil and temptation. Tell Him that pride has never become you, that you rebuked the disobedience of the First Fall of man. Tell your Savior that His time has ripened in you, and therefore in all the universe. Do not fear to declare that He waited too long, that your forbears and loved-ones suffered for centuries waiting for the Son of Man to reclaim His Kingdom. And, He will look at you with eyes of pity! He will consummate all things you learned in the Sacred Scriptures. My children, tell Him in the last hour everything you are hoping for now. Empty your hearts into Creation's basin. Be honest and sincere, and fall to your knees in thanksgiving that the Messiah has arrived to take you to your everlasting home, to the Glory of the Promised Land. I pray that you will prepare your testimony because My Son has lent you His receptive ear.

My faithful ones, what you hear next will help you finalize the meaningful purpose in the moment you were conceived in your mothers' wombs. If you can, imagine the Love in the eyes of the Son of Man peering at you with full awareness of everything you conquered in His name. He will commend you with so much compassion in His Sacred Heart that it will look like the father and the prodigal son being reunited after a thousand-year search in Earth's time. My children, I must warn you that you might have to wait before His response becomes clear because He will be weeping in joy, speechless to see you, and for you to see Him. His breast will be saturated by streams of happiness, and His feet standing in the tears He has shed since you were first baptized in Him. Your Savior will indeed attest that your baptismal gowns are beautiful to behold! And, He will appeal to use them as banquet cloths for the Feast to which your souls are led. He will dry His tears with them and thank you. And, He will thank you again. My children, I daresay that there will be still another dramatic pause because the Son of Man who redeems you will thank you once again. And, why such effusive adulation? Because you stayed the course during your tenure on Earth. You kept the faith and bore the burdens of mortality with the dignity of the highest orders of Angelic Courts. You will know that you did the Dominions proud, and the Principalities too! You will see the reflection of your souls in the Blood that Jesus shed for you on the golden streets of Paradise, on the very place you shall stand. He will speak about this famed destiny that you have been seeking, and about your reward and fulfillment, and the sweetness of the victory that you shall have won at last! My little ones, My favorite part is still to come. Your Servant and Savior will then tell you about His Mother!—the Mother to whom He bequeathed you from the Cross on Good Friday. He will remind you about My humble deference to His Passion and Crucifixion because I knew it meant the final riddance of your corruption and condemnation. I knew that it would close the fissure between Heaven and Earth, that it would amend the rolling ages, that it would heal the breach that has long caused the living on Earth and Triumphant in Heaven from seeing one another with the reciprocal vision of our Triune God. On another day, perhaps the Feast of Easter, I will tell you what else He will confirm. My Special son, it is with hope that I speak to you because I give you strength for the continuum of years. I wish you to know that your brother by whom you are praying bears the love for you that is no less proficient than Mine. Thank you for taking care of him. Thank you on behalf of Heaven for taking such good care of him! You are both well and are earning favors for the Kingdom of God..."

Sunday, November 9, 2003
The Dedication of St. John Lateran
2:01 p.m.

"With peace and hope I arrive at this holy place to bless and pray with you. When you feel My presence, you know that I am showering My radiant Son upon you so you will be absolved by the power of His Sacrifice in the Light of Paradise. Thank you for reciting the Sacred Mysteries of the Holy Rosary with honest faith and regularity because the Lord summons you to be pioneers in the proliferation of Christian Truth. As you know, the Jubilee of the Rosary that recently ended has been a gift for suffering-humanity. My beloved children, I ask you to pray the Rosary with the same devotion as you have for the past fourteen years. I have told you that these are days of good fortune. Yours is the mission to heed My call in ways that others have yet to comprehend. Your obedience has been the ushering of untold millions to the Cross, and your reward in Heaven will be great. On this Feast of the Great Basilica, remember that the passing of the centuries has not amended or altered the Sacred Truth that God has revealed to the world in Jesus, and Creation is humbler for His promise. When you ponder the millions of poor sinners who once walked the corridors and naves of those mighty Churches, it should bring you to recall the swiftly-passing ages during which God is purifying and redeeming His people. Be happy that Jesus was born a Man and your Savior! All the world should be jubilant beneath the Light of His Paschal Resurrection. This is your Redemption! This is Salvation! Come to Jesus to be saved! My two princes, I speak to you briefly because I know that you will have a week of tedious labor. Thank you, My Special one, for buying My priest from India a winter coat, earmuffs, thermal clothing, and galoshes. Bless your soul for sharing your gifts of plenty. There is nothing I can say that would help you understand how grateful is God. And, twelve years ago, your brother told Jesus that he would gladly wear two-dollar shirts and hand-me-down breeches if God would send him one priest in need of the clothing you bought Father Samuel yesterday. As you see, his wish was fulfilled by your kind generosity. My Dominion Angels wished for another opportunity to indicate their loyalty to you, so they produced your lost document that you were seeking. It was in a place that neither of you would have looked for months..."

Sunday, November 16, 2003
St. Margaret of Scotland [AD 1045-1093]
1:08 p.m.

"Jesus is the Light of life and the Conqueror of darkness who preserves you from death. He is the expiation for your sinfulness. In Him, you owe no debt to the Father for the wrongs you have done. This, My children, is the best news you could ever hear. I am pleased to have participated by birthing the Savior of the world into Creation because, like My Son, I love you infinitely. I have been asked by several seers whether Jesus prays. Of course He prays. His entire Being is a prayer to the Father so your souls will be redeemed for Eternity. He prayed while walking the Earth in sinless Flesh, and He prays for you now at the Right Hand of God, that you will perform His Holy Will. Do you remember the prayer to the Father that He taught you to repeat? You offer it during the Holy Sacrifice of the Mass, when reciting the Sacred Mysteries of the Holy Rosary, and as an integral part of the petitions you lift for the healing, sanctification, purification, elevation, and Salvation of humanity. Be pleased that you have the opportunity to speak to God with such power. Believe that He hears you with the Love that blooms from Jesus' Sacred Heart. My children, you are a fortunate people because you are the chosen beneficiaries of Jesus' Crucifixion and Easter Resurrection. Everything good for which you have pined will be granted you in Heaven if you pray from the heart in Jesus' name. So, pray with Jesus and Me. Help us beseech the Father to soften the hearts of lost sinners everywhere, that they will understand that human Salvation comes only through the Cross. No mortal man, woman, or child can be redeemed unless they accept Jesus Christ as their Savior. I assure you that this is as real and necessary as the air you breathe. What happens to those who refuse to believe? What is their fate and final destiny? The answer resides in the Sacred Mystery of Jesus' Divine Mercy. The prophesies He told Sister Faustina are true, and they are occurring in your lifetime. When you fear for the Salvation of souls, commend them to the Divine Mercy of Jesus, and trust that He hears you. I ask that you despise no man among you, rather realize that many are affected by evil influences. Everyone has the opportunity to accept the Blood of the Cross, but whether they will have sufficient time before the Son of Man comes in Glory is yet to be seen. Please pay particular attention to the Scriptural readings for the Holy Mass today, and you will see it written from the hands of those who listened with care to the Wisdom of the Holy Spirit. My Special and Chosen ones, I have praise for the goodness you are affording your brothers and sisters. As difficult as it may seem, many of your friends are close because you teach them about the perfection that Jesus is seeking. You hold your composure under the pressure of those who disbelieve that perfect human love can be achieved. I am proud of you and happy for them. Now, you will enter the next phase of your witness for Jesus, continuing your work here at home. Thank you, My Special one, for reaching-out the way you do. You are often seen as the hero of the moment, and rightfully so. The Earth appears to be lacking in heroes. You are determined in your Christian commitment, unyielding in defense of the Truth, and commissioned to accept the buffets that come from those who falsely purport to uphold the dignity of others in their struggle for righteousness. They expose themselves as hypocrites. Thank you for praying the Rosary to reverse the infiltration of evil in academic institutions. And, bless you for taking care of Timothy; it means so much to Me. Although you do not hear them, I am listening to the Angels who are declaring that it means a lot to them too!..."

Sunday, November 23, 2003
Feast of Christ the King
2:39 p.m.

"Now comes your Holy Mother to share the Good News of the Salvation of humanity in Jesus Christ the King. With the Son of Man as your Savior, you rest in the assurance that perpetual, sublime, and ethereal peace is yours. It gives Me hope to pronounce that the Father is pleased with Jesus' Sacrifice so you may join the Heavenly Hosts. The Sacred Mysteries about which I speak are fulfilled, and your Redemption is inevitable. My dear children, I am referring to spiritual hope and extolling the fact that the transformation of the Earth into the image of Heaven is ongoing. I realize that this is difficult to detect because of the harshness of your detractors and adversaries. Perfection and piety are not readily apparent amid the corruption that stains the world. However, each second that passes, every instant and hour and all the cumulative years are moving toward this day. I repeat the promises that I have made during the centuries. My words reflect the Truth that the Kingdom of God is at hand. When you hear the wailing of the unrepentant, know that they are signals of the End Times. There have been wars and natural disasters, famine, pestilence and outright sorcery, but these are remnants of the passing world. The Virtues of Providence are succeeding, being cast toward you from beyond every new horizon by the Son of Man. You sense it in your piety, feel it in the depths of your hearts, recognize it by the perception of the intellect, and know by your sacred baptism that you belong to Christ. The ages are fleeting, but Eternal Salvation never expires. Your successors will commit your remains to the dust, but the Son of God will raise you from the grave. How could any soldier of good fortune be more elated than to know that this is imminent? I have called on My messengers to be beacons of Light to counter the darkness of those who have no love. I am joyful that you have complied, without exception, and that you will soon revel in these things. As the Church celebrates the Feast of Christ the King, remember that Heaven is a Kingdom of Glory, honor, sacrifice, service, humility, faith, love, hope, beauty, and loyalty to the Mother of God who is speaking to you now. Your filial obedience is the maximum beauty about which Saint Paul spoke with profundity. My gladness and admiration are inexplicable because they are fruits of the sublimeness of My Immaculate Heart, the beauty that your souls have become in Jesus' Crucifixion. If there was ever another term to describe My dear children, it is definitely patient. There has never been a messenger or seer who did not learn to wait in joyful hope for the Coming of the Son of Man. This is not only your calling, it is your sacred duty to God and your gift to the world. Those who have seen My face and heard My voice are the chosen offspring with a new perspective about life, about human existence, and about transcending the bonds of mortality unknown to other men. Wisdom is in the Prince who sits at your side, and His Mother is your Advocate on your behalf. I ask you to trust your hearts to believe that God commands His Creation. The Holy Spirit is your narrator when you become speechless. And, when you receive the Blessed Sacrament during the Holy Sacrifice of the Mass, you are partaking of the Bread of Life. The Eucharist is physically, spiritually, and simultaneously the Most Blessed Trinity. Your faith in the Sacred Mysteries is your escape from harm, and your enlightenment, good fortune, healing, and eternal joy. As has been confirmed by the Saints, the Body, Blood, Soul and Divinity of Jesus Christ is the antidote to death. I beseech you to remember the values and virtues you have learned from Jesus along with your brothers and sisters in the Church, and with the hope and trust that the economy of Christian Salvation instills in your hearts. I commend you to Jesus for all that God Wills for you. I have told you that you are not only those who pray with Me, you are My prayers. I ask My Son for His blessings on the Earth and His Divine Mercy upon those who need it. Thank you for heeding the conscience of the Holy Spirit, and thank you for responding to My call.

  My Special son, I am honored to be with you and your brother because you uplift My soul in the way of the Archangels. You give Me hope that humanity has not surrendered to despair. I see you laboring in Jesus' vineyard without counting the cost. For this, you will always be Special and Chosen in the mind of God. It is raining outside. The birds and animals need fresh water; and the rains are providing it, along with giving nourishment to the soil. You, however, are brine in the drink of Jesus' enemies. Could you describe the look on their faces? Yes, it is fear, as though they have been doing something wrong. I urge you to remember this expression because it exemplifies those who die without having reconciled with God. William, many of them have known a long time that they are on the wrong side of history. Be thankful that most will not remain this way forever. They will be received by Jesus gladly, and they will not be afraid when seeing the Father whom they shall glorify. The Lord is grateful, and you are blessed. What if you were a priest? What routine would you have? A priest has a pulpit every day, and you have one as well. It is called your heart, and you must deploy it in every sense to call upon the Holy Spirit to give you strength in times of trouble. There is eloquence in your voice that says you are hopeful, but it is contradicted by a subtle reticence. You tell Me that you try to be more happy, but you do not know how. You should have concise perspective in all cases, but I am concerned about your spirit spiraling into depression. If you do not clarify your faith in Jesus by elevating your hopes in Him, your future will be dark. I realize that you are concerned that not all of your brothers and sisters are receiving the messages I have been giving, or they are not paying due homage to the Cross. These are important matters, but I am limited by the temporalness of the Earth to address your pain. How many ways can I say that I love you? You are pitiable when you are sad.

The perspective you require can only be attained when you see what you had after it is rescinded. This may be the next series of events, however God chooses it to be manifested. It is you who shall determine how the Lord will shower His Light upon you for the good of your spirit. You alone must decide. I am pleased when anything occurs to lift your heart so you know that you have no reason for despondence. *(I asked how God can pay so much attention to one particular soul.)* Because He is a Father who loves you, and He knows what is best for you in preparation for His Divine Kingdom. He does this by overwhelming you with such affection that your consciousness cannot grasp it..."

Sunday, November 30, 2003
Feast of Saint Andrew the Apostle
10:28 a.m.

"Dear children, you are held deeply in love at the center of My Immaculate Heart, and this is where you remain. I watch over you during uncertain hours so your lives will be blessed with the bountiful protection of God. Please remember to pray without ceasing for the ills of the world because Creation becomes a more holy place when you ask Jesus to intervene. I have spoken about the specificities of the Church, its holiness and ullage, and I have broadly referred to the expanses of human life. The intention of this message is to tell you that I am with you in all ways. I am your Matron of Guiding Light who wants no harm to come upon you. Children, whenever you see terrible things happening, it is brought by the sins of men, and I urge you to pray for their conversion. Ask Jesus to lead them to Him so there will be no sorrow. Whenever I speak to you, it is always from the purview of Wisdom. And, what about Wisdom? Is it not the sacred knowledge that leads you on the pathway of Heaven's righteousness? Is it not everything that supports, fosters, and maintains your desires to become like the Messiah of God? When we speak through the miraculous events that He deigns, can you not recognize that His Wisdom is the source of our intercourse? We shall pray until every illness in Creation is eradicated. Together, we beseech God to bestow His blessing on the Christians who are His living harvesters on Earth. There is intense challenge in the claims that I am making, and great consolation too. It should be your hearts' desire to set things right. You should pine for the amendment of everything that is not in alignment with the Will of the Father. He can hear you; He knows when you sit and when you stand, and His Angels are your advocates through the toils of life. However, many of My children ask, '...why us? Why would our Patriarch come to us?' The answer is Love, dear children. You were created in Love, you are sustained by Love, you shall be judged according to the Gospel of Love, and your soul will be granted Salvation by the Love of the Father. When I speak about the reciprocal instincts of Heaven and

Earth, I call upon you to defend this Love. Tend to Jesus' sheep, and feed His hungry lambs. When you do this, the meaning of Divine Truth becomes clear to you. My Special son, how pleased I am to speak with you. You are much more happy than when we spoke a week ago. I am here to pray with you on the last day of the month. I bear the glad tidings of Jesus and offer His blessings upon the Advent Season. This is an anticipatory time. Thank you for keeping the perspective that the world tries to destroy. I appreciate your trust that Jesus has the ability to bring you fulfillment. I am happy when you are happy because when you are not, you lose sight of the hope that Jesus has placed in your heart. Please remain joyful knowing that He is making the Earth the best of all possibilities for its transformation into the likeness of Heaven. You had a good week enjoying your time away from your workplace, observing the secular Thanksgiving. You know that your brother takes his business seriously because he sees the effect it has on your Apostolate. If you watch him, you will see that he analyzes the conditions that must be addressed to attain these goals. He uses the term 'tenacious.' This is how he is when he has an abundance of work. Without you, he would have no tenacity. He would have no goals or objectives. He would have no life or purpose. This is why he is dependent upon you, much like a child. You are his reason for living, and you shall reap a great reward for the aid you are affording him, and I mean this sincerely. Your Mother has no words to express how grateful God is for helping your brother endure the years. Your writings are holy, elevated, insightful, and filled with edification for your lost brothers and sisters. Yes, I hold the title of your first work deep inside My Heart. When the Children of Light read your manuscripts, they will have the courage to shed their apprehensions and be valorous soldiers in the struggle for holiness and purity. You must be assured that God does His best work with humble people in remote places, and you and your brother are two of them. Your brother's literature review lacks the simplicity that the world requires because of the integration of intellectualism with the piety that keeps so many close to the Cross. You must recognize that the abstract readings, heretical class sessions, massive amounts of research, and endless pages of typing keep your brother exhausted most of the time. However, his university experience will cause him to be no different than he was before the process began. Thank you for reciting the Sacred Mysteries of the Holy Rosary and for allowing Me to speak with such candor. This is a nostalgic time of year for you, for your brother, and the entire world..."

Sunday, December 7, 2003
St. Ambrose, Doctor of the Church [AD 340-397]
2:59 p.m.

"Dear children, the Second Sunday of Advent brings more opportunities to remember everyone who needs the cultivation of the Holy Spirit in their hearts so they can be sanctified and made responsive to the Nativity of Emanuel. I ask you to seek His blessings for the impoverished and enlightenment for the millions around the globe who do not understand the purpose of Christmas with faith. I have told you during My previous messages that Jesus' Nativity has nothing to do with materialism. It is about freedom and the call for humanity to be liberated from the temptations of the physical world. I am praying for your conversion to His Sacrifice because the principles of self-denial are given to the depths of the heart there. Advent is about anticipating the Birth of your Salvation. It is about the miracles of Heaven. When you give yourselves to the Virtues that are excelled in Christianity, you will see Christmas not as a time to exchange merchandise, but to practice contrition, servitude, and mutual forgiveness. How many times must the Mother of God say that the western hemisphere has a skewed sense of reality about the Feast of Christmas? I implore My children to return to the innocence of Jesus' childhood, away from the diversions of secular capitalism. I speak to you because I care about your future, not only about the next months and years, but your immortality. The Sacred Scriptures are replete with warnings about being sown to the Spirit and not the flesh. The Beatitudes in My Son's Sermon on the Mount recount the requirements of those who are worthy of His Kingdom. Will America ignore the faith that Christianity demands? I have sorrow because many of My children defy the real meaning of thanksgiving by spending the following month purchasing superfluous materials. It is only hypocrisy, and it comes at the expense of the impoverished and neglected. The Mother of Jesus Christ whom the Church venerates is consistent in Her words. Let go of the Earth and join the march for life. Release yourselves from the bondage of products and engage your hearts in Heavenly Love. Resolve to pursue the prophetic beauties of Truth. The hours are short, I have said this for generations. If you consider human logic, you will know that time has never been more brief than at the present..."

Sunday, December 14, 2003
St. John of the Cross [AD 1542-1591]
Doctor of the Church
2:55 p.m.

"Salvation is an evasive prospect if your hearts are closed, but if you accept Jesus' Crucifixion, your union with Heaven has already begun. My dear children, we speak about the Light by which everything is revealed because you are God's disciples, and His holiness becomes you. Thank you for reciting the Rosary and embracing the piety to which you are called. Your relationship with the Father is founded in the faith that He bestows upon you. Today, we celebrate the Feast of a jewel of Christianity. What does this mean? How does someone become a Doctor of the Church? You know that every Saint is a practitioner of pious hope and holy obedience. I assure you that to become a Doctor of the Church is more involved than being an ordinary Saint, but if you extol everything that Jesus asks, you shall become Doctors of the Beatitudes. Be with the Lord in all good things; prophesy in His Holy Name, live the mandates of the Apostles Creed, preach soundly and simply, be loving, humble, caring, compassionate and generous, and you will be Doctors of the Church because under the auspices of the Most Blessed Trinity, you are the Church. Your Immaculate Mother has come speaking during Advent to awaken your consciences to the Messianic Truth. The anticipation you felt when you were youngsters about Emmanuel should be the same in preparation for Jesus' return in Glory. You have known that these years in history are declared the Second Advent for this reason. I am accepting of My children. I am blessed to be the Immaculate Conception, and even more blessed because My children are responding to My call in such identifiable ways. There is much to feel good about as Christmas 2003 approaches. There is a great amount of work to finish for the purification of humanity, but see how far you have come! The words and actions by which you are fostering human conversion is a gift to the Kingdom of Heaven! Let us be grateful that the Holy Spirit is flourishing within you for the refinement of God's Creation. And, My Special son, never before in Christendom has such edifying writing been placed onto the page as that you are giving Jesus. You must know that this is true. It makes Me shed happy tears to realize that there is such sanctification in your spirit that everything you have poured into your labors will induce those who spurn Jesus' Crucifixion to finally convert to Him. It will soften the hardened of heart and thaw those who are frozen by indifference. You can do no wrong when you offer your years for evangelizing God's Kingdom. My words express insufficient gratitude for everything you are doing, but this is the reason I come, and it is the substance of what I have to say. I am confident that My messages are humanity's spiritual poultice that I spoke about in January, and you know that you and your brother have exacted a more principled approach to life than you might have otherwise employed. Your Mother has been sustaining you! Your intentions, supplications, and recitations of the Litanies, especially the Holy Rosary, have been your suppliers of Wisdom. Jesus' Passion has been your strength and peace. The Holy Eucharist has been your Sacramental Bread. All these gifts from Heaven are culminating inside you to make your lives sweet to the palate of humanity. You will see when Spring 2004 arrives that there will be many favorable fruits born of these. Your obedience has been the procuring of this goodness. I have told you time and again that I cannot succeed without you. The accomplishment of Jesus' mission is manifested in you for eternity, and God and the Celestial Court are thankful. Eye has not seen nor ear heard the Glory that is awaiting you in Heaven. Thank you for accompanying your brother to the movie theater last evening. The point is not whether it was an appropriate motion picture, but you re-entered your relationship with the culture of your nation and participated in the things that make you mid-American people. You live normal lives in many ways, but you are sons of the Immaculate Queen who intercedes on behalf of Her adopted children. Can you see that My messages are in answer to the novenas of the contrite generations who have gone before? They prayed for modern miracles, and this is why I am speaking. You represent the hopes of millions of Christians from the past, the present, and the future. I shall remind you how happy I am that your life is unfolding with such Grace. You are healthy, prosperous, holy, humble, and compliant on the pathway to Heaven and living with your best friend and fellow messenger. How could life be better than this? I only ask that you remember that you are blessed. I exhort you to be patient, knowing that every time you rise from your slumber is an opportunity for the world to receive the Good News of Christianity. I will bless My children in other regions of the world. Be comforted knowing that Jesus adores you, that you are one in the Cross. And, thank you for taking care of your brother. O' how grateful I am that you are tending to him! All the Doctors of the Church could be no more gracious, receiving, loving, and supportive than you are of your brother... There are two Sundays remaining in 2003, and you sense the reflection of your travels through time..."

Sunday, December 21, 2003
St. Peter Canisius [AD 1521-1597]
2:48 p.m.

"To the Church-Militant whom I love with endless joy, I pray for humanity and your future in anticipation of your arrival in Heaven. This Fourth Sunday of Advent is an opportunity for you to reflect on the gift of Salvation that My Son has bestowed upon you by His Crucifixion as you contemplate the sublimity of His Nativity. You are raised in the Paschal Light of His Resurrection and united in His Sacred Heart that upholds your hope, courage, and maturity in faith. Many times you have cited the Visitation in your intercessions and remembered that your souls leap with jubilation knowing that you are saved. As you pore over the years of weekly messages that I have given on behalf of the lost around the world, remember that My gratitude for your obedience in accepting them to the benefit of your brothers and sisters is an inexhaustible blessing. I have told you in times past that Christmas is meant for simplicity and solemnity. I have reminded you that the Birth of Jesus is about giving others your heart, and I have warned against the materialism that darkens your observance of Christmas in the United States. I wish that you will forever remember that I call you to pursue holiness over and again because to understand your faith with perfection, you must loosen your grip on the physical aspects of mortal life and reach for the Messianic Truth who has freed you from sin on the Cross. I have often spoken about God's timing and His timelessness, and many are they who have responded to My call. My little ones, I promise that everything I have conveyed in My messages is true; every prophecy will come to pass, and every enemy whom I dared you to conquer will fall. Yes, throngs of them have already been cast into the shadowy Abyss because of your obedience to Me. It is for these reasons that you must elevate Christianity as My army of children. There will come a time when you will sense the imminence of the triumphs depicted with epochal artistry in motion pictures, and I promise that this will move you. Your journey will be complete, and your souls will be raised to the greatest ecstasies ever known. I pray that you trust Me as I declare that this is true. My Special and Chosen ones, I appear in this home as a satisfied Mother. I have transcended the veil of human exile, having passed from Heaven to Earth for the conversion of humanity. I assure you that if you persist in your labors, you will recognize that victory is yours. This Advent and the Feast of Christmas you will soon celebrate offer humanity more ways to realize that holiness prevails over Creation. While you wait for the conversion of your brothers, do the work that Jesus asks you to complete. Do not be dismayed by temporary feelings that have nothing to do with His Kingdom. Remember the role of the Angels and Saints in your work, for they gather around you to ensure your success. Ponder the beauty of Heaven residing in your hearts, and you will find comfort from within. Partake of the Most Blessed Sacrament with the assurance that the Holy Eucharist is your Salvation, and you will be fulfilled. Let Wisdom be your inspiration to make the nobler choices in life, and Salvation will find its way to you. Everything you will attain is founded in your holiness, whether it is the refinement of the Earth or your eloquence honed by decades of suffering. I assure you that the Holy Spirit is the Wisdom that allows God's people to be convinced that Jesus has conquered evil. It is written across the chasm of the ages by the Blood of the Lamb and inscribed into Creation by your pious works. Christmas is a time of remembrance not only because of the nostalgia of your youth, but because of the innocent children you have become. When you call out Abba! Father!, the Creator of Heaven and Earth hears you. Even in your darkest hours, He binds you ever closer to the courage that you find in Jesus. Even people of indomitable faith have despair at certain moments in their lives because they know that the world is not responding to the Wisdom of God. They see deplorable suffering and inequity, and children without food, clothing, sanitation, and shelter. These holy ones cringe at the sight of wars and diseases, and they weep at the thought of someone forsaking the integrity of their faith. I promise you that everything that drives the people of righteousness into despondence is offset with valor and resilience, for no villain can detain the children of God in the darkness forever.

My little ones, have I not felt the angst, unease, and apprehension that you endure in your lives? Did I not witness the Son of Man spurned, persecuted, and Crucified? Thus, I have compassion for your torment in the vineyard of the Lord. I understand what it is like to see Perfect Love rejected and disdained. Therefore, I speak simultaneously from the purview of Eternal Life and human experience. I assure you that the dreams you are harboring are emblematic of your belief in God, and they are within your grasp. If only you could gain a sense for this, you would never fall to despair again. It is obvious that your days seem fraught with peril and are lastingly cruel; the same was true for Jesus. He is with you, and He reigns in you. You never walk alone; the value of your loyalty is priceless to Him, and He will grant you endless favors before the years are through. I have told you that the mainstay to peace is patience. Of all the deficits that afflict My children, patience is the most prominent, but you cannot be blamed. I yearn to see the end of human corruption more swiftly than anyone who ever lived. Having entered Heaven and received My Coronation, I tell you with the precision of Eternity that despair is unwarranted. However, without your trust, without believing what I am saying, I am unsure that you can personify My claims. There is no sadness that your faith cannot overcome. My precious ones, can you see how happy is your Mother who has been given your lives and souls? I know that I am a good Mother because it is the way God created Me. And, you are all good children when you heed My call and work for the conversion of lost humanity without counting the cost, without tallying the score, and without peering behind to see if you have advanced a longer measure to the finish. There is untold peace in your allegiance to the Lord, and you have been faithful. There is no reason for despair. William, I hope you will approach Christmas with the perspective of the Angels, for it is a season of joy, and you are accorded signs to strengthen your faith. Thank you for giving *Morning Star Over America* to your friends for Christmas. Your petitions have been delivered to Jesus. Can you see that My words are like soldiers on steeds pouring over a hill? This is how God utilizes them for the conversion of humanity and vanquishes evil through the Triumph of My Immaculate Heart. Please summon the intercession of the Holy Innocents to precede My final appearance of 2003. I have distinct things to say on the 13th anniversary of My messages, February 22, 2004... Please be consoled that Christmas has come, and pray for the lost and forsaken. I love you..."

Sunday, December 28, 2003
Feast of the Holy Innocents
2:26 p.m.

"Now, children, your Mother has come for a concluding message in 2003, and I shall continue in 2004 with your kind permission. We are amassing together a bounteous trove of supernatural communication that will inspire the hearts of lost sinners to seek Salvation in Jesus on the Cross. I am telling you that many people have yet to find their spiritual bearings and life's direction. They have lost the meaning of human existence in all the distractions you have cast aside so your souls are vested in holiness. I speak about the Sacred Divine because it is by the Divine that you are sanctioned. My dear ones, you have been traveling a glorious boulevard since February 22, 1991 that is bending the course of history. As you know by the anthology of messages that I have given, no ear has heard or eye seen the gratitude that the Mother of God has in Her Immaculate Heart for those who accept the Cross. There will be many more. There will be millions more! As you leave 2003, remember how you offered it to God in deference to His Will. Never forget how special you are, how intriguing is your curiosity about Heaven and the Afterlife, and what the future will bring that it would not have held without your compliance. While there will be time for speeches about the accomplishments of men, you should realize that yours are still being written because your work for Jesus is unfinished. I will speak to you in 2004 so we can upend the lives of the lost souls who have not a clue about the meaning of Truth. If anyone believes he cannot be perfected in the Holy Spirit, let him hear the words of the Mother of God. Please tell them! Tell them, My children, about the awesome wonder and Glory of Heaven! Be attentive in your sojourn because the years pass swiftly by. It will not be long before you shall bask in the Light of Paradise with Me and the Angels, and Jesus will hold you with the tenderness of His Sacred Heart. Have hope every time you wake in the morning because the hour about which I speak is near. When you ponder the condition of human spirituality, you see that there are masses of the Christian faithful worshiping God in the way Jesus prescribes. Bishops around the globe have led their flocks to repentance, contrition, holiness, and prayer. These descendants of the Apostles have a great amount of work to accomplish in this modern age. There are enemies of Christianity who would see them fail. However, you are among the millions who stand beside them in love. I urge you to support Bishops and priests everywhere in the way you have in the past. On the Feast of the Holy Innocents, it is imperative that you pray in union with the Bishops for the end of infanticide. Little has been done to curb abortion, and there is a great deal more to do. It begins in the hearts of mothers! We must implore women bearing children in their wombs to allow them to be born! I seek your assistance in prayer and speech to teach them the essential lesson about the sanctity of unborn life. The Church reserves this Feast to remember the little ones who were stillborn and those yet to be born. It is a time of prayer for humanity to espouse the preciousness of life. When you recall the thoughts of Mother Teresa about ending abortion and replicate her sacrifices, God will hear your call for the protection of the unborn. Why do I ask this with urgency? Because there seems to be an atmosphere of sloth in America about the subject of human life. Unborn children are aborted for convenience because their mothers will not accept the burden of rearing them. I assure you that none of the Holy Innocents is forgotten by Jesus. I have told you that grotesque will be the chastisement upon the devil's henchmen who are taking the lives of the unborn from their mothers' wombs. Let us pray that God intercedes swiftly and justly, as only He can do.

    We commemorate the Feast of the Holy Family in the Church's Liturgical Year. How can a family be complete without its unborn children? We must pray for the end of abortion and the culture of death. My Special and Chosen ones, we move into another calendar year at the middle of next week. The work you are completing is sublime. We are making the difference that God expects from us. The Catholic Church is stronger, its people holier, and its mission clearer through everything you do. Have I not told you from the beginning that your labors for Jesus would bear these fruits? What would your lives be if you had not lent them to the conversion of humanity? Your goals and objectives are being accomplished because your vision is clear. Can you not see that the will of indifferent people is an impediment to everything you are trying to achieve? Do not let them stop you! Jesus will bless your lives even so! They cannot prohibit you from effecting the changes for which you were born so the Kingdom of Truth prevails. I assure you that you are warriors and stately princes in these things. And, is it not clear to you that the Victory about which I have spoken is inevitable? This is true because of Jesus' Sacrifice; and in His Paschal Resurrection, Heaven has already won. By accepting your mission at this hour, you are victors as well. I bear the Good News that there are no wasted moments. Even in your idle times, God loves you as His creatures. He calls you to rest at sundown because tomorrow there is much more work to do. The Angels by the tens-of-thousands hover over you while you sleep. You are not alone because your soul is encompassed by the Grace of God. These are pleasant themes, and you are dutiful servants. I hope you realize that you are blessed to be honored as the Children of Light. My messages are beautiful, but I could not have given them to humanity if you had not agreed. Your prayers are the reason these manifestations are occurring. My Special son, I did not choose you. You have chosen Me! I came on February 22, 1991 and you complied, while many others declined because they would not let go of their material lives. They were battered by temptations of the flesh to which they conceded. However, you and your brother remain pure of heart, mind, body, and soul. When the world as you know it passes-away, you will see everything I am telling you. This has been a year of achievement by you and your brother because you have remained united. Each of you is the other's self. I cannot describe how strong your union is, and I believe you see it as well. Please remember to pray for Mary Jane. She will soon come to live with Jesus and the Saints..."

MORNING STAR OVER AMERICA

The New Millennium
In the Year of Our Lord
AD 2004

* *On December 5, 2004, Our Lady began revealing names of some of Her children from Christian history who are presently Saints in the Kingdom of Heaven, although they have yet to be canonized by the Magisterium of the Roman Catholic Church. One purpose of this delineation is for everyone to realize that the Church's official recognition of Saints is an authoritative declaration of fact regarding the citizenry of Heaven, rather than a conferment of deliverance. Our Holy Mother wishes the world to know that millions have achieved the blessedness of Paradise who will never be recognized by the Faith-Church on Earth. Therefore, none should fear exclusion from the Kingdom of God because they will not be hailed in the eyes of the Church. These Saints' names have been denoted with an asterisk.*

Sunday, January 4, 2004
St. Elizabeth Ann Seton [AD 1774-1821]
3:11 p.m.

"Let us pray as we have for many years last passed, acknowledging that the conversion of lost sinners is incomplete. I assure you, My children, that the souls who are bound for Heaven are aware that the Earth is lost in turmoil, wrought by the sins of humanity, but that Jesus has reclaimed you for His Kingdom. Hence, it is inevitable that the cultivation for which we are yearning will ultimately come. This is a new month and year, and you have decided for God. I bless and pray for you before His Providence because I realize that you know Him as He sees you. Please be careful to keep warm during this bitterly cold January. Saint Francis of Assisi was known for saying with levity that he did not mind the inclement air as long as there were sufficient amounts to breathe. Today's civilization makes it possible for you to bear the harsh elements with comfort. Always remember that to be safe, you must live prayerfully. My children, I rededicate humanity to the Divine Mercy of Jesus as our prayerful mission for 2004. I ask you to remember the great Sacrifice that Jesus offered the Father 1,971 years ago so you might take your rightful place in Paradise. When you look back at 2003, please recall that you worked with the dedication of saints so the arrival of the Son of Man will find you worthy of His Grace. Be assured that My appearance here and My messages of encouragement are evidence that He is pleased by your accomplishments. It is said by optimists that hope springs eternal. While this is true in the context of your exile, there will come a time when you will no longer live by hope without proof or faith without seeing. As of this week, you are another year closer to this reality. My dear children, you have always recognized that I am an eternal being because I am the Mother of God. Jesus has offered Himself so you will be moved in righteousness to give your lives and souls, indeed, your whole being to Him. This is how His Kingdom is fulfilled in your linear time. I also know that you are content in your sacrifices because you have made your mortification one with His Crucifixion. Let no man tell you that there is no perfection in the goals you have set forth to transform the Earth into the image of Heaven. When you live in the likeness of Jesus and emulate His Divine Love, you are not only perfected, you are made spiritually flawless. I am happy for this beyond all telling. I direct your eyes and ears to the plight of the suffering in 2004. I ask you to pray for peace in places where there is only war, and remember how helpless you would be without the guidance of the Holy Spirit. Offer your obedience with the empathy of the Angels to the little ones surrounding you who have no one to lead them to the good and truthful path. How do you remain simple in love and take-on these magnanimous chores? You must turn to your Mother for help. I have given you the Christ and offered you reason for life. Thank you for having responded to My call.

My Special son, it is with great affection that you see and hear My presence for another year, and I offer a gratitude from the Father that cannot be weighed. The work that you and your brother devote to Jesus is nothing less than beatific. I am happy that your book is going well and that you have chosen to incorporate My previous messages in its text. Do you recall that I asked you never to worry whether anyone might believe that you are embroiled in negativism or that you appear to have no hope for the conversion of the world? When you are speaking about the erroneous aspects of humanity, you are tilling the soil of their existence. You are redressing the grievances that God holds against those who are unfaithful to Jesus. Surely you are His blessing before men, beckoning the lost to raise their hearts and admire the Creator who gave them life. If you wish, you may employ the use of levity in your new book in the likeness of the Saints. You know already by having lived over 42 years that without a sense of humor, no one can win the fight against depression. Jesus has long admired your capacity to laugh at things that are worthy of laughter, your ability to fight with resilience when the struggles are intense, and react with compassion when you see His people suffering. Deep inside your heart, and that of your brother, you must be pleased with yourselves for everything you are giving Him. He has claimed you for Heaven in every sense of the term. Once you lay-down your mortal flesh when delivering your soul to God, you will recognize many things that you are encountering now. However, you will be satisfied because you will not endure the aging of the body; the aches and pains of stress, focusing your eyesight to see, and the incessant ways that the physical frame must be maintained. There is no reason for you to have anxiety about the knowledge you have of the future, and every reason to exalt the praises of the Lord for making it true. There is so much Divine power and Grace that fills your lives that you may be unable to comprehend it before you are with Me in Heaven. I am happy because you are happy. I know that the world batters your spirit at times, but please search for new hope, and pray for the people who did not believe you in 1991 because they must accept Jesus on the Cross. In a hypothetical sense, the end of time had come when the events of 1991 unfolded, and these people saw what they had done. They have asked not to relive the opening of the messages, only their share of the suffering of Jesus in reparation for not embracing what I came to say. If they had not retreated when they did, you would not have the privacy to accomplish your work. Can you gain an understanding of this? I tell you that the universe is unfolding as it should. If we could convince men and women to relinquish their desire for committing sin, our mission would be complete. Until then, we go forward with your cooperation and the Truth of God. You will not arrive before the Throne of Judgment and be forced to admit any violations against His Divine Love..."

Sunday, January 11, 2004
St. Theodosius the Cenobiarch [AD 423-529]
2:22 p.m.

"This is a crucial moment in history in which the Countenance of Eternity is being shaped. Know that you are participating in the making of Saints of many sinners and that your aid on behalf of the helpless is of unparalleled service during these difficult ages. Be honored that you have been chosen. My children, I plea to millions of people to turn to the Cross for Salvation because there is no other redemption for man. We enter 2004 with confidence that those around you will know that your work is from God. You have detractors, but your supporters are far and wide. The allegiance of Christians is overwhelmingly in favor of the faith you have in Jesus. You will see. You must believe that the words I am saying are true. Thank you for being so kind to God's creatures. I remind you that you are given miracles because they reaffirm that you must remain together, working for Jesus through the Heavenly Hosts, although you do not require evidence that I am guiding your lives. Your faith is strong and your loyalty to God will sustain you through the trials to come. If you should be called to sacrifice even more, you will prevail. My Special son, I am protecting you in ways that you have yet to see because you have enemies whom you have never met. Why are they so opposed? Because you love Jesus, and they despise Him. They espouse darkness, while you are a child of Divine Light. Please keep the Purple Cross as the signature of your Apostolate. I see that you are addressing a letter to the newspaper about the Kingdom of God versus capitalist materialism. The former is the Eternal City, the latter will soon be vanquished. I admire your writing these documents to support the sanctity of the Most Blessed Sacrament in the way of the Bishops. I applaud your actions. It would be appropriate if you placed the title of your Apostolate below your name. I appreciate your patience when others act belligerently against the Catholic Church. For you, and during this time, violence is not an appropriate response. When the Bishops deny Holy Communion to politicians who refuse to uphold the dignity of human life, they are doing the Will of God. This is not violence, it is Jesus' Divine Mercy. Do you see that the Bishops are imitating the righteousness of Jesus by refusing to permit Catholics who support abortion to receive His Eucharistic Body? You have longed for these things, and they are beginning. However, please pray for these Bishops because they are subject to ridicule. Their actions are saintly, My child, and so are yours because you foster the arrival of God's Kingdom and serve those who cannot help themselves. The baptized Christ and those who are baptized in Him belong to the same Eternity. As you celebrate the Feast of Jesus' Baptism, remember that it is possible to remain as pure through the Sacrament of Penance as you were the instant you were christened. Thank you for being devoted to My Immaculate

Heart, for taking such good care of your brother, and for trusting Me when I say that this year, many astounding things will happen..."

Sunday, January 11, 2004

Mr. Barry Locher, Editor
The State Journal-Register
One Copley Plaza, P.O. Box 219
Springfield, Illinois 62705

Re: Response to Bishop Burke Sanctions

Dear Editor,

    The Sacred Host of the Original Apostolic Church which we, as Catholics, receive in Holy Communion is the pinnacle element of our spiritual unity. Our partaking in this Bread of Life is our oath, our surrender, and ultimately our being, which we humbly offer in testament to our unity in body, in spirit, in mind, in ideal, in community, and in conviction.

    Notwithstanding our detractors and critics, this Universal Communion remains the outward communal act of a people sincerely trying to rise in holiness who have forfeited their own ideas and instead now conform themselves willingly and sacrificially to an incontestible wisdom and perfection that is celestial realms above us all. Those who have made the confession that confers the blessed title of "Roman Catholic" upon their soul remain in communion with that miraculous benediction only through their faithful abandonment to all that the Roman Catholic Church professes dogmatically and to the ethics that She maintains pastorally.

    So, who are these people who have unilaterally decided that it is somehow illegitimate for a reverend Minister of this Universal Communion, His Eminence Bishop Raymond Burke, to rescind the privilege and blessing of partaking in the Treasure of our Faith from individuals who present themselves publicly as Catholics, yet knowingly adopt positions that are an outright assault against human life, a violation of the virtue of the title they bear, and a lie overshadowing the promise of unity they have made to their fellow parishioners? Oh, if the leaders of every faith would be of such courage!

    The more disturbing question is whether America has become a nation wherein its citizens are terrified at the prospect of an elected official being a person who is held accountable to the dictates of faith. Well, if that time has finally arrived and those seeking office must abandon their profession of wisdom, virtue, and holiness in order to be acceptable to the media and the masses, then we have crossed the threshold into the darkest hours of the annals of American history.

Sunday, January 18, 2004
Saint Prisca [3rd Century]
3:01 p.m.

"You are assured, little children, that small victories lead to huge triumphs, and that everything you offer Jesus in humility will be extolled by Him before the Father in cascades of Glory. When you pray from the heart and speak the Wisdom of the Holy Paraclete, you are the excellence of beatific human love; you are the essence of perfection in an imperfect world, and you make the Bishops beam with gratitude that you belong to them, that you are the shining stars above the rest of their flock, and that they can trust you to know that the Salvation of man is only a brief time away. You speak the Truth and embrace Jesus perfectly because your spiritual awareness is refined. You hold-out nothing to comply with the Will of the Father because you realize that He is the Glory forever to come. My children, you are fashioning the future during the present and rewriting history by the goals you have planned. I do not expect you to comprehend the mystery in all this, I only ask that you believe Me when I assert that the ancient ages from which this world has blossomed belong to you. Your modern existence is the capstone of the hopes of the billions of people who have passed on. And, beyond this, for all the shining hours and towering mountains, for all that is worth seeking in the Divinity of God, you are there for the suffering and groveling poor in the image of the Son of Man who commissioned you as His principals in a Creation that is in too many ways as blind as a wolf in a blizzard. Know that everything is reconciled in Jesus, and that your gift of pious faith with which the righteous breathe is the loveliness that has sustained the hopes of hundreds of generations. You have inherited the world for the sake of rectifying it, edifying its societies, evangelizing God who has manifested it, and praying in thanksgiving that yours is the charge of chastity and peace. Your Holy Mother bows to offer you a kiss of gratitude upon your cheeks down which too many tears have fallen, for happiness and from sadness, in the hope that you will know that you have been bequeathed to Heaven by My Son. You have been claimed and recollected for the same Glory that brought Him to lay down His life and rise again from the Tomb. You live an esteemed faith that was given to you before your fathers were born. You belong to a humanity that is only now realizing its dreams of greatness, its power, and its strengths. You are the property of the Maker of All Good Things who knows you not only for who you are, but the Saints you are about to become. My Special son, what great light has come to the Earth by your contributions to the Church. Your letter to the masses that appeared in the newspaper is the subject of discussion in thousands of households. *Who is this man who speaks with such eloquence, they ask? What is it about him that he has come to know with such trust and faith that the Holy Eucharist is the Body, Blood, Soul, and Divinity of the Son of Almighty God?* They realize by the throngs because they have come in great numbers to see what is The Morning Star, and have discovered that it is Me. They are opening their eyes because of your laudatory claims that I have been instructing you in issues of faith and morals for years. The laity knows, the clergy is now seeing, and your Bishop accepts. How can I thank you for the holiness that you are pouring-forth over this land? How can God repay you for offering your faith and belief in Him? You have the sensation of the Glory that the final hours of time will bring. I give you My solemn promise that everything I am saying is true. If you hold Me close as I hold dearly you and your brother, you will see that the unfolding of the future will lead inevitably toward the defeat of everything that opposes you. I have never said that you would not be persecuted along the way. And, God has not told you that your pathway will be strewn with flowers. Does this sound familiar? I only wish for you to remember that within the Triumph of My Most Immaculate Heart resides your victory over the world. You already know this, and I am pleased that it is everything you hoped for. Indeed, see the golden shorelines and bright lights! I came prepared to speak for hours, but I know about matters of practicality. You have gained a great blessing from God by your work because so many are reading your letter about the Blessed Sacrament. I wish for you to ponder for a moment that the media were forced by the truth of your words to concede to your request to print your letter. Eloquence, indeed! You are the honor of your hometown and family. So, take this day and place it in your flask of gladness because it will be accompanied by thousands more. As you see, your brother is putting a great deal of work into his assignments for school, but he knows that it is a quickly passing event, that he must make the most of it. If you continue on this pathway in your writing, in your prayers, and with the passage of time, you will see that you will transform the media you so despise into the vehicle for Jesus that you have made it today. Your brother must study, and I ask you with emphasis to underscore his efforts by requiring that he allow you to critique his articles. See the opening at the end of the tunnel, and know that anything you do is another step toward the future about which I speak. You will know with what importance this plays in your favor. I also realize that you are planning *To Crispen Courage*. You must be pleased that you are writing it so well. I ask only one favor today. I have told you that it is a worthy task to admonish humanity the way you are doing in your manuscripts, but you must not allow this approach to be the subject of your discussions every day. Focus on more positive issues as much as you can. Jesus keeps you in His company because you understand deep inside your heart that you are loved. Thank you for working in His vineyard of the Earth..."

Sunday, January 25, 2004
Conversion of St. Paul, Apostle [d. AD 67]
2:44 p.m.

"My children, elation and gratitude best describe the way I feel about your holy lives and purposeful prayers. We are remaking the face of the Earth by the Wisdom of the Holy Spirit and the Divine Love that God created us to be. We are awakening sleeping souls to the Good News of Salvation through Jesus on the Cross. It is a cold, blustery Illinois day outside your doors, but you are unfazed by its inclemency because you are focused on your mission of peace. When you research the annals of history for the presence of Heaven's Light, you will find it shining most brightly from within your hearts. Today, I have come to pray beside you with the intercession of Saint Paul because your brothers and sisters are still ignorant of the Truth. We ask Jesus to reside among them and give them holiness and strength. You read and hear about the terrible casualties of the horrendous war that I told you would ensue in My September 16, 2001 message. This senseless killing is a function of the greed, vengeance, and paranoia of America. There are hosts of reasons why this war should not have been prosecuted. Please remember the innocent victims who are dying at an alarming rate there, and the countless numbers who are suffering in agony in the other conflicts around the globe. My children, imagine what it is like to be in a place where your friends to whom you are devoted reminisce about their childhood during one hour and lay dead on a battlefield the next. This is what is happening. Senseless fatalities and brazen aggression are the enemies of peace and love. I tell you that there is no freedom for humankind being gained by the military action in the Middle East. The war in Iraq is not about democracy, but about profiteering, greed, and retaliation. When you ponder the reasons why your fellow countrymen are being killed and their deaths being concealed by your government, this is the time to reconsider what it means to be called a benevolent state. As Patroness of the Americas, I ask My children of all faiths to pray for the cessation of wars and conflicts wherever they may be. Indeed, I harbor high hopes that these battles will soon end. Now, to My children praying before Me, I combine My supplications with yours for the holiness of humanity to be manifested with dispatch. You are garnering a wider notoriety for your lofty words and admonishing writing. Accolades will be shared about you in the anterooms of municipal halls, in consistories, and among pious people everywhere. It is unnecessary for you to see and know about these things because the accomplishment of your goals has never centered around public approval or collegial acceptance. Make no mistake about it; there are hundreds-of-thousands who consider you to be an enemy of pluralism and secular diversity. And in this, you are unified in the Sacred Heart of Jesus. You are the modern heroes of righteousness about whom Saint Paul wrote in his letters. I ask you not to be boastful of your valor, but humbled that this virtue is sewn into the fabric of your lives. It is a gift from Almighty God upon which He will call time and again. You are living in an age of anticipation, one during which you are preparing the world for the Second Coming of Jesus Christ. Your oral testimonies and religious parables describe Creation the way God wants it to be. Inside your hearts resides the vision that He seeks from every man, woman, and child. I return to this place because you are answering the call to holiness, taking the Truth of the Gospel seriously, and ushering in the New Dawn of the Son of Man with the kindness of princes. Be assured that you are blessed in this life and throughout Eternity by your service to the Lord in the vineyard of the Earth. If not for seeing clearly, you would be lost, but you have chosen to see through eyes of faith that the Kingdom of God is everlasting. There has never been any question about this. Now, your active participation is aiding its arrival into the societies of the globe. Thank you for playing the part you have been chosen to serve.

    My little ones, I ask you to remember the thousands who are forced to live outside in the cold. There are homeless paupers dying from exposure in places where leaders hover around fireplaces with marble mantles. We have spoken over and again about the inequities and lack of sharing of the commodities of a globe with plenty for everyone. We have prophesied the gruesome future of politicians who have chosen to defend the scourge of abortion, and those who will not tend to the poor. America has entered another year of tawdry politics where millions of dollars will be spent determining who is allowed to sit on its titular throne. Politics have never been the answer to the errors of humanity. Democrats and Republicans are demons in disguise! They are secular sorcerers! Only those who surrender themselves and their future to the Holy Gospel of Christianity are the salt of the Earth! The stench of politics has wrought wanton greed, destruction, licentiousness, hatred, division, and wars of naked destruction against innocent nations for far too many centuries. I ask you to refrain from entering the debate about politics during this year of 2004 because it is only a distraction from your work for God. There has never been a cause for the sainting of a person who told humanity that he or she was a politician, but that he or she made decisions and took action that directly reflected the Holy Gospel. You must become Christians primally and in all other things. This is the request of the Mother of God for Her children. Do you understand My desires? And, do you recognize that it is not because I wish to censor your freedom in your country? The only exception is the day in November when the collective conscience of America speaks because it is an exercise in participation and exemplary of the acclamation that will occur at the end of time before the Throne of God. However, the latter shall be a wholly spiritual and judgmental one. Thus, you need not be too eccentric about hurrying to change your television channel just because they are speaking about politics. I ask that you do not engage these fora or study forensics about secularism that keep America's citizens so divided. I know that you have been busy praying and writing during the past several weeks to the benefit of humankind. The Angels offer their intercessions, and the Holy Spirit is your guide. You are speakers and practitioners of the Sacred Divine upon whom many will depend before the ages are through. Thank you! I am so pleased by your progress that I lack sufficient words to describe it. I will simply remind you that you are blessed. If only you knew what state of grace this implies, you would be jubilant beyond all telling..."

Sunday, February 1, 2004
Saint Pionius [3rd Century Martyr of Izmir, Turkey]
2:21 p.m.

"This moment of peace during which I speak is the remarkable signature of conciliatory Grace between God and mankind. I assure you that He hears your prayers as they are lifted into Heaven upon the plinth of My intercession. Thank you for trusting Me, My children. Bless you for heeding My call, for delivering the message of conversion and Salvation to the love-hungry world. Yes, you hear My voice, transcribe My words, and transfer them to those who are lost in darkness. Now as you see through the Wisdom of the Holy Spirit, you are echoing the same passages of Divine Truth that I pronounce to you. What does this mean? That you have become not unlike the Saints before you whose hearts were open to this Truth. You stand undaunted by threats of hatred and disdain that originate from your secular peers. You care not whether you are allowed entry in cliquish circles where people of high means celebrate their wares. I give you My promise that you own the riches of Creation by sharing the Love of God with everyone you know. You attest to the fact that human privilege is not in owning material wealth, but being in possession of the future of joy and happiness that Jesus has promised. Therefore, you must realize that these days are yours to pursue and to wield the bounty of the Grace of God to which I refer. Children, this is the month in 2004 when you shall celebrate the completion of 13 years as My humble messengers. Year 14 will come, and 15, and so on until the Lord says that our work is through. I tell you that the greatest benefit of your dedication to Me has yet to arrive. You will leap with joy and smile broadly because you will see that by giving yourselves to Jesus through My Immaculate Heart, you will achieve everything for which you have pined. Indeed, I have given you beautiful messages throughout the past 13 years, and I know you will deploy them for the advancement of the conversion of humanity in ways known between yourselves and the patriarchy of the Holy Spirit. I have not given sentence fragments or the parsing of words, I have offered lofty speeches that you will deliver to your lost brothers and sisters before the end of time. And, they will weep in gladness to sustain you, just as you have been elated to be loyal to Me. You might wonder why there have been times during which I have spoken so prolifically, and others when I have been concise. The answer is because I understand your length of days, the precision of the hours, the strength of your spirit, and your work planned for tomorrow. I have come to enlighten you, not to wear you down. I speak of uplifting the Earth in spiritual revelation, not always of chastisement. I wish for you to know your Mother as your Matriarch of Peace, to turn to Me when you are lonely and afraid. I expect that you will call on Me for help during times of duress, and these are the reasons I speak to you and intercede for you before the Cross of Jesus. God wills that you turn to Me the way Jesus did when He walked upon the mortal Earth. My dear ones, Jesus is still as dependent on Me in your day to awaken your slumbering hearts so that you will invoke the Holy Spirit to usher the Kingdom of God into the world. Please grant My Son the gift He desires. Give Him the best of yourselves, the noble chambers of your hearts, and the deepest strength you can muster. My Special and Chosen ones, this is precisely what you are doing. To the former, there was a time when you could never have written with the overpowering brilliance by which you are authoring your manuscripts. However, you gave yourself to Me. You said 'yes' instead of 'no.' And, the fruits of your compliance are sweet to Jesus' taste. You are giving Him the harvest of human souls by His agony on the Cross to Heaven that awaits you. It is true that the Holy Spirit creates your works because you can scarcely read them without weeping from joy. This is the fulfillment that I am seeking in you. Weep all you must, for this is what I have come to achieve. I wish to turn your sorrow into joy, and this is irrefutable proof that the Mother of God is succeeding. This month will bring the beginning of Lent, and it is imperative for My children to receive the Sacrament of Confession. We have spoken about this at length in past years. The Sacrament of Reconciliation is your union with the holiness of Heaven while you reside in earthly exile. Thank you, My Special son, for doing everything I have asked for the last 13 years to perfection. We will speak more about this three weeks from today. Thank you for placing your life in the sanctity and protection of My Immaculate Heart. You remember that this is the anniversary of the loss of the Columbia travelers. You often say that every day is the anniversary of something. It seems that humanity recalls only the solemn and poignant things. Here is one from 1968. You are seeing a vision of a point-blank shooting during the Vietnam war that shocked the civilized world, a moment of infamy, exposing the corruption of man. *(Our Lady mentioned the picture of the officer who executed a Viet Cong prisoner before a contingent of journalists.)* What do you feel when seeing this vision? Repulsion, horror, and repugnance? Yes, all of these. This is what God endures when witnessing the world's wars. Humanity regularly refuses to heed the call of conscience that I have summoned for hundreds of years. My cherished son, you are mitigating these issues. You are making the Lord happy;

you are alleviating His sorrow; you are lessening His grief, and you are consoling His Crucified Son. Please repeat the quotation that bloomed from your heart last evening, and record it in this message, *...and may the hues of our future rainbows never be blanched by the sting of old fears that shall no longer abide.* This is the hope through which you are offering your Savior comfort and rest. You have given Him your heart, and this is what is most important. I wish to offer you the most compelling words I have ever said. The Son of Man will come calling with gifts of kindness for the sacrifices you have made because you are blessed beyond your own imagining..."

Sunday, February 8, 2004
St. Jerome Emiliani [AD 1481-1537]
3:18 p.m.

"Now, I come to visit My children who are laboring in earnest to offer My messages of Love and conversion to humanity as they are dependent upon you. Today is February 8, 2004. It is special because it connects linear time, past and future, and represents another installment of your daily lives where the Lord has deigned to bring you to perfection in the Sacrifice of His Son. It provides a venue for recollection, preparation, and perspective. You have lived many years under this date, but none as unique as this. I tell you over and again that the newness of life is repeated once the morning breaks the eastern horizon. Let us be happy and joyful, and let us sing with jubilation that someday you will be coming home. I give you My promise that I will do everything in My power to strengthen your resolve, clarify your faith, and refine your focus. I will pray for you and with you. My Christian sons, Creation stands waiting for the fruitful completion of your work during these cold winter days in Illinois. Your homeland is prepared for the piety that you are recording in your manuscripts. Humankind is the beneficiary of your determination to succeed in your emulation of Jesus. Therefore, let us think about them in prayer. Remember the millions of people who have no one to comfort and protect them. Pray for those who are dying in battle and for their families who mourn them. Ask the Lord to heal the thousands who are becoming disabled, blinded, lamed and afflicted by the waging of war, by disease, famine, and the darkness that has overcome the continents of the world due to human sin. Lift your hearts to Heaven in memory of those who have died in the process of living for others. Remember the Saints and Martyrs of the Church who offered their mortality for the Salvation of their brothers and sisters. Yes, My children, there is still plenty of praying to do. You can take solace in the fact that you see the aging of the Earth because you are young and simple in your attitudes of faith. You know right from wrong because the Holy Spirit is instructing you. You have chosen the better course of life because you are practitioners of

Divine Love. This strengthens you, it gives you reason to proceed, it gives you hope, and it provides redirection and maturity. We pray for everyone to come to the Cross so they can know the worthiness of the righteous Truth you have embodied. February brings the anticipation of a new Spring which will arrive next month. This is your time to make a difference before the Dayspring of Jesus' Return in Glory. I ask you to cast away everything that causes you sorrow, and pray for the lifting of burdens that sadden you. Let God be God, and He will raise you on the path of holiness where your spirit will never be brought to despondence again. I am your Mother of Perpetual Help, and I come seeking My children who are crying-out from their impoverished shells. I will leave no helpless child behind. I wish to offer your souls to Jesus, and your open hearts will make it so. I herald the Good News of Salvation because this is the Will of the Father who sends Me. I am the Mother of Redemption. I am your Eternal Queen!

My Special son, how awesome and holy is the writing you are penning in your most recent chapter of *To Crispen Courage*. It makes me weep happy tears to see the Holy Spirit in your heart guiding your thoughts and words so the final product of your piety will be the conversion of millions. I ask you to ponder what your brothers and sisters around the globe are doing this day. How many of them are writing about the Crucifixion of the Son of Man and His Sorrowful Mother? There are not multitudes or thousands. You are one of a few in six billion people who are penning your memories about the Mother of God. This should not make you sad, but elated and pleased that you are exalting the revival of human life, that of the intercession of the Mother of Jesus Christ and the blessings that God is bestowing upon humanity through the Sacred Mysteries of the Holy Trinity. You do well because you choose life well. You see righteousness clearly because your heart is ajar. You are sanctified because you have become holy. You yearn for the coming of a perfect world because through these years with your brother, you are helping purify it. You are fashioning a life of goodness to share with humanity because you began on the foundation of miraculous Truth. You said yes, and this has made all the difference not only for you, but for millions who will be brought to Paradise by experiencing the supernatural eloquence of your works. Can you imagine the reception you will have in Heaven? Are you aware that its inception has already occurred, and that you are the passing of only a few years from seeing it firsthand? We go forth in hope and happiness. I pray for you and your brother in ways that are beyond your comprehension. How I love you! You must know this, you must realize this by now! And equally important, you and your brother have proved your loyalty, allegiance, and love for Jesus. Every day that expires is another step toward eradicating the influences of evil in your midst and around the globe. This is why your brother's work is so complementary. Through the decades, his writing has become like yours; commanding, concise, and purposeful. The Lord works through your lives. This is how the New Covenant Gospels were written by the Holy Spirit and dictated to Saints Matthew, Mark, Luke, and John. My Special son, I wish for grand happenings as the Mother of God. I pray for world peace, for the end of suffering, for the propagation of Christianity on every continent, and for the helpless to be given due care wherever they may be, in the womb or already born. And, I wish I could find the words to thank you for everything you mean to Jesus and to the Redemption of the human race. If there was anything greater I would wish, it would assuredly be this. For now, I can only say 'well done' and ask you to accept that I truly mean it. Someday, you will see this simple accolade blossom into a celebration of gratitude that will overtake the Earth. I promise that I am speaking the Truth. Please pray for those afflicted with congenital birth defects. Many of them may not be healed over the years, but they learn to cope. This is the way broken people survive in the temporal world. It has always been the same. And, perhaps coping is a form of healing; it is overcoming adversity by telling the affliction that your love for God is greater than anything else. Healing involves these visions that we have discussed before."

Sunday, February 15, 2004
St. Sigfrid, Apostle of Sweden [11th Century]
4:27 p.m.

"My children, you celebrate time-honored traditions and memories, and My messages are among them because they remain beyond the ages. I speak about human love that transcends all imagining, and of Truth outlasting the expanse of perpetuity. I embrace you as My sanctified little children, and I commend you to the sacred beauty of the ethereal Absolution that is bestowed upon you by none other than My Crucified Son. Today, I speak about much more than simple new beginnings. I wish to tell you about the brilliance of a billion suns breaking past the horizon so that all the world will realize what unity lives inside the sovereignty of God's Divine protection. The sublime purpose of My speaking to you is as it has always been, that humanity will finally comprehend that shared nobility and common sacrifices are products of your fruitful existence in God. Your duty and mission should be to one-day, and for all and everlasting, become assimilated within and consumed by the Most Blessed Trinity. Being mortal on Earth is not just a station, it is a process. These are your defining days to make the difference that the generations before you could have only dreamed of accomplishing. God has brought the prospective of the 21st century to bear upon your shoulders, and the hopes of an entire humanity and the strength of its nations are dependent on your response. Will you walk by faith and trust in His Light? Will you turn away from sin and implore your brothers to follow? Do you believe in the Profession of Faith to the limits of your being? Provocative orators from past centuries pined about the world to come, the one they would be unable to perceive from their side of time. They spoke of yearning for the healing of a broken Creation which has been bequeathed to you. My children, millions upon millions of them died before realizing their dreams, and I have come to ask you to offer their dreams back to them. I am urging you to search beyond breaths and tolls, and books and bells. Your Mother has come beseeching the children who were given to Me by Jesus on the Cross to take back the righteousness you hold so dearly from the secular thieves who are slowly but surely stealing it. What will come of the future if you decline? Will there be any beauty left in Creation beneath the rainbows I have promised? Has the pricelessness of the heart been supplanted by the distractions of materialism and lust? Your Mother comes weeping in jubilation, and yet filled with sorrow because My lost children are turning away. Not another child in its mother's womb will be aborted from its shelter if the world's Christians refuse to allow it. Why the silence? Why the indifference? Why, oh why, do My children turn their heads as though it is none of their concern? God help you! There is no such thing as same-sex marriage! There are no values to accompany decisions being made by the cloaked representatives of Satan in America's courts! I hope when you hope because I understand My children's frustration. I have seen the end of time, and I have witnessed the horrible annihilation that will befall peoples and republics that refuse to practice the Commandments of God. I have already seen the awful bloodshed and heard the wailing and screaming of those who are responsible for the apostasies that are occurring in America today. When I urge you to dream, I am not referring to a slumbering indifference or casualness. I am speaking about an awakening of the conscience of men, women, and children alike. I ask you to imagine with all the hope in your hearts what human life can be when everyone understands the implications of Divine Truth. Love is neither liberal nor conservative, nor is it left or right. True Love is knowing and believing rightness, and refusing to espouse everything that is wrong. Love is not social disenfranchisement or the power to attract the mobs. It means being little in the simple things that will usher-in a new age of sacrifice. Love means understanding the motivations of all the James Robert Kennedys* of the world, and reaching-out to communicate with them through the healing of the Cross. Love means losing when everything else is on the line, and winning when it is the last thing expected. Love means handing-over the spoils of victory to the competitor who finishes last. Love means declining the splashy interviews, the confetti, and the strobing lights. Love means giving everything to help your brothers triumph, and then allowing them to see you working even harder in God's vineyard when they come to offer thanks. There are no laurels upon which you can rest! This is not what your life on Earth is for. I repeat to you that living is not a product, it is a process. Every minute of the day, every hour, every dream, every hope, every tear, every moment that you walk and speak in the language of Jesus Christ is your imitation of the Providence of Heaven. All the physical issues to which you attend should be for this purpose, and for enhancing your spiritual faith, and that of your families and community of friends.

God has been good to you. He has led you from the desert and nourished you with the Manna of Life. He has surrounded you with an environment capable of sustaining you for decades and generations. He has spoken to you through the Prophets, taught you through the Wisdom of the Holy Spirit, admonished you by the howling of Nature, and became Incarnate in the Flesh of His own Son. What is a Mother to do? What must I say? You are given the present-hour to speak on His behalf so that, should there be any children of your children, and children of theirs, they will know that Charity, Love, and Hope abide with them because you cared enough to preserve everything you could possibly learn about God for their future. I am the Immaculate Conception. Do you know what this means? Do My people stop for an instant to consider what manifestations have come before them in the Dogma of the Immaculate Conception? If nothing else, please spread the word that a Perfect Creature has come calling upon humanity to turn back to God. The assailants against pious goodness, hope, purity, and charity that are running rampant in the United States must be crushed. Tell them, My children, about My Sacred Heel. Show them the holy relics depicting the Mother of Jesus Christ stomping the head of evil into the ground. I must and I already have. I hold so much hope for My children because, as I have said, I have seen the end of time. I have seen your ultimate victory inside the Triumph of My Immaculate Heart. This is why I ask you to be happy. The process about which I have spoken today is unfolding more quickly than many are willing to admit. They are not blind, but are refusing to see. The process of human life is unwinding, the good and bad. I know that you feel blessed to be participating in a way that is enhancing God's Kingdom. Please do not worry. Although you are filled with angst about the things that have gone awry, I am confident that the righteous among you will ultimately succeed. My Special son, next week will bring the date of February 22, 2004, which is thirteen years of My messages. They have not been just any thirteen years, but the most productive that you and your brother have lived. This is not My doing, it is yours. I am comforted that you trust in the clarity of your own wisdom to place things in perspective, continuing to cling to the higher purposes of God. I am pleased that you understand what efforts are put into making people champions and how awesome it is to see a spaceship rocket into the void of outer-space. I am not disappointed by your interest in them, but millions of others do not understand that everything in which they are participating is transcended by the spiritual realms. Jesus has asked Me to bless you for taking care of your brother. You have paid his passage through school, fed and clothed him, and stayed close to him in the hope you share for the changing of the world. Do you remember that I promised that you would have a definitive effect on defeating one of the most nefarious institutions on Earth, the American media? If you stay the course that you are traveling, write your books, be patient while your brother finishes his studies, place the events of your workplace in perspective, and accept the hours of life as they pass, you will defeat that monster! I have told My messengers at every shrine that has been officially recognized and those that have not that I cannot succeed unless My children consent to help. Too many have refused in the past, and this is the reason why there is such darkness on Earth. You are walking by faith, and there is no clearer way of seeing. Thank you for being such a good listener, writer, and spiritual child..."

James Robert Kennedy is an individual portrayed by Cuba Gooding Jr. in the motion picture 'Radio,' an account of how one man's compassion changed the life of a developmentally disabled person and the hearts and minds of his hometown.

Sunday, February 22, 2004
Feast of the Chair of St. Peter, Apostle
2:36 p.m.

"Ah!—Mine eyes have also seen the Glory of the Coming of the Lord! And, He is filled with splendor, Mercy, kindness, absolution, compassion, Wisdom, charity, peace and Love! I have given My Son to humanity that you may be saved. On this auspicious day in the lives of My Special one and Chosen one, I continue to offer My Intercessory Grace because you are My pious little helpers in the conversion of the world. What does this mean, 13 years? What implications does My miraculous presence here with you offer to the lost? With your help, I am offering guidance, sustenance, support, and Truth to the people whom God has regained in the Crucifixion of Jesus on the Cross. Every single person in Creation needs a mother. I am your Mother! I am the Immaculate Conception and your Queen of Heaven! Come unto Me for nourishment and consolation, and I will feed you the Love of Almighty God in the Second Person of the Blessed Trinity. I ask you to no longer be afraid of the perils of the world—be wary of them, but no longer fear the things that cannot harm you from the exterior of your soul. You belong to the Resurrected Son of Man! How happy you must be to know that sin has been wiped from the face of the Earth. My little ones, we have brought Light and joy to countless hearts over the expanse of the past thirteen years. In Communion with the Church, you have grown in faith and trust that the Will of God is the purpose of your lives. You have overcome hardship, temptation, persecution, and the despair which comes with the rejection of your families and friends. You have given of your spiritual and physical labors so that human suffering can be alleviated. You have sacrificed your lives so that the hopes and dreams of untold numbers of your brothers and sisters can be fully realized. And, most of all, you have loved in the likeness of My Son. You are one in the genuine affection that God has for His Creation because you have said yes to your Mother of Perpetual Help. My message to you today is that we will continue into the future in the knowledge that your work is yet unfinished. I ask you to give My blessing and Love to My little Mary Jane and Laura, and to all the hundreds and thousands who know that this is your Anniversary Day. Feel free to publish this message for the masses and throngs who have been silently praying for you at their bedsides to conclude their days. Remember with fondness how they have stood beside you in faith. Honor with your own blessing the tens-of-thousands who have read your books, especially those who are heeding the call of My messages. You are not alone—you were never meant to be alone. You are all one in the Holy Spirit, one in heart and soul in your participatory attendance at the daily Holy Sacrifice of the Mass, and certainly one humanity in your supplications, petitions, and prayers.

Please tell your Bishop that I am not unmindful of the tremendous burden that rests upon his shoulders as the leader of his flock here in this Diocese. Tell him that I love him. Indeed, tell him that the Mother of His God is protecting him with the power of all the Angels! It is peace that Jesus gives you; and I give you Jesus. I ask you all to place the power of human suffering in greater perspective. Realize that once there are no longer any sinful acts by humanity, suffering will cease. This is why it is so urgent for you to continue to pray and work for the conversion of the world. Pray for the elimination of the extremism in America and worldwide that is making such a mockery of human decency. When you do these things, My children, you will see that the world and all its people will become united once again. For that purpose, for the mission of your lives, and for the happiness of your future, I commend you all to the Grace and Sanctity of The Divine Mercy of My Sacrificed Son—The Christ—who is your shield and protector. As you enter this 2004 Season of Lent, let your sacrifices and almsgiving be a reminder to you that you are the people of a God who is filled with charity and forgiveness. And, for one of the few times in the history of the world, allow the manifestations you see as reflections of Truth in your remembrance of *The Passion* to take you closer to complete understanding of the power of Perfect Love. Thank you, My children. Thank you for saying with complete abandonment that you will stand by your brothers and sisters until the last day is done. Remember the words of St. Paul, that you can stand with eyes aloft and hope elevated when you see your Savior's Holy Face and tell Him that you have fought the good fight, that you have finished the race, and that you are begging with every sense of contrition in your soul for the Crown of Salvation that awaits you. This is a happy day, My children. It is a Rite of Passage that this Anniversary should come, and that you should still be here with Me, praying and hoping for the cultivation of the world. Be hopeful and happy because the reward which will soon be dispensed to you will be great. This, My Special and Chosen ones, is My message for you today. It is My commendation that you continue to realize that you are succeeding in the existence of human life. I will be here with you long beyond the end of the mortal ages. Indeed, I will be with you beyond Eternity, your Everlasting Life in Jesus. Thank you for having responded to My call..."

Sunday, February 29, 2004
For the Poor Souls in Purgatory
10:55 a.m.

"Now comes your Immaculate Mother to pray with you for the conversion of lost sinners and the healing of the brokenhearted. My children, this is a leap-year message about contrition, servitude, and self-sacrifice for the 2004 penitential Season of Lent. Your labors are inundating the Lord's vineyard with Wisdom, and your wholesome lives manifest charity around the globe. God sees your work in Jesus as the exalted fruits of change for His Kingdom. Thank you for persevering in faith that the Son of Man will deliver you to Heaven. Today, I am touched and overjoyed that Christians everywhere are culling the noblest from their hearts and consciences to assuage the torment of others' suffering. While Jesus told Creation that the poor will always be among you, He admonishes you to help lift them out of poverty onto the plateau of dignity. When you give of yourselves, your wealth, and the prayers you offer for them, you lead the sacrificial lives that mean so much to the poor. In response, I intercede for you because I know that you are heeding My call and placing My messages into practice. To cause the Mother of God to smile places you in good standing before Jesus. Thank you for helping Me reach humanity. I have urged My children to pray for the Poor Souls in Purgatory who cannot help themselves. Remember that they are calling-out to the Faith Church on Earth for your holy blessings and intercessory petitions. Pray for them in your morning matins and primes and before you recline to sleep for the night. Imagine what agony they are enduring because they desire to enter the Light of Heaven, but cannot secure it on their own. If you embrace their plight in communion with My intercession, Jesus will hear our petitions and allow them to savor the Eternal Life they shall find in Paradise. Thank you for helping them see the Face of God with indescribable jubilation. There are many other reasons to pray during the Season of Lent. The scourge of abortion must be eradicated not only from public laws, but from the hearts of expectant mothers. You must always recall that the purpose of your lives is for love, and this is why I come to you, to strengthen your love and ask you to raise your concern for wayward sinners. I have told you that prayer for your brothers and sisters is one of the greatest gifts of consolation and peace that you can offer them. Love is about factual healing, and healing is about thanksgiving. The mission to which you have been assigned brings great holiness to the world because humanity becomes united in the sanctity of the Cross. There have been many authors who have written about individualism and your right to be liberated from the burdens and encumbrances that are heaped upon you by the malfeasance of other men. There is true liberty in Christianity because you are freed from sin, and yours is the honor of helping your brothers break free from the bondage of their own transgressions. Humanity is reluctant to forgive sins if you do not believe that it is possible for someone as powerful as God to forgive them as well. Your espousal of the Holy Gospel is important in teaching your brothers and sisters about the expiation of human corruption in Jesus' Crucifixion. My children, Lent offers as many opportunities to learn about yourselves as the people living in your presence. What do you suffer for the Lord, and why do you suffer? If you place these questions in the perspective of the Cross, you will see that it is so that all can be saved, not just the people you celebrate and admire. If there had been sufficient prayers throughout the ages, do you suppose there would have been such horrible wars, ethnic cleansing, and terrorist acts like that of September 11, 2001? With the rhetorical nature of My question, you should realize that prayer for the spiritual conversion of humanity must become the highest priority of your lives. Wars and terrorism are not punishments from God, they are the result of a lack of cohesion among the Earth's diverse peoples. I am here of God's accord, and I have spoken to you so the Holy Spirit can manifest in millions of hearts the intense desire to see humankind united beneath one sign of hope, the Holy Cross of Jesus Christ. If everyone believes that it is possible for humanity to become perfected in Him, then you will accomplish it. This, My children, is among the goals you must achieve. Share the knowledge that your souls have been sanctified in Jesus' Blood; instill this hope with all the encouragement you can muster, and your lost brothers and sisters will imitate your holiness. Elevate your petitions to Jesus through Me, and I will help you pray..."

Sunday, March 7, 2004
SS. Perpetua and Felicity, Martyrs [d. AD 203]
3:58 p.m.

"My children, I implore your intercessions for world peace in a crucial way because God is inclined to allow the battle for wayward souls to ensue with great ferocity. What does this mean? How can humanity sustain these awful struggles? You must remember that you are called to the Holy Cross for strength, courage and Wisdom, and you are asked to follow the footsteps of

Christ. In doing so, you realize the sacrifices that are required to secure a meaningful and lasting peace. Sadly, the conflicts of these days have little to do with Christian evangelization or goodness, but are about imperialism and profiteering. This brings an opportunity to magnify your intentions for the alleviation of human suffering in ways that are remedial for its poorest victims. Their perspective is one of frustration because they are not accorded the transparency that flows so prevalently in the Free World. Innocent people in distant lands are seeing their homes destroyed and children massacred without warning. What do they make of this unimaginable horror? You identify with their feelings of chaos and fear. Please pray for the end of war, for those who are suffering its neglects to know that they will be freed from strife. The pathway to peace is to pursue the campaign for righteousness, not partisan bickering or financial gain. We celebrate today the birthday of a humble man who came to Heaven on January 31, 1997. Jack Smedley was acquainted with many Illinoisans, and he lives with the Angels and Saints, breathing freely the peace of the Dominion of the Lord. Why do I refer to him? Because his destiny has been fulfilled; he was raised by Jesus' Crucifixion to the summit of Truth. He endured countless adversities to prosper his message of simple service, humility, and the giving of his life for the dignity of his family and friends. Yet, he did much more. He gave of himself so his enemies would know him as a child of God. I call you to invoke his intercession through the Redemption that Jesus bestowed upon his soul. My Special son, you know that this is the Season of Lent, and Jesus asked you for a moment last Wednesday to feel what He suffers when humanity spurns His Sacrifice. Imagine the sorrow Jesus undergoes when He sees the sinners He has saved turn their backs on His Passion and Death, what He thinks about those who scoff at The *Passion of the Christ* that has been bequeathed to the nations through the power of the Holy Spirit. It is clear that you understand how others demean the purpose of this artful screenplay. Indeed, you have seen for yourself that they are wrong. I tell you these things, and yet I ask you to have faith in your brothers and sisters' capacity to change. Be patient while their eyes are opening to the vision that you have witnessed for years because it is a profile in suffering, conversion, and repentance. It is another manifestation of the wisdom spoken by Robert Kennedy Jr. last Wednesday evening. He was honored to receive your gift. He cherishes your kindness, and he will come seeking you someday. You listened to his oratory about the same concept of civility that you have learned from Me. You heard him revel the works of many you cited in your previous books, names like Lincoln, Whitman, Dickinson, and Merton. You have addressed these people's ideals because they held a single thought in mind; they shared the hope in which you likewise believe that humanity must be more devoted to God. Be gratified that you have placed your thoughts onto the printed page for the world to see because it lends emphasis to the fact that Jesus is guiding your way. We speak of the requisitions of God from His exiled flock, not that you must pay the debt for your transgressions against Him because Jesus has acquitted them on the Cross. However, the Father will call lost sinners to account for their indifference and to believe that Jesus has redeemed them. Even in all the suffering that the Lord allows, He is never meanspirited or cold-hearted. Thus, there is no lack of mercy in your castigations. Jesus inspired *To Crispen Courage* to touch those who decline to open their hearts in any other way. Be joyful in your work and realize that it is another titan, another pillar upholding the Kingdom of God on Earth..."

Sunday, March 14, 2004
St. Leobinus, French Bishop [6th Century]
3:58 p.m.

"As your journey through Lent continues for 2004, I ask you to remember that your strength is your faith, and the signs for the long road ahead reside in your Love for Jesus. As you emulate that great devotion for the purification of humanity that My Son has for His created people, ponder anew how He felt while the world awaited His great Passion and absolving Sacrifice. You have often considered the Feast of Christmas as the happiest time of the year, but I wish for you to also pray deeply about the imminent Easter Triduum that you shall celebrate in a few weeks' time. Your Lord sees every trial and tribulation that you face during your walk of mortality upon the Earth. Indeed, He has been there before you. He knows of the darkest hours of your grief and loneliness, and how you are tempted by the forces of evil to leave the pathways of righteousness. Remember Jesus' responses when He was tempted in the desert. Man does not live by bread alone. Hold deeply in your heart the certitude by which Jesus remembered the reason why He was born as Man. Hold inside your thoughts all the ways that My Jesus stayed with you, even until Death. And, ponder the many ways that He recalled that the Holy Spirit was within Him while He completed the course for you. He said to Creation in the desert that God could not be tempted to forsake the people He came to save. Yes, please always acknowledge this commendation of Love that He continues to bestow upon you as you live-out the days of Lent 2004. It is wholly true that you must become like Jesus in order to accompany Him back to the Light of Paradise. Let no mortal man ever try to persuade you to believe that you are incapable of perfect Love. I have told you on a number of occasions that you will be ostracized for embracing the Truth of Christianity by your fellow sinners. You will be cast-away as dreamers and zealots. Your faith will be looked upon as the making of fanatics. However, My children, please stay the course with Me in assuring your detractors that you belong to the same Christ who is the meaning of life and the making of your seamless perfection from this life into the next. I have given you the benisons of a grateful God because you have not yielded to the forces of doubt that accompany so many along your journey through Lent and through human existence entire.

When you pray for the cultivation of the world during this Holy and Sacrificial Season, I ask you to remember to ask Jesus to rescue those who are being punished for their faith. Ask Him to deliver the downtrodden back to the sweetness of their dignity again. It is not too late for you to ask God to end abortion with swiftness and jurisprudence. I know that you often wonder how it can be true that so many unborn children have died in a land which purportedly so values a single life. Americans somehow believe that unborn children are expendable commodities that can be destroyed at the will of its doctors and the faithless mothers who bear these tiny ones in their wombs. And, yet, others are known as criminals if they inadvertently take the life of a child in the womb whose mother 'intends' to bring it to birth. How can the former be called a practitioner of the medical profession and the latter a murderer? The Truth and Light about the sanctity of human life is that an unborn child is a living human being from the very moment God places a soul inside a mother. There is no room for debate in the matter of protecting the sanctity of unborn human life. This Season of Lent is an appropriate time for all My children to ask God to end the scourge of abortion once and for all. Christians everywhere should band together in a united front against the enemies of unborn human life. You should marshal your forces to protect the innocents who ask with silent anticipation for the opportunity to be delivered to birth. This, My dear ones, is My special request for you today.

And, to My Special and Chosen ones, I realize that you also understand the value of the sacrifices you make during Lent and for the whole of the Liturgical Year. You recognize the cleansing power of the Rite of Reconciliation and the peace you feel inside because you are so good. Thank you in all ways for living the holiness that I have so invoked you to embrace. And, My Special one, I wish to tell you something that your brother said to Me and the Angels as his bedtime prayer last night and upon awakening again this morning... I tell you this now so you would know that this is a serious dedication that he is offering to you with the intercession of Me. He said in his prayer that he has seen generations of awesome people come and go before him. He has seen the summits of the mountain ranges at the U.S. continental divide. He has seen the whitecaps of the Atlantic Ocean from thousands of feet in the air. He has seen the ancient cities of places like Dubrovnic in all its elegance, and all the cultures which have come together there. He has been to the summit of miracles at Medjugorje and also here. He has seen healings and conversions with his own eyes to rival no other age. And, he says that he has even seen the face of the Mother of his God. However, in all of these things, My Special one—of all the miracles that anyone could hope to see in a span of 50 years, the most profound and heart-touching is the way that you love him.

This eclipses anything and everything that he has ever seen, heard, or experienced. Jesus' legacy is alive and well in this 21st century world in you, and Creation is all the more blessed because God has given you life. And, you are sharing that life with your brother in a way that has miraculous overtones that not even I could impress upon his soul. This is his gratitude, My Special one. He shall always say 'yes' to Me and to your Savior not only of his own accord in Love, but because of the example that you have placed before him. When you get to Heaven someday soon, you will also see with great clarity the gratefulness that Jesus has for you. Jesus can rewrite history and reverse the effects of time. He can amend the course of human existence even after the annals of history are through. I wish for you to remember this all the days of your life. Why? Because Jesus will amend the course of human events based upon the lives of people like you. By simply living the way you do, with all the hoping and reaching-out to the poor, and praying with such dedication everyday, you will see upon your entrance into Paradise that many of the things you are concerned about now will have not even occurred.

My Special one, you can see that I am speaking to you of miracles again. Yes, I am referring to the miraculous manipulation of the times of Creation by the God who fashioned it. My Son can do anything He pleases with His Eternity and with His people. I ask for you to remember during the times when you are disappointed that history will be rewritten by the holy things you say and do. It will take all the power of the Saints among whose number you will join in many cases, but I assure you that goodness and purity will prevail. Women who have fallen to the temptations of lust will become virgins once again. Priests who themselves became victims of the forces of Satan will see that they were chaste all along. No one will have ever starved to death, they will have simply fasted for too long. I am speaking to you on this day in March 2004 about that remaking of the world—that breaking of a New Dawn that you say should have already come, the one that was meant to be. I come today, My Special son, to give you hope anew that your life in dedication to Jesus is of vital importance to the Son of your God Most High. Never despair, always be steadfast in hope, and know that Jesus is always near. And, where there is Jesus, there is the Holy Spirit, and the Mother of them both! Thank you for believing the miracle that is still unfolding before you now. Thank you so kindly for believing in Me, for understanding that God has given His humanity to Me as My children. Be confident in what you believe to the depths of your heart... I have completed the message that I came to offer you today. I am sure you can see how happy I am with you and your brother... Remember that no greater miracle has your brother ever seen than the way you Love him. I offer you both My holy blessing for today. ☦ I will speak to you again next week. Thank you for your prayers. I love you... Goodnight!"

Sunday, March 21, 2004
St. Serapion the Scholastic [4th Century]
2:33 p.m.

"My dear children, when Roman Catholic priests invoke the blessing of the Holy Spirit upon you at the conclusion of the Holy Sacrifice of the Mass, they pray that your thoughts are pleasing to God and your hearts sincere. In the hundreds of thousands of words I have stated during these years of miraculous messages, their crux is summed by what these priests say. It is My prayer for humanity too. I ask you to ponder as the Season of Lent ensues what it means to have thoughts that are pleasing to God. It is clear that you see best when you understand His righteousness best. I realize that there are numerous distractions from your lives of faith, especially here in America, and there are other matters that are simply indescribable through human language. When you do not know the meaning of a term, you use the dictionary. Paradoxically, what helps you learn? Other words. You learn new words by comparing them to ones with which you are familiar. This is called the use of synonyms; and oftentimes you discover the meaning of something by its opposite, or antonym. Hence, when I tell you that you should internalize Beatific Love, you must employ the Fruits of Love to comprehend it. God has created your hearts so they can draw the connection between the mortal and the Divine by knowing the correlation between earthly existence and Eternal Life. Jesus is the venue, the Way through whom you more wholly understand the nature of your being inside the Dominion of God. The Providence of the Will of the Father has paved the way for you to return to Heaven through His Crucified Son. You appreciate the power of Jesus' Passion by suffering yourselves, and you actualize the meaning of Love by becoming perfect in Love. Therefore, I ask you to open yourselves to the possibility that this is achievable in your time. Can you become Saints while residing on Earth? This is yet to be seen. However, you can be crowned Saints the moment you take your last breath, and this is what Jesus expects. Your becoming Saints in the way of those who have passed into Glory is dependent upon the life you lead and the way you accept the divinity that God implants inside your hearts. My children, there are wide and varying opinions about the intentions of Lent in the Liturgical Year. Some view it as a time for self-denial, greater almsgiving, and momentum of prayer; and they see it rightfully so. However, others see Lent as a time when God looks at them disdainfully or when they are supposed to feel less than dignified compared to other times of the year. As for the latter, God does not wish for you to lessen your hopes for happiness or your accomplishments simply because you are observing Jesus' discernment in the desert. The purpose of Lent is to help you become more prayerful, to open your eyes to the world's suffering, and to induce you to let go of the material world and grasp things that are spiritual. When Ash Wednesday's decree is that you are dust and will return to dust, this does not imply that you have no value before the Father, it simply means that you will leave nothing spiritual behind when you die. I pray for a happy death for My children. I hope you understand the purpose of suffering from the purview of the Cross and recognize Sacrificial Love as being as benevolent. Truly, I ask you to place the Season of Lent in this context because I am setting your sights not only on the Crucified Christ, but also the Resurrected Christ. The purpose of My intercession is to raise you before Him as My blessed, purified, and cultivated children, fit for presentation to the Father in the Wounds of His Messianic Son. I urge you to remember that you are worth the price Jesus paid for your Redemption. There is joy in this, and primordial deliverance and maximum fulfillment.

    I come to this Illinois city to speak to My children about the springtime of hope and renewal inside the Sacred Heart of Jesus. The thawing of the Earth has begun, and I ask you to recognize the parable of Nature and your life in Jesus that is posed by the Lord. How do you offer your lives to God in Jesus' likeness? You become as much like Him as possible. You utilize the Fruits of Love to personify the meaning of Love. This is not a covert, philosophical, deeply theological series of events that is knowable only to certain intellectuals and biblical scholars. It is the simple plan that God has outlaid to seek the lost and forsaken to become part of His flock. Being open to Truth does not imply that you will never know what it means to be rekindled in Jesus. Your Mother is a simple Handmaid who seeks the millions upon Earth who have never known God, and to convert those who see Him as a random quantity separate from their animated being. I seek in you the openness of little children. These are the reasons for Lent, My praying ones. And My Special son, you are opening new doors of opportunity by preparing the record of your background. There is a subtle anxiety that comes with change because you meet people unlike those with whom you interacted in your formative years. There are different perplexities, strange environments, and a part of you that is emotionally attached to more familiar surroundings. You are required to relearn to fly instead of calling on your natural instincts. Are you sensing some of these things? The alternative is to stop dissecting the decisions of others with whom you work. Perform your labors; bring home your salary, and live in peace with the knowledge that anything that goes wrong cannot be blamed on you. On the other hand, there is a mammoth world around you that you can engage. Remember the perspective I asked you to adopt. These may be prime times for those who reject the holiness about which I speak, but they are drawing their dying breaths. Their propaganda is in shambles, their authoritarianism is drab, their spiritual indifference renders their opinions irrelevant, their haughtiness is in its last throes, and their legacies are worthless. Watch them die; watch their obstinance suffocate, and be pleased to see it. You are positioned as if on a glass elevator on its way up, and you can peer across at another glass elevator on its way down. You and your friends are rising, and your adversaries are falling. This transition is occurring, but you believe that circumstances are in stasis. You enjoy a vibrant life of reason, hope, and justice. Your enemies are descending to their defeat, and God is positioning them for the impact. Watch them die. Goodness is on the rise and injustice is destined for the grave. The expiration of the years causes you to feel insecure, but you must allow God's Creation to unfold. Are you one who would have prohibited the soldiers from driving the nails into Jesus' Hands? What did He say that day? Get behind Me! And, since you live the Resurrected Christ, you are seeing the last actions of the evil He destroyed. You understand in the same way that Pope John Paul II has lived his life. God's Plan is unfolding as it should. You are on the pathway of the Passion with Pope John Paul II and all righteous people who want every tint of evil wiped from your presence. In the meantime, there are sinners to convert to Christianity. I have said this time and again. I appeared by apparition to Pope John Paul II and told him the same thing. You must allow God time to lead His Triumph through My Immaculate Heart. Please keep your spirit aloft and remember that the Truth prevails in Eternity. You are a good boy, and I love you beyond your comprehension. Thank you for taking care of your brother. The two of you comprise a gallant unity against the forces you despise. Thank you for facilitating the eradication of evil and praying that it will be done..."

Sunday, March 28, 2004
Saint Tutilo of Switzerland [10th Century]
2:40 p.m.

"It is with magnified hope and adulation that I pray with you as you nestle in your little room, asking the Lord to convert your lost brothers and sisters to the Cross, heal broken humanity, and ensure the nativity of the unborn. Together, we realize the Will of the Father through the Divine Love that we share in Him. How do you know what it means to remain so true? The answer is to be in agreement with His wishes. Thank you, My children, for giving yourselves to righteousness, to the warmth of the human heart that brings consolation to many through the end of days. You are not isolated, My children, and you are never alone. You are strong because your vitality is bolstered by the Wisdom of the Holy Spirit. You are not hopeless because the Love you receive in the Sacred Heart of Jesus is your expectation that your mortal lives will culminate in the victory of all victories—the Triumph of My Immaculate Heart. Today, you heard your pastor speak about the imperative of forgiveness, without which no dissension can be reconciled. I have spoken about this since February 22, 1991 and embodied the providential signs of human coalescence since My Immaculate Conception in My mother's womb.

I ask you to give your hearts to Me so I can shape them into florid bouquets worthy of adorning the mantles of Heaven. My kindness is revealed in My dedication to you, and yours through your compassion for your prodigal brothers and sisters. Do not desist, dear children! Never surrender to the darkness or loss of vision that befalls those who refuse to turn to Jesus for relief. High are the mountaintops and deep are the valleys! The reach of your insights is far because you possess Divine Truth to see beyond your own environment into the excellence of Eternity. We are speaking about the intersection of your earthly existence and Everlasting Life. Can you sense this miraculous undertaking that God ordains for the purification of His people? You touch objects with your hands, and the sighted examine them with their eyes, but I ask you to see Paradise through the conversion of your souls. Should someone read *In Our Darkest Hour: Morning Star Over America*, he will know that God is the Ruler of Nations and Jesus the King of Creation. The Earth at its finest is their handiwork because the perpetuity of your Salvation is ensured. Perhaps not within your immediate sight, but the world is converting, and you are the reason. My Special son, I come for the beauty that you permit Me to see, and I recognize God's Kingdom by your actions. While men adore His gracefulness in the architectures of Nature, I see the gallantry of heroes in your inspirited heart. Please remain undaunted by the disharmony of the world. Jesus is with you in the Holy Eucharist. Thank you for leading an exemplary life. Remember that you are forever My obedient child..."

Palm Sunday, April 4, 2004
St. Isidore of Seville [AD 560-636]
10:12 a.m.

"My children, I appear physically and spiritually in your midst to advance the cause of human conversion in a world still marred by sin. Today, we observe Jesus' entrance into Jerusalem and His impending Passion, and we pray that the modern Earth receives His sacredness with promise, compliance, sincerity, and honor. Little ones, you have seen supernatural events unfold on many feast days while enduring the casualties of ordinary time. These are gifts from God who has never forsaken you, He who seeks your acceptance of the Gospel message as your journey to the Cross is manifested. Today, there is much indifference toward My Son's Crucifixion and multiple offenses against His chastity. Like a young child, I console Jesus during these times as He sees the wars and impurities that sinners decline to renounce. His Sacred Heart is aching, as is Mine, over the desecration of the holy relics that God has placed around the globe as signs and wonders to strengthen your faith. If you believe in them, gladness will brighten your future upon these lands where you were birthed as imperfect babes. I shed copious tears because not all My children accept Salvation in Jesus' Blood on the Cross. Yet, I am emboldened by the faith of Christians who practice humility, good will, and servitude among men. If humanity understood what it means to offer a timely apology, a gesture of kindness or mutual absolution, the communication between you would be filled with pardon and peace. God asks this from you, that you shall become united in the Messiah who dignifies your lives and saves your souls. He commends you to the strength that is garnered by your prayers, and He offers the subsistence of the Blessed Trinity as your guide and protection. You receive every awareness about Eternal Life through the Wisdom of the Holy Spirit. Indeed, the fullness of your genius is given by Jesus Christ, the Perfect Man and Incarnation of the Father whom you exalt. I pray for My children on Palm Sunday. I ask you to recognize that the signs and blessings filling your years are purposeful beyond all telling. They are manifestations of God's Love for the people He has deigned to save. My Special and Chosen sons, thank you for your dedication to your peers, for your charity, and for charting a course to the unfettered Grace of holiness. You are in the world, but belong to Me, and therefore to Jesus. With all the majesty of My Immaculate Heart, I offer My appreciation for your help in everything I have asked. Yes, as the springtime comes and the breezes blow fair and the peonies bloom, remember that My Love is as clement and benign. I realize that you seek new ways to glorify God, to admonish those who violate His Will, and to advance Christianity on every corner of the globe. I cannot overstate that your reward in Heaven will be intense. Your eloquence and poetic images, your emphasis on the Sacred Scriptures, and the tenderness you offer the suffering prove that you are already the Saints you shall be in Heaven and God's instruments on Earth. Your Mother is touched by your desire to remain in My presence during these perilous times. I beg you to harbor hope for change because it will come, but too many of your brothers and sisters are still unprepared. The Return of the Son of Man will arrive more like a flash of lightning than the blooming of a flower. The signs you see are of His preeminent Grace, and they foretell that the culmination of the ages is near. The Children of Mary are positioned on the favorable side of history, and Jesus will soon appear and take you to your eternal rest. As for Christians, Saint Luke proclaims, ...*I tell you, He will judge in their favor, and do it swiftly. But, when the Son of Man returns, will He find faith upon the Earth?* [Luke 18:8]. God will pour Glory upon those who accept Me as the Mediatrix of Heavenly graces. I am the Mother who nurtures My children to spiritual health. It makes My Heart glow with satisfaction that you are praying for the conversion of humanity at the same time I intercede for you before Jesus. As you celebrate Holy Week, allow the Holy Spirit to be your enlightenment in the thoroughness of Heaven. Live-out the promises you made for Lent and reaffirm the commitments you offered My Son. Renew them often so the sanctity of human life can be sustained, even as the New Heaven and Earth are configured in fulfillment of the Scriptures. Holy Week is a period of reflection for Christians because you are united with Jesus in spirit, faith and practice, no matter how vast the distance between you. Come to life and be fruitful among the disciples who believe that the mortal Earth must defer to the Kingdom of God, for this is where your Salvation reigns. Thank you, My Special one, for fighting for this Truth. Stay with Me and know that you are in My infinite embrace. Let not your heart be troubled by dark things because they are from the dying past and will never be one with the beginnings that you have found in Jesus' Sacred Heart. Easter is a time for joy, renewal, enlistment, Resurrection, promise, hope, healing, and Grace. All of these belong to you because you are obedient to your Mother of Perpetual Help. Enjoy Holy Week as a blessing from our Creator, and take comfort praying with your brother to sanctify the Earth. Thank you for being united with him..."

Easter Sunday, April 11, 2004
St. Stanislaus, Bishop of Cracow [AD 1030-1079]
10:56 a.m.

"My dear children, on this Feast of the Paschal Resurrection of Jesus Christ, the Son of Man, let us pray that every flaw will be eradicated from the hearts and minds of God's creatures. Only then will nations live in peace; only then will there be hope for lost sinners. Your Mother is pleased that you have chosen to observe Easter by praying the Holy Rosary for the conversion of humanity. I have spoken in years past about the jubilation brought by the Resurrection of Jesus from the Sepulcher, and you are aware of the new life that this brings. Never forget to keep your spirit drawn to the Light that comes from the Feast of Easter! Even though your bodies grow old and frail through time, your Salvation is an endless gift from the Father. When you look around the globe, you see only few signs of hope and new life, and death and destruction. There is untold tyranny, oppression, poverty, disease, pilfering, murder, and licentiousness. My children, these things are real wrongdoings. They are manifestations of man's imperfection. Even as I urge you to be heartened because of the abundance of Easter, I also ask you to reach-out in prayer for the less-fortunate. I told you on September 16, 2001 that there would be another war that would spawn more casualties, that there would be thousands among the dead. You are seeing this happen not because you did not deliver My message sufficiently, but because God knew that humankind would refuse to turn away from vengeance. There may be greater carnage to come. I pray that it will be averted, but signs indicate that the obstinance of secular partisans is causing more degradation in lands far and wide. I ask you not to be despondent that lost sinners refuse to heed My call. Do not foster revenge against those who reject the Holy Gospel that I extol because the people responsible for foisting suffering on their peers will eventually judge themselves. Be confident in your service to Jesus and your allegiance to the Holy Spirit who provides your Wisdom to succeed. Be joyful in this Eastertide because you hail from Truth; you are My blessed children, and you belong to God of the High Kingdom who manifested the Triumph of My Immaculate Heart. My little ones, it would be easy to succumb to the grief that engulfs you. It might even be tempting to surrender the mission that I have asked you to complete. I understand your propensity to be despaired by the calamities of the world. However, your hope and My intercession are interwoven to sustain your trust in the Paschal Resurrection of My Son. If you give in to the darkness, then you do not comprehend the meaning of Divine Light. I recognize how you might say that it is easy for the Mother of God to declare that the world will have a happy ending because I am already in Heaven. I ask that you place yourselves in My Immaculate Heart, and your spirits will foresee Salvation. Never mind the defeats you suffer. Cast-off the deception that victories never come. Remember that the world swims in turmoil, that it stumbles over its own ineptitude before the mightiness of God. The inconsistencies between the happiness of Easter and the battlegrounds of Earth mark the distance between hope and reality, and I implore you to adopt a fresh vision based upon hope. I seek your willingness to usher-in God's Kingdom by not allowing sinful men to make you believe that the Earth will always be this way. This message is about creating an atmosphere of change, the catalyst of miraculous revelation that makes every individual realize that they are special before the Seat of Wisdom. This change evolves slowly, even by the hour, so that you rarely sense its presence. Let not the world burden you or make you lose faith in the Kingdom you are promised by the Resurrection of Jesus from the Tomb on Easter morning. My Special and Chosen ones, your prayers are received and answered. You belong to Me, and I acknowledge you as among the holiest ever to be vested by the profundity of God's Domain. As difficult as it may seem, this should be sufficient to keep your spirits aflame until the end of time. Thank you for helping your neighbors walking the Earth with you, for not being absorbed in intellectual materialism, and for not being mired in political divisions. Your steadfast focus on your mission is admirable. You know by My messages that I ask you to extend your lives beyond this day in time. Can you anticipate the promise with which I speak? Do you understand why I trust humanity, despite the circumstances around you? This is founded upon Eternal Truth, your source of perfect knowledge; and it is to this that your hopes are anchored. You have succeeded in the mission that Jesus asked of you. Anything more is added blessings. Everything you have done since *Morning Star Over America [first Diary]* is beyond the expectations that Heaven could have foreseen. You will discover as you age that you will be more mellow toward certain issues, and your mind will be trained on the spiritual things we pray about. Next week, I will speak about the Divine Mercy of Jesus, and how important it is for sinners to seek His forgiveness..."

Sunday, April 18, 2004
Feast of Divine Mercy
2:33 p.m.

"Now, My cherished children, I speak about the gift of Divine Absolution that Jesus bestows upon repentant and contrite hearts. I bring the Good News of eternal forgiveness because you emulate Jesus every day. Christians who practice their faith dutifully are tempted to perceive others who are lukewarm with eyes of disdain and indignation. However, even with all the errors in the world yet to be mitigated, God still loves you with infinite power. In all the obstinance through which lost sinners approach daily life, Jesus still offers His Divine Mercy to the penitent. Therefore, I call upon you to remember Sister Faustina, and always live the humility, sacrifice, and servitude that she gave Jesus during her earthly years. Faustina has been in Heaven since the moment she handed her soul to the Lord in death. Her hallmark is one of suffering for the conversion of wayward sinners, and the messages in her Diary are replete with hope. Jesus asks you to remember this day because His Divine Mercy is for those who seek to begin life anew. It is possible to be rebirthed in the spiritual beginning that He promises because His Crucifixion and Resurrection have expunged the effects of human sin from the shadows of the Earth. And, the Sacraments are given for the sanctity of those who receive them—for blessing, nurturing, vision, peace, and interior contemplation. This Feast is about many great things that are wholly and uniquely centered in the forgiveness that God mandates from His creatures. I am prone to declare that obstinance is the conduct that you must conquer in yourselves and pardon when seen in others. When Jesus commends His peace upon you, He does so in the knowledge that you are not only holy in a factual sense, but that your progress will ratify your righteousness on the final day of your lives. What is this power that is so intense? It is love! It is Omnipotent Love that is founded and fashioned within you from the moment you are baptized. My children worldwide celebrate today's Feast as the capstone of Easter because the Divine Mercy is the reason why God raised Jesus from the dead. All the Glory and providing of Heaven reside in the Divine Mercy that Jesus gives those who believe in Him. My Special and Chosen ones, it goes without saying that this Feast is also about you because you have become an innate part of God's Plan. You have relinquished your will so that His Will may be done. At every moment, you have said 'yes' to helping the suffering, lonely, impoverished, and afraid. These are the fruits of your own miraculous love that are touching people everywhere. I know that you understand My words when I say that your victories are only now beginning to occur. And, to My Special one, thank you for your charitable kindness by giving $100 to Annie Zara whose wallet was stolen by a thief. As your brother said, she will be a great intercessor for you soon. She has been exiled on Earth for 90 years, and her repatriation in the land of happiness and perfection is near at hand. She will bring with her the gratitude that she is holding for you today and offer it to God for the healing of the world. Can you see that your having found her empty wallet on the street was ordained because Jesus knew that you would make reparation for her loss in His honor? You are fulfilling the Will of God and have received a sign that He is pleased by your awareness that others are in need. It is proper for you to share your thoughts with Me. *(I told Our Lady that it is increasingly difficult to see the Earth being lost in the darkness of human sin.)* What recent incidences have brought you to such a conclusion? *(I reiterated my hopes for purifying the Earth in every way Jesus desires, but it feels as though only few are trying. It is a sensation of being isolated from humanity.)* Being a Christian around lukewarm Christians is a lonely business, while other people swear no oath to religion at all. Do you recall Mother Teresa traveling through periods of darkness? Do you remember the sorrowful writing of Sister Faustina when she said that she felt like she was the only individual on Earth? It is not self-serving to have these feelings, nor is it the desecration of your faith. This is normal in the process of your spiritual growth. Why do you suppose Pope John Paul II donned his athletic shoes and trekked through the mountains, valleys, and fields? Because he has told God the same thing you are telling Me. There sometimes is a darkness that overcomes everyone who is perfectly united in Christ and who sees a world that does everything it can to reject all that you hold dear. What would you tell the Lord about the way you feel, given the opportunity that has been accorded? *(I spoke to Our Lady privately.)* I tell you that there are many things that are left to you; this is what Jesus told Sister Faustina. One of the precepts is that your state of mind is a function of the power of your faith. Happiness begins in your trust in Jesus from deep within. If time is a burden or the voyage of life seems too far, it is because your faith has entered one of those holy places along the way where you say 'Lord, please end this now.' This is not an unholy line of thinking, although it is not always helpful. Do you believe that you are alienated from everyone you know, and this is your source of loneliness? You are speaking about the spiritual relationship that you desire to enter with every acquaintance and those you will eventually meet. These are appropriate aspirations, although you are clearly in a state of Agony in the Garden in your spiritual life, just as many Saints before you. I will ask Jesus to give you peace and comfort throughout your years with Me at your side in these hours of spiritual torment. Please allow Me to remind you that you have been a giant among men, and I am grateful for all you have done. I shall never forget your service and kindness to help usher the Kingdom of God into a world that is in such need of change. 'I was not loved enough by humanity' is the sentiment proclaimed by the Son of Man who surrendered His life to save them from damnation. Do not be ashamed to say the same thing that He told the Father in Heaven. On this great Feast when you have laid bare your soul in honesty and integrity, I thank you on behalf of all the Saints who have suffered deeply and painfully on the hallowed ground upon which you walk with such dignity and grace. I will be with you from this moment forward, and with your brother whose fiat first set your work in motion. You have every right to stand-down if your soul is tired. Of all things, I wish for you to be happy because I love you more than your capacity to know. And, as you begin a bright future, I offer an addendum that makes Me smile. It is that your brothers and sisters, regardless of who they are, what they have confessed or where they live, will come to Salvation because of Jesus' Mercy. This is pardon and Justice, forgiveness in every form, the elimination of ancient grudges, the reconciliation of generations, the eradication of vengeance, and the arrival of the new beginning that was initiated long before you were born and will endure forever beyond your passage into immortality. Jesus is glorified because you are sharing His grief. He will give you rest and peace because you are a Christian soldier. Thank you for responding to My call..."

Sunday, April 25, 2004
St. Mark, Companion of Saint Peter [1 Pet. 5:13]
4:41 p.m.

"With overwhelming joy, your Mother speaks to you because I see the glow of righteousness issuing from your hearts. You realize that the permanence of the Cross of your Salvation is as perpetual as the Divine Light of Heaven. Today, My little ones, we celebrate the Feast of Saint Mark who has written the Holy Gospel from the Paraclete of God. Will you thank him for his allegiance to Jesus and the Kingdom of Heaven in which he has become a citizen? I bring you holy tidings of remembrance from all the Saints in whose company you will reside. I call My children to prayer because another tragedy is about to befall America. And, I ask you to petition for the souls of the tens-of-thousands who have joined in protest against the sanctity of human life from the moment of conception until natural death. These people are clearly lost. They are selfish and arrogant, and filled with pride because of the illegitimate choices they demand in the name of secular liberty. Under no circumstance is the abortion of a living unborn child sanctioned by God, even in the case where the life of a mother is at risk. I have spoken in this home for years about the necessity for people to abandon the culture of death that has become the norm in the United States and other nations around the globe. If anyone should inquire whether I have pronounced My sentiments upon offering the Eucharist to anyone who does not support unborn life in every sense, action, thought and deed, tell them that it is a grave mortal sin for someone to espouse policies that foster abortion. Jesus will judge them swiftly and harshly. Let there be no confusion about what I am saying. The right of the unborn to continue life is mandated by God. Anyone who deviates from this is living in contradiction to His Will. And, it is better for them to have a millstone tied around their necks and be hurled into the seas than to bring harm upon God's unborn innocents. I assure you that the testament of the Heavens can be no clearer than this. Thank you for taking this message to your brothers and sisters. My prayerful children, I offer My Immaculate Heart because there are many changes being made to create a holier world. I realize that you feel this in your hearts, and you can see where the debate about the Church and state is ongoing. The fact that the discussion of worthiness to receive the Blessed Sacrament is occurring is an auspicious sign. We pray that American Bishops and the 47,000 priests under their patriarchy will be undaunted in their conviction that a culture of life must be maintained. There are many good things happening, My little ones. There are awesome events underway! To My Special and Chosen sons, you have witnessed these changes, and you envision the dawn of the reckoning that is about to unfurl. No matter what happens before the end of time, remember forever that you are on the right side of the battle. You are participants in the reign of Jesus over His people and the reconciliation between God and humankind. How much I have wished for you to seize this day, and that you hold each other with the grasp of friendship that you have shared for over 28 years. Like Saints Mark and Peter, you are companions in the war against Satan, compatriots of a country that is being cultivated in the furrows of justice. Thank you for allowing Me to speak with such urgency. And, My Special one, you see the task you share with your brother of writing the ecumenical dissertation for his school. Even though the title is ecumenical, the goal of his thesis is to propagate and exonerate Roman Catholicism before all other religions to the dismay of the critics of the Catholic Church. This will be subtle in places and quite obvious in others. There is no way I can place into words how jubilant this makes Me. This is the free exercise of Roman Catholic Christianity in the United States of America. Thus, hearts will be opened, and sinners will see the Light of the Risen Christ! You have offered many blessings that will convert millions to the Cross. I realize that this is a mystery, but you will see that everything I am telling you is true. And, for all the issues about which I have spoken today, this message will be brief. My purpose is for you to know that I am overjoyed by your faith in Jesus..."

Sunday, May 2, 2004
St. Athanasius, Bishop and Doctor [AD 297-373]
1:59 p.m.

"My children, your Immaculate Mother asks for your contemplative prayers for the transition of humankind into the spiritual health to which the Heavens are nurturing you. Redeeming Grace is living inside your hearts and within the grasp of your hands so that by the strength and Wisdom of the Holy Spirit, you may lift your lives into wholeness and purity. This is the month of May 2004, a time when Creation is groaning from the afflictions of human sin. But, you know that Jesus has made reparation for your offenses. He has forgiven you, and He asks that you move forward and sin no more. What does it mean to be liberated from sin? This is the question every soul must answer. It is the mission of your lives to respond to God by realizing that you are made worthy of Heaven when you hand-over your spirits in death. I address this pivotal moment in your existence because at that final hour, you will judge yourselves against Jesus' Crucifixion. Billions of people before you have leapt headlong into His Holy Arms in contrition and thankfulness because they realized that they were unable to see the Father without Him. One day, My lambs; one day every soul who breathes will be asked to make that fateful decision about Eternal Life or never-ending perdition. I pray that you will choose the Blood of the Cross as your Everlasting Redemption. I wish for My people in every region to conclude that war, corruption, impurity, and materialism are not natural to a soul that is destined for Paradise. The mayhem that has come at the opening of the 21st century is in direct contradiction to the Will of the Father. So, why is it occurring? Because an exiled world of lost sinners insists upon rejecting the Holy Gospel of Christianity. One at a time, however, Jesus is converting you. Even though you cannot see it with your eyes, each of you is being transformed into a creature of stately promise so you will be known by God upon your passing from the Earth. It is a remarkable distinction that so many paupers are teaching the affluent the true meaning of honor and charity. How ironic to see cities and nations where little children are asking their elders why such horrific suffering is taking place. And, what is the response of these adults? *Because we are free to do whatever we wish under the power given to us.* Today, I am asking them what power? What do they presume their foundation of legitimacy to be? I assure you that they will have no defensible response. Please inform them that the Mother of God says that they have no real power other than that which is given to them by My Son, and it is to be utilized to humble themselves before Him and beseech His forgiveness for their extravagant lives. Today, My Special and Chosen ones, I bring you the peace of the Holy Spirit because you are living in the condition of Grace to which I am calling you. When you have referred to the national statue at your eastern shores bearing the inscription ...*Give me your tired and your poor*, you are taking literalness into higher domains. You are asking your brothers and sisters to spiritualize the principles of giving as you practice your Christian faith. The secular definition of goodness has little to do with the sacrifices, communally and individually, that Jesus asks you to make. You are good when you give what you have so there is nothing left for you. Goodness is in protecting the dignity of unborn human life. Goodness is about absolving those who have offended you of everything they have ever done. Indeed, should you see them living in sin or embracing positions of heresy, or if you hear them blaspheming the Holy Spirit, goodness implores you to chastise them to the limits of Divine Law. I know that you are challenged and encouraged. You see the imperatives in My messages, and you realize that every person created will ultimately hear every syllable I have uttered before the world is through, be they already deceased or walking the face of the globe. The essence of true goodness mandates that you publish what I am telling you. My Special one, I need not remind you what a moment of transition this week is for your brother's work at the university, for the inferences that will be scrutinized in his ecumenical research, and for the peace of heart that you are gaining anew. The year 2004 will usher many new beginnings, and pleasing ones, that will indicate to your soul in silent Light that everything you have ever wanted will eventually come to be. I tell you over and again that Jesus will rewrite human history at your fondest command and the Will of God. Be confident that you are on the righteous path of His goodness and Grace. The blessing of the Holy Spirit is upon you! *(Before we began the Rosary to receive Our Lady, I looked out the window and a large group of rabbits were sitting outside, all staring into the bedroom from which I was looking.)* Creation itself has known that you would be writing with creativity, and this is why the little rabbits have been assembling on your lawn. They even stare into the windows to see from where the Divine Light is shining! If praises could express My gratitude, please accept them now for proofreading the extremely irrelevant document your brother prepared for his schooling in the past few days. You are embarking toward the day when his degree will be conferred. You must realize that divinely, spiritually and mystically, you are fathering and fostering the propagation of Truth over the world. You will better understand this in the future, and I ask you to believe Me today..."

Sunday, May 9, 2004
Mother's Day [secular]
St. Pachomius, Abbot [AD 292-348]
2:04 p.m.

"This, now, My children is the time during which I ask you to be attentive to My words because I am offering you the holiness and Wisdom of Almighty God. We pray again by continuing to seek in Him the granting of everything on Earth that will make humanity pure. This is Mother's Day—a time when millions who have birthed little children are honored for their faithfulness to the duty of bearing new life into the world. Would the Mother of God not be remiss if I did not magnify My Son's call for the protection of the sanctity of all life on this day? I come to you in happiness because My children are honoring Me not only today, but during the entire month of May. This is a unique opportunity for My Church to realize the gift of human Salvation and for the Grace that makes you whole again in the sight of Jesus. When Christians speak of remaking the face of the Earth, the call for the transformation of the human heart is the essence of doing it. I commend you to prayer today and always because this is how Creation is changed. Prayer is the means to achieve the spiritual goals that you have outlaid in your parishes and homes. The true meaning of loving God is to pray to Him for assistance both now and at the hour of your death. I intercede for you because I am your Immaculate Mother. Thank you for staying at My side for so long, because it is only through your faith that I can succeed. My little ones, it must be apparent to you by now that I am nurturing you to spiritual maturity that you may wilfully call yourselves to duty and service for Jesus. I shall never leave you or allow you to stray from beneath the protection of My Sacred Mantle. However, you must know by now that your spiritual maturation means that you take upon yourselves the choices, decisions, and actions that will mend the divisions between nations and peoples. It must become necessary for you to do these things of your own accord and under the Wisdom, guidance, and leadership of the Holy Spirit. My duty is to rear you in Love, and yours is to reflect the Fruits of Love in the most profound ways while you live your mortal lives. How happy I have become to see so many who are, indeed, taking the reigns of Christian responsibility and servitude so that the wounds caused by human sin can by healed by your acts of contrition, reconciliation, and unity.

My Special and Chosen ones, it is obvious by now that I come to speak to you with words for the entire body of humanity, but I wish mainly to address My sentiments into the depths of your hearts to display My undying Love for you. So many years you have prayed with Me for the cultivation of your brothers and sisters, and so many millions are becoming the beneficiaries of your dedication to Me. You must also know by now that many things culminate in victory for you, and that it is only a matter of time before you see them come to fruition. If there is one more word added to the series of faith, hope, love and charity, it would be the invaluable purpose of patience. I have told you on multiple occasions that humanity is undergoing a vast, wide, far-reaching, and varying reconditioning of the heart that ofttimes takes years to proceed. And, it is during those same years that your Love for God is growing, that your understanding of the purpose of human life is becoming more clear. And, it is during these same years that you understand that every day of your lives is another step toward the Christian perfection to which Jesus has called you. Always believe you will achieve it! Never concede to the relativists who insist that there is no such thing as moral Truth! Fight against the enemies of the Cross who do not accept that the Crucifixion of One Man has mitigated the sins of an entire humanity. Rise-up against the many in your midst who believe that 'compromise' is a better subsistence for the mortal world than Divine Revelation, for there is no compromising the fact of Love that Jesus has laid-out before the world in the Holy Gospel. There is no ambiguity in His Beatitudes. There is no room for liberal interpretations of the very conservative exhortations which proclaim that the Gate into Heaven is a Narrow one! I arrive with great joy today because I know that My Church stands on the Rock of Truth that cannot be amended by time or the musings of mortal men. When I tell you that Jesus has given you the power and authority to speak on His behalf from the pulpits of the Roman Catholic Church of Christianity, please know that this is bound in Heaven as it is bound upon the Earth. Do not seek pride for the sake of pride, but be extremely proud of your Roman Catholic heritage. Hold fast to the traditions that have made Saints of the millions who have served so dutifully in centuries past! Never surrender your knowledge that Roman Catholicism is the Church that Jesus Christ intended His Church on Earth to be—and no other! Why? Because He wishes you to partake of the Holy Eucharist and the Holy Sacrifice of the Mass simultaneously. And, this can be done only in His Church, only in the Roman Catholic Church, under the guidance of the successor to Saint Peter, himself.

My Special and Chosen ones, I have decided to tell you these things today because you are about to begin working on a project that will seem altogether too ecumenical for you... And, My Special one, can you now see the commencing of great things that have come to be in the past thirteen years because you have given of your human will to Me? I ask you to continue to do so because you will continue in the line of Marian Saints who are praying for your successful journey through life with your brother in the Church. Indeed, these are happy times because time, itself, is a passing element that you are utilizing to its greatest potential. You love and are in Love. You see well because your sacred vision is clear. This is why all ultimate victory belongs to you, and it is also the essence behind My proclamation to you that Jesus will someday rewrite the history of the world. It is a very beautiful day where you live in your homeland of Illinois! I wish for you to go outside soon and enjoy it, and that means My message for you today is nearly through... The ecumenical work you are about to prepare will predispose thousands more to the Grace and beauty of the Roman Catholic Church by implication...

You must be elated at this time by the continuation of your union in the Holy Spirit as you write additional pages in *'To Crispen Courage.'* It is a great and holy work of Christian Love and admonition. The mortal world so needs that approach...during the present age. Do you remember the story that Fr. H told you today about the little boy who donated his bone marrow? Please put that story in your next book and attribute it as being My request. Let Me assure you that you are attending Holy Mass at a very sanctified parish that is under the care an endearing priest. The story of the little boy is one that is reflective of My Jesus! However, My Jesus did die! Thank you for all the hours you are spending writing about the way the world ought to be... Do you remember what your brother told you that he wrote in his brief farewell in his 1976 annual book? The crux of the matter is that, even at age 22, he was imploring humanity to set-out to deal with the sheer crisis of human nature. The acts about which you speak, are among those that make-up that collective crisis. Ultimately, the entire body of error is the product of human sin. If all the world would come to Jesus, they would rise and sin no more. Thank you for praying so piously with Me today... Thank you for traveling to the Saint Augustine Cemetery last Friday... I was there looking down upon you! And, just as I did that day, I now give you My holy blessing of perpetual Love. ☦ I love you. Goodnight!"

Monday, May 17, 2004
St. Paschal Baylon [AD 1540-1592]
7:23 p.m.

"Remember that Jesus loves you, little children, and nothing will drive your hearts asunder. Reflect upon the genius by which God became Man through the Divine Incarnation of His only begotten Son. I urge you to train your focus on the Cross when you do not understand the purpose of suffering, and there you will see the perfect Sacrifice that has made your pain united with the Savior of the world. Today, your spirits and thoughts should be enlivened by the knowledge that your Savior is forbearing with majestic patience while the Earth is purified. Imagine what it means to have the patience of God. I come to you joyful and hopeful that you will honor the Mysteries of the Church with enhanced vigor, even as you see such desecration by its enemies. All I have ever wanted, My lambs, is that you would accept the plentiful Redemption that My Son is offering. In doing so, your fortunes will change. Your goals will stand tall as you sojourn through time. Why would your Mother tend to Her lost children in such a way that values your will? Because I trust you to enunciate the Wisdom and teachings of the Holy Spirit. I do not worry that you will be caught by the snares of the devil because inside the sanctuary of My Immaculate Heart, evil cannot reach you. I usher-in the renewal of the innocence that many have squandered to motives that have nothing to do with righteousness. When I say that My gratitude is yours, you can be confident that your Mother is pleased by the procession of events that define the goodness you have espoused. And, I implore My American children to fulfill your oath to protect unborn life, to nourish the hungry, clothe the naked, shelter the homeless, and free the captives. America prospers at the expense of the health and dignity of paupers unknown to you in foreign lands. You waste your resources for illicit purposes and ignore the opportunities that Jesus accords to tread the noble paths of self-sacrifice. My children, the United States of America is the most selfish, materialistic nation ever to exist in the annals of the created world. You have the lowest moral standards of any people to inhabit the Earth. How can you possibly suggest that God has shed His Grace on you? Why do you invoke His Name in everything you commit that defies His Will? Why all this blasphemy? Why the licentiousness? Why the corruption? Jesus has provided you the way of goodness, Mercy, and Light. This is May 2004, a time when the Spring has opened and you honor the gift of motherhood. As I have said in recent days, how ironic is it that such a republic can celebrate mother's day when over 50 million unborn children have been killed in their mothers' wombs during the past 31 years? How can this be true? How can it be reconciled with your faith? I wish for My children to learn to see your lives from the reverse side of time so you can muster the strength to forego your selfish ways. Imagine what it is like to be judged by the Son of Man for the wrongdoings you are perpetrating against His innocent creatures! I pray for you because so many are indifferent toward the prospect of posthumous life. I am a Mother of compassion who wishes you to know that a reckoning will come in your time. The signs foretold at My shrines will appear. The unsighted whose vision has been promised will begin to see. However, My little ones, once these manifestations unfold, it may be too late for many to change. This is why I seek your participation. It is the reason all souls must repent, pray, fast, and search for peace. War is not the proper response to aggression. Divine Love is the answer. Perfection reigns in forgiveness and absolution. These are extremely crucial days for humanity. Why would My Son tell you that you must prepare for the coming of His Kingdom if it were not true? Why did He say that for some the End Times will arrive like a thief in the night? What about the parable of the master returning to the house when those inside least expect it? You are told these things to steer you away from spiritual apathy. They are premonitions that the Wrath of the Lord is an omnipresent rectifier of everything ill in the material world. Will you join Me in praying that God's anger lasts only for a moment, and that the Divine Mercy of Jesus will inundate your souls?

My Special one, how pleased I am that you and your brother continue living beneath My Holy Mantle. These are the grand days that precede the Glory which is to come, that has already arrived, for which you have long prayed. Never have I told you anything that would impugn your dignity. Never have I predicted that there is reason to lose hope in the Triumph of My Immaculate Heart! I know that you fight every day for happiness, and you often fail to win that battle. Remember the faces of all the strangers you saw graduating at the University in Champaign. With what great hope they have lived! And, most of them will serve in benevolent ways to assist the developing world, but at what cost? Did they adopt their plans to enrich their own lives? There was a bittersweet pall over the auditorium because the permanence of their parting was so stark. You sensed this in 1984 when you graduated from college. These are part of the temporary things that I told you about in 1991. However, the Kingdom you are augmenting shall never ebb. There will never be a time when you will lay down your righteousness because perfection is your goal, and I am more honored by five minutes of your work than the entire four, six or eight years it takes someone to earn an academic degree. You and your brother are two wings that keep My hopes aloft for the sanctifying of Creation in the way of the Crucified Son of God whom I carried in My Virgin Womb. You are doing this for Me! It is obvious that the mission you have accepted is eventful; and you know where it is leading, when it will end, and why you are asked to commit to certain acts of faith. Asking your brother to relocate the capstone from the theater to the gateway at Saint Augustine Cemetery is an opportunity to sense his penchant for artful design, and the relic will serve a specific purpose in the work you are doing. God wishes you to live-out your lives in His Plan, not seeing what part everything you do plays until the last. Do you begin viewing a motion picture in the middle before watching its earlier acts? The answer is no, and this is why the Lord asks for your faith and trust during your exile. Imagine what it is like to see the world as the Mother of God. What sorrow I overcome to arrive at this holy place in joy. I do so because of the gladness you reflect upon Me, and because you make Me feel welcome. Please invoke the Saint of Eucharistic Congresses whom we honor today..."

Sunday, May 23, 2004
St. John Baptist Rossi [AD 1698-1764]
3:08 p.m.

"A world that is well prayed and purified will open itself to the miracles that God is pouring forth upon His Creation, and I come seeking modern disciples of Christianity to make this come true. I urge you to invoke the seminal beginnings of your faith, of accepting the Truth as revealed in the Gospel, your allegiance to the Apostles Creed, and your obedience to the commands of the Thrice-Blessed Paraclete. My cherished ones, you have come to an age where the primal essence of human conversion is coming to fruition. By all means, look around and see the signs. I have told you that the footprint of humankind has been a tortured one. I have asked you to pray on bended-knee for the Mercy of your Savior. It is with honesty and openness that you must come in contrition to the foot of the Cross for everything enlightening about the details of human life. You perpetually ask, ...*where do we go from here?* The answer resides in your hearts because there you can already reach across the chasm of mortality and begin your relationship with Eternal Life. My children, all knowledge, understanding, reason, faith, justice, and perfection are revealed by your union with Christ Jesus. In Him, there are no unanswered questions. There are no diseases that cannot be cured. There is no darkness to demean the Light. Today, the collective soul of humanity stands atop a towering mountain whose summit spires amid the clouds. You look outward with the courage of warriors because you are the disciples of a Resurrected Man. I ask you to place your purview from that pinnacle to good use. Raise your spirits and accept the Promise that has been foretold and the dignity that is yours. You wish for reprieve from your disciplinary sentences. You seek not to judge lest you be judged. You do not feign allegiance to the Lord and turn your back some other way. If you are to remain one in Him, you must keep your oath to these virtues despite the vexations of the present hours. Let no war discourage your desire to sign parchments of peace. Allow no misgiving to raise your doubts in the dutiful faithfulness of Jesus to chastise and console you. If you are to become Children of Mary during these latter times, you must break-out of your shackles of fear, intimidation, and darkness. You must be revealed to Creation as the makers of a renewed joy that no man among you has ever thought to fashion. Even though you are helpless on your own, you can rightfully achieve these things by the power of My Crucified Son. Consider everything for which you have prayed. What in the name of Heaven would you change? The answer is simple. You would transform suffering into happiness, sadness to joy, licentiousness to purity, and darkness to Light. You would have your lost brothers and sisters reject the lies of Satan like a flinch from a prick. You would preserve the goodness of the Earth for the Glory that is to come. You would defeat the adversaries of the Cross by running them through with their own spears of arrogance. Indeed, you would make the Earth like Heaven before the sun sets on this Sabbath Day. Therefore, My children, the Mother of God is telling you to pursue these things forthwith, in all the trust that you are presently succeeding. Know that the Lord is God; and God is present, and God is in you, and you are in Him. Realize that the ameliorative power of sublime resolution is alive in each of your holy hearts; created, molded, and remade in the likeness of the Most Sacred Heart of the Messiah who was Slain to save your souls from the endless agony of Hell. Teach all and be all to the ignorant and obsessed. Be healers of broken sinners whose physical bodies you will never touch. Call out to kings and captains perched on their thrones at home and abroad, all of them ignorant of the Eminent Truth that will force them to their knees. Laugh heartily at their obstinance. Pray for them as they cry-out on their descent into the belly of despair. Tell them that their insolence is an account of their crimes against the innocent, that they will damn themselves unless they heed My admonishments. Ask them to have mercy on themselves when the fullness of time arrives, lest they choose to squall in the fires of Gehenna forever. The Immaculate Mother of Jesus Christ has come to raise the brows of the poor and lonely, and to tell everyone who suffers grief and pain that victory is yours. Jesus is your birth anew! You are the sharers in the Glory of Emmanuel who was born among you to manifest your peace. The Matriarch of Creation is here. The Mother of God pronounces favor upon My children because I witnessed Jesus' Crucifixion. I awaited His Resurrection from the Tomb, and I was there when He ascended to Heaven aboard a cloud. I have rejoined Him, and we see the Earth from Eternal Glory. The world beneath us is rotting because it is corruptible, but it has been redeemed, and God gives you the capacity to repent. Heaven offers you Jesus Christ! Everything you will ever need is personified by Him. This is where you discover the keys to perfection. It is in Him that you attain perpetual happiness. My Special son, I tell you of My delight to speak with you. I am elated that you receive Me, that I might appeal to My lost children through you. We pray with hope that all the things I have told you will come to pass. Yes, all these are proof that you are living the Will of God. I will return on the Feast of Pentecost. Please remind your friends about the Mercy of Jesus. My dear child, thank you for being so receptive, and bless you for exalting the Lord's Triune Love. If anyone inquires how tall I am, tell them that I am sufficient height that the summit of the universe looks up to Me. And, the Lord's Kingdom is infinitely higher than the mountains about which I spoke today..."

Pentecost Sunday, May 30, 2004
Saint Joan of Arc, Martyr [AD 1412-1431]
3:31 p.m.

"Taking time for prayer to memorialize everything that touches your hearts is to adhere to the principles taught by Jesus. You are expected to remember the blessings you have received, the tragedies you have faced, the sacrifices you have made, and the gifts you offered to your brothers and sisters. I am your Mother of Absolution who urges you to be mindful of the benefits of personal reconciliation. If there had been more pardoning throughout history, there would be no need to grieve the war dead being elegized in cemeteries today. My children, the world is cruel because sinners make it that way. Evil legions seduce good people into doing malevolent things. We pray that even with the memory of your departed loved-ones, you realize that life goes on, both here and in Heaven. We call upon all who hear our voices to join our ascending acclaim so the Saints resound your prayers. We ask the Lord to bless you through My intercession, for it is My honor to heap kindness upon His people. I ask you to pray especially for the intentions about which we have spoken for thirteen years. Given that you are predisposed to the Kingdom of God, know that it is prospering in Christians like you. There is healing and goodness by your prudence. There are leagues of esteemed people wishing that the Earth would be pious and pure. There are Doctors of the Church in your presence, and time and history reveal who they are. I implore you to be happy not from blissful ignorance, but because you are confident that Jesus is leading His flock to Salvation. Feast on the Providence that the Holy Spirit plants in your hearts. Become cultivators of Light over the darkness of the netherworld. And most of all, know fervently that time is near its end. What you bequeath to the ages will be judged by your loyalties to the Creator who fashions them. Will your legacy be of peace and justice, or war and inequity? Let us pray that as time runs its course, you will see these things as building blocks of the unifying accord that the final hours of humanity will see. I remind you that My blessing upon the Earth is God's Incarnate Son, and there is nothing more sanctifying I could offer. In Jesus resides every healing you require. His Wisdom is the faldstool where you kneel to address the Father, arrayed in Deific Light. His Sacrifice is your Fount of Divine Mercy. His Gospel is your blueprint for Everlasting Life. My children, Jesus is living and breathing in your company. Remember that Saint Joan of Arc refused to surrender to the heretics who persecuted her. She led an entire army with the miraculous graces that she knew came from the Father. The proverbial long gray line of warriors who fought for her realized that she was commissioned by the Savior of the world to defend His Kingship. I wish for all Creation to hear what I am about to say. Your Mother of serenity has the ability to dispense to the Earth the same justice as Saint Joan of Arc by My words and deeds. If necessary, I will dispatch an army to slay the enemies of Salvation. But this time, no heroes will be burned at the stake. The billows will be the leaping flames of God's Wrath. He will elevate Me before humanity that has denied My role in the Redemption of lost sinners. I have told you that the Triumph of My Immaculate Heart is here. Not unlike you during this Memorial Day, Jesus has decisions to make. Will He return with anger, or will Paradise relent? Will He toss unrepentant souls into the Abyss, or pull them to His breast? Will He allow the victims of sin to become the battlefront against the rogues of the world, or will He offer a pass to the guilty by the forgiveness of the afflicted? Jesus depends on the Faith Church to make these choices. If you pray for Divine Mercy, it will pour from the skies like rain. Should you ask for Absolution, it shall be granted. This is how crucial these years are for man. My Special son, thank you for knowing deep in your heart which decisions Jesus would rather make. It is Absolution and Mercy because God is loving and forgiving. As you realize, Christians play a unique part in opening Jesus' Sacred Heart to receive the humbled and contrite. I fear that the rest will fall to the fate that befits them, but please do not mourn them. Whatever you do, please do not mourn them. And, thank you for writing about the issues facing the nations and how Jesus would act if He were seen by your brothers and sisters the way they see you now. Bless you for harboring hope that your Morning Star book will convert to the Holy Cross the souls about whom I have spoken in this message. However you choose to make its format more practical is something to pursue. The Feast of Pentecost is an imperative reminder that the Holy Paraclete lives with virtue in your heart, as in the Church. Your openness to dispatch the revelations that will mend the world is nothing less than priceless. I have told you that June is dedicated to Jesus' Sacred Heart. His Truth shines brightly as you extol the excellence He prefers..."

Sunday, June 6, 2004
Saint Norbert [AD 1080-1134]
4:24 p.m.

"My holy children, let us be appreciative that the Lord has accorded another opportunity to pray together as we celebrate the Feast of Saint Norbert. I ask you to imitate all the Saints because they fashioned their lives after the compassion of Jesus. Today, you see a continuously changing world of hopefulness mixed with pockets of despair. The wars that are being fought on many fronts both physically and psychologically are painful for everyone. The Great Battle for Souls is the one in which Christ is invested. Hence, I visit you again to encourage your pursuit of everything that evangelizes humanity. Be friends of your brothers and sisters with affability and grace. Remember the summons to prayer that God implores you to answer. I am the Immaculate Conception to whom Jesus requests you to listen. Whenever you do these things, you will see your lives flourish in a more fruitful light. I love you in ways that you have never imagined. If you station yourselves beneath the protection of My Mantle, you will react to the impulses in your hearts that have to do with the reciprocity between God and His people. Thank you, My children, for responding to My call. The challenges that lay before you are never insurmountable. The tasks to which you are assigned can be achieved through the determination of your goodness. Many of My children kneel in prayer and ask why their days are so repetitive. Do they not know that each new hour is another ordained time to open the entrance of Paradise for tens-of-thousands who do not know God? Can they not see that the Spirit of Truth is available at their simple call? Sometimes I weep in sorrow because humanity refuses to employ the power that God gives to those who love Him. At other times, My tears are of joy because My children are praying and working for that great unity which the world finds in the Sacred Heart of My Son. Even though I ask you to remember this every day of your lives, I especially call humanity to greater devotion to Jesus' Sacred Heart during June. My Special son, this is the summer of compounding awareness and Wisdom by which you shall lead your brethren to the Cross. I have seen how you contemplate the infinity of God's genius. I know when you weep in joy from the beatific measures that you are taking to brighten the lives of the brokenhearted, the poor, dejected, and forsaken. Your heart senses that you are coming of age in your life in Jesus. No more do you become despaired because of the infidelities that overwhelm other people. You help them rise in jubilation by the gift of your faith. You are recording the images of the Kingdom of Heaven from within your soul onto the printed page, and this is more mighty than the sword because Jesus will ensure that everyone from this day forward reads what your heart has to say. He will make this another avenue for their understanding of Heaven's Light. You are participating in and contributing to the cultivation of God's children in ways not seen before these times. The pressure was intense on the Saints to prosper the message of Salvation, but there are now incalculably more distractions for the unchurched to overcome. You are eliminating the roadblocks by reflecting Jesus' Gospel through modern venues. The more you praise Him, sufficient inroads will evolve. This is the reciprocity about which I have spoken. The fair weeks of 2004 have arrived with beams of hope because you have not conceded to temptations of the flesh; you have not desisted in your intent to maintain inner-peace; you are determined to reach the summit of holiness, and you have declined to give in to your associates for another way of life. God knows these things; Jesus manifests them in you, and humanity will stand down with deference before the sublimity of your faith..."

Sunday, June 13, 2004
St. Anthony of Padua [AD 1195-1231]
Doctor of the Church, Hammer of the Heretics
3:55 p.m.

"My little ones, on this Feast of Corpus Christi, I call you to hunger for the righteousness of God. Be near Him in all things, pray for His Divine Mercy, seek His Salvation, please the purposes of His Will, regain the dignity your forefathers forfeited, purify the intentions of your hearts, enrich the lives of your enemies, seek the conversion of the lost, emulate the piety of the Saints, embolden the tepid to be strong, emblazon your future across the horizons, garner the faith to succeed, admonish the faithless in your midst; and above all things, love Jesus, as He is your Savior and King. I tell you again today, as I have given the world warning for centuries, that they who hold fast to their belief in the Most Blessed Sacrament and receive Holy Communion with penitential contrition shall be granted Eternal Life in Heaven. My children, your Redemption is this clear and simple. If you can muster the courage to fight for the Truth of Jesus' Holy Presence in the Bread of Life from the Altar, your Salvation in Heaven is assured. Your Mother realizes that there are many transgressions which have yet to be mitigated. There are treacherous life-plans that need to be altered. There are captives in need of release. Yes, there are countless other sins which need to be ended. But, I tell you over and again that all goodness that will purify Creation to the best of all things is found in the Sacred Body and Blood of My Crucified Son. Imagine the strength of belief of the Church throughout the ages, that She has offered the gifts of Bread and Wine to Her priests. Of anything else you can ponder in your mortal lives, think about this Consecration of humanity to the richness of Salvation by God's chosen priests who are humanity. The victory of peace over war is found in the Holy Eucharist, the healing of the sick is located there, the conquering of the darkness by God's Holy Light is manifested in the Most Blessed Sacrament. My children—My Church—your dedication and devotion to Jesus in the Most Holy Sacrament of the Altar is this important in your lives.

Today, we also pray for those who are leading their brothers and sisters away from the Traditions of the Church. Pray intensely for those who are desecrating the Holy Relics of the Catholic Church in the name of modernization. Pray for the souls of sinners who are perverting the Truth of the sacred Banns of Marriage in the interest of diversity. Be compassionate toward the ignorant and enraged against those who are perpetrating outright heresy and error for financial gain. These are strange and frightful times for good Christians everywhere, but all who come to Me shall be granted shelter during the imminent storms. Bring to Me your most finely fashioned dreams and I will make them all come true. Give unto Jesus your most impossible hopes and He will grant you your hearts' desires. I promise you today above all the other promises I have made—I am speaking on behalf of your God! I carry the commission to make clear to the world the infinitude of His Glory. I bear to you the Good News of His Holy Will. No humanity anywhere else in or outside of Creation could be more blessed than that which resides on the face of the Earth. I assure you of your good fortune in Jesus, and I tell you with all the sureness of His Resurrection that your Divine Life for which you have long-prayed and suffered gladly is nigh at hand.

My Special son, I realize that you seek in your brothers and sisters the holiness that has engulfed you. They have yet to know and hear from the Mother of God. Feel compassion for them because of this, and know the high status of your own good fortune to have been granted such a gift. I call upon your very soul to speak to your heart, and reciprocally your heart to your soul, that all things are occurring according to God's Plan—as difficult as this may be to comprehend. Your prayers and sacrifices, the intensity of your Christianity pouring-forth into the world, and the miracles that your own miraculous life is manifesting are indeed opening the sleeping eyes of the rest of the world. You often seem to wonder how your Mother can come to you with such great hope and happiness. I sense in your heart the impressions that I could wield My awesome power more widely and prominently. I only ask you to believe for a time that I truly am—I truly am in ways that you have yet to understand. Bear with Me in the same labor that I bore your Salvation into the material world 2,004 years ago. You will soon see the fruits of your labors in rather obvious ways, with overtones that will expand the elements of time and space. You will sense that sacred unity for which you have always pined between the living and the dead. You will begin to have thoughts of the sweetness of your brothers and sisters instead of the oppression by which they are controlling the Earth. And, your perspective will turn to your own sure realization that the End Times have come. Your vision and your tenor will be of reflection, compassion, encouragement, willingness to sustain and be sustained; and that simple, beautiful, confident, and precious sense of accomplishment will be yours. You have seen this in My predictions which have come true. You have received these things by your own making—by toiling and not counting the cost, and by believing in our work together when only few others would accept. Thank you, My precious little one. Thank you and your brother to whom you have given the greatest of yourself for many years.

I have offered you words about Jesus in the Holy Eucharist because He has been the receiver of your supplications for the entirety of your years. Ever since you were a tiny child in Saint Augustine Church in your little village home, you heard the Sanctuary bells peal to tell you that a Divine miracle was about to occur. This was the Consecration that has preceded your own consecration to My Immaculate Heart. This is Jesus' having physically given you to Me. And, I accept you, I want you, I cherish you, I pray for you, and I will someday see your dutiful and obedient little soul in Paradise with all the Angels and Saints forever to come. You will bring your Baptismal Gown back to the very Holy Spirit who once handed it to you, fully intact and utterly unstained. This is a promise that I make not only to you, but to the God who created Me as well. I have given you the bounty of My Immaculate Heart here today because this is what we do. I offer My Grace to you in a way that the nation of America shall never be worthy to receive... The pageantry of the last week in the death of Ronald Reagan was about the inevitability of death. I am offering you a celebration of Eternal Life in Jesus that has been prefigured since the Dawn of the Ages. I wish for you to not ponder the figurative images of black caissons and mourning widows. I wish for you not to dwell on riderless horses with inverted shoes. No—I wish for you to draw your hearts into that great and noble triumph of humanity itself being borne on the withers of God's own Secretariat carrying His people back to His awaiting arms—so far ahead of the claw-footed world that neither wind nor lightning could ever hold you in arrears. This, My son, is what you are doing for God here on the Earth, and this is why you will ultimately stand inside the circle of victory with champions' flags waving overhead and a quilt of fresh carnations blanketing your soul... I offer you now My holy blessing for today. ✞ I will speak to you again next week. Thank you for your prayers. I love you. Goodnight!"

Sunday, June 20, 2004
St. Sylverius, Roman Pontiff [6th Century]
3:49 p.m.

"Good afternoon, My Christian children! Thank you for kneeling to pray with Me for the conversion of the world. While the mayhem of fortress America brawls outside your doors, we ask the Lord to clear the avenues down which you travel to find the efficacy of His Love, that you prevail in all things for which you have prayed since you were young children. I ask you to look openly to the future so that reparation can be offered for the wrongs of humanity for the Glory of God. God does not ask for restitution for the errors of sinners, but He wishes for proper mitigation to be made in Jesus' likeness so at the last moment of Creation, men will raise their heads in consolation that anything they may have done to impugn His Kingdom will have been addressed. Today, I ask you to continue the mission of peace to which you are called, that you will pray for peace every day. Too many of your brothers and sisters do not comprehend the meaning of peace because they have never given Jesus the opportunity to bestow His blessings upon them. I have told you in years past that peace rests in the solitude of your heart when it is given to prayer. This Dove of Peace is timid, but the courage of Christianity in your hearts accords Heaven the manner to dispense the strength humanity needs to survive in a world of turmoil. There is vice and greed in your midst to rival no other age. Impurity and violence are overshadowing what few honorable pastimes you enjoy. As I implore My children to be piously reverent in Jesus, I expect that your contemplative recitations include a look at your lives, a daily examen of the ways you approach existence as you rise from your slumbering nights. It is not unachievable for you to come full-circle in the Grace of God because it is in His Grace that your years began. When you ask Jesus whether He might be pleased with your acts, does He not respond that they be your emulation of Him? He resides within and among you because He wishes for Creation to be united in the fullness of Divine Truth. If this were not possible, He would not have been born as the Incarnate Son of Man on Christmas Day. Wisdom is made manifest when you embrace this knowledge and Truth about which I speak. In weeks to come, you will see more outright evil arise from the dungeons of American politics. You will hear promises that will never be kept. There will be vague attempts to justify illegitimate wars. Women and their political cohorts will clamor for their right to continue killing the children in their wombs. Your Mother is urging you with this message to avoid the rancorous partisanry, posturing, platitudes, and patriotism of American politics because they are only distractions to your Christian piety. By the time this message is revealed to America, the decision about whom will serve will already be made, and you will know that My words have come to pass. Affix yourselves to the immutable Truth of God's Kingdom, and you shall never fear the diabolic acts of the secular void because you will be nourished by the Holy Spirit. Your souls will sense a comfort that the physical Earth cannot offer. The center of your being will perceive the perspective for which you have yearned all the days of your lives. Only in this piety will you understand the virtuousness of Heaven. Be jubilant that you are destined for Redemption, and the awareness that victory is near will reign abundantly in you. Everything the Saints proclaimed will make sense. Every sacrifice that God asks you to make will become clear through the sanctioning of His Divine Plan. When you honor the Most Holy Trinity, you pay homage to the Thrice-Blessed Creator who sustains your lives. I beseech you to enhance your union with Him by offering sacrifices on His behalf. I cannot make you happy in this life. I will deliver you to Jesus, and He will give you fulfillment. Please allow your Mother to lead you down the path of righteousness where you shall greet this peace and joy.

My Special and Chosen ones, I wish you could see from the eternal side of existence that you have presently achieved your fondest hopes and dreams. The absolutely profound writing that you are composing consists of the sound of the opening of the doorways of opportunity for millions more to learn about their Salvation in Jesus. They will comply with God's justice and propriety. Rebuking your lost brothers and sisters about their vain ways is an act of mercy that you are bestowing upon them. This is the kind of reparation that Jesus is asking you to ensure. Sometimes you are traveling too close to temporal avenues to realize the Providence you are revealing to humanity. If you will look with deep humility and modesty at your labors, you will see the overwhelming powers they possess. Jesus is pleased by you and joyful for you. What does this mean? It certifies that He knows how you will judge yourselves come the end of time. You will be merciful toward your future for the lives you are giving Him. You will be piously proud to have honored the Mother of God in everything I ask you to do. You have shed the world and donned the Divine Light of Christ. What else could the Immaculate Conception require of Her children? What else? As you number your blessings, do not forget that they consist of offering your own will in alignment with that of the Father. This is a benediction that He dispenses to you as much as your faith. You are My holy sons who have clung to your dreams in the knowledge that My promises would eventually come true. They are occurring, My dear ones. The peace and Grace of Jesus Christ is being given to you as each new sunrise dawns. I am happy because you do not oppose the things that Jesus asks of you. You tell Him that He may do whatever He wills, and this is key to your good fortune and the origin of the auspicious times ahead. I ask you to recall all the things I have told you when you need comfort and consolation. My Special son, did you ever believe you could write with such profundity? The elevated, mystical composure about which you are speaking comes from the Angels into your writing because you are deeply devoted to them. Please do not compare Jesus' admonishment of a world that He often chastises with ranting. The testing and tempering of your thoughts is the reason your writing has reached the pinnacle of perfection. Can you sense the Triumph of My Immaculate Heart in which your lives are situated becoming more apparent? You are on the right side of immortal history. Always remember this because it will be of consolation in many dark hours that will befall your tormented brothers and sisters. You will comfort them by telling them everything I have said about joy, peace, victory, conversion, and Truth. Yes, these are propitious times. You will succeed in everything you do because you have the patience to see the process through..."

Sunday, June 27, 2004
St. Cyril of Alexandria [AD 376-444]
Doctor of the Church
3:08 p.m.

"There are so many poor souls who are begging for prayers, little children, that you would be remiss if you forgot them. I solicit your abilities to be strong, sincere, and fervent for those who have no way to provide for themselves. This is a grand day in the destiny of Creation because you are working feverishly in God's vineyard to expose all forms of affected piety. Jesus is with you as your guide and counselor. I assure you that your station within God's Kingdom is blessed by your good offices and intentions. These are not just difficult times for the faithful and faithless alike, they are determining how the parameters of human judgment shall be measured according to the Father's Will. The decisions you render as a chosen people will someday be reconciled against everything you have ever known to be proper in the tenets of your religious beliefs. I urge you to look with perspective upon the Final Judgment and the specific, daily decisions you make because the latter of these things determines your life's record. Be trusting and know that you are My children, that you are doing everything I have required of you. Be pleased with the prayerful lives of those with whom you pray during the Holy Sacrifice of the Mass. Consider all the missionaries and foreign-aid workers who leave their homes and families for months on end to alleviate the suffering of the victims of wars and poverty. Here in America, there are pockets of children in impoverished neighborhoods who are forced to live in cardboard boxes and drink effluence from street sewers. All around the globe, it is the same. The division between rich and poor has never been wider; leaders of nations and their governors have never been more greedy. These are among the problems that I address to those who have the capability to help with kind compassion. My children in distant places from your homeland often wonder how they will secure their next meal, and suffer the pains of hunger when unable to find it. Your country has a windfall of plenty, and God mandates that you reach beyond your own borders to share your life-sustaining commodities, not bombs and weapons that destroy them. Next Sunday will be a momentous secular holiday in the United States, but what are you celebrating? Are you observing imperialism and isolationism? Does pride make you ignorant? I ask you that when the Son of Man returns to the Earth, will He find faith in the United States of America? Or, will He discover that the American populace has invested its future in luxury and greed? Does the Constitution give you license to live in direct contradiction to what is required by the Holy Gospel of Christianity? These are times for you to wonder what it means to have freedom in a nation that is imprisoned by the impious struggle for monetary assets. You have been rightly told that Communism is an unfair system, but can you not see that in many ways Capitalism is as dark? You claim the freedom to spurn the admonishments of the Prophets, both the ancients and the new. You depend on avarice to speed you to another appointment to garner more funds or be entertained. Hear! The Mother of God implores you to break free from the idolatry of consumerism. Give your purpose to the Holy Spirit of Wisdom and charity. Americans must be aware that God will never bless a country in which it is legal to kill children in their mothers' wombs! I have told you on a number of occasions that horrible chastisements will befall the American republic. And, I remind you that this is true, that absent your repentance, contrition and conversion, it is utterly inevitable. Government leaders and legislators who condone abortion and who oppose initiatives to help the poor should prepare for the punishment they deserve. It saddens Me to foretell these things, but there is no escaping the fact that My Son is a fair Judge, and His is the Judgement that condemns the acts of the blasphemous.

My Special son, I wish not to cause you any anxiety, but I request that you publish this message in 2008 so those responsible will discipline themselves and amend their ways. By the Lord's providing, you will do this. Ironically, I appear before you today with pleasant overtones. I sense your frustration because people will not live responsibly. They have a far distance to travel to understand human life the way you have come to know it. You have not seen the proverbial top of the stockpile compared to the innumerable people who have not the slightest notion what holiness is. Everything righteous is attuned to reason. What Jesus desires is present in the conversion of every heart. Be at peace knowing that the best of all possible outcomes is imminent. This may not appear to be the case, but I am telling the truth. Be confident that Jesus cares so much about wayward sinners that He will gather His lost sheep through any means. This has always been the same. Thank you for supporting your brother in his studies and holding him when he weeps. He is exhausted from everything that the world and all who detest him have heaped upon him. You are moving toward 14 years of messages, and this is a long time to suppress his will, causing intense pain to his spirit. Your mission has gained a valued effect. It is forever of Jesus, and God is glorified by your faith. Thank you for remembering the refugees in Africa; your prayers are the way to change things. *(I asked Our Lady to intercede for them.)* I will do as you ask. The Lord provides miracles, and this is the reason Americans are free to practice their faith. Heaven takes care of Christians. Remember the Passion that Jesus endured, and that His disciples are suffering mightily. You are living His Paschal Resurrection; and in this, you have won the war. The persecution that pierces human hearts cannot impale the Mystical Body of Christ. Please do not worry, everything will be all right..."

Sunday, July 4, 2004
St. Elizabeth of Portugal [AD 1271-1336]
2:34 p.m.

"Of all the greatness possessed by the Lord, the greatest is Love! My children, I have come today to speak to you about this Holy Love which is the bastion of purity, goodness, and peace that your souls are silently seeking. I have not come today to speak about patriotism or secular freedom because the greatest chains of bondage known to humankind have come from the hatred that is espoused by governments around the temporal world. In and of itself, individualism is not freedom. If quoted out of context, Truth is not freedom. And, if used for sinful purposes, emotions and affections that bind men's hearts together are also neither the producers nor result of freedom. I wish to speak to you about Love today because it is the core of the freedom that the world can neither give nor ever take away. What of this Divine Love? Why should you accept it? Why should you emulate it? Why should you embrace and extol it? The answers to these questions require your openness to accept your helplessness before Jesus as contrite sinners whose only means to Everlasting Life is in Him. Your personal and social consciences are founded in the One Truth that is God in Him. I wish for you to ponder these things because the annals of history prove that you are helpless to discover the true meaning of freedom on your own. You cannot reach perfection of your own accord. You cannot survive either physically or spiritually without the intercession of Heaven. Those who choose to deny this are already dead. So, while you see and hear the fireworks displays around America today, remember that you are only a self-serving society of selfish rogues whose materialism will be the reason you shall never own the Grace from God you proclaim to possess. If you do not turn your hearts and minds to the spirituality that you require to see the world the way it is, and indeed how it should be, you will never be granted that Perpetual Light of Divine Salvation. The colors red, white, and blue have nothing to do with the perfection of the human race. They are a collective symbol of imperialism and idolatry. They are the three vices which keep you imprisoned in a nation without conscience. They are the three swords with which you are lancing your own dignity. But, what will your peoples say when told that the Mother of God is displeased with the insolence, audacity, and selfishness of the country over which She reigns as Patroness Saint? Can 287 million people understand that what lies within your borders, save the Roman Catholic dioceses, has nothing to do with faith, trust, hope, prayer, and deliverance? And, what about those who refute what the Catholic Church teaches? Ask them precisely what it is they are protesting against!

I realize that it seems to be such a contradiction that I tell you that I am displeased with the conduct of the people of the United States, and yet I come to you as a happy Matriarch of God's Creation. I am happy because I already know the outcome of the world. I have seen the Victory of the Cross which has come to fruition within the Triumph of My Immaculate Heart. How could anyone be sad when they know that this moment is at hand? I am asking you to look at the Earth with a new perspective, to realize that it is your temporary home, and see for yourselves that your impending deaths are your release from the bondage of human mortality once and for all—only inside the Crucifixion of My Beloved Son! I have ofttimes told you that Jesus' Sacred Heart is filled with Mercy, and His Judgment is one of understanding. He knows the temptations that lure you in other directions, and He also knows the ones who are trying to take you onto another path. He has already amassed a stockpile of millstones and created a cauldronous fire for those who reject Him at the last. My purpose here today, as always, is to assure you that there is hope for the millions who yet do not understand the power of the Cross. In that Cross, you will discover the ultimate fashioning of true freedom in the way that God wishes you to be free. Knowing this to be factually true beyond the capacity of any of His creatures to refute, I come to you with joy and in the expectation that, in your good capacity to reason, you will accept the Crucifixion as expiation for your sins. If you will only give yourselves time in peaceful pondering to comprehend what I am saying, you will know why there is time, and why you are in it. I have told you this long ago on many occasions, during a special series of messages in the opening months of 1991.

My little Special and Chosen ones, I understand that you are also happy along with Me because you realize that everything I am telling you is true. You have learned nothing new in My message to you today. However, I wish to reinforce My Love for you by asking you to take some of My words to the outerworld societies that will not listen to other modern Christians. You give of yourselves to Jesus because you know and accept everything He has given to you—Grace atop of Grace that are juxtaposed to your other efforts—and gifts that you offer in accordance with the obedience of your own personal will. You shall be granted sainthood for this! I tell you with the fervent Love in My Immaculate Heart that the future belongs to you, that you have already conquered the element of time and your enemies, too. And, if only you will find in yourselves that your timely discussions about the perils and evils of the world are not an undue focus on the negative, you will become happier as you live-out your daily lives. It is alright to see what is happening, but please do not become distraught that they are not changing quickly enough that you somehow internalize your own spiritual fatigue. I wish for you to be wise in the way you view the horrible aspect of the material world. See what is happening, discuss possible solutions, pray for them to come, and be happy that God has given you such recourse in Him. This is one of the venues to freedom about which I am speaking—not in a secular sense, but in terms that will strengthen your trusting relationship with Jesus and with God. You are wise little children.

You have stood by Jesus through countless agonizing moments. You have never once surrendered your faith. These things cannot be said about very many people! You shall be sainted for this! My children, in all of these things, you should be happy along with Me. Why? Because My happiness is not full unless you are happy with Me. If the Mother of God can see the countless ways that My Son's Sacrifice is being ignored and desecrated and still come to you with a smile on My Face, surely you can muster the joy to know that anyone who is guilty of these things is being conquered by the obedient gift of your lives... I will continue to speak to you if you will allow it... Thank you again for your prayers; this has been a very good day. I offer you My holy blessing now. ✞ I will speak to you again next week! I love you. Goodnight!"

Sunday, July 11, 2004
St. Benedict of Nursia, Abbot [AD 480-547]
3:49 p.m.

"My dear ones, it is imperative that we make the most of this extraordinary experience that God has accorded to reflect upon the fashioning of vigilance and fairness on Earth. Our designs and desires must complete His Will, and yours is the duty to ensure that you abide by the Gospel so that it is fulfilled in your day. My Immaculate Heart emanates eternal joy because My children are heeding My call to holiness and Truth. We have spoken of the eagle's flight and remaking the world into the likeness of Paradise. What does this mean? How can a planet so restricted by boundaries mirror Heaven that is so infinite? The answer must be found in your acknowledgment that Divine Love has no parameters, and that your imitation of Jesus can set the globe afire, freed from the burdens of mortality. You are to strive by virtue of the Holy Gospel for the everlasting freedom that cannot be constrained by a geographic orb. We wish for everything that is of holiness to engulf the essence of humanity as a collective species because the world is chaotic and filled with disunity, but mostly because it is not your final resting place. Give Me your hearts, and I will take you to a place called joy! Offer Me your hands, and I will wrap them around the circumference of Truth. I wish for you to understand that the concepts you use to describe certain feelings are actually physical places for people who know God well. Always and everywhere do they see their destiny before they should die in Him! How enlivening to realize that a journey can be complete before it has ever ended. With what jubilation you welcome tomorrow, though it may not have yet come! Imagine the majesty and eloquence with which you will address the Father of Creation in whose sacred presence you shall bare your souls. Is it possible to nurture in your hearts the all-important miracle that will come to you at last? God reminds you that it is. He is creating inside you an indomitable manifest of infinite power! This He has already given to you in Jesus Christ, faithfully and forthrightly alive in your hearts as the Holy Paraclete. Where else would you go?—one Apostle was heard to ask. Why depart the Grace before which you stand? The bountiful future is yours, and a good one when you stay with Me, beneath My protective Mantle, until the sum of your days finally ends. Let us dwell upon the Immaculate Triumph to which the Saints of old subscribed. Turn your faces outwardly like blooming flowers. Can you visualize the warmth and compassion that flows from the Sacred Heart of Jesus at the Right Hand of God? Does this Grace not invite you to be raised in the same manner that Christ be lifted up? You are not only commanded to be simple, but to be like Emmanuel in whose Sacrifice you are preserved. There are Mysteries aplenty to accompany you on your journey through life, but none of them is shorn of the perfection that through your faith you see the culmination of the world, the same end that is your initiation into Salvation. What seems mysterious is the fruit of your faith, returned to Heaven from whence it came. My darlings, you must concede to the Dominion of God so you will no longer question His Kingdom in this life. Accept what shall come with joy and obedience, and through your concession will arise the daylight you have been seeking. I have told you that 'I wish.' What does this mean? It is more than just yearning for something you cannot see, for I have witnessed your souls bound for Heaven. I saw them with mystical joy at the Annunciation. I ask you to amplify this renewal. Be excited because the sadness of Earth is passing away. Be carolers of honor, service, vision, and peace. Be the voice for the Saints whose faith resonates through the archives of time. Become doers and dreamers who will stand erect on the last day and say, 'We win!' Go to Jesus Christ for the sustenance you require, and you will know the meaning of life. Then you will stop wringing your hands, wandering barren fields and darkened corridors, searching for your dignity, for it shall be found in the legacies of the slain warriors and dying pilgrims you see lingering there.

Look for the sun in the pit of the night. See your reflection in the pools of Martyrs' blood as they evangelized the Cross to nonbelievers. Your holiness is the dressing for their wounds; your love is their remembrance. Your suffering spells death for the enemies of the resurrection of men. Give Me your tired and your poor, indeed! This Final Colossus says bring Me anyone who is broken, and the Lord will make them whole again through the Crucifixion of My Son. No ailing man or beast of prey whose weakness, malevolence, or ulterior motive is stalled in time can disavow the Queenship of the Immaculate Mother of God! And, this victory I offer you as your health, happiness, and strength to see the arrival of the Kingdom of Heaven in your day and time. Remember Me for this, My children! Remember that I am a Mother who speaks while you are yet mortals in the flesh to urge you to repent. Remember when you get to Heaven that it was the Blessed Virgin Mary who advocated your Salvation with the determination of a lioness. Humble yourselves before Jesus, and God will restore your tortured spirits to their fullest, and more, and more! Christ is your liberating Messiah, your elevation, the eloquence of your speech, the longevity of your faith, and the reason you live. Let your hope shine like a billion suns descending to the Earth, awakening humanity from thousands of decades of sloth, indifference, and spiritual ineptitude. Let the biblical Revelations fall like rivers from your tongues and speak of the ecstasy for which every mortal seeks, granted at the Throne of God. I give you My pledge on this eleventh day of July 2004 in the year of My Son that everything I have said is true. And, through the intercession of Saint Benedict, may you set-out with fire in your eyes and trust in your hearts because someday, the Savior about whom I speak shall return. It will be to the delight of the faithful and the anguish of those who spurn Him. My Special son, thank you for another occasion whereupon I have given you a message. I know that you will wield it like a saber against Satan and those who would attempt to denigrate the fineness of your faith. Thank you for your prayers, and thank you endlessly for taking care of your brother. Always remember that I love you. When everything else is agreed, please remember that the Mother of Jesus Christ loves you..."

Sunday, July 18, 2004
St. Bruno, Bishop of Segni [AD 1049-1123]
3:59 p.m.

"Jesus' Holy Wisdom shines forth through your lives when you walk in His Sacred Light. Please maintain your hopes and keep your spirits high because so many good things are forthcoming that you will be unable to number them. My curious children ask the question...When? My answer is that 'when' is irrelevant to Christians who know that their Salvation in Jesus is preordained. In time, tens-of-thousands of doubters will search for comfort upon realizing that the Kingdom of Heaven is nigh, and they will ask...Already? What will you tell them? This is the crux of the agent of time. If you honor My 1991 Easter request to '...tell them now,' you need not worry about the rest. Telling them means living the way you have for the past thirteen years. You tell them when you author manuscripts that may not be read for several decades. You are telling them when you fashion your lives in reflection of the Cross. However, your brothers and sisters are listening not decades hence, but in the present hour. I offer you hope because your victory is worthy of the anticipation you espouse. I remind you that all the images I have given in hundreds of messages are elements of this same Truth. Every word you have written is a keystroke on the piano where you harmonize the sanctification of humanity. Your melodies are the dreams of your hearts, so do not dismay that you cannot immediately grasp the miracle that has come upon you. Remember that God is purifying you, not the contrary. We work, pray, and sing because we are overjoyed. You give yourselves mystically, materially, and spiritually because your future lives in the Afterlife. Do not let the world expire without remembering that it is here that Salvation began, born from your Mother. Your Redemption is a manifestation of the holiness you were given when you surrendered your souls to be immersed in Jesus' Blood on the Cross. Your spirits can see this through the themes of divinity that God superimposes over your years of consistent faith. I am speaking about the supernatural, mixed with the purification of your humanness. Once these intersect, you have achieved your Christian purpose. My Special and Chosen ones, I offer intense praise for your allegiance. These are wondrous times during which you are gaining deep perspective about the remaking of the Earth into the likeness of Heaven. Can you see that this has been growing in you? I am pleased by the labors that you are offering God's faithful in your witness for the Church. I urge you not to be afraid or bitter during the fortunes of time. Remain steadfast in Christ! Your lives are in transition. Each new day, you are elevated and magnified in piety and Grace; and if you are loathed by your brothers for this, then you are more the blessed. Therefore, stay the course of righteousness, and the ecstacy that your hearts pine to realize will come. *(I was given a quote recently by Archbishop Fulton Sheen. "Ridicule is the tribute that mediocrity pays to genius." The Truth of the Gospel is the genius of which this Saint of God was speaking.)* This has been a summer of changes, none of them ill; and you are coming of age in body, mind, and instinct. You foresee the fate of lost sinners who reject My messages or do not care to hear them. And, people have sought to know you better, even those who have known you since you were children. Your young sister came to visit because she wishes you to know that she harbors no animosity against your work. She trusts what you say because you are genuine in your faith. The rest will soon follow. If you offer them patience and some of them a wide berth, your family will stand beside you in the unity for which you have prayed. I ask you to be hopeful in the knowledge that what I am telling you is true. What would the Lord have you do? Where else would you go? To whom would you turn if not Jesus? It is clear that the Blessed Trinity is your source of resurgence, and you would pursue no alternative. In this, believe that you are acceptable before the Omnipotence of God. You are regained in the Sacred Heart of Jesus by reason of His Sacrifice on the Cross..."

Sunday, July 25, 2004
St. James, Apostle and Martyr [d. AD 42]
3:22 p.m.

"The glorious ministration of the ages teaches you patience on your earthly journey, along with willpower, fortitude, perseverance, and the determination to overcome the abstract ruses employed by the enemies of the Cross. While their lives are gilded by shallow piety, you are dedicated servants for the Kingdom of Everlasting Life. You have been told by orators before you that everything about life swims and glitters, that the stability of existence comes from the Holy Spirit stationed resoundingly in your hearts. From the arching blue skies to the seafoam greens that buoy your maritime vessels, everything benevolent originates and will capitalize in the Dominion of God. The Alpha and Omega was birthed from My Womb as the infinity of your Salvation in one Incarnate Child. You will digress in thought and action as many times as you breathe during your lives, but you will not see Heaven unless you proceed through the Crucifixion of Jesus Christ. When humanity ultimately comes to peace in this; when you finally understand that this passage represents freedom over captivity, you will know that your work in Jesus is worth every moment you offer in His name. My dear ones, too many of you ask God, 'Why a cross? Why the Cross?' The reason for your mortification is so you will accept the Sacred Mysteries of Jesus' Life, Death, and Resurrection. The way you underscore your lives and the dedication you invest to repair the broken world is the begetting of your resolve in the reconciliation between God and humanity in the Cross. Therefore, placing your comprehension of the Cross in the form of a question is misguided. You must remember that God has no beginning, that He perpetually exists. Likewise, the Cross is the forever-prescient vehicle for the conveyance of human sinners from exile on Earth to paradisial excellence. God prefers that you not inquire, but that you commit; and this is compulsory for your reunion with Him. He desires not your curiosity about the thesis of life, but that you become the best livers you can be. You are special people to whom He gives the finest of everything He has made. The traditions of the Catholic Church, the Holy Scriptures by which you propagate your faith, the Sacraments that make you whole, and the Holy Spirit who sustains you are His constant reminders that you are moving into His quiet Light. You grow in trust and conscience by living-out the Apostles Creed that sets you apart from those who do not accept Salvation in Jesus' Blood. You study scholarship and philosophy on a regular basis, and man's pedantic lectures keep you focused on the careening, evolving, and passing of the Earth. However, your heart is more important! Jesus calls you from the heart and into the heart. He commends you to sense the urgency of the bounty of the heart that keeps you one in immortality. Inside you lives the virtue and

Wisdom to take you beyond your parting hours, into the Eternal by which you are blessed. Place your hearts in the presence of God, lest you fall over the precipice of indifference to a death from which you shall not rise! Cease living only for the temporal world and the physical norms by which it is framed. Fashion your thoughts and actions around the perspectives of Eternity, for it is immortality that you seek. God has given you a benignly beautiful planet on which to prepare for entry into Heaven. He gives you clear skyways and cool breezes. He issues the rains that make your foodstuffs grow. However, when you respond defiantly to His Will and perpetrate acts that bring a lack of peace, you turn the forces of Nature against unsuspecting people. You manifest global destruction and violence, and you make the Dove of Peace frightened to remain in your midst. Therefore, I ask you in remembrance of Saint James to acknowledge God's Sons of Thunder! Do not forget that His Apostles are living in His Kingdom that has come to Earth. Call on Saint Michael as your safeguard when you feel threatened. Most important, remember to seek comfort in Me, your Immaculate Mother, who will always be your Advocate. I secure My happiness knowing that I am your Protectress!

My Special son, where can your Mother begin to tell you how pleased I am by your life? How can I give your brother due praise for working so diligently on his academics to sustain the credibility of your labors? The two of you are the likenesses of James and John. Your reflection is of Jesus who is humble and courageous, who is the presence of God's delight in a world that shuns His miracles. I have told you that you should not have feelings of pride that come from accomplishments, but believe everything I am saying to you, that you are living the succession of events that tend to your honor in the Church and before humanity. Be happy that God has made you blessed. Be filled with gratitude that He has given Me to be your Mother. Be elated that the Angels feel duty-bound to remain with you during the day and night to guide you in the Wisdom of the Holy Spirit. Immerse yourselves in the knowledge that the Will of the Father is effected by the advice you offer your friends and peers. Thank you for playing the part of peacemakers and mediators between Heaven and Earth, that you are entrusted with the longings of Christians to procure the blessings and vision they need to embrace righteousness and peace. Be confident knowing that your arrival in Heaven is a brief matter of time. My Special one, this fall will pass quickly, the year 2005 will come, and you will awaken the slumbering conscience of humanity even more with the greatness of your works. You are moving through time more swiftly than you know. Thank you, and remember that this would not be possible without the invocation of your trust. Bless you for accepting the Wisdom of the Holy Spirit in your heart..."

Sunday, August 1, 2004
St. Alphonsus Mary De Liguori [AD 1696-1787]
Redemptorist, Doctor of the Church
3:08 p.m.

"For every fruitful reason, My children, you know that the power of God is invincible. You give of yourselves that He might be glorified, that His Kingdom shall overwhelm the Earth, that Truth will be the vision of humanity, and that you shall live with Jesus and the Angels and Saints upon the completion of your years. When your Mother speaks of righteousness, I refer to these things. We seek the interior spiritual enlightenment of your brothers and sisters because it is here that the refinement of the conscience begins. All ambiguity about the purpose of your existence is eliminated in understanding the conversion to which you are called. Is this a temporal attribute? When speaking of the Corporeal Acts of Mercy it is. Mainly, however, Heaven summons you to grow into spiritual beings because this is where Salvation lives. You ponder all the grandness that you shall ever become. You dream about your future. You contemplate the complexity of your potentials. In the final analysis, you wish to forecast the future during your unfolding lives. God gives you this ability in Divine Love when you accept Jesus as your Lord and Savior. He offers you His mightiness and foresight, allowing you to reach for new ways to introduce the miraculous essence of Himself in the manifestations of your holiness. This, My children, is vibrant faith! You will never be greater than Jesus, and you shall never become more powerful than God. However, the Father and the Son are declaring that your goals can be just as legitimate, your goodness can be just as refined, the perspectives with which you see Wisdom just as clear, and the perpetuity by which Paradise shines can be given to you now. You need not wait until death before realizing the parallels you share with the Savior of men. Therefore, I pray that you will pray. I urge you to heed the call of the Saints to the austerity that made them venerable in Jesus' eyes. If you tender your lives to this kind of greatness, everything else for which you have been created will flow like waters from a fall. My children, if there were any other reason for life than for you to become like Jesus, God would have revealed it to your predecessors. When you wonder what it means to encapsulate the hierarchies of joy, do you realize what happiness is? To feel the comfort and consolation of the breath of God giving you peace, are you prepared to receive Him without a whit of bitterness? Think about these things during your contemplative prayers. Wonder with hope how you will become an integral part of the lasting jubilation that is about to ensue. What role will you play? You are each individual particles in the higher calling of sanctified humanity, and Christ Jesus wishes to take you in hand. Reciprocally, if you lift Him up before the world, He will draw humankind unto Him. This is where your unity reigns. This is the endearment you are seeking, while you may not yet know it to be true. The Sacraments ensure your piety, magnify your Absolution, console you when you are mourning, sustain you during times of distress, and are your Heavenly Light in the darkness of the ages. Jesus asks you to be worthy of them not only for the sanctification of the self, but the good of humanity. There are too many divisions of culture, politics, wealth, and ideology around the globe. Will these be alleviated before the Return of the Son of Man? The answer is clouded. However, this does not imply that you should cease trying to be one humankind as a collective, peace-filled league of nations before the Earth is through. America is embroiled in a partisan debate as I dictate this message, and few are speaking about the spiritual values, the sanctity of unborn life, the suffering of the poor, the dignity of the aged and dying, and the stature of the soul in the eyes of the Lord. The only issues about which you are hearing are who will be best at prosecuting wars, whom will further the continuance of infanticide, what elitists are adept at bankrolling dollars, and what weapons are built to ensure the isolationism from the rest of humanity that the United States espouses. God deigns Me to intercede as Patroness of America so that in the end, My intercession will spare lost sinners from being subject to perdition. I advocate for your Salvation as I do for everyone who permeates the boundaries of the Earth. However, the more important issue is how you will judge yourselves.

The matter centers around the purpose of life that is given to mothers and fathers. Where do your priorities lie? Do the people of God who live in America intend to stay in cocoons of indifference for the remainder of their years? Where is the courage that you promised to wield against Satan when you vowed an oath to the Profession of Faith? To what creed will you tell the Wonderful Counselor you conformed when you stand before Him at the Final Judgment? And, most crucially, what will you say when He inquires about your allegiance to the Cross? Heaven forbid that you petition His Mercy and confess that you believed it not important. Therefore, I call you to share the lives of the Saints to the degree that you imitate them. I ask you to reflect on your dedication to God as opposed to the plight you suffer to prove it. One of the most critical questions before the world is, *Who are the children of Mary?* Turn to Saint Louis de Montfort and discover the answer. Seek the origin of your power! Know the capability that God gives you to expunge evil. Then, My children, come to Me as you pray to God, and you will comprehend the necessity of My messages. You will not only internalize the urgency of their content, but ingest the essence of everything that makes them a concordat in the conversion of humanity. Thank you, My Special son, for hearing My pleading. Thank you and your brother for the modest lives you are leading for Jesus. If I shall be given the opportunity to speak in the waning moments of time, I would bless you during each one because you are of the innocence that the Lord asks His disciples to be. You are the genius that enlightens lost souls.

And, the virtues you accomplish are the transformation not only of the nations, but a world that is burdened with peril and corruption. Listen not to those who will minimize God's miracles. Lift-up the many who are reaching for Jesus in childlike ways. And, be humble and happy that you have been chosen to play such a pivotal role. My Special son, you are enviably strong, as I have reminded you. Thank you for the love and dignity that you are giving your brother. You are everything that sustains him in his earthly life. I know that your happiness is worth the hope you have mustered while you pour-out your life for Jesus. Your brother has asked to hear the words that have launched a thousand hopes before. *'Roger, Morning Star, roll program.'* May your dreams be as lofty as the stars!..."

Sunday, August 8, 2004
Saint Dominic [AD 1170-1221]
Marian Visionary, Confraternity of the Rosary
2:13 p.m.

"Welcome, little children, into the sanctuary of My Most Immaculate Heart where you will find eternal consolation and the Maternity of Redemption. I seek in you the piety that was given humanity when Jesus was born in Bethlehem, the same innocence and purity, the same openness and simplicity that can be offered only by a blameless child. Will you give yourselves to holiness so all Creation can be remade through Jesus' Sacred Heart? Heaven is boundless and endless, and yet it is stationed inside the Sacred Heart of the Resurrected Messiah. I give you solemn assurance that you will find the peace and happiness for which your souls have yearned within the radiance of the Divine Mercy that Jesus is offering during these fleeting decades. Your Mother comes not only in Grace and gratitude, but to remind you that all hope that is built on the strength of Wisdom is arriving with expeditious pursuit on the face of the Earth. You are upright in Jesus when you accept the righteousness that God seeks of you and when you become that same holiness for those who surround you. You are servants and actuaries of the Lord's Divine supremacy over the whole world, remembering that you must ward off the temptations that draw you into sin. I have informed you that you are sinners who are uniquely capable of disavowing sin. In this resides the purpose not only of the ages, but of all that is eternal, so you will begin every day with the knowledge that your lives have been taken wholly into the presence of the ever-living Savior of the world. Wish with Me that all who hear My voice will heed the call of conscience, that they will take an intricate look at themselves, that they will realize that Truth is made manifest when you comply with the Commandments that Jesus asks you to obey. This Truth is reflected in your sacrifices on behalf of suffering-humanity, for the poor, the reckless, the recluse, and for the millions upon millions of simple people who are mortifying themselves for the greater good of humanity. Yes, you hear stories and parables about the kings of men. And, your hearts are moved to tears knowing that these kings take pity in caring for their people. However, no king can transform the Earth into the Kingdom of God without bowing before the true King of Creation, Jesus Christ. My children, endless are the hours you have pondered the mysteries that surround you. Your thoughts and actions collect you into one ensemble of consciousness on the surface of the globe, but Jesus wishes to know whether your intentions are sufficiently beatific to be in harmony with the Cross. There are many venues through which you serve Him, and His Will is that you lift-up humanity in the most profound ways while exercising your faith. This charity must be clearly authentic. You must take control of your lives by placing them in Jesus' hands. And, why do you suffer thereafter? Because you know that personal sacrifice and self-denial are synonymous with Christianity. You realize that Jesus' Passion and Crucifixion are catalysts for your desire to perpetuate the Glory of the Father. Christians are honored to suffer because you know this to be the way Creation is transformed. If you wish to see humanity perfected, become perfect absolvers of your brothers' faults in the way that Jesus forgives them. I am not speaking about a symbolic gesture such as ceding territory upon which you would never walk again. I am referring to allowing your comrades access to the catacombs of your hearts in which the quadrants of your plans reside. Give to the poor sufficient alms that you exchange places with them. Enrich the means of the impoverished by making yourselves beggars for God. Walk not only in the shoes of the downtrodden and brokenhearted, give them your sandals and carry their sorrows. Be the pleading Christ who prayed in the Garden of Gethsemane, taking confidence that the Will of the Father is with you. Never loosen your grip on the sanctifying Cup that has been your conversion for twenty centuries. If you heed the messages of the Mother of God, I will give Him your petitions along with My prayers, and the world will be healed overnight.

    My Special and Chosen ones, you know that I come with anticipation that you will live with happiness anew. All the negativity and sarcasm upon which you choose to dwell in the physical world is unwarranted. It is unholy, unseemly, and unfounded. It is the work of the devil to which I implore you to refuse to concede. Do not surrender to the despair and hopelessness that evil is peddling. Your lives and spirits belong to the Mother of Hope, Queen of the Triumph, to the King of kings, and to the Most Holy Spirit to ever reign in the seeable and unseen realms. You are many ways at the beginning of your lives, and always near their end. Why not accept the perspective that I have been teaching you for years? Why not rise and try again? Why not practice more hope? These are the things I ask from you. You are loved more than you have the capacity to comprehend while you live on Earth. Your future is brighter than a nova ablaze. The fulfillment of your dreams is just beyond the horizon of your prayers. And, the Lord will bring them to you in full if you desist in your unrest and lack of hopefulness. Thank you for allowing Me to say these things, for you are the great hope for millions who are unwittingly dependent upon your pious works for the enlightenment they need to accept the Blood of the Cross as expiation for their sins. We are a people not only of eternal hope, but sharing that hope throughout the world. The time is near when you will be required to be sequestered because of the fanfare around you, and that is the moment when you will be burdened. These are your hours of social mobility and anonymity when you travel at your leisure with the knowledge in your hearts that victory is yours. You never have to wonder what the outcome of Creation will be because the Mother of the Lord has already told you. This sets you apart from the billions of other souls on Earth. Be humbled that you have been invited to help. My Special son, I wish to share something that I have never imparted that has to do with thoughts you have entertained, and the question '...if the Holy Mother was displeased with Me, would She say so?' Do you remember this? The answer is that I would tell you so you always know My sentiments about your conduct..."

Sunday, August 15, 2004
Feast of the Assumption of Mary
3:53 p.m.

May you prosper the Gospel of Jesus Christ through the Blessed Virgin Mary!

"My children, this High Feast is for you! It is the making of your holiness, your obedience to the Holy Spirit, the nature of your self-denial, and the origin of your desire to live as selflessly as Jesus all the days of your lives. I wish for you to lend yourselves the reflection that it is not without your sacrifices that the world is sanctified. When you pray for the arrival of the Holy Spirit, your purpose is to amend your hearts so you will become the likeness of Jesus for humankind. Your faith is wholly found in your ability to seek the best of yourselves so many who are lost will follow you to the Light of Salvation. You are learning that there is much being said about communication between religions in the world. However, do not be misled by people who say that the Holy Cross is not the Redemption of humanity. Such lost souls are working for Satan. When you visit other religious persuasions, be wary of anyone who would focus your sights on material things and false prophets. Creation has always witnessed prophets, but there is only one Messiah, one Savior of your souls. This Savior, My children, is Jesus of Nazareth. As you observe, recognize, and celebrate this High Feast, remember that the Son of Mary is the only begotten Son of God. Jesus prophesied His own Crucifixion and

Resurrection so that the Sacred Scriptures would be fulfilled. The Archangel Gabriel came to Me, a lowly Handmaid of the Lord, to announce the favor of God for His Mother. The Child from My Womb is your Redeemer; there is no other. His Sacrifice on Mount Calvary is the expiation for your sins that God accepts for your entry into Heaven. The admittance of your eternal souls into everlasting life has been manifested by the Crucifixion and Resurrection of Jesus Christ. I assure you that you must remember that Jesus is your only Salvation. Hence, as you visit other religions and speak about what they believe, know with confidence that if they do not praise Jesus Christ as the Savior of humanity, they are not living in accordance with the Will of God. They are lost, and they must become Christians to be granted lasting Salvation when they fall asleep in death. Today is about My Assumption into Heaven. The Church has been faithful in living the ordination of the heart that is given you by God to realize that I did not die. My children, I shall never die. And, it is for your Redemption that Jesus laid down His life on the Cross so you can pass from mortality into Paradise without being subject to the punishment of your transgressions. Will you remain inside the protection of My Immaculate Heart so I can lead you to the Man from Galilee who has given you Salvation? I shield you beneath My Mantle in ways that you do not comprehend. The Celestial Court of Angels that surrounds Me offers you friendship, comfort, and guidance. Your petitions are heard by Jesus and given ascension by the Holy Paraclete. I urge you, My little ones, to pray for the conversion of lost sinners to Jesus, and for the end of abortion. Pray for the intentions of Pope John Paul II and for the episcopates of the Bishops and Cardinals. When you search the Earth for signs and wonders of Heaven's presence, remember the leaders of the Church who have promised obedience to the Holy Father. Life as you see it is a difficult process not only because of the enemies of the Church, but because many within the Church are denigrating its Traditions. Did Jesus not say that the world would not contain all the books required to record everything He accomplished? The Lord speaks to humanity with compassion and guidance through Pope John Paul II and the Prelates who remain loyal to His Pontificate. The Catholic Church is sovereignly living, vibrant, and healthy. The Church is the source of your piety and your reason for experiencing your conversion. And, God asks that you make your confession through the Church, that you receive the Holy Sacraments in your willingness to become Christians in the lineage of the great High Priest. The plan has been laid before you so you will understand how to live faithfully, peacefully, piously, and sacrificially. I assure you that your happiness resides in these things, and you must trust that it does.

My Special son, this is the Feast that first touched your heart and brought you to the realization that I have come to claim My children. It was fifteen years ago that you did what I am asking all My children to do, to become humble in the presence of the Lord in all you say and do. You consecrated yourself to Me and Jesus in the wonderment of the mountaintops of Medjugorje, and you have never turned back. You have kept your promise to the Creator of the ages. You have prayed like no one else I have seen. Your heart has been molded and shaped into the dignity of Jesus. You reflect His Truth, compassion, and admonition with the adeptness of the Saints. This should make you happy. You have told Me that you love Me. This is the source of My gladness because I know that your love for Me means that you comply with the tenets of your Christian faith. You will never be led astray by people of other religions. You shall not be asked to become a martyr to prove your allegiance to God, but He has urged that you burn-out your life for Him as an advocate of Divine Truth. This is why your brother and you were given the gift of life. I am interceding for you in ways that you cannot yet know, but you see signs every day. You are My gift to Jesus when your mortal years are through. O' how awesome it will be to give you to Him and hear Him tell Creation that He knows your souls! It is with this anticipation that the Heavens see you and your brother manifest the artworks of your lives. The orchestration of your Christian talents that you are playing for God is sweet to His senses. The brevity of life is difficult to overstate, and you will someday see that your smallest gifts to Christ have been profound. The Lord has fashioned a design through the powerful suffering of His paupers in America to annihilate the evil empire of capitalism. You are facing the beast head-on with His Holy Word. You are driving the Sword of Triune Justice deep into places it has never pierced. You are conquering the enemies of human Salvation that Jesus pronounced dead from the Cross, knowing that it would be you who felled them. This is your purpose, and Jesus is your strength. Everything you and your brother are doing is worthy of the Fruits of the Crucifixion. There is destiny, hope, clarity, devotion, and longevity in every reason why you and your brother are alive. It may have been simpler for Me to implant this message in your consciousness fifteen years ago in the Yugoslavian mountains, but I desired for you to learn firsthand that human love can be that same message contained in a sequence of events unfolding below the Heavenly Court with dramatic conviction. Your commission is that you are listening to Me. Your obedience rests in the venues you have been given to touch other lives with the eloquence of your thoughts. These last fifteen years have been the reflection of the revelations of Jesus for untold millions who would otherwise not have known Him. You are rescuing your lost brothers from the pit of despair. You have augmented My messages by embracing Me as their origin. On and on, day after day, you have deferred to Christ Jesus so His Kingdom may come. Thus, I bless you with the consistency of the Angels and Saints on the Feast of My Assumption. Some of the last words you will hear on Earth and among the first you will receive in the heights of Heaven are, 'Thank you for taking care of your brother.' There are no expressions with which I can describe the magnitude of this contribution to the Church. We pray atop our prayers that the epic battle for souls will be one in which you may deploy your righteous pride for selfless reasons, all who are the Mystical Body of Christ, so that the selfish pride that was shown in the Garden of Eden by Adam and Eve will be forgotten. Indeed, the storied conversion of the Earth and all souls who shall live in Paradise will be a revelation that no one will want to miss! Thank you for enlisting My modern Saints from all walks of life to stand beside you when that time arrives..."

Sunday, August 22, 2004
Feast of the Queenship of Mary
3:45 p.m.

"Love is the Dominion that gives you liberty, My children, the miraculous exhilaration of unceasing dignity that God bestows upon you. I promise you the affirmation of My Heart and Womb because your Redemption is the hallmark of My supernal being. I am the Immaculate Conception and the Queen of Creation, and I thank you for the florid crowns that My children offer Me today. Your souls require a King and Queen; and Jesus is the King of kings, and I am your Queen of Heaven. I hope you understand that My prayers are not only in union with the Church, they complement the holiness and precepts of the Church to remake the face of the Earth. I pray for you fervently, hope for you demonstratively, aid your piety with Maternal intervention, and seek from Jesus the great and final Pardon that is the deliverance of sinners to Everlasting Life. I am the Mother of God, the most esteemed Benefactress you will ever know. If you will comprehend this, the meaning of holiness will become clear to you. Jesus shed His Blood on the Cross to cleanse you of sin. He suffered the indignity of public Crucifixion so you can live in immortality. God raised Jesus from the dead so that you may be given the Fruits of His Resurrection. In these Sacred Mysteries rests the surety of your faith that stretches beyond the years. Hence, your unity with the Most Blessed Trinity demands that you concede to the Will of God for His people because He has the prerogative to forgive you through Jesus' Sacrifice on the Cross. Even though you see this as a Sacred Mystery of untold proportion, it is the Truth that is discernible by your souls. If you honor Me for no other reason than this, the Glory of Heaven is perfected in you. The work of your hands, the meditations of your hearts, the intensity of your outreach, and the petitions that you lift before the Son of Man are your labors of love, giving you all the inspiration and excellence that your spirits desire. I am hailed as the Matriarch of Christendom because beneath My Mantle resides everything holy that God ever created. I am your safeguard and shelter in times of trouble because I bear the Messiah of the New Covenant in My Bosom. I welcome you to join My Son in the hospice of My Immaculate Heart because no evil can harm you there. I implore you to heed the admonishments that I have given humanity throughout the centuries because I have seen the Coming of the Glory of the Lord. I invite you to approach Jesus in My presence for everything you have ever sought from the Father. Always remember that My Womb was the Church's first Monstrance. I beseech you to trust Me by believing that your future in Heaven is shaped by My outstretched hands. I see clearly, My dear children, because My vision is of God's Truth, and I offer you this sight in Jesus. He died to reveal His Love for you. Jesus elevates Me as the Queen of Heaven and Earth because He is My Divine Son, and this same Divinity is attainable by you. Do not be afraid; do not recoil from the perils of the Earth; never concede to forces trying to dilute your faith, and especially do not lose the trust in yourselves that you have gained through the strength and Wisdom that Jesus has deposited in your hearts. When you pray upon rising for the day, remember to thank the Lord for sharing His Eternal Light along with the morning sun. Look to the horizons with hope at the early hour of dawn and at dusk when His splendorous artworks adorn the western skies. If peace eludes you at times, know that the silent perpetuity of His unconquerable Love springs from within. Look inside your hearts for peace, and Jesus will enter there. Anticipate the future with relief because there is lasting Justice at the intersection where His Crucifixion meets the end of the world. Do not despise your brothers and sisters who hate you for everything you give to God because they do not understand the meaning of life. Forgive them seventy-seven times, then seventy times seven times, and then more than you can calculate. In essence, little ones, hold no grudge against those who have sinned against you, and neither will Jesus sustain any resentment toward you.

Every week, My Special and Chosen ones, you kneel at My feet. You are of the union of believers in the long gray line of soldiers who keep pouring over the hilltop of the ages like cleated warriors, one after another reminding Jesus that no amount of suffering or persecution can destroy your allegiance to Him. He died for you on the Cross of Mount Calvary, and He knows that this is where you are nurtured. You attend the Holy Sacrifice of the Mass daily to receive the Eucharist because you desire to remain one with the Redeemer of the lost. Thank you, My children, for being so dedicated. When winter arrives, you will finish another year of messages for recording in your diaries. My sons, whatever happens on Earth, I will employ the Grace to continue speaking to you. If one of you is suddenly or inexorably taken to Heaven before the other, I will share with you the same signs that I have accorded in the past. The venues and languages may not be the same, but you will know that it is Me. All I ask is that you trust Jesus; pray to Him that you will remain together for decades to come, and our work will proceed with the same undaunted righteousness with which it began February 22, 1991. My Special son, how kind of you to have shown the passers-by the Crown of flowers on My statue in front of your home. Subtle graces like this make the mountains tremble.

This is the simplicity of children that makes the Lord weep from happiness. And, thank you for the brilliance by which you are helping your brother collect data for his thesis. It appears that you have performed a thorough analysis of the problems that need attention around the globe. God hears your prayers for peace. Thank you for avoiding the politics that have poisoned the atmosphere in America. What they are trying to do is convince the electorate who is the better prevaricator. The entire spectrum is so corrupt that it defies description. Thank you for not getting involved. You belong to a hierarchy of principles that glorify Jesus. *(Our Lady mentioned an opossum that wandered into the yard near where we were seated last evening who was a little too close for comfort.)* The opossum frightened you! I can understand why you were startled. After all, an opossum is not a benign looking creature. Thank you for amending the ways of lost souls by lifting your petitions in your prayer room. Your brother helped you pray with such intensity that towering walls of oppression came tumbling down. I hope you remember the tremendous contributions to the Church by Saint John whose legacy will preface our next message... Never forget that I am beside you, that I am the Queen of Heaven who prospers your convictions..."

Sunday, August 29, 2004
The Beheading of John the Baptist
3:04 p.m.

I should be baptized by you, and yet you come to me.
Matt. 3:14

"The remarkable faith by which you lead your lives is itself a gift from God in whom you prevail. My cherished ones, Jesus gives you everything you need to be confident in His Grace. He provides strength for perseverance, nourishment for indomitable valor, Wisdom to choose pious paths, and the Seven Sacraments by which your hearts and souls are sanctified. You should forever remember that the holiest sacrifices for My Son are those that bind you to Divine Truth, and that your death does not end it. I speak about the faith that makes you whole because you live with true righteousness in a world that lures you to its opposite. Long are the columns of enemies who demand you to abandon the tenets of Christianity for secular humanism and atheism. However, you shall never yield to these forces. You will always be the children of Light, extolling the Kingship of Jesus Christ to the lost. We remember today the Martyrdom of Saint John the Baptist, one who condemned the heresies of pagans. He offered himself in humility and kindness when pressed into service as Baptizer of the Prince of Peace. With the Holy Spirit above the River Jordan, he fulfilled the prophecies of the Sacred Scriptures. You likewise do this by accepting your part in the Plan of God to be His disciples for Triune

Love in your homeland and around the continents. I offer you My beatific intercession so you will succeed in making yourselves worthy of the blessings you receive from God, and for those you dispense on His behalf to your brothers and sisters. This is an opportune time for you because the summoning of the Holy Spirit to take abode in your hearts is happening every moment of the day. Add to this inspiration your veneration of the Holy Cross. Ask the Lord to give you a new heart of compassion for those who are aching. Ask for a clearer vision of things around you, and be leery about people who are forcing decisions that affect you. Place your motivations in the perspective of the Catholic Church because it is the proprietor of Truth. The Roman Catholic Church informs the Earth where other persuasions fail. The Sacred Sanctuary of the Roman Catholic Church in Saint Peter's Basilica in Rome is the focal point for all nations to seek the solace and vision that 21st century humanity needs to survive. Call on the infallible judgment of the Holy See for all decisions about faith and morals. If you wish to know what Jesus Christ has to say, ask Pope John Paul II to speak. I remind you that the cup is running over. Whatever you are doing that is not for God, bring it to cessation. Everything you are giving to enhance His Kingdom on Earth, multiply your works with intensity. The stench of secular pluralism is repugnant to everything holy. Millions upon millions of people are aligned against the Roman Catholic Church. I am telling you that if you ask Jesus to defend you in defeating them, He will do it. Jesus will dispatch the Orders of Angels as your guides and protectors. Call on the Communion of Saints to be your intercessors before the Throne of God. He so loves when they honor Him. The Heavenly Court has the arsenal you need to conquer the adversaries of Christianity and the Salvation of the world. Take up your Rosaries in prayer and send everything evil around you into the fires of Hell. Call upon Saint Michael the Archangel to wield his Sword of Justice against your enemies, and he will slay them with a Starlit Slash. O' how Saint Michael wishes to destroy everything that stands between your souls and Heaven! And, pray with Me that all peoples in every nation will convert to the contrition and humility that will take them to Confession. Ask God to rebuke their pride and strip them of the haughtiness that keeps them from accepting the Holy Gospel. In memory of John the Baptist, call your fellow Christians to defy the edicts of secular kings. Become servants of Jesus Christ instead of earthly rulers. My children, if this sounds like spiritual mutiny, then you understand My words correctly..."

Sunday, September 5, 2004
Blessed Teresa of Calcutta, Foundress [AD 1910-1997]
3:06 p.m.

"To forward our agendum of piety for humanity, we value our time to share our devotional prayers. Little ones, do not worry that you might fail to hear God's response to your petitions. Lift them anyway. And, do not be concerned that your brothers and sisters might scoff at your dedication to Me. Honor Me nonetheless. Pay no mind to people who say that your lives are predetermined by fate from the moment of birth. Expect miracles to happen even so. God is not only the Maker of human life, He is the sculptor of everything by which you shall be blessed. He knows the ills and travails that befall you, and He will reshape the future if only you will submit to the Omnipotence of His Will. I ask you to remember that God wants for you the best of all things in your Christian lives through the Divine Love by which you were formed. Given the opportunity, He knows that you are capable of achieving mighty goals in ushering-in His Kingdom from the quaint valleys of your lifestyles. This is why I implore you to respond to My call with your hearts, because the charitable heart is the facilitator of every perfect act on Earth. The Holy Spirit reigns in your hearts; Jesus takes residence there, and God brings the refinement of your lives to perfection within you. My little ones, success does not imply that you will never endure fatigue, loneliness, rejection, or despair. It does not mean that you will see the immediate products of your labors. You honor God best by trusting Him to know in advance of your prayers everything you are going to say. Even in this, ask Him anyway. The foundation of your Christian Love is the platform upon which your stature in Jesus is constructed. You take your first strides toward holiness there. You give families and nations venues to establish their legacies of peace and good will there. Hence, when all is said and done, you will know that the vision of hope and Truth that you have promised Jesus and the whole Earth will be positioned within distance of your resurrected souls. And, the foreground of your loveliness will be the first place your children will wish to play, knowing that beyond the foothills and mountaintops you have deposited the best of everything God gave you to bequeath to them. I ask you to become part of the mystical nobility that will make you legends of the holiest age of men to ever walk the face of the globe. We pray not only for these things, My children, but that you will accept the suffering inflicted upon the disciples of Jesus, as no other age shall withstand it for you. If Creation is to change for the better, be givers of the future to your progeny. Be founders of vocations, missions, and societies. Establish an unprecedented era of purity by which your descendants may live. Sow the seeds of righteousness in every land and walkway so they will literally take to their knees in remembrance of your allegiance to the Crucified

Son of Man. This is what the Commandments and Beatitudes are all about. If you cannot sense the reason for complying with them at the beck and call of your conscience, do it for those who will mourn beside your lifeless frames at the solemnity of your wakes. Be not only heroes of the Cross, but makers of legacies so prolific in goodness that the Saints will wish to have inherited their wisdom from you. There are nutrients for robust beginnings for humanity in this, My children. There is faith, Light, and hope for better tomorrows. You do not know the day or the hour when the Son of Man will render time obsolete before the backdrop of the ages. This is why I implore you to be ready for His arrival. I have spoken here for months and even years, calling you to prepare yourselves and your households for the Master to return. I have summoned you forward with lighted lamps in expectation of the Dawn of the Messiah because not only is His coming nigh, but also is your Judgement. The latter is a source of anxiety for those who fear God without realizing that trust is the larger portion of their faith. I pray for you, My children, that you will become holier by the minute because this bolsters your assurance that Jesus will dispense Mercy upon you. Be unafraid what He may require before your lives are through. Give to Jesus everything He deigns you to accomplish for His Kingdom of Glory so you will stand with confidence at the conclusion of the years, prepared for God to deliver you to Salvation as your just and due reward.

My Special one, I hope you will remember with millions worldwide the holy life of Mother Teresa of Calcutta. I realize that you admire her for her service to the poorest of the poor in India, her allegiance to the Gospel, her veneration of Me, and her trust that God adores His Creation. You have a powerful intercessor in Heaven in Blessed Teresa of Calcutta. She is a Saint before the Throne of the Father who is about to be canonized by the Church on Earth. I have told you that there are billions of souls in Heaven who have not yet been sainted by the Church, and these are your elder intercessors. I speak about the Providence by which God allows the Communion of Saints to be your advocates in Paradise. It is fitting that you respect their service, recall their legacies, and walk in the foreground of piety and Grace that they have bequeathed to you from generations gone by. They are your cohorts and companions laboring beside you to sanctify humanity from the immortal side of time. You are a loyal legion of people in whom the Lord places His righteous intentions for the nations of the Earth. Thank you for helping your brother work on the thesis you will finish in the next ten days. As you can see, the brilliance you have added to it, the exceptionally innovative way of comparing the hearts and minds of men, is something that he could never have developed alone. This is the proverbial last straw of unsurpassed intelligence that will convince not only your Bishop, but Bishops everywhere, that you are on their side in espousing the spirit of Pope John XXIII's Second Vatican Council. The College of Cardinals has not revealed to humanity that whomever shall come to them with a framework to reflect the ecumenical vision of the last four Popes will find good favor among them as the Church's princes in the modern era. It seems that you have accomplished a great deal of late, and I hope you are not becoming too tired. Thank you for preserving your health. Can you sense the unfolding of the grand things to come for you and your brother in the next several years? I bless you every hour and guide your footsteps in Jesus. I support you beyond your fondest imaginings. Thank you in advance for remembering Me this Wednesday on My special Feast and for your prayers and modesty. The fall will come quickly, and you will relish the beauty of autumn..."

Sunday, September 12, 2004
Saint Guy of Anderlecht [d. 1012]
3:11 p.m.

"This wonderful and fulfilling time we spend together, My children, is a joy for Me. You lend Me high hopes, the Mother of Jesus who sees the Father's Face, that My children are mending their ways and understanding the essence of Holy Love. You are like flashing beacons in a world that is palled by darkness. If only humanity will turn to Jesus, the meaningful reason for your birth would become apparent with unequivocal clarity. We desire to perpetuate peace instead of war, honesty instead of shame, and compassion rather than retribution. Your Mother is heartened not only by the progress you are making to foster the Kingdom of God into the Earth, but for My Son's acceptance of your sacrificial gifts offered so unselfishly on His behalf. Indeed, there are multitudes who still cannot see the perspectives that I have given you through the years because they are blinded by materialism and lust. The burdensome earthly plight that has become the curse of suffering souls is aggravated by the malefactors of evil. I bring Good News for you! Listen to My messages, little ones! Jesus Christ is the manifestation of your happiness. He is reason for your hope! These are not empty promises from God whom you cannot yet see, they are His Word in the Son of Man who has already been seen. I remind you about the essential element of time, the component that helps you comprehend the brevity of your exile on the Earth. I offer My motherly advocacy and premonition of the End Times, and everything prudent you must accomplish before your days are complete. And, I dispense the benign succor and tenderness of My Most Immaculate Heart. Your decades need not be laden with duress and sorrow. You need not weep endlessly through the night, wondering from where will come your imminent revival. Your deliverance is in My Crucified Son. Your future has been won by Jesus' Resurrection from the Tomb. Though these may seem mysterious to you, they are Sacred Mysteries of the Love of God nonetheless. It is by your faith that you believe; and this is the gift that God gives those who are loyal to Him. My

Special and Chosen ones, I know you remember that My Queenship inspires the offering of My requisition for the benediction of Jesus' Mercy. I call upon Him to have compassion on the people who do not yet understand. I wish for you the knowledge and Wisdom that take your hearts and thoughts to the realization of flawless peace in which untold millions before you have died. Thanks to your obedience, you are attaining this Wisdom. There are insufficient days and years in mortal time for Me to tell you everything you could know about Jesus' life. Together, we are creating an insight of what it means to anticipate Heaven, if not comprehend what it is like to be there. I have told you that this pining for Absolution is a hunger that is satisfied by the heart. When you see the perils and travesties of justice that are ongoing in the world, you are filled with righteous indignation. Wisdom helps you see clearly and provides the means to respond. Jesus dwelling in the depths of your hearts is the reason you write as visionaries. The Holy Paraclete is supernally embedded in the eloquence of your manuscripts, the substance of your petitions, the hopes you nurture for things to come, and the good fortune with which you make them manifest. These are the reasons why you are Special and Chosen. If you are to be the disciples that Jesus asks of His people, remain the way you are. You are achieving it; you are giving Jesus every reason beneath the sun and beyond the stars to know that His Word and His presence are alive in you, and thus implanted like a seed beneath the soil of your spiritual excellence that will blossom during the final hours of the world. Please understand that I am searching for words to tell you that God is filled with gladness about the arrival of Jesus in Glory because you have prepared Him such a clement place to return. Be humbled and filled with gratitude that the Lord has included you in His Dominion of Grace. Never forget everything I am telling you. Please always remember that every joy in His Sacred Heart is bound to the fruits of your prayers. My Special one, thank you for tending to your brother, for remaining beside him through the years, and for the sacrifices you have extended to raise him to dignity as a messenger. I am enjoying the manuscript you are compiling for *To Crispen Courage*, and I know by the tears in your eyes and the hopes in your heart that your writing is divinely inspired by the Holy Spirit dwelling within you. Your holiness will expel the devil that is prevalent in the world. It is the antidote to the immorality that has befallen humanity in the wake of their sins. I do not extend My congratulatory adulation mildly, so I beseech you to realize that I am sincere..."

Sunday, September 19, 2004
Saint Januarius, Bishop and Martyr [d. 305]
2:32 p.m.

"Heartsongs and sanctified melodies of holiness are sung in this home by Christians whose faith is the reason for Jesus' joy. Do you know what this means? Do you realize the implications of your consecration to the Savior of the world? Your service, piousness, prayerfulness, and obedience have far-reaching powers that transcend not only these difficult times, but have isometric impacts beyond the Earth to offer good tidings for lost sinners. My little ones, you are more than frail mortals living parenthetically inside the element of time. Your prayerfulness changes the course of human events. You are part of the Mystical Light that has overwhelmed time and space, so that in your Christian devotion, you are creators of a supernatural benevolence. I assure you that you are wielding this power, else the Lord God would have dispensed His Wrath upon those who are persecuting the Church. O' for humanity to comprehend the eminence of this Mercy! If you ask Jesus to forgive your offenses against His Kingdom and amend your ways, He will bring healing to your hearts and upon your lands. Jesus does not require you to work miracles, for He is the Miracle Worker. He is pleading that you become His practitioners of unprecedented goodness, honor, humility, and contrition. He seeks in you the same heroism that has already delivered countless souls into His presence by martyrdom and sainthood. Be wary against false prophets who say that the purpose of life is for material pursuits. Ponder with discretion the things that the affluent offer you to patronize them, lest you follow them into the flaming pit. Do you recall that I am the Mother of Good Counsel? My advice is that you remain poor for Jesus in every way He prescribes. Prosper by the example of the Saints. Storehouse your treasures in Heaven, and they will await your arrival. I ask that you gain a sense for the Sacred Divine that gives you the ability to recognize the right paths to follow. I am with you on this sojourn of life, the lonely one you travel, from My station in Heaven. Heed My words of warning about avoiding the temptations of the Earth that hinder your vision of the Kingdom of God. It is near not only because the fulfillment of the Scriptures demands it, but because at long last, the moment has arrived according to the prescience of the Holy Spirit that fell like tongues of fire upon the Apostles. My angelic ones, what does this mean? How does this speak to the virtues of faith and perseverance? Do you know that you are the Children of Mary in these Latter Times? This makes you more than mere mortals. You must become brave in your faith, steadfast in justice, clear in your mission of Truth, and willing to endure anything the Lord asks you to suffer. You must succeed over your enemies with prayers of inflection and invocation. The enemies of Salvation live all across the globe, cloaked in other religions and holding high sectarian and secular offices. Satan has infiltrated places that were previously impenetrable by his wily fiends. Be on guard with Rosary in hand, and pray like no other generation for Jesus to strike-down your enemies, for the days to come depend upon your petitions. My children, never be afraid. Be wise about shielding yourselves and keeping your souls free from stain, but harbor no fear. If it is accolades that urge you to comply, then I extend God's deific thankfulness. If uncertainty makes you reluctant to lead, then know that Jesus encourages you. He asks you to be adept in spiritual insight so you can instruct your children how to avoid the onslaught against their purity that is happening now. There is no doubt that there are ongoing wars and insurrections. However, as grotesque as they are, goodness will always prevail. If you are true to the Cross, you will be victorious. It is a forgone conclusion and mathematical certainty. My Special son, you are about to embark on an historic and conclusive week. You will observe your 43rd birthday tomorrow, and it will be a blessed day for you and the rest of humanity. I ask you to carry this confidence with you when you address the professors at the university. Be poised, congenial, charming, and informed. I know you will do well, especially in proving to the group that the academic credit your brother is seeking is worthy of conferment. Thank you for your willingness to intercede. I am honored that you are the dutiful one who is worthy of your title. There is no way I can overstate the immensity of this accomplishment for your brother and you. In the passing of eight weeks and the penning of four more papers, your brother's experience at the university will be through. Thank you for everything you have done to assist his writing, proofread his assignments, discuss issues between sessions, appear in November to howls and scowls, uphold his dignity when his heart was heavy, and for paying the bills. This is your milestone as much as his. And, he will utilize its fruits to enrich your life and make the best of what it means to Me. You must live-out the course that God has planned for you that will fulfill your portion of the Cross. Would it not be hypothetical for Me to answer your question when God has yet to reveal His Will in a way that glorifies Him? You have always been strong and wise. Bless you for saying your prayers on behalf of humanity and for the cessation of wars in which thousands are dying. Pray for your country, My child. Pray intensely for your country. I implore everyone to remember to pray for the end of fighting around the globe. There has never been such a thing as a civil war..."

Sunday, September 26, 2004
SS. Cosmas and Damian, Martyrs [d. 303]
2:37 p.m.

"You are My fortunate children because your souls are chosen for Heaven. You will go there because you are obedient to your Savior. I bless and thank you for professing the selfless charism and humility of the heart that has brought such Christian edification to humanity. Your mission has always been about creating venues through which the Holy Spirit can touch the lives of My wayward children. I assure you that the fruits of your labors are sweet to Jesus' palate. He wishes for you to recognize the high regard in which He admires you for enlightening His prodigal flock. If you aspire to be great in honorable things, keep doing what you have been accomplishing for years. Today, it is My privilege to tell you that your petitions for the poor souls in Purgatory are resulting in their entry into Heaven. Your sacrifices and deeds manifest change in Creation beyond the Earth. You are part of the sublimity by which Jesus' Light is emblazoned into the hearts of those who are consumed by darkness. It is important for you to realize that the problem is more than a deficit of clear vision for sinners who refuse to love. They have an innate deficiency in the awareness of how to be holy. Due to your prayers, their souls are apprised of the Blood of the Lamb that they may have some share in the Salvation that the Lord grants to all. I urge you to remember that this is a death-defying gift. Be pleased that God has chosen you to be His instruments. Feel the Grace by which you are solicited. My dear children, it has been fifteen years since you traveled to Medjugorje, and I wish to remind you that you were holy people before you departed to that miraculous site. Medjugorje gave you renewed vigor to believe in miracles in a way that you had not known, and it opened your hearts to the possibility that the Mother of Jesus Christ might appear to you. I am here! I embolden your confidence to know that you have always played a role in God's Plan for the conversion of lost sinners. You have been blessed to live in a nation that permits you to pray and propagate your religion in a public way. You were given to parents who understand the meaning of charity and sincerity of the heart. I beseech you to remember with thankfulness all that God has given you because it will help you remain steadfast in faith as you enter the final years ahead. In this sense, your new world view is your friend and companion. My little children, My Special and Chosen ones, I know that you can feel the imminent joy and sense of accomplishment that comes with waking each day in the good favor of God. You are on the pious side of human history and the vastness of Eternity. I assure you that this is the result of your desire to know God. This is not blind curiosity, it is your hunger for Divine Truth, and the Lord is feeding you. You are maturing in His Providence in the likeness of the Saints. All glory and honor to Christ Jesus for providing the example of what a Saint should be! You are learning well, My children; you are living exemplary lives. My second purpose in appearing to you today is to listen, to hear what you have to say about your station in life, about the sentiments of your hearts that you wish to share with your Mother. *(I commented on the number of people who are stopping to relax on the porch with us.)* Can you not detect the decency that they feel here? Your Wisdom and vision about the Omnipotence of the Lord is a profound sensation for them to behold. They recognize Jesus in you. They wish to become like you, behave like you, think like you, air the intelligence that springs from you, and become good friends like you and your brother. This speaks volumes about your desire to help those in need, even people who are capable of deigning for themselves. You know how to communicate well with them because I have given you means through which to enter their hearts. Grand benisons are poised in the offing. As future years come, you will see more and more that your life is culminating exactly as it should. You are blessed because you worship God. Do you remember what He declared about those who love Him? What was it that no eye has ever seen nor ear heard? Billions of people throughout the ages would call themselves blessed beyond fathomable miracles to be leading the lives of you and your brother. Yes, you have fair weather to sit on the porch and relax. Always be careful not to become victims of incidental crime. Thank you for praying for the betterment of your country and conditions in the world. In just over a month, the American political process will conclude, and if anyone asks in the future whether the Mother of God told you for whom to vote in the presidential election, tell them that I said that neither was fit to serve because they refused to extol the Gospel of Jesus Christ in their words and deeds. They declined to exalt the Truth that will set the captives free. Thank you for praying with Me over the years. I know that you will never leave Me because I shall always be with you... Please invite your lost brothers and sisters to recite the Sacred Mysteries of the Holy Rosary..."

Sunday, October 3, 2004
St. Thomas of Hereford [AD 1218-1282]
3:33 p.m.

"My little ones, the elation you feel with the prospect of seeing Heaven is the fashioning of the Christian inspiration of your souls. I ask that you anticipate Redemption not only with this joy, but in the knowledge that in Salvation, you will receive everything your hearts desire. You will presently join the Communion of Saints and bask in exhilaration before the Throne of the Father. Today, I request you to pray for suffering war victims around the globe. Pray for the dying and the thousands of refugees from Sudan and Iraq.

Realize deep inside your hearts that if it had been the Will of God, these tormented people would have been you. How can the Mother of Jesus Christ be hopeful speaking to you in light of these wars? Because I know that through your petitions and intentions, hope is brought to the anguished. Indeed, enduring peace will soon prosper because My Son hears your call. God acknowledges the entreaties of His pilgrims, and He realizes that by answering your invocations, you will have good lives. Famine, lust, languishing, disease, violence, and infirmity are eradicated by your pleadings. Therefore, I ask you to pray, pray, pray! Be children of Light who are conquering the darkness of human sin by your love for God. Imagine a world in which there is no war. Think of far-off lands where there would be no more suffering children if only the more affluent nations will not be such isolationists. I tell you that these contemplations will bear fruit if you implore Jesus to make it come true. We pray together as the ages expire to bless humanity with peace and justice. Thank you for responding to My call. My Special son, I will speak to you briefly because you are planning too much activity in one day, and I wish for you to have time for leisure to enjoy the Sunday afternoon. I remind you not to push your daily itinerary. My message is the same whether or not I speak aloud, that I love you beyond all imagining. My intercession during these times is of import for the work you have taken on. I wish you would realize that your tranquility is based upon knowing that I am capable of speaking during any moment of your life. I am pleased that you chose the motion picture that you witnessed last evening. The miracle of the Blood of Jesus is a good message for the hundreds-of-thousands who saw the program. My Special son, can you see that God sometimes allows for pragmatic explanations surrounding His designs? Do you know why? This is where the exercise of your faith is most resplendent. Indeed, premonitions regularly precede such miracles. You may remember that there were miraculous manifestations that came before My first messages to you in 1991. In other words, the human soul is prepared for the supernatural before the fullness of such events is observed. This offers needed conditioning for those who might otherwise be so apprehensive that they would disbelieve because of fear. If one is predisposed to receiving miracles, which is what My experience with you and your brother has been about, then the heart will open more willingly. Hence, your good deeds and righteous works are preparing millions for the Triumph of My Immaculate Heart. This is the eternal dynamic through which the Lord works, even to the point that there are beatific elements of awareness that induce reparative prayer, religious scholarship, posthumous bequests, and other vibrant gifts that indicate that the Holy Spirit is intrinsically present. Please pray that the Lord gives you and your brother plentiful Wisdom, good health, longevity, prosperity, and Eternal Salvation. Thank you for your devotion to Me and your affinity for Jesus' Most Sacred Heart..."

Sunday, October 10, 2004
St. Paulinus of York, Bishop [AD 584-644]
2:35 p.m.

"My children, the remarkable progress you are making on your journey to the City of Truth is an achievement for the whole of humankind. You carry with you the blessings of the Lord who is not only grateful, but who shines Holy Light on the shadows beneath your feet. It is imperative that you be consumed by this Light so you will choose the nobler courses before you. Be glad in the knowledge that Jesus is with you during every step. He asks Me to tell you that many are the times when He has sculpted and provided for your success. He has watched His disciples from On High, situated at the Right Hand of the Father. My children, when you ponder the great works ahead, all the things you will accomplish in your lives, imagine foreknowing the outcome of your prayers. Think of what it will be like to look backward in time and review the impact you have had. Perceive your achievements through your spiritual prophesies as Jesus knows them. Heaven is glorified by your faith, encouraged by your perspectives, and comforted by your compassion. God is praised by the reciprocating intercession of your holy works. If you want to see the beauty of Divine Love, look deep in your hearts and ponder how brilliant God implores them to be. Indeed, when you imagine the Messianic Gospel coming to fruition within you, there will be no more wars. You will not be hungry of heart, mind, soul or body because your sustaining Grace is the Son of Man. Today, I invite you to see Creation through Jesus' eyes and be overflowing with gratitude for the good deeds that His people are committing. You are in this number. You have been taunted on several occasions to disavow the audacity that comes with faith, believing in miracles, and adoring the Lord. However, My little ones, righteous pride keeps your lives focused on the Holy Cross and victory over death in Jesus' Sacrifice. Pope John Paul II told the adolescents at Cherry Creek State Park in Denver, Colorado to proudly proclaim the Gospel of Christ from the rooftops. He was referring to the benevolent pride of realizing that you are Jesus' Mystical Body on whom God's favor rests. Why have I told you this, My children? Because I do not wish for you to be disconcerted when people say that you are territorial Christians. Upholding the Commandments and complying with the Beatitudes, and requiring others to do so, is no sign of arrogance; it is assurance that the repentance and purification of humanity must come in your age if your lost brothers and sisters expect to be as enlightened as their converted ancestors. Worry not that you are perceived as too animated in your Christian example by your friends. By all means, demand it not only of yourselves, but likewise from them. My Special and Chosen ones, it gives Me abundant joy to know that you do not concede to accusations that you are elitist in your faith and the sharing of your love. When you implement the Will of God, you do so with the commitment that His Kingdom will be more abundant for your lives. You are the Children of Mary of the present age. Be proud of your role in God's Plan. Clothe yourselves in the sacred and beautiful that you are given to safeguard your chastity. When Jesus commands that you return your baptismal gown free from stain, He means precisely this. Let no sin preclude you from calling upon His Divine Mercy. Fear not that you will be turned away. This is the message that I am asking you to deliver to the world. And, you will refer it to ears that will hear for the sake of the Redemption of their souls. Meanwhile, thank you for praying with Me and living the humility that the Mother of God has come to know in you, not because you are worthier than others, but because you believe Me. It is obvious that you have put your destiny in the Sacred Heart of Jesus. There are rewards and accolades awaiting you at the appropriate hour. For today, live the holiness about which I spoke earlier in this message. See yourselves as Jesus sees you. Be assured that you are participating in the culmination of the world, that you will take your place in Jesus' presence when He claims the Earth in Final Judgement. Thank you for acknowledging that not everything He seeks is done in one day or a week, or even twenty years. You are participants in the Triumph of My Immaculate Heart in the way that thousands throughout the centuries have served, with anonymity which shields you from harm. This is ordained by God. Remember that the crux of My message is that you live in peace, that you expect that the greatest of all things has yet to unfold, and that you will be present when My Immaculate Triumph is won. These facts are as irrevocable as the Truth can be..."

Sunday, October 17, 2004
St. Ignatius of Antioch, Bishop and Martyr [d. 107]
3:43 p.m.

"Here you are, My little darlings, glistening like diamonds amid the Earth's brutality, praying to erase the darkness. Whenever you hunger for the Manna of Life, turn to the Holy Eucharist. I remind you that the Blessed Sacrament is your Wisdom and strength. My children, I come admiringly because you are faithfully discharging your duties as Christians, and Jesus hastens to dispense Divine Mercy upon many who have spurned Him. I have spoken of the debts that humanity has accrued not only of each individual, but of the Mystical Body of Christ. What are some examples of these debts? It is clear that you owe gratitude, reverence, and thankfulness to the Communion of Saints who helped lay your foundation in faith and wash the waste from your eyes with the blood of the Martyrs. The Angels are a colony of intercessors whom you cannot see. Most importantly, never forget to exalt the Sacrifice of Jesus on the Cross because the Crucifixion is the reason your sins are absolved.

I urge you to be overflowing with gratitude for human life and the opportunities you are afforded to pay homage to God, the Father of life. Your years are saturated with wonders and blessings, and your souls are warmed by the flames of Truth falling on you from the hearth of Paradise. You possess keenness of the intellect, compassion, knowledge, and logical sense that tells you when to act and speak, and how to make amends. The swiftly passing seasons mesmerize your consciousness because you are too preoccupied with the intricacies of life to notice the reprising brilliance of the sun. The prolific Joymaker and Master of the Ages offers you a berth of freedom from which to make decisions about industries and avocations. The Lord gives you plentiful food and a fertile Earth upon which to prosper. All Glory and thankfulness belong to Him, My children. Everything you are and will ever become are gifts from God. Hence, I implore you to return to the center of your faith while there is still time. Put away the distractions of the world and turn your backs to temptations of the flesh. Never mind that you are ridiculed, but prepare for new battles against your enemies. Give of yourselves to God with such deference that your entire constitution is spilled before the Cross. I assure you, My little ones, that this is where you encounter the essence of human existence. This is the beginning of discovering why you were born as babes in the wombs of your mothers. Every question that is worth answering is reflected in your response to the call of God for you to worship Him. There stands the origin of the meaning of life. And, when Jesus asks you to suffer for your brothers in His likeness, He enlists you in His battalion of disciples, invoking the power of Easter that thrives in you in memory of Lazarus, saying...*hero, come out!* He kneels on the foot-stones of your hearts like a curious child peeking into a fox's lair. See His jubilant Face as He looks into the innocence of your glowing eyes! *Come out and live with Me!* He declares. Jesus invites you to join Him at the pinnacle of human holiness. Be His confidants by lifting the poor to the dignity they deserve. Raise My Son's Sacrifice so high that the Blood of the Crucifixion can be seen above the summits of Nepal. Then, America will believe, and Mount Saint Helens will have heaved its last. Remember My daughter who urged a nation consumed by itself to look up and out, into your sisters' eyes and your brothers' faces.* The morning has dawned, My children, and I assure you that Salvation is waiting. Put away the sins of hatred and division. Cast aside the call for freedom of choice. Let unborn children be birthed, and bestow clemency upon death row inmates in their prison cells, or the Son of the Most High will condemn you! And, when He does, you will be forgotten forever, rightfully so. My children, if you do not turn your culture of death into a culture of life, your souls will be lost irrevocably to the depths, and the Lord will heap another eternity on top of the original one. Your Mother pleads with you to disavow your wicked ways, convert your hearts to the Cross, and take refuge inside the Sacred Heart of Jesus Christ.

Jesus told humanity at the Ascension that the Kingdom of God is at hand. His disciples have been warning you for generations that the Kingdom of God is nigh, and 1,971 years after the Crucifixion, His Mother is saying that not only is the Father's Kingdom at hand, it is present and knocking on your doors. Will you heed the call of the Mother of God? Will you give Me the honor of knowing that your compliance is the answer to My prayers? I harbor hope that My children will be delivered to Heaven because I am the Matriarch of Christianity and Mother of the Messiah who expunged your transgressions. Do not make more of the world than the simplicity by which Jesus commends. Repeal your curiosities about the spheres that rotate in the cosmos or how many ages have passed since God placed them there. My Son will not be interrogated. He will not allow you to dissect His infinite genius because there was never a moment when He did not exist. And, He will not divulge the secrets of His supremacy because He wishes not to steal the thunder of your discovery of Divine Truth inside your hearts. You possess the ability to magnify this Light. It is the Dominion about which I have spoken since I was old enough to know. Let not your hearts be troubled, Jesus says. This is a summons for you to permit Him to engage your lives and expel all that is evil. It is your mandate to be as loving as you can be. The Earth is a swirling cauldron of mania and fashion, distractions and impressions. You are a better people than you are revealing, and God calls you to prove that you are worthy of Heaven. My Special son, the legacy you are establishing will awaken sleeping hearts. I assure you that you need not be concerned where next to place My messages in a published text. Your first Diary completed the task that I commissioned from you and your brother when I first appeared. Everything you accomplish hereafter complements that masterpiece of spiritual ingenuity. My messages are to teach you that there is no reason to be impatient about the way the Earth is ending. They are meant to offer hope that the followers you are leading to Jesus will cheer like echoes from a stadium. You will make the final shot at the buzzer and win the game. Your brother will toss the last pitch and strike-out your opponents. I not only bless you for welcoming My intercession, but for believing in Me and opening your hearts in a providential way. Thank you in the meantime for accepting these things in faith... I will speak to you next week on another grand Feast, and I pray that you continue to be appreciative for the gift of miracles by which your piety is sustained..."

* *Reference to the poem Maya Angelo recited at the inauguration of President William Jefferson Clinton.*

Sunday, October 24, 2004
St. Anthony Mary Claret, Archbishop [1807-1870]
Missionary Sons of the Immaculate Heart of Mary
2:51 p.m.

"Greetings on this sweet and holy Feast day, My children! I bless you with harmonious Grace because you are the beneficiaries of the wondrous and prolific presence of the Holy Spirit in your hearts. This gift is yours because you are loved by Jesus in ways that you do not fully comprehend. I have ofttimes spoken about the power you wield by His Love, that your volition allows you to know through your thoughts and actions that you are worthy of the Eternal Absolution Jesus has granted. Your petitions are proof that you accept Salvation in the Cross. The way you live in peaceful accord with your brothers and sisters instills the beauty that has grown in abundance through your compliance with the Holy Gospel. Today, we celebrate the memory of someone who holds Me dear to his heart. I wish for Creation to know that he who venerates the Mother of God is dearly beloved in the House of the Father. I protect you at all times, and I will intercede for you before the Son of Man. I beseech the Divine Mercy of Jesus through the Holy of Holies. I shall carry your concerns and wishes forever as we are united in the brilliance of Paradise. One day presently, My little ones, you will know that formulating your prayers was itself a gift from the Holy Spirit because you cannot yearn to see God without His placing this desire in your hearts. You cannot wish to be loved unless you realize that Divine Truth is the finished product of a perfect human life. You cannot hunger or thirst for righteousness unless the Holy Paraclete helps you open to believe in the Lord's primacy. These are unending interchanges between Heaven and Earth that keep your faith engaged. It is not improper to ask God for more of everything that helps you defer to Jesus, for such things are not redundant wishes. Offer to God your heart! Call on Him when life makes you stumble, and Jesus will steady your footsteps. Kneel prayerfully before the Cross in contrition, and you will become as statuesque as kings. Then, when you sense the barbs of temporal life threatening your souls, you will know that My Son will sustain you. You will feel the tranquility of God's presence within you, and you will betroth the conference of peace that accompanies you all the days of your lives. My Special son, I cannot express with syllables how much you mean to Jesus. There are no terms to aid your understanding. You are beautiful in ways that are inexplicable, especially after the passing of 43 years. Thank you for remaining united with your brother who is anxious to comprehend the honored demands of Christianity. Be glad that you are blessed to be together. You are living peacefully in this bucolic place; challenging times for the world, but peaceful here. I extend My solemn promise that I shall be your mainstay in whatever endeavors you pursue, despite what the future holds. The solstice approaches rapidly as the months continue to expire. We hope that 2005 will be a blessed year for you and your brother. Pray that God gives you peace, longevity, unity, prosperity, and Redemption. I know through the context of your devotions to Jesus that Heaven responds to your intentions. You are reconfiguring your residence into the design that you have preferred, and it is important to acknowledge that your brother's studies have not interfered with your work. I am aware that you pursue short term objectives and long term goals, and I pray that the Lord binds them into fruition. The most vital issue is that you remain poised when preparing for Salvation while on the Earth. Your years in exile should not be burdened by dreariness because you live with transcendent awareness and affirmation that God's promises are true. The main ingredient of your confidence is patience. I have told you this before. I will conclude My message because I wish for you to enjoy the day. I will offer lengthy dictations during the wintertime when you are forced indoors by the inclement weather. Thank you for being united with Jesus, and bless you for your allegiance to Heaven. Most of all, thank you for taking good care of your brother. Nothing you shall ever do will render you as blessed as the support you have given him... I will speak to you next week when we remember the Saints! Be prepared to receive unexpected blessings..."

Sunday, October 31, 2004
Vigil of the Feast of All Saints
3:44 p.m.

"Filled with eagerness to hear the strains of Wisdom, you gather at My feet to pray for humanity. I am with you to the delight of the Angels and Saints on this Vigil of All Saints to herald the Good News of Jesus to lost sinners through the benefaction of My Immaculate Heart. My children, there is no more weeping or mourning in Heaven because the tears the Saints shed filled the Ocean of Mercy where the Sacrifice of Jesus sails. The Martyrs left in their wake your buoyancy, your conveyance to piety through their legacies. I ask you to remember the Saints with the same consecration by which you honor Jesus. Think of the persecution they suffered for the Kingdom of God. Derive your courage in the knowledge that their valor paved the way for your holiness. Thoughts you would never have if you lived a million lifetimes were inscribed in their private diaries and homiletics. A means for sharing the Love of Christ with the whole of the nations is bequeathed to you in the estates of the Saints. My little ones, if you wish to know your Savior to perfection, study the reasons why the Communion of Saints never denied Him. Place yourselves in their circumstances through the annals of time to see why they never relinquished their faith. Allow your spirit to embrace their memories, to be saturated by their consanguinity with the sanctification of the soul. I speak of the Saints whose intercession you invoke with the passing of the day. My prescription for Divine Love forever excelling is not only in your empathy for their agony, but your imitation of them in espousing the servitude, goodness, charity, and purity that has taken them to the apex of Creation. It was never easy for them. Human life was treacherous at their every waking turn, and their enemies tried to kill them in their sleep. Their bloodshed was the begetting of untold blessings for you from God. Their martyrdom is the aroma that keeps your souls safe from malevolence. I wish for you to open your hearts and keep them ajar for the rest of your days so that through the intercession of the Holy Spirit and the Saints, you will receive the awesome Wisdom that has created such a backdrop for the sanctification of the world. Beyond the envelope of time, the Saints are living in Heaven with Jesus. His long suffering disciples of good faith and hope have arrived in the daylight of Paradise. They are the children of God, and of Moses, Abraham, Isaac, and Saint Joseph, My spouse. They are the brothers and sisters of Christ the King. They are the fruits of Jesus' Sacrifice of Redemption that will usher the newness of life to you. I have asked you to ponder the extinction of the years, to meditate upon the transformation of human existence into immortal life. And, I have told you that Jesus has prepared a place for you, unbounded and free from every encumbrance you could possibly conceive. Your Mother is entreating you to strive to become among the billions of Saints in whose honor we are praying today. They have not all had Masses said for them. They were not lauded in public on the downtown square. Many of them are unknown to the world. Most are anonymous men and women who accepted Jesus as their Savior on the last day of their lives. Millions did not know they had an opportunity to see the Light of Paradise until the Angels revealed it. My children, most of the Saints who bask in the Light of Glory were people who lived in shanties, who were paupers without any clothes, who had no families to care for them, and nary a penny to place into the coffers of the Church. Hundreds-of-thousands of them could not read or write, let alone possess the gift of a Holy Bible by which to hope for the resurrection of their souls. Still, they are among the fortunate ones. They are the people of God, children of righteousness, servants of peace who did no harm, who honored the Father in ways that only He has known. Their names never appeared on the Broadway marquees. They never held a microphone, never stood on a platform or stage, and at no time had a high-ranking chancellor say 'he was a mild and stately man.' I speak about everyday people who perhaps committed an error once in their lives and were placed inside cold, dark prison cells. Now, however, they are as honorable as the Pope. I speak of human beings who were disdained for being ignorant, who seemed lacking the proper rearing that might satisfy the elitists in the neighborhood. My children, these Saints are your colleagues for infinity to come, so tender your hearts to the Divine Glory that was given to them. Become known to Creation as operatives of God, as the reciprocal anonymity of the countless unheralded Saints! The Mother Church need not have canonized them in Saint Peter's Square for you to recognize them as heirs of the Sacrifice of Christ. The next two days are an opportune period for you to reclaim the dignity of the people you see every day through the dignity that was lost by Christians of generations past. I am happy because I can sing the accolades of the Saints with irrefutable knowledge that you will soon join them. When they arrived before Jesus, every one, and saw the reason He is allowing the Earth to evolve beneath the Light of the Crucifixion, they declared, '...thousands of years hence will probably never be enough!' They wish He would stand with patience until the last mortal child on Earth is conceived before He breaches the starkness of the ages with His Justice. However, Jesus will not wait until then. His Second Coming in Glory is close at hand. Your children and their children will see the manifestations preceding the end of the world. The new skyscrapers you will construct in replacement of the old will be felled this time by the power of Divine Grace in the Person of Jesus Christ. He will physically appear and wipe them from the face of the globe with the waving of a hand. Indeed, He will say, 'Be gone again! Let no one honor you as the summit of success!' The Son of Man will command you to bow before Him, shine for Him, love for Him, die for Him, and rise anew in Him to the sounds of the deafening thunder of invincible Love, the same piety and righteousness that groans from the conception of your birth. My children, you are situated on the plateau of the conclusion of the ages, and you do not even know it. Your souls are a whisper of the Angels away from seeing the battle-scarred faces of the Martyrs and Saints. Your capacity to perceive the smile of the Father is only a blink of an eyelash from here. What was once a steel girder separating Heaven and Earth is now only a strand of wire upon which a funeral dirge can be played. My children, I adore the Saints! The Saints love Me, and they love you, and they live on to fight for the Kingdom of God with the power they prayed to have during their darkest hours on Earth. The Father is informing you through the Communion of Saints to seek this power through them, from the Sacraments of the Church, through the intercession of the Holy Spirit, and by your dependence upon and filial consecration to Me, the Immaculate Conception, from whom all graces from Heaven to humanity have flowed.

My Special one, I have been speaking to you for an extended period of time. I know that you will accept this because you love Me in the lineage of the Saints. I have told you that I did not come to you and your brother in 1991 because you were more deserving than others, or that you have marked some achievement that would have sent 10,000 soldiers of My Blue Army into the squalid quarters of the world. I came to you because your hearts were open, because you could look at a relic of the Saints and wonder what it might be like to be so remembered by the faithful who will inherit your legacies when you die. I came because you were not among those anonymous millions who were unaware of the capacity of the Holy Spirit to capture the brilliance of men and utilize it to sanctify the Earth for the Kingdom you will see. I came because you were not kings with subjects to claim, judgements to render, and fortunes to disperse. I came here because you are My children; you are among those whose names will be hailed with the Apostles and Martyrs, with Saints Peter, Paul and Andrew; James, John and Thomas, Philip, Bartholomew, Matthew, Simon and Jude; and Linus, Cletus, Clement, Sixtus, Cornelius, Cyprian, Lawrence, Chrysogonus, John and Paul, Cosmas and Damian and all the Saints. I came to you because I knew you would sacrifice yourselves for the conversion of lost humanity, sparing nothing and concealing nothing that would leave a soul behind, in honor of Saint John the Baptist, Stephen, Matthias, Barnabas, Ignatius, Alexander, Marcellinus, Peter, Felicity, Perpetua, Agatha, Lucy, Agnes, Cecilia, Anastasia, and all the Saints. I came because I realized that your holiness has rendered you fit to be called the Children of Mary of the Latter Times, that you would thunder through the world like warriors on mighty steeds against the enemies of Divine Love. I came to you because you shined above the rest like Saint Timothy and Saint William, and Peace and Justice, like everyone and anyone who has ever said that they understood what the Incarnation of God was about. Therefore, I thank you for upholding the unparalleled standard, that mark of distinction that shows the world that humility and servitude are still alive. It is with this Love that I speak to you with kindness and Grace, and I ask you to remember that the Saints can hear your voices in the night. They understand your desire to snap your fingers and make the adversaries of Heaven disappear. And, they know that you realize that war is never simple, especially the heated battles of righteousness. One day, My Special son, Jesus will give the nod and you will have more than the miraculous power you are seeking from the Holy Spirit. You heard the history of America where some 60,000 patriots and confederates died on a battlefield in a course of hours with single-shot arms. And, you have known cities where over 100,000 people perished because of ordnance dropped from the bomb bays of two warplanes. These things are true; they are real suffering known to man, but they were not spiritual battles that changed anything. They did not ensure your right to worship God as you please; they were secular annihilations that have allowed millions in their wake to reject Salvation with outright impunity. Indeed, the power that will soon be given to you and My other messengers is that of the spiritual devastation of the enemies of the Cross. I am speaking about the power of Divine Revelation that will cause God's adversaries to turn their weapons on themselves. And, this is not the new war, it has always been the only war that has ever mattered in the annals of the histories of men. So, be prepared to savor a victory unlike you have ever seen. Wait until your Holy Mother is through! Wait until God raises all the Popes from their tombs and places them back in power as the leaders of the nations of the continents for a thousand years. Wait until you see the grand finale that the Lord has planned for the Legions of Angels who are fluttering around you with and without the shining of the sun. You will see why they gleefully laugh every time they are allowed to be heard by human ears. They know that their role in the paramount conclusion of time will be one of singing and dancing in a way that will be seen by all who have lived in the gruesomeness of wailing and gnashing. I give you My promise that in these solemn cities where your predecessors walked, you will witness the dramas play out where everyone whom you ever thought lacked the Holy Spirit will come counting on you. And, you will look outside your door and see the Lincoln cortege the way you always imagined it to be, not bearing the remains of a slain president, but carrying the unimaginable holiness of a nation that has forgiven the one accused of gunning him down. Yes, you will see forgiveness as though it is a touchable thing, blessed with the Blood of Jesus Christ. You will see with your eyes aglow a matter called 'unanimous perfection through the Glory of God' as the Mystical Body of Christ is seated in the flowerbed at My feet. The Church Militant, the Church Suffering, and the Church Triumphant will be united before the vision of all Creation so that you will know the part that each of you played. Then, to satisfy those who have always prayed without knowing, Jesus will tell you what He will do with the Key He is holding in His hand to complement the one He gave Saint Peter during the Messianic origin of the Earth. If you wish to speak about gladiators, legends, and kings in intelligible terms with enduring screenplay, envision yourselves as these. My Special son, your recitation of the Holy Rosary keeps you attuned to receiving My messages. I will summon the Saints about whom I have spoken to intercede for you in every way you desire... We shall go forward with the work that Jesus has given us to do. He is your Salvation, holding the future in His hands..."

Sunday, November 7, 2004
St. Herculanus of Perugia [d. 547]
3:31 p.m.

"From the ethereal realms of Heaven, I descend to the physical Earth to be your adviser and comforter. I offer you the vision that has been yours since you were given sight of Jesus in the manger. Today, I remind you to pray for the poor souls in Purgatory whose freedom depends on your petitions. Through space and time, their pleas are heard for you to remember them during the Holy Sacrifice of the Mass and when you recite the Holy Rosary. And, come Christmas this year, multitudes will be allowed admittance into the New Jerusalem because you love them sufficiently to ask the Lord God to grant them beatific rest. I understand the plight and oppression under which you are living. Creation is being stirred by the Truth of God as He watches your conversion unfold. The holier you become, the more humanity is perfected by the Cross. Soon, every goodness will be seen, and everything within your morality and consciousness will manifest the indisputable miracles of Jesus' Crucifixion and Resurrection. I have told you that if not for the influence of time, you would already realize this. For now, you have work to do. There are millions of lost sinners to reach, countless masses who do not know about the paradisial Truth that illuminates your paths. Too many innocents are suffering at the hands of secularists who boast about their fairness, but refuse to practice it. I ask you to remember these victims, that their faith will be sustained through their torment, but not in vengeance. Their perseverance is the begetting of a peaceful coexistence between societies of different beliefs, and the exercise of your Christianity gives them spiritual drink. You must effectively portray Jesus within you through the Holy Spirit.* You should harbor no ill will against your enemies, but pity them for their ugliness. Jesus gives you incentives to know that courage and enlightenment are gifts from the Holy Spirit, and you must pray for them. Ask God to dispense His Wisdom upon you so you will understand that righteousness reigns. You will discern the blessings for which to pray next week and next year because the universe belongs to you when you pray from the heart. This is the spirituality to which I have summoned you for centuries. Will you give your hearts to the Mother of God? The excruciating pain being endured by the poor in America and foreign nations is reprehensible in His sight. Lawlessness and the desecration of Christian relics push His Wrath to the limit where He will pulverize the perpetrators. Is there no fear of Justice? The Earth has deteriorated from respect between republics to an atmosphere of bloody competition for goods and services. Weapons of mass destruction have fallen into the hands of despots who will not use them to ensure peace through strength, but for naked aggression. It is clear that the grave dangers to unwary lives must be addressed by makers of good will. The tactics of the United States to destroy other countries will haunt America until the ending moment in time. My children must be aware that you are not immune to retribution. This is not something that should strike paranoia in you, but preparedness for the horrible days to come. Why not call upon Me, the Immaculate Conception, as your Protectress against vengeance by your enemies? Without My blessings, you would already lay in ruins. Recite the Rosary to invoke My intercession during periods of duress. These are perilous times because your secular leaders are ignoring My call for holiness. Your forefathers could not have imagined the destruction that would come during the first half of the 21st century to the democracy they carefully built. They could not have foretold what it would feel like to see so many pillars of freedom plunge into oblivion through the apathy of their successors. Jesus is a charitable Savior. He is the Master of kindness and unity, but if it is war that you must study, He will not impede it. If you pray for peace, He will grant you the berth to number the blessings of your children. You must turn to Him to enlist the intervention of the Father's Kingdom before the nations will be healed. My Special son, I assure you that the manuscript you read to your brother will pierce the ears of everyone alive. Do not assume that your work will have no effect. There are soul-searching, heart-rending parables in *To Crispen Courage*. Such refrains shall be echoed by those who will go to Heaven. It is difficult to bridle your pride when you are doing such holy things for people. Offer your gratitude to God for giving you the Holy Spirit as your ecclesial tutor, and be humbled before Jesus for pressing you into service. I promise you that the days will culminate in the final victory about which I speak. This year will bring a revealing Advent for the eternal Salvation you are defending. I cannot overstate the progress that the Kingdom of God enjoys because of the service of you and your brother. My Son is asking for the full compliance of Creation within His Grace, and this takes time to complete. Please forewarn humanity with certainty that they are being called to purification to prepare for the reappearance of Jesus in Glory. Thank you for being Heaven's courier. I shall close by urging your brother to embark on a trip to McKendree cemetery to honor the memory of the people buried there. This will satisfy the request of the Church to pray for the faithful departed, especially during November..."

* *Saint Paul stating 'Christ alive in us!'*

Sunday, November 14, 2004
Saint Lawrence O'Toole of Ireland [AD 1128-1180]
3:28 p.m.

"Jesus sees every microscopic fiber of morality and goodness inside your mortal souls, little children; and like the mustard seed, He helps them grow in you so that you become the giants of sainthood that God has always wished you to be. I speak to you today with great hope that humanity everywhere will heed the call of the Holy Spirit to receive openly and willfully the Grace which has become your sustenance on the Earth and the Love of Jesus that is your strength during times of trouble. We pray together that the righteousness about which you speak on occasion will also continue to flourish on a societal basis so that nations and continents will accept that transformation which is the call of holiness. I ask you to never surrender to the grudgingly pale babbling of relativism that is trying to take your faith away. Ignore the call for allegiance to any persuasion of politics because you owe no loyalty to any authority other than God. Remember that there are many seasons in the world that historically come and go—a time to live and a time to die, a time to reap and a time to sow, a time for mourning and a time for dancing. You must know that the Mother of God is telling you now that this is the crucial time in human history when pious people everywhere must band together beneath the Holy Cross and defend the Sacred Scriptures, even unto your deaths. Pay no mind to the radicals who say that a certain gender is worthy of a pagan movement of equal rights. Denounce those who proclaim that abortion is not a mortal sin. Heap much pressure on public figures who are calling for the social acceptance of lesbianism and homosexuality—for these are the workings of evil. Collect your consciences inside the Most Sacred Heart of Jesus and He will protect them there, He will give you the Wisdom you need to see past the prevailing winds of sacrilege that are attempting to keep your piety down. Jesus has given you to Me as My holy children. I will not abandon My children to the wretches who are trying to take you down errant pathways, away from the purity and sanctity that you have gained in Jesus. I will protect you from harm if you will remain steadfast in prayer with Me for the conversion of lost sinners, for even these sinners must be told the Truth before the last day is done. I wish for you to accomplish this, My children, lest they be lost! Remain in prayer and meditation. Pray the Holy Rosary every day.

Today, I wish to also set your sights on the great Saints who have gone before you. This is the month of November, a time when you should especially call upon the deceased who have risen again in Jesus to be your intercessors. Soon, you will enter the Season of Advent once again and the arrival of another new year. Can you not see that time is passing-by very quickly now? It is inexorably marching toward that Final Battle that will end the ages and present to humanity that most crucial opportunity for everyone to return to the fold of the blessed. These are not just passing days in a perpetual world of endless time, they are critical times during which you must pray for God's help. Ponder the contributions of the generations before you, those who have continued to build-up the Mystical Body of Christ on the Earth. Give yourselves the opportunity to be one with them across the chasm between time and Eternity by remaining in unity with the Apostolic Church. You already know that mortality does not end human life, it only changes it. The continuation of the goodness and propriety that you begin here will not conclude here. Therefore, be careful to choose the pathways of righteous accord. Never mind how you may be chastised by those who do not believe in God. Ignore the crowds who scoff at you for your allegiance to Jesus Christ. Lend no ear to the enemies of the Holy Cross in which humanity has gained Eternal Salvation. You are the people of God now! You are the maintainers of Justice around the globe. You are the visionaries who have blazed new pathways of peace where pagans everywhere have denounced your faith as a signal of weakness. Your faith has already destroyed them! By that same faith, you have already been saved. And, through your suffering, so have the souls of the enemies of God been bleached and cleansed of the corruption that would have otherwise kept them from seeing the Face of God and the Light of Paradise.

Your Mother is asking you to give the millions who do not know God an opportunity to greet Him and know Him in you. Walk with your spirits so aloft that the many who pine for a morsel of your righteousness will need to look upward for their reward. Be the peacemakers that Jesus has asked you to be by defeating His enemies with your kindness. Hold your souls next to the Flame of Righteousness and see that Good Grace emanating from you. Do you remember that your Immaculate Mother has promised that, someday, all those who wonder why you are so happy to be Christians will eventually envy you? This time has come. Yes, the world is changing by virtue of the demand for change that has grown from the conscience of Christians around the world. I assure you that you hear of change for the sake of holiness because new voices are being heard for the recapturing of purity and Light. This has nothing to do with borders of nations, politics, elections or who is fortunate to live in the most prominent white house. It is the inner-spirit of a collective humanity who has decided that it has seen enough of the perversion of the Gospel of Jesus Christ. Roman Catholics around the globe must lift-up the Papacy to the nations as the example of human perfection on the Earth. All Revelation and Truth comes from the Roman Catholic Church. When God says 'Be now My vision,' He is saying 'Be now My Roman Catholics!' Strength for your journey comes from the Most Blessed Sacrament. Wisdom and power are given to you when you receive the Holy Eucharist in Communion. It has been said that no state or people own the Truth of God. However, the Truth of God is revealed to humanity through the Roman Catholic Church. Should anyone on the Earth wish to place their soul closest to the hearth and Heart of their Living God, they must come to the Roman Catholic Church. There, they will be warmed in spirit and given the Wisdom to know that miracle of Vision which was given to humanity when Jesus ascended into Heaven. Do not shy away from proclaiming everything I have told you today to anyone who will hear. To those who will not, pray that God will have Mercy upon their wretched souls..."

Sunday, November 21, 2004
Memorial of the Presentation of Mary
4:33 p.m.

"O how I love you, My cherished sons. I bring the blessings of our grateful God for your distinction in the work He has given you to do. We set out long ago to mend a world that is painfully broken by the sinful actions of men. Years, dates and seasons later, you see that righteousness is prevailing in places where Divine Love was never given the opportunity to flourish. We have restored decency and humility in many quarters of the Earth; we have filled faithful hearts with energy, and we shall continue as long as the Father deems it necessary. I assure you that the miracles He has wrought will become apparent to all. I give you this promise from Heaven. I have told you that our prayers and your good works precede this peace. You escort lost sinners to the Fount of Divine Mercy by your example, and this is a source of gladness for them. We ask Jesus to heal the brokenhearted and touch hardened hearts. We seek His consolation for the grieving and comfort for the dying. We ask Him to dispense His compassion on the suffering poor, those who lie in hospital beds with crippling diseases, and the tens-of-thousands who have never been told that they are loved. Be at peace with the knowledge that this year has been another installment toward the growth of the righteousness of men. Give the Lord an opening, and He will usher-in the blessings for which you pray. He will clear the eyes of the blind and allow them to witness what you have seen. These gifts are not the result of magic, they are the profits you have gained in the Providence of Truth. I wish you could know in your hearts the profundity of the triumph you have won in Jesus' Sacred Heart. It would seem that there are too many distractions that keep you from envisioning the joy and peace that the Holy Spirit brings, but when you pray, they arise in fullness. My Special son, I see that you have contracted a virus at your workplace. I realize that it is little consolation, but such has a detoxifying effect on the body. You are being cleansed of foreign elements through the alertness to which your system has been called. I know that you will feel better in a few days time. Thank you for remaining indoors while you recuperate because it is damp and cold outside. And, you know that a week from Wednesday will begin another era for you and your brother as his studies at the university are concluded. You will enter winter with a return to many of the same holy acts that you performed prior to June 2003. Even through the heaviness that his academic studies have been, he has proven to skeptics that he is of stable mind, lending sufficiency to your work. And, you may change other things such as attending the Holy Mass at the Blessed Sacrament parish. This will stir fond memories and restore a sense of continuity to your lives in Jesus. I know that you have sacrificed plenty to remain loyal to your pursuits. You have been separated from your family and forsaken by your friends. While this pains My Immaculate Heart, you will know in time that you have done everything right. Please remember always that you are loved and admired by God..."

Sunday, November 28, 2004
St. Stephen the Younger, Martyr [AD 714-764]
3:33 p.m.

"Good afternoon, My dear children! You are the glow of the ages for many whom you have yet to meet. These are glorious times because enlivenment has come in your day through your obedience to Me. Today is the 333rd day of 2004, and there are 33 days remaining. Your union in Jesus finds you on track to make this one of the most prosperous for the conversion of humanity as any you have heretofore lived. Your Mother is pleased by your multi-dimensional approach to life, that you engage the spiritual bedrock of Christian Truth that supports your holy acts. The Dominion of God hovers around you, as it has in past ages for the Saints who nurtured and propagated My Son's Kingdom. When people live the Truth, which is your visionary life, there need not be a debate about how much piety one should aspire to achieve like the conversation you heard this morning on the television program. Life is precious, and life should be protected from the moment of conception in the womb. Likewise, no one has the authority to take another life for crimes they may have committed. Capital punishment is a grave sin against Heaven. When you approach social justice with thoughts of forgiving and being forgiven, you will be aligned with the mission that Jesus has assigned you. From men toward other men, there are no unforgivable sins, and humanity is commanded to absolve those who offend you because this is the way the Son of Man asks you to live, and it is the example that teaches future generations how to survive. The accomplishment of the holiness that Jesus requires is contingent upon your willingness to forgive those who trespass against you. When you ask God to pardon you, expect that He demands you to do the same for your brothers and sisters who have maltreated you. Is this a sacrifice for you? The answer rests in comparing the forgiveness you are asked to offer with Jesus' Crucifixion on the Cross. My children, yours is the easier task, but one that is as wholly important. I urge you to direct your course of life away from competition for power, political gain, and material wealth that is the mantra of the United States. If you believe that God sheds His Grace on you, then you should live like it. There is no Grace for a nation that fosters the killing of unborn children. There is self-aggrandizing pride by its people, and there is no legitimacy before the Throne of the Father for the acts you perpetrate to hold your independence. Indeed, there is no Grace for a nation of military might that kills innocent civilians by the thousands in foreign cities with impunity. You are not the peacemakers that Jesus requires you to be, and a sure and definitive discipline is awaiting you. There is no Grace shining on a nation that allows its weakest members to live in abject poverty and with illness without healing. These are the things that make the United States a cursed land for wealthy independents who claim to be benefactors to the paupers of the world. The United States creates more pollution to the air, land, and seas than any nation in history. Unwitting people around the globe are being exploited so America can stockpile its military and industrial resources. This, My children, is far from the home of the brave that Jesus expects to deliver. The affluent in America and those who support them are legions of white-collar hypocrites whose destiny is less than enviable. I am Jesus' Immaculate Mother, speaking on His behalf. The Father who gives life is as displeased with the United States during this hour as He has ever been with any state, society, or republic whom He has disavowed through the ages. My children, your time for obedience has come. You will find no solace in your booty when the Son of God takes you to task. America will fall to its knees and beg Heaven to relent in the suffering you are about to endure. Then, you will realize the meaning of agony the way

Jesus suffered on Good Friday. My Special son, I do not wish you to be unnerved by the warnings I give. You will dispense this message to your countrymen in 2008. Millions of your brothers and sisters will hear, and whether their reaction is compliance or scoffing remains to be seen. We shall remain united in the guidance of the Holy Spirit and tell them what Jesus demands. At the last, the prayers of the faithful will determine our success, and I have every reason to know that victory is ours. I have told you this before. Can you see the descent of the United States into the dungeon of secular humanism? And, can you see God's response to this crisis? Jesus will prosper the work of the disciples who are devoted to Him, and they will be shielded from the onslaught that will befall the adversaries of Christianity. There are many tests that must be passed by those who claim allegiance to the Cross. Your lives were not meant to be comfortable, and this is why you have chosen the sacrificial way. As you have stated, the burden and the yoke leave you none the worse for the wear... The future will ratify my prophecies today... Thank you for celebrating Advent with hope for the conversion of the world..."

Saturday, December 4, 2004
Blessed Ivan Sleziuk, Bishop and Martyr [AD 1896-1973]
5:23 p.m.

"My beloved little children, this is so much a time of Grace for you that you cannot grasp its magnitude. You are living an epoch that throngs of people before you have prayed for, the opportunity to be teachers of agnostics and serfs, mentors for doctors and philanthropists, and examples of human servitude for the millions around the globe who do not know what Christianity is. These days are filled with mystery and miracles; they are your opportunity to capture the Wisdom which has thus far transformed the Earth by the power of God into a plateau of cohesion and understanding beneath the Holy Cross of My Crucified Son. Dwelling within you is the effusive and flourishing efficacy of Eternal Paradise. You are heralding the revelations of God by allowing the Holy Spirit to thrive in you. If you ponder what this means for humanity; if you take the broad envisionment to see the perspective that I have given you through the years, you will know that you are new creatures beneath My Holy Mantle and are no longer imprisoned by the darkness you have always feared. You are preeminently and pervasively the Saints who have yet to step across the threshold of mortality. And, with this comes great responsibility. The two of you have touched so many hearts that it is beyond description. In a matter of 554 days, your message of conversion and the example I have asked you to set have reached the hearts of the lonely and forsaken, some of whom are highly esteemed educators and administrators. Magnificent challenges are being made by people to accentuate the goodness you have come to know.

Indeed, slowly but surely, the flowering of holiness that I have dispensed upon this place and within your hearts is growing to wider parameters. And, people who are close to you are asking not whether they should believe you, but whether they can trust themselves to become worthy of the inspirited Wisdom residing in you. I have told Creation about the final ages in which miracles will beget miracles, and the Children of Mary with high-arching faith will restore the dignity of lost souls. These are those days about which I was speaking. This is the starlit beginning, the throat of the joyous melody that I told the Saints in years past would come resounding across the chasm of time to intersect history and the future with unparalleled urgency. My children, you are participating in this masterful plan, the culmination of the hopes and aspirations of the billions who lived before, anticipating the Triumph of My Immaculate Heart. Jesus has told the world that weeping would be turned into laughter, and mourning into rejoicing. Tears shall be changed into cascades of freedom for societies who for centuries have been buried beneath the rubble of oppression and anarchy. Anything and everything that has ever seemed wrong in your hearts from whence you were little children will be redressed so you shall not take a negative thought into the final moment of life. Many ask whether this could be done, but it is happening now! You speak of becoming the stabilizing element in a world torn asunder because you have been conditioned to be wise in the Sacred Heart of My Son. You live and do well because you are His voices who whisper comfort to the ears of the bereaved and shout the Truth of God's Wrath to the unrepentant. You were given a hearty commission that is fashioned by the Justice of Christ, and you are fulfilling it with precision. Hence, do not question the Will of the Father as you travel this road of victory. Never permit the journey to give you reason to doubt the destination. I assure you that we are everywhere changing the essence of human existence because you embrace the miracles that are given you with the same loyalty and allegiance to Salvation that took Jesus to His Crucifixion on Good Friday. My Special son, I am so pleased that I am nearly beside Myself. When I tell you that these are days of anticipation, I promise that you can take this as fact. I realize that you have questions that you would like to ask as the recipient of additional information, and you are deserving of answers. I desire for you to have them. Remember that you have done everything you have been chosen to accomplish. As you know, this bears a higher mystical meaning than you can detect, but you will see more clearly in the ensuing weeks. Thank you for your obedience to the Holy Spirit through which you are given the vision to see the heights of Heaven from your purview on Earth..."

Sunday, December 5, 2004
St. Harlan De Canter, Hermit [AD 1490-1577]*
2:29 p.m.

"My dear ones, you need not possess hypermnesia to recall Jesus' words of righteousness given to humanity twenty centuries ago. When I asked for miracles on your behalf, who could have known that the greatest would be Me? Through your faith, you believe that I have borne a Savior from My Womb to the Earth, not only as your Redemption, but the model of holiness and service by which you are blessed. When I speak about signs and wonders, I invoke your trust that they are gifts from God, and that you will act upon them. You must see them as seedlings of fruit in your lives so that in the wholeness of Christianity, you can alleviate the suffering of the poor and bring purity of heart to the millions who are trapped in the bowels of evil. I realize that your existence is a perpetual struggle against the elements, the injustices that burden the landscape, and your own frailties. There are other triple-headed beasts about which other visionaries have written, but they originate from the same place. All despair and inequity are products of the lack of human faith in the Dominion of the Lord. Trust that God is leading you to the Promised Land through the valleys about which you were forewarned. You speak of shadows and death as though they are something to fear, but this need not be true. If you taut your conscience according to the Gospel, you will have strength, courage, and insight at the foundation of your heart. Hence, I ask you to never surrender the anticipation that you have established as the stairway of ascension upon which you are approaching the Throne of God. Heaven dispenses countless graces to assist you along the way. If this were untrue, Jesus would have told you. Indeed, if this were not true, I would not be here, conversing with you now. God loves you beyond all telling, in dimensions you cannot fathom. While your days are like leaflets in a book, the boundless Paradise to which He calls you will leave you reclined in castles of joy, not that you will never see darkness or death before then, but they will no longer matter. You must remember that God has no beginning or end, that everything chaste has always been perpetual. Human knowledge in compliance with Divine Wisdom is inherited by you. Jesus requires you to be prodigies of love in His likeness, something that is entirely achievable. I am not speaking about your capacity to recite the Periodic Table of Elements by heart or compose orchestrated symphonies when you are ten years old. I am referring to recognizing the difference between God's goodness and the malevolence of the world. I am describing your proficiencies to be holy in the face of the dereliction and rampant temptation that you fight at the dawning of every day. I speak about never-minding your losses in situations where winning would take you no closer to Salvation than you were before. My Special son, it is My honor to speak to you because I love you. You and your brother fight the loneliness of isolation because you are loyal to Me. This is no deprivation, but the essence of Christian sacrifice. Peace and joy live in this home, at least when the two of us convince your brother that all is working toward the conversion of the lost. I give you signs and wonders because you know from where they are derived; you appreciate them, and you do not dismiss them as coincidences. Do you remember that Jesus was not seen as a prophet in His native land? The fulfillment of the Scriptures is complemented by My intercession and the Grace of God's Love. Your brother accepts signs with greater assurance from you than from the Angels. Imagine the incongruity. Tell him what I am going to reveal to you now. Do you recall April 24, 1995 when he was struck by lightning? And, you are aware of the role that the phenomenon of 333 has played in your lives since the 1970s. If your brother asks whether the 554 days he spent at the university was his doing, tell him that it was the Providence of God. Nine years after he was struck was day 333 of his tenure in school, April 24, 2004. One cannot plan this or attribute it to chance. This is another sign that your lives are on course. You are entering Advent with holy thoughts and pious intentions. I am jubilant that you and your brother are My children, united in My Grace. You have been praying for a long time, and the signature 33s have been revealed to you for 28 years. And, from where do you believe their origin has been? Yes, from the Cross on the mountaintop in Medjugorje... Please never forget that My Love for humanity is indispensable..."

Sunday, December 12, 2004
Our Lady of Guadalupe [AD 1531]
2:59 p.m.

"With the peaceful reign of Jesus Christ, I come on this Feast to pray for the conversion of humanity to the Holy Cross in which you have been reconciled. My Immaculate Heart is elated because My children are remembering Me in Masses, cenacles, holy hours, and devotional prayers. I blessed the world in the 1500s with My apparitions to Saint Juan Diego, a miracle that is manifesting pious graces to this day. If nothing more you have learned from My maternal intercession over the generations, please remember My call to prayer. Your homage to the Father, your gallantry toward the Mother Church, and your Christian humility are fruits of your petitions. These are not clement times to live, but in Me you have a gentle Mother whose kindness has led many to Redemption. Indeed, the conversion of the millions in Mexico, the eradication of the plague, and the witness that these miracles have wrought are proof that your response to Divine Love is more than a gesture of conscience, it represents the deliverance of humanity to holiness and consecration. Therefore, I come bearing blessings of peace and joy. I bid you to become like Jesus through the benediction of the Increate Truth that is growing inside you. With this plan for the future, you prosper in the anticipation that your Salvation is close at hand. When you recite the Holy Rosary, remember the Saints and seers of miracles. Realize what these people and these manifestations mean for you. If you approach Me in prayer, I will take you to Jesus. And, if you elevate Jesus before humankind, He will raise you to the Father. I promise that the Holy Gospel lives in everything I say. If you exchange peace and absolution with those who violate you, God will declare you free from your own transgressions. Prayer is the key, little children. It is your compliance with the Apostles Creed by which you obey the Commandments and agree to His requests. I ask Jesus always and everywhere to make this happen. Now, My Special and Chosen ones, I wish for you to underscore your success with the realization that in Me, you are more than sanctified because I am in union with the Holy Spirit who resides at the center of your being. I have asked My 20th century seers to become like Me by emulating the Love of Jesus. Everywhere you are comporting with My wish; you are living the Will of God. Be content in the knowledge that you have done this. You are not only My messengers, but also My miracle workers for the souls who would not otherwise engage the presence of the Lord. Do not desist in fighting the struggles you face because they will soon come to an abruption. As you have been told that you know neither the day nor the hour when the Son of Man will return in Glory, remember that the Triumph of My Immaculate Heart will culminate in that same resplendent moment. Have no despair that you endure occasions of darkness, for they scatter in God's Eternal Light. Never mind the castigations that you receive from pagans because you are children of the New Eve. Remind them that you are devoted to Me, that your love for your Mother has taken you to heights of holiness that you could not find elsewhere in the world. Tell them of the prescience that God has implanted in you, your knowledge that your souls are bound for Heaven. This was true for Saint Paul, and it is your future as well. I would not remain with you to share My messages if I did not know that you will live in Paradise with the Angels and Saints. Be sure of your success and more patient with your critics. I concede that this is easier to say than for you to do, but come the end of time, you will know that it has been worth it. You are not alone; you have never been alone. Remain beneath My Holy Mantle where you bask in the Light of the Sacred Heart of Jesus, and your lives will evolve with higher meaning. This is the Grace of the Lord shining upon you.

My Special son, you are moving toward the last day of 2004. As I have told you in past weeks, you have every reason to be assured that history will record this year to be one of your most endearing and productive. There are people who see you and your brother treading the Earth with peace and grace. Thousands whom you have never met know your names. I ask you to proceed in anonymity because it allows you to finish the work that Jesus has given you to do. I see facets of your lives in ways you cannot comprehend. The strength you lend your brother to be more receptive to the Holy Spirit is evident in the prayers you raised to Heaven yesterday. I will explain further. There are several reliefs laying beside you that depict sacrificial acts of holiness and the edification of the hapless world. Please reach for them, and I will describe what I see. The first is a portrait of a disciple of God holding a relic of one of the greatest Saints to ever breathe. His name is William the Conqueror, and he lived in the United States, born to modest rural parents in AD 1961. Pilgrims by the thousands sought him for advice and to pray before this relic, said to have brought forth healings and miracles for the sick and those with tepid faith. He has since been honored for his devotion to the Blessed Virgin Mary who appeared and spoke to him with candid spontaneity, dispensing thousands of pages of journal entries about the Catholic Church, the conversion of humanity to Christianity, and the culmination of the End Times. The second relief has two parts. We see this Saint situated beside one of his companions and the relic that brought the Providence of God to bear upon the wicked of the Earth. The image you are seeing is your courage; it is your love for Me; it is your vision and strength in your life with Jesus, and it is the miracle by which you have slain the dragon of impudence that has laid ruin to so many lives. You impaled the evil that has taken throngs of God's children down the road of impiety. The next relief is when you told Jesus that you are in control of your future by giving yourself to the Will of the Father, a promise you have kept to this day. There is a Scepter of Truth above your head that will not permit a tint of doubt to depose you. And, the relief to the right bears the plaque where you affirmed the Letter of Saint Paul in I Timothy 3:16. Your deference to Me, your love for humanity, your allegiance to the Cross, and your foretelling of the future uphold you in the Eternal Glory that is at hand; and you are the backdrop upon which the Son of Man has scripted His Word. The final relief is the grandest of all. It is an image of power so strong that it can rescind the ferocity of a million ballistic missiles. It was engraved into the world to prosper humanity's purity and wholesomeness, so much so that the Saint whose image appears to the right has come calling upon you for Wisdom through your commission from God. You enlivened her heart and caused her to manifest a spiritual movement in the Americas that brought untold numbers of Hispanics to convert to Catholicism. I am dignifying the Earth's iconography of Christian values, and I assure you that humanity will see these relics of your dedication to the Lord. Before that moment arrives, please regale them with My message today where I have celebrated the gifts you have given through the years, the sacrifices through which many will be converted, that the Will of God is done. These things carry multitudes of intentions that simple writing cannot capture because you are invoking a faith that is miraculous in itself. I am joyful on this Feast because all is not lost. Darkness is never unchallenged in Creation. The Children of Mary are emitting beatific light. I assure you that everything you are doing assists in the reaffirmation of the founding of the Marian Movement of Priests. Your struggles for Jesus sustain their purity and the reparation that has been made. Now, instead of clergy succumbing to Satan's deceptions, you are feeding his hounds poison for which there is no antidote, driving his dogs' carcasses into the grave. There is deliverance in this that you will discover soon. Rather than evil hovering like vultures over priestly vocations, you are despoiling the devil's appetite with a lethal dose of righteousness. It is the same with Jesus the Sacrificial Lamb who was Crucified for humanity, even though He has always been free from sin. You have expanded your knowledge about the role of the Church in the sanctification of the Earth, and you have come far in defining your own spiritual identity. I delivered your petitions to Jesus during your midday prayers on December 8th. You look so peaceful in the Church of Saint Aloysius. *(During noon Adoration, I told Our Lady that I was present for everyone who could not be there, presenting their petitions.)* We have spoken at length today because you accept My messages with charity, and I feel welcome here..."

Sunday, December 19, 2004
St. Anastasius I, Pope [Son of Maximus, d. 404]
3:01 p.m.

"We pray that the Holy Spirit permeates the hardened of heart so they are comforted by their rebirth in Christ. If you pray with Me, He will touch them, and they will be healed. I described in My earlier messages the difference between the knowledge of God and the Wisdom of God. The transformation of knowing Him to becoming one in His sacredness is manifested by your conversion, sowing the seed of edifying Grace in your spiritual consciousness. You have come to the last Advent Sunday of 2004, and you call upon Emmanuel to remain in your presence for everything you seek from Heaven. Jesus is always and everywhere your King, and I promise that in Him, justice, peace, and decency are yours. Advent is your hope for Glory, the stirring of the heart, and your receptivity of the arrival of Jesus to close the ages. You have always known that the human heart is simultaneously fragile and permanent, and your exuberant fidelity to Christianity helps you reach across the expanse of time to see your place in history. God will collapse the ages into a single moment, and you will see the face of Heaven. What will He find you doing? Will you be cavorting with reptiles or soaring with eagles? You search for treasures that Creation has hidden that appear to elude you, and they are found in My Son. Jesus is more than the Child you honor on His birthday, He is Mighty Lord and Master of the New Jerusalem. Call on Him, the Son of the Most High, for favors from the palms of Sacrifice that bathe your souls with forgiveness. How can it be true that O' Israel is this blessed? Because you are clothed in Absolution by God's generosity without end. This is the way your forefathers lived who have been raised into the Eternal Kingdom. When you sense antipathy in your hearts, enlist the Holy Spirit to be your guide, your reason for life, your strength and rest. Christmas is about the call for peace in nations foundering in war. It is Heaven's call for Jesus' disciples to be deployed. Your acceptance of the Will of the Father cannot happen unless you embrace the Man from Galilee in whom your Salvation is manifested. When you do, you will finally understand the principles of life and your station in perpetuity. You will know the basis for the creation of men, and how you are justified in the Messiah. You will have grasped the Sacred Mysteries in which your souls shine as the centerpiece of your faith. My Special and Chosen ones, I will offer another message in 2004, and you will enter a new year learning about the enlightenment of the heart in a context of sacrificial benevolence. This will occur because obstinate sinners will open their lives to Jesus, not before more destruction has been perpetrated by those who are lost, but open their lives they will. All the catastrophes in the world cannot place a blemish on the certainty of your Christian faith. Let the heathens concede to the bombastic errors of human blasphemy, but this will do nothing to diminish the piety of the children of God. You must be stouthearted and long-suffering; such strength is your accolade. The scowls that you see on the enemies of the Cross are enigmatic, but gleeful smiling and spiritual equilibrium overwhelm every heart that is consecrated to Jesus. The Triumph of the Cross and the Triumph of My Immaculate Heart stand in Biblical harmony. The Church is prospering in places you cannot see. Look not only with your eyes because Salvation is beyond your sight, that humanity has hungered for these sources of joy since your ancestors were babes. The pains that suffer your spirits are eradicated in the Crucifixion that gives you forgiveness. The holiness that makes time irrelevant fashioned the world, and this is the hand of the Father in everything He does. Not unlike your forbears, you are preserved by the sanctity of His Kingdom through which you shall be raised in Jesus' Resurrection. Hence, you are citizens of the present and inhabitants of Eternity. Your souls are situated in the world, but they are traveling toward their final resting place.

Therefore, My Special and Chosen ones, do not dismay at the unrest in your midst. You are seeing remnants of the depraved evil that first attacked Jesus in those who claim to be Satan's minions. Many will die of their own accord, others caught in the guillotine of Justice, and more will be converted as the holiness of My children is ultimately unleashed. Why are impulses prone to evil only vestiges of the corruption that felled Adam and Eve? Because Jesus defeated Satan by His Crucifixion. Many claiming to be wicked will scamper like mice when evil forces are turned against them. Do you recall My words that God's children do not know enough about hatred to hate? You are seeing lost sinners embracing a culture of death and impurity being festered by remnants of evil, but they will be awakened by the realization of their inability to extricate themselves from the path to Hell. Some lead lives of dysfunction and chemical dependency, but they will come to see their helplessness to orchestrate their destiny. Others will find that success is not what they expected. There is goodness in them, but also materialism and conspiracy; and these are issues that Christians reject. Secular fortune can be an appalling paradox for souls sown to the Spirit of God. Remember that age is no presumption of wisdom. Can you sense the sublime Grace present in Christians? The poet you once cited said that the romance that the world exists to realize will be the transformation of genius into practical power. You take this still further by explaining that holiness is prescribed by your faith; genius is the Providence of God, and practical power is your ability to scrutinize life through Jesus' eyes. You seek perfection in what the Lord deigns, declares and allows, which is a divergent position from the writer's existential premise. Most see your need to quote him, knowing that you are capable of foreseeing the connection between the internal being, which is transcending of existence, and your compliance with God's Will through the Roman Catholic Church. Recall what your brother posited about the flippancy of the human spirit, that it is God's cushion between being and doing. You complete this circumference by proving that people can coexist with ordinary fate and pursue Redemption at the same time. There, your being supercedes the physical frame; and in doing the Will of God, you have already permeated the veil through which you will pass at the moment of death. You shall live with the Lord who gives life, who sustains your faith, and who perfects your good offices in the Blessed Trinity. Sadly, the storied 'everyman' on the street would believe that you are deluded because you speak about a world that is upside-down, while he thinks his is upright. Like a billion Roman Catholics around the globe, you are correct, and everyman has it wrong. Your mission is succeeding in the unseeable realms that I have described, although it seems nonsensical in the musings of other men. Advent and Christmas accentuate the impotence of secularists to understand the Incarnation of the Redeemer of humanity. There is contradiction in their ways. What is their conduct during Christmas? They procure and receive material gifts because they can see and touch them, and place them in their homes. But, when one inquires about Jesus' Nativity, they look as if to say, ...*where does that apply? How does the birth of the object of someone else's faith affect how my children see me as a good provider when the season comes for me to prove that I have the capacity to give?* You see the skewed perception that perverts their meaning of Christmas. *Yuletide? What?*...and on and on. You know in your heart that Jesus resides there to be given to humanity every instant in time. You and your brother are like orchids blooming from His Kingdom because the secular world is so ugly. This is among the reasons why God created you, because you are sightly before the Angels. This will seem more apparent when you are given opportunity to see time from the other side of life. For now, your trust in Jesus confirms your role in advancing human conversion. Lastly, I hope you know that everything you hold dear about this home lives in your hearts, not in the plaster and lathe. You may continue living here if you wish, or you can seek other accommodations. I do not want you to feel immobilized just because you hold My intercession in such high esteem. Love is the shrine you seek, and Heaven is your birthright that the heart pines to know. You will have a good week in advance of Christmas, and you will anticipate the Feasts of Saint Stephen and the Holy Family. Hold deep in your heart great appreciation to God for His having given you these things, and then place your sights beyond them, to the origin of this Grace; to the living, loving, breathing essence of perpetual perfection in which you have invested the legacy of your life and the destination of your soul..."

Sunday, December 26, 2004
Feast of the Holy Family
Saint Stephen, First Martyr [Acts 6-7]
3:02 p.m.

"Bringing the majesty of Heaven to this holy place, I have come for a final hour in 2004 to pray for the Eternal Kingdom of God to dispense health and favor upon humanity, but the world often resists this overture with pride. My presence is a manifestation of the power through which Jesus has bestowed miracles upon you for centuries. While you employ faith to accept them, it is imperative that you internalize these blessings as having greater import than proving that Heaven exists. Your commission is to propagate others' faith with yours and assist them in believing from the heart that the Lord loves them beyond reproach. I am happy to confirm that you are achieving these goals. You are celebrating the Octave of Christmas, and your joy is replete in the knowledge that Christ Jesus has come to sustain you. This is foretelling of the closure of the ages because in Him, you are assimilated by His Kingship that gives finality, Truth, and forgiveness. Christmas is a good time for holy people. You commemorate the years by the things you do. For some, it provides the only moments of affection they ever experience. When you consider that orphaned children suffer year round; and if you call upon your Christian conscience to comfort them, then the Feast of Christmas has served its highest purpose. Heaven calls on you to share the Christmas spirit the whole year through. Sadly for many, secularism lures people away from this happiness and causes them to forget the joyous beginnings that Christmas brings. We pray that everyone understands that Jesus about whom we speak is not only the Incarnate Son of God, but the deliverance of humanity from Earth's last revolution when its soiled framework expires. What better gladness could you wish for than this? I have spoken about the Corporeal and Spiritual appearance of the Man-God in the Manger, and I have regaled humanity's joy at the arrival of the Messiah under the starry skies. You should welcome this excellence, the Child of Bethlehem who reveals that there is an entire New Creation of peace in the Kingdom of the Lord. You might imagine the Christmas messages that I have given to seers throughout history because I am the Matriarch of Redemption, and I assure you that the Holy Spirit gives Me providential Wisdom of prefigured eloquence so profound that the hardest of heart are brought to tears. Why is this so? Because they realize that the heart is not for transient idols, but for comprehending Christian hope, conversion, sanctification, and Salvation. The human heart is not so much a function of the body as it is your unity with God. Peace be with you!—the heart says, reflecting its repose in Jesus' Incarnation. Good will to those who touch the heart! We shall never cease speaking of the heart, My children, because it is the sacred repository of Divine courage in a dangerous material world. The constellations you see at night are there because God wishes you to envision your place beside Him. The midday sun is a reminder of your warmth for the poor, for hurting children, and the broken and afraid. The evening horizon echoes your solemn Amen, invoking compassion in the image of the Son of Man. When it rains outside, God is telling you that the Earth is inundated by His Dominion. When you see a rainbow after a storm, this is Christ the artist, assuring you with all the hues in His Sacred Heart that His beauty reaches around the globe. Christmas is about humble people in little places who become slayers of giants. It is about seeing beyond the seeable and accepting without proof that the Holy Spirit informs the contrite. Christmas means comforting the dying and lifting the infirm. It is for redressing grievances held by those who see you with contempt. The Child of Bethlehem is the Messiah on the Cross, and His Sacrifice endows your conscience every day.

    We have prayed over and again for the poor souls in Purgatory, that they be released into the ecstasy of Heaven; and by the miracle of Christmas, this is done. Imagine what it feels like to be freed from this bondage, taken from the darkness into the Light, given drink in the desert, and led to a campfire at the summit of a mountain during the most inclement blizzard of the year. Imagine a son seeing his father approach him after a lifetime of insolence, hearing him say 'I love you' for the very first time. Imagine warring nations coalescing under the Cross, and criminals and prosecutors sharing the same meal. Christmas is the birth of the reconciliation between Heaven and Earth in the same way that the prodigal son returned home to his family. Reach for the fatted calf because the memories and blessings are coming to pass. All this began with the Nativity of Jesus Christ who opened His eyes and said...*So, this is it. This is the place I came to bless. These are the people I was born to redeem.* I ask My children to grow your faith the way Jesus grew in strength. Receive His Wisdom and acknowledge that your time has come. Be empathetic! Strive for your reward! Touch the hem of His garment and be healed. Lead holy lives. Pray for the return of your Redeemer with the urgency with which He asks you to tend to your brothers and sisters. My little ones, your Holy Mother is pleased because I have seen the Triumph about which we speak. The occasion that you will reach the Promised Land is an irrefutable fact. Be of cheer because your Salvation is at hand. To My Special and Chosen ones, I will speak to you in the future for scores of days. I will appear in 2005 and ask you to proceed with the same exertion that the Lord sought in 1991. You are children of Light and My cherished ones; you are examples for the rest of humanity. You are opposed on many fronts, and yet believed by millions. They will not tell you this, but I have. I see your march through time; and with all reason by which your faith outlives calamity and error, you are favored sons of God. Your love for His people is the opposite of their indifference to the timelessness of Heaven. Your payment will be magnanimous, so let nothing subdue your hearts. Allow no one to foist despair upon you or make you feel worthless before the fortunes of men. You are prophets in precincts around the world, and your images are being hewn in the mountaintops of the ages, one heartbeat at a time. If you pray for empowerment; if you hope to be remembered for everything your brothers sought from God, then live as you have been living. Pursue the piety you have offered with the freshness of the universe. Know through the fabric of your being that Jesus prospers in you, and you in Him. Your destiny and His Easter Resurrection are inseparable. This is Christmas, My children. This is what I mean that Christmas has come into the world. As you live the final ages, raise your hopes like a glistening sword against the perils of the Earth. Wear your faith like a crown; display your allegiance to the Son of Man on your lapels, and receive the spoils of war. Emmanuel! God is with you! My Special son, I have great hope because you are serving Jesus with loyalty. You know when evil lurks in your midst, and you make the decisions that preserve you from harm. Remember that secular humanism stands in direct contradiction to the Kingdom of God. You know this to be true, but pagans tend to forget as though Satan will somehow prevail. However, in a world flush with Christians, they will assemble upon a foundation of goodness so there is no foothold for evil. Humanity requires someone to reprimand unbelievers and invigorate the faithful, and this is your Apostolate. My Special son, I offer My messages because you are eager to receive them. Thank you for remaining beside your brother, comforting him, giving him food and shelter and a place to lay his head. Bless you for being the most important person in his life..."

MORNING STAR OVER AMERICA

The New Millennium
In the Year of Our Lord
AD 2005

Sunday, January 2, 2005
The Epiphany of the Lord
2:44 p.m.

"We embolden your experience in exile to ensure that your acclimation to holiness and manifest Glory is consistent with heroism and perseverance. As you offer your intentions for AD 2005, please remember Mine as well. The incidental misfortunes, the catastrophic tragedies, and the inordinate callousness of life that befall humanity are consequential in that they heighten your motivation to assist the afflicted. Prove by your generosities that you pity the victims. Pour-out your hearts and grow your charity lending support and healing. I have said that your petitions suspend the forces of Nature. Can you see the ferocious destruction that results from a lack of prayer? We are together so the world can be healed through the edicts of the Holy Gospel. Why do I speak about the final ages? Did they not begin upon the Incarnation of the Son of Man? We seek the creative instincts and remedial architectures of humanity to mend broken families and repair fractured lives. These gifts are accomplished by your holy intentions and good works, and reaching out to strangers in innovative ways. I call on you to shear yourselves of every restriction and inhibition that keeps you from offering others everything in your possession to ease their suffering. God permits tragedies to unify the Earth. He desires the East and West to recognize suffering in the way of Jesus' Passion. This is the meaning of sacrifice and reconciliation. When you share these virtues as one people, you will no longer be divided over political differences and cultural ideals. God gives humanity sufficient opportunity through oceanic earthquakes to prove that you are worthy of the blessings you seek. Give Him ample evidence that you are like the Christ Child whose Nativity you just celebrated for another year. Reflect His brilliance through the darkness, and produce harmony where there is discord. Your opportunity to be like Jesus has never been greater. I urge you to kneel in prayer before the Blessed Sacrament because you are enlightened during Eucharistic Adoration. The Holy Father brought you a challenge this year to open your hearts to the Manna of Life so you would defer to the Will of God in more ways. Modify your thoughts so your deportment complies with His decrees in the Sacred Scriptures. Imagine what the Saints would do if they were present among you. Celebrate their memory so you will wish to eliminate the deprivation under which others suffer. This begins in your dedication to and Adoration of the Holy Eucharist. Be heartened knowing that God has given you the Grace of faith to believe this, and approach life with the foundation of service as the purpose of your days. My children, millions of souls weaker than you have done so, and the world is better for their faithfulness. Do not allow this process to end in your age. As your Mother, I seek in you the blessedness I knew of the Apostles and disciples who lived with Jesus, walked alongside Him, preached the Gospel, and endured the torment that agnostics heaped upon them so His Kingdom would be revealed. You possess the courage, venue, vision, and ability to forward the charge that has been placed before humanity by Jesus' followers from every age because you are communicants of the Holy Eucharist that fed them the Truth of Salvation and kept their consciences clear. I mourn for My Son during the Holy Sacrifice of the Mass, and I pray through the Sacred Mysteries. As you come of age at Mass, your spirits are cleansed by His Blood. Be grateful that you are forgiven and counted among the chosen who will be handed to the Father and the mansions of Paradise through Jesus' Crucifixion.

My Special and Chosen ones, I offer My greeting and thankfulness for your consecration. Heaven is your reward, for you know what holiness means. *Thank you for defending your Roman Catholicism last week because it represented your anticipation of yesterday's Feast. Few are the places where I can hear the words, 'I have seen the Virgin Mary. I have shared the beauty of Her Immaculate Heart.' These are acclamations from a humble Christian who knows that My Immaculate Heart will Triumph over any aggression against the Catholic Church. Thank you, My Special son, for your veneration. Your friends were proud of you because they saw someone who refused to concede to secular relativism. Your presentation on December 31, 2004 on Stanford Avenue will live as one of the greatest testaments for Divine Truth in the annals of the world. And, it was simple because you have so given your heart to Me that speaking the Gospel comes natural to you. There is no opposition to My Matriarchy that can withstand the witness of My Children of the Latter Times. As your brother aptly said, be not proud in a way that felled Adam from the Garden of Eden, but proud that you stand on the right side of time and the compression of all histories. This is not only the opening of January, but a new year when multiple benedictions will come. It is difficult for some people to contemplate the arrival of another year and wonder what they might contribute to life, to the furthering of peace, the treasury of Salvation, and amending the ways of sinners. Your Apostolate has addressed these matters for fourteen years. I have asked you to tread this path for righteousness' sake and the millions who do not know God because righteousness is a self-sustaining good. There are many lives brittled by destruction and rancor, and your pious works remind men where the emollient for their hearts resides. You are blessed, loved, and admired for taking such good care of your brothers. I am grateful that your prayers are making a difference in the conversion of humanity, not only in your proximity, but the millions worldwide who read your writings. As I have said, it is rare that a disciple of Jesus and seer of apparitions becomes honored in his homeland, but you will be embraced by your peers as time unfolds. The Mother of Jesus deplores curiosity seekers; and like sending-forth the seventy-two, I look for warriors who are willing to forgo their own accouterments to prove it. I search for those in gated communities who dare shed their luxuries so the downtrodden can be raised to the summit of dignity..."

Timothy and I had an evening dinner with a group of people where the integrity of the Catholic Church was on trial before a secular humanist intellectual who has no conscience about splaying his militant defamation of the Church before anyone and everyone under his influence. It is ironic how Christians are pressured to remain quiet during such onslaughts in order to maintain a peaceful decorum in such gatherings. My brother and I feel no such pressure. Our Lady responded to the fact that we were unafraid to engage his diabolical audacity in order to gracefully set straight the record of history and contemporary events, including Her miraculous intercession.

Sunday, January 9, 2005
Feast of the Baptism of Our Lord
St. Adrian of Canterbury [d. AD 710]
3:01 p.m.

"Now comes your Blessed Mother from Heaven to speak with compassion and urgency about the conversion of human souls in the Blood of the Cross. Dear little ones, you know that I have given you several years of messages about Love and righteousness, and My mission blossoms from the Heart of the Father. You are refurbishing the Earth through your virtues. Thank you for responding to My call. You speak about Angels who come to your assistance because they are your helpers through the years. These Angels will accompany you when you die to the undimmed Trinity of God's Glory. You cannot get there alone. It is inarguable that your soul must be washed by Jesus' Blood before you are allowed entry into Heaven, and My intercession precedes your beatific rest in His Resurrection from the Tomb. I was there when they scourged Him, and I saw the Sacrifice that He withstood for your Salvation. Your spirits are marked with the Sign of the Cross when you offer yourselves to Jesus. This is how I recognize you as My children. When you anticipate the Angelic greeting about which I speak, you will know that you are at the threshold of seeing God's Face. What a joyous moment this will be, one apropos for infinity! This is why your pious works, service, and contributions to Christianity are of grave importance. You have only so much time. When you pray for the Providence of Truth to infiltrate your thoughts and actions, the Holy Spirit guides you through the darkness. The Third Person of the Trinity saturates your consciousness with Grace and takes hold of your lives. Then, as you live and breathe, you know that you are fighting for Jesus. Is this too difficult for believers to comprehend? Only if you refuse to give everything to the Father. The purpose of your will is to ensure that it magnifies His. My children, when you ponder the Baptism of Jesus in the Jordan, it must give you new hope to approach the Sacred Mysteries that you celebrate to this day. What becomes of the future is dependent on the Penitential Rites you receive. You must unify yourselves in the Divine Plan that the Lord gives humanity through the Sacred Scriptures. Moreover, you must become immersed in the Blood of the Cross and remain loyal creatures who are freed from every stain. This is a critical manifestation of your commitment and a narrow and difficult pathway to follow. The dailiness of life wears you down and clouds your vision from the sanctified road upon which Jesus asks you to travel. Walk beside Him! He is always and everywhere present for every person, during every hour. This is the Omnipresence by which you are sustained in strength and perseverance. Let no man exploit this righteousness or cause you to go astray, for it is in this that the purpose of your journey becomes clear. Always remember that your Mother sees your existence in every dimension, and I know where you might stumble. I also rebuke your enemies, and I realize that you do not always see the refinements you require for your daily examen. Pray for My intercession, and you will travel with surety. Offer the Rosary for peace, consolation in your hearts, the coalescence of your families, and for healing and protection. I am your Mother of Perpetual Help, and I assist you in the perilous times that you encounter on Earth. Mine is the distinction of offering My Motherly Heart that God intends to share. Together, we have overcome the obstacles that inhibit your progress, and we avail you to the blessings that Jesus dispenses to your requisitions in prayer. My Special son, I am elated to speak to you as I give My second message of 2005. I see that you are working forthrightly with your brother through the parameters of time for the encouragement of the faithful and the admonishment of the lost. Please be the mentor and guide to sinners who call on you for spiritual help. You know by now that there are many auspicious moments to come for you and your brother... I have told you that I appear in the world to stir the conscience, heart, and soul of My children to recognize God in the Blessed Trinity so you will actively pursue the righteousness to which Jesus speaks. This does not place the will of men in abeyance. The water is in the well, the gold is in the mine, and the Crucifixion is stationed in time and Eternity for the taking. God is providing the opportunity to convert, but men must accept of their own accord. You are an obedient and resplendent child, and you often weep. My beloved son, you have surrendered your home, your family and friends, and have suffered your reputation to remain beside Me. You have made deep sacrifices to see that your goals are met. I promise that you will stand before God when He calls you to Heaven and be overjoyed that you have accomplished everything Jesus asked. You must be confident of this!..."

Sunday, January 16, 2005
Saint Marcellus I, Pope [d. 309]
2:47 p.m.

"These times are nettlesome to your spirits because you live at the front of battle against evil forces that are trying to dampen your faith in the Kingdom of God. I wish you grand blessings and valor in your struggles because I have seen the outcome of these engagements. You must remember that your mission is to be true Christians, and your conveyance to victory is the Holy Cross. My children, God has manifested the Sacred Mysteries that were foretold by the Prophets so you will be purified and healed. You have learned that the Lord is your strength and refuge in times of trouble, and these are those times. It is clear that you must have untrammeled sight, and you must establish a means that will transform this vision into decisive action. You must strive with your hearts and hands to become strategists for Christ so your lost brothers and sisters will respond to the Light of the Gospel. If you persevere in your faith and realize that there will be periods of darkness, that Creation is riddled with these things, you will place them in better perspective. By your willingness to act on this insight, you will prevail against the nefarious forces trying to stymie your progress. *Come unto Me all who are weary, and I will give you rest.* This is the promise of Jesus. Find solace in embracing the Divine Wisdom that God implants in your hearts. If you do not, little ones, you will become bitter and impatient, and you will collide with the very darkness that you are trying to conquer. Thank you for centuries of progress through your inflection of your forefathers' faith. You are blessed to accept the writings of the Doctors of the Church. Do not allow your hardships to cause you to surrender your role in the inexorable journey toward the hour of reckoning. Be strong links in the chain of congruence with your predecessors so time will be connected by the unity of your trust in Jesus' Word. My Special son, I am pleased with you and your brother because I know that since last week, you invoked a new perspective to keep you uplifted as the years expire. See time as though it is a passing parade, although you are moving with it. Feel convinced to bid farewell to your burdens, and look forward to the challenges facing you ahead. Be not fearful of change, in fact, embrace it with all the courage you have been given in the power of the Holy Spirit. You and your brother have forged a standard of holiness that cannot be expunged. No matter what happens from this day forward, that legacy cannot be destroyed. The Earth has been sanctified by your exhortations. You must believe that every creature has a purpose in the Kingdom of the Father. Ever since your soul was deposited in your mother's womb on Christmas Day, December 25, 1960 the world has been brighter. Your brother has been a blessing for those who have come to know him with affection. God knew that your union would advance His

Kingdom on Earth, and he led your brother's family from the south in 1956 to be near you in the heart of Illinois. Like you, he was conceived as a gift to humanity. The date of May 28, 1953 will shine in history for many who have yet to permeate the veil of time. He lived in Alta's womb eight months and was born thirty days early to advance the mission of Saint Angela Merici. God lent you to the Earth as ambassadors of His sovereignty, as messengers for His Providence, and disciples for the humility and simplicity that are wrought through your emulation of Jesus. You were Specially Chosen to serve in the Lord's vineyard so tens-of-thousands would repent in the aftermath of Adam's Fall. I am honored by your deference to God's Will and your consecration to Me. Creation will know no greater Love than the Sacrifice of Jesus to deliver you into Paradise, and My Heart is of this same perfection. I birthed the Victim of the Cross because, regardless of what some theologians suggest, I knew your potential before the Throne of the Father. The Annunciation was My desire that His Will would come, for I am the Mediatrix of all Graces from Heaven. I claim you and your brother as more than idle children. You are participants in a way that few before have shared. Take these things I am telling you to heart, for they will be consoling in later life. I am inspired that you have written with such Truth and eloquence over the preceding fourteen years..."

Sunday, January 23, 2005
St. Emerentiana, Martyr [d. 304]
2:54 p.m.

"Working through the miracle of your lives, you are ushering the Kingdom of God to the masses. My children, how can I tell you of the esteem in which you are held? What words can express Jesus' thankfulness? The signs and wonders for which you have prayed are converting manifestations for the many who do not believe, but you yourselves are their greatest blessings. The fruits of your lives are the changing of hearts and the mending of ways in places you have never seen, in lands whose names you do not even know. Your Mother is calling you to a vast continuance of this gift to humanity by renewing your pledge to the Sacrifice by which your lives are sustained. Tell Jesus that even though you see the poignance of the past, you are willing to cultivate the immediate future so it resembles the Paradise from which all goodness flows. If you pour-out your lives like a libation; if you replace your imperfect will with God's Divine Will, if you concede that you oftentimes wander in shadows to reflect greater Light, you will know that you are attesting to the Glory of the Father. Is your vision not clarified by conquering the blindness of others? You are sanctified by helping Jesus purify the Earth. Your hearts are sealed by the gifts of consolation you offer to your brothers and sisters. The miracle through which you were given life and the sustenance by which your existence is enhanced is wholly a manifestation of your trust in the Resurrection of My Son. I have asked you to be ombudsmen for Jesus to societies who have not begun to seek Him and to be the valor of Truth to those who reject His Promise of Eternal Life. My children, God may rebuke them for their obstinance, but it is they who will repudiate themselves. This is why we must reach them through our prayers, and especially your Marian works. Suffering is rampant everywhere, and the alleviation of this agony is the reorientation of the world to the Holy Cross. If you wish humanity well, pray that everyone comes to the Cross for the fateful criteria by which they will finally be judged and adjudicate themselves. Today, we remember to pray for the unborn, the poor souls in Purgatory, for the victims of tragedies, for purity of the flesh, heart and mind, and all the traits that make men holy. Remember those on their death beds and the unsuspecting numbers whose lives will be taken in wars and fatal accidents of all kinds. We wish for the millions who are hungry and who suffer disease to be fed and healed. In essence, we pray that the consolers and helpers of humanity will themselves find strength to bear the burdens that have been heaped upon them by the happenings of these times. With all these intentions in our hearts, we turn to God in supplication. We ask Jesus to hear your petitions and respond to My intercession on your behalf because we are a family with bonds. There is no stopping the affinity we have for Creation. And, when someone declares that you can be perfect regardless of the odds, that person speaks the echoes of the Holy Spirit. Humanity is perfect when you try your best, not whether you win or lose. You become God's champions by entering the fight, not by demanding the prize. My dear children, My Love is so overwhelming that if it were described as a point of Light, it would pierce worlds a billion universes from here. I am the Mother of the redeemed for the Earth and skies, and I have been watching your progress with compassion and patience. I herald Jesus' Crucifixion, and I urge Him to be merciful upon you. Indeed, when you have seen Jesus, you have seen the Father. I am the Mother of Jesus and God Almighty. I have called for leniency when they have prescribed punishment. My Grace has soothed their vengeance against a cold-hearted humanity that ignores the Sacred Scriptures. I do not wish retribution to be inflicted upon My children just because you are spiritually blind. God has given Me the latitude to teach you the intercourse between Heaven and Earth. This is why I have come. You do not obey all the rules, and I intend to make them known. If you do not listen; if you refuse to heed My call, and if you decline to be informed about the Justice of God, then your future will be grim.

What would the Father have you know of Justice? What investment does He hold in your conversion to His Son? Why does our God of the Ages come to you through miracles and Sacraments, and in Paraclete and Nature? Because He wishes you to realize that you are lost, but in Jesus, you are found.

The Sacred Heart of My Son pines for you to accept Him of your own free will, not because He will force you with warnings of doomsday, and not because you are bribed by dreams of grander delights than Heaven can provide. My children, there are no greater things than Heaven! I ask you to take this as Gospel Truth. Nothing your souls or thoughts could imagine can be fulfilled anywhere but in the Paradise to which the Holy Spirit is leading you. The satisfaction of your hearts is found in the supernal Kingdom that is sung in Gregorian chants, not in university halls. The perfection for which your spirits thirst is in the Chalice of the Holy Sacrifice of the Mass, not on the ocean crests upon which you sail to reach a horizon that will never come. I assure you that most of your efforts boast of vanity, your hopes of conquering an enemy called death that you will never defeat on your own. I am asking My children to see beyond the tragedies of the day by being so in love with the afflicted that your response to their agonies precludes their pain. Remember the eloquence of your spiritual growth, and know that it transforms your actions into seeable deeds of mammoth holiness. You often hear speakers reflect that if they wrote a history about these times, let them say that they lived among giants. Tender your hearts to the perpetuity of God, and He will make you the legends of your age. It is not in the secular void that you will find yourselves champions, but in the noble love you return to Jesus by gathering His sheep. My Special son, I cannot sufficiently express how happy I am to see you beside your brother today. I am joyful that you are patient with him, that you understand that he does not always do things perfectly. I send the Archangels because your writing confirms their intentions for the world. You see clearly because your vision of Christianity is concise. I have told you time and again that your closeness to your brother is dependent upon how you love him, and you are loving him with the dignity of the Saints. This is why My Angels call so often with such joy. This is why they offer their helpfulness, because your brother is weak in as many ways as a struggling child. He has been publicly rebuked on so many occasions that it pales your workplace like a walk in the park. However, he is still here. He is strong in the issues he knows to be crucial for everything that matters to Heaven. He realizes that there are no messages unless he spends his years with you. You will know the fullness of this when you see Paradise at the beginning of your Afterlife. You have foreseen it here, but you are still behind the veil. It is not that the Lord does not wish you to be in Heaven, but He needs you as servants in His earthly Kingdom. It is no more difficult than this. Let us go forward with the hope you have held in your heart since My messages first began. I am with you, and I will never leave. You may share the content of your text so the Angels can applaud. *(I read aloud a passage from my writing about the callousness of many American women; those who have disavowed their marriages through material and egocentric pretenses, and those who have procured abortions devoid of conscience. I told Our Lady that it was disheartening that God created such beautiful creatures and engendered them with the mystical capacity to touch men in the most profoundly personal ways, but when men surrender the tenderest places of their hearts, many women administer unbearable psychological retribution, selfishness, and emotional abuse in return because they have become lost in the material seductions of the world, destroyed their own spiritual happiness, and then refuse to any longer engage their beatific responsibility to lift the world one man at a time.)* This is a proper description of some females. You may parenthesize it when we are finished and add it to your manuscript. Tell the world what you told Me today, and My response is that no man has ever sought to have an abortion..."

Sunday, January 30, 2005
St. Raphus Buchanan, Martyr [AD 1553-1601]*
3:16 p.m.

"Where there is darkness, light; where there is despair, happiness; where there is suffering, health. I desire you to emulate the glories of the Saints whose hearts bled for righteousness over lands that were awash in sin. I bring tidings of peace and joy because Heaven is peace and joy. Your soul's fulfillment and the purpose of life is in God. How many times has your Mother told you this? I offer hope in assuring that your spirits will soon repose in the blissfulness of Eternal Light. By faith, morality, service and humility, you are reconstituted forever. The unending nature of your being is stationed beyond the constraints that define your mortality. Your love for Jesus and His for you make your mourning become the Daylight of Justice that is inundating the Earth. We pray for the transformation of humanity to good-heartedness. All equality and dignity are discovered in and disseminated by your response to the Holy Spirit within you. Change for the sake of change is rarely progress, but converting human hearts in allegiance to the Sacred Heart of Jesus has eternal ramifications. I give you His Love as I speak to you for another day. When in your petitions you ask the Lord for inner-peace as the mainstay of your excellence, He will give it to you. Little ones, we reside together beyond the annals of world history in the sanctity you know to be Divine Love. The highest peaks of holiness about which I spoke many years ago are within your reach. You are looking forward to everything that needs to be seen. You are marching toward the end of time, and there is jubilation in this because the dormancy of the Earth is passing away. Do not fail the calling of the years! Be glad in them. Embrace them. Place your hopes beyond them and your future in the Eternal. I ask you as Christians to be united as marshaled soldiers against the influences of evil that are trying to pilfer your holiness. Do not be deluded by the eroding of time. You are imminently immortal people now! Live as though the Scepter of Eternity has been passed to you. See Glory in the years by reconfirming your faith in honor of Jesus. My Special son, I offer My gratitude for the awesome ways that you please God and invite His people to envision the pardon He has promised. You need not include it in your diary unless you wish to, but the Angels have mentioned to your brother about a writer from the last century named Antonia Machado. He was a philosopher who wrote many poems about living with transeunt vision. He once said, '...traveler, there is no path. Paths are made by walking.' This is how I see your life upon the ground. You are laying the way for many of your successors to find the path to Jesus by the legacy you leave them. Before your birth, there were untold other people who took to their knees in prayer and humility to prove that they were in compliance with the Dominion of God, and you and your brother are in agreement with their cause. All brilliance and beatitude are encompassed by your thoughts, words, and deeds. These are not hollow compliments from a body who is happening by, but discernable acclamations from the Mother of God. It was only hours ago, it seems, that I told you it would be another new month and year, and now that beginning has come and gone. Time will deceive you because you assume that it is slow in passing. Can you imagine continuing your work into fifteen years, and then twenty and thirty? By that time, you and your brother will have given your peers a magnanimous deposit of books and articles about how you knew that it was Me who appeared to you three decades before. The calendar will tempt you to believe that Jesus will not return in your day, but remember that your journey through time is swiftly passing. The elderly and infirm stare at the ceiling above their nursing home beds, wondering where it has gone. This is why I call you to patience, for patience is the virtue that allows you to put the element of time into a perspective in which even itself is circumscribed. You are growing older and wiser in the Thearchy of Salvation, and God will have you employ this goodness to the exaltation of His Kingdom before your life is through.

  Thank you immensely for nurturing and comforting your brother as the days and weeks expire. Timothy has made it clear that it is not only for Me and Saint Joseph, and the Communion of Saints, and even the Father in Heaven that he lives, but also for you. Your brother's allegiance is to you. He tells Jesus every day that you are the solace in his life, that you are the best friend any person could be so fortunate to meet. And, given everything you have done for him in Jesus, he has that right. He has the authority to admire you as much as you adore the Most Blessed Trinity and the supernatural ways that God dispenses His Grace. These are much more than marvelous times to be alive, they are purposeful times. How saddened you might have been to have lived in the 18th or 19th centuries when humanity was a hundred more years removed from the Second Coming of Jesus. Now, you live at the threshold of this supernal event that encapsulates the entire architecture of Creation. Be filled with joy that your contributions to God are being united in a timeless way with the legacies of the Saints from ages past. Yours is the capstone and pinnacle to the foundation of holiness that they laid in many regions around the globe. From this point in time, and from your place on Earth, you are connecting the past, the present and the future by forging venues to praise God who gives life. You have been handed leverage so profound in His Kingdom that I daresay you have yet to behold. The power you will wield before you close your eyes in death will defy death, itself. I promise that these things are true. You have a vibrant faith and lasting loyalty to the King who wears the Crown of all crowns. I am pleased to tell you that good fortune will soon be pronounced upon your work for humanity to see. These, however, are the times that you will pine to regain. These simple days and quiet hours you will plead to return. So, savor them now because a great change will come to your life before your earthly journey is ended. You came to Medjugorje with gladness in your heart and with loyalty and trust in Jesus. I could never have let you depart those foreign shores without blessing you and your brother through Viscka to give you the commission to grow Christianity in the West. And, as you see, that same Western Hemisphere from which you came and to which you have since returned is in need of spiritual help. The Sacred Scriptures are being fulfilled in your time, in this place. Indeed, you are despised and rejected among men, but do not stop to stone the devil's dogs. Take the nobler course and remain focused on your work. It is true that the enemies of the Cross will destroy themselves. Remain above the fray and do your writing, praying that the conversion of hearts that Jesus seeks will occur before more lives are soiled..."

Sunday, February 6, 2005
St. Florence de Chelone, Virgin [AD 912-977]*
2:26 p.m.

"I am here, the Mother of the Victim whose Sacrifice has made your peace with God. With joy and prayerfulness, I anticipate the conversion of humankind to the Holy Cross upon which He died. My children, can you see the reciprocity between Heaven and Earth? You ask the Lord for His blessings, and He endows you with every good thing because He depends on you to trust Him. He requires your loyalty and faithfulness in good times and bad. What would you tell Jesus if He appeared before you? How does humanity approach such unapproachable Light? You meditate on these thoughts during the penitential season of Lent. My Heart's desire is for you to comprehend the peacefulness and sense of duty that you are expected to tender the Kingdom of Heaven. You see, yours is more than the role of standing in wait, you are summoned to be active in your labors for the conversion of wayward sinners. God has revealed to you the path and destination in Jesus. Your course is clear, your determination is sound, and your commission has been sealed. These are the times that make you aware of the critical nature of your compliance with the Holy Gospel as your lives relate to the present and the future. If it is true that the most portending passage in the Sacred Scriptures is 'The world as we know it is passing away,' then should you not be concerned about the world that will supplant it? You have the venue and capacity to realign the nations into a union of fairness and wholesomeness. Through your prayers, you are making the changes that holy people wish to see. Harden not your hearts! Do not become embittered by the torment of aging. I tell you over and again that time is deceiving you. There is little time for idle things; you must take-on the ideas and motivations that assist Jesus in recreating the world to be like Heaven. This plan is found in the Holy Bible. Surely you know by now that everything you must learn to be saved is in the Sacred Scriptures. And, Grace too. Yes, the Grace that engulfs you with righteousness and Truth surrounds your souls like an ocean of clouds. From the wombs of your mothers are born the greatest people you shall ever be. Please allow Jesus to grow in you so you will flourish in time and become the Saints He sees in you. My Special and Chosen sons, I ask you to be grateful for the progress of these months. The new year that has arrived is unfolding with promise and consolation, if only you will recognize it. There are more resplendent circumstances arising than you could anticipate. And, as you read My messages from earlier years, you sense their impact. Imagine if you were hearing them for the first time. This is how they will awaken the somber world. It is the way you will ultimately realize that you have done everything in your power to convert your brothers and sisters to Christianity by completing My wishes. I am honored to be here today, as briefly as I will remain. I wish for you to go outdoors and enjoy this Sunday with caution so you will not be harmed. Remember that the two of you are mature children filled with Wisdom, but let not this bring you to boast before neophytes who are yet growing in the Truth. Indeed, employ pity and admiration for them because they are walking toward Heaven not only sightless, but without the supernatural guidance through which you have been blessed. My Special son, I will offer you some overwhelming messages soon, and I wish for you to live the entire duration of this year with confidence that you are doing everything I have asked. Remember when you watched the depiction of Jesus raising Lazarus from the dead in the motion picture, and there was a sense of urgency throughout the land. This is the way your work will rouse the conscience of millions of sinners before your life is through. I am prophesying this because you are required to live in faith like everyone else. Even those given a glimpse of Heaven before they died said that they were unable to grasp its magnificence while still in mortal flesh. It is not that you are tethered to Earth or held captive by reasons unknown. You and your brother are servants whose tenure in God's vineyard is unfinished. As I say, time is deceptive, and you will soon wonder where it went. Live your years to the fullest, and remember that life is a process, as My Angels attest. Your writing is of indispensable importance to the conversion of men. Thank you for buying the motion pictures and watching them because it is all for the Glory of God. I assure you that these are miraculous times that you could not have known without your obedience to Me..."

Sunday, February 13, 2005
St. Catherine Dei Ricci, Stigmatist [AD 1522-1590]
3:04 p.m.

"My little ones, while so many in your midst look skyward to discern what type of thunders the heavens choose to roll, you turn instead to the Seat of Wisdom for eternal knowledge. I invite you to continue to share the glories of Paradise from your position in mortal time through My intercession, until the moment when you shall join all the Saints in that lasting benison of unending Light. I come to you with great joy and hope today in the realization that My people on Earth are bringing great cultivation to the world. You are changing the face of the Earth by embracing the Truth of God's Kingdom. Therefore, you are making this a special season of Lent for 2005. Please remember to include all the needy in your daily prayers, especially while you recite the Sacred Mysteries of the Most Holy Rosary. And, pray for Pope John Paul II as well. Yes, he does lead the Church with the vision of perfect Love in his heart. There will be no greater pope to live in your age, My children. Please heed his call to holiness, and defer to him in all ways. Protect his legacy to the death, and follow his teachings as you would the Word of God, Himself. The Holy Father is making his valedictory speeches as these waning days of his life continue to pass. When you think of peace and justice, remember that Pope John Paul II has been a prince among you for the elevation of the poorest of the poor. His call for peace is written everywhere, and only the just among you have chosen to respond. I ask you to stand-up for him when you hear the heretics of the world attempt to impugn his good name. All of this is the espousal of your own testament of righteousness on behalf of Jesus Christ. My Jesus mandates a Creation filled with purity and the decency about which He has spoken for centuries on end. He calls for your service without recompense, for humility despite the unsightly face of your enemies, and compassion even for those who persecute you. You are the children of this final age of time who are growing the sacred vestiges of the Saints for your own successors to pursue. When you recall the magnanimity of the sacrifices that the early Christians made, ponder how easy it is for you to live-out your convictions today. Here, especially in America, you enjoy the freedom of speech and expression. May the words of your mouths and the meditations of your hearts be acceptable in the sight of Almighty God.

My little ones, when you ponder the illnesses of humanity on physical terms, consider also the spiritual agony that is overwhelming the Church. It is true that you fight the enemies of relativism and secular humanism. There are oceans of heretical thought around you that are attempting to dilute the Truth for which you stand. I assure you that you have the strength to swim against the tide. You are given the power to walk atop the crests of egregious error that are facing humanity, and you will survive the fight with valorous courage. I ask you not to wade too deeply into the abysmal debate that is taking so much time away from others who could be accomplishing God's work. There are certain messengers who have been chosen to engage the enemies of the virtues of the Cross and to admonish sinful humanity for its errors of commission and omission. I call upon these seers and chosen ones to continue speaking the Truth with Heaven's acclamation as your guide. I am the Mother of God. I give you assurance that My intercession throughout the ages has been a way station of strength and guidance for many before you. Call upon Me during these perilous times. Be not afraid to repeat *Mother, I need your help.* Jesus has given Me the commission to comfort and console His Church during these present hours of trial and persecution. He has allowed Me great latitude in telling you the impending events of the future that will correct the course of a misguided humanity. My children, I take My role in the conversion and redemption of humankind very seriously. Why? Because I wish to see each of you at My feet someday in the beauty of Heaven. Give Me your hearts and minds, and make every action one with the Divine Will of God. If you become like Jesus in every way, you will succeed.

My Special and Chosen ones, I assure you of My continuing participation in your lives as the future continues to unfold. The miracles of My coming here would be wasted, it would seem, if you had not decided to live in compliance with My wishes. But, you have obeyed, and have consented to be My workers in the vineyard of the Earth to make all Creation a better place. How can two words 'thank you' be sufficient to express My gratitude? The coming 'morrow and all the rest of your days are an expression of God's happiness with you. We do not concede to the deadpan slowness of the element of time because we realize that every ensuing moment is critical in the remaking of the future of man. Every thought you entertain toward that goal is another blessing for the Earth. Whenever you sit down and write-out your faith and love for God's people with pen and page, you are praying for the re-arrival of the Son of Man. It may not be clear to you now what I am saying to you, but someday soon, one day in the very near future, you will realize what a blessing you have been..."

Sunday, February 20, 2005
St. Reinaldo Lorenzo, Hermit [AD 1423-1501]*
5:33 p.m.

"If you extend your hearts to Me, I shall comfort you. I will give you reason to be hopeful about your resolutions to bring human conflicts to an end. I tell you this because I am elated that you have placed your lives beneath My Mantle. I am pleased because you have turned to Me for protection. This is the summation of My message. You will this week conclude fourteen years' service to the Father by consenting to be My messengers. I thank you, and I love you. Let us go onward with the sense of accomplishment that is imbedded in your thoughts. There you have it. I have given you one of My briefest messages because I wish for you to enjoy the evening. Thank you—O thank you for living-out the purpose that Jesus has held for you since you were little children. I am with you, holding your Savior in My arms..."

Sunday, February 27, 2005
St. Stanislaus Diogenes, Martyr [AD 1313-1362]*
3:01 p.m.

"Please permit Me to remind you, dear children, as you enter your 15th year of service to Heaven as My seers, that you are building-up the Body of Christ with every lost soul you convert to Christianity. I come to you as the Patroness of your nation to give you sustaining hope. Please always remember that you should call on Me during moments of spiritual darkness in your lives. No one is immune to the burdens that prevail upon Christians over the years, but the perspective that I offer in My messages is sufficient to help you comprehend the brevity of life. My intercession should be evidence that the end of the ages is nigh at hand. Do you remember that I once told you that if you wish to ask questions, you should ask why you are asking so many questions? This does not presume that you are not curious about the implications of your existence on Earth. God wishes you never to cease invoking His Divine assistance. You who are so blessed by Jesus to have been saved by His Sacrifice already have the knowledge about the meaning of life. Jesus is the meaning, and you are the elect to whom He has promised to give His Truth beyond the end of time. While I realize that it is not pleasant for you to live sacrificially, all your gifts to the Kingdom of God, especially during the Season of Lent, help you understand how sorrowfully and passionately Jesus agonized for you. It is true that some of the bloodiest suffering in Creation affects the human mind, as well as the body. What sorrows are carried by the soul, and what angst is borne by the wounded spirit! Those who are despised among you would much rather endure physical affliction because such pain can be addressed with an analgesic, while mental oppression demands the willpower of spirituality. Jesus has assured you time and again that He is the mending of your infirmities. He is the healing of your body, mind, and spirit. This is usually misunderstood and unaccepted by worldly psychologists who blame the ills of the Earth on fate and chance. They do not see the evil that causes human deficits because they are too blinded by it. My children, My lesson today is that you know that you are fighting against the devil who holds your lost brothers and sisters in darkness and physical pain. The human part of their nature is both corrupted and corruptible, but it can be transformed into purity, beauty, peace, light, and health if they comply with the Will of the Father, if they turn to Jesus for strength and Wisdom. God has given you the Holy Spirit whose consolation I am offering now. See those who are lost with pitiful eyes, and do not disdain the ones who do not understand. It is the sinners in your midst who claim to accept Christianity but refuse to live it who are most in danger. As you enjoy the Year of the Eucharist, receive the Most Blessed Sacrament praying for these souls, with petitions to God, asking Him to intercede for hypocrites who lead lives of licentiousness and debauchery. When offering the Communion Prayer during the Holy Sacrifice of the Mass, remember everyone who asks you to pray for them. Place their whole being inside the Sacred Chalice, and implore Jesus to preserve them from harm. There are fundamental priorities about which I spoke in My first messages that will never change. When you ask the Holy Spirit to touch the hearts of the faithless, Jesus will do it. When you seek the intercession of the Angels and Saints for lost sinners, they will proceed. God anticipates your prayers and hears your petitions for the poor souls in Purgatory. Jesus stands with you in your desire to rid the Earth of evil. Among all the things I have asked you to never forget, please know that your prayers offered in silence and spoken aloud are recorded in Heaven, so pray that people change. Ask Jesus to knock on the door of their hearts until they let Him in.

Today, I would like to speak to you about the condition of the Church in America. I wish to convey to you the deep Love that Jesus has for the priests and religious who are trying to fight against such a reckless culture. It must be made clear to Americans everywhere that those who are accused of being violators were victims before they were claimed to have victimized others. All are victims of the same evil that has been an enemy of human Salvation since the beginning of time. I stand by My priests. I believe in the powers of contrition and absolution. I call upon the citizens of the United States, especially those with prosecutorial powers and members of the media to stop feeding on the weaknesses of their mortal brethren like sharks and vultures. No one is immune to the temptations of sin. How can it be true that secular institutions claim the moral high ground when it is their own lacking in righteousness that has exacerbated the problem? They have created a monster over the past forty years, and now are complaining that there is a monster on the loose. Therefore, do not be disconcerted at the purification that is ongoing both inside the Church and outside. However, collective America should not single-out a particular person as an 'example' of evil in your midst. You will be very surprised come the end of time to see where evil is really lurking around you now. It is not in the convents and rectories. It does not exist the first place you might imagine. No, My children, the greatest evil is found where human beings refuse to stand beside other people in their weakness, but instead, stand-out in arrogant pride and point fingers as if to say they, themselves, are free from sin. Does humanity not recall the reluctance of the people in the Sacred Scriptures to stone the woman who was accused of adultery? Let Me tell you now—all of modern secular America is guilty of adultery! Humanists and relativists of all stripes are groping the innocence of holy people everywhere by lying to them for capital gain, backslapping their patrons in the name of fortune and fame. They cannot be betrothed to their religious faith and to the material world, too!..."

Sunday, March 6, 2005
St. Palomar Dubois, Hermit [AD 1116-1177]*
3:01 p.m.

"My children, the dimensioned and wondrous love that you share between you in the Holy Name of Jesus is a miraculous sign for the world. We hold in our hearts the great fortune of knowing perfect holiness, and it is My desire to bring your lives into full perfection in it. Therefore, I have come today to speak to you with overtones of humility and patience, sanctification and purity, and self-denial and almsgiving. Your search for the meaning of human existence culminates in your awareness that the Lord is the source of life; your souls are His possession. As your forbears pondered 'What God hath wrought,' you should remind your contemporaries that He gives you the sacred impressions of benign deliverance from your difficulties. He is the essence of knowing about the purpose of living. And, you must respond in-kind by reveling before the nations all you have learned about sanctity and coalescence. I harken the olden days, before the industrial and communication age allowed you swifter contact with your peers and peoples in far lands. Humanity had a simpler fortune back then. Now, however, dispatch is the pride of the hour and a mysterious movement away from the simplicity that Jesus had taught His first followers. You must counteract the busy means of life that your friends are leading by calling them to the stillness of peace. Ask them to restore in them what is lost, the obedience to Redemption that their forefathers knew. This is no doubt an advanced age, but it need not be one that is less holy. God allows you to move forward through your ingenuity and inventions, but not at the expense of simplicity. Humanity is redefining the 'art of war' to the point that fewer are dying in the process. My little ones, there should be no war.

There should only be a determined diligence by humankind to unite in a shared vision beneath the Holy Cross. God has given you the human nature of Divine Wisdom in Jesus to be your example, but how can you emulate Him if you will not follow Him? There is a grand challenge ahead for the people of this final century. Surely it resides in the sustenance of your bodies, the health for which you pray, and the successes of your progeny. However, it also rests in your hopes for the future laid beyond your generation, and even after the cessation of mortality on the Earth. You must search with innate fineness the meaning of self-mortification and the purpose of Lent. Look at the Son of Man! It is true that there is a lackadaisical view that blinds Americans about the deficiencies in distant lands. The culture of death in the United States is one of grotesque sinfulness that stands in direct opposition to the Will of God. I have told you that your country will suffer awfully for these things. The fate of your children's lives will be a dark and gruesome one because of the infidelities of today's parents. I wish more of My children would recite the Hail Mary in places other than a football stadium. I call you to earnest prayer on behalf of the suffering and dying. I ask you to look upon the lives of the impoverished, and upon looking, do something to alleviate their indigence. Too many people in America are complaining that the Mother of God speaks only of humanity's errors. I urge these souls to remember that it is not for accolades that Jesus calls them to serve. My Son asks you to be His likeness in the poor quarters of the world. See in other lives the poverty in which Jesus was born, and lift them up the same way He calls you to elevate Him! Many prayers are needed from you. Countless holy believers are being persecuted because of their faith, especially in America. Priests from every parish in the United States should rise smartly to the pulpit and hail their allegiance to Me. They should devote holy hours during the Exposition of the Most Blessed Sacrament for the conversion of lost sinners. Indeed, they should resolve to receive as many penitents as possible through the Sacramental Rite of Confession before the Son of Man returns. I have told you before, and will repeat it here. I stand by My priests with gratitude. Anyone who brings harm to one of My priests is in true peril before the Lord. My Special son, I am absolutely overjoyed to speak with you. You know that I am the Mother of Jesus; you know that you are welcome at My side through the innocence of your heart. You heard a secular king say last evening that he had come to reclaim his throne and recover his birthright. Your birthright is to remain a messenger for the Matriarch of Creation, for the Queen of Heaven and Earth. You are playing your portion well. The destiny of humanity is assured by the Sacrifice of Jesus on the Cross, but their will to accept Him is brought by the goodness and obedience of Christians like you. You recite hopeful prayers, and I am pleased by the life you have chosen to pursue. You and your brother will be repaid commensurate with your sacrifices for the Lord..."

Sunday, March 13, 2005
St. Euphrasia, Daughter of Antigonus [d.420]
3:08 p.m.

"My beautiful children, I take this extraordinary occasion to speak shed of the constraints of time to remind you how inspirational is your eagerness. I bring good tidings and fond wishes from Heaven and the Providence and blessings for which you have prayed. I intercede on your behalf to Jesus for His influence and advocacy on your sojourn of life. I ask you to pray for the unborn and the millions living in destitution. Lift them to dignity. Ask God to ease their pain by creating new frameworks to redress their plight. I have spoken about the marketplace of illusions called secularism, and poverty is one of its debasing effects. Secularism perpetuates divisiveness and death, and this is why I call humanity beneath My protection to the Covenant of Eternal Life. Secularism is on a path of annihilation and extinction, but your souls are accorded the opportunity to live in perpetuity in Heaven. You must come to Jesus! You must turn to God for the Wisdom of the Holy Spirit. My dear ones, your sanctification and Salvation are procured through Jesus' Blood on the Cross, and simpler men than those who will hear these words have understood and accepted Salvation in faith and trust in Him. I summon you to this life, to this affirmation, so you will allow the Son of Man to rescue you from perdition. Do whatever is necessary to avoid the cruel acts of partisan bullies and radicals who author sectarian violence. As you pray during this Season of Lent, remember everything that is missing, the benefits that would mitigate the agony of the poor. Ask Jesus to vanquish their poverty by enriching their lives with the profits of your petitions. Your faith and good works will heal them and lead them to the freedom that you seek in Him. I urge you to remember in extemporaneous ways to call on the Holy Spirit to convert lost sinners. Do this in addition to your everyday contingent of prayers. Ponder visions in your heart of the way the world ought to be, and ask Jesus to make these images real. I assure you He will do it. The Earth must become an enclave within the higher Kingdom of God. The pain endured by poor people in backwood villages is alleviated by your charities. My Special and Chosen ones, I offer My heartfelt gratitude for the way you pray with the Archangels for the radical reorientation of humanity. You need not worry that there will be insufficient time to culminate your works. God will ensure that every word you write and every meditation from your hearts teach the multitudes about Redemption before your mission concludes. Nothing you say will be concealed from anyone given life, retroactively to the centuries before you were born. This is the mystical gift that the Lord bestows upon those who believe in Him. Jesus' Countenance shines upon them from the skylines of Paradise. This is what Sacred Love looks like, My Special son. It is overflowing with consolation, appreciation, consecration, unity, solidarity, and good will. Please be at peace in the piety you live, and remember why. It is because you allow the Holy Spirit to breathe on you, while you are discharging your duties according to your station in life..."

Palm Sunday, March 20, 2005
1:46 p.m.

"This special day is made even more holy by your dedicated prayerfulness on behalf of God's people who are chosen to suffer in exultation of the Cross. On this Sunday, as you honor the King of kings who was welcomed into Jerusalem only to be slain for the sins of the world, place your own sorrows in Him. Know that your enemies are despising Jesus when they speak ill of you, and be glad to partake of the Passion of the Son of Man. You shall inherit His just Resurrection! My children, you have many reasons to thrust your spirit of thanksgiving onto the world stage. Christianity is much the better for your embracing it, and Catholicism remains contemporary as you extol the Traditions of the Church. I have asked you on more than one occasion to decry the movements to modernize the Roman Catholic Church. Remember the Saints who fought to keep holy the great relics that have been handed-down to humanity from Saint Simon Peter to Pope John Paul II. Trust with all your being that Jesus is pleased by your faithfulness, because maintaining your allegiance to the Traditions of the Church connect you not only with the First Apostles, but with everything the Faith Church will discover come the end of time. You can no doubt sense this circle of continuity in which you are living, the chain of loyalty in which your lives are links, from the Birth of Jesus in Bethlehem to everything you can imagine to facilitate His Kingdom before His Glorious Second Coming. I have asked My children to be not only God's people, but God's holy people. Comprehend the spiritual continuum manifested by the faith you hold so dearly in your Crucified Lord with that same Christianity reflected by your predecessors in faith. Each time a priest offers the Holy Sacrifice of the Mass, he codifies the union of the ages with God's Christological Truth. You are one with every other person who is rescued by Jesus from the perils of death. And, by virtue of the consistency of the Sacraments and the Grace of the Holy Spirit, all time is one in Him. The millions of anonymous Saints who have died heretofore reside with you now in the resilient power of the sanctity of God. They are your counterparts in the Mystical Salvation of humankind, and I ask you to call upon them for Wisdom and guidance. Should you desist in sparing some sense of hopefulness for the sorrowing among you, please recapture your spiritual strength and rise above the darkness that keeps you from seeing the jubilation of the Holy Spirit clearly.

Today, I have come to thank you for the faithful service you are giving to My Son. I ask you to realize the blessings you have been accorded by Him in the works of peace and justice you are so lavishly bestowing upon this broken world. For all the corruption and the effects of human sinfulness that you see every day, I ask you to place your sights upon the bright imaginings that keep your hopes aloft. It may be true that you cannot return to some places here in this life that once brought you broader reflection and consolation. However, I assure you that harboring fruitful fondness for life's perspectives in your hearts will ensure that you will live those great moments again—even if after you have completed your journey of mortal life. You are bound for Heaven, and happiness cannot escape you there. No elation is beyond your grasp. No hope is left unfulfilled. You should remember that life on the Earth is a preparatory process whereby you are amended and changed, and your souls are bolstered by the awesome commission of Jesus Christ to manifest perfection in you. There will be many great discoveries before the Earth is through that will convince even the hardest of heart that God loves them. There are revelations yet to be unveiled and miraculous signs from beyond the skies and past the tortured silence of the heavens that will perpetuate unparalleled belief in millions of lost souls everywhere. I ask for an enhancement of your patience while these things come to pass, knowing that many of them may occur after you have come to Heaven. Knowing that the world is now being purified and cultivated should always give you hope. The delight of your faith, itself, is allowing the Will of the Almighty Father to be done in His own time. Pray to always be in union with Him as the generations come to a close. God will provide the signs and wonders to assure your Christian eagerness that you are on the right path.

And, what of these signs? What is it about the world that lay in wait, hoping for discovery, rediscovery and resurrection? Does it include the thousands of shipmates at the bottom of the seas, burdened by the unwary darkness their lost captains could have never fathomed? And, will you be visited by strange and unheralded vestiges or extraterrestrial beings as signs from Heaven that the Son of Man is near? I tell you today that such are not necessarily the signatures of the Final Ages, but they comprise the cosmic paraphernalia of a transfigured universe poised for the grand closing of the chasm between humanity and the Creator of the Universe. Indeed, what of these signs? Will you decipher cryptic messages or discover hidden sequences in manuscripts and ancient artifacts? Your Lord would have warned you in advance of the testaments of His Truth even so! You need not search the chambers of the world to discern the culmination of time. You only need Jesus Christ! Every sign, every message God ever gave the world about the transformation of humankind from 'lost individuals' to 'found people' is clearly revealed in the Nativity, Life, Passion, Crucifixion and Resurrection of Jesus of Nazareth. He would have you translating cryptic messages as a matter of course if He thought it to be significant in the greater Providence of the Plan of God. But, Jesus is God's message, and the messenger, too! He is the full accord you seek between this world and the next. He is the genius whom God has dispatched to teach and inherit the Earth; and by His Holy Sacrifice, He has made the world complete. Jesus has brought the dominion of God to bear over all the lands sprawled across the latitudes by His Father before the ancient days began. He represents Heaven, both in Wisdom and premonition, to everything that was lost when Adam and Eve were first cast down from the Garden of Eden. And, His invitation is for humanity to begin anew in the justification that has been wrought by reason of His Divine Love; that this same humankind, now healed, shall be perpetuated before God's unapproachable Light. I assure you of this—My Jesus will succeed at the last. He will make of the world what He chooses, and He will lethally destroy and craftily repair Creation according to His vision of the perfectness of life. Being in unity with Jesus means understanding one's place in the universe before the backdrop and purposes of Heaven. And, if any man wishes to be brilliant in the ways of great novelers and expeditionists, he should come by simple understanding to defer to the Son of Man in all things true. He should embrace the beautiful with profundity and obedience, and with a stellar heart filled with the prescience of the majesties of God; for it is in these things that you will discern His willingness to ratify your peace and good wishes on platforms of silver and gold.

Therefore, My message to you today, My little ones, is a sublime dictation of happiness and Truth. I call upon your deftness of spirit and knowledge of Love to be always and everywhere aware of the slow transpiring of human conversion that your work is benefitting. Be fond of Me, and love Me dearly. I am a benevolent Mother and charismatic Queen who calls upon you to espouse that Christian romance which softens the hearts of the stoic and tenders the lost to the absolution of Jesus so wilfully given to the forgiveness of men. I ask you to pray fervently for the conversion of the world as you begin to celebrate the Easter Triduum. My children, as you can see, I have come today to assure you that Jesus is with you through your trials and tribulations, and in your suffering. I bid you a very good day on this Palm Sunday. Why? Because this is the Feast of Palms, the palms laid beneath the pathway of the King of Creation. You realize with great imagining after the passing of centuries that these palms would lead the path of the suffering of My Son. Please accept the text of this message that is given to you heretofore as My intentions for you and the world.

Now, I wish to continue speaking to you in a consoling tone. There is, indeed, a dark pall that comes over the human spirit at times. It is one of helplessness and fear, one of questioning and lack of understanding. Sometimes the human soul feels so out of control of its future. I assure you that Jesus and I are closest to you during these times. You are My lovely and living children, and you are faithful to My call... Can you see how even the most simple hearts among you can be attacked by evil, and in a way that feels uncontrollably dark? It is true that you have fought such a fight before. You see, when someone is in such a state, their sense of perspective is factually destroyed. Their ability to conceive happy thoughts is impaired. And, even when they muster a sign of happiness, they see it only as a self-imposed ruse to cover the truth. There are millions of people the world-over who are suffering this now. And, they include not only the poor and abandoned, but many who have simple and productive lives. You see that the 14-year-old prodigy could not conquer the darkness that overcame him, and he took his own life... I offer you now My holy blessing for today. ☦ I will speak to you again at the great High Feast of Easter! The Paschal Mystery will be complete! I love you. Goodnight!"

Easter Sunday, March 27, 2005
1:59 p.m.

"To know the Paschal Resurrection of Jesus, My children, is to comprehend the Sacrifice that liberates your souls. I speak about the timelessness of Easter as an event when you consecrate your rebirth into sanctity, purity, and forgiveness. A Sepulcher amid the rolling hillocks was chosen to receive the Slain Messiah's Body, and He was raised to outshine the sun. Those who accept His Crucifixion and Resurrection as their reconciliation with God, their hearts are inspirited with marvelous intuition and inviolate Truth. You are the beneficiaries of a supernal blessing and a priority of existence transcending the world. This is a prerequisite for you. This is the moment when you actually realize that all things are possible with God. Wonder not whether you warrant this benediction, My little children, for there is nothing you can do to earn it. You are remade through conversion and Salvation because God loves you, even to the death of His Only Begotten Son. I hold you in My Immaculate Heart and feel the joy in your parishes. I pray for you during Easter, taking your petitions to Heaven. You have mourned the suffering of Christ, and now you rejoice forever. This is your hope for the remainder of your lives. Always remember that the Paschal Resurrection of Jesus is the Good News that gives you the means to live with momentum and purpose. You partake of the Eucharistic Body of Christ and are united in Him. How is it true, some ask, that humanity has been this blessed? Humility, contrition, and turning away from sin place you in the enviable posture of being fed the Fruits of the Cross and the Holy Spirit. Now, you share the spoils that My Son has won in His victory over Satan. Therefore, when you attend the Holy Sacrifice of the Mass, see the Savior whose Crucifixion has reconciled you with the Father. Jesus has been Crucified, and will never die again. He has been raised from the dead to perpetually reign. My lost children must believe the significance of this salvific achievement by the Son of Man. Today's Paschal Feast offers them the impetus to unite geographically and spiritually. You are given unique ways to reach the impoverished with a refined definition of Christian poise. You should elevate your spirits to heights that have never occurred to you. The Holy Child of Bethlehem has brought you this tenable means for uplifting humanity through the articles of your faith. If you will unify your hearts with His during this time of Christian conversion, you will know not only how to be righteous, but the reason why it is important. God wishes you to recognize Love when you see His Sacred Face. He wants you to shout out *Papa!* when the Angels usher you into His presence, and you must be humble when you get there. This is why I implore you to excel in Jesus' image. If you are like Him during this life, Heaven will envelop you when you surrender your soul to death. Easter provides humanity an awakening invitation to pray fervently for a more intimate relationship with the Holy Spirit. You know that Jesus was raised from the Tomb and is inclined to bestow good fortune upon those who believe in Him. There are insufficient words to describe these Easter Mysteries in practical terms, but the simplicities you practice, the way you invoke My intercession, and your requisition of the Holy Spirit allow you to accept like unassuming children. Your hope is justified and your sights are cleared in the reliance you place in God, both here and in the Afterlife. I implore you to never fear the future. Jesus seeks in you a rejuvenated faith that transforms your lives into an epic of spiritual trust never before seen in the history of the world. Be stouthearted and do not concede to temptations of the flesh. Hold fast to the mandates of the Gospel, and you will be blessed; you shall visualize what true forgiveness is. My Special and Chosen ones, I have a deep sense of gratitude because you have contributed a great deal on the Lord's behalf to this embattled world. The plateau of Grace on which you stand and your endeavors on Earth are gifts from Heaven, as is your reciprocal love for God. When the Mother of Jesus says that She is pleased by your lives, you are in good stead before Him. I pray for your safety, I call for your patience, I plead for your obedience, and I promise that the days are passing as they should. They are doing so because you have allied your will with My Son. You have confirmed your atonement with Heaven through Jesus, the Triune Redeemer from Nazareth, who gives reprise to human hope that is yielded through no other creature conceived. My Special son, I understand that you are honored to do your work, and I see your joy in knowing that God's Will is done by your friendship with the Angels. Please pray for your brother, that his spiritual darkness is lifted. Thank you for sharing this Feast with him and taking good care of him. I promise that the love you are offering Timothy makes you like the Christ for whom Easter is celebrated. There are scarcely any means to describe your stature in the Lord. Please remember your petitions next week for Divine Mercy Sunday..."

Sunday, April 3, 2005
Feast of Divine Mercy
2:46 p.m.

"Through the intercession of Saint Faustina, your prayers are delivered to the Messiah and given utmost consideration according to His Will. My children, I speak to you as the Matriarchal Fount of Divine Mercy, even as humanity brawls with an alarming and acutely disconcerting lack of spiritual peace. I ask My dear children to turn to Jesus for diplomacy, consolation, and forgiveness. You must know that the Divine Mercy Chaplet is your means of praying for the absolution and tenderness of heart that you seek in your lives. My humble ones, I realize that you pray for the gifts you require, for the compassion that the Lord dispenses, and for the awakening of your spirits to everything He commands. It is right that you should give Him thanks and praise for the goodness He designs. The bounty of Jesus' Mercy is as timeless as Paradise and closer to your hearts than you assume. I pray with you for the bestowing of the petitions you raise to My Son. The most imperative urgency of this Feast is to pray for the millions who are unaware of the Justice of Heaven. Remember those who are ingrained in sin, and ask Jesus to preserve them from its horrible grasp. You know that the Lord despises sin, and anyone who remains in sin is separated from the Divine Grace that sanctifies His earthly flock. Millions of prayerful people are offering this Hour of Divine Mercy on behalf of their relatives and friends, even for strangers who do not know God. This is also what I seek from you. I understand that you have brought Me a list of petitions for this Feast of Divine Mercy according to My instructions from your last message. I shall ask you to recite them presently. However, I first desire that you reflect upon the majesty that has been given to you through the relationship we have developed over the years. Your obedience to Me in living the Will of God is in itself a mystical prayer for suffering humanity. You must recognize that your embracing of My intercession is a part of the Divine Mercy that Jesus is giving to the world. Thank you for being powerfully merciful to lost sinners by receiving Me in this place, by your persistent attentiveness to My call for the conversion of human hearts to the Holy Cross, and your patience in a world that is wracked by the transgressions of men. I assure you that you are mitigating the errors of these people by your consecration to Me and the mission that the Lord has given you to complete. We pray because God loves humanity. He sees above and beyond the purview that you hold from your station on Earth. His wish is the best of all good wishes that you could hope to attain in the span of a natural life. I urge you to remember with the faithfulness of the Saints that God is a benign Creator, that He dispenses every good thing to those who love Him, and that His Will is done when you accept the blessings and graces that He extends to His suffering flock. Now the day has reached the three-o'clock hour where you live, and I will hear the reciting of your petitions for the intervention of Heaven. Thank you, My Special son, for lifting these heartfelt intentions to the Throne of God through the Divine Mercy of Jesus. These are holy requests you seek; they are venerable prayers for a broken humanity who is only now becoming aware of the willingness of My Son to dispense His forgiveness to sinners who feel unworthy of His pardon. And, you should understand that it is not only your will that manifests these petitions, but the Wisdom of the Holy Spirit helping you see clearly the distance humanity must travel to reach its new beginning in the Sacred Heart of Jesus. As you think about your prayers on this special day, be reminded of His messages to Sister Faustina and how difficult it was for her to engross the words she had been given. Realize the magnitude of her participation during the 20th century, that she was asked to do the bidding of the Holy Spirit under intense distress and failing health. These are among the reasons Jesus chose her as His earthly messenger. Sister Faustina possessed every attribute that all men shall have before they enter Heaven. She invited Jesus here as He inquired why humanity spurned His Sacrifice, while His intention is to preserve your souls from Hell. Jesus approached Faustina knowing that she would comply in My image at the Annunciation of the Archangel Gabriel. This is what makes Saints of ordinary people. It is when God's disciples commit to His Holy Kingdom without question or knowing in advance how certain tasks will be complied. This is the obedience that brought the Apostles to be Christian Martyrs. It is the abandonment of the self and of your own volition that is present in the Saints, those canonized by the Church and the billions who have traveled anonymously beyond the bonds of Earth into Jesus' hands. Yes, making Saints of wayward sinners is what conversion does. I come to lift-up the lowly, guide the lost, inspire the indifferent, and manifest in meek people the mightiness that will make them visionaries among men in your time and for the ages. It has been said that moral courage is a rare commodity; and this may be true in some places, but not here. Not in this house! Not where the Mother of God speaks! Let there be no equivocation about it. Anyone who venerates the Immaculate Mother of Jesus is living a paranormal existence that is blessed by the Savior of the world in ways that are incomprehensible by secular societies. You are My Children of the Latter Times whose hearts are one with the Angels. You are Salvation-seeking activists whose prowess cannot be matched by modern armies and war machines. Under My maternal care, you are the living aroma of Heaven's Scent, of Jesus' Nativity, His ministry, and His Sorrowful Crucifixion and Glorious Resurrection. You are patrons of righteousness in this new century of Christendom, and you will not fail the King of kings. I herald the Divine Mercy of Jesus because I birthed Him into your presence, and I bring peace wherever He sends Me. You are vested with the authority to censure heathens who have little regard for the Dominion of the Lord, and I commend you to strive for the excellence that will cease the transgressions of sinners who will someday thank you for their priceless faith.

My little ones, it is painfully obvious that Satan is still cruelly poisoning the Earth. There is nothing new in telling you this. But, as horrible as it seems, the issue of your existence is more transcending than to simply watch Creation suffer under his oppression. In the Sacrifice of Jesus, and by virtue of His Resurrection from the Tomb, you are empowered to ask God for anything you wish to receive, and He will grant it according to His Will. This is what this Feast is about. And, even though you are tempted to dissect the basis of His Will, suffice it to say that whatever He allows and whatever you yield, know that it is to His Glory and for the Christian conversion of men. Today, there is another Saint and intercessor for the Church. Saint Pope John Paul the Great of 1978-2005 will be an historical hero until the end of the world and beyond the calling of Eternity. He is with Me in the company of Jesus, along with his predecessors into whose presence he went with ecstasy. He knows what your spiritual battles are about. His pursuit has always been for the sanctity of life, and his message from Heaven is as sure as ever. Do not be afraid! I have taken My Pontiff into My embrace as I hold you who are still exiled on Earth, fulfilling the Plan of God. I nourished him with a Mother's Love, and his devotion to My Immaculate Heart was his comfort during innumerable agonizing days. He endured extreme mental anguish because millions would not heed him, but he is now satisfied knowing that the sacrifices of Roman Catholics are altering the course of history. Your lives will be all right, My children! Jesus has expunged everything about which you are afraid and all things you mourn by His Crucifixion on Mount Calvary. And, the gladdest man is not the Saint who just arrived in Paradise, but he who remains on Earth, living-out his faith knowing that the promises of God are true. Yes, Karol is with Me, and he is praying deeply and devotedly for your success in dimensions that he could never have imagined. God is listening to him, as always, and He is honoring your petitions, especially on this Feast of the Divine Mercy. Thank you, My Special and Chosen ones, for being My sons. Redemption becomes you! See beyond the struggles of the day, and know with confidence that Jesus sustains you. Tend to your life's struggles with perspective; continue your work with Me; write with the prolific beauty that reigns in your hearts; and most of all, trust your Immaculate Mother in all things. I have given you Christ, and He is all you need to survive. You will witness the majesty and pageantry of the Church as Masses are offered for Pope John Paul II. We shall see whom the Holy Spirit chooses to be his successor, and I pray that his flock will be equally as devoted to him as they loved Karol of Krakow. Thank you for your prayers on this auspicious Feast..."

Petitions to Our Lord Jesus Christ
on the occasion of
the Feast of Divine Mercy
April 3, 2005

1. Grace, wisdom, composure, strength, and courage to the man who will become our next Pope.

2. For the grandest reward for Pope John Paul II in Paradise this day.

3. For the continued union of Timmy and me in our consecration to the Sacred Heart of Jesus through Our Holy Mother.

4. For the Second Coming of Jesus Christ in Glory.

5. For the healing of humanity from every illness and disease, physical and spiritual.

6. For the capacity to live with the dignity and strength of Pope John Paul II.

7. In thanksgiving for my life and the grace with which I have been blessed.

8. For the conversion of those lost in worldliness and materialism.

9. For the conversion of the rich and haughty.

10. For spiritual blessings of revelation upon our families and friends.

11. For the grace to continue my writings and articulating Our Lady's wisdom to the world.

12. For protection for the Roman Catholic Church from all diabolical forces, both inside and outside the Church.

13. For all those with whom I work, asking the intercessory guidance of Saint Francis.

14. For the mystical mobilization of all the angels and saints to provide assistance in the transformation of the Earth.

15. For the release of all souls in Purgatory, and deliverance of those who would be otherwise bound for the fires of Hell.

16. For the culture of Life to again flourish in America.

17. For the permanent end of abortion forever.

18. For an increase in vocations to the priesthood.

19. For courage and strength for Bishop Lucas and Cardinal George, that they may trumpet Our Lady's intercession as the *Morning Star Over America*.

20. For the protection of the integrity of my brother and me for the sake of Our Lady's work.

21. For our health and longevity together.

22. For the restoration of the lives of those addicted to substances and alcohol.

23. For the leaders of our country to return to the wisdom of the Holy Spirit.

24. For the conversion of everyone outside the Catholic Church to join us at the Altar to receive the Body, Blood, Soul, and Divinity of Jesus Christ in the Holy Eucharist.

25. For the Triumph of Our Lady to come to its summit.

26. In reparation for my sins of arrogance and haughtiness, impatience and slothfulness.

27. For the unity of all marriages, that husbands and wives would know the love that exists in Your Heart.

28. For the realignment of women's identity in America, that they may take-on the beauty of the Most Holy Virgin.

29. For the guidance and resources for my station in life.

30. That every person may feel the love that I have felt deeply in my heart.

31. For the protection and sustaining of the faculties, senses, and physical systems of my brother and me.

32. That we will succeed in every way and through every dimension in our example of Jesus and our witness to the Most Blessed Virgin Mary.

33. How could I forget the poor? For the least of these, that they may be lifted to the heights of Heaven and Earth.

34. That the world would begin to meet my feet and the desires of my heart.

35. May Satan be chained in the Abyss forever, never allowed to bring the twinge of sadness or disappointment to any human heart.

36. May violence and hatred be extinguished.

37. For the end of war and protection against global disaster.

38. For the conversion of the Muslim world.

39. For true peace and unity among the nations.

40. For the supernatural intercession of the Archangels Michael, Gabriel, and Raphael, and the Dominion Angels.

41. For the capacity and opportunity to heroically engage this world for the sake of the Gospel.

42. To be united perfectly with the Sacred Heart of Jesus and the Immaculate Heart of Mary in union with Saint Joseph and my brother Timmy.

43. For the public, ecclesial approval of *Morning Star Over America* by His Excellency, Bishop Lucas.

44. For the grace to never sin again, to remain in communion with perfect Love throughout the Earth and the rest of Eternity.

I ask these things as the basis for all that I hope both the world and myself to be. I pray for the world to flourish into its infinite dimensions of holy Love and manifestations of grace from the foundation of the Beatific Vision between the Sacred and Immaculate Hearts. Please take us all to Heaven soon. Please come in Glory to set the world aright. I love you with all my heart.

Sunday, April 10, 2005
Saint Fulbert, Bishop [AD 952-1029]
2:51 p.m.

"My children, this message is My prayer for you to God, that you might be enlightened by the Wisdom of the Holy Spirit. And, your response is your prayer for humanity, that your brothers and sisters will come to know Divine Love in the way Jesus taught. Through all the innocence and sublimeness that have become your character in the Lord, you are the faithful followers of miraculous Truth, so much so that you have been isolated from the worldlings who would delay their Christian conversion to another time. You see that your prayers are reciprocal to Mine, and still in unison. We wish for the same things to come in your day so the future will unfold with peace. For certain, it is true that violence and poverty are rampant in the northern, southern, eastern, and western hemispheres. Why is this so? Because not everyone has accepted their lives of sacrifice and humility found in the Holy Gospel. We have yet to finish the mission of encouraging them, and this is why I speak to you. I come for the purpose of addressing humanity-whole, but I also speak to you personally about My intentions for your Apostolate and My gratitude for dedicating your efforts to My Son. There is no question that I have allowed you to see many miracles; and these are not the last of the gifts I come to dispense, but signs and graces to keep your hopes alive. I have permitted you to witness manifestations of supernatural substance because I implore you to never forget that the Kingdom of God is preeminently evident. You are called to be the perfect likeness of Jesus, although you are yet sinners in the flesh. I have told you that even though you have a propensity to sin, it is not inevitable that you do. Your devotion to Me speaks volumes about your determination to remain sinless in your emulation of Jesus. He will help if you ask. The Holy Spirit is your guide during moments of temptation and your discernment when you have decisions to make. Perfect Love is natural to you if you give yourselves to everything pleasing to God. Every person must be true to his own measure, realizing that there are circumstances of extraordinary distaste that pervade your lives. Call on Me, little ones. Even though you may never hear My answer in audible terms, call on Me, and I will lead you to the holiness that My Son has provided. I am the Mother of the Resurrected Savior who knows no bounds of Mercy for the repentant. Jesus understands human temptation. He realizes the magnitude of the fight against the appeals of the flesh and the materialism that distract you from your spiritual lives. I have asked My children for centuries to avoid the temptations that draw your attention away from the Cross. This is why you must live more modestly and exercise prudent judgement in worldly affairs. Remember that Creation is not comprised simply of the things you see, but the wholly magnificent spiritual order that you cannot yet see from your station on Earth. You are called to be spiritual creatures, and your destination is Heaven where spiritual beings live beneath the vaults of the Father. You will be given a perfect body when you arrive in Heaven, when the excesses of Creation are purged. Now, however, you must call on the Holy Spirit to enable the goodness in your heart to become the likeness of Christ. My children, how humbly you live, and with what veneration you are obedient to Me! I come calling for your prayers because I know that you will not desist in fighting the good fight about which Saint Paul spoke. You should remember that time is brief, that opportunities for making a difference are few, and that you have only so many hours in the expanse of the years to exalt the Kingdom of God. You are emboldened and commissioned to herald the New Covenant where it has never been heard, and where it is rarely heeded. This takes a great deal of might because you are despised and rejected, and mocked and ridiculed. When you are, know that you are succeeding. Beware when pious men speak praisingly of you! And, be not afraid that godless people might impugn your good reputation in the marketplace or the secular commons. You are on the right side of history where the sheep are spared by the Lamb of God who takes away the sin of the world. On the last day, you will see that your labors have been worthwhile. I promise that everything I have told you is true. My Special son, I bolster your confidence that Christ Jesus trusts you to pen and publish His words in unity with the Holy Spirit. He realizes the sacrifices you have made, that you are not living the amenities that your friends enjoy. However, is it not true that moderation is in keeping with the Will of God for all mortal men? This gives you pause to pray for people who live more extravagantly. I am not suggesting that they are unsalvageable or that their Redemption is in jeopardy because of their ignorance of Truth. Most of them do not sit on Church pews praying for the poor and return to homes worth hundreds of thousands of dollars. These sinners are not the primary targets of your work. It is the hypocrites about whom you write, the ones who boast in social circles as being charitable and given to the enhancement of paupers' lives. You know who they are, and they will be rebuked by your words. Every time you publish a book, it is a stepping stone for lost sinners to walk to *Morning Star Over America* where they will find the rendezvous with destiny that so many have spoken about. The more books you publish, the more steps they will take toward conversion. When approaching your neighbors on the Lord's behalf, make decisions based on the atmosphere of the times, the nature of the circumstances, and the conditions by which you can best propagate the Holy Gospel. I will be with you wherever you go. I pray that your wishes come true, and we shall know God's Will according to the turning of the years. You are given latitude to preside over the judgements you have the capacity to render. The fullness of My messages will be revealed in time, especially the passages concerning the conversion of the lost..."

Sunday, April 17, 2005
St. Harriet Bethany, Virgin [AD 1829-1886]*
2:42 p.m.

"The broadness of God's gratitude is spread over your years, My children, in remembrance of the great devotion you have accorded His Kingdom on Earth. If His Dominion could be given a face, it is assuredly poised with confidence and certainty that your work is attuned to His Will, that His expressions of sympathy for those who suffer are being poured over them by your pious lives. You are the esteem with which Jesus is mending the hearts of many who would otherwise feel forsaken. They are being awakened in the newness of Eternal Wisdom by their trust because they realize that your dedication to their Salvation is the legacy of all Christians now being bequeathed to lost sinners in your day. I wish you could comprehend the boundless expanse of timeless beneficence you are giving those who are unaware of the graces God wants them to receive. They often do not pray because they have never been told of the magnitude of its purpose. They are too timid to beg your intercession and that of the Angels and Saints, and they must be taught and motivated, converted and inspirited. Through your lives, I am able to touch them and unite them with Heaven through the Most Sacred Heart of My Son. O' how I love My people! How many ways has Jesus proved His Sacrificial Love for the creatures whom the Almighty Father deigned to give the breath of life? The number is endless, and the human family is only now coming to realize most of them. Yes, mystical gifts and charisms, blessings and miracles—all for the outcome of opening the hearts, minds, and consciences of your brothers and sisters who do not know God. Please remember that you have the power to help them in their struggles against the world. You can lead them from temptation of the flesh and give them strength in the fight against the throes of materialism and greed. You tell them that I am their Mother, and they agree with you in numbers larger than you have the ability to recount. Many people who become converted in spirit, heart, mind, and soul are so elated that they have not sufficient words to tell you how it feels. You are mindful of their suffering, so please know the victory they inherit once they have been set free from sin in the Blood of the Cross. My little ones, My Immaculate Heart sees a world that is impacted in unprecedented proportions by the passing of John Paul the Great. He made a lasting impression on the temporal side of Creation by serving in God's vineyard with devotion and distinction. I realize that My children grieve his absence among you, but I ask that you understand his elation in having come to Heaven to be with Jesus and Me, and the Angels and Saints. My dear children, John Paul the Great is a Saint because he exemplified the divinity of Jesus for billions. He fought against the rampant secularism that is an enemy of the Church. He lifted-up the poor, set the captives free, stood fast for the Traditions of the Church despite the ranting of the liberalism trying to tear them down, and he fought the good fight against illness, assault, and aging. I assure you that John Paul the Great built a Church that is more proceeding than the one he inherited. He was the right Pope for his time, and his warning is for you to never be afraid. Do not fear the beast trying in vain to devour the holiness in your hearts. Do not fear the wolves of atheism prying at the door. Prostrate yourselves before the Holy Eucharist and make your lives the image of the Cross in the same way he placed himself in this posture to fend-away the murderers who came for his life in its prime. Karol was successful in evicting them from his presence because he invoked the Cross spontaneously. This also, My children, is his message for you. Do not be afraid because the Holy Cross is God's signature of virtue. Do not be afraid of anything that might appear to you in the form of usury or promises of wealth because, in your hearts, you know these things to be vacuums. Do not concede to temptations of the flesh because you understand them to be pursuits that will take you from the spiritual realms. And, My children, do not be afraid of the enemies of your Salvation because the Holy Spirit has grounded you in the faith that makes your Redemption inevitable. In all these things, you must have trust and courage to realize that you have already fought the great battles in giving your souls to God. You are Christians now, and good ones; and this is the step that has secured your Eternal Life in the Celestial City beyond the Firmament. My Special and Chosen ones, I offer My intercession before the Cross of Jesus for the intentions you hold in your hearts. I give you My promise that your supplications have been galvanized through the intercession of the Saints. As you know, God loves the Saints; He adores those who hold fast to His sacred principles with fondness. You are facing the militance of human strife that you have overcome by your loyalty to Heaven. How could anyone be more enlightened than this? Your petitions and good works, humility and servitude, and your determination to succeed are serving humanity well. Your compliance is important for the sanctification of humanity, and the events of this week will be of great magnitude for the mission of the Church. Remember to savor the magnanimous power of the Papacy in the ensuing days. My Special son, I cherish you beyond all telling. You make Me happy when you are happy, and I am sorrowful when you feel sad. I am elated that you are in service to Jesus for the cultivation of the Earth..."

Sunday, April 24, 2005
Dedicated to the Papacy of Pope Benedict XVI
2:58 p.m.

"...a bright light flashed around us and a deafening clap of thunder exploded that made us both cringe... Glittering sparks engulfed his entire body and a bright ball of fire flashed from the top of his head. The electricity made a crackling sound as it encircled him in a brilliant glow... I know that an incredible cloak of protection is safeguarding our lives. There is no doubt that it is the Mantle of the Blessed Virgin Mary."
William L. Roth Jr.
Morning Star Over America
April 24, 1995

"Now, My little children, you are living in the year of Pope Benedict XVI, and your journey toward Heaven is much closer than when it first began. I am the bringer of Great News in that you have continued to be chosen to enlighten your brothers and sisters about the supremacy of God and the provisions He has made for your exculpation and deliverance to the mansions of Paradise. As you ponder how the future months and years will unfold, I ask you to pray for the intercession of the predecessors to My holy Pope Benedict XVI. Indeed, call upon the strength and Wisdom that took Saint Peter to martyrdom in the name of human absolution. Today has been dedicated to the installation of Pope Benedict XVI, and represents the opening of Eternity even wider for the conversion of lost souls to the Grace of Almighty God. Jesus has planned for His Church to live into its present hour since the beginning, and it would be too rhetorical to assert that the Papacy of Benedict XVI will be more brief than that of John Paul the Great. As you have moved past the age of 40, both of you have been allowed to see the many transformations of the modern era that will lead to the culmination of all the ages. You have seen histories of terrible wars and the burdens that have been placed on innocent lives. You have fought against the evil forces that have besieged your ancestors and tried to take from them that very peace for which your hearts still yearn. Throngs of agnostics have assaulted your characters, and evildoers of all stripes are yet attempting to bring ruination to your good names. Even in the wake of these things, I ask you to bear forward in the acknowledgment that your victory in Jesus has already been won. There is great hope in the world today, little ones, because the Shepherd that Jesus has chosen to lead His flock is a tried and true Roman Catholic Christian who will not change his stripes according to the direction of the wind. My Pope Benedict XVI comes from a lineage of courageous fighters, and his honorable service to the Faith Church on Earth will be so admired that he will be long hailed as one of the greatest Pontiffs to ever reign at the Holy See. Therefore, this is a very good day for Heaven and Earth.

I ask of My children today that you pray for My new Pope. Ask Jesus to keep his spirits always aloft and give him the Light of Justice as his guide. Pray that no one would ever attempt to take him from this world until his service to God is through, and that Jesus will uphold his dignity as in the greatest servants in the days of old. Please tell humanity, My children, that Pope Benedict XVI has the kind and gentle heart that is most reflective of Jesus than anyone who has ever been elevated to the Papacy. He loves…O' how this Pope loves Jesus' people. He understands the oppression that befalls those who live in places where human freedom is oftentimes ignored. He has held fast to the Faith, he has been a pillar in a wavering world, he has fought the good fight against the liberal forces wishing to dilute the Traditions of the Church, he has suffered greatly over the inequities between peoples and nations, he has given his life to the spreading of the Holy Gospel, he has prayed like none before him for the conversion of the lost, he has been unselfish in giving to the poor, he has been the most reflective about God's creatures since the great Saint Francis of Assisi, and now, at long last, he has become the Vicar of Christ on the Earth! He is more than your Holy Father now, he is the very imitation of the Son of Man incarnate in the world. And, how I love this Pope! How My Immaculate Heart pines that My people will embrace this Holy Father with the admiration of the Angels! He is My Pope! He is My gift to you! He is your intercessor to the Hosts of Heaven by his very invocation. His blessing will grant you the Plenary Indulgence that can shake the worst evil from the depths of any man! I ask that you give him your hearts, your souls, your spirits, and your dedication. Love My Pope like you love Jesus, Himself, because he will lead you during his brief Papacy to the foyer of the Promised Land of everything you have ever wanted from the Throne of God.

My Special and Chosen ones, you have witnessed on April 19, 2005 that majesty, mystery, and mysticism of the Roman Catholic Church in the election of the 264th successor to Saint Peter. And, he has presided over an installment Mass in the past few hours that moved the heavens to tears of joy. His homiletics are utterly profound pronouncements of Eternal Truth that issue from the lips of God. When you think of every impassioned admiration that you held for Pope John Paul the Great, prepare to treble that fondness, love, and devotion for Pope Benedict XVI. He is the future of your faith in the Church, your vision of human Salvation for all the world, and your source of ecclesial guidance for his tenure in Rome. Watch carefully how he is received as he travels the world. Pray for the protestors who might heckle at the utterance of his name, because they are under the influence of evil legions. I know that both of you are true to your trust in Jesus and the infallibility of the Holy See. It will not be difficult for you to continue in your seamless service to My Sacrificed Son under the guidance of your new Pope. Your work for Me is yet incomplete. You have many more prayers to recite, miraculous messages to record, and contemplations to write. You have countless other lives to touch, hearts to soften, eyes to open, and souls to convert. This is the mission to which God has assigned you, the one you have chosen to accept, and the reason you will someday rest in My Arms in Heaven with Jesus and all the Saints. I hope you understand the importance of your continuing to decipher the difference between what the world defines as good and what your hearts tell you to be Fruits of Goodness. You see clearly because you have been accorded the vision to see Heaven clearly. Let not your hearts be troubled by the calling of the flesh or the seduction by your friends to lend to other pursuits. Your goal is the reaching of Heaven and helping your brothers and sisters understand the reason for their seeking that goal as well.

    I will ask you to tell Me what it felt like to see, hear, and witness the events in Rome this week when the new Pope made his appearance. I wish for you to try to capture your feelings in words based upon the heartfelt victory that you have just described because, in a small way, that is the same elation humanity will feel upon the Return of Jesus in Glory.* Do you remember that His Return will be announced like a surprise gift by the Holy Spirit just prior to His breaking through the clouds? 'I announce great joy to the world! Habemus Papam!' And, with these words, your souls have again been granted the Protection of My Immaculate Heart from a Pope who is deeply devoted to Me and who has venerated Me as His Mother since he was first able to utter audible words. Send the word forth, My children, that this is My Pope! You have, indeed, witnessed this week the beginning of one of the greatest pontificates in the history of the whole of Roman Catholicism. Be grateful to the Lord for bestowing this great gift upon humanity! As this humble servant labors in the vineyard of God, humanity will indeed walk more gracefully to that Glorious Resurrection that Jesus has given to you all. My children, I end My message today with the same joy in which I came. I commend you to the service of Pope Benedict XVI and the Divine Mercy of Jesus. I remain your Protectress and Benefactress. Please continue to emit the jubilation that is befitting of your obedience to Me... My Special son, you know that I tell you things that are awesome to hear; but what you have seen from Rome this week is awesome to behold!... I give you now My holy blessing in the Name of the Father, the Son and the Holy Spirit. ☦ Be of great joy! Habemus Papam! I love you. Goodnight!"

* These sentiments were recorded in *To Crispen Courage*.

Sunday, May 1, 2005
Feast of Saint Joseph the Worker
5:03 p.m.

"With holy anticipation, I speak on this evocative day of Grace. I come that the Spirit of the Lord will seek out the lost and convert the wicked, and I call you to devotion to Saint Joseph because his intercession yields great favor in Heaven. The Saints and Archangels harbor you from life's storms, and they bring you the resilience of spirit and trueness of heart that the world cannot give or take away. With your participation, we will convert millions more to the Cross. It is prudent to usher lost sinners to the Crucifixion where they will see the Sacrifice which has brought renewal to the obsolescence of the Earth. My children, My joy would be incomplete without your service, and I come to offer the emolument you deserve. My Son does not call you to be loyal to the world, only to Him and to the graces that render you close to God. Your gifts of prayer and sacrifice make a difference that you cannot see, but please offer them anyway. I deliver signs, wonders, and words to complement your faith, and you recognize them through your trust. I told you November 17, 2001 that one of these prefigured events will happen on 05-05-05. Remain together in My presence because you will learn about many issues prescribing the configuration of the Earth before the Second Coming of My Son. Prayerfully scrutinize your mortal existence and think about the times when your predecessors lived through poverty, strife, warfare, and fending-off the elements. Your years are comfortable compared to the struggles of their age. By the Lord's desire for you to honor Him, He placed you in this generation, in this century, so you will transform the United States into the holiness He commends it to espouse. There is so much progress to discuss about the sacrifices you are offering My Son that it is difficult to start. Suffice it to say that you are the imitation and reflection of Jesus for humanity. You are the hope of millions for their enlightenment in the spiritual realms to which you have given your lives. My little children, you know that God's Kingdom is replicated in your hearts when you defer to the Holy Spirit. The Pope welcomed into Heaven on April 2, 2005 once declared that you are not expected to match God's Love, but to understand it, to internalize it, and realize that Jesus is the Manna of your Salvation. You will make mistakes along the way; you may fail to comprehend the meaning of manifestations given to cultivate your faith. However, you are always beloved because you are pearls in the fathoms for whom God searches to treasure your affections. As this new month arrives, I ask you to manifold your prayers for mothers, especially whose children are in their wombs. If it seems long that the Lord has not responded to your petitions to end abortion, imagine the difficulty He is having converting mothers who reject Him. Jesus died for them, and your sacrifices are the

Pauline profits that lead them into conversion. Be not frustrated by the lack of response from people who disbelieve Christianity. Pray for them, and God will grant them forgiveness because of your intentions, especially those offered before the Most Blessed Sacrament. And, to My Special and Chosen ones, I have never doubted that you have never doubted that I love you with overwhelming power. I understand that you discuss and contrast the messages and images I give you with the conditions of the world. You must be strong of heart so you will not become embittered by the world. No one alive understands more your exasperation about the wrongs and evils in the world than Me. Imagine the sorrows of My Immaculate Heart as I witnessed the Passion and Crucifixion of Jesus. O' how difficult it was for Me to receive His Body in My lap on Good Friday. I made it through, dear children, for the same reasons you will survive and prevail over your enemies on the Earth. I knew that Jesus told us the Truth about His Resurrection from the Tomb. I ask you to remember the sense of impending victory that I embraced as I saw My sacrificed Son that day. I knew that the sinners of the world would not have the last word. By all means, I knew that The Word, the Son of Man to whom I gave Birth in Bethlehem, would emerge on Easter Morning to the shame and chagrin of everyone who hated Him, to the people who crucified Him, and to the pitiable sinners who knew not what they were doing. He forgave them all because they were bringing the Salvation of humankind to Creation, even in the error of their ways. Their intentions were not benign; their work was the work of evil. But, God turned this evil into good.

My Special son, I support everything you do because I see your heart, and I know when you are thrust into despair. I pity you and pray for you when you are distressed. The grief you endure is of the same darkness that plagued the Saints. Your periods of sorrow are nothing new. You have the presence of mind to retrain your thoughts and invoke God's peace to elevate your spirit, often in a matter of moments. This is a mark of courage and faith. It is your love for Jesus, for Saint Joseph, and for Me that is unprecedented in many parts of the world and through the centuries since Pentecost. I am gratified that you control your emotions. You are an example for those who are motivated by your books and speeches to offer themselves to My Son. It is urgent that we pray for My adopted daughters around the globe, especially in America. Some are headstrong and given to false freedom that lures them into sin. Wives nag their husbands with demands about menial matters, and when their husbands recoil in search of a sense of dignity, their wives call them unfaithful. This is an irony in America. They play on men's affections, coaxing them into having compassion, even with their wives' stony hearts. I shall remain steadfast in upholding your dignity. The experiences you have had through the years give you vision to write passionately about the gender conflicts dividing the American Church. God does not condone females to be priests. Even so, they resort to demagoguery to coopt decisions that belong to priests, bishops,

Cardinals, and the Holy See. You may reflect upon these things, but it should not be an exercise in bitterness or revenge. I wish not to supplant your experiences with inordinate ideals, but that you learn about your faith. It is crucial that you ensure your protection, safety, and security wherever you go. You are sometimes reckless with strangers in parking facilities. It should be apparent that these occasions come with unexpected responsibilities that you would rather avoid..."

Sunday, May 8, 2005
Mother's Day [secular]
2:52 p.m.

"My dear ones, the Angels appear with wings aglow, and My Immaculate Heart burns with Love for you! I am encouraged by the piety of the Church and the Sacred Traditions that have made its mission so successful. I dedicate today's message to all who bear children in their wombs, that they will ensure that their babies are given proper postnatal care. I come joyfully because in the strains of your tongue, God gives Me eloquence to pronounce your Salvation. I speak every language in the world, and His Love is the same in each one. When I refer to the peaks of human holiness, you know to lift your lives in search of the purification of the heart. When I speak of peace flowing like a river, you find that it is placid, plentiful, nourishing, cleansing, and beautiful. I have spoken of the spires of piety to which you ascend and the plateaus of righteousness from where you reach with grappling hands to rescue your lost brothers and sisters. Your Mother has spoken about charity and hope, that your trust in Jesus gives you a sense of survival that prevails over any darkness and everything that degrades you as Christians. I have enjoyed dictating messages about cultivation and conversion. We have spoken about war and peace, lust and chastity, and of the Fruits of the Holy Spirit that make your lives complete. I do this because I am the Lady of Perpetual Help. In many ways, you see the content of My Most Immaculate Heart because you are privy to the sanctity of the Truth. You are challenged to live one day at a time and moments in sequence. This is as it should be because it gives you the opportunity to decide for God. These time passages, when engorged by your fealty to Jesus, become stepping stones on your journey to Heaven. I often call you to invoke the intercession of the Saints because they are of great help in framing your vision of Omnipotent Love. They breathed the same air and tread the terrains that allowed them to conquer their temptations. Your imitation of them foretells holy events as the end of time draws near. Thank you for the awesome flowers blooming from your hearts, the pining and longing wishes that you see through the bounty of the Cross. You are fortunate to be Christians because it places you among the chosen ones whose purpose is more than rapt in stoic symbolism; you are active servants in God's Kingdom. The angst you feel knowing that only few respond allows you to see the larger number who have answered Me. I remind you, My children, that secularism is an archenemy of the Church. You are saved by your loyalty to Jesus and embracing the Commandments and Beatitudes that took Him to the Cross. You will be despised and rejected when you live His reflection because those who are enamored by the world cast aspersions against your spiritual foundation. You are blessed not to be them, and I seek your prayers for the conversion of lost souls through the Sacraments of the Church. I believe this will happen, and this is why I am heartened by your faith. Consider the circumstances since My apparitions began. Millions more are visiting My shrines. And, when their hearts open to My intercession, let them return because their curiosity is indicative of their hunger for the intervention of God. If anyone asks about the miraculous manifestations of the Mother of Jesus Christ, tell them that I go everywhere My children reside, in the broadness of day, in skyscraper windows, images jutting from trees, and below trestles where the poorest of the poor assemble for the night. I offer them comfort and sow in them the seed of hope because I am the Mother of the Lamb of God who consoles the brokenhearted. My Special son, I cannot overstate My gratitude for your kindness. Your 2005 manuscript is a revelatory work of genius that will usher your brothers and sisters beneath the protection of My Mantle. I know that you shun such compliments because of your modesty, but I ask you to remember My appreciation for your consecration to Jesus..."

Sunday, May 15, 2005
Feast of Pentecost
Saint Isidore the Farmer [AD 1070-1130]
3:04 p.m.

"My good wishes become your blessings on this High Feast of the Church. I am impressed that you understand the emancipation you receive when the Holy Spirit enters your hearts, as well as the prescience and perseverance that help you avoid impious circumstances and aid you in bleak moments in history. When you think about the Holy Advocate, the Third Person of the Trinity, you are required to enlist your faith because the Spirit of the Lord is not seeable with human eyes. Unlike Jesus, the Holy Spirit does not have a perceptible frame, but it is the Spirit that delivers you when you are lost, when you stray into unsavory purlieus or other nether paths. The Dove of Peace aligns you with the Will of God and the holiness that Jesus implores you to espouse. The Holy Spirit allows you to know Me as the Mother of God, and you respond in obedience to His voice living at the center of your hearts. This is the way you realize that the adversaries of Christianity have an erroneous perception of life, that they are inept in battling immoral forces. The Advocate from Heaven shapes your meditations so you know that your Absolution is derived from your immersion in the Blood of Jesus. Hence, when you die, you will see that you have lived through Him, with Him, and in Him since you gave yourselves to Salvation through the Sacrament of Baptism. I repeat everything for which you pray because I see the obstacles you face. It is obvious when you are taunted by people who reject the Holy Spirit. I invoke your patience during these times, and not just the kind that allows you to cope, but patience that brings you to cast aside questions about the idiosyncrasies of other sinners. I speak with you because I am concerned about your happiness and the way you take too seriously the nonsense of the secular void. My Special son, it moves Me when Jesus allows Me to appear to you because I know that you appreciate My calming presence. I am partly responsible for your overexposure to the negative aspects of life, but I do not intend for you to be the watchdog of human morality. Everything you have written about the corruption of the United States is true. It is commendable that you pray to end social injustice. By all means, remember the Triumph of My Immaculate Heart! I have made you a roaring lion, charging the ills of the world, but you see yourself as a yelping puppy focused only on the problems that violate God's Truth. This is causing anxiety in your life, and your brother is doing the same thing. I trusted God during Jesus' Crucifixion because I was your example. When you look around, you see millions of people who detest everything for which Jesus stands, but we must ensure that they know the effects of their actions. Life is like seeing a motion picture a single act per day for years, and this is why you are impatient. Man dissects the events of history a crisis at a time, often one hour at a time, over decades and centuries. You know about the victory of Jesus on the Cross and His Resurrection. You are one of the fortunate people who sees Creation the way the Father wants you to approach the perfecting of humanity on His terms. I am committed to teaching you this lesson according to His timetable; not Mine, not yours, not the postman's, not anyone other than God. It is clear that you feel as though your soul is trapped inside a gristmill, and no number of superlatives can describe your discontent. I cannot tell you when the end of time will come, but I have seen its effects. Jesus will not predict when Heaven will assimilate the Earth in Glory, but He knows what He will accomplish once God sends Him back. These are the Mysteries by which you live the faith you have promised to practice, and they are inherent in your participation in the mission of the Roman Catholic Church.

    Modern Christians are not too timid to overwhelm the Earth because you have been victorious in the same war against demonic forces that Jesus killed on Good Friday. By your duty and compliance, you accept the task of satisfying the recommendations of My Son in your day. When Christ looked out from the Cross of Mount Calvary, He saw all the centuries combined through the end of time, but there was no milestone by which lost sinners could earmark this vision. He was seeing beyond that demarcation, past the conclusion of the Earth. When He said 'It is finished,' He was seeing farther than human eyes could witness, well into the Eternity that He knew His Sacrifice would deliver you. Yes, you have spoken and written about the way Jesus' Crucifixion catapulted your sights past everything that would inhibit your progress toward Heaven, including the periods of spiritual darkness that have haunted the greatest Saints who ever lived. And, without these parenthetic intervals of suffering, you would not understand the magnitude of the Divine Light that is engulfing you now. There exists nothing that could be called a necessary evil because evil must be exterminated. The intent of My words is to clarify that in these grave times, you have the right to boast of the greatest role in the heated fight for human conversion. You are dousing the flames of injustice while they are most fierce. You are waging a war against impurity that has never been as far-flung, either in practical terms or the conceptual continuum of history. You have grown in multiple ways since you were a child, something you have in common with everyone. Your body has developed into adulthood; your cognitive skill was honed according to your environment, and your spiritual awareness has been given you by the same Holy Spirit I mentioned earlier in this message. The latter two are the only traits of your being that you will take on your passage into Heaven. And, this means that they are fixed in time and after time; and you must safeguard and maintain their integrity until you go out to greet Jesus wearing your baptismal raiment upon His Return or when you die in the wreck of this world and set eyes on His Sacred Face. This leaves the first of these to keep pure to the best of your ability. The human body can withstand egregious abuse through the years, short of suffering some illness or other manifestation that God asks you to carry. And, whether or not you believe it, you have the capacity to maintain your health by decisions you make and the way you are receptive to the warnings of the Holy Spirit. Lest this message take on metaphysical overtones reserved by New Age philosophers, I wish only to remind you that God sustains your inner-peace and physical strength if you allow the world to unfold according to the time line that He has established. I do not know its point of reckoning or discernable date on your calendar of years, which does not affect what day it is, but I do know the consequences of the Second Coming of Jesus, His Return to the Earth in Glory; and I know that it is destined to occur this century. When Jesus told the Apostles that it would be in their day, He meant that the hour in which you live is their day. All time will be one upon His Return, including Good Friday and Easter Sunday. What makes this message different is that I am telling you that Jesus will Return in Glory in this century, a statement that I have never announced to the previous twenty. I told the seers at Medjugorje that there will be no more messages after theirs because the end of time is near, and I am telling you the same. This, My son, is why your work is so crucial to God's Plan to convert lost sinners. It does not imply that the lives of the Saints were unimportant. Your contribution to the conversion of humanity actually augments theirs. People who were seen as peons in nondescript places are now stationed with Me in Heaven and know the ways in which you are achieving astounding success in offering your Christian witness to the 21st century Earth.

My Special son, please never give up hope. Continue with the courage and dignity that became yours in Jesus' Paschal Resurrection. Allow Easter to be your tenacity in ways you could have never imagined. Do it for all the Jeff Buhls who need you in this world, for a fair maiden named Julia* who is waiting to see you in Heaven, and for everyone I hold in My arms. If you are despaired, remember this 2005 Feast of Pentecost, and know that I have impelled you to rise above the fray. Renounce the negativity that has darkened the lives of sinners who have no trust in God. Be aware of the right and wrong of the world, but do not allow the wrong to make you unnerved. We have already won! The Earth as you see it is passing away, and a New Creation is poised to take its place. No one has better faith than you, and I am simply asking you to use it. There is so much more good we need to accomplish, but it is you who must work in the Lord's vineyard beside Pope Benedict XVI. If you call to mind the day you saw the Mass of the Resurrection for Pope John Paul the Great, contemplate the contrast between the sadness the world felt when the pallbearers carried his casket to the entrance of the Basilica and when they turned it to the crowd for a valedictory ovation. Remember how the bells pealed and the hundreds-of-thousands cheered in every language. They knew they were witnessing the passing of an era in history that is not likely to be seen again. Yes, compare this with the happiness they felt for the arrival of Pope John Paul the Great in Paradise to rest in Jesus' arms after 84 years in exile. To dwell on the historical imperatives that unfolded that day, and to remember the renewal you wrote about when Pope Benedict XVI was elected and appeared on the loggia for his inaugural blessing To the City and to the World—these are the new beginnings about which I spoke in My opening messages in February 1991. They are more than visions of the heart that make your soul feel timeless; they are perceivable scenes of Heaven played-out on Creation's floor. They are signals to give you hope and to sustain your faith. They are paranormal gifts from God that help you realize that in many ways your hearts have already reached the mansions of Paradise. God is asking you to wait a little longer as the epilogue of the Earth plays out. Your life is in total agreement with Jesus' life, and you are part of the entourage that will welcome the Return of Christ the King. Your role in the drama of history came here with your brother. The gift of your lives has been worth the wait, and you will see that these are the best days in your service to the Kingdom of Salvation..."

*A reference to a very kind, lonely, but homely, elderly woman from my childhood whom many heckled and shunned because of her eccentric nature.

Sunday, May 22, 2005
Feast of the Most Holy Trinity
St. Cyril van Demeter [AD 1746-1805]*
3:06 p.m.

"May the Grace and Peace of the Holy Spirit be with you always! My dear ones, I bring you greetings on this Feast when the Church celebrates the Sacred Mystery of the Most Blessed Trinity. You know that there have been untold ways that Doctors of the Church have attempted to portray the Trinity. I showed you years ago the visual example of one eye seeing three distinct parts. And, you have become familiar with the phenomenon of 111 that is one quantity comprised of the tripling of the same digit. The Father is in Heaven with Jesus the Second Person, and Third as the Holy Spirit on Earth in your hearts. My children, Jesus is your Salvation, and the Spirit ratifies your conversion by the love you proclaim. If you remember these things until your death, and if you see in Christ the forgiveness of your sins and the deliverance of your souls to Heaven, then you will understand in essence the origin of the Church. Theologians can explain themselves arguing the rest. Saint Patrick also offers his rendition as a servant of God when you recall the Blessed Trinity. He loves you with the immensity of the Holy Spirit. All the Saints do. You are given an intriguing knowledge of Truth in Jesus, and you are vested with the opportunity to share in His Love for the purification of the world. This is a process that has mandated more than one generation to complete. The writings, lessons, and teachings you give your successors are important for their sanctification. Your recollections and orations of Christian peace are blessings for the heirs you leave behind. And, My Special son, this includes the wonderful new book you are about to publish about the courage humanity needs to survive the tribulations that come upon those who remain true to Christianity. Especially beautiful is the Conclusion to the book that is the perfect ending for the thesis you have proposed. I exhort you to work on it steadfastly, that you inspect it with your brother to make sure there are no presentational anomalies. You are generating a respectable deposit of religious codices for your library. When historians look at the bibliography you leave them, they will see the beauty and harmony of your devotion to Jesus through Me. When you hear about passages in commencement speeches and attribution is given to you, do not be surprised. You have fashioned a theological framework that honors God's miracles in the Salvation of the world. Indeed, it will seem miraculous that you had time in the span of one life to garner such a comprehensive understanding of the Kingdom of God. Yet, they will see from your renderings that it is elementary. Just as there are contradictions in the physical realm, many have seen that the deep thoughts, imageries, and eloquent parables you employ speak to human love so benign that a child can understand. Is this not what Jesus asks of them? My son, this is how America can staunch the bleeding of so many broken marriages. What is the cause of their breakdown? The constant negativity upon which couples focus. It is all right to survey the inequities of life, but it is counterproductive to dwell on them every day. There are too many issues that occur in marriages through the years that are counter-intuitive to the reason people become betrothed. Such blessings as trust, patience, deference, kindness, and forgiveness seem not as important as time passes. The concepts I have just related are virtues that cannot be seen with the eye, but they compose the basic elements of a loving relationship in everyday life. There are toxic forces trying to drive people apart, often with success, that must be eliminated from marriages by the spiritual vision contained in the writings you have given humanity from your humble heart. It becomes habitual to accept abrasive relationships as some sort of inevitable evil over the course of time, but there is nothing inherent in conflict that makes it a component of an amicable marriage. There are poisonous effects in poor relationships that appear as original problems. Husbands and wives focus on irrelevant matters and wonder why they are not at peace. Do you remember that love is patient, love is kind, love does not judge, and the rest? When couples dwell upon love and ignore the complexities of the secular world, they will be led to the Divine Light that allows them to see the reason for their differences. On a broader scale, how do officials who represent public institutions reconcile their decisions when they run contrary to the teachings of Jesus? How do they extract themselves from this dilemma when they lack the courage to stand against the immoral majority? 'I don't know what I am going to do.' This is what they say while collectively rejecting righteousness based on their strength in numbers because they feed off one another's indifference. This is the mentality that preceded the Crucifixion of My Son. In other words, any one of them could choose differently and singlehandedly brunt the effects of their unanimous error, but they say instead, 'surely our constituents will not condemn us all.' This is how warriors are slain and Martyrs created, why Christians are imprisoned, how the Holy Gospel is pushed aside, and why souls condemn themselves upon seeing the Son of Man when they die. They conspire with the mob instead of upholding the Truth. Jesus died to absolve humanity as one body, but He judges you as distinct individuals. I say this to impart how important it is for every sinner to become the likeness of Jesus and remain in the flock at God's feet..."

Sunday, May 29, 2005
Saint Maximinus of Trier [d. AD 347]
3:19 p.m.

"Let there be no illusion that the Will of God to remake His creatures could ever be subverted. All who are devoted to My Most Immaculate Heart know that the historical events of this age portend the serious consequences that will befall anyone who declines to embrace this mortification. We speak of trust and counsel between Heaven and Earth because these are times of tribulation for the Church. I wish for My children to turn to Me for consolation as human error causes untold calamities around the globe. I will intercede for you by invoking Jesus' Sacrifice to induct your souls into Heaven, so it is with undivided interest that you should heed My call for prayer for lost souls. By doing this, you will be given the gifts for which you have prayed. There is danger in the world, but no reason to live in fear. While sunrays may be illustrative of Heaven's delight, contrary to popular belief, thunderheads are rarely an authority in forecasting God's anger. He remains with you despite the troubles you bring upon yourselves. You should seek the approval not of the wealthy, but of the poor, while consoling the afflicted and realizing that Jesus commends your conversion, warrants your purification, and facilitates your consecration. The Earth is like an embryo for the fusion of the excellence of men and the Glory of God, a gestation of refinement and renewal that draws you to the Word of Truth. We seek your personal atonement through your religious resolve and apostolic zeal because you are the disciples whose humbleness helps Jesus amend your lives. Christians accept this fact. The Church believes that the Earth cannot much longer endure the recklessness that humanity imposes. Your faith teaches you that there comes a reconciliation of all things; now is the time when you must answer the call of God to serve Him alone. Today, I implore you to pray for those who oppose righteousness and shun the Divine Mercy that Jesus wishes to share. The Mother of God is recruiting legacies for the virtues your forefathers offered Him during their earthly years. When Jesus seeks their fitful replacements at the closing of the ages, He will discover you. He gives you strength to take the reigns of love in your hearts and become like the holiest Saints the world has ever known. This way, you will be their comrades for advancing Divine Love to the far corners of the globe, to the fractured and forsaken, and the millions who aspire to universes unknown, crying-out for modern miracles of Biblical proportion. I am confident that you will succeed because your holiness cannot be suppressed. Always and everywhere, you are destined to be like Jesus, to lead and serve, suffer and absolve. Be forgivers of your enemies, and every offense you have committed shall be forgiven of you. Place your sights beyond the larger picture about which philosophers and theologians hypothesize. Effect a transformation of humanity that surpasses the dimensions that your vision allows you to perceive. Remember that the circumference of Christian righteousness is not a measure of expediency. The Father has fashioned these times to evoke your compliance with the Gospel and the present-day demands of His Kingdom for urgencies specific to your age. Some people refer to the evolution of man in a context that is bereft of credence because they fail to allow for the residue that every generation leaves behind. The evolution you should be addressing must be of spiritual cleanliness, responsible conduct, heeding the Commandments, living charitably, imitating the lives of the Saints, denouncing material goods, and training your sights on benevolent things. You have an incumbent responsibility to make good on your oath to the Apostles Creed to which your faith is sown. Atop of this, you are asked to harbor no fear. Never mind the wolves howling in the darkness and clawing at the door. Pay no attention to the antics of Jesus' adversaries, for He has vanquished them. Love not life in the flesh, for it is passing. I am calling you to a higher standard and a new meaning for living. I yearn for your comprehension that human existence is transitory, taking your spirits to the Salvation you anticipate and the unparalleled sanctity expected of you. Today's Christians are asked to be bolder fighters than those of old because you must battle more cunning enemies than they faced. You are spinning through the revolving doors of industrialism, continental trade, and mass-communication. These are viable means to share the Gospel, but they have also been perverted by evil wiles to lure unsuspecting people away from the Cross. The message of Christianity is the same as in days of yore, and you must be active to ensure that it reaches the remotest places where lost sinners have gone to hide. My Special and Chosen ones, you are privileged to record My messages, and it is My honor to be here. Never have I seen a whit of pride in you. Share compassion for those who scoff at what I say, and pray in thanksgiving for the faithful ones at your side. Many blessings will be given to them and their children. Pray for the new converts who have come to know Christianity and everything Jesus expects of them. Of all the prophecies in the Bible, God does not reveal the day or hour when the Son of Man will return, and surely you recognize the genius in this. You are on the righteous path; you are accomplishing the work the Father asked you to do. Heaven will provide for you and your brother. We have conducted a good conversation today, and you are aware of the intercession of the Angels. I can do little without My children praying, helping, and obeying. As we continue through June, seek the intercession of the Sacred Heart of My Son. Thank you for dedicating your lives to the cleansing of the Earth..."

Sunday, June 5, 2005
Saint Boniface, German Apostle [AD 680-754]
3:02 p.m.

"I appear before you, My children, because you believe that the Lord God does things right. You know the plight and massive confusion in which millions worldwide agonize and the conflagrations that haunt their daily lives. They are held in prisons of hatred built by the cruelty of other men, predatory thieves, and governments that favor only themselves. I ask you, My honored ones, would you judge the Earth with mercy? Given the diligence of holiness and the capacity of man to become the reflection of Heaven, would you stop the clock and declare My work complete? There are sinners who do not simply reject Christianity, they lack understanding because they are shorn of their innocence by thugs exploiting them as products and possessions. They cry-out for justice, and I wish this would occur in a single day. The enemies of Christianity, many I have mentioned whose souls will be cleansed by fire, stand like roadblocks to this righteousness. We dare take them down with a simultaneous force of Grace, one that Creation has never seen. We must destroy their facade and erect a fortress around the globe, fashioned by love and situated on the foundation of Christian Truth. We see the ease by which most Americans live; often ignoring the impoverished, oppressed, and detained in foreign lands. Those holding them captive must be stopped, and this requires time. I have spoken to My Medjugorje messengers since June 1981. Imagine this. Why have I still not erected the permanent sign there? Because I see more souls to usher to the foot of the Cross, people whose contrition is growing, whose love is blooming in their hearts, and whose participation in the conversion of humanity is required. You know that time serves their transformation into the likeness of Jesus, a modern miracle for sure. You become like My Son when you observe the Father as the Master of timing, for He knows the hour of Jesus' Second Coming. My Special son, regardless of what you believe, this has been a good week. Even at the pace of the mindless world, several things have changed. You have grown in wisdom by your feelings about the manifestations of God. Your spirit has been enhanced by multiple degrees of understanding about the punishment that Jesus has suspended throughout the years. Let us see what He does as the end of the ages arrives. Whom will He include in His Kingdom? Who will be condemned? These are among the questions facing the world. It is crucial that your children learn right from wrong, receive a good education, become invigorated about faith and morals, and look to the future with hope as they plan their vocations in life. These things come and go, and they change with cultures and times, but the Will of God to receive them into His flock of disciples is a process that has lasted for centuries. It is obvious that secularism is the worst enemy of their conversion. I have told you this before. I give you signs and wonders, and you muster a vision to see blessings from Jesus by your spiritual curiosity. There is no doubt that one issue with life is that it is so daily, but you must see each dawn as an opportunity to bloom in the fascination of God. His omnipresence is ever-living and apparent through the working of the galaxies, but you see only a sliver in the course of one day. Rising in the morning is your time to prepare, to plan something special, to pray for the sinners who do not share your beliefs about Heaven. Have pity on the greedy and mercy on the obstinate. When I speak of casting them into the Abyss, it is a moment when they give their final response to the question 'Do you accept Jesus as your Savior?' It is important to remember that this may come tomorrow, whatever the inclination of God. As I say, this could be My last message, or they might proceed beyond the decade. The Father will expose His intentions in time. You must adhere to His sacredness, serve in His vineyard, and watch Jesus feed His flock His Eucharistic Manna as long as God allows.

    This has been a happy week because you better comprehend the role of the Angels and how I have dispatched them through the centuries as My emissaries. I have sent them to teach you how to preserve My image before the nations while I have been more candid than anyone would believe. My mission is to convert My children to the Cross, to Absolution in the Blood of Jesus; and you have graciously offered to help. I have requested My messengers around the globe, especially sites in the production 'Marian Apparitions of the 20th Century,' to offer My intentions in a way that elevates the posterity of My station. Therefore, you know the reason why the Angels are aiding you. My children, you belong to a contingent of creatures who are willing to turn-over your lives for the Salvation of humanity. You do not go out on the town or waste funds for lucrative entertainment. You are not addicted to alcohol or drugs, and you care little what influential people in high places think of you. Your work has always been about changing humanity for the better, for praising Jesus before the souls whom I have mentioned heretofore, and assuring yourselves and your peers that Divine Love is the reason for human life. You are to be awarded a high commendation for living this way, and you will be repaid a hundredfold a thousand times over. The injustices you see are often the result of personal misunderstandings, conflicting interests, eccentric minds, and destroyed self-images. You rarely deal with malevolent persons, but ones who are hurting in ways that others do not know. This is why it is important for you to be patient. Patience, prayer, love and patience—patience! My Special son, your life is the quilted fabric with which I wish to cover the Earth in Grace. In a larger sense, this is the way you will see your contributions to God at the end of time. It is not a matter of how many particles are extracted from air pollutants, who offends whom at their workplace, or how noisy it becomes along the thoroughfare. I sought you out because you are decent in the ways that God wishes Grace to be personified. You are the essence of goodness, peace, integrity, charity, and selflessness. If these things could be seen with the naked eye, you are the picture the world would observe. I am asking you to hold on a while longer, until the Son of God sculpts humanity into the greatest likeness of Himself that could be rendered. There are heartfelt crescendoes that occur during the passage of the years, but not enough about the things you wish to see. Sow your spirit to the brilliance of My Crown! Internalize what it means to defeat the deception of time before you undergo its extinction. Counteract the drudgery of the world with a jubilation that would make men envious of you, one so curiously and peculiarly founded in the Holy Spirit that theologians would wish to dissect your soul to see what makes you tick. As you know, I am limited by the spoken language to tell you how immense is God's Love. I could take you to summits where you could set eyes on the grandest beauty Nature has to offer. I could reveal the victories you are about to achieve in multidimensional display. I could charter the Saints to travel with you when you exit the door tomorrow. I could appear in the sky, at the east portico, in the local Chancery, down the block where the poor people live, and at America's National Cathedral. But, these are not the things that increase your trust or change the Earth. You already know that I am beautiful, and you are not looking for applause or personal fame. You seek only the simplicity of Divine Love, the charity of heart and conscience that urges lost sinners to become Saints. O' how many people arrived in Heaven and said that their years on Earth were too few in number to accomplish everything they wanted to do for Christ! Therefore, I wish for your home to be one in history where I can finish My work to its fullest, not preempted by the suspicions of naysayers or the enemies of Christianity who are lurking at every turn. I pray that I have made the case for your patience, that you will enjoy the Angels and feel that you are living as I have asked. And, My Special son, thank you for continuing to help your brother. He has invested many hours not only in the secular university to aid the credibility of our Apostolate, but in all your efforts. He calls forth the Spirit to be his succor and strength. He had a bad day yesterday; he was despondent and did not know why. He wanted more answers from God, and God asked him to wait. Finally, you became his peace by telling him that everything is all right. You offered him comfort by assuring him that the Angels will augment your work by helping in ways that are beyond your capacity to know. He feels better because you are better. Thank you. And, it was apparent that his gift became your gift when he swatted a wasp through the veil of mortality, creating another butterfly in Heaven.* This was a miracle that helped him through the day. Please permit Me to tell you about his bedtime prayer last night. He said that he did not yearn for fortunes. He does not want the world to end in a flash while there are still so many unprepared. He does not even wish the return of his loved-ones who have come to be with Jesus. He prayed only that you would be happy. That is all. He wants your peace of mind, but he does not know how to get it.

The Angels assure him that his life is on course, that you are doing well, there is peace in your hearts, and of all the blessings he has been granted, you are his greatest gift. And, please know that I see you as such..."

We were sitting on the front porch enjoying the evening when a wasp began menacing us. In a stroke of grace, Timothy reached out and waved his hand at the wasp as it passed as if to help him along his way, but not to hurt him, and the tiny creature miraculously disappeared in front of our eyes. It was not even a question of 'where'd he go?', he just vanished. I simply giggled and said 'thank you' because it is representative of the miracles being manifested in our lives in union with Our Lady's miraculous intercession.

Sunday, June 12, 2005
Saint Conrad Mont Jasper [AD 1514-1588]*
3:16 p.m.

"My children, I bring peace to your hearts through My Immaculate Love, and you receive it with eagerness and piety. It is a blessing to appear before you and assist your prayers for humanity during the grand transformation of the Earth into the divinity of Heaven. We pray to the Sacred Heart of Jesus. You know that He pines for the immersion of lost sinners in His Ocean of Mercy, and we ask the Father to bestow His healing upon those who suffer for the sake of righteousness. Will you pray for your brothers and sisters who are persecuted for their faith? I speak to you today because it is the Will of God. You are more than beautiful in His sight. The gifts you offer His Kingdom make the heavens rejoice. My Special and Chosen ones, I desire you to know that your holiness is articulated by many around you, by people who have read your books, and the Angels and Saints who share the Glory your hearts feel. Admiration is growing for your service to Jesus. I urge you to be modest and simple, and practice the humility that has fashioned your lives. I cannot recount the favor you have found with God because there are insufficient words, although I will offer some departing sentiments for today. It is not enough just to follow your feet or watch with disinterest the obsolescence of the years. You must pursue the innocence of the heart. You live in a world that is defined by lines, boundaries, limits, and prohibitions on your actions and the environment, but no one can impose restrictions on your thoughts, affections, and emotions. Always remember that impiety, blasphemy, and the desecration of the sanctity of human life will eventually force the rupture of the American way. You must not become hypersensitive to every off-putting circumstance, but likewise never act casually when you see an exercise in discretion being impugned. Trust in oneself must come from within; it is never slipped over the Earth's transom by unknown sources, not by osmosis or carrier pigeon or by accident, but through faith in the Providence of Heaven that cannot be seen with your eyes. The values that sustain you are vision, valor, righteousness, prayer, contrition, loyalty, and truthfulness. Human spiritual conversion is founded principally upon repentance, and behaviorally upon moral prudence. I shine My Love on a land whose dreams greet the blooming marigolds and morning glory, whose towering steeples pierce the atmosphere where unity begs to be shared and brotherhood enabled, sanctity redeemed, and chastity underscored. Do not tarry in responding to the summons of the Lord calling you to obey the ordinances of propriety in the magnetism of Truth. Stature, prominence, honor, and character are all meaningless without the invocation of Christian faith; they are like trees without roots and battles with no victors. There is no such thing as conscience without principles like charity, self-control, sacrifice, prayerfulness, and love. Your dignity, foresight, courage, and poise are all dependent on your comprehension of the Lord's intercessory Grace. The sincerities of the heart are lacking and inadequate if you do not have trust in Him. Many Americans say that they do not know God, and they have a tendency to believe the worst of what they hear about strangers. My dear children, I come to give you perseverance greater than the fabled phoenix and more powerful than reparative holocausts. God loves you more than you know. Your faith throughout the centuries has been esteemed, resourceful, bold, and resilient from quill and parchment to pulpit and amphitheater, but a closed heart and soiled conscience allow no room for healing in a world of broken promises. Hence, never forget that you have untold numbers of advocates to assist your conversion. The Saints will sail the darkest nights to uphold you. By His own Incarnation, Jesus said that He would rather live in poverty among you than reign in His riches without you. He instructs humanity that moral fortitude is not ingested or absorbed, it comes from within. Thoughts do not become ideas until you reach a conclusion, and affection does not become love unless you share it. To succeed in history, you must disarm your enemies with kindness, smile through their antagonism, be infinitely patient, and never once compromise the Truth. Always realize that virtuousness, purity, honor, servitude, and charity are the descendants of Christian obedience..."

Sunday, June 19, 2005
St. Romuald of Italy, Hermit [AD 950-1027]
10:31 a.m.

"With gentleness and kindness of thought, I urge you to pray for the solace of Jesus as He invites you to teach humanity about spiritual fertilization. You are more than conquerors, do you remember? You have become practitioners of faith in the New Covenant between God and man, and it is always with tenderness that I speak with you as you give rise to the mission to which you have been assigned. My advocacy is situated deeply at the center of your works because I am aware of the agonies you undergo for the sake of the Cross. As difficult as it may seem, you must understand that the Will of God is urgent in your everyday lives, and you are defending the prevalence of His Word, speaking the Good News of Salvation that millions have declined to believe. Some ask whether there are consolation prizes for the misery that accompanies the lives of Christians. Is it not enough to know that you are blazing the trails that are reaching the hearts of wayward sinners who would otherwise be damned? Surely you realize that God is pleased by your faith, even in the darkness that buffets your consciousness during the day. Consider the metaphoric parables that Jesus addressed when He walked the Earth. They were not polemics about secular odds; He told humanity the Truth about the goodness of the human spirit, the opportunities for growth that would change the world for the better, and the reconciliation between Heaven and Earth. Where in all of this could there be room for alternative opinions from the sinners whose fate rests in the Mercy of the Creator who gives them life? Humanity needs to look back to the beginning of time and reconsider the journey of the soul, recalling the reason Adam and Eve were exiled from the Garden of Eden. Then, one must remember that God wishes humanity to be repatriated to that Glory as the sequel of celestial joy. Jesus set the example for the way you should live. He was displeased by the world He saw 2,000 years ago, and is not impressed by it now. However, He sees your desire for hope and potential for holiness. He believes in the preservation of the human heart, even while He knows whom is in His flock, and who will follow Judas Iscariot. Feel gratified that you are His disciples; you are His sheep. This should give you peace beyond any form of imprisonment, rejection, humiliation, or ridicule you might face in a thousand lifetimes on Earth. I wish you could send your spirits across the cosmos and see the world the way God sees it. You can if you pray. I wish you could know in what good stead you stand under His Throne. I wish you could see the gathering of Saints who are peering upon your lives with the giddiness of children because you are holy, you are serving, you are suffering, and you are trusting Jesus. What good fortune it foretells when someone inquires whether you are Christians! What tidings it would bring for the Lord to hear those sacred words from the people He has converted and nourished with faith! Indeed, how joyous are the Saints who proclaimed their allegiance to Christ as their final act. Some were even martyred because they knew their homeland of freedom lay on the other side of time. My little ones, there is a high degree of possibility that you will never be asked to be martyred, at least not in the physical sense. Yours is a life-long spiritual martyrdom enduring the longevity of years in a world that despises the Church, the Blessed Trinity, and your witness to the Gospel. Yours are days of servitude and humiliation in a whirlpool of secular repugnance where your bidding for the Son of Man is unwelcome. Do you remember that Jesus told you that you should be happy when men utter slanderous remarks against you as you magnify His Word? These come in ways that are unhearable as well, through body motions, facial expressions, and the conspicuous absence of popular people in places you attend. Deep inside your hearts, My dear children, you know this. At the core of the Christianity that you came to serve as tyros was planted the seed of righteousness that is blooming in you now. The years have been your friends, not your enemies. Your maturity in holiness is a fruit of your long-suffering love; and I beg you, do not forsake this shining future now.

My Special son, I hope you do not allow your brother's negativity to cause you any pain. He harbors great defiance against the media and how smug people treat those who are loving in Jesus' image. He has been rejected by your city for employment, by public schools and social agencies, and many other places because he comes into these fora with a vision that cannot be explained in worldly terms. This is his primordial essence; it is his constitution. He refuses to conceal his spiritual identity just to procure gainful employment in the secular realm. I wish you could know how seamless it would be for him to matriculate into the labor force due to his poise. He prays to be here with you until the conclusion of his years. You have ratified his life in more ways than I can explain; and most important, you have legitimized his acclamation of February 22, 1991 that I came speaking to him in the middle of the night. For this, you shall be profoundly rewarded. You will garner the merits of Heaven that have been allotted to Saints like Joan of Arc, Pope John Paul the Great, and many more. You will be situated at the right hand of the Father, and I ask you to move forward in the knowledge that each day is new, that every moment is more important than the previous as you march to your union with God. As the innate portion of your lives, keep the hope about which you speak, knowing that it shall be fulfilled in Heaven and on Earth. You suggest that you will have to wait for the end of time before your dreams will come as though there are centuries left of the existence of the world. You give My Immaculate Heart greater gladness by accident than most people do intentionally. I urge you to exalt man's anticipation of the sacred promises of My Son. Never forget that humanity is being pardoned every hour you live. Everyone who offends you, all those you see violating someone else, all the people in every corner of the globe are being absolved as time ticks by because of the way you pray. You are the precious emulation of Jesus, the Son of Man, the Son of God, the King who is your Savior. The aging of Creation, the befalling of inequity, the expiration of injustice, all of these things are happening while you endure your mortal days. The elevation of piousness, the feeding of the poor, the purification of the wicked, the finding of the lost, the birthing of the unborn, each and every one of these manifestations is occurring now. You must remember that what you see with your eyes and sense with your consciousness is only a fragment of multiple planes of human transformation that are happening simultaneously about the world. You are privy to them when you aspire to the greatness of simple men, of anonymous servants of the Cross who have gone to their graves with no one to mourn them or notice their absence. Your passage into history will be of notable record to humanity. You will be honored as an orator, a charismatic child, a pious Christian whose Marian works, teachings, preaching, and admonishments led countless sinners to the Sacraments of the Church. There will be flags waving and trumpets reporting when you die. Weeping clergy will repeat the same words to the clamoring bells that tolled for the eternal emergence of Pope John Paul the Great—*kings and paupers bowed before him as he bade his final farewell to the humanity he loved.* This is your championship; this is your reward. You will not be interred by a fence in a country cemetery with only a wooden marker to keep the world abreast of the death of someone they did not know. You will be lauded. And, this makes your responsibility great to be the master of your emotions, the controller of your sentiments, and the stronghold of your sights. I commend you to the Holy Spirit for guidance, and I pray that you live as I ask. My son, if only you could know that you are your best self with the Spirit of Jesus in your heart, you would see the Earth in a brighter light. Never mind the wars and contusions that dampen the egos of lesser men. Focus on the change you sense at the center of your being, of a world that has been conquered, of the conquest of the remaining ages that has yet to be protracted, and the endless victories you have already won for the sake of the Kingdom of God. Therein rests your consolation, and in this resides your awareness that the universe is unfolding as it should. My Special and Chosen ones, you are both so beautiful, but you fight the identities that have come to you by reason of your being reared in America. You have been taught sports competition to exclude others from the celebration of your joys; you have been given an education in the workings of capitalism; you have been forced to bow to a three-colored flag; you have been taught to believe that fighting is better than compromise; you live in a society where buying and selling are the gist of personal exchange, and you have been given the impression that Christianity is a subset of secularism rather than its demise. Therefore, when you look at yourselves with impatience, remember that you are products of your environment, and I am trying to open your hearts to the Glory of God. You have been living around relativism that is diametrically opposed to everything for which Christianity stands. Be kind to yourselves, be more attentive with your thoughts, be gentle in dissecting your lives, and you will arrive in Heaven with a smile across your face. I tell you these things because they are true. Thank you for your prayers! I am elated that you seek My intercession because you know that I will respond. We shall celebrate a prayer of thanksgiving on the anniversary of My Medjugorje messages during the ensuing week. While I wish for you to live the future, I will say that 2006 will be the beginning of the revelation of a miraculous sign..." *(25th anniversary of Medjugorje Apparitions.)*

Sunday, June 26, 2005
St. Juliette Marquis Barcroft [AD 1454-1522]*
1:27 p.m.

"While you are often disconcerted by the poignancy of life and events that bring you to reflect on the past and shape the future, please remember to uphold those whose spirits have passed through the veil of exile, the poor suffering souls in Purgatory who hunger for your remedial prayers on their behalf. I recommend them to the Divine Mercy of Jesus as you pray. My little children, today is joyful because I extend My intercessory graces across the Earth so you will accept God's Kingdom more intimately. We pray because the Lord is stirred by your petitions for the world's lacking. Jesus' Sacred Heart is consoled by the conversion of lost sinners, and He wishes that you proceed through Him on behalf of the tormented and afraid. I lift them up as they enlist My intercession. It seems as though the days are passing swiftly. The years are depleting, and all who accept the Cross are marching toward the foyer of Heaven. The Angels are your chaperones who lead you beyond the temptations that may cause you to falter. You have broached the midpoint of MMV, but you know that your mission is incomplete. I beseech you to remember My intentions in communion with yours; and if you do, the Lord will hear and respond with the same precedent that raised Jesus from the Tomb. He will dispatch the Holy Spirit to reign in you, and He will make you appointing to His Kingship in ways you never knew were possible. He will rescind the burdens of mortality and grant you the buoyancy that you sought to lift the Earth. Thank you for yearning for the completion of these things. My Special and Chosen ones, I speak to you because you wish to receive Me, though I have no specific message for the world today. I am honored because your devotion keeps you close to Me, and you look forward to the coming of the promises that Jesus made to arrive in your day. These are revelatory times during your lives of Christian virtue. Good things have occurred, many more graces to take your hearts to ecstatic joy. I pray that you do not become the reason for your own sorrow. Do not allow the world's complexities to bring you down. Please remember that the message of Christ is of success and not defeat. His Crucifixion has removed the sins of humanity, and His Resurrection proves that you will reap these blessings in your time. *(I spoke to Our Lady about a personal concern.)* My little child, you have made a statement that Jesus said 1,972 years ago. You speak about humanity who is not heeding the call of their Mother. Most are unwilling to accentuate the miracles that God gives the world to enhance their vision. This is why they are rigid and stoic. The point is that the more supernaturally they live, the more accepting they are of the Holy Gospel. Hence, they are forced to relinquish their material possessions and offer sacrifices they would not ordinarily make. Others essentially believe that the less they know about Christianity, the better. For them, the Holy Gospel is an archaic superstition that only pilgrims of ancient days followed. This is why I have come. It is justification for My messages. When God said that He will make all things new, He was also speaking of nonbelievers' dead faith. I have come to restore the vibrancy of American Roman Catholicism that is riddled by apathy. I will succeed through consecrated people such as you. I shall make the difference that cannot be manifested by anyone else. The important matter is not whether you are tired of the unappeasable greed plaguing the West, but that you do not permit its lack of charity to plunge you into spiritual darkness. If you allow this to happen, you will cripple your mission for the Kingdom of God. I need your trust that what I am saying is true, that everything you have learned from the Scriptures since you were a boy is near at hand. This is why I direct your focus upon the Church. I am making you aware of the ominous nature of things to come, and that you must participate in God's Plan to avert the catastrophes that will happen in the absence of the holiness of other men. Their intentions must be unified with the Will of the Father. Please remember that it is one thing to be physically or emotionally exhausted, but to be spiritually distraught must be immediately addressed. Turn to Jesus, and He will preserve your peace..."

Sunday, July 3, 2005
Saint Thomas the Apostle
3:12 p.m.

"With gratitude, your Holy Mother seeks your prayers for the conversion of humanity. I convey good wishes from Heaven and reassurance that your work is on course. Today, we pray with united hearts for the poor and lame, especially in foreign regions with orphaned children. When in meditation and contemplation, remember the victims of natural disasters, political oppression, and the sufferers of crippling and fatal diseases. You are My children whom I have nurtured since your conception, and I know that you care about the graveness of sin around the globe. If you pray with Me in union with the entire Church, erring conduct will cease. Employ the insightfulness of the Saints when you encounter the grueling aspects of life. You protect your faith by attending the Holy Sacrifice of the Mass and rededicating your lives to the Providence of God. You know the sacrifices you have made to prepare for the confluence of the ages, and you witness to humanity the perfection of the soul that is befitting of the sainthood you shall inherit. I offer your hearts the intrigue and palatable joy of Heaven, the uplifting peace that Jesus dispenses to those who exalt Him. My Special son, you have accomplished many good works through My intercession over fourteen years. Some messengers view their experience with disproportionate negativity because humanity appears not to be listening. In this land of personal freedom, you practice Christianity without obstruction. You acknowledge God's desire to transform His people through the Truth that He asks you to uphold. When counting your advantages in the United States, include your ability to force change for the better without being throttled for your beliefs. There are malevolent forces that defy your works and attempt to sever your connection with God. This is why I urge you to be careful but unfazed when relaying My intentions. You are faced with scant persecution compared to seers elsewhere, and this is why I have given you and your brother broad latitude to express your faith. You are beneath the protection of My Holy Mantle, and you must evangelize the Gospel in ways that promote the liberty that your forefathers preserved. Father Jozo could only pray while he was imprisoned; and in America, denunciation is not beyond possibility for My Marian seers. When I warn you to choose wisely, I ask you to follow the guidance of the Holy Spirit by judging the harshness of the world. You must never stop pleasing God and responding to His call. You have never violated His trust, and this shall not change. God is grateful for your holiness. This is why He cares, and it is why I come in thanksgiving to visit you. The Love of Jesus is inside you, and you know what you must do before time is gone. Consider the blindness in which others live. Most go to their death unaware of the avenues to bring change for righteousness' sake. However, a great many do know, and their lives are fair compared to the anguish that you and your brother have known. The Earth groans beneath the burden of human corruption, but you are decreasing its effects by telling lost sinners about Jesus' Blood on the Cross. Especially in this country, those who are guilty of blasphemy will be felled by the Justice of God. You set this in motion where Jesus commands. You may not read about it in the newspaper or hear it on the street or inside the foyers and vestibules of homes and churches, but the cultivation about which I speak will come. God makes it clear that He does not send Me to supplant the judgement of My children, but to complement your lives with His vision of Grace. After watching you through the years, I realize that you deem it irrelevant to see your name displayed in marquee lights. You do not require a calculation of how many sinners you converted yesterday. There is nothing absurd about your desire to end every kind of injustice, but the free will of man disallows this to occur. I have asked you to pray and serve as My messenger for the masses, and you have agreed without condition. However, other Americans are unwittingly entangled in materiality because they do not have the conscience you possess. Their parents taught them to be claimers; their young children are indoctrinated in systems that promote polytheism and pragmatism as the basis for social understanding, and the culture of America offers little hope for enhancing their relationship with God. Again, you and your brother are rectifying these issues in a provocative way. You are never disconcerted by the fads of your time; you maintain your devotion to Jesus without being distracted by your peers, and you hold true to the Catechism of the Church because your faith is refined by the Holy Spirit. You spoke about a group of priests who abandoned their vocations. Even in cases where they brought matters on themselves, they are victims of the wreck of this world. They were attacked by evil in ways that caused them to sin because they could not fight the temptation. They sullied their names because they could not see clearly to avoid the enticements of the flesh. Through My intercession, I am restoring their lost dignity. The mark on their souls is still there, and they will return to fight for lost sinners. They may be afflicted by the wounds they have suffered, but the Father will heal them, and Jesus will place them before the faithful in full clerical regalia to testify how difficult it is to follow the narrow path. They understand more than most what it means to be debased by the ravages of sin. Please join Me in praying for them, and know that I am not issuing a hollow promise when I say that they will don their priestly vestments like gold-crest robins being freed from a cage..."

Sunday, July 10, 2005
St. Stanislaus Bavaria [AD 1126-1155]*
3:03 p.m.

"How awesome is the moment when I appear before My children with holy hearts to pray in the name of the Lord! My wishes for the conversion of humanity will come to pass because of the petitions of the faithful. My little ones, we know that the consequences of human strife move people closer to God, but you must realize that God does not induce strife, but takes it away. Sinful humanity is the origin of suffering, and Heaven abates the pain. If My children do the bidding of Christ, agony around the world will disappear. Jesus is your shield and strength; and the Holy Spirit longs to give you Wisdom, but you must open to receive these gifts from the Almighty Father. He requests your intercession with Heaven over the years. We speak of benevolence and the Christian conscience in the context of the heart because it is through these manifestations that you pray. All moral teachings are gifts from My Son through your acceptance of His requisite decrees. If you do not believe that Heaven exists, your soul will likely not go there. I pray that My children hope in the fact that the Earth is not your final resting place. Be eager and anticipate your passing through the veil to the presence of the Heavenly Hosts. You are closer than you have ever been, but are you prepared? Does each of you know the meaning of contrition and wilful obedience? Do you understand that sacrifice is your testament to Truth? My purpose is to call upon My children to make you aware of the transformation every soul must make to attain the great holiness which informs you about the ways that are crucial to God. Never mind the trappings of the Earth or how you feel, what your temperatures are, how many possessions you own in your homes, or where the next secular field day might be. Turn your thoughts to the critical issues for the fate of humanity, the integrity of Wisdom that inspires the heart, and how you will give yourselves to Jesus so He can utilize your existence to advance His Kingdom. My dear children, I remind you about the prophylaxis of Divine Love because it preserves your life; it is the protection of your faith through the mediation of the Lord. You are cleansed and befitting to be Saints when you strive to do good. It is not something you inherit by your station on Earth or the imminence of death. Becoming Saints is not an inevitability unless you know that you can procure the blessing of Heaven. And, in this, you are perfected by the Holy Spirit. You must answer the call by setting-out to be the holiest you can be during your exile on Earth. I will help you live as Jesus teaches. I will satisfy your faith and nurture your strength for the journey. Can you see that I love you to the Infinity you will someday live? This is why I am happy. I realize that My children are aware of their power to welcome Jesus at the door, to reprimand sinners in His name, and discover together what the Glory of Heaven is about. The best largesse you can leave your heirs is your humbleness, your comprehension of the majesties of Grace, and the hope you have espoused. You exude the image of Jesus when you teach them to forgive, when you ask them to extend a helping hand, and when you foster their courage to never be afraid to accept the signs from God that He is dispensing in your age with unprecedented regularity. My Special and Chosen ones, when the Earth is done and the numbers told, you will see your Apostolate as a motivator for change. It is more than your reflections about My messages and intercession, it is a reminder to the world that civility and transformation are true and tangible facts. It hails the prerogative of God to sanctify any creature He chooses and make Saints of the most grotesque sinners to draw the breath of life. It evangelizes the Scriptures with preeminent Light to the unsuspecting world. My Special son, I have wept happily about your new book because you prepared it exactly the way I asked. You have spent hours formulating your thoughts and penning them with care, and you must surely be contented by its outcome. I wish for you to listen closely. I will elevate your book for the Kingdom of God. Jesus will raise it before humanity as being conceived through the power of the Cross, but if He does so sooner rather than later, you will lack anonymity to finish your work. You must be patient for the creativity of your mission to run its course. This is why you become despaired when you see people behaving impiously. I will tender your book to Jesus, and He will hand it to the Father in gratitude for you and your brother, with confidence that this book will join your other manuscripts as having magnanimous influence on the conversion of the world. May I urge you to consider what it means to be patient while Jesus prepares His flock? Thank you for understanding what My messengers have endured and for sharing your trust with your brother. The Holy Rosary helps you remain close, and it touches Creation in dimensions you have yet to see..."

Sunday, July 17, 2005
Saint Christine Whitehurst [AD 1738-1803]*
3:14 p.m.

"Your perfect submission has brought you Absolution, My little ones, and the faith you profess with your tongues is persuading lost sinners to reach for the Cross. The Spirit of God can permeate the darkest crevices and heal the deepest wounds. He wills that you partake of the Crucifixion of His Son, that you witness the price of your Redemption and comply with the mystical laws and charismatic mandates of the City of Light. My children, I wish you well because I understand your struggles. I am aware of the fight to uphold your dignity in the secular void. I am also aware of the enemies of your faith, and that you value the inner-strength that guides you during the perils of life. I come in hopefulness with the desire for you to remember that the Lord calls you to worship Him through the miracles by which you are blessed. His is a summons to prayer with the urgency of the Holy Spirit, for you to persevere in the oppression that you encounter on the heathenish Earth. The holiest things you do go unnoticed by most men, and this reflects the Will of the Father. Where is it written in the Scriptures that you stand before the world as flamboyant as peacocks for your devotion to Christ? Since it is not, you are touching Creation in the ways Jesus would have it. I assure you that no pious gift remains unrewarded. God is repaying you now; what appears to be arbitrary advantage is often His prefigured Grace. In the coliseum of human events, you are asked to trust everything Jesus teaches, while not always knowing why things happen in certain sequence. I remind you to walk by faith as you prevail in your Christian lives. With this faith and your good offices, the holiness of the ages will come. May no creature either living or dead cause you an ounce of exasperation or moment of dying hope. Let the curricula of the centuries be eclipsed by your goodness so beautiful that your enemies will see your love as heavenly as the stars. Aspire to become enlistees under the command of the Risen Christ. There are no surplus answers to the problems of the world, so obey His commands the way He hands them down; then you will understand the omnipotence of Truth. Then you will hold a grasp on the last bastion of beatific brilliance, the Wisdom that is of old, the God of Abraham and Isaac, the God of your fathers, the Kingdom that has sustained humanity through disasters, droughts, and monsoons for thousands of years. It is not a sign of weakness to confess your mistakes; and somehow, saying 'oops' is not enough when a heartfelt apology is due. My children, the honesty of humanity is formed with the heart where your courage is nurtured from when you are babes. It is said that most heroes are born, which may be true to a degree, but giants of Christianity are created in the heart. By the sin of Adam, you were thrust into exile, but by the power of Jesus' Passion, Crucifixion and

Resurrection, you are inspired to act in alignment with Prudence. The brothers and sisters of Jesus know that their time has come. The elect of the New Jerusalem realize that these are the concluding ages of men. I recommend you to the surety that I speak, and seek your commitment to the Sacrifice by which your Salvation arose. Christians who are devoted to the Mother of Jesus are so engulfed by the Holy Spirit that the Saints of old hail you from the mansions of Paradise. *'What we would have given to know the urgency of the hours,'* they are prone to say as they entreat the Father in your regard. These are not only cataclysmic times, they are culminating times when the Son of Man is poised to arouse His flock in such jubilance that you will wonder how it could be real. He knows your strife and ratifies your actions. Jesus praises you by the indulgences you receive. He is your prescience, strength, and resilience when you are tempted to defect. My children, it is not that your eyes cannot behold this, but that you may not believe it to be true!

Today, we pray for a globe that has been broken for longer than you know, a world that is splintering into pieces. You serve the sacrifices that your Christian predecessors have made to canonize their beliefs. Catholics have been handed a torch that was ignited on Easter Morning, the Paschal Resurrection when Jesus was raised from the Tomb. You carry the fire of faith, goodness, and trust with veritable invincibility for a Church that has suffered many pains. Like Jesus, the Church is being crucified by its adversaries, by the relativism about which I have spoken, by cruel legions claiming an oath to Satan, and by the indifference of the secular crowd. I say, let those naysayers come! The Church is under siege by the enemies of the Salvation of humanity, but such will not prevail over the power of the Cross! No opponent of the Will of God to repatriate His people into the Land of Promise shall live to tell it beyond the parameters of time. Given anything that shall come, God has already succeeded in bringing Creation to perfection. Time will bear this out. I promise you that history is on the side of the Catholic family. See that your sustenance is your belief in the Supernal Truth! Know with relief that Jesus is alive and dwelling in your midst. Build-up His Mystical Body as you grow your faith. Never mind the enemies, ignore the buffets, and stand tall in the face of your detractors. No tempest can flush you into the pit as long as your faith remains strong. Let plight and plunder do their worst against the children of God, and you shall rise against them! Let the enemies of Messianic Truth clamor with impudence against the Roman Catholic Church, and My people will slay them all. You have been given an example of the prowess of My Motherhood in Saint Joan of Arc. I come as the New Gabriel to announce that your battles for Truth and the clairvoyance of your spirits have been commissioned by God. You must be aware that the night is almost spent, that your station in the brilliance of Heaven is only moonbeams away. Live with trust that these are ominous days for your enemies, and auspicious ones for you.

My Special son, I wish you high hope for the accomplishment of your work. This is a good time because you have not surrendered to the world. You and your brother are guarding your friends by pursuing the goals we have laid out, the ones we spoke about years ago. Your hearts are sturdy for Justice and tendered to the poor. Your courage is of the Ancients, from the Throne of the Father whom your forbears revered. I often weep; most times with thanksgiving. The latter is My sentiment today. It matters not what the savvy think about you. What matters is that you have written your testimonies across the ages, that you created them of permanent record in the annals of men, that you catalyzed the sanctification of the wretched by maintaining your own purity. Believe that your part in the Father's Kingdom has succeeded not just because I am telling you, but because your heart knows that such magnanimous miracles from the Mother of God could never be in vain. Even in the case that you pursued another life, your contributions to the Church will live on. If you were to recant every word I have said, if you conceded under threat of martyrdom, there is no way that My messages could be destroyed. I assure you that your mission for the Redemption of humanity has placed a mark beyond the sanctioning of time. The Morning Star is irreversible, irrevocable, and permanently here. Thank you for your faith, for your beauty and charity, for your trust in the Incarnate Word, and for living-out your years in the Wisdom that flows from the Sacred Heart of Jesus. I know that you love Me, and I have always realized that you are My child. Be not dismayed if the dailiness of life seems difficult, for it shall pass swiftly, and the New Springtime of Love about which I speak will come to you at last..."

Sunday, July 24, 2005
St. Bristol de Royale, Martyr [AD 1081-1122]*
3:06 p.m.

"Let there be no mistake, the battle between good and evil rages on in this world, but you are shielded beneath My Mantle where Jesus hears your ecclesial prayers. We seek God's blessings on the victims of the struggle for righteousness, and conversion for the adversaries of Redemption and the perpetrators of ill will. My children, it is imperative for you to remember that the poorly conceived works of lost sinners are rarely their own making, but their inability to be spared from the stratagems of unchecked evil. If the Earth were in unanimity for Christianity, there would still be differences about how to practice it. Even so, there are other societies that are still opposed to the Cross who do not comprehend the mystical union of Love and Sacrifice, and who are unwilling to accede to the power of God to transform Creation. We join Saint De Royale in approaching Jesus to provoke purification and cultivation where there is no peace, where good men and women turn their backs on their brothers and sisters, and where the dying consciences of their peers are causing spiritual blight and blindness around the globe. The true conversion of the heart is more than a placement of focus, it is the protraction of benevolence in the face of hatred against the reign of God. Look around you, and you will see countless examples of piety and good works, but these are not lauded before the nations. Jesus asks you to discount the public accolades that prouder men require for their acts of righteousness. You are asked to be kind, anonymous servants in the vineyard of the Lord. Thereafter, your names shall be inscribed in the Book of the Living. As I speak, I call for your cheerful acceptance of your role in human conversion. I ask you to bear the burdens of mortality with poise and conscience, to see in yourselves and others the virtuous attributes that make you reflections of the life of My Son. Wear the yoke of mortification with humility and grace, for it is barely heavy. Give yourselves to the best of all things unique in the reorientation of man to the Resurrection that Jesus has so profoundly secured. If you declare yourselves defenders of Virtue, you must not become deeply involved in debates and issues that stir the passions of secular throngs. Trust in the Will of the Father, and you shall be given the peace of the Holy Spirit. Today, it is also important that we pray for the refugees of wars and oppression. Let us remember the starving and those suffering from crippling and fatal diseases. Pray with Me that God will heal them, that He will release them from the burdens of infirmity that bind them to their pain. We wish to include the victims in your nation and around the world who are battered by hatred and violence. And, most of all, we pray for the priceless unborn children who are growing in their mothers' wombs. Even as the debate continues about the American scourge of infanticide and the Supreme Court appointees, we must pray that every expectant mother values the precious life that is blooming inside her body. I call upon you to recite the Holy Rosary to stop the mortal sin of abortion, and I know you join Me in asking God to eradicate it from the Earth. I also recall the random bloodshed of adolescents at the hands of street gangs and other criminals. The selfishness that breeds these acts is too gruesome to describe. Chemical dependency is one of Satan's ways of luring good people from the path of righteousness, and this is most observable in America. Yes, we have much praying to do, My children. In the future, when you see that your petitions are making a difference, you will be convinced that your participation has been worthwhile. Thank you for responding to My call.

    My Special son, it gives Me elation to know that even in your fragile nature, your resolve to complete your work for Jesus remains strong. You have the heart of a lion and the steadfastness to see the journey through. Do you not know that all this will have a suitable end, that it is the heightening of My intent to prove to the skeptics that My children are conquerors for Christ? It lends Me great joy that you accommodate the power of hope, that it is your acknowledgment to God that you know the reason for the sanctification of man. It is your union with the purity of hope in Jesus through His teachings, Passion, Crucifixion, and Resurrection. You are heralding the means to the Salvation of humanity by your existence in the world, by your deference to the Gospel, and your obedience to the Holy Spirit in everything you do. This makes you a proprietor of the Earth in your day, one in whose grasp the keys to Paradise are availed by your allegiance to Pope Benedict XVI. As you live the year of his reign, know that countless Saints before you share your goals for the refashioning of Creation into the holiness of Heaven. You walk in the shadow of extreme numbers of legends among men who were unknown to the peoples of the nations for anything other than being ordinary. Let God be the judge of whom among them is most worthy! This decision does not belong to the secular elite or those whose wits are engrossed by the repartee on the stage. I give you My solemn promise that if you and your brother continue to persevere in your work, you will prevail over any enemy who dares to raise his ugly head against the Providence of God. The weeks and months will expire, and you might search for evidence of this, but I assure you that a timely victory has been deposited in your future. You will chasten your detractors with the substance of your prayers. You will annihilate your adversaries with mere thoughts of justice. And, the Glory of the Father you wish to see will unfurl before you, showering upon you and like-minded Christians the knowledge that the battle about which I spoke moments ago has already been won. If you think about this in the context of the Cross, you will understand. If you place your perspective in the purview of the infinite ages that will eventually assimilate your spirit, you will realize that your enemies have already been vanquished by the exhaustion of time. No matter what befalls you, regardless of what may be revealed by the garishness of day, never minding the despicable cruelties that crawl from the repugnance of night, you should always be inspired by the Triumph of My Immaculate Heart. You are a participant in the process. With your brother and all My seers and visionaries, you have been given a reparative warranty for which you should be grateful. You have never failed to discharge your duties with idealness and care..."

Sunday, July 31, 2005
Saint Ignatius of Loyola [AD 1491-1556]
3:12 p.m.

"It is your faith, My children, that inspires Me to come to this holy place to speak of the awesome wonders of Pristine Love, to implore you to move forward in the veins of hallowed Salvation, to unify you in the Sacred Heart of Jesus, and to remind you that the world is at the conclusion of its long journey home. I ask you to bring everything virtuous when you come to Heaven, all that makes you Saints and the intentions in your hearts that are in compliance with the Will of God. You are separated from everything corrupt by His Divine Revelation, and your spirits must be prepared to enter Eternity that is not of this Earth. For all the hoping you do through the years, none is more important than your desire to see God's Face and touch the archways of Sacred Truth in whose presence you shall never be afraid. For all the years that are fleeting and conditions that change, the Providence of God is perpetual. I commission you to go onward as absolvers of your brothers' faults while Jesus redeems their souls. I call you to reflect Heaven in your lives and accept the pardon dispensed from the Glory of the Cross. You can do this, My children, because you are not impotent. Anyone whose thoughts can stretch from the atom to the solar system is capable of knowing human love as the most indomitable force in the universe. This is your endowment from the Father. In Him, you are subscribers and developers of hearts filled with goodness to convert sinners of all sorts, from lettered doctrinaires to whiney simpletons. You are beset by inhibition at times, but you are invincible in the Christ who has loved you to the summit of the Cross. When you see His beauty in the architectures of your designs, you are near the threshold of Redemption. When you have a knack for excavating the root of all moral wrongs, you have tapped the origin of perfection. Love, selflessness, prayer, piety and servitude will take you there, as does generosity. It is from these gifts, these intentions, that you grow to be servants of the Christianity born of My Womb. We have spoken about exacting details and permeating vision. We have prayed that all men will see. And in this, My children, we must ensure that every ear is lent to the pathway of salvific peace. It is not fashioned by politics or greed; it cannot be fostered by the settlement of public affairs, and it is never wrought in appeals of the flesh. The Wisdom and Prudence about which I speak are fruits of Eternal Love that only God can give, and you must be openhearted to receive them. My dear ones, you are the darling echoes of the Earth in whose hands have been laid the most imperative aspects of genuine faith. You have been passed the baton of holiness that prevails in the Faith-Church to transform your brothers and sisters into the most extroverted disciples they can be. You should not only be examples of Jesus' life, but students of His Gospel. You must chip the barnacles from the spirits of forlorn sinners who lay in the depths of their own despair. You must break the indifference that is strangling ordinary people, that they will grow to extraordinary heights in devotion to God. I implore you to fight the good fight that makes these changes, even from the corners of your rooms. It is certain that not everyone has access to global exposure. Your names will likely never appear on city keys or your images seen on billboards along boulevards, but the silent warriors for Christianity are experts in the motives of human conversion. You are seeds growing like thunder to strike the gardens that your friends will consume in their final agony. I wish you could gain a sense for this in your life. I speak to humanity in ways that elevate your hopes about things to come. I hear debaters in institutional halls, speaking of promises they cannot keep. I see their actions that betray the pledges they have made. And, I wonder why they do not call for the reconciliation of their conscience with the Truth of Almighty God. I look with pity upon the victims of ill fortune, and I pray for the changes that must be made. Calling on wayward sinners to be freed from such devices as dependency, lust, and perversion implies that it is you who must rise to assist them. I implore My children to decide for God and choose the righteous path where your destinies are blessed for the goodness you perform and the piety you extol. I ask you to reach deep into the catacombs of your holiness, and the world will be a better place. My Special one, you are providing a vast opportunity to reach others because you pray with Me every day. It is obvious that your desire is that the Will of God be done, not to allow adversity to command the moment, and that conversion will come to Creation in a wholly reparative way. Heaven is served by My children who aspire to the holiness of you and your brother, who hold to the tenets of faith, and who pray for all good things to come. As I have said, you are to look for your spiritual elevation beyond the Earth, but you are not yet called to depart it. If this seems a contradiction, consider that Jesus reminded those in His midst that by seeing Him, they had likewise seen the Father. What wealth was possessed by those who believed! What distinction of life came to the men and women who accepted His counsel! Anything worthy that can be said of the benevolence of humankind is attributed to the Sacred Heart of Christ. You live in a nation where decisions are rendered about war and peace, life and death, riches and poverty, cleanliness and filth, and the future versus the past. Please rise above the fray and recognize that some arguments exist only to divide people one from another for financial gain and for the distractions that lure innocent people away from God. The Christian conscience that prevails over your decisions separates you from the rest. If you were to see the expanse of time from its end, you would know that many issues about which publicans are arguing are irrelevant... Please pray for everyone who does not speak of forgiveness during their lives..."

Sunday, August 7, 2005
Saint Pope Sixtus II and Companions
2:58 p.m.

"Through the brilliant salutation of God, little children, I have come to pray with you for the coalescence of Americans. I enter your presence to bless you by the divinity of the Holy Spirit. Together, we know the Will of the Father, and we exalt the Truth that is overwhelming the consciousness of men. We ask Jesus to inundate the entire universe in His Passion and Grace, that no man is lost to the netherworld. Today, I request your prayers for the unborn, for the end of famine and pestilence, and the conversion of dark hearts to Divine Love. It is imperative that unknowing people from all walks understand the freedom in Christianity, the opportunity for their spirits to soar in the ecstasy of Eternal Light. Heaven is not far from you, My children, and the conversion of humanity can neither be long in coming. How do I know this? Because the moment is ripe for the Master of the house to return, for Jesus to rescue the destination of His disciples from the jaws of the predatory world. With Him, I call you to renew your profession of faith and baptismal vows. Think of the ways He would have you better serve the lonely and oppressed. Imagine the possibilities derived from your determination to set the world aright through your faith in the Cross, by your sacrifices and goodness, by your compassion for the poor, aging and suffering; and by your desire to live-out your brief years in prayerful anticipation of His arrival in Glory. I have spoken of Christian nobility and the revelations of the conscience, and I speak today about the courage and valor you must invoke to bring them to pass. It is appalling what secularists will do to take you from Me. Indifferent people attempt to deceive you into false temptations, and they deliberately time their acts to coincide with your duties for the Lord. Indeed, they reserve the best of the day for themselves and reach you only after they have satisfied their craving for the worldliness of life. We pray in unison that they will be repudiated, that they will come to you at the dawn of first light for encouragement to become more holy. I am the Lady of Wisdom who exhorts you to cultivate the furrows of sanctity and prayerfulness, to stay the course that you have honorably advanced. My Special son, I shall not speak at length because I realize that you require rest. Thank you for remaining with your brother and facing the monotony of the weeks. With the work you accomplished for Jesus, you have fulfilled your ecclesial requirements for this weekend. Can you sense the invincible power that is growing in your hearts? It takes trust for others to believe, but their faith becomes new knowledge and an unfailing reminder that nourishes their curiosity for Truth. You are succeeding in the timeless expanse of Creation. You are invoking the Eternal Wisdom about which I speak. Many are not doing so, but they are moving toward the vestibule of the reckoning of the ages with you as their friend. Their favor with the Lord is widening..."

Sunday, August 14, 2005
St. Maximilian Mary Kolbe, Martyr [AD 1894-1941]
1:54 p.m.

"My dear children, I must speak about the urgency of your prayers for the victims in war-torn nations around the globe. Pray for peace! It is important that you offer your petitions for innocent people who lose their lives and others whose villages are destroyed. Pray that food reaches the starving who are afflicted by the ravages of military conflict. Jesus watches men make war while it is the effect of their hatred, but He asks you to perpetuate peace instead. Please allow your faith in the Holy Spirit to discipline you! Ask the Lord to supplant the pendulous pacts of nations with lasting good will and fervent righteousness. My dear ones, you are the living, breathing tabernacles and monstrances of holiness. Present in you is the exquisiteness of the Most Blessed Trinity, the Father, Son and Holy Spirit, by virtue of your reaffirmation of Easter. This is a beatific mystery that you do not comprehend in your physical state because you lack posthumous eyesight. If you turn to God and seek His inviolate intervention, your holiness will lead you to His Kingdom of Truth. Therefore, I ask you to be consecrated to righteousness in an outward way so you will live for Jesus. Choose the scrupulousness that heals the brokenhearted and mends the divisions separating races and nations. When you pray for these things, God will know that you wish to be His. You will understand how He commands you to live, that His Will is the constituting and protraction of a culture of life around the globe. When you speak of Christian preferences for international unity, please remember that you are taken there by embracing the Cross and your sacrifices and charity for those in need. The autumn will soon be upon you, and wintertime will follow. Will there be world peace by then? The answer is no, but it need not be this way. You must traverse the chasm of the ages to enlist the Prince of Peace who was born in the Bethlehem manger, and reserve your place on the Mount of Olives. You must honor the Lord's call to be like the peacemakers of generations past. You must remain one in Him by embracing the Crucifixion of Mount Calvary in your hearts. Remember that Jesus asks you to be champions of unity and agents for the preservation of human rights. Included in this, My children, is the goal for people to live free from the oppressions of war. A Feast in the Roman Catholic Church will be observed tomorrow, and I offer My maternal blessing upon My children on the Feast of the Assumption even as much as Christmas. Jesus urges you to turn to His Mother for consolation and counsel during these years of fighting between factions. He seeks in you the humility to accede to the Will of the Father in ways that make you the apostles of these latter times. If you invoke the Holy Spirit, you will share Heaven's profits; you will be filled with Grace and Love, and you will realize the importance of the spiritual and social cohesion that Christianity requires. It is true that you do not know how to pray as you ought, but you must try. If you apply for Jesus' guidance, you will be inspirited with the knowledge of Justice. You shall be given the prescience about which the great orators have spoken. You will have eloquent hearts in the likeness of the Angels and Saints. Please dedicate yourselves to working closely with one another to achieve equality. If you do not understand the unity to which you are called, read the Sacred Scriptures about self-denial and servitude. Then, you will know that to deny the self is to elevate those around you, to tend to Jesus' sheep in the way He desires. I wish you could awaken tomorrow and find peace, but it takes time. Pray with Me, and you will be bold. Humble yourselves, and the Lord God will bless you. Deny yourselves, and the Son of Man will preserve you, each and everyone, for the sacredness of Paradise.

My Special son, I was reflecting moments prior to speaking to you today about your awesome experience on the mountain in Medjugorje 16 years ago this evening. You must realize that the touching of your soul changed your life. Many people fail to see signs from God because they decline to believe in Him. When He speaks to them, they harden their hearts. Do you know why? Because they are callous about the inequity of the temporal world, a deprecating existence that humanity has created on its own. I have told you that lost sinners are inclined to blame injustice and immorality on God because they have done little to eradicate it. They are cynical about Divine Truth because they refuse to understand what Redemption means. This has never happened to you. You have always believed from your childhood years that there exists the Divine Light of peace and justice that you cannot yet see. You have known since you became aware of your station in exile that your soul was not truly home. This has been a gift from the Grace of God, but it has also been your willingness to seek Him from an early age. Even in your pre-adolescence, you knew that poverty and war are wrong. You believed in your heart that there are greater heights to be pursued, and this is why you were awestricken by the space flights of your youth. You looked beyond the realms of man for the stars that brightly shined, ones that seemed to fashion themselves into discernable images as if to be connected like dots. You made yourself a glowing star, an inner-peace grown to magnanimous heights inside a civilization that only seemed to survive by preying on itself. The Glory in you has always been that of Jesus; it has always been to yearn for spires and pinnacles that were fashioned by the Providence of God. My gentle one, you and your brother are attaining these things. As painfully slow as it might seem, you are reaching those glittering stars, beyond the Moon, permeating and pervading the universes in one holy swoop, to bring to the nations the singular Truth of Jesus Christ. I am ecstatic to be with you during these years as your Mother and intercessor to help you understand that the human race cannot cease pining for everything that comes after life. My child, when I saw you on the side of the mountain 16 years ago, I found more than a soul who was hungry for Salvation. I recognized the incarnation of sublime potential just waiting to be unleashed. I spied thousands upon thousands of pilgrims who came curiously close to God, but few who were thirsty for His Wisdom. You are among the ones willing to savor more, and Jesus saw you there. The Angels and Saints saw you there. It was your own initiative that kept them with you because they had strangely seen one so much like them who still walked in human flesh. I wish you well on your sojourn through the remainder of your earthly life, and I pray that it will be an extended one of peaceful accord. I cannot tell you the hour when Jesus will return in Glory, but I can confirm that He has already laid claim to the bravery of your heart. Heaven lives in you, and humanity knows it. Divine Love prevails in you, and the Lord sees it. Truth, peace, and human dignity grow through you, and the Angels celebrate it. Someday soon, your work will be lifted before every nation and government that ever existed in the history of the world; and the entire collection of continents will respond to it. Please know that you are loved, and you are attended by the endearing Wisdom of Jesus who waits in joyful anticipation for the command of God to Return in Glory. And, I would be remiss if I did not mention your brother. God declared that someplace in time He would create a soul who loves you as much as Jesus, and thus He gave you Timothy. He has accorded you your own reflection to share. Your mission is as inviting as the gates of Paradise. Be joyful in your life's vocation... Do you remember that miracles precede the Saints' canonizations? Your writing is as inspirational for the Mystical Body of Christ as the Grace that created the Martyrs. You are doing God's bidding. We love each other beyond time, and soon, Eternity will abound for all..."

Saturday, August 20, 2005
St. Bernard, Abbot and Doctor [AD 1090-1153]
2:16 p.m.

"My children, you exude a perplexing piety to those who do not know God. You are a mystery to worldly people and a source of curiosity for your peers who question your source of happiness. I come to resound the inherent Wisdom from which your goodness flows, the solace and fortitude you gain from the Holy Spirit. These are auspicious times because you have given Jesus the best of your lives. You decline to embark the tangent pathways that have led others from His Grace. Wisdom calls you to be placid during periods of duress, and you are asked by the Holy Spirit to remain calm at the onset of social tension. The love in your hearts teaches you to separate yourselves from the fray by knowing where Truth exists amid global and personal crises. It is this penchant for peace that I bring you, the maturity of faith I teach you. It is true that there is stress in the world caused by malfeasances of the mind, political corruption, selfish oppression, and spiritual blight. For countless years, I have asked you to disavow the hypocrisy that you see in the lives of others, to imagine the existence of humankind from the purview of God. You gain strength knowing that your struggles are few, in your awareness that everything shall pass in the exhaling of the ages. It is true that you mourn the inequities that have overcome humanity; this is a fruit of the compassion in your hearts. And, you yearn for the strength to usher the changes that the Church says must come. If you could force the instantaneous conversion of the world, would it account for the reorientation of man's collective will? It is imperative that the children of God come to the Cross on their own. They must approach the Son of Man wilfully, with predisposed repentance. This is the finishing of the universe, when sinners suddenly comprehend their need and desire to be holy. It would not be such a miracle if Jesus coerced the conversion of souls because it would be a disservice to the ability of people to change. Souls receive Salvation because they attest to His Love and Truth, not because they are constituents of a supernatural transformation in which they play no part. It is clear that time is of the essence, but it is more crucial that lost sinners pledge to the Cross of Christianity of their own accord. This is the Lord's desire for His flock because they are famished for righteousness. The Wisdom about which I speak has multiple facets, more than we have discussed in the messages you have received. However, the vital trait of Wisdom is that the Holy Spirit inside you opens your lives to sacred dimensions. My Special son, it was 21 years ago tomorrow when you said 'through this door walks the freedom of the soul' in speaking about the grave of Timothy's mother. Tomorrow will be the twenty-first Sunday of the year, the date of August 21, and twenty-one years since you issued those prophetic words. Since that moment, you have seen that the freedom of which you spoke can be garnered on Earth for those who believe in Jesus. The Holy Spirit enlightens you as much here as in the City of Truth. Humanity cannot yet see its golden streets, flaming mountaintops, or silver-running streams. Your eyes may not yet reflect the Scepter about which the Prophets spoke. However, you harbor the Love of Jesus in you now; you speak with the power of God across the meadows and valleys of the Earth, and you sense with the anticipation of ultimate victory that the Son of Man is incarnate in you. You have all the imaginings in the history of histories at your fingertips when you pray from the heart for Jesus' Resurrection to guide you through the plight of your years. This seems sparse consolation among the repetition of the days and the endless barrage of conflicts that pummel your peacefulness at times, but I call you to realize that such conditions are created by human anathemas who do not share your inspiration in the Wisdom of the Lord. Have pity on them! Do not harbor disdain! Realize that you know our God of peace in your heart, and refrain from allowing their conduct to pull your spirit into the darkness. You have the faculties to know that every error you see is passing, to be supplanted by perpetual gifts of Grace, Peace, and

Light that know no end. My children, you are envied by the ages who hoped to see God before their time expired. Saints and Doctors of the Church would have given limb and fortune for the modes of communication and transportation that you enjoy in this century. And, they are obliged that you are lauding the Divine Love that helped them live, that consoled them in their final hours, and that now and hereafter shall be your guide to blissfulness beyond your tombs. As innovative as the world is, you cannot rescind the Sacred Mysteries of human Salvation that remain unfazed by the bombardment of time. The Earth cannot produce the Grace that comes from Heaven to lift you to the gladness you seek. Only the Holy Spirit is this source of happiness. Only the Crucifixion of the resurrected Messiah is your means for the Redemption of the soul. I am aware of the difficulties you face. I recognize the indifference of your counterparts and the blasphemy of your enemies. If you take them seriously, you will be distressed into spiritual atrophy, and your faith will suffer. Pray from your hearts for peace. Know that the presence of God is the humility in you, the dignity that I have been asking you to accept for years. Can you see the progress we have made, or are you perceiving your lives with such blind introspection that you fail to acknowledge the triumphs you are winning in a divinely upward way? You know what I know to be true, that humanity is not long for this world. This is one of your assets in your struggle for holiness. It is your consolation when it seems that the enemies of Jesus are profiting; but they have lost, they have already been sentenced to the depths. My Special son, I am pleased that you kneel to pray, that we share the values of servitude that have been the principles of your life. I try to lift you up in the Truth about which I speak because I wish you to know that any criticism from others is unfounded. They do not understand the Way of Love with the obedience of your heart. You are a child of Mary, the Immaculate Mother of God! There is no better sanctuary available to men than to rest beneath My protective Mantle. Please do not fear the future. Let no one dampen your joy in the Triumph of My Immaculate Heart..."

Sunday, August 28, 2005
St. Augustine, Bishop and Doctor [AD 354-430]
1:59 p.m.

"I speak with assurance of sympathy, compassion, and encouragement. I am your Mother who understands your doubts and fears, and I sense the anxieties that bring hesitance into your hearts. I pray to the Most High Priest that you will receive an interior tranquility like you have never known. I planned this message for today to honor Saint Augustine because I knew that you would need comfort. Human history can repeat itself, and you have withstood the test of time through appalling parallel events. You have seen desperate acts by people who have leapt into the limelight because of their crimes and perversions. To whom do they turn when they lack trust in others? What can be said in a world of six-billion people about those who prefer the empty darkness or humanize creatures and objects for companionship? You must approach them for Jesus. Please respect your elders even as you admonish them when they are misguided. There is no substitute for experience. One can be born with intelligence, but knowledge is always learned. Christians must ensure the proper interexchange of information that prospers the Good News of Jesus on the Cross. I promise that My Immaculate Heart is filled with Divine Love, and My Mantle gives you protection. It is highly obvious that you understand God's Will, and you know what Jesus expects as you work in His vineyard. I beg the Church to maintain your composure. In your interaction with the secular world over the years, you have endured battles without end. You have fought hatred, heresy, desecration, and impiety. These engagements have left you scarred, but not alone. I call you to muster courage through your prayers and to forgive one another's faults. My little sons, God stationed you together to do My work, and you have consented valiantly. You should place your displeasure with secularism in perspective so your hearts will not be troubled. I hope your spirits are not tormented by your friends and neighbors' indiscretions. Remember that everything I have told you about Heaven and Earth will be revealed. Yes, realize with certainty that you have given yourselves in ways that were previously untold. I am grateful for your devotion to the Lord, and I am immensely thankful for your obedience, knowing that your response has taken you from life's amenities. To you, My Special one, goes the accolades for your faith and support of your brother. His has been the easy part. He told you what he has heard and seen, but it is you who trusted him. Your brother is often overcome with emotion because he does not want to lose you. He recalls that you brought him into the Church. You have been his friend for three decades. You took him to Medjugorje. Everything that constitutes his awareness of God and the righteousness of life is attributable to you because you are Jesus' example. You have supplanted his mother and father. You are the counselor of his soul. You are his kindred spirit, his brother in Christ, his compatriot, and everything you could imagine that would have come from his family. His gratitude is unsurpassed in the annals of the Earth. I say these things so you will know his heart. He admires your imitation of Jesus in the patience you extol, your gentleness, capacity for reason, civility, and kind mannerisms which prove that you are filled with the Holy Spirit. You are trustworthy, honest, faithful, charitable, self-sacrificial, and wise in Truth. For these attributes, you have won your brother's heart, respect, and loyalty. You shine before the Angels. Where else would Timothy have turned when he heard My voice calling in the night? You are the one who believed, and this makes you the conqueror of humanity's indifference. Yes, his has been the easy part. *(I asked Our Lady how to avoid being ensnared by*

American capitalism when disseminating our writings, and why it is so difficult to evangelize the Holy Gospel for someone without a religious vocation.) There is a temporality suggested by your question that speaks to marketing. If you have a commodity that people are knocking on your door to procure, it is not as pronounced. If you are overly aggressive in a secular way, it contrasts with your spirituality. Saint Paul saw this after his revelation on the road to Damascus and placed secularism in proper context. He made himself poor to remain a disciple the way he said, but these are different times. Your environment requires the interweaving of your work with your religious beliefs to induce others to convert. More simply stated, lay persons take part in the labor force to remain self-reliant while at the same time teaching others that miracles happen to private individuals as well as in the Church..."

Sunday, September 4, 2005
St. Winifred Voltaire, Hermit [AD 1236-1298]*
1:58 p.m.

"On this day, My little ones, I comfort you and offer the prompt succor that uplifts your hearts. Please remember to pray for the poor victims of the tropical cyclone that overwhelmed the southern gulf of the United States since My latest message. I have warned you that unexpected tragedies happen when people are unprepared and when they do not fend for the most vulnerable who often become caught in the throes of these events. God will bless those for whom you pray. He will deliver the displaced to safety and heal the sick and wounded. Will you join Me in asking the Lord to come to the rescue of the thousands of hurting people? Thank you for having responded to My call. Also today, I urge you to pray for the victims of international wars that are being prosecuted around the globe. Indeed, millions are adversely affected by global conflicts, suffering misery that is heaped upon them by circumstances beyond their control. We must be sure that they are provided for, that Jesus hears our pleas for their relief. When it seems as though the Earth is becoming more broken and divided, and when your lives appear to be tattered and upended, this is when you must appeal for the assistance of Jesus the most. Call on the power of the Divine, the indomitable Love that brings you all the help you require in this life. If it is protection you need, ask the Son of Man to shield you. Moreover, plead for Heaven's Wisdom and Truth, for guidance in discernment, and for the spiritual valor that allays your fears. Ask Jesus for vision and perseverance, for the ability to see beyond your sorrows and apprehensions, and for trust and unstoppable faith. My angelic ones, you know that your future depends on the intensity of your prayers. If you ask Jesus to help you, God will dispatch hope into your lives without delay. Whether you are in physical pain or mental agony, Jesus offers support for the journey. Lift your petitions for the sake of the thousands whose lives have been shattered by the hurricane in America. Extend My condolences and intentions for the victims whom no one would help. Through your prayers, their future will be bright, and they will be healed. To My Special and Chosen sons, I understand the difficulties you have faced during the years, especially the pains burdening you at present. God deigns that you cope with misfortune at times, and He knows your needs and desires. Please pray that Jesus gives you peace of heart and mind, good health, and everything that makes you happy as long as you live. We have been searching for the transformation of humanity for a long time, and I ask you to join Me in praying that the Father will allow us to continue into the future. Your written texts and spiritual masterpieces are blessings for the world, guiding beacons to humanity lost in its own darkness. Your counsel to the wicked is to become repentant. You speak for Heaven when the Holy Spirit inspires you with Wisdom. We shall pray during September for everyone who will enter winter without food, heat, and shelter. And, we pray for the hundreds-of-thousands who will have insufficient wraps. The indignity of the suffering poor is a pitiable sight. You must understand that people do not choose to be poor; they are thrust into poverty by economic systems that ignore those of little means. Jesus told you that the poor will remain with you, but He did not say they would be so numerous. If you pray that those in power will share their profits equitably, the scourge of poverty could be halved before the end of this decade. You should realize that there is great wealth concentrated in few hands. Pray that the Gospel is heralded on a massive scale so equality is manifested. These are the reasons you live. We wish to end poverty and disease by softening human hearts. My Special son, I am pleased that you are looking forward to additional projects to evangelize the Kingdom of God. If given the venue and sufficient time, what would you say to the citizens of America about the suffering that is being forced upon the victims of natural disasters and wars, something that would comfort the afflicted? Think about what context you would put floods, hurricanes, tornadoes, earthquakes and the like to help your brothers and sisters comprehend their place in the unfolding events of the modern world. And, when seeing nations with such victories, spoils and rampant poverty, there are sufficient citations in the Sacred Scriptures, in the Roman Catholic Catechism, the writings of the Saints, and other codices to prove that the former are taking part in degrading the human race. I would like for you to ponder these things in broad parameters so you might begin your next book in this vein. You may pursue personal goals that make your life meaningful. I do not want you to assume that our work is insignificant just because you are doing other things. I will always be with you, praying for you..."

Sunday, September 11, 2005
Commemoration of U.S. Terror Attack
2:31 p.m.

"With solemn meditation, you kneel in the presence of the Lord to pray with Me for the purification of humanity in the Cross of Christendom. I wish for you to believe that there is no higher purpose for your faith than to strive toward the Salvation of sinners. You must remember that your contemplative thoughts and intentions are the begetting of world peace, and your actions and good will bring about the charities that rescue tormented societies from the turmoil they endure. Today, we remember not only the victims of wars, but particularly the attack on the United States mainland four years ago. Americans must ask themselves the question whether they are a more peace-loving people than 48 months ago. Are you willing to build unity with the Middle East nations? Are you more tolerant and compassionate, or does your government seek vengeance and profit? I told you on September 16, 2001 that the most honorable way to remember your loved ones is to seek the unification of nations and to share your wealth. Imagine the Divine Light your loved ones see in the presence of God, and what they would say about the oneness of Heaven if they were allowed to return. Too many Americans are shifting blame instead of sharing blame. There is no one person or group who can be cited as the source of terror in your midst. It is caused by the corruption of humanity. Your Mother has called upon you to find reconciliation beneath the Cross upon which your Salvation was sealed by Jesus. There, you will understand mutual sacrifice and the dearness of Preeminent Love. Why do I ask My children to seek the Divine? Because anything not Divine is unworthy of pursuit. In the Divinity of God resides your foresight, healing, reconciliation, peaceful accord, mutual compassion, and zeal of heart. God does not want His flock to be divided. Instead, He urges you to be one mind and spirit in Christ. After all, it is dignity not unlike His that humankind seeks. If you love in the perfection of Jesus, if you challenge yourselves to become the reflection of the sacrificed Lamb of God, you will gain the vision you need, the ability to see past the pressing ages and into the Eternity that will absolve you. My children, America suffered a tremendous loss four years ago, but you must make the most of it for your children's future. There is no permanent goodness in the fight for temporal things. Buildings and skylines come and go like falling stars. I implore you to seek the unwavering power of the Spirit of God in you, the Justice that can never wane. If you wish to receive every semblance of potential that you assume human beings can become, see the gentle giantness of the Holy Trinity in you! Accept and believe that you are those heroic hearts that are spoken about in cordoned inaugurations and valedictory speeches. Know and understand that the trivialities of the day's politics are irrelevant in the grand perspectives of God. Cast off cravings that make you believe that you must be someone worshiped and feted before the masses. It is in this simplicity, My little ones, that you find the fairness that overcomes the inequities of the world. Creation is refined and remade through the robust nature of these simplicities, not by the random commotion you generate for the sake of history. Saints would not leap onto a public stage and proclaim who they are, they would linger humbly at its foot and recommend whom you should become. Giving and forgiving imply that the self is diminished in pride and enlarged in humility. If there is any other message you should take from today's Gospel, it is that others are elevated before God when you tell Jesus that they are worthy to be there. I call upon the hailed and justified, the pure and extravagant, the ignorant and the learned, the honored and shunned, and the known and anonymous to touch the hem of the garment of the Son of Man and become healed of everything that ails you, all that impairs you cognitively, spiritually, and physically. My Special son, it gives Me happiness to speak to you. Your prayers mean so much to Jesus; and your love is holy, just as Jesus is holy. We pray for you and your brother's longevity. Be suppliant for your country, especially the victims of disasters, for the unborn, the impoverished, and those afflicted by wars. I speak about Jesus because it is by His Light that you are led; it is His Light that you reflect. Your brother seems concerned about the prisoner being held in a concrete cage with no windows and only one hole in the door. Those who do this are of the same corruption that caused him to commit his crimes. He is kept there by vengeance, the same revenge that Jesus denounces in the Gospel today. Can you sense the seriousness not only of the way this convict is being treated, but that it is by those claiming to be Christians? The latter is the blasphemy that the Lord promises to punish. The prisoner can be absolved, and he will at the end of the ages. It is obvious that those who are holding him like an animal need to reconsider their approach to the teachings of God. They do not understand the Scriptures they claim to follow.

Let us consider the concept of perspective once again. What did you learn about Mother Angelica last evening? Church officials refused to acknowledge her work, and others declined to help, but she made an indispensable contribution to humanity anyway to magnify the Kingdom of God. And, what about the seers at Fatima, Lourdes, Medjugorje, and other shrines? What are their charitable gifts? What occurred during their lives? What is growing in the hearts of the Medjugorje visionaries? And, what of the Marian Movement of Priests? What conclusion can be drawn from these blessings? The secular void is your enemy; there is no doubt about that. Jesus discovered in His earthly years that miracles yield little results. Unimaginable tragedy and human suffering have converting power. My beloved son, there is no such thing as restive frustration to Christian mystics. You have the means and capacity to manifest the amendments you seek. As for the genius of God's timing, not even I foretell the essence of that. I am not frustrated, I will never surrender, and I will always believe that everything I have told you about the world can change. There is nothing wrong with maintaining your hope; it is a gift from the Holy Spirit to inform your heart every day about the premise that change comes from the inside of humanity. This is where you are working; it is the core of your vision; it is the reason millions of souls will be saved. If you are expecting the Earth to look tomorrow like a fifty-year-old automobile with a dazzling coat of paint, you should rethink your perception. The change you must seek has been growing from within the conscience of humanity since the lives of the first Saints. There is one thing you do not know, and that is how pleased you make Me when you consider these things. You decry the physical errors of men, you cringe at the thought of unholiness, you pray for the betterment of societies, you yearn for the veneration of My Queenship, you seek from others the innocence of children, and you know from the depths of your spirit that the arrival of God's Kingdom is only sunrises away. I will provide another example. I appeared to a young boy named Rawly Sebastian and told him who I was. He was eight years old, and I asked him to keep a journal of all the good things he saw in his life as best he could. I told him I would return to see what he had written. Seventy-two years later, when he reached 80 years of age, I returned three days before he died. He had compiled over 3,000 pages of notes of peaceful acts, prayerful gifts, holy recollections, and the names of hundreds of friends he had known in whom he was sure that the Holy Spirit of God had lived. In essence, I asked him to view the world through a straw and focus only on the positive traits of humanity that he could have known with far more critical overtones. He appeared before Jesus convinced that there was little sin on the Earth. However, what was his contribution on a higher scale? His work had little bearing because he ignored the tragedies that plague the lives of most people. My sole purpose in appearing to him was to raise this issue today. I have similarly summoned you and your brother to scrutinize the world through a straw, but based on reality commingled with the miraculous. God has requested you to remain in an environment where you understand the capacity of men to be holy, but you see them constantly fail.

You have been asked to record the terrible record of history, an accounting of the transgressions of participants in the physical realm, one much greater than the narrowness that Rawly saw. Therefore, your suffering is deeper than his; your feeling is sharper, and your desire for change impacts your state of consciousness every hour of your life. I have never wished to draw you to sadness or anxiety by the things I have asked you to do, but I am responsible for the way you perceive humanity. My promises and predictions have you sitting on the edge of your seat, waiting for the last miracle to arrive that will allow your brothers and sisters on all the continents to see their existence through the lens I have availed to you. Your growing lack of patience is focused on the hope you have almost lost. I am the cause of your wonder, I am the reason you are awaiting the balm of relief from the bottom of your heart. I have told you for over 14 years that it will be a little while, and everything will be all right. I have asked you to believe with the faith of the Saints that your life is a manifestation of the Resurrection. My Special son, I have told you nothing less than the Gospel Truth in everything I have said. Sometimes the clock is your friend, then it becomes an enemy, and then it appears to be your friend again. I am suggesting that time is for gestating the holiness in humanity from the interior of your hearts. This is where you are working; it is the source of your prayers. Exterior changes that set free the captives, discipline the arrogant, and make millionaires peasants once again are happening now. Please trust Me in this; the world as you know it is dying. Dawn does not break like the tripping of a switch. It is a slow, progressive process, and one that you cannot always see when you are focused on the diameter of a straw. The hope I fear you might lose is the hope you cannot know only casually. It is the hope in all that is yet unseen that I ask you to retain. Years and buildings and workplaces do what they must to sustain the citizens of Earth, for they are timely matters that perpetuate your movement toward the Eternal Divine. I am asking you to reclaim your spiritual peace, your innate desire to fend off the challenges that pester you from morning until the pit of the night. Imagine the Earth situated in Creation where there are no hours or schedules, no reports to file, no superiors to please, and no cubicles to enter. Happiness is located in this sustaining knowledge at the center of your heart, the Wisdom by which you were birthed in the world to help Jesus manifest the perfection of men. Realizing this makes you more confident of yourself, and to the greater imagination of the Angels who surround you, the ones who cheer your every move, the ones who fly to God like butterflies and ask how He could have made a creature so loving as you. They fawn over the faithfulness by which you stand beside the Passion of Jesus; they are awestruck by your determination to see your journey through, and they weep over your perseverance because they are happy to see so many in the 21st century serving like the Apostles of the first. I have told you that I cannot make you happy in this world, but I can ask you to be satisfied because your labors will complete their purpose in the Redemption of human souls. So, go out and discover new roles to play; find a new position of employment; build all the dance halls you wish; go wherever you desire on the planet that helps you endure the repugnance of the night. I only ask you to recast your spirit into a hopeful light where joy and contentment matter in the deepest recesses of your heart. Build and grow, and sustain and work. Lift and possess, and aspire and avow. Do what you do simply with the Sacred Heart of Jesus as the timbrel of your ways, with the sanctification of the Earth as your goal, with the Light of the Holy Cross as the reason you see. My Special son, there are millions of worlds to conquer and billions of suns that shine. There are life forms on other spheres in universes that have their own issues to solve. But, this is the humanity upon whom you must concentrate, the people of the Earth where the Savior from Nazareth shed His Blood. He tread the pathways where you are yet blazing trails. He loved and suffered before you were born, but you were with Him where He walked 2,000 years ago. This is the genius of the God of your fathers, the God of Abraham, at whose behest you have been placed here to live, serve, and die. This is the time and these are the messages that you will look upon in Heaven someday as the seed of your accomplishments, that day when you will have all the answers to the questions you hold in your heart. A Man once thought that the Cup might pass Him by, but it never did. He was more determined than afraid, and more prepared than He knew. In all things, this is what God seeks of His disciples. He desires the sense of reality in men that everything they thought was impossible is occurring today. There are groanings and wailing, and the gnashing of teeth, and there are problems whose resolutions may not come in your day, or perhaps they undoubtedly will. These are the reasons your prayers matter. If all the Saints who have lived before you had their way, they would never have questioned an hour; no person in their presence would have been afflicted; no woman would have died during childbirth, and every sinner would be living in Heaven by now. However, these same Saints are stationed with Jesus with nothing but praise on their lips for the Messiah who saved them by the Crucifixion through which God has sanctified the world. I am not being evasive to your concerns. You are blessed, and you are blessing humanity. Having said everything I have told you, I wish to repeat that these are not times like the earliest Saints encountered. Prevailing upon you are extraordinary circumstances ushering-in the culmination of the ages. This is why your work is the reconciling bookend for the constancy of life. Please understand that I am telling the Truth, and you will see in due season. I promise that you will be elated that these days are playing out precisely as they are..."

Sunday, September 18, 2005
St. Cyprinus de Blanchette [AD 795-857]*
2:49 p.m.

"When in your prayers you remember the lost and forsaken, be assured that the Holy Spirit dwells within you. I again ask for your supplications especially for unborn children who await their birthday and for impoverished people who have been displaced by strife and environmental calamity. I have hope when you pray for your brothers and sisters because it is a signature of your trust, a signal to God that you know He will respond. When you see sinners suffer the pangs of mortal militance and ask Jesus to be their help and consolation, you are building up His Kingdom; you are favoring the flawless piety that is prevalent in you, and you are opening wide the gates of Paradise for new Saints to enter through. Today, My dear children, I ask for your petitions for those who are persecuted for their faith, especially Christians who are oppressed in nations where religion is not allowed. Jesus hears you, as I have said, and He provides the means for His brothers and sisters to worship Him in ways that are pleasing to God. I am happy to know that your holiness is their conveyance to the free exercise of Christianity. I have warm and welcome memories of the ages when My children have worked together for security and good will. I recall the decency that has been nourished by hearts of love and the willingness of My faithful children to sacrifice themselves in so many ways to alleviate the suffering of the poor. This individual and social conscience is ailing in America because secular humanists are leading your little ones away from the Holy Gospel. I have made this point before. However, the prayers you are lifting today, along with the incalculable petitions that are placed before the Almighty Father by Catholics around the globe, are making a difference. You are stemming the tides of defiance against the Good News of Christianity; you are creating better venues for the Holy Spirit to remain, and it is with intense joy that I appear with you, knowing that the Earth is cultivated by the meditations of our hearts. I wish that millions more would recite the Holy Rosary to help humanity. Jesus desires that you depend on Me for edification and guidance. I pray from My Immaculate Heart that people on every continent will understand that turning to the Lord in contrition is the key to achieving world peace. My Special son, I ask you to remember how great is My Love for you, and I will be with you to celebrate your birthday. Please do all I have asked to assist your longevity. You must eat more healthful food, and you have an exercise device to keep your body strong. This is especially pertinent during wintertime. Thank you for sending *To Crispen Courage* to the recipients who will read them during the next several weeks. It is important that you keep a record of the books you send. If you place this list in your brother's possession, he will enclose it in Sister Faustina's Diary during his recitation of The Divine Mercy Chaplet. He lays her Diary face-down on his heart while praying the Chaplet of Divine Mercy during his Holy Hour. And, he prays for your career, for your longevity and good health, and for everything you have asked Jesus to give humanity. I assure you that you understand the nature of My conversations with My other seers. We speak in terms that reflect the issues I am sharing with you. You are a true gentleman who serves with faith; and to embrace My apparitions is a function of your belief and trust that God is permitting you to experience miracles through your honesty and loyalty. You are interacting with Heaven in degrees that require openness to believe, and this blesses you in ways you do not comprehend. I have remained with My Medjugorje seers to hold their attention and sustain the piety I have deposited in them. Imagine what an historical event it would be if they compiled a detailed accounting of our relationship and gave it to the Church and humanity at large. You have said veritably ingenious things about the intercession of the Saints, the Angels, and Myself. How can Christians be so blessed(?)...you once asked rather rhetorically. I assure you that the benediction for humanity is not that the Mother of God appears to you, but that these seers accept the mission to which they are called. This is more than manifesting miracles before the human eye, it is your compliance that the Lord God has sought since the Mosaic days. Indeed, to have pilgrims in the millions believe these visionaries is an extension of His exemplary Grace. I pray for your intentions as your books enter the hands of your Roman Catholic peers. This week will bring the continuation of *Supernal Chambers* that you are penning from your heart. The manuscript is a work of charity for the world from the center of your holiness, from your spiritual conscience to the unconscionable Earth. It will not seem as chastising as your last book, but a more amicable one lifting the dignity of Christians in Jesus' Resurrection..."

Sunday, September 25, 2005
Saint Mitchell Morales [AD 1774-1832]*
3:06 p.m.

"To offer humanity My maternal blessing, I pray with you in high hope that your brothers and sisters will gather at the Cross of Salvation. I adore this home so filled with peace. I search high and low to find My children, just as Jesus in the Temple. My mission would be incomplete without you because you aspire to the holiness of the Saints. You do God's bidding and deliver the Gospel of the Fairest of the sons of men to far regions where many unconverted sinners live. The Most Blessed Trinity is a three-masted galleon fighting valorously for you on the rolling seas of life, and blessed are the Sacraments that Heaven provides. Jesus rewards you for your faith. It is your humble hearts that He indoctrinates and your souls He redeems. There is no conceit in you, and you will have no ill-gotten fortunes to explain when you arrive in His presence. Yes, this will translate into a welcome ceremony upon your passing. I remind you to practice the steadfastness that will bring your efforts to fruition. You have been told by theologians and lyricists that God sees you from a distant Heaven. While they have honorable intentions, they should realize that Heaven is not that far away. I have said that Salvation is just beyond your sight. In the spirit of your love for Jesus, you can feel Redemption from where you stand. You can enlarge all the horizons of human endeavor, even immortal ones, when you allow the Holy Spirit to accompany you. Imagine all the places where you kneel to pray; and Jesus wishes you to do so. However, He also asks you to pray for locations you do not see that are inhabited by malnourished children. The Lord calls you to remember the poor in foreign states. Extend your hearts to places where the bravest among you fear to tread, and ask the Holy Spirit to go there and touch their lives. When we pray to transform sinners into Saints, God will change them. Wherever you see and hear of injustice, error and inequity, ask Jesus to intervene and you will see the gifts of the Holy Gospel in identifiable terms. I am grateful to My children who pray the Rosary for the conversion of the world. My little ones, you must empower your brothers and sisters to amend their ways. While it is possible to engage those in your company with the message of repentance, you must expand your piety and the intentions of your hearts around the globe to families and peoples you may never meet in this life. I have told you that humanity is one nation divided into many factions. The world is too large, it would seem, for you to imagine changing everyone. This is why you must hope with magnification, so your petitions become greater than the problems for which you are praying. When you allow your souls to magnify the Lord, lost sinners will come to you; they will esteem and emulate you, and they will seek holiness in you because you are reflective of the Kingdom of Truth. You know that those around you are curious. When they witness your actions and words, allow them to see the visions of Paradise that I have seen amplifying from you. Be soft and tender, and caring in mercy. You have been vested with righteousness to lend God's people a perception as beatific as the Holy Cross. This is the clarity of your commitment; it is your promise that you will forgo the luxuries of life to heighten your brothers' allegiance to Heaven. Sinners will inquire if suffering is inevitable, and you must tell them that it is dependent on their response to Jesus' Sacrifice. He is the Man-God to whom Christians defer, and I am the Patroness of prayer. I beseech your supplications that are worthy of the intervention you seek. Even the most simple prayer is sacred in the mind of the Lord. It is your essential sign that Salvation is present in your heart.

My Special son, it gives Me gladness to appear in the land where Abraham Lincoln lies buried. It gives Me joy to come to you who were blessed by a Roman Catholic Bishop on this day in 1992. Even your home was blessed. You see this house as an abode that has shielded you from the elements. Your hearts are the habitat of Christ, and you are the beneficiaries of the episcopal benison that was given here thirteen years ago. I know that you pray and hope that your work will flourish in your time, and I urge you to trust that this is ongoing at the center of your lives. Imagine the first Saints who did not have the benefit of easy modes of communication. Even those of younger years knew that their legacies would not be known until after they died. However, they did not work for themselves. They did not ask Jesus to tell them the score because they knew in their hearts that their Christian service would benefit the Mystical Body of Christ in timeless ways that they could not see. And, along these lines, the Saints ask you from Heaven to live with this same surety. You are a confident child in many ways, and I assure you that your trust in the Divine Providence of God is well placed. It is true that you are despised by humanity's indignance; and you are treated with indifference by friends, slighted in social circles because of your beliefs. Congratulations, your Christian faith has been validated! You are on the right course; your trust in Jesus is advanced, and you are augmenting the work of the Martyrs from centuries ago. I reassure you that I support your efforts in the measures you pursue. I want you to feel wholesome, and I wish your heart and conscience to realize that I have no opposition to your daydreams. You have given your life with your brother to Jesus in ways that are unprecedented by most people in America. I understand that you do not wish to move from beneath My guidance. Indeed, I can teach you better in matters of faith and morals if you are not oppressed by secular trends. You rely on employment for sustenance, but when it becomes a vexation to your spirit or violates your sense of dignity, then it is time to make appropriate changes. God recognizes your plight and has compassion for the dailiness of life. Laboring in His vineyard is a horrible burden if you feel impugned by the lack of piety of other men. Let us pray for His Wisdom to inform and guide you, and we shall see what transpires. You enjoy relative peacefulness in your American homeland, and these are auspicious days for Christianity during extremely difficult times. Please pray for the longevity of you and your brother, and for happiness and peace. It is not selfish to ask God for prosperity and good health. Your Salvation is assured. I know that you love Me; this has never been in doubt. You have loved Me from your mother's womb!..."

Sunday, October 2, 2005
Feast of the Guardian Angels
1:28 p.m.

"It is through the efficacy of purity that you share the Wisdom of the Holy Spirit by following Jesus' example in your thoughts, expressions, and devotions. I persistently ask you to heed the call of the Father by becoming united with Him. My little ones, today we celebrate the Guardian Angels, and each of you has one to protect you when you live prayerfully. It is important for you to remember that God asks you to walk with concordance and choose the paths that keep you safe. Ask Him to station the Angels at your side, for they follow His commands. You contemplate world events when the Roman Catholic Bishops gather to address Church issues. Everyone should pray for Christ's Prelates as they shepherd their dioceses, particularly when they are amassed as one assembly. And, pray for Pope Benedict XVI, that his flock will be obedient to the Holy Spirit speaking infallibly through him. You are exhorted to respect the encyclicals of the Holy See by your humility, and pray when the Pope addresses the Bishops. Support the Cardinals of the Church whose hearts opened to the Spirit of God by electing Benedict XVI to the

Papacy as the Vicar of Christ and Successor to Saint Peter. I have referred numerous times to the intentions of My Immaculate Heart, the decisive ones that are most dear to Me. If you see the world through Jesus' eyes and with the clarity of the Holy Cross, you will know upon whom you should ask the Lord to dispense His forgiveness. On this day, there are millions who need our prayers for health and virtue. It is obvious that you are aware of them. I also ask you to pray for the Church Suffering in Purgatory, that these souls are granted admittance into the Light of Paradise. You have the faculties to ask God to end their purgation and send them to the Glory in which they become your intercessors. My Special son, I concur with the pity that streams from your bountiful heart for your lost brothers and sisters, so much so that I sing in thanksgiving for your holy acts. It is a gift for humanity to ask the Mother of God to touch Her little children. Please stand upright knowing that Jesus is glorified, that He recognizes in you the attributes that sanctify the world. I say this not to embellish your self-image, but proof that the Kingdom of Heaven blooms through your faith. Many are the moments when I speak in tones of encouragement and pour accolades upon you for honoring the Father, but I realize that you do not require it; you only wish that humanity would convert. Adulation flows from you to Jesus and your Mother, and for the suffering poor who are living in stark conditions around the globe. You are amending their fate through your prayers; you are correcting their course by giving them courage to see in themselves the dignity of the Lamb of God. And, I pray for the Diocese where you live, that there will be sufficient vocations, ones that hold sacred the Traditions of the Church and who are devoted to Me. Together, we will pray until prayer is needed no more! We wish everyone well who enters the Sacrament of Matrimony, that they will be faithful to their spouses and ask Jesus to bless their families. It is difficult for marriage to succeed here in America because there are too many distractions, too much materialism and idolatry. The hedonism of the Western culture that you often repudiate is a burden for Americans to overcome in imitating the lives of the Saints. However, we know the outcome. Conversion is attained because righteousness has claimed victory! My Special son, beauty, wonder, peace, holiness, consolation, and awe are built into your manuscripts, and I am happy that your brother offers a Holy Hour every day. He recalls the intentions known to Me for ending the injustices that the Church condemns in the secular world. I pray for the healing of your spine, your happiness, longevity, good health, prosperity, unity with your brother, and success converting lost sinners to Jesus. Christendom was born prior to your conception, but you were given life to prosper Salvation before the Second Coming of the Son of Man. Thank you for having responded to My call..."

Saturday, October 8, 2005
Saint Simeon [1st Century]
Luke 2:25-35
4:29 p.m.

"The grand divinity you procure in the brilliance of the Holy Spirit is worthy of your faith, My children. I beseech you to seek the Lord in all things, to choose what is commendable, and remember that the continuum of human history must elevate Jesus in all ways. Please acknowledge your capacity to know when to act and how to cast out the devil trying to bring your piety down. The brazenness of humanity's inequities and wrongdoings clarifies your opposition to them as you comprehend the vastness of your own holiness in contrast to the corruption of the world. What frustration comes upon My children who suffer their sinful brethren! It is right that you recognize their need for conversion because it adds emphasis to your efforts. I promise you that Jesus knows about the unfairness you feel. His Crucifixion brings all error to end, so pray that wayward sinners will come to the enlightenment that is given them through the Holy Paraclete begging admittance into their hearts. My Special one, I offer unique perspectives about why things occur as they do, speaking in narrative terms. And, the image you positioned in your Rosary room accurately depicts the way I have appeared to you and your brother since February 22, 1991. I fold My hands in prayer and turn My thoughts to your petitions. I am your Advocate before Jesus, and you should request His assistance for all your problems during your earthly years. I am pleased by your holiness and grateful for the blessings you offer His Kingdom..."

Sunday, October 16, 2005
St. Margaret Mary Alacoque, Virgin [AD 1647-1690]
10:56 a.m.

"Undaunted by the blight and egregiousness of the secular void, you work in the Lord's vineyard to convert lost sinners to Christianity. My children, I offer you the best blessings in life, that you will know the Peace and Grace of God by remaining open in every way to receive the Holy Spirit. You inherit power and enlightenment with the Lord's Paraclete shaping your thoughts and actions and sculpting your speech to persuade your friends to turn to Him. Today, you heard the parable of the coin belonging to Caesar and the choice that Jesus asks you to make. It is the premise that befits the often-stated allegory that the Messiah came to comfort the afflicted and afflict the comfortable. God's intercession allows you to see distinctly the urgency with which humanity must awaken in advance of the Second Coming of Christ. You are fortunate ones who comprehend the meaning of humility, sacrifice, self-denial, compassion, and forgiveness. It lends Me great anticipation to speak to you because you know what I come to say; it is all about the repentance of humanity. How many parables can be told about the corruption of prodigal men? It would seem an infinite number that attribute the responsible heart to supernal beauty. I call on you to finish your work, the mission that Jesus sustains. The preaching, charities, lifting of your petitions; all this is exemplary of your trust in Him. When you feel daylight while approaching Jesus, this is the Eternal Truth that cannot be concealed. You have corrected vision in prayer. You change societies and nations by asking God to touch them, and their response to Him is what our work brings forth. We seek people who thirst for justice that they do not know where to find. We are achieving our goals, My children, because you have not surrendered your spiritual resolve. I alluded last week to evil influences that pervade innocent lives and the vengeance of Satan against Christians who oppose him. Jesus is your example for the way you must deny evil. There are no secret pacts between God and the devil to persecute His flock hidden behind the veil of time. The echoes of the years remind you that Satan is dead, but agnostic sinners do not realize this fact. They repeat the horrendous lies they are told by other nonbelievers. They are radically indifferent because they are too selfish to practice love. Sinners who do not accept the Cross are anti-Christ. They have two identities; the first is a malevolent beast they cannot control. This is the one they feed, the monster craving their condemnation. They starve their second identity, their capacity to be perfected in the image of My Son. None of My children know enough about hatred to hate. It is spread through subliminal devices, and this is the unholiness we are praying to stop. Satan coopts the ignorant and diverts their attention from the Cross. Darkness attacks Christians in an attempt to lure them from their faith, wanting them to surrender the battle and take the easier course. Timelessly and indomitably, the Crucifixion of Jesus of Nazareth has neutralized evil from controlling anyone who desires Salvation in Heaven and piety on Earth. As I have said, the fight is more than conquering evil, it is rescuing sinners from its clutches. Evil will never turn into good, and it must be avoided. Accepting the Cross reverses its damning effects. This is how the Saints saturated the Earth as missionaries and Doctors, and it is through this that your souls are hewn into the Cornerstone of the Church. Indeed, it is from this faith that the disciples of Jesus remold the architecture of the universe by their intentions and works—giants like John Paul II, William the Conqueror, known as William the Great. You are more perseverant than anything that befalls you with mental anguish or physical pain. God is glorified when you stand with Jesus through the pains of life, for it is in this that you reap immortality for millions of souls. Thank you, My Special son, for praying for the conversion of the world. Your holiness is undimmed because you reflect the Light of My Son and manifest His Kingdom..."

Sunday, October 23, 2005
St. John of Capistrano, Priest [AD 1386-1456]
3:29 p.m.

"When men on Earth genuflect in prayer, your Immaculate Mother is there bearing the Son of Man in My arms. It is God's wish that your desires be fulfilled, your dreams realized, and the intentions of your hearts commended by the Victim on the Cross. My little ones, tumultuous times accompany your conversion to the Kingdom of Light. Your predecessors were long suffering; you are blessed to have known them, and they now intercede for you as you uphold the sacredness of their values and the integrity of their trust. With you has been deposited the healing of broken sinners to end the ages in the Sacred Heart of Christ. To you has been given reason to pray with hopefulness, walk with compassion, see with enhanced vision, and rise in the morning knowing that the arrival of the Son of God is near. When men yearn to attain spiritual actualization, they refer to the eternity of the soul. They celebrate their conversion, Salvation, and the invigorating Grace that brings forth the enlivenment of the heart. I urge you to multiply your loaves to feed the bonds between Heaven and Earth. Ask God to touch the world with the grand magniloquence that is His to speak, to usher to this age the graces that will turn every nation to the heavens in holy acclamation. Pray that your brothers and sisters become inspired to such degrees that they hunger for the Sacrifice of the Lamb of God. The times are rare when pagans ask for assistance because they are encased in cocoons, and permeating their walls of indifference does not seem significant to the unchurched. Unfortunately for them, this partition exacerbates their ignorance. Elitism and separatism are enemies of Christianity. Your Mother asks you to remember them in your Masses. And, pray especially for the souls in Purgatory. We do this because human creatures are one in God in Three Divine Persons. You have known that peaceful victories are as honorable as triumphs in battle, and it is good when differences are resolved by the conscience. You also know that suffering for the sake of suffering has little meaning, but suffering for the sake of the Cross is cleansing for the Earth. When I ask My children to turn to Jesus instead of the world, I beg for your recognition that Heaven is your final reward. The Gospel is as alive as the Saints. I am seeking more from you today. Allow Jesus to guide you as though you have no other will than His. Consecrate yourselves to His return because it may happen before you fall asleep in death. There has been an expectation of Jesus' Coming in Glory for twenty centuries. Encounter the final ages with unity. Go about your chores knowing that you are downstream of time, that the pendulum has swung toward your sanctification and swept away everything dividing Heaven and Earth. You are counting the hours before the Second Coming of Jesus by tending to your faculties; and before you realize it, the

Master will be here. Will He find you guarding His Kingdom? Will there be sinners consumed by insolence in need of conversion? Christians have been aiding the holiness of others for 2,000 years. I am not an alarmist, and I do not speak in desperate tones, but I urge you to greet Jesus with abandonment and listen for the voice of the Archangel Gabriel to whom I gave My Fiat in the most crucial hour for humanity.

My Special son, it gives Me pleasure to appear to you because you know the intensity of the honor. You kneel for My messages with the innocence of a child. You recite the Hail Mary with sincerity, with a pleading heart that would change the world in an instant if you could. You have more questions about the condition of humanity than I have provided answers. You want to hear about how devilish acts will be excised from the Earth before many of them ever occur. However, I have said that your work is forward thinking for the spiritual reckoning of your brothers and sisters, not for spending time commiserating with your friends about why God allows certain things to happen. Your sense of faith defies the questions you raise. Wisdom and knowledge are yours as the future unfolds in the Grace by which you are saved. The darkness that enshrouds the globe is destroyed by the magnification of human coalescence. There is a mystery in this that is elusive to your thoughts. As much as I wish to teach you how to better understand human perfection; and you will know soon enough, I promise that rivers of knowledge are flooding the Earth's atmosphere from the oceans above the Firmament, and they are inundating you now. The whole world will be enlightened by this deluge, the coming of the Divine Mercy about which Sister Faustina wrote. Light, goodness, chastity, healing, faithfulness, justice, peace, and Truth—all of these things have supernal meaning that is broader than men have ever known. You live in the age of dogmatic revelation where Jesus will take you by the heart and lead you to the Promised Land. Perhaps many will not die before God deposes the history of the Earth. Do you recall the passage about men falling in ecstasy? What an awesome prospect for the deliverance of souls! What a commendation for your spirit to see Jesus arriving in a blaze of Holy Light like the Fatima Miracle of the Sun. Be of cheerful heart that God may ask you to complete your life early so you can see the implosion of the world from the purview of the Angels! These are glorious times not only for pure faith, but the way it dovetails with the Plan of Salvation. Do you realize that there are numbers of accomplishments being achieved by My people? The Roman Catholic Church is being revitalized as we speak. And, *Supernal Chambers* will touch the hearts not only of the poor, but unbelievers who are waiting for a sign from God. His intervention is timed by the Grace of His Will. There is nothing that shall come too late, even the healing you seek from Jesus. The Lord leads you to those who can mend your brokenness. Finally, I wish to speak about a group for whom we must pray. They feel socially imprisoned at their workplace because they are often treated with disrespect, and they have children to feed and disabled relatives who require their wages to survive. They are being browbeaten by capitalism. This is what leads your friends to say that they are tired of giving their paychecks to their wives in such a stagnant existence. It seems pitiable that they have no sense of worth greater than a mule. This is why your neighbor lost his employment. He could not enter the same building every day to the same heaviness, speak to the same colleagues, and carry-out the orders of his superiors like a workhorse. Millions are caught in these conditions by their lifestyles. I ask you to pray for them, that they will appreciate being healthy with a means to raise their children. Pray for their superiors to have compassion for the laborers under their employ..."

Sunday, October 30, 2005
St. Veronica Collier Dunseth [AD 1739-1801]*
2:13 p.m.

"I come with the peace of the Lord to speak about the joy of Christian Love in a world that reeks with malfeasance. I bring you the benignity of perfect Light so you will join the ceaseless strains of jubilation engulfing you now. My children, it is possible to discern the Will of the Father through the holiness of the Church. If you employ your faith, you will know the Wisdom that binds together the days of your lives into a unity of understanding. Remember that God wishes to claim your souls for Heaven, and your journey through life is a process toward that goal. Somewhere between the cradle and the catafalque, Christians undergo a solstice of the heart where you are perfected in Grace and Truth by the Messianic Gospel. This is like the photograph of history we spoke about. Focus on the impulses and influences that prepare your lives and make way for the arrival of your souls at the Throne of the Father. This is the essence of your belief; it is the reason you have taken the oath of repentance and professed your faith before the Blessed Trinity to be guided by the Holy Paraclete to Salvation in the Cross. It is not necessary that you enter the mind of God to perceive His purposes. The Saints did not live shorn of flesh and blood and a skeletal frame. Could you have recognized them by their meditations without their having publicized them? The response to this question is obvious, and it relates to knowing the Lord for what He has done. He is our Creator, and we His creatures. His is the sacred vision of all the universes combined, and you are compliant seers. Make what you will of the hypotheses of professors and theologians about the designs of Heaven, but each and every one of you must join the Mystical Body of Christ. There is responsibility in this, and undescribable beauty, and an instinct that is genuine and everlasting through the trueness of your heart. I am the Mother of God who calls you to propagate His Kingdom without seeing it in advance. Allow the clarity of your faith to moderate your sight. No more perfect trust can there be than for you to accept the Will of the Father with obedience and humility. It gives Me happiness to know that His creatures defer to Jesus without counting the cost. My Immaculate Heart is filled with accolades for the children My Son has warded Me, that you are praying and completing the tasks that God expects of you. There is no pride in Me, but I hold you with affection, fondness, and appreciation for committing to the work of the Saints. You see clearly because you shun matters that distract you. I implore you to call on the Saints with confidence that they will intercede for you. I have been revealing the names of certain Saints who have yet to be canonized by the Church, but they are among the redeemed nonetheless. Today, I identify Saint Veronica, and she will be near every child of Christian faith until the end of time. Soon, you will know the contributions that each has made, and their necrology is a priceless relic of Christian heritage. Ask the Saints to pray for the brokenhearted, for those who do not know God, and the poor and innocent. Summon them by name to be your companions with the Angels, especially Saint Michael the Archangel, who defends you in battle. Then, when your friends inquire where is their Lord, their Master and mankind's desiring, you may remind them that He is waiting for their prayers. Heaven assists you in this life, and Jesus asks that you will turn to Him. Paradise lives in your presence, calling in silence with the majesty of Absolution from the lips of Truth. My Special son, you know that the Holy Spirit helps your healing and the preservation of your happiness, and you do things to complement this process. You make wise decisions about your safety and protection, and seek the efficacious sources that ensure your good health. Many Christians are tempted to question the Will of God, but you must realize that He does everything perfectly and allows tragedies to happen for the sanctification of His people. This is what Jesus' Crucifixion is about. Everyone eventually tastes the bitterness of the Holy Cross before they die; and if they repent, they will drink from the Cup of Salvation without it passing them by. The resurrection of the departed soul makes it worth the cost, the salvific flight of all sinners in union with the Paschal Resurrection of Jesus on the Third Day. It seems apparent that your faith helps you through the darkness and allows you to understand that all things work for good for those who believe in Him. I am appreciative for the petitions you lift for the souls in Purgatory and for the end of abortion, and I know that you reap the benefits of the prayers that others are offering for you..."

Sunday, November 6, 2005
St. Rosetta Purcell Eisenhower [AD 1711-1767]*
3:01 p.m.

"Lift up your hearts to the Triumph flowing from Heaven, giving you hope on Earth! Be joyful that God has prescribed for you the Spirit of Wisdom, that He gives you yearning for the Judgement that sets you free in Paradise. We pray that billions of souls will call upon the intercession of the Saints and understand that the holiness of your forbears has overcome their corporeal mortality. Thank you, My children, for the gift of your lives. God is glorified, and I am grateful that you work for the conversion of humanity. I speak about the Saints because their souls have already entered Eternity. They rest in perpetuity with the Hosts of Heaven who adore them unconditionally. I again ask you to remember the poor souls in Purgatory, those who need your prayers, especially during the Holy Sacrifice of the Mass and the recitation of the Most Holy Rosary. When you ask the Lord to pity them, He will free them from their encumbrance. God will admit them to the Eternal City and grant them the joy and peace that you seek from your station on Earth. It is fitting that you remember their families and friends who survive their passing. There are likewise countless mourners grieving loved-ones lost to wars, famine, disease, and violent acts of Nature. Please remember them to God. Your compassionate petitions bring them consolation and strength. And, as you move to the end of the Liturgical Year when you shall honor Christ the King, give yourselves to the stated purpose of your faith, to the living and Omnipotent power of Divine Love that provides for you. When you raise your prayers, reach outwardly and consider that you are one of a larger people, the Mystical Body of Christ, and that you bear the responsibility of praying for people whom you have never met. They are bombarded every day with horrible struggles, unrest, malnourishment, betrayal, physical aggression, disunity, deprivation, murder, and abandonment. I beseech you to resolve to ask God to alleviate these scourges from this planet. Remember everyone who suffers to elevate His Kingdom. I speak of the highest pinnacle reached by the soul because this is where you will spend the fullness of Eternity. Your position and duties in this world are passing, but you must remain true to every moment in your life's work. It is notable to wonder what lies beyond the horizon, but I ask you to maintain your focus on the workings of today. When Christians think about whatever is excellent, whatever is pure, whatever is holy, honorable and compliant with Truth, you refer to your ability to train your sights on the infinity of your future at the same time you cope with the specificity of the present. I have asked you many times to confront issues that can be changed in your lifetime to make amends with God. The outcome is wholly dependent on the goodness you accomplish today. And, as I warn you that time is short, I am not requiring you to relinquish your life's goals in these times. Do you remember that the Sacred Scriptures tell you that Jesus will enter His Kingdom unannounced? Let Him find you working in the Lord's vineyard where you live. Allow the Saints you admire to look at your asceticism with hope for the rest of the world. Give the Angels the answers to their prayers, that humanity will be like them in simplicity and innocence. Reach for the heavens by taking the hand of your brothers in this land. My children, I ask you to be single-minded in a multifaceted Creation, and offer yourselves in every way for the advancement of the Kingdom of God. Many changes have come to Earth since your messages began almost fifteen years ago. Humanity has aged and the Church has grown. Your sense of purpose has been enhanced by the awakening of your spirituality. These are good amendments that have fashioned in you greater hope for the Salvation of the world. Deep inside the brokenhearted lives a longing for Jesus' Wounds. Where pious men and women desire the Feast Table of God's forgiveness is the craving of which I speak. You peer at life as though you are looking through a portal and seeing images that you never knew existed. There are parameters to your being that are exceeded by your spirituality. There is no genuine love without perfect sacrifice, and you are called to invoke Jesus' Crucifixion as evidence of this. If you could see the future, what would you wish to know? Many have spoken of a triumph over death that is free of scars. In light of your Christian knowledge, you know that this is not possible. There is no deliverance of humanity absent the Crucifixion of Jesus Christ. And, this is your profession. Your scars may not be manifested by physical assault, and your flesh may never be pierced by a saber, but your spiritual martyrdom is within the Will of God while He seeks in you the reflection of His Son. Those who dance through life shed of sorrow are not as close to the Son of Man. Your mission is to join Him in the Agony in the Garden of Gethsemane where He prayed with awe preceding His Sorrowful Passion. There was nothing ignoble about His thoughts. His meditations were indicative of His humanity, His capacity to understand the human spirit and the random trepidation that accompanies the lives of men. True devotion means overcoming these throes with perfect love so that when God asks for your trust, you will know that His perfection has come to fruition in you. Fear is real, and people who are afraid are not weaklings that would rather not fight for the holiness they espouse. The Saints throughout the ages lamented what might become of them, but the Holy Spirit came to their aid and gave them courage and perspective to see the resilience of their faith. For them, their greatest witness for the Kingdom of Heaven was as instinctive as their consent to die. They laid down their lives defending the conversion of unrepentant sinners.

Thus, My darling children, I speak during the month of November when the Church fetes the Saints and dares imagine that they were once like you. They discharged their duties and tended to their chores with reciprocity, thanking God for the breath of life, that they would be worthy to someday stand in His presence and celebrate His Glory. It is with this same faith that you shall prevail over every adversary. Yes, this is the faith that will bring you to Heaven. It is this faith that allows you to become conquerors of your impulses, to vanquish anything that tries to bring you to despair. Angels, powers, glories, sunrises, blessings, Sacraments, prayers, beginnings, victories, and everything else that God has offered you along these lines rules in your favor. The universe is unfolding within the grasp of the Son of Man. He is in command of all, and He will never allow anything to happen that does not prosper His Kingdom. Your compliance with My intentions and the Holy Gospel by which you live is fashioned by your trust in the Will of God. It is true that the artistry of your lives oftentimes seems too abstract to understand in practical terms. If you believe this, it implies that you are open to the Providence of Heaven. However, if you constantly search for logic in Christianity that you discover in mathematical quotients and physical lines, your faith will look like the hypocrisy that so many doubters have lambasted along the way. The summit of your perfection is to deposit your life in your religious faith, not the converse. To comprehend the splendor of Heaven is to realize that the Lord demands from you innovations and actions that you never dreamed you were capable of achieving. Heroism in Christian virtue means that you are willing to defer to the Wisdom of Jesus Christ, just as He taught during His earthly ministry. There is no honor in questioning the pervasive persistence of the Holy Spirit to evoke the best in you. The reverence that God is seeking is your loyalty as you withhold your curiosities with the perseverance of the Saints, and there is not a soul on Earth who cannot accomplish this task. My Special son, you must know that the Angels and Saints surround you and your brother, that the Dominion of the Father inspires you in moments when you seem not to understand. What you have said and written on behalf of the conversion of humanity is unsurpassed by the majority of people who have populated the Earth. I present you the gratitude of Jesus that He knows you deserve. He realizes that you are doing God's work not to reap His accolades, but that His brethren will turn their faces toward His Holy Light. He will wield His ordnance with the intensity for which you pray. He will give His people their fill in due season, but they must hunger and thirst for the righteousness which is the source of their sustenance *(Psalm 63)*. Jesus eagerly responds to the prayers of all the Popes from the past 2,000 years, and the millions upon millions of Saints who have conveyed His Divine Love in backwood places around the globe. His most impassioned desire is to bring conclusion to the inequities that you see, to force His enemies to endless torment in the jowls of the fiery Abyss. He wishes all the Mother Teresas on Earth to have thousands of her likeness to assist in healing the broken nature of impoverished humanity. He asks God the Father with as much appeal as you employ to turn Him loose on the world, to allow the conquest of the centuries to ensue, to open the floodgates of Holy Justice, and permit His faithful disciples to expunge the adversaries of the Cross from existence. I have said that there is fairness and expectancy in your yearning to see these things. Your hopes are well-founded, and your vision for the culmination of the ages is precisely as the Son of Man has seen. Jesus is not waiting for humanity for slight reasons. He is the Master of timing, and He knows the best hour to strike. No creature is His match, nothing can diminish His righteousness, no fiend can rescind His dignity, and no person in the universe could ever usurp His place as the King of all kings. I am pleased because you have never surrendered the delight of your heart in Me. You know within Me the Fiat that is sought from My children, and you have seen the blessed Pieta where My Immaculate Heart was stricken with mourning and grief. I kept asking myself, *what has this Child of Mine done?* And, the response by the Holy Spirit has always been the same, *He has saved the entirety of humankind from the cauldron of Hell.* My Special one, you must understand that not even the devastation that befell Me that day could dampen the happiness of knowing that you and everyone in your likeness would have unabashed hope. I am telling you that life is never easy because the righteous course is always the most difficult one. Indeed, it has been this way since the fall of Adam. And, the return of humanity to purity, the restoration of God's people to a state of grace, is a process that is based upon the Crucifixion of Jesus. You are given years to hail Him, to replicate His perfection, to immerse yourselves in that Sacrifice, and to remake the face of the Earth by everything you know about the Glory of Heaven. Inside you resides the Wisdom that God knows can alter the course of history, that can change those irresistible tides that always seem to fell the hearts of men. Living within your heart is the same power about which you have spoken so nobly and eloquently in your books. The strength, courage, perseverance, Truth, Light, Wisdom, and faith that the Almighty Father has written about in the Holy Gospel are present in your mind, heart, soul, spirit, and body. I exhort you to utilize these things to recognize why God seems to be taking so much time to mend the ills of the world. Imagine why He is delaying. Consider what He must be thinking as so many faithful Christians around the globe in convents and cloisters ask Him with a collective plea, 'what are you waiting for?' Peek inside the Sacred Heart of the Master of Creation and try to comprehend the paradox in wishing to slay the goats before sunset tonight while still allowing the Divine Mercy of His Sacrifice to take its prefigured course. Come with Me to Heaven for a moment in the depth of your heart and consider the oxymoronic conditions that exist in the exhilaration of the Saints who realize that they are living beatific ecstasy in Paradise while still knowing that the Church Militant on Earth is in such dire straits. How can these postures be reconciled? And, what about the hearts of saintly Christians like you who are praying for the Wrath of God the Father to strike down the enemies of the Church with a force so powerful that they would not even know they were poised in time? Is this not another dilemma?

God wishes that lost sinners would convert with hasty contrition, and Jesus is pleading for the Church to pray for it to come to pass. What, then, does He do with His promised Divine Mercy? What of the wretches in brothels and taverns who will learn about their compassionate God in June of next year? What about the mothers contemplating abortions who will be stopped by the prayers of the Saints before they arrive at their doctors' doors? And, what of the adolescent boys who are wishing to become priests in the lineage of the greatest Popes whose dreams would wait for another day? If God preempts their hopes before He permits them to heal His sinful masses, would Heaven not suffer from lack of their tasks? These are not imagined circumstances that might happen someday, they are remnants of holy hours from sequestered nuns, friars, priests, brothers, and lay people all across the Earth. 'Oh Jesus!' they say. 'Please do not allow the world to end until our prayers rescue that pitiful woman we heard about the other day, the one beneath the railroad trestle whose living is made by the profits of her flesh.' My Special son, God thinks people like her are worth the wait. And, in the process, more souls far from Him are committing sins of their own; and their confession, conversion, and repentance are needed to induct them into the Communion of Saints. Remember that Jesus did not come to convert the righteous, and He is not concerned that you will leave the grace of His presence. He is still fishing for men, for those who are slaves to the wrongs of the Earth. He hungers for souls to save in the same way you yearn for His righteousness to end the militance of human corruption. He knows all about capitalistic transactions, impurity and obscene fashions, and the trickery that is employed to bilk innocent workers of their hard-earned wages. All of these have already been consumed by the Justice of the Cross. The grievous error He wishes to eradicate has to do with matters of the heart that are blasphemous to God. This is why there is time, and this is the reason you are in it. Your work is mitigating the sinful nature of human flaws and eliminating the blasphemy too. So, never mind the despondence, and be careful about judging the torment of dignified men. I wish every injury could be healed in the next twenty seconds, and I pray that not another abortion would happen from the time it takes to say this to you. But, engaging God is a process for Creation; it is a critical intersection of the will of humanity and the Divinity of Heaven. You have articulated this in as many beautiful ways as the Archangels aspire to pronounce..."

Sunday, November 13, 2005
St. Frances Xavier Cabrini [AD 1850-1917]
2:40 p.m.

In Memory of the Man-God, Sovereign Prince of Peace

Embodiments of grander things, God's signature foretells
Principles wrought into timelessness, toll Saint Peter's bells
Deigned to bless the wayward world, His Christological Son
Past cynosures, palls, and parapets, the generations run
We harken paths and paleology for hints of moral good
And crucify the placidness where simple Truth once stood
We know the Earth was saved by a Bloody Crimson Tide
Of a Messiah whose ordained Justice will avenge infanticide
Peace and goodness, Light and Love—the clarion call of God
With lukewarmness we deny our sins with a simple wink and nod
Prophets, kings, and profiteers have trekked these ancient lands
That Christ reclaimed in agony with thorns and nail-scarred hands
Our spirits are starved for loveliness and never-ending peace
A gift to be dispensed to us when all world wars have ceased
Where are all the gallant leaders whose solemn oaths procured
The legions of foreign nations that have for centuries endured?
Mine eyes have seen the Glory of Tabernacle Choirs' songs
Where Angelic Hosts and saintliness fill Paradise with throngs
Disquietude and depravity are taking rampart, fort, and hill
With onslaughts of vain impurity that haunt our children still
God's people bear the dailiness of hatred, horror, and malice
With the Love of Christ's martyrdom in a Sacred Host and Chalice
We have been delivered from temptation, the serpent, and the Fall
By our Savior who suffered mightily from lashes, nails, and gall
So let us denounce the impudence that keeps us bound to sin
And heed the call of the Mother of God to convert and begin again.

William L. Roth Jr.
11/10/2005

"Your reverential prayers for spiritual abundance and the transformation of humankind rest with favor in the sight of God. I promise you that He hears your sacred pleas for the Divine intercession of the Saints and Angelic Hosts, for the assistance that brings you courage and virtue, and for perseverance to fight the good fight that only Heaven can provide. Today,

I have appeared to remind you of the happiness that I feel for your help and support in touching your brothers and sisters with the Wisdom and Grace of Jesus. I will summon all My children before time is through, especially those who are waiting for the slightest utterance from the Mother of God like anxious piano strings sitting idly by while God plays-out the symphony of human conversion through other lives. There is no question that Christians everywhere will play a key role in the final hours of Earth, and the hopes and aspirations that the Holy Paraclete has implanted in the hearts of the faithful will be utilized in the concluding battles of time. For now, I seek each of My children to prosper your faith, to pray unceasingly, and to be watchful for the signs of the Glorious Return of the Son of Man. It is factual, My little ones, that everyone whose soul will live in Heaven begins their delight on Earth in spiritual and transcendental ways. You believe that you are bound for Salvation; you will have a vision of the world you depart and the Paradise you enter when you pass through the veil of exile. During this month of November, I ask you specifically to pray for the faithful departed souls in Purgatory. Call on the intercession of the Church's moral giants, the servants who are yet in the militance of earthly life and the Saints of the Church Triumphant. The darkness of mortality will never be so impermeable that you cannot see your way clear to accept the exculpating Blood of Jesus. He is your help and shield, your rock of Wisdom and protection during times of trouble. Call upon the intercession of Saint Frances Xavier Cabrini from her station in Paradise to intervene for the poor and helpless in America. Pray for the intercession of Saints Matthew, Mark, Luke and John; and for Saint Ignatius, Saint Ambrose, Saint Padre Pio, and Saint John Paul the Great. They will help nurture your Christian piety because they pray for you to be with them in Heaven. They have seen the reason for your faith; they have been granted residence in the New Jerusalem where there is no suffering or pain. Remember always that the purpose of your years is to attain the Salvation that they now see with a broadness and keenness that their own faith always knew to be there. My Special son, thank you for writing the poem for Jesus on Thursday. It is a heart-touching rendition of your allegiance and fealty to Him, your way of fashioning the substance of your love for God in tangible terms. It may be true that modern-day people do not read as much as their predecessors, but they enjoy poetry and works of art. Indeed, your poem is rich in both of these. I have spoken about bright days and revelatory moments. Deep inside your spirit, you know that you have surpassed the faith of your forbears; you have given of yourself in ways that pale the woes of millions. Do you and your brother recognize that your mission is on the same auspicious course that it was in 1991? As difficult as time is to comprehend, it continues to be on your side. Imagine what you would have thought if I told you in February 1991 or briefly thereafter that I wished for you to write a dozen books, some nearly 700 pages in length, about My current intercession. You might have viewed such a request with dubious skepticism. And, you would have wondered about the relationship between its spiritual and practical applications. However, you have prevailed in composing such works because you have stood by Jesus patiently and endearingly. You have allowed God to be God, as I asked in My initial messages. You and your brother have stared-down the world by taking life one day at a time. For these things, you have found immense favor in the sight of My Son. You have created a blessing for the future world beyond that of most mortal men. You are playing your part in the reconciliation of the nations to secure a lasting peace that blooms through the Triumph of My Immaculate Heart. You have played robust roles in the ultimate consequences of the Judgement of God. If you will allow it, if your persistence continues to be as strong as in the past, you will find yourselves stationed at the rostrum upon the closure of the world with the Saints and Angels who are appreciative for your servitude. They know that you have a great deal to say to the harried Earth, that you lift-up humanity who has suffered so egregiously the devices of Satan, that your hearts overflow with sympathetic strains for the victims of the injustices that life has laid at the feet of impoverished Creation. You will receive the opportunity to stand on the podium and have your say, even as you are effecting the changes for which you have prayed and long suffered. As I told you last week, I am your Protectress as you do the work of Jesus in this life. There is more to My intercession than placing petitions before the Cross of Jesus. I not only share the sentiments of your prayers, I amplify and magnify them with harmonies of Glory and peace. When you utter a sentence in supplication for the world you wish to see, I declare with emphatic dissertation before Jesus why your desires should come true. I add distinction to your sanctity; I further your causes by reframing them with the Wisdom of Heaven that you are coming to know. The homilies and writings of the Saints resound throughout the world and the ages of men; and yours are no exception. I have told you that millions will be converted by your works and prayers, and I wish to reconfirm that this continues to be true. It is an inevitable and irrevocable fact. As I elevate your gifts to the Lord through My messages, please hold My intentions deep inside your heart and never forget that everything for which you pray will arrive. Time cannot dilute or destroy the substance of your hopes. Jesus hears you, and He embodies the righteousness for which you strive. I assure you that in God's Providence, He will ratify your vision with His Triumphant Plan. Thank you for hearing My words. I concur with your petitions for strength and good health. As you grow older, your body reflects the element of time. Some things occur as a part of aging, others by incidental forces. Please do not take your medical care for granted. When there are issues that arise, you must tend to them. My children, the staple of your faith is to realize that God's graces rain down upon you like heavenly dew to bless you in the good you accomplish. You are sustained and guided by the composure you yield from that faith, by spreading the Gospel through your words and deeds.

I acknowledge that you have been noble in this, that you have stood by My miracles when others turned away. You have been My obedient children, servants for God's people, and ones who do not analyze His Will. You have challenged the faith of others, tested their allegiance to the sacrifices Jesus asks them to make, and caused them to be true to the Creed they promised to obey upon their baptism. I am the Mother of God whose kindness and sureness cannot be impeded, and I understand the gifts you have given the Kingdom of Heaven. You are exalting Jesus' Crucifixion and finishing the race, and I pray that you will remain with Me while God purifies His Creation where billions of mortals have lived. My Special son, thank you for kneeling to pray with Me when you could be outdoors among your friends, taking-in the world. I beg you with a Mother's Love to never leave Me..."

Sunday, November 20, 2005
Feast of Christ the King
1:43 p.m.

"Even desert orations flow with the living waters of God's eloquence when delivered in honor of Jesus. I speak with compassion and happiness on this Feast because Christ is the King of Creation, and I am His Mother in whose arms you are embraced. Please pray with Me, My dear children, that sinful mortals will turn away from their wicked lives and see goodness, righteousness, pleasance, peace, purity, and Grace by receiving the Holy Spirit in their hearts. If the Earth is to be remade; if humankind is to be whole in the sight of God, then everyone far from Him must search for Jesus of Nazareth as their Redeemer. Indeed, the matter is more than the innocence of a Child-King who was martyred for your Salvation. Jesus manifests the inspired heart and outward actions by which you should live in exile and in Heaven. He is your conscience in complying with His mandates, in knowing in advance your response to unholy conditions that fall unexpectedly. Your souls need Light to grow, and Jesus is the Light of the world. Soon, you will enter the Season of Advent, another opportunity to celebrate the miracle of Jesus' Incarnation in a way that allows you to comprehend the Sacred Mysteries of your Salvation. It is true that God would have you bow before Christ the King to pay Him homage as your Savior and witness before His Throne, and He also asks that your allegiance be that of loyal subjects, knowing that you must reflect His Light and be filaments of Truth. Some ask how it can be true that you imitate the King of Creation by being His servants. The answer is that your nobility resides in your contrition and self-sacrifice, that you are kingly in spiritual stature and deserving of Heaven by which you have been blessed. What homilies could be rendered on the Feast of Christ the King! And, Jesus is worthy of the adulation and honor you give Him. Does He not also call you to His piety and simplicity, His willingness to sup with paupers in order to sympathize with their plight? Does Jesus not ask you to see Him, the King of Creation, in the least among you? How can this King be in the poorest of the poor? Because He is Holy Love, the Power of powers that allows you to subscribe to the honorable service by which you are sanctified. You may never be kings in this life, but your imitation of Christ the King takes you to the height of heavenly princes in asking God to grant your prayers and the pardon of sinners. He urges that you seek from Him the reprieve for all peoples to whom He wishes to dispense Jesus' Divine Mercy. Today, My little ones, I also ask you to perceive this moment, this time I speak to you, as of high importance because time affects you, and your movement through mortality quickly passes by. You are growing wiser in matters of forgiveness every day that dawns. You make the best of the hours by being prayerful in reproaching humanity. Everything that will make you Saints is being commissioned in you now, all that takes you to the comfort of Jesus' arms. Never mind the barrenness of doubters who oppose your faith. Pay no heed to the sensationalists who attempt to make your work for Me a fad for fame or profit. You are the children of Mary, the chosen whom God has deigned to accomplish His charitable feats at the opening of this new millennium. Spoils and praise have rarely altered the course of world history, rather courageous actions of pious men whose sights are set on the victory of the ages in which you are participants. It is clear to many who understand the Truth of Christianity that the finishing of the Earth will be its transformation in the Love of Almighty God. Nonbelievers are in grave danger before the Throne of Heaven. They are lost and distracted by the physical aspects of life and the concept of secular freedom, of a humanism that will take them nowhere in death but the pit of perdition. We hope and pray that they will open their hearts and see with faith that Jesus Christ is the reason for their lives; He is the destiny to be pursued and the Face of Heaven. My Special one, I am grateful to speak with you when I appear. We have done much good in the decades you have lived on Earth, and the depth and spiritual beauty of *Supernal Chambers* is another example of the piety you extol by your obedience to Me. You ask the question why, how you are able to write with such profound overtones, and the answer is because you practice your devotion to the Mother of God. The images that blossom from your heart are the fruits of that loyalty. You have asked for time to pen your thoughts about God's relationship with humanity, and you are receiving your wish as you create your manuscripts. Can you see that I am urging you to proceed with gladness and assurance, that the Angels are your advocates in accomplishing these things? You are never alone; your labors will forever be accorded the company of the Holy Spirit. Now, I have accomplished the purpose of My message today. I wished to speak to you with appreciation and ask you to pray dearly for the lost and brokenhearted, for the aged, the ill, and the millions afflicted by wars, famine, disease, and family dissension. Things are going well for you, and they will continue as long as you hold in your heart your allegiance to Jesus. Have I reminded you how I love you? I wish to repeat it. I know that you love Me by the sacrificial life you are leading. And, I do not wish to diminish any of the gifts you have given God, but the grandest of them has been taking care of your brother. Someday, you will understand the magnitude of this gift. If only one soul is won for the Glory of God, then it will have been worth the cost..."

Sunday, November 27, 2005
First Sunday of Advent
1:32 p.m.

"Wishing you peace and holiness, I speak about this 2005 Advent Season with the requisition that you humbly submit to the Will of the Father. You are My dear children who are compliant with My desires to pray for the conversion of lost sinners. You have manifested these intentions with love, and Heaven welcomes your petitions. You pray resolutely and implicitly for miracles to come to the lives of the faithful and to prodigals who are distant from God. My children, you hail from a heritage of disciples whose faith has advanced the Gospel of Jesus around the world. They passed to you the lighted torch of Truth to offer your successors, to assist in sanctifying your brothers and sisters as they endure their exile. There is suffering and pain around the globe. If you join Me in praying to Jesus for the alleviation of this agony, He will respond. My little ones, please be chaste in your thoughts and truthful in your ways. Realize that America is not well. Remember that Christ Jesus is the only Man whom pain and suffering did not change. This is an opportunity for the providence of suffering, to know that it softens callous hearts. It excavates humanity from indifference and allows the Holy Spirit to call you to empathize with Jesus' Passion and Crucifixion. You know that your daily prayers make a difference. I call on you to trust that the Lord is providing for you in everything you undertake. As you prepare for Christmas, tender your hearts to the Child Jesus for courage, strength, Wisdom, and health. Know that the Holy Cross absolves you the same way that Jesus accorded His Divine Mercy to your ancestors. Always recall that Love is kind and charitable, that the Sacred Heart of Jesus is filled with compassion and Absolution for those who believe in Him. This, My children, is your fountain of hope. My Special son, I take advantage of your receptivity to the Holy Spirit, knowing in your heart that your work is never in vain. God will dispense untold miracles to assist humanity in accepting your writing as a gift from Heaven to convert lost sinners to the Cross. One of the ways this will be done is that I will cite various passages from your books to priests and Bishops. This is why it is more crucial for you to prepare your manuscripts than for everyone to know who you are. In the fullness of time, I will appear to certain Cardinals in the Catholic Church and read excerpts from your books, even if years from when you published them. This will lead humanity to the date of February 22, 1991 and the commencement of your apostolate. I pray that you believe that it is more prudent for you to serve anonymously, else you will need sequestering to finish the work that Jesus has assigned to you. Your mission with your brother is touching the human heart en masse so the Earth will be Christian. Sinners will follow their dreams to My Immaculate Triumph with anticipation and trust, even if they suspect that their lifelong experiences take them nowhere, somewhere, or everywhere. At least they will try. This is all I ask. I am overjoyed that you stand with Jesus and the legions of Angels and Communion of Saints, that you are loyal to God's Kingdom, and that you dedicate your life to propagating His Word. I told you several years ago that your work is beautiful because you are beautiful. There are incalculable reasons for you to move forward with hope because your aspirations for the purification of men are coming true, despite appearances to the contrary. We pray that you have a pleasant Advent Season in advance of the Christmas Feast..."

Sunday, December 4, 2005
St. John Damascene, Priest and Doctor [d. AD 754]
3:24 p.m.

"With modesty and poise, you kneel before Jesus to explicate your longings to the Father in whom you have irrevocable trust. It is your belief in holiness that will heal your lives and make the world a better place. We pray for the conversion of millions to the Holy Cross, that they will understand that their spiritual identity is seated in Jesus' Sacrifice. Thank you for staying with Me, and please accept My benediction in honor of your admiration for the Cross. The lessons I give you tell of the Glory of Redemption; My messages seek your hearts as long as the Father allows. He summons you to adhere to His Will during your sojourn through time, knowing that you will be required to sacrifice mightily. I implore you not to worry about the value of your personal reputation. Be unfazed that you are indistinctly prepared for the things God asks you to do. We pray during Advent that you will have a growing anticipation of the Return of Jesus in Glory, that you will be ready in ways that have never occurred to you. The Light of His Love shines brightest when you submit to His Will in all you say and do. Embrace the self-denial that is mandated from you in memory of Jesus' Passion and Crucifixion. I have heard My children say on recent occasions that time seems to pass too quickly for them to complete everything they are required to do. My response is that you are asked only to live for God. Accomplish the mission of being good Christians, and there will be sufficient time to address other matters. Align your priorities according to the Sacred Scriptures, and your pleasures will be derived from them. Of all the important issues I have discussed with you, the most crucial is that you pray, for there is no substitute for prayer. It is your true communication with the Heavenly Father, and is evidence of your commitment to do His bidding in His vineyard. Advent is a time to reassess your achievements in the virtues of faith, hope, love, and charity. The years offer you opportunity to lay your lives alongside the Saints, with the legacy of those who were committed to the conversion of lost sinners with the temperance of Jesus. The goals you establish for yourselves, as lofty as they seem, are within your reach through the facility of your prayers. Remember the intentions I have described to you, and those for your families and friends. As Christmas approaches, ask Jesus to give peace and healing to those whose lives are hurting. Call on the Holy Spirit to guide you in prayer, to give you notice of wrongdoings that need to be rectified in your midst and places unknown to you. Humanity suffers, little children, because not enough self-avowed Christians bow their heads and ask God to mend their lives. Selfishness, greed, catastrophes, and morbidity can be stopped if you ask Jesus to intercede at your behest. I have told you in many places around the globe that you do not realize the power of prayer, that God awaits with anticipation that you will turn to Him during your hours of need. His Providence necessitates your reaction if Salvation is to include every soul. Please pray for your comrades to commit to Him, that they will come to the Blood of the Cross, that they will look deeply within themselves and see the void that Jesus fills with piety and Grace. You speak of the wars, famine, decadence, and violence that are overtaking the world as though you are helpless. However, the power to bring cessation to everything that contradicts the Love of God rests within you, in the intensity of your petitions. The Holy Rosary is your requiescat for the faithful departed; it is your diplomatic faculty to create a peaceful accord between peoples and nations. Where there is war, there is lack of prayer. Where there is lack of prayer, there is war. You know the transition between the world you see and the one you wish to see. I cannot overstate the need for you to pray the Rosary and the litanies that the Church teaches to deliver your intentions into the presence of the Father with urgency.

  Sinners who practice error are exacerbating the pain of those they oppress because the Children of Light will not act. Jesus implants spiritual conversion in you, the Holy Spirit of inviolate Truth, to amend everything about Creation that opposes the Will of God. Your Christian conscience should teach you that you are helpless without Him, but you are not weaklings because you have accepted His intercession. I implore you to make the most of this time to seek the uplifting of humanity in Jesus' Resurrection. I beseech you to perceive the world as I see it, knowing deep in your hearts that all is not as it seems. There is hypocrisy in some who profess to be religious, and outright malevolence in those who do not. The reconciliation between Heaven and Earth is ofttimes filled with torment because worldlings are reluctant to release their grasp on cruel habits and material goods. Lives in ancient lands are composed of suffering brought about by the extravagant consumerism of the United States. The outcome of this unfairness is the root of the destruction of societies at the price of tens-of-thousands of lives every month. My children, I invite you to observe the larger picture of existence and widen your perspective about your purpose on Earth. One starving child over the expanse of the globe is one too many. And, millions more have no access to medical care and nourishment. Oh—that another Mother Teresa of Calcutta would come forward for the impoverished indigents of India! I pray that a more conscience-prevailing government will arise in the United States, that the civilians of America will look with outward love instead of inward greed as they wake from their slumber in the morning. If anyone asks why the Mother of Jesus scarcely speaks with levity, tell them that the reason is found in the lives of the affluent who reject with disdain the sacrifices they are enlisted to make for the Kingdom of God. There are times when I would say that God is amused by the theatrics of men, but how can He be humored by the horrors that plague the innocents around the globe? How can I speak about tranquility when there exists such devastation? There is confounding pandemonium on Earth, and the eradication of suffering is the most important achievement to be accomplished today. My Special son, I speak to you with joy because you take My messages to heart. You are immune to many temptations because your conscience keeps you focused on the Cross. You exert piety in your life that is lacking in millions around the world. Every time you pray, each time you ask Jesus to intervene in ways that must be addressed, another life is touched. There are too many in America who live brazenly in their relationship with God. You and your brother are making amends between humankind and Jesus in ways that you will someday view with consolation. I realize that you know the meaning of Christmas; this has been the same since you were a young boy. As I told you in past years, the admittance of the poor souls in Purgatory to the Light of Heaven is dispensed generously during Christmas. I am pleased to tell you this because you understand what it means to them. The Church Triumphant is the goal for humanity! I shall never stop asking you to carry the Light of hope in your heart, no matter how dark the hour. Please offer prayers for broken families, for the survivors of those who have been killed in battle, for orphans, and that husbands and wives embrace each other with the matrimony they validated at the altar..."

Sunday, December 11, 2005
St. Damasus I, Pope [AD 304-384]
1:58 p.m.

"My prophetic children, My presence in your midst resounds of the virtuous lives you are leading in accordance with the Will of God. Not only are you holy, you are actively pursuing the eternal sanctuary of Heaven. I pray that you achieve your success, that untold numbers of souls will convert to the Cross. It is not only that you have donned the raiment of Christianity, you have shed secular excesses in ways that others envy. You share the joy, peace, and beauty of Jesus; your souls are disposed to the Wisdom of the Holy Spirit that is given to God's creatures of good will. Therefore, I speak to you, My Special and Chosen ones, that you might have spiritual aplomb during life's battles. I offer My messages to emblazon your hearts. You realize with assurance that Paradise is glorified and the Archangels rejoice in your company. I tell you simply that Jesus loves you in dimensions you have never foreseen. I love you, Saint Joseph loves you, and the Heavenly Hosts acclaim your talents. Your supplications, devotions, suffering and sacrifices, and the petitions and intentions you raise to God give you a pious sanctioning derived from Jesus' Sacred Heart. Today is a time to celebrate your goodness in ways I have not clearly articulated because humanity is broken and you are helping them to be healed. When the Lord created the gift of compassion, He crafted it by such works. These are traumatic times, and your brethren suffer the ill-effects. Thank you for taking care of them. I promise that you will look with awe at the manifest of Eternity and see your names inscribed there. I offer My oath that I will greet you with warmth, thanksgiving, praise, and honor. We have shared an awesome experience dwelling upon the Kingdom of God and the Christian conversion of humanity; and if it is His Will, we shall continue into the future. As I have said, My appearances here lend God's imprimatur to your reflections. Your writings, lessons, teachings, parables, and poetry will be heard by every person to enter the Glory of Paradise. I have spoken about the ways Jesus showers accolades upon His disciples and Apostles. I have given you a peek through the window of death to see the precision by which you are following the laws of your faith. Yes, I adore you, My children. This is what My messages say. The Advent Season continues to unfold, and the Feast of Christmas will follow. I again ask you to pray for the poor souls in Purgatory, for stopping abortion, for purity and chastity, the end of poverty and disease, and for world peace. Thank you for residing in this home, away from the thrashing of the streets and the distractions they bring. When you say the Hail Mary, it is like hearing Angels' songs. You recognize the intonation of Jesus' gratitude in the Angels. As you see, these are perilous times. America is at the brink of moral bankruptcy, but your holy lives stand in contrast to that cataclysm. You are the defenders of the faith that will be spread over the whole of Creation before the ages are through. My Special one, no one knows your soul better than Jesus, and I understand the tenderness that reigns inside your heart. I share your desire to cease the impurities and injustices on Earth. I pray for you, and I ask your Savior to respond to your petitions. There is no exhausting Jesus' Divine Mercy, especially for those who have the farthest to travel to piety. Indeed, the Lord God intends to sanctify them. With faith and prayer, Jesus will transform your enemies, even those who deny His Kingship..."

Sunday, December 18, 2005
Fourth Sunday of Advent
3:18 p.m.

"With splendorous joy and the magnitude of God's Love, I speak to you on this gracious Sunday of Advent to remind you of the impending return of Jesus in Glory, and I beg you to find in your hearts the impassioned courage by which He has regained the world. Let it be declared about My children that you are hopeful people whose sights are set on the grander perspectives of virtuous Truth, that you know the brilliance of Heaven through your tenets of faith, and that you bid welcome to the Dawn of the Eternal Ages with the same fidelity with which you cultivate the framework of the years. When it is said that men search for beacons in the night, that ships are guided by lighted shoreline towers, your eyes are given venue to see the Will of God by becoming the likeness of His Son. Your courage springs from whence your fears are banished by the immensity of your love. If you wield the Glory of Truth in the ways I have taught and according to the Holy Gospel, you will resound the tenor of the final ages with eloquence. Deep within your hearts rest the troves of pious riches that are pining to emerge. If you pray, you will know when to speak, what to say, and how to behave. Many are the times when My children have been accorded the opportunity to take to the populations of Earth the ecstasy and elevation of Heaven. The Holy Spirit dwells within you to encourage the embattled world with a sense of valor, knowing that the victory of the Cross has thrived in you. I implore you to pray and imitate My desire to see history through. I stand before you with compassion and diligence to enlist the Children of Mary to fight the good fight of holiness, even to the point that you are despised for Jesus' sake. Your reward in Heaven shall be great. Speak truthfully to yourselves, accepting that everything the Prophets said will come to pass. Do not be deluded into believing that there are not wars yet to be fought. There are perilous, malevolent villains who wish for My children to cower from the forces that contradict God's Triumphant Life. They would rather see you falter and be impugned. It is only by succeeding in the campaign for righteousness that these evildoers are vanquished. Dear children, I have spoken of color and light, value and sense, dutifulness and verity, and wonder and happiness. I have given you parables and images about the infinity of Heaven, anything I could say to direct you toward the prospective of Eternity. I speak because My children are listening. Christians around the globe are heeding My call to holiness, sacrifice, and to that special humility that lends your obedience to the conscience of God. You may be lanced in your battles, but never felled. You might be mocked and ridiculed, but you cannot be stolen from the haven of Paradise. Even the flesh of your body can be racked and ruptured, but your spirit belongs to Jesus. I assure you that these things are according to the Scriptures, that the Apostles and Martyrs knew that to live for Jesus was to die to themselves. When you ask for blessings in your lives, for your families and friends, and for the conversion of lost souls, remember that all these have come through the Passion and Crucifixion of My Son. They have been given to humanity through a providential Sacrifice that you must embrace, obviously not match, but one that you must sacramentally accept. We pray that you are open to the Will of the Father in ways that overcome your weaknesses, that broaden the horizons of your vision to include manifestations about which you have never thought. As you know, the spontaneity of selflessness is such that you are not always prepared for its unexpected tolls. I speak of the human heart in the context of the holier life of humanity because all peoples are united in the Holy Spirit who takes residence within you. The heart is the focal point of Divine Truth; it is the instrument with which you comprehend the Glory of God. When you relinquish fame and fortune, let this be the reason. Never cease your desire to become poor for the sake of the richness of the Lord's Kingdom. My Special son, it is with high hope and genuine happiness that I speak to you. You listened to the Gospel reading at today's Holy Mass with such adoration for Me that I was moved to tears. Remember that the Archangels are your defenders where you live, both temporally and spiritually. You see the crests of life with gladness because you know the lulls and valleys cannot last long. You train your sights on the Light of Paradise because you realize that the darkness is passing away. I wish for My children who are lost in the world to adopt your way of living, your penchant for pursuing the Truth, your long-suffering anticipation of the Second Coming of the King. I beseech you to continue this interaction with God. Keep your hopes aloft with Me, knowing in your heart that Heaven is just beyond your sights, that the Saints herald your success before the procession of the ages, and that Jesus lives in you for the fruition of your work. In a few weeks' time, you and your brother will finish fifteen years with Me. What does this mean for humanity? How has it changed your hearts? These are incalculable effects that only the culmination of the Earth can measure. Suffice it to say that many seasons have bloomed not only of Nature and the universe, but of the sanctification of the human heart over the continuum of time. The young people whose names you do not know will be converted by the fruit of your labors. And, just as you would have it, they will hail the Mother of God in illustrative terms, and you and your brother will be examples for them. They will realize that you have given all praise to Jesus. For everything they shall discover about decency, purity, modesty, and prayer; for all they will learn about justice, piety, sacrifice and peace, they will give the accolades to the Holy Spirit of God who is speaking through Me now. If you culled all the annals of Creation into one crescendo and added the most evocative valedictories you could imagine, this is what will occur when every soul sees Jesus encircled by His friends, disciples, and messengers upon the end of time. My Special son, as much as you pine for this to come, you will not be prepared for the elation you will feel. Let us pray that 2006 is a year of health, peace, good will, and happiness for you and your brother as votaries for the conversion of men..."

Sunday, December 25, 2005
The Feast of Christmas
2:37 p.m.

"The Peace of the Lord has entered the world! My children, you have been given the opportunity to testify to living anticipation through My Messianic Son. Your lives are complete in Him. Today, I pray for you with the honor and joy that you procure in the Prince of Peace, realizing that you pour-out your lives for His Kingdom with sacrifices you have endured through time. My blessing today is accompanied by My request that you lead ameliorative lives, declining to engage in debates that do not advance human holiness. Two of the notorious enemies of peace are negativity and social competition. I plead for the Church on Christmas to depart from the causticism in which many are embroiled because it only brings discomfort to your hearts. Ponder the Christmas Mysteries and Jesus' perfect life. Imagine the hope He holds in His Sacred Heart for the souls He came to redeem. If pessimism had been intrinsic to your faith, the Biblical Apostles would never have stood steadfastly; they would not have been convinced about the growth of the Church. In America, negativity alienates citizens for power and profit. Pitting one group against another for material gain is an enemy to the peace Jesus asks you to extol. Therefore, please accept My wish that you do not dwell on negativity because it is vexatious to the spirit and serves no righteous purpose. And, I have spoken on several occasions about the futility of competition. It is important that you approach others as your associates and not your opponents. Even when they persecute you for your faith, forgive them knowing that they will eventually come to the fullness of God's Light. I offered a Christmas blessing at Medjugorje today, and I spoke with prayers for unity around the world. Here, in your humble home in Springfield, I call on humanity to disengage from the sarcasm that casts a pall on your daily discourse. Exemplify the highest principles of indelible faith; place adversity in proper perspective, and look to the future with hope and tranquility. If you do this, your lives will be happier because the Holy Spirit will reign in your hearts. The rote nature of your days threatens your progress. Those who demand your service in workplaces and in your families do not understand the depth of the sacrifices you make to satisfy their requests. I ask you to rise above the fray, avoid the brinkmanship that legitimizes your persecutors, and know that the Victory of Truth will prevail at last. Although this may be difficult for you, it is important to consummating your mission, and it is necessary in preserving your peace of mind. You are ardently pious in ways that you do not even know. The Lord looks at you with pity, compassion, and appreciation because of the grueling cadence of your lives. If you rise above the commotion, you will enjoy the peace that Christmas brings. How rudimentary is this concept! Remember the Light of Christmas, its call for forgiveness in the heart and around the globe where believers recollect the imperatives of faith. Even though Jesus' Nativity was centuries ago, His legacy as the Child of Bethlehem still gives you the consolation you have always sought. Jesus the Teacher and Crucified Master remains with you as My Resurrected Son. And, the Holy Father in Rome, Pope Benedict XVI, exhorts his flock to remember that Christmas is a time for prayer, not consumerism. Please celebrate it with the expectation that it should make the Earth glisten like a priceless gem. And, most important, be at peace with the vocations to which you have been called. I am the Mother of the Church, and I urge My children to give the best you have to offer. I am the Patroness of America who calls on the West to renounce materialism and embark on the journey of Christian sharing. If you do this, you will be inundated with benedictions, and you will feel less anxious about future events.

My Special and Chosen ones, it gives Me hope to speak to you because you appreciate the resplendence of the Nativity. You realize that Jesus' Incarnation brought the Holy Gospel to humanity. You are My stately sons whose mission is underscored by your own resolve. Thank you for responding to My call. Please accept My gratitude for staying the course through many difficult times. I send the peace of Christmas into your hearts, and I beseech you to accept My blessing for your consecration to the Cross. My messages address the conversion that I offer humanity during this new millennium and about My Fiat to the Archangel Gabriel centuries ago. They instill the invigoration of the spirit that was absent before Jesus was born. I carried the Son of Man in My Womb with an expectation for wholesome change that Jesus fulfilled during His ministry. I was the world's Living Advent as Jesus grew in My Womb. My trust was in the Will of the Father, and My hope was fashioned by My full obedience. What did it mean that Heaven came to inhabit Earth in a sinless human frame? For what other purpose had the Archangel come if not for awakening the dead? I was not disconcerted by Gabriel as some historians believe. I was relieved because I knew that My time had come. The purpose of My being echoed through Creation when Gabriel spoke, and I had no apprehension. I was inspirited to inquire how I was to bear the Messiah while knowing no man, assuring the world of My virginity and Jesus' deific conception. I knew the answer; it is recorded for the Church to preach. Even in these present times, the joy of My Immaculate Heart resonates the reason for My birth. I knew that I was with Child so billions would be saved; this is the narrative that foretold the coming of Christmas. My gift to humanity would be the Savior of lost sinners, the birthing of the Wonderful Counselor who ushers repentant souls to Paradise. I contemplated the moments to come, My Virgin Motherhood, and the Wisdom I extolled. When it was inclement during Jesus' Nativity, I knew that this was the beginning of His life of suffering. When I pondered these things in My Heart, I accepted that it was to the betterment of the Earth. The Christ Child was born of My Womb into a world that trembled more than He did. It was as though the sanctity of all creatures came springing forth like a tiny bud or little flower. I saw compassion and Mercy before Me with eyes of forgiveness. I knew that the Lord had performed a miracle, and this beatific blessing prevails today. Light came to end the darkness with sanctifying Grace, and Love dared to annihilate the hatred of men. Graves would be emptied, transgressions expunged, and peace would overwhelm the mountains and valleys with blessings deeper than the Great Flood. Jesus' Nativity was the birth of the divinity that had eluded the hearts of humanity for thousands of years. This, My children, is why I was humbled when Christ was born. My focus was tending to this Man-God who had been deposited among you from Heaven. I was filled with the same joy that was conveyed by the Archangel Gabriel upon the Annunciation. The Prince about whom I spoke at the opening of this message was born on Christmas, and all who accept Him will be absolved. Thank you, My Special one, for heralding the refrains of Salvation during your earthly years. I am elated that you touch the hearts of your unfeeling brothers and sisters. Nothing will impede your success..."

The Morning Star of Our Lord, Incorporated
Other Available Titles

In Our Darkest Hour
Morning Star Over America
February 22, 1991 - December 31, 1992
Volume I

In Our Darkest Hour
Morning Star Over America
January 1, 1993 - February 22, 1997
Volume II

At the Water's Edge
Essays in Faith and Morals

When Legends Rise Again
The Convergence of Capitalism and Christianity

White Collar Witch Hunt
The Catholic Priesthood Under Siege

Babes in the Woods
With a Little Child to Guide Them

To Crispen Courage
The Divine Annihilation

Supernal Chambers
A Resurrection Prayer

Morning Star Over America
The New Millennium
AD 2000-2002

See copyright page for ordering information.

www.ingramcontent.com/pod-product-compliance
Lightning Source LLC
Chambersburg PA
CBHW070715160426
43192CB00009B/1198